D0455717

RESISTANCE OF THE HEART

INTERMARRIAGE AND THE ROSENSTRASSE PROTEST IN NAZI GERMANY

BY NATHAN STOLTZFUS

W·W·NORTON & COMPANY · NEW YORK LONDON

For information about permission to reproduce selections from this book,
write to Permissions, W. W. Norton & Company, Inc.,
500 Fifth Avenue, New York, NY 10110.

The text of this book is composed in Aldus
with the display set in Optima
Composition by PennSet, Inc. Manufacturing by The Haddon Craftsmen, Inc.
Book design by Jacques Chazaud

Library of Congress Cataloging-in-Publication Data

Stoltzfus, Nathan.
Resistance of the heart : intermarriage and the Rosenstrasse
protest in Nazi Germany / by Nathan Stoltzfus.
p.   cm.
Includes bibliographical references and index.
ISBN 0-393-03904-8
1. Jews—Germany—Berlin—Persecutions. 2. Holocaust, Jewish
(1939–1945)—Germany—Berlin. 3. Interfaith marriage—Germany—
Berlin—History—20th century. 4. World War, 1939–1945—
Underground movements, Jewish—Germany—Berlin. 5. Berlin
(Germany)—Ethnic relations.   I. Title.
DS135.G4B476   1996
305.8'924043155—dc20   95-50107
CIP

W. W. Norton & Company, Inc., 500 Fifth Avenue, New York, N.Y. 10110
http://web.wwnorton.com

W. W. Norton & Company Ltd., 10 Coptic Street, London WC1A 1PU

1 2 3 4 5 6 7 8 9 0

Dedicated to
those at Rosenstrasse
and my parents

The world is too dangerous to live in—not because of the people who do evil, but because of the people who stand by and let them.

—ALBERT EINSTEIN

Then I reflected that everything that happens to a man happens precisely now. Now. Centuries of centuries, and only in the present do things happen. Countless men in the air, on the face of the earth, and the sea. And all that is really happening is happening to me.

—JORGE LUIS BORGES

We must try harder to understand than to explain. The way forward is not in the mere construction of universal systematic solutions, to be applied to reality from the outside; it is also in seeking to get to the heart of reality through personal experience. . . . Human uniqueness, human action and the human spirit must be rehabilitated.

—VÁCLAV HAVEL

NOTE: *Some of the names in this book have been changed.*

CONTENTS _____

ACKNOWLEDGMENTS   xi

INTRODUCTION   xv

  I: Hitler's Theory of Power   3

 II: Stories of Jewish-German Courtship   17

III: The Politics of Race, Sex, and Marriage   41

 IV: Courage and Intermarriage   50

  V: Mischlinge: "A Particularly Unpleasant   57
      Occurrence"

 VI: Society versus Law: German-Jewish Families and   65
      Social Restraints on Hitler

VII: Society and Law: German-Jewish Families and   76
      German Collaboration with Hitler

VIII: Kristallnacht: Intermarriages and the Lessons   *98*
        of Pogrom

 IX: At War and at Home: *Mischlinge* in   *112*
        Hitler's Army

  X: Racial Hygiene, Catholic Protest, and   *124*
        Noncompliance, 1939–41

 XI: The Star of David Decree: The Official Story and   *150*
        the Intermarried Experience

XII: The Price of Compliance and the Destruction   *162*
        of Jews

XIII: Plans to Clear the Reich of Jews—and the   *192*
        Obstacles of Women and "Total War"

XIV: Courageous Women of Rosenstrasse   *209*

 XV: Protest, Rescue, and Resistance   *258*

      EPILOGUE   *279*
      NOTES ON SOURCES AND DISCOVERY   *289*
      ENDNOTES   *299*
      BIBLIOGRAPHY   *355*
      INDEX   *365*

ACKNOWLEDGMENTS

The pursuit of this history of protest and regime has brought me a rich network of friends, acquaintances, and experiences. Many persons have given me assistance as experts and friends.

Professor Raul Hilberg and Dr. Sybil Milton were helpful, particularly at the outset of my research, and encouraged me to write the Rosenstrasse Protest story in the context of intermarriage during the Third Reich. Dr. Milton provided me with the best materials from the Leo Baeck Institute, and Professor Hilberg always (to my astonishment) made himself freely available on the telephone as I asked him for overall perspective, archive information or for key but obscure facts and figures. Richard Breitman became just as helpful in identifying essential primary sources and criticism. Professor Ian Kershaw also generously gave his time on several occasions to talk, read, and make valuable suggestions, as has Professor Hans-Ulrich Wehler.

For scholarly critique, I have had the generous assistance of the best in the field. Omer Bartov, David Clay Large, Klemens von Klemperer, Robert Gellately, Peter Hoffmann, Peter Hayes, Herbert Strauss, Herbert Kelman, and Walter Laqueur have helped me identify and analyze key problems and strengthen arguments. I am grateful to my dissertation advisers at Harvard, Professor Charles S. Maier, and also David Blackbourn for invaluable overall perspective. They have pointed out what I would have overlooked and inspired me with their grasp of detail and mastery of scholarly works. Professor Franklin L. Ford was most supportive as well, and I was very fortunate to have studied with him just prior to his retirement from teaching. John Torpey, Kristie Macrakis, John Borneman, Elizabeth Boggs, Peter Wyden, Nikola Baumgarten, Maya Dummermuth, and Rishona Zimring have also read and commented with care on parts of the manuscript.

For their editing advice, I am indebted to Jack Beatty, Lisa Austin, Mechthild Küper, and Karl-Heinz Jansen. Special gratitude goes to Ed Barber, my editor at Norton, for his hard work to improve the style and emphasize the narrative line of the book. Eike Geisel and Shepley Metcalf provided me with important media and publishing contacts, for soliciting further information. My agent, Rosalie Siegel, has always been there as an ally to encourage and make the right connections.

One of the most rewarding adventures of archival work is meeting scholars, such as Professor Werner Schubert, J.D., who pointed out relevant Nazi laws on marriage and intermarriage. For access to court trial documents in Berlin I am grateful to the senior prosecuting attorneys—Balke, Severin, and Steglich—for granting me access to trial documents still at the Landgericht and Kammergericht (District and Supreme Courts) in Berlin. Walter Griebel, the senior prosecuting attorney from Frankfurt am Main, became a collaborator and friend, as we shared information on former Nazis as historian and prosecutor respectively. For interviews with Berliners about their experiences in the Third Reich, I am indebted to Hans Wieneke and the Charlottenburger Heimatsmuseum. In Jerusalem Professor O. D. Kulka made available records of the Reichsvereinigung der Juden in Deutschland (Central Organization of German Jews), before I was given access to all of them in the former East Germany.

While I lived and researched in the former East Berlin, Dr. Albert Wollenberger made me feel at home and interceded with officials to help me gain access to materials in the *Giftschrank*, before the wall fell. Hans-Oskar Löwenstein de Witt provided me with his apartment in Tel Aviv while I did research there, and Gad Beck of the Berlin Jewish Community was a friend and counselor on matters relating to Berlin's Jews during the Nazi period and thereafter.

I thank various funding sources, especially the Harry Frank Guggenheim Foundation and the Albert Einstein Institution. The Fulbright Commission, originally, and then the Albert Einstein Institution and IREX (International Research and Exchanges Commission) granted me invaluable funding. The Friedrich Ebert Stiftung, Rabbi Everett Gendler, and the Harry Frank Guggenheim Foundation contributed generously to the final research and writing stages of this work.

I owe a very special gratitude to Dr. Gene Sharp, who, as the founder and president of the Albert Einstein Institution, pointed me toward research on the Rosenstrasse Protest, gave me some initial ideas and perspectives for its analysis, encouraged me when the effort seemed naive and out of reach, and then helped me secure funding to carry out the research in Germany and elsewhere. Given so much priceless assistance, I only hope the reader will not perhaps expect more from the book.

INTRODUCTION _____

BERLIN, FEBRUARY 27, 1943

Hours before first light a battalion of SS men, local Gestapo agents, and street policemen fanned out across Berlin in a fleet of three hundred trucks,[1] to capture the city's last, unsuspecting Jews. Leading the charge was the Leibstandarte Hitler, an SS unit of select tall blond soldiers whose small advances against the Red Army had briefly fanned hopes of German victory, at a time when the Wehrmacht was largely in retreat. Some of the SS troops on Berlin's streets this morning wore the decorations of valor in war.[2] But their mandate this Saturday was to make Berlin "free of Jews." Jews still working in armaments factories, as well as intermarried Jews (Jews married to non-Jews), were the primary targets. In black uniforms and steel helmets, armed with bayoneted rifles and machine guns, the SS cast a grim image intended to put fear in the heart of anyone who might protest or complain about the arrest of these last, relatively well-connected Jews of Berlin. The Gestapo's code name for this massive arrest (which has often been called the Factory Action) was the Final Roundup of the Jews, and for thousands this was the beginning of the end.[3]

Without warning or explanation, the SS and Gestapo fell upon the workbenches of the "Jewish crews," driving them without explanation onto the waiting furniture trucks. The victims, clad in thin work aprons, were not allowed the time to pick up their winter coats or their homemade breakfasts and lunches. Clapping their hands and shouting, "Faster! faster! Get a move on!," the SS drove the Jews forward with the butts of their guns. Pregnant women and men too old to jump onto the trucks were tossed or shoved.[4] Dozens suffered broken bones.[5] All over Berlin the Gestapo was seizing Jews from work, home, or the street. Anyone wearing the Star of David was grabbed and put on the trucks. Even Jews who were just in Berlin to visit were taken.[6]

Crammed with dimly visible human shapes, the trucks began rolling up in long columns at five makeshift collection centers in the heart of Berlin. The vast motor vehicle garage of the Hermann Goering army barracks in Berlin-Reinickendorf and the riding stables of the barracks on Rathenower Strasse had been temporarily emptied. The amusement center Clou on Mauerstrasse now also served as a grim holding center for arrested Jews, as did the synagogue on Levetzowstrasse and the Jewish Community's public and youth welfare administrative center, at Rosenstrasse.[7] Some Jews were also brought to the former Jewish old people's home on Grosse Hamburger Strasse, a regular collection center for those newly arrested Jews about to be sent to the camps.

Every collection center was a theater of brutality and fear, hours of horror on this Sabbath never to be forgotten by survivors. One who escaped remembers that terrible moment as a truck rolled up to discharge its human cargo. The doors sprang open, and "an older lady streaming with blood fell unconscious into our arms. Behind her a girl, perhaps seventeen, tumbled from the truck, blood streaming over her face. She was followed by a man bleeding from a leg wound. He supported his wife, whose dress was torn to shreds. They were people who had 'tried to defend themselves' the SS explained, laughing. A young SS rogue stood there laughing and photographing the scene."[8]

Panic reigned. Women shrieked for their children, who waited for them at home. Infants, plucked from homes while parents were away, screamed for their mothers and fathers.[9] Married partners who worked at different factories were taken to different collecting centers, half insane with fear for their loved ones.[10] People begged to be transferred, for a swallow to drink or a bit of straw to sit on. Freezing in their thin clothes, hungry, beaten, and without water or toilets, many sought the escape of suicide. An eyewitness reported, "People plunged through windows, threw themselves under cars, or took poison (Vernal or Zyankali, which particularly cautious persons always had with them); it was horrible, an unimaginable chaos."[11]

In the midst of this anguish, the SS and Gestapo, some with horsewhips, sorted out the Jews who were married to German non-Jews, along with their *Mischling* children (in Nazi Germany *Mischling* referred to anyone of mixed race, but it generally referred to persons of part German, part Jewish ancestry). These were shoved again onto the omnipresent trucks and removed to the four-story administration building of the Jewish Community at Rosenstrasse 2–4. Deportation executive Adolf Eichmann had ordered these persons separated and sent to Rosenstrasse to make it appear as though they were to be sent not to death camps but to labor camps in Poland.[12]

On Saturdays Jewish workers normally got off work at around 2:00 P.M. When on this Saturday, February 27, 1943, they did not return home as usual, those with German spouses began to worry and to call around for information to the police, the factories, each other. Some of them received information through a "telephone chain" formed to alert one another of danger and passed information along to other Germans in intermarriages.[13] Soon many knew their loved ones had been imprisoned at Rosenstrasse, a one-block street in the heart of old Berlin. Women hurried to this street now, one by one or two by two, to get any further information or to bring their loved ones bread, cheese, razors, and toiletries. Most of the Jews arrested were men, and the overwhelming majority of the Germans in search of them on Rosenstrasse were women.[14]

By the time Charlotte Israel arrived at Rosenstrasse "there were already about one hundred fifty women there. Through a trick I determined that my husband was [interned] there," she recalled. "I asked the guard for the potato ration cards, which Julius had. Then I received them too! On the back he had written very lightly, so that I could read it when I held it up to the light, 'I'm fine!' Other women demanded a house key, or food ration cards, to confirm that their husbands were there. The women began calling out their demands right there on the streets."[15]

Rosenstrasse was one of Berlin's oldest streets, one block of cobblestones that cut a narrow strip through the line of downtown offices and residents.[16] The streetcar passed over Rosenstrasse on its way to the famed Alexanderplatz, several blocks away. By the early twentieth century Rosenstrasse was bordered by the Jewish Scheunenviertel, the center of poor Orthodox Jews, recently immigrated from the east. Directly to the north was the main Jewish business section of town.

Between Rosenthaler and Oranienburger Strasse, the home of Berlin's oldest synagogue, stretched shop after shop of Jewish department stores, textile and fabric shops, and other retailers.

For the Jewish Community, the building at Rosenstrasse 2–4 was the center of community social services, a barracklike structure of five and one-half stories with little in the way of ornamentation, lined with evenly spaced, rectangular windows. Here the Jews clothed their destitute, fed their hungry, healed their sick. Here the relatives of the Jews deported suddenly to Buchenwald in June 1938 gathered for solace and information; here the victims of the Kristallnacht Pogrom, returning home after terrible weeks in concentration camps in late 1938, were received by the Jewish Relief Committee, clothed, given medical care, and reunited with their families.[17] The community held the public mikvah here.[18] Now on this Sabbath the narrow offices lining the long hallways were groaning under the weight of prisoners. Outside, five armed SS men in black uniforms lined the space between the arriving women and the building's only door facing the street.

As the first rumors of the arrests coursed through Berlin, Germans

Rosenstrasse 2–4, the Jewish Community's administration building, where intermarried Jews were interned under SS guard during the Final Roundup of Jews, beginning on February 27, 1943, and the site of the protest by their non-Jewish family members.

Employees, in 1934, at Rosenstrasse 2–4, a public and youth welfare administration center of the Berlin Jewish Community.

married to Jews flocked to Rosenstrasse. Arriving alone or in pairs, they found themselves among a small but growing crowd. One woman appeared with her brother, who wore an army uniform and was on leave that week. Three other soldiers joined him, and together with them he approached an SS guard. "If my brother-in-law is not released," he told the guard, "I will not return to the front." The SS man pushed him back and threatened: "If you don't leave on your own accord, you will be carried off."[19]

As the early darkness and chill of a Berlin February night descended, some women stood huddled together, miserable but seething. Some had known Rosenstrasse 2–4 over the years as one of the most important houses of the Jewish Community. Some came from old, even noble German families who viewed SS men as upstart impostors.[20] Adamantly they demanded their husbands back. Several women boldly approached the SS intruders and began to complain. Their words grew more and more angry. Who did the SS think they were? How did they come to separate them from their family members? What crimes had their husbands and children committed? After all, as racial German citizens they were entitled to rights. "If you don't let us in, we will come back and make trouble," someone said. "We will bring a battering ram and break through the door!" Before departing for the night, several women made a promise among themselves to meet at that same spot early the next day, to make a noisy public protest.[21] They knew that arrested Jews were customarily held for two days in collecting centers before being herded onto the trains from which few, if any, returned, and they had to take action fast. It was to be an unprecedented demonstration of open German resistance to Nazi persecution of Jews.

Annie Radlauer reached Rosenstrasse early Sunday morning. As she got off the train at Bahnhof Börse, she could hear a noise swelling up from the direction of Rosenstrasse, three blocks away. The closer she came, the louder it grew, until she could make it out: "Let our husbands go. We want our husbands back! Let our husbands go. We want . . ." Several women stood arm in arm in tight groups; others walked up and down in front of the house, hoping to see a husband or child show in front of a window. And again the crowd broke out in a chorus: "We want our husbands back!"[22]

Day and night, for a week, Germans married to Jews staged their protest. One witness wrote in 1945 that the crowd grew larger until the street was "crammed with people."[23] London Radio called the scene an ongoing demonstration procession, with women continuously arriving to join the protest or leaving to take care of other family or work matters. As many as six hundred or more gathered at once, and thousands had joined in by the protest's end.[24] On different occasions armed guards commanded, "Clear the streets or we'll shoot!" This sent the women scrambling into surrounding alleys and courtyards. But within minutes they began streaming out again. Again and again they were scattered by threats of gunfire, and again and again they advanced, massed together, and called for their husbands, who heard them and took hope. According to one witness, the "accusing cries of the women rose above the noise of the traffic like passionate avowals of a love strengthened by the bitterness of life."[25] One protester described her feeling on the street as one of strong solidarity. Normally people were afraid to show dissent, fearing denunciation, but in the square they knew they were among friends. A Gestapo man, impressed by the display of protest, was forced to see his unquestioning loyalty to the regime in a new light. "Your relatives are out there protesting for you," he told one Jew. "They want you to come back. This is German loyalty."[26]

By the fourth or fifth day of the protest a widening rift had developed within the RSHA, the agency responsible for the administration of the Final Solution, on how to handle the unruly crowd. A Gestapo chauffeur on duty during the Final Roundup reported to a postwar court that he had overheard conversations about the controversy. Rival centers of power (*Machtgruppen*) had issued contradictory orders to their subordinates.[27] More than forty years later this was also how Joseph Goebbels's deputy Leopold Gutterer remembered it in an interview. The SD (the intelligence arm of the party within the RSHA, which monitored civilian morale and played a key role in the administration of the Final Solution) had orders to deport the arrested Jews, Gutterer said, but "it wasn't united about whether they should overthrow the protest by force or whether they had to find another solution."[28]

Fearing the forced separation of intermarried couples would cause

Leopold Gutterer, Goebbels's top deputy at the Propaganda Ministry, was also the Third Reich's official director of mass rallies and liaison between the Propaganda Ministry and Reinhard Heydrich's RSHA. In recommending Gutterer for a promotion, Final Solution executive Heydrich wrote in 1940 that in press, radio, film, and general propaganda, Gutterer had "in every way conceivable" made appropriate administrative responses to the "wishes, impulses, complaints and irritation" of people overheard by police agents. The Reich Security Office now worked more closely with the Propaganda Ministry than did any other ministry, Heydrich enthused. The author interviewed Gutterer, mostly on tape, for five days (although he had made a career of deceiving the Germans, Gutterer was credible where his self-interest seemed to coincide with the truth).

serious social unrest, the Nazi leadership earlier had "temporarily exempted" intermarried Jews and their children from the Final Solution, over the objections of the RSHA. In the fall of 1942, however, the regime made plans to complete the Final Solution in Germany. Most of Germany's remaining Jews were in Berlin, and most had been temporarily deferred from the deportations because they were from Jewish-German families or because they worked in the armaments industry. Goebbels, the Nazi party's gauleiter, or district leader, in charge of Greater Berlin, planned a massive action at the end of 1942 that would forcibly deport intermarried Jews without children. He arranged for Hitler's bodyguard division of the SS, the SS Leibstandarte Hitler, to assist in this effort, and in advance of the action he forbade all the editors of the Swedish press in Berlin to report on it (as a neutral country Sweden was still permitted to have its journalists in Germany, while Goebbels kept his eye on them).[29]

Outwardly, debate within the RSHA hinged on how to deal with the protest, so that the Jews from Jewish-German families could still be deported. In the background was a bigger rift. The top leaders—especially Goebbels, Hitler, and to a lesser extent Himmler—were afraid of domestic unrest, especially during war. Lower-level officials generally lacked this perspective. At the RSHA, in fact, Eichmann had actually responded to Germany's plummeting military fortunes in early 1943 by expanding the categories of persons to be deported from Jewish-German families.[30] But now women had reacted to the arrests of their Jewish relatives with an around-the-clock street protest, and Goebbels was under pressure.

Since 1926 Joseph Goebbels had been the party gauleiter of Greater Berlin, where he founded his own weekly newspaper, *Der Angriff*, to rail at the Weimar government and promote National Socialism. In public speeches Goebbels's deep, booming voice proved almost equal to Hitler's in spreading the cause. Greatly impressed, Hitler in 1929 appointed the slight man with a clubfoot and glittering eyes propaganda leader of the party (replacing Heinrich Himmler), and his efforts, particularly in the year preceding the Nazi takeover of power, were decisive, as he revitalized the party for each of its election campaigns.[31] Six weeks after becoming chancellor, Hitler appointed Goebbels Reich minister for propaganda and public enlightenment. Goebbels was a master of modern propaganda techniques, becoming in effect dictator over German press and cultural life and spreading assaults against the Jews.

Joseph Goebbels's job was to generate total popular allegiance to National Socialism, a position that was strengthened during the war as the task of maintaining public morale became more critical. His position as gauleiter placed him directly in control of the fate of Berlin's Jews, but his charge over public morale lent him influence over domestic Jewish matters in general. Goebbels was particularly influential in the sensitive matter of intermarriages, sharing as he did Hitler's concern with social unrest while also enjoying the Führer's close confidence.[32] He preferred to solicit voluntary rather than regulatory compliance with Nazi racial policy by presenting images of a citizenry so hostile to Jews that the regime was actually obligated to take extreme measures. Along with public propaganda, he used street crowds to turn Germans against Jews and intermarriages.[33]

In his tireless struggles to align popular opinion with the will of dictatorship, the man who usually wore an oversize trench coat relied on deceptions, secrecy, and manipulations. Goebbels was especially adept at manipulating the images of National Socialism through the mass demonstrations and rallies. "No other party was so astutely aware of the unifying force of symbols in mass demonstrations and as an expression of solidarity."[34] Knowing the majority had little tolerance for standing out in a crowd, Goebbels used mass gatherings to control behavior. In a crowd, he said, little people feel powerful. At mammoth political rallies each person experienced "a kind of metamorphosis from a little worm into part of a big dragon."[35] And if worms joined together into a dragon, Goebbels could become the dragon master, creating unity under the swastika. He thought that "we cannot have too many demonstrations," for as a means of exhibiting and gathering mass support, demonstrations were "far and away the most emphatic way of demonstrating one's will to govern."[36]

Goebbels was a curious man, most interested in throngs. When he heard of the protests on Rosenstrasse, he might have had his chauffeur drive him the half dozen blocks from his gargantuan home at the Brandenburg Gate, across the Spree River, to the edge of the throng swelling outward from the center of Rosenstrasse. Under his organization, mass rallies and demonstrations had become a regular feature of the German state, used both to exhibit and to recruit public support of a mass, unified movement. This form of politics was so powerful the Nazis guarded it jealously. In May 1933 a law (For the Maintenance of Public Quiet and Security) banned public demonstrations without prior police permission,[37] and in December 1934, to quell further its fears of non-Nazi crowds, the dictatorship even banned all public gatherings other than "ancient, traditional . . . processions and pilgrimages."[38] Given his view that demonstrations were effective weapons in the struggles of power politics, Goebbels considered the law that banned mass public gatherings in May 1933 an important cornerstone of the Nazi takeover and consolidation of power. The crowd of women calling out for their Jewish family members was an "unagreeable scene," Goebbels wrote in his diary. "The people gathered together in large throngs and even sided with the Jews to some extent," he complained in his March 6, 1943, diary entry.[39]

In March 1943 Goebbels had his eye on the war and the fate of the Reich. The Sixth German Army had just collapsed at Stalingrad, its entire range of equipment along with 209,000 soldiers totally lost.[40] What's the difference between Germany and the sun?, a joke circulating in Berlin asked. The reply was that the sun comes up in the east, while Germany goes down there. Nevertheless, the propaganda minister had appeared to whip up enthusiasm for an even harsher war. Just nine days before the Final Roundup of Jews Goebbels had delivered his speech calling for Total War. In the cavernous Berlin Sports Palace he had repeatedly shouted out the question "Do you want Total War?" and the thunderous Yes! of the audience echoed across the Reich via the omnipresent radio, the new mass media and propaganda mechanism Germany possessed more of, per capita, than any other country. In that same speech Goebbels had also railed long against the Jews. By deporting intermarried Jews, however, the regime risked antagonizing non-Jewish Germans and injuring public morale. Although not all Germans related to Jews were their friends (many, in fact, tried to avoid their Jewish relations in order to avoid trouble for themselves), there was nevertheless a circle of Germans closely related to Jews whom the regime worried about; they would complain and perhaps spread rumors about the disappearance of their own Jewish relations.[41] The secrecy that the regime strove to maintain around the Final Solution would thus be threatened.[42]

In early 1943 the machinery of the Final Solution was operating at full capacity. In 1942, the year of massive death, 2,700,000 Jews were killed (compared with 1,100,000 for 1941 and 500,000 for 1943), while 7,978 Jews arrested in the Final Roundup had been or would be deported.[43] More than 50 percent of these were immediately gassed and burned, while the hard labor alternative for those who lived was intended only as short step preceding death.

The rescue of Jews by their German partners demonstrates the courage—and the compromises—of a resistance limited to defending its own families. Who were the Germans married to Jews, and why did they openly disobey one of history's most ruthless regimes? Why did they choose to suffer the relentless persecution, uncertainty, and heavy stigmas of intermarriage? These Germans were part of the regime's "Master Race," so-called Aryans.[44] What could have motivated them to risk even life itself, rather than divorce?

On the other hand, how are we to understand the decision of Joseph Goebbels, the Nazi party authority for Greater Berlin, to relent to unarmed street protesters and Hitler's concurrence with this decision? What Nazi concepts of power, what other incidents of opposition, and what historical circumstances help explain this release of some seventeen hundred to at most two thousand Jews?[45] Why did they survive, officially registered with the police while receiving government food rations? Jewish-German intermarriages were continuous advertisements against Nazism's basic race creed, public figures of dissent. Their children were troublesome mixtures of "Master Race" and Jew for Nazism. Why, then, were they not the first Jews sent to death, rather than the ones to survive? By war's end intermarried Jews constituted 98 percent of the surviving German Jewish population.[46]

MARRIAGE VERSUS FAMILY, MARRIAGE VERSUS REGIME

The Rosenstrasse Protest was the singular incident of mass German protest against the deportation of German Jews. It is hard to imagine an act more dangerous for German civilians than an open confrontation with the Gestapo on the Gestapo's very front doorstep. This book is the history of that brave confrontation, told through the stories of those who made it happen. It examines the protest as a climactic event in the lives of those who protested and also as part of the complex of events and circumstances that surrounded the climax of World War II. Thus the book is a history of the regime's struggle against intermarried Germans, for the Rosenstrasse Protest was just the culmination of their hard struggles. For the ten years leading up to the protest, intermarried Germans openly offended the entire spirit of the regime and on occasion disobeyed its laws. The state was ruthless. Yet these intermarried couples, on the whole, were resilient. It was the resilience of the intermarriages that led Goebbels in 1942 to describe them as "exceedingly delicate questions."[47] How could he extract them from the social and economic fabric of Germany?

In the early twentieth century intermarried Germans were individualistic and self-defining. Many of these couples were secular, living in big urban areas where norms were less restrictive, and lifestyle possibilities more varied. Even as the trend toward intermarriage reached its peak, only a tiny minority of Germans married Jews. In many cases these Germans braved the wrath of their families and other institutions to marry Jews. The history of intermarriage in Nazi Germany is not one of family triumphing over regime, but of a regime forcing Germans to choose between their birth families and those they had built as adults. Losing family and social approval was wrenching, but continued marriage often led to strong unions and identification with the Jewish side of the family. As social and institutional pressures grew, intermarried couples learned to rely on themselves and each other to an unusual extent for their sense of meaning and identity.

By the time Hitler, Goebbels, and the Gestapo took their turns at trying to get intermarried German women to abandon their Jewish husbands, they were already well versed in resisting threats and sanctions from their own families, friends, neighbors, and strangers. During the Holocaust the Gestapo immediately arrested and deported any intermarried Jews whose German spouses died or requested divorce, and intermarried Jews suffered the taunts that their partners were about to divorce them. "Your wife might well divorce you," a Gestapo agent told one. "One doesn't pair a racehorse with a workhorse."[48]

In the decades leading up to the Third Reich, Jewish assimilation in Germany had taken the form of intermarriage. In 1904, 9.3 percent of Jewish men who married, and 7.7 percent of Jewish women, married outside the Jewish faith. Between 1910 and 1913 these averages increased, respectively, to 13.5 percent and 10.92 percent, while the war years, 1914 to 1918, saw further sharp increases to 29.86 percent and 21 percent.[49] In 1933, against the grain of the new politics, this trend was still strong, as 44 percent of the German Jews who married chose non-Jews. In 1934, with the tide of Nazi propaganda and persecution rising, this number fell to 15 percent,[50] and in September 1935 the Nuremberg Laws prohibited further intermarriages altogether and nullified all marriage engagements between mixed couples. As of June 1935, some five hundred thousand people stood on the membership lists of Jewish communities in Germany; approximately thirty-five thousand of these lived in intermarriages.[51]

Up until 1941 and the ban on Jewish emigration, intermarried Jews left Germany in slightly lower percentages than German Jews in general. Two-thirds to three-fourths of intermarriages in pre-Nazi Germany consisted of Jewish men and non-Jewish women.[52] Men were more mobile than women.

Furthermore, most of the Jewish-German couples who married after Hitler took power were also German women and Jewish men.[53] As the persecution and propaganda against them spread, Jews had more reason to seek security in intermarriage. At the same time, however, the state added regulations to discourage more Germans from marrying

Jews. Most of these early regulations aimed directly at intermarried Germans levied sanctions against job opportunities, measures that affected more men than women. Beginning as early as June 1933, the civil service began to discriminate against intermarried Germans, and industries and professional associations followed the state's lead by also prohibiting intermarried Germans from either taking employment or receiving promotions. Thus some intermarried German men faced career restrictions while others—entrepreneurs or those working for independently minded private firms—could largely escape these and were more prone to stay in Germany than those who lost employment. The threat of losing a job or chance of promotion affected men more than women. Also, because Jewish men who intermarried tended to be from the middle class, they caught the brunt of state and private regulations that prohibited and expelled Jewish employees. Non-Jewish men with Jewish wives, however, were somewhat less vulnerable to this loss-of-income pressure to emigrate.

Thus, after Hitler took power, fewer German men married Jews, while it was still possible, and more German men than women divorced their Jewish spouses under the Third Reich.[54] Because the large majority of intermarried Germans were women, and because these women were part of "Jewish households"—married to men subject to every measure of the anti-Jewish persecution—the story of opposition by intermarried Germans is largely (but not only) the story of German women married to Jewish men. "If ever the song of German loyalty has been justified then it applies to the non-Jewish wives of Jewish husbands," writes Ernst Bukofzer, a Jewish lawyer who survived the Nazis because of his wife.[55]

The Nuremberg Laws, which prohibited all further intermarriages, had stopped short of nullifying existing intermarriages between Jews and Germans, in deference to the social and religious sanctity and privacy of marriage. Thus in 1939 there were still about 30,000 intermarried couples in the German Reich and its Czech protectorate area. Almost 1 in 10 Jews was married to a non-Jew.[56] At the end of December 1942 the number of intermarried Jews was still 27,744.[57] By mid-1943 intermarried Jews were virtually the only officially registered Jews still in Germany. As of September 1944, there were 13,217 registered Jews in Germany; 12,987 of these lived in intermarriages.[58] Virtually all, if not every one, of these intermarried Jews survived.[59] Thus some 98 percent of officially registered "full" German Jews who outlived Nazism did so in intermarriages (and intermarried Jews were more likely than other Jews to have escaped official registration altogether).[60]

These intermarried Jews were disturbing to Nazi ideology and power as no other Jews were. National Socialism considered inter-married Jews as so-called full Jews objects of extermination. (Full Jews, according to the Nuremberg Laws, were those with either three or four Jewish grandparents.) German law made sexual intercourse between non-Jews and Jews a punishable crime called *Rassenschande* (racial shame, indicating racial pollution), but mixed couples actually lived together openly in marriage. National Socialists claimed Jews were so inferior they should not be permitted to live among their fellow Germans. But intermarried Germans daily and publicly bore great sacrifices for their marriages, an open dissent troubling to the Nazi myth of flawless German unity. Their noncooperation threatened the social and political unity of the nation. Furthermore, and especially during the later years of the war, the German leaders strove to increase the German birthrate.[61] The most radical Nazis claimed that a German woman who had sexual intercourse even once with a Jew became infected and was no longer capable of bearing a racially pure German.[62] And rather than produce children deemed of positive value to the Reich, they gave birth to an ambiguous mixture of Master Race and Jew—the *Mischlinge*, or mongrels. Some Nazis thought the peculiar mixture of *Mischling* blood caused them to be especially threatening and politically unreliable; others argued that the precious half of their blood that represented the Master Race entitled them to live side by side with racial Germans. So the repercussions of intermarriage even reached into the state's decision-making process, disrupting the rote obedience of official Germany with many tedious debates and discussions.[63]

Under the logic of "racial purification," intermarried Jews should have been the first Jews to be isolated and expelled from Germany, and the regime set out immediately to separate them from their German relatives. Beginning as early as in June 1933, with a law requiring candidates for the civil service to prove the German identity of their marriage partners, the regime took numerous steps to encourage Germans who had married Jews to get divorces and abandon their Jewish family members.[64] A burgeoning number of laws and regulations restricted the rights and opportunities of intermarried Germans. The regime turned from mass propaganda to the social and economic pressures of career penalties, to legal restrictions and police threats and arbitrary arrest. Intermarried Germans endured great uncertainty about the fate of their loved ones, especially during the deportations. As of April 1939, intermarried female Jews without children who had been baptized as Christians were required to move into houses occupied exclusively by Jews, indicating that their fate hung in the balance. Some intermarried couples thought they might actually starve on the reduced (already meager) rations for a household with Jewish members. Perhaps these great pressures and uncertainties increased the divorce rate among intermarried couples during the first years of the Reich.[65] Some divorce was the norm, and a few intermarried couples might have gotten divorced under old divorce standards, rather than under the racial difference reasons of the new regime. But on the whole intermarried German women did not divorce.[66]

At least since 1933 the Nazis saw intermarried Jews and *Mischlinge* as their "certain victims."[67] But by 1942 Goebbels acknowledged that the problem of isolating intermarried Jews and their *Mischling* children was an "extremely delicate" matter.[68] He referred to the complexity of extracting intermarried Jews from the German political and social fabric, family by family, without ruffling popular morale. In matters of delicacy the "little doctor" fancied himself the expert, for delicate matters were often best handled by the lure or threat of propaganda —resulting in "voluntary" consent—rather than with the blunter instruments of law and force. Goebbels, like Hitler, referred to problems of public morale as "psychological problems"—problems of aligning public morale with official policies through "sophisticated" propaganda.[69] But intermarried Germans had personal, everyday experience with Jews, and most did not readily fall victim to propaganda's abstract evil depictions. It was through intermarriage that Germans had developed feelings for Jews, Himmler complained near the end of the war.[70]

RESISTANCE OF THE HEART

of Germany's military defeat in World War I are basic sources for understanding the regime's fear of noncompliance and public protest in this case. The role of simple terror to explain both the consensus the Nazis achieved and the lack of resistance they encountered has been overemphasized, as Robert Gellately has indicated in his groundbreaking work showing that the regime needed the everyday cooperation of the people in order to enforce its racial policies.[1] The arbitrary use of police force, the Gestapo, and the concentration camps were always the backdrop of the Third Reich, yet the regime sought (and received) noncoerced mass support as the best means for achieving its ambitious goals. Brutality and repression, in fact, increased Hitler's domestic popularity if they seemed to promise "peace and order."[2] A diminished reliance on coercive terror to explain Hitler's domestic control reduces the expectations that the dictatorship would use force against all types of opposition.

The Nazi party recognized that in the age of the masses no government could survive long "without the consensus, whether forced or passive, of a broad social stratum."[3] Seldom, if ever, did National Socialists challenge the idea that all power derives from the conscious consent of the racial people. In *Mein Kampf* Hitler says that popular support is the primary foundation of political power: "The first foundation for the creation of authority is always provided by popularity." With this support in hand, political leadership must then employ force, "the second foundation of all authority," to stabilize its power. Political power established through popularity and stabilized with force, however, would never be enduring until it was supported by social traditions, that final cornerstone of power. A popular authority, stabilized by police force and aligned with popular traditions, "may be regarded as unshakable," Hitler writes.[4] For the Thousand-Year Reich Hitler envisioned, neither political manipulation nor force could change social traditions quickly; one could not "suddenly take out of a briefcase the drafts of a new state constitution" and impose them by command.[5] The basic task, then, was to secure the conscious consent of the people. "The movement will have to direct its fight entirely to winning the broad masses," Hitler wrote in the mid-1920s. "No matter, therefore, from which standpoint we examine the possibility of regaining the independence of our state and nation, whether from that of the preparation of foreign policy, that of technical armament, or from that of battle itself, there remains the preliminary winning over of the great masses of our people for the idea of our national independence as the presupposition for everything."[6]

Mein Kampf did not constitute a programmatic plan for the Third

I

HITLER'S
THEORY OF POWER

The regime encouraged the social isolation of Jews, but only the German people could accomplish this. The Holocaust built on earlier phases of anti-Jewish measures achieved only with popular compliance and assistance. Genocide was not the only possible result of Nazi race ideology, but popular participation in racial identification, denunciations, and expropriations encouraged the regime to introduce further more radical anti-Jewish measures. German Jews whose non-Jewish spouses died or divorced were sent to death camps along with other Jews. German Jews the regime could not isolate socially, however, generally survived.

Intermarried Germans rescued their partners with noncompliance and protest, defenses that seem extremely weak in the face of Nazi terror. The regime did not use physical force, as part of any general policy, to control or punish intermarried Germans. Why?

Both the Nazi leadership's theory of power and its interpretation

Reich, yet Hitler's theory of power did not change. Also, the theory of power in *Mein Kampf* was that of the Nazi party as well as of Hitler. The statement introducing the party's twenty-five points (from April 1920) implied a direct correlation between mass support and political success and indicated that the continued existence of the party depended on whether it had carried out popular will. "We realized as early as 1919 that the new movement has to carry out, first, as its highest aim, the nationalization of the masses," Hitler writes.[7] In the years leading up to the Nazi takeover the party leadership remained committed to winning power legally, at the polls. Outsiders tried to provoke the party to attempt another coup d'état, and the party's SA storm troopers were eager to do so. Hitler restrained the SA. For the party leadership, campaigning for power was not only a means of gaining the levers of state power but a means of gaining the support the party knew it had to have in any case.[8]

Once in power, Hitler and the party did not alter their basic theory of power. Hitler's search for a consensus continued after the Nazi party made an alliance with the conservative elites and after that alliance was shuffled off in favor of fascism. In public speeches Hitler spoke clearly of his reliance on the people, especially as war approached in the late 1930s,[9] and he could not allow his image as Führer to deviate much from the one Germans wanted.[10] For war, Hitler (and Goebbels) thought the continuing support of the people was at least as important as the caliber of armaments.[11] Reich Minister Alfred Rosenberg, the Nazi philosopher of race whose job was to govern in the conquered eastern territories, argued by mid-1943 that Baltic peoples must be wooed with good treatment and racial status approximating that of the Germans. Goebbels, ruing the way the Wehrmacht had squandered its reception as liberator when it invaded in 1941, concluded that the regime had "hit the Russians and especially the Ukrainians too hard," adding that "if they are treated right, something can be done with them."[12] Hitler agreed with these pragmatic assessments. In mid-1943, after ten years as ruthless dictator and in the midst of barbarous warfare, he reiterated his theory that "one cannot rule by force alone." Reflecting on the problem of German rule in the conquered eastern territories, Hitler added that "force is decisive, but it is equally important to have this psychological something which the animal trainer needs to be master of his beast. They must be convinced that we are the victors."[13]

In Nazi theory, terror was a means for controlling the fringe once the majority was amenable. In practice, National Socialism benefited much more from Germans who cooperated voluntarily than from those who cooperated rather than face torture or the concentration camp. There was no general law requiring Germans to denounce Jews, yet even the dreaded secret police relied extensively on unpaid collaborators, ordinary Germans who chose to side with the police, although not coerced into doing so. The enforcement of racial policies "required the cooperation or collaboration of 'ordinary citizens.' "[14] Denunciations from the general public in fact were arguably more useful to the Gestapo than the regime's own spies.[15]

More common in achieving accommodation than death and imprisonment were pressures of economy and society, jobs and status. True, the regime maintained control not just through acts of terror but through the "atmosphere of terror" surrounding the draconian, arbitrary terror. Even friends thought they must "betray each other in order to survive."[16] The desire to be good, rather than cause trouble and stand out in the crowd was also behind this self-policing. Out of "kind neighborliness" some Germans warned friends against standing out as nonconformists. It was not necessary for the party itself to tell others to fly the swastika, subscribe to the party newspaper, or raise an arm in the submissive one-armed salute because ordinary Germans did this, " 'letting [others] in on what one had to do.' "[17]

Many Germans went well beyond what career interests or survival demanded to assist the regime. By September 1935 the regime prohibited sexual relations between Germans and Jews, and in October 1941 it prohibited all "friendly relations." In each case, however, the public had already been denouncing this behavior to the police, well in advance of the laws that prohibited them.[18] There was no law requiring the Germans to denounce Jewish-German couples for having sexual encounters, but in July 1935 the police reported "numerous denunciations, since "the public has been enlightened through the Nazi press and is now keen of hearing, keeping a watchful eye out for Jews who go around with blond girls."[19] In 1938 Reinhard Heydrich, the later executor of the Final Solution, argued successfully against establishing Jewish ghettos within Germany because "today the German population . . . force[s] the Jew to behave himself. The control of the Jew through the watchful eye of the whole population is better than having him by the thousands in a district where I cannot properly establish a control over his daily life through uniformed agents."[20] When the regime made a trial deportation of German Jews in October 1940 (more than a year before the general deportations in Germany began), Heydrich had their German neighbors studied attentively. The main point of his terse two-paragraph report on the deportation was that the surrounding populations had hardly noticed.[21] Certainly the regime was far more anti-Semitic and murderous than the Germans in general. Yet in part for truthful reasons, the regime claimed the legitimacy of truly representing the racial people. As the prestige of the Führer expanded to encompass each of his great new achievements, the regime grew confident that with such broad general support the public would also support its anti-Jewish policies or at least not oppose them.

Nazi propaganda also indicates that the regime preferred to convert Germans to its cause, using force against fringes that could be identified as criminal. Goebbels was in charge of winning the people, and force, in Hitler's language, could only "stabilize" this consensus. The regime was careful to portray anyone sent to a concentration camp as an enemy of the people; Goebbels discontinued using reports of terror in propaganda when they found "no uniform reception among the populace."[22] At his inaugural press conference as propaganda minister, Goebbels made the lofty claim that "it is not enough for people to be more or less reconciled to our regime, to be persuaded to adopt a neutral attitude towards us. . . . [The regime] will not be content with 52 percent [of the people] behind it and with terrorizing the remaining 48 percent but will see its most immediate task as being to win over that remaining 48 percent."[23] Successful propaganda turned persons into fanatics, for according to Hitler, strong beliefs made strong soldiers, and a person who believed a lie fanatically was stronger than someone who held to truth tepidly.[24]

As the regime advanced, however, it adjusted to the banalities of everyday life, gradually accepting accommodation from the vast majority rather than fanatical support from everyone.[25] Despite the Nazi slogan claiming that the "common good" took precedence over "individual good," the regime did not change the Germans into a community of selfless persons.[26] Social practices circumscribed the dictatorship's actions. Because the Germans did not fully internalize Nazi norms, the leadership was "forced to settle for external compliance."[27] Both the regime and the people discovered that they could get along if the regime met the people's basic needs, material and otherwise.[28] If the people did what it required without complaining, the regime could carry on, an indication that passivity was also a form of complicity.

Social unrest and noncompliance, however, the regime tried to avoid like defeat. Goebbels as well as Hitler thought of mass disobedience as a force so powerful it could topple a government. Goebbels wrote in 1940 that "examples show that the public attitude can throw

a government into misadventures, which in the end leads to the destruction of the state."[29] Hitler went so far as to claim that "a National
Socialist, as a means of exercising power, has a duty to disobey those
in authority who are unworthy of power"[30] (an insight unfortunately
lost on Germans of the Third Reich). Hitler worried that trade unions
could force approval of the demands of workers through repeated strikes
and wrote that any "economic concessions" to the working class would
more than repay the regime if this helped win the broad masses.[31]

Hitler's interpretation of the 1918 revolution and Germany's loss
in World War I forged his fear of mass noncompliance and protest.
His main source of anxiety was the German workers. Workers, he
thought, constituted the backbone of the home front unrest of 1918,
stabbing the German Army in the back.[32] This interpretation of revolution and unrest is key to Hitler's thoughts and actions.[33] The party's
theory of power flows naturally from it and Hitler's commitment to
"represent and promote the interests of the people" (especially the
workers and not counting the Jews).[34] Hitler was convinced that the
will to fight determined who would win the war, and his fateful decision
not to retreat in the Battle of Stalingrad was influenced by his distaste
for the damage to civilian morale that retreat would cause.[35]

Goebbels also believed Germany lost World War I because the
people lost the will to fight.[36] He feared strikes so much he preferred
not to publish reports on those in enemy territories. This was unusual,
given his often shrewd exploitation of any evidence of domestic disaf-
fection in countries at war with Germany.[37] Public protests or strikes,
by showing that opposition existed and by offering an unambiguous
way to express it, could gather momentum quickly. While still the
outsider, the Nazi party itself had benefited by causing unrest. According to Hitler, it was directly after the party had demonstrated its
power to shake the status quo by throwing the entire city of Berlin
into "extreme agitation" that the old ruling elite decided to make him
the offer to build a coalition government as Reich chancellor.[38]

Once becoming the dominant movement and symbol of power,
the Nazi party would even compromise principles to prevent social
unrest. Nazi leaders considered mass public gatherings a unique, powerful form of politics that they must monopolize and exploit fully.
German mass protest was the most effective form of arousing Hitler's
and Goebbels's fear of unrest. It is arguable that Hitler placed too much
confidence in the strength of popular unity and feared social unrest
unduly. Yet his perception of power determined the kinds of actions
he allowed to sway him. Mass protest, potentially powerful within any

government system,[39] was forceful against Hitler for reasons unique to National Socialism.

At Rosenstrasse, protest stalled the machinery of deportation, a story that appears bright against the more common pattern of German compliance. Much compliance was due to passivity or social conformity. Some cooperation was coerced. The experience of intermarried couples suggests the Germans did not fully exploit their chances for noncompliance, which might have slowed the regime's translation of race ideology into genocide. The standard of opposition set by intermarried Germans is a high one, well above that required during any ordinary time. Yet many Germans, far from standing out in opposition to the regime, were not even able to resist collaborating with the regime, at least when it coincided with their own interests. Like research on popular collaboration, the history of intermarried Germans helps correct the view that the regime extorted anything it wanted with terror.

The history of noncompliance and protest by intermarried couples provides illuminating examples of social restraints on the dictatorship. They were not cowed by either the Gestapo or the social atmosphere of terror. Their most common, persistent noncompliance was their refusal to divorce despite enormous social and police pressures. Beginning in June 1933, laws and regulations aimed specifically against these Germans prevented them from working or hobbled them on the career ladder. In 1938 the Gestapo began directly pressuring intermarried Germans to divorce with sundry threats and promises. To one Berlin Jew it seemed like a "miracle" that Germans married to Jews "withstood with utmost strength of will and resistance the temptations, insults, and threats" heaped on them by the Gestapo in its attempt to have them divorce.[40] As members of "Jewish households" German women suffered in some ways more than some Jewish women married to German men, living in "Aryan households." These German women bore administrative discriminations (like inferior housing) as well as police harassment, such as random house searches, resulting from the Star of David having to be placed on the outside doorposts of Jewish households as of March 1942.[41] German men married to Jews were expelled from the military in April 1940, and by October 1944 intermarried women worked in separate forced-labor task forces, while intermarried men were forced into hard labor for Organization Todt of the Armaments Ministry.[42]

Tragically, intermarried Germans feared their neighbors as well the police. They learned to live as outsiders, unable to celebrate Hitler and German military victories. Fear, whether of standing out in the crowd or of arbitrary Gestapo power, caused the parents and siblings of intermarried Germans to expel them from their homes. One Jew frankly admitted that when it came to harassment from neighbors and others, his non-Jewish wife had endured more than he had.[43]

Yet as long as they remained married, they could generally reckon with a common fate. Public entertainment and social opportunities for intermarried couples dwindled, with the so-called Jewish ban prohibiting Jews from concert halls, theaters, motion-picture houses, museums, exhibition halls, athletic fields, and bathhouses.[44] In a society where so much centered on marriage and family, it was problematic to exclude a Jew and continue professional and social relations with the marriage partner. A university colleague of an intermarried German wrote that because of "the particular circumstances in which you live, we will not be able to have you over anymore."[45] For the non-Jewish spouse of an excluded Jew, it was even less tenable to retain active memberships in social groups, such as clubs, than in professional associations. And in Germany of the 1930s, especially in villages and small cities, "the real social cohesion was supplied by clubs."[46]

One of the earliest, most basic steps toward the separation and deportation of German Jews was racial identification. Germans might have refused the regime's questionnaires about "racial" identity. Instead they researched their family trees and took to the regime's "Aryan Identification Cards" with alacrity. The churches, which possessed the essential records for this research, made their records freely available. Entire congregations joined together in researching their ancestries, often out of pride to be so German more than out of fear of noncompliance.[47]

Beginning in 1933, many German professional, social, and religious groups adopted the Aryan Clause of the Law for the Restoration of the Civil Service, expelling Jews, sometimes also imitating the government's lead by excluding or discriminating against intermarried Germans as well.[48] Even the massive German Faith Movement adopted the Aryan Clause and expelled Jews. On January 17, 1934, the interior minister wrote that the "very strong public interest" in eliminating Jewish influence had resulted in the wholesale appropriation of the Aryan Clause by cultural and, above all, private business organizations.[49]

This kind of "voluntary, preemptive acceptance" of the regime was prevalent.[50] Opportunism was just one of a whole range of motivations underlying popular accommodation, but Germans who actively denounced Jews or expropriated their property often acted out of self-interest. The regime tried to create and control social norms, but it was easier for it to begin controlling behavior through the co-ordination of its own goals with existing social behavior. Stereotypes identify Germans as sheep, citing unquestioning obedience as the basis for Nazi crime and aggression. Germans, however, were capable of following their own self-interest like anyone else.[51]

The dictatorship attempted to control all avenues to wealth, status, and even social survival. Jews were cut out, and the regime rewarded those who helped exclude them. Although there were no laws requiring pubs and other businesses to prohibit Jews publicly, many businesses across Germany banned Jews (in some cases because of threats of boy-cotts from Nazi party organizations).[52] Entrepreneurs in many places hung signs marking their businesses "Aryan." Following the official boycott of Jewish businesses in April 1933, German businesses proved so ready to continue boycotts that the Propaganda and Economic min-istries tried to restrain them (for economic reasons). Nevertheless they continued until the interior minister, nine months later, issued an order of restraint against them.[53]

Denouncing Jews or their German partners to the police was a common way for Germans to support and encourage Nazi racism ac-tively. The regime in fact relied more on denunciations in the enforce-ment of racial policies than in other areas. Not content with holding the levers of state power, it pushed into traditionally private spheres and attempted to rearrange social relationships fundamentally. Regu-lating race and health required the control of day-to-day life and personal habits. The number of paid police officers and agents was especially inadequate considering the enormous variety of newly crim-inalized activities in Nazi Germany. The regime could never muster enough police voyeurs, for example, to patrol the streets and bedrooms for violators of its ban on sexual relations between Germans and Jews. Racial policies could be enforced only with the assistance of unpaid snoopers and denouncers. Nearly three-fifths of the Gestapo case files in the district of Würzburg were initiated by tips from informants whose motives "ranged across the spectrum from base, selfish, personal, to lofty and 'idealistic.' "[54]

In the Frankfurt am Main region Nazi authorities relied on de-nunciations in order to draw intermarried Jews into the destruction process. Following denunciations, intermarried Jews were arrested un-der so-called protective custody orders, prosecuted as criminals, and sent to hard-labor camps, where they died, or to the death camp at Auschwitz. The goal of these arrests in early 1943 was, as an integral part of the so-called Final Solution, to "clear the area of Jews," according to a postwar German court.[55] To "clothe [their deaths] in a form that appeared to be legal," these intermarried Jews were murdered as individual lawbreakers. Even at this relatively late date, German authorities considered this appearance of legal procedure necessary, since these Jews had "relatives and friends among the *Volksgenossen*," the German people.[56] But initiating these cases depended on detecting breaches of petty regulations in the course of a Jew's everyday life, which required not just more uniformed police but the denunciations from a wider public.

The desire to eliminate competition or acquire resources was a frequent motive for denunciations, especially among the old German middle class of self-employed shopkeepers, artisans, peasant proprietors, and professionals.[57] It was not unusual for German employees of a Jew to position themselves to assume their boss's business while watching it slide to collapse. In order to promote their own cause, "sales personnel, craftsmen, and factory owners did not shy away from denouncing their competitors as 'not Aryan.' "[58] Entrepreneurs generally did not lay off others until all Jews had been laid off (again in some cases party organizations cowed them into doing this). The so-called Aryanization process depended on Germans willing to buy out Jewish businesses at a fraction of market value. Germany's largest bank, Deutsche Bank A.G., helped the regime expropriate Jewish businesses and secure economic control of conquered territories. To advance their careers, bank employees joined the party and threatened to denounce Jewish sympathizers.[59]

Discrimination against Jews and intermarried Germans in the workplace was especially threatening to men, who, more typically than women, sought careers or were family wage earners. Tragically some men faced with leaving either their Jewish wives or their jobs divorced their wives (a number claimed it was the only way they could support their children).[60] Women also were not above such behavior, as shown in the striking case of the leader of the League for the Protection of Motherhood, whose careerism led her to divorce her Jewish husband, so that nothing would "stand in the way of a brilliant future in motherhood services."[61] Considering their burdens, it is astounding that only a tiny minority of intermarried Germans got divorced (a mere 7 percent, according to one recent calculation).[62]

Denunciations reached a peak in 1941, when there was still no sign of German defeat on any horizon. Hitler seemed unassailable. The regime's unprecedented successes legitimated it in popular opinion.[63] Many Germans never thought of noncompliance as a possibility. In the case of denunciations it was not ideals but Germany's falling fortunes that curtailed voluntary support for Nazism.

The Gestapo was not a force independent of the people but was of the people and relied on the people. Civilian cooperation with the regime provided early evidence of *Selbstgleichschaltung* (voluntary integration). The Nazi takeover of power was initiated with "vigorous thrusts from the party" but "completed voluntarily and spontaneously," according to one former member of the Gestapo.[64] "Seldom had a nation so readily surrendered all its rights and liberties. . . . There were certainly many camps taken by force, but even more simply surrendered."[65] Hitler and the party were greatly encouraged. It was only the great positive response "of the masses from below that lent fresh courage to the new rulers, strengthened their own drives, and inspired them with the ultimate audacity they needed to go all out."[66]

The Nazi regime built on popular accommodation and acclaim and translated its race ideology into genocide in interaction with the German people. With the help of denunciations, social bonds between Jews and Germans were dissolved, and it became possible to enforce racial policies. Although the Nazi leadership later pursued its racism to the extreme of genocide that it did not trust the public to accept, support encouraged the regime to tighten the vise of anti-Jewish measures to the point of publicly dispossessing and expelling German Jews, the point at which the state could better hide from popular opinion. The rescue of Jews married to Germans suggests that the regime's ideology might never have developed into genocide had the German people not attained for the regime a social isolation of the Jews, the prerequisite for deportation and mass murder.

The problem of collaboration, by which the regime lived, points to the problem of dissent and resistance, which it encountered only rarely. If its secret police depended so much on collaboration, to what extent could the regime's power have been challenged by noncompliance and public protest?

The historian William Sheridan Allen writes that the regime, with all its means, could not convince German villagers to give up churchgoing, because "no matter what their Nazi leader told them, Northeimers would not stop going to church, because that was what they had always done on Sunday."[67] In fact, popular actions in Northeim could actually determine the regime's actions, even on that issue of fundamental importance anti-Semitism. The reactions to the 1938 Kristallnacht Pogrom in the town of Northeim "was so openly negative that it was the last public anti-Semitic incident in the town."[68] Thus not only could the townspeople express their dissent, but their dissent also determined the regime's course.

To maintain popular compliance, the regime made numerous concessions, for Hitler thought that "to win the masses . . . no social sacrifice is too great."[69] The dictatorship "tried to keep the morale of the people in the best possible state by concessions," writes its former Nazi armaments minister, Albert Speer. "It betrayed great concern over a loss of popularity which might develop into an insurrectionary mood."[70]

Were violence and police force always effective, there would have been no need to abridge Nazi ideals and make concessions. Flushed with their success in resisting official efforts to remove crucifixes from schools, Catholic activists asserted among themselves "that every anti-Catholic action of the state must remain unsuccessful if the Catholic people stand united together."[71] They made this pronouncement in 1936, yet the Rosenstrasse Protest, not a Catholic action, is the best illustration of its truth during the Third Reich.[72]

A number of authors have focused on Catholic history to uncover the influence of popular opinion in the Third Reich,[73] while others have investigated the working class to show that Hitler's perceptions of unrest were key to his decisions.[74] The Rosenstrasse protesters, who assembled neither as workers nor as Catholics, indicate that the threat to public morale could be exerted outside the church and the working class and that it was influential enough, once, to pressure the regime into releasing a limited number of Jews. Open, united German dissent was a (life-risking) challenge, spoiling the official image of consensus and showing that dissent was possible. Intermarried Germans showed that popular protest could still be successful after 1941–42—that is, even during the period when popular trust in a final German victory had grown thin and there was "an acceleration of violence and terror."[75]

Were the very few cases of public opposition successful only because they were rare exceptions, because they represented challenges to the regime that it could not meet with force, and because they did not oppose the regime in its entirety? If "ample evidence shows that Hitler drew back whenever he met public resistance,"[76] how are we to know where the regime would have drawn the line had there been much more such behavior?

The regime made concessions when it calculated that the popular support it could thus maintain was more valuable than the immediate implementation of its policies and goals. Nazi leaders considered the politics of mass mobilization a peculiarly National Socialist form of exercising power,[77] they used mass rallies to demonstrate and increase their party's support, they banned all other public demonstrations as a means of consolidating their power, and they gave way to mass popular protests. The regime wanted people to surrender their individual identities in exchange for an identity focused on Führer and state. With the aggregate energies of the people, the state would become something great. Each person could then in turn take pride in the state and build a new identity around it.

But there were obstacles to this scenario of the state and a collectively subservient people. In Germany there were institutions, and there were traditions. Each institution had its own self-interests—purposes and goals not always matching the interests of the regime. State power, Hitler wrote, can guarantee law and order only when laws coincide with the dominant world view and way of life.[78] The problem for Hitler was that the party's radical program required deep social changes, fundamental reinterpretations of the value of human life and society hardly achieved with police force. Basic values that had been accepted and reaffirmed over hundreds of years were now to be changed. If the Nazi state could rescript society with Nazi values, asocial behavior would become that of an enemy of the state. A closely knit community would shun asocial behavior, so that the state would ride the force of social norms. Propaganda would work more effectively here than coercion. Yet Nazi propaganda too—even during the regime's peak of popularity—worked best at emphasizing already existing norms and values and could not push society quickly, if at all, in a direction it was not already heading. Attempting to define the nation racially, the regime encountered the opposition of partners in a venerable social institution: marriage.[79]

In the view of Nazi leaders, greater ambitions demanded greater popular support, and ironically, it was their most ambitious designs that cut most deeply against popular customs, habits, and traditions. This is the heart of the matter. The fundamental Nazi ideology and in turn the prized Nazi policies cut against the grain of social traditions the Germans could not part with. The regime had to hide programs it knew the people would reject—for example, racial hygiene requiring divorce, maiming, and murder. Nazi "Euthanasia" divided families between victims and healthy Germans, causing protests that curtailed this racial hygiene program. The intimidation of dissent within a dictatorship so widely accepted and terroristic was offset by policies that affected personal lives.

The historian Ian Kershaw, however, concludes that popular pressures never hindered the overall effectiveness of the Nazis to govern.

Hitler's popularity was so great that it neutralized dissent until 1944–45, when Hitler began to look like a loser, and the escalation of terror, in reaction to the crumbling popular consensus, limited resistance to those willing to expend their lives.[80] Furthermore, some historians have asserted that protests against just one aspect of the regime actually stabilized it, by letting off steam that might have otherwise built up to a level capable of a more general challenge to the dictatorship.[81] Yet in considering the social limitations on Hitler's dictatorship, these historians have not closely considered the implications of Jewish-German intermarriage.

The noncompliance of intermarried Germans, by the time the deportations of Jews in Germany began, had caused a conflict between Nazi ideology and perceived policy options, influencing Hitler to hesitate. Hitler did not like to be publicly associated with divisive matters. Rather than make public pronouncements on intermarried Jews, he gave vague and contradictory orders on whether to include them in the deportations, from behind the scenes, and to his confidants only. Despite attempts by high party and SS officials to include intermarried Jews and *Mischlinge* in the deportations, Hitler acted to defer them temporarily from the Final Solution in 1941 and 1942.[82] Perhaps by 1942 he had begun to think that deporting intermarried Jews should wait until after the war.[83]

But true to his style, the Führer awaited the right moment for including them, the moment when he sensed that this could be done without endangering morale.[84] Thus in 1943 his signals on intermarried Jews wavered. Had their German relatives not protested, the Jews imprisoned at Rosenstrasse would have been deported in early March 1943, and Hitler would have been happy to be rid of them so soon. Yet Goebbels reported that Hitler understood his response to the "psychological" conditions of unrest that caused him to release the intermarried Jews.[85] Three months later, however, Hitler gave a very different signal to Himmler. While meeting with Himmler at Obersalzburg, the Führer agreed with Himmler that the Jewish Question would have to be resolved radically, regardless of the unrest it caused.[86] At the time of this meeting, in June 1943, Jews in intermarriages were the only group of remaining officially registered Jews in Germany. Despite Hitler's pronouncement, intermarried Germans rescued their partners from certain death, and they posed a challenge to those who stood by or actively assisted a regime as it made its way toward committing the greatest crime in history.

II

STORIES OF JEWISH-GERMAN COURTSHIP

Love won't change the history of the world, but it will do something much more important: teach us to stand up to history, to ignore its chin-out strut. I don't accept your terms, love says; sorry, you don't impress, and by the way what a silly uniform you're wearing.

—JULIAN BARNES

Hitler wanted the people to learn to collaborate, and he taught this lesson with a system of rewards and sanctions. Yet it was the regime's pressures that caused intermarried Germans to disobey. The few altruistic Germans who actually assisted Jews began their resistance in a small way, growing into their roles.[1] This course of growing to meet demands was also that of intermarried Germans. There is an old German saying that if you say "a," you must also say "b." Some individuals and institutions at first accepted or collaborated with the regime in a small way and then, perhaps reluctantly, increasingly compromised their own identities as the regime advanced, gathering up more and more support (thus making it more and more difficult to organize resistance), and by the end of the twelve Nazi years, many who had wanted to go only a small distance with the Nazis or thought they would accept Nazism to only a limited degree were actually fully complicit and fully compromised. Psychologically the course of these who started out with the regime and found no place to draw the line is a match with that of the intermarried Germans who, over time, were forced to say no to the regime again and again. "It was under the Nazis that I learned to defend myself," said Charlotte Israel. "It was during the 'Thousand-Year Reich' that I grew into that."

This history of the Rosenstrasse Protest begins more than a decade before, with the stories of those who protested and how they had come to marry Jews. These Germans had not married their partners because they were Jewish, but unlike some other Germans, they had no prejudices against Jews. That difference seemed insignificant to Germans who married Jews, but it eventually cut them off from their home families once anti-Semitism became the official language. Elsa Holzer's parents and sisters disowned her for the remainder of the war, after 1941, and cousins who had been dear friends suddenly went to embarrassing lengths to avoid her. Because of her Jewish fiancé, Wally Grodka lost her mother and her young daughter, a pain she has described as the worst blow of the Nazi period. Charlotte's mother was anti-Semitic, and her sister married a member of the SS. Both became desperate to stop Charlotte from marrying Julius, breaking off all contact with her, and Charlotte never did recover her relationship with her sister. Her brother became a party member, but she has forgiven him because he remained her friend during the Third Reich. Just as the regime relied on society for the enforcement of its racial laws, so too nonconformists like intermarried couples found support on occasion from neighbors, colleagues, or strangers.

MODEL GERMANS, "ARYAN" AND JEW

Charlotte Israel now lived in Zehlendorf, a prosperous neighborhood of West Berlin, where she had three rooms on the second floor of a small apartment building. At eighty years old she was still blond and easily delighted, in appearance a traditional German hausfrau, with proper seasonal decorations on the mantels, mottoes of folk admonitions on her walls, and padded patterned carpets on the floor. She was a charming host and storyteller, and it was easy to forget that she sometimes needed a wheelchair now. She was proud of what she did during the Third Reich and felt like an "unsung hero." Once, years after the war, she attempted to write her memoirs but completed just twenty pages, breaking off on that day when the Gestapo took her husband and she began the week of protest on Rosenstrasse. From the current German government Charlotte received a small pension as one of the "persecuted" in Nazi Germany. She remained convinced, however, that "my enemies have more." She was unable to listen to her husband Julius Israel's music because it was recorded on old 78-speed discs, and she could not afford to repair her old system. But, she admonished, "One cannot live permanently with thoughts of revenge."

Charlotte Israel was convinced that her "Aryan" good looks helped her protect her Jewish husband during the twelve Nazi years. At that time she was tall, blond, and athletic, the physical embodiment of the Nazi racial ideal. Charlotte recalled shyly that the SS had wanted her in one of its *Lebensborn* maternity centers, the program conceived to assure the strength of Germany by allowing SS men to reproduce themselves with women like Charlotte.[2] But by then Charlotte had other commitments.

Like Elsa Holzer and Wally Grodka, Charlotte illustrates how loyalties led to political action when the regime tried to interfere with personal life. These women considered marriage their own business, not that of the state. In the Germany of the 1930s women were expected to look out for husband and family, just as husbands typically took responsibility for having jobs and earning money. Charlotte, Elsa, and Wally are Germans who might not have opposed Nazism had they not married Jews. They were not especially political, yet all portrayed independence and strength.

When her father died in 1926, Charlotte was just sixteen, and Berlin was the city of the cultural avant-garde. Charlotte's sister went out almost every night into the cabarets on Friedrichstrasse or the newer pubs and dance halls along the gaudy Kurfürstendamm, but Charlotte went to sit on her father's grave. She felt herself fill with strength there, she said, and kept going back for most of a year. On her father's grave she tried, finally, to tell him everything.

Even during his lifetime Charlotte throve on his idealized memory. She remembered the day in early August 1914 when Germany declared the war that became the Great War. Her father was a translator in Belgium and never lifted a gun to his shoulder, she said proudly. On his rare visits home he told her stories from his company and taught her the truths he had learned to live by and meant to pass along. "Don't ever speak evil of a nation, religion, or group," he said. "Judge only the person. Every race has good or bad people." When he finally came home for the last time in 1918, he was sick and waning. In 1926 he died. Charlotte's mother, widowed at thirty-nine, grew listless, on many days unable to open her small hat shop in the upscale Charlottenburg section of Berlin. Pension checks from her husband's employer continued for just three months.

Charlotte had high aspirations and dreamed of opera training. But she quit school and went to work cutting and sewing men's clothes. During the First War women had entered the job market in unprecedented numbers, and in 1926, with the German economy doing relatively well again, the number of women in the job market continued to rise. Germany, with Berlin in the lead, boomed into a consumer society with a vengeance. The reduction of the working day to eight hours, the trend to have fewer children, the increase in female employment outside the home—all these factors led to more people with money and more time to spend it.

But Charlotte gave all her earnings to her mother and sat with her baby half brother in her spare time. Perhaps the memory of her father still kept her looking inward. Her mother worried that she wasn't normal since she never went out with men. It was as her boss that Charlotte first knew her husband. She met him by answering a newspaper ad for a seamstress. By the time she saw the ad it was midafternoon, and she knew that to get a job, she should appear for an interview the moment the shopkeeper opened the doors. But the Israel tailor shop was a mere twenty-minute walk away, and the day was lovely. "Sorry, the job has been pretty much promised," the short, handsome man leaning on the counter said. But Charlotte knew he was interested. "What does 'pretty much' mean?" she asked.

Even before Nazism, Charlotte's relationship to Julius was protective, for he was crippled, a victim of childhood polio who hobbled on a cane. He stood a head shorter than Charlotte. His shoulders and arms, overgrown with muscles that compensated for his lower trunk, were those of a weight lifter. With one arm grasping a doorknob, he would stretch out his other arm like a bar of steel so that his six-year-old niece, Inge, could twirl and swing from it like a gymnast. Julius's bent form, however, did not deter the artist. He loved the piano and played as only a connoisseur could.

Julius had grown up hundreds of kilometers to the east of Berlin, on the shores of the Baltic Sea in an East Prussian fishing village near Königsberg, where his father owned a small fishery. Julius's first jobs were bedding the horses and driving the team to the town market with the day's catch. Mrs. Israel bought a piano and, when Julius was six, started him with a local teacher. Six years later she sent him to Berlin to study piano and composition at Berlin's renowned Sternsches Konservatorium, and in time he played recitals with career musicians and even performed on radio, the amazing new electronic medium that reflected one's professional achievement and brought fame. By the late 1920s Julius was playing in Berlin's hotels, bars, and restaurants and was, as Charlotte recalled, "much loved, regardless of whether he played German or Jewish songs."

But Weimar Berlin spilled over with the famous and the ambitious—musicians, painters, and writers who had streamed there from all over Europe—and when Julius was turning thirty, his uncle Jitzak, a practical man who feared that a *klezmer* would never find a wife, persuaded him to learn the retail clothing business. Julius continued to perform music during the weekends and evenings. Like Charlotte, Julius was an unwilling tailor with a passion for music. Yet to Charlotte this is the way it was meant to be. "If his uncle had never advised him to learn a practical profession, I would have never met Julius," she said. "And I have never regretted meeting him, even though I went with him through the inferno of the Thousand-Year Reich. I have never regretted it."

When she met Julius, Charlotte didn't realize he was Jewish. "Israel" was the name above the shop door, but she had never learned to look for what was Jewish. "Jewishness didn't bother me in the least," she recalled. "To me, Julius was a person." Charlotte's mother, Mrs. Press, was different. Before the Nazis came to power, Mrs. Press tolerated Jews, yet beneath the surface there was a carefully maintained notion that Jews were different—different in a way that drew gossipy discussions with her own non-Jewish kind, whispered allusions to the Orthodox eastern European Jews of the Scheunenviertel, with their flowing beards and weird diets, and rumors about the assimilated secular Jews, who just made money and weaseled their way into positions of power that really belonged to "Germans."

Charlotte was eighteen, and her boss thirty. As she remembered it, she immediately took over some key chores, impressing him with her business savvy, cleaning the place from top to bottom, and throwing out old inventories. Julius Israel was an artist, not a businessman, so Charlotte looked after the money. Julius was a man, she remembered thinking, so he wasn't aware of the dirt and disorder so noticeable to her fastidious eye.

The question of whether this particular relationship would become a romantic one was in the air from the beginning. "He was impressed with my ability around the shop and my whole style," Charlotte said. "But he never trusted himself to tell me so. He didn't think I could be interested in him because he was crippled." But because she spent so much time at work, and because the only telephone Charlotte had was there, Julius soon knew all about her lonely personal life. When they did begin doing things together outside work, they preferred going to movies or quiet cafés or listening to music. For Charlotte, a seamstress whose domineering mother was a shop owner, Julius represented autonomy and upward mobility, the top of the work world as she had experienced it. He was also, in her opinion, much more conscious of German society and politics, the reasonable and informed voice. She was in love with him. "For me," she said thirty years after his death, "Julius was my gospel. Everything he said I believed." If Julius, as she claimed, was already as wise to what the Nazis and their growing power meant for him personally, then Charlotte also represented some safety to him.

At home she kept her happiness with Julius a secret, hoping to avoid sarcastic comments and interference. At first she stayed late at the office with him or went to quiet cafés. She loved to hear him play, but getting out the door without a full explanation to her mother was not easy. Once she planned with Julius to see the film *Count of Monte Cristo*. That evening, when she explained to her mother that she was leaving the house to see a movie, she didn't dare say she was meeting Julius. "That's a great idea, *Monte Cristo*," her mother replied. "I think I'll go along." Charlotte was nervous when she arrived in the company of her mother in front of the stately old movie theater on Bismarckstrasse across from the opera. But once Julius arrived she acted as if she had just happened to bump into her boss by chance and suggested to her mother that "by the way, maybe all three of them should see the film together." In 1931, when Charlotte wanted to announce her plans to marry a Jew, it was her mother, not the Nazis, she worried about. "Of course I was anti-Nazi—very much so," recalled Charlotte. "But I never foresaw what Hitler would bring." Politics bored her. She always considered family her personal domain, the center of her responsibilities. (The risks she took during the Third Reich, though, were taken not in defense of her jurisdiction as a housewife but out of a sense of devotion to Julius.)

Despite her courage in facing the Gestapo later, she still spoke of Julius to her mother as only her boss. She could tell strangers. One evening Julius played at a fine restaurant on Schlossstrasse, named for the summer castle of the high-spirited Prussian queen Sophia Charlotte. Charlotte couldn't afford the price of admission to hear Julius, so she sat outside on the street's median strip, shaded by trees and lined with benches like a spacious veranda. A couple emerged from the restaurant and came her way. As they voiced their admiration for how well he played, she couldn't resist telling them she was going to marry Julius, she recalled, pride still in her voice.

Finally she hit upon a scheme. Her mother, Charlotte said, floated loosely from one political position to another as quickly as opinions floated in and out of the room. Standing up for an unpopular opinion was not one of her strengths. Mrs. Press would do anything to avoid the embarrassment of being different. With this in mind, Charlotte calculated that the best way to muzzle an angry response was to break the engagement news at a large gathering of relatives. On her twenty-first birthday she threw a party and announced that her boss was also her future husband. "To my relief, my mother didn't object then," she said. "But later she did, when I wanted to marry. That was in 1933. We should have long since been married, but I wanted a beautiful wedding, and we had to earn the money for it first."

For Charlotte, the Nazi years arrived as unexpected as accidental death. She continued to ignore politics, even though political parties, under the guaranteed freedoms of the Weimar constitution, sprang up and proliferated. Social Democrats, bringing politics into even the most

Julius and Charlotte Israel.

private domestic spaces, passed out bars of soap with the inscription "Vote SPD." The Communists labeled the Socialist party chairman a "soap artist," and for the election of May 1928 the Communists took electioneering to the stage, with the production of a musical. They also produced a film, hoping to interest the increasing numbers of Germans who, like Charlotte, avoided politics but went to the cinema, one of the new forms of mass entertainment of which Berlin was an important world center.

The Socialist, Communist, and National Socialist parties—parties of the workers and the masses who were just coming to expect a voice in the political process—often used demonstrations as a political instrument. Before 1933 mass rallies became for National Socialism "a theatrical and aesthetically organized experience."[3] To focus the people's attention on National Socialism, Goebbels wanted to monopolize the forces of mass rallies for National Socialism. For Leopold Gutterer, Goebbels's top assistant at the Propaganda Ministry, the regime created a position for the orchestration of mass party rallies and events.

Gutterer, four years younger than Julius and eight years older than Charlotte, was already extraordinarily successful in his Nazi career by 1926. Gutterer, a country lad with strong Catholic roots in the Black Forest region, had met Goebbels while Goebbels was studying at Frankfurt am Main and simultaneously organizing publicity for the Nazi party. Gutterer described a major street demonstration in the late 1920s pitting the Nazis against one of their main rivals, the Communist party. The Communists had planned a demonstration in Gutterer's region of Hanover, and he set to work to organize an even greater demonstration of Nazi popularity, on the same day in the same square. Gutterer described the scene that day as fateful and hair-raising, a great clash of two powerful forces, which siphoned the winds from the Communist sails as workers streamed to join his party. It was a war of nerves and a display of popularity, performed as if the election outcome itself depended on it. When he ascended the platform, Gutterer bragged, he spoke into his bullhorn with a voice that, joining with the roars of minions, drowned out the Communists!

At the time Charlotte and Julius were dating Gutterer was also in love. When he came with his wife to Berlin in 1933, he moved into an apartment on Kaiserdamm, several blocks from Charlotte and Julius. But unlike Charlotte and Julius, the Gutterers, profiteers of the Third Reich, were still living together in Germany in the early 1990s.

In Berlin Gutterer organized major Nazi crowd pageantries, including huge holiday bonfires and parades (National Labor Day and Harvest Thanksgiving Day) and the Berlin Olympics. From behind his bookcase he produced a large black-and-white glossy photo of himself at the Day of the Workers Führer Rally, riding in the Führer's open limousine beside Hitler, streets lined with saluting multitudes. When President Field Marshal von Hindenburg appointed Hitler chancellor on January 30, 1933, the Communists staged further demonstrations, notably in the eastern German city of Breslau, while Hitler and Goebbels unleashed their own rally in Berlin. Goebbels, who called Hitler's appointment as chancellor "the great miracle," envisioned the march as "an unending stream of people . . . SS men, Hitler Youth, civilians, men, women, fathers, children in their arms, raise them to the Führer's window."[4]

To Charlotte, the streets full of saluting Germans came down to one thing: They hated Jews and wanted to smash everything she valued. She remembers running in the other direction whenever she encountered the frequent SA marchers. While others stopped and held out their arms in salute, Charlotte "looked for an entryway or house door to disappear into, until they were past. I never once held my arm up! I always forced myself not to. I made a vow to myself back then: 'I will never say Heil Hitler.' "

The former Gestapo man Hans Bernd Gisevius, who portrayed the Nazi takeover as a combination of force and popular "devotion, enthusiasm, not to say fanaticism," emphasized how difficult it was for any one person to resist the public supportive actions for Hitler. Even doubters were "sucked into the torrent of joy and hope" evoked by the élan of a party that promised relief, finally, from national humiliation and hardship. No one wanted to be last, so everyone rushed to be first and at the front. The SA assisted the "spontaneous *Gleichschaltung* mania" with brute force, by smartly slapping anyone who did not salute as the SA columns marched by. In such a situation even "staunch individualists" gave in and held up their hands, telling themselves that they were merely going through the form, to get by, while others were crass enough to be true believers. But as Gisevius pointed out, this did no good at all since "no amount of mental reservations detracted from the external victory of the movement."[5]

When the German Reichstag burned on February 27, 1933, Hitler convinced President von Hindenburg that it was part of a Communist revolutionary plot, and Hindenburg declared emergency decrees that abridged the rights of citizens, gave the police arbitrary powers, stifled the press, and outlawed public meetings that threatened vital state interests. Many Germans actually welcomed the demise of their rights under the Weimar constitution, rationalizing that this was necessary for the restoration of order and the destruction of the Communist threat. Hitler's popularity following this abrogation of their rights actually increased.[6]

Julius's family was stunned by the new politics and police powers, but not because they were Communists. Charlotte's father, a Socialist, had been much less patriotic than the Jewish family Charlotte was to marry into. Julius's family loved fin de siècle Germany and had honored the kaiser. In Germany the so-called Enlightenment and the triumph of the principles of the French Revolution had ripened into business, artistic, and professional opportunities for Jews hardly paralleled in all Europe. A huge portrait of President von Hindenburg hung in the family dining room of the Israel home in Charlottenburg's Kantstrasse, where they had moved from Königsberg. Pictures of relatives who had died or been decorated in Germany's service during the Great War flanked that of Hindenburg, Germany's most recent military hero. "Julius's family could be loyal to the kaiser," said Charlotte, because "they didn't have to separate Jews and Germany."

Charlotte first experienced the brunt of Nazi politics as family hostility. Her brother, Stefan, younger by three years, joined the Nazi party. Julius didn't feel welcome at Charlotte's house, and again they met mostly at his shop. Increasingly Charlotte was at home with Julius's family. Greatly exacerbating the family rift, Charlotte's older sister married an SS officer, who was utterly contemptuous of Charlotte and "her Jew." To Charlotte, her new brother-in-law was "a great big Nazi, a hundred percent Nazi, a fanatic," who always wore his uniform and never missed an opportunity to greet her with "Heil Hitler." "Have you forgotten how to speak?" he demanded when she ignored his greeting. "No, it's only that you don't understand my language," she replied.

Since the Nazis were in power, Charlotte avoided any talk of Julius with her mother. Julius, knowing the pressure Charlotte was under at home, was afraid she would leave him. Since the late nineteenth century radical German racists had demanded a ban on sexual relations between Jews and non-Jews. Heinrich Himmler regarded the mixture of German and Jewish blood as particularly dangerous.[7] In 1931 the Nazis had begun requiring their elite corps, the SS, to follow strict rules for preventing "marriages outside of race." Each applicant had to prove that he descended from racially pure "Aryans" since 1880. Julius had read *Mein Kampf*, Hitler's manifesto in which the future Führer writes that the Germans, to fulfill their destiny of world supremacy, had to remain undefiled by sexual intercourse with other races, especially the Jews. "For hours the black-haired Jew-boy, satanic joy in his eyes, waits for the unsuspecting [Aryan] girl, whom he defiles with his blood and thereby robs the nation," Hitler says. The state would have to regulate marriage to prevent racial mixing.[8]

WEIMAR BERLIN AND SMALL-TOWN AUSTRIA

Charlotte Israel never met Elsa Holzer, not before or after the war, and had it not been for the Nazis, they would have hardly had much in common. But with the Nazi takeover their decisions to marry Jewish men became a political matter, and their fates were drawn together until they joined at Rosenstrasse. Like Charlotte, Elsa did not know Rudi was Jewish when she began dating him, nor would it have mattered.

Forty years after her husband's death, Elsa Holzer's story was still about him. Their twenty-seven years together determined the longer years without him. Rudi led her not only into intermarriage in Nazi Germany but also into forty years in Communist East Germany. Elsa, a short woman in a Socialist-sparse row house flat, was convinced that love of money and possessions is treacherous yet was clearly happy for the lox and goat's cheese that were available only since unification and the West German D-mark. She grew up and spent the war years of her marriage in what became West Berlin, but in 1946 she and Rudi followed his Communist ideals from their home in what in postwar Berlin had become the American sector of the city to the East Berlin Soviet sector.

Elsa remembered Rudi in words she used for highest praise: "open-minded," "logical," "a soul." The heavy engraved plaque beside her door still bore his name—Rudolph Holzer—in baroque, old German script. "Have you ever thought of changing your name?" I wanted to know. "Neh," she answered without hesitation. "For what reason would I have changed it? He's my guardian angel. I didn't want another husband. We understood each other. I tell you, something like that you won't find again. But for my husband I would have scrambled up a tree!" With her near-ninety years, Elsa laughed, picturing this. "Well, maybe so," she said, growing serious as she realized what she had just said. "With my crooked legs I would never make it. But I would *try*." Her laughter, coarse and heavier now, came in deep groans. Hours later, as she walked me to the door, her joints stiffly resisted the stairs' steep descent. "It's impossible for me to get to the door anymore." She laughed. "But I can't live without trying! What one can do to change things for the better, that one should do." Then, while she waited with me at the bus stop, our conversation turned again to the Third Reich and "the battle," as she called it, to keep her husband from the Gestapo. "You won't believe what a person is capable of when in danger," she said. "You do something then that you will never achieve again."

Interviews with Elsa usually proceeded in swings. One minute she was passionately telling her story. The next she was shouting that her story was entirely unimportant, that she was as used up as an old treadle sewing machine and had had enough of life already. Graciously she allowed me to be there.

In 1929, when Elsa married Rudi, it was not the Nazi party but the churches that she thought she was opposing. It wasn't Nazi politics but the economy that friends saw as the reason for questioning the marriage. It was not at all the fact that Rudi's bride was non-Jewish that caused Rudi's father to complain but the fact that she had no dowry to undergird the family business. To Mr. Holzer, his son's bride was a "clothes rack" around his neck, a force that drew Rudi away from rural Austria and the family business to Germany and faraway Berlin.

Elsa's memories of life before Rudi were faint. Tales of Rudi's early life came more easily to her now than her own growing-up stories. With the help of family photographs stored in a collapsing pile in the top drawer of the living room end table, she recalled her early years and lingered over a picture displaying the occasional beach outing the family made to Berlin's Wannsee. Mother, father, and three daughters sit in polite order at the Berlin resort that several decades later was host to the infamous Wannsee Conference called by Final Solution executive Reinhard Heydrich.

Hard nose-to-the-grindstone work, though, was more characteristic of the Klose family than was pleasure. Elsa's father was of the stuff the kaiser and army might depend upon: nationalistic, obedient to superiors, and authoritarian to underlings. He treated his family like a personal fiefdom. Mrs. Klose meekly abided his tirades and tantrums, rising at five each morning to begin the household chores. When she was older, Elsa would clench her fists and imagine that in her mother's place she would yell back. Fortunately for Elsa her father was often out of town. He was one of Germany's earliest electricians and was often gone for up to three weeks at a time, on trips to bring electricity to homes and businesses around Germany.

Like millions of other schoolchildren across the kaiser's empire, she was schooled in nationalism and patriotism. Anti-Semitism, however, she says she never encountered while growing up in Berlin. When World War I came, Elsa was ten. The Klose family lived in the heart of the oldest part of Berlin, on Brunnenstrasse (near the Rosenthaler Tor and Rosenstrasse), where Elsa attended public school. The kaiser's birthday was celebrated as a holiday from classes, and particularly nice weather was known as "kaiser weather." Now in war Elsa, like other German youngsters, was caught up in the national mobilization of morale and war matériel. "We had correspondence with the sailors, at school, and we knitted caps and wool scarves for them," Elsa remembered. "We went collecting for them too, so that new submarines could be built. And Mom had to cook marmalade and bake pastries for the soldiers. Then we had to pack things together for them in school." Strong home front participation in wartime was an German tradition dating back to the early eighteenth century. Now, as under King Friedrich I, women and children proudly put on the military uniforms of their fathers, brothers, and husbands. "During the war we always wore the sailors' uniforms." Elsa continued. "Even at home. Then there were caps, ringed with bands, with the kaiser's signature. We didn't think it was unusual at all to have school students participating in the war effort as well." Often during the war they had no school classes at all, Elsa said, adding that she preferred not to go to school anyway.

By the time of her confirmation in March 1918, the mood in Berlin had turned sour. Germany, which had seemed to be on the verge of winning the war, was suddenly being pushed back. At home women unwilling to bear the privations of war any longer led angry street protests against the war and the scarcity of bread and were rebuffed by the kaiser's police. Nearly everyone had friends or relatives who were missing or killed in the war. When the war ended in November 1918, fighting continued on the streets of Berlin, as the Spartacists battled the centrist Socialists for the Communist Revolution they hoped to usher in. "There was fighting and shooting, right on the street," Elsa, the veteran of five German regimes and governments, recalled. "In my life there has always been some kind of excitement or other. When I was young, that was just great, but now I just want rest."

In 1923 Elsa was still living at home when the German hyperinflation hit. To ease the financial burden at home, Elsa took a job at the Berlin division of the American firm Kodak. She was soon one of the few women working in Kodak's management.

One night her younger sister, Ingrid, had an invitation to attend the Berlin Printers' Ball. Their father refused to allow Ingrid to go without Elsa as chaperone, and Elsa of course refused to go. She was a very private person, introspective rather than partygoing, and she insisted on staying home. "I will *not* go," Elsa remembered screaming, adding that at her home there had always been plenty of conflict and shouting. She recalled fondly and in wonder now that she came within a hair's breadth of not going. By the time Ingrid convinced her to go, Elsa was in the mood for anything but dancing with the city's printers. At the dance she thought she would do her job as chaperone sitting on the sidelines. But a well-mannered man with round glasses and a quizzical grin, who first danced with Ingrid, asked her for a dance. Dutifully she agreed to one dance, and as she recalled, the young man tried to dance too close to her. All in all it did not go well, she thought, so she was surprised when he pressed for more. Still feeling contrary about the evening, Elsa insisted to the young man that she was too short to dance well with him, that Ingrid was "lighter on her feet, and prettier too." "You're right," her suitor replied. "Ingrid dances lighter than you. But I like you better than her."

"If I hadn't gone that night, I would have never met Rudi," Elsa said, delicately now, as if far away. "Life hangs on silk threads," she said, and then repeated the words again, as if to hear their truth one more time and think about it. "One small turn, and the road ahead is totally different. And some say they have control over life. I don't believe that."

To Elsa, the Berliner, the narrow Austrian valley where Rudi grew up seemed suffocating. Rudi Holzer was from Sankt Johann, a town on the Salzach River deep in the mountains.[9] With his new car, the first in the town, Rudi's father could speed to Salzburg, forty miles away, in just over an hour and a half. To Elsa, the majestic peaks surrounding Sankt Johann were high walls, damming out the new and more progressive ways of life. The villagers were Catholics who congregated in clusters under the rule of priests and bishops, and to them Rudi's Protestant friend from the north was strange. Elsa remembered them as anti-Semitic. "Sankt Johann was an anti-Semitic nest," she declared. "In Sankt Johann they never married 'others.' Every group had its own style, and in that nest everyone knew who was Jewish and who wasn't. The Austrians are more anti-Semitic than we are here in Berlin. The church down there in Austria had more power than the emperor. Rudi had experienced anti-Semitism already as a child."

When Rudi was growing up, the entrepreneurs in his village were Jewish. Different, they had also become indispensable: the wine dealer, the department store owner, the porcelain trader, and Mr. Holzer, the local publisher. These were secular Jews, Jews who knew themselves primarily as merchants and traders. Like his neighbors, Mr. Holzer neglected Jewish holidays, had his children baptized at birth in the local cathedral, and went with his family to Catholic services. Sankt Johann had no organized Jewish community. Rudi's mother's family, although Orthodox Jewish, made no point of talking about it when young Rudi was there, and his father's four siblings all had married non-Jews. "Rudi didn't have the least clue about Judaism," Elsa remembered. "Of course he wasn't circumcised. At home nothing at all was said about being Jewish."

The Holzer family's conversion to Judaism, in fact, had been a coincidence. In the early eighteenth century a group of Czech Jews fleeing a pogrom in their Bohemian hometown had escaped south to Lower Austria. One family found shelter there with a family by the name of Holzer, and the Holzer son fell in love with the guest family's daughter. When talk turned to marriage, the bride's family required the young Holzer to convert to Judaism. Through the centuries the Holzers had held fast to their adopted religion, and Rudi's father had married the daughter of a rabbi.

Soon thereafter, however, Rudi's parents brought the family's Jewish tradition to a close. Generations after the first Holzer had turned to Judaism, Rudi's parents converted back to the religion of their chosen

Rudi Holzer (*standing*)**, at age eight, with his mother, father, and grandmother.**

home. When Mr. Holzer fell so ill that the village doctor feared for his patient's life, the local priest had paid an obligatory visit. "Sorry, Mrs. Holzer," he said, "but in my district your husband cannot be buried. Not in the Catholic cemeteries. He isn't Catholic; he's Jewish." So Mr. Holzer requested baptism, received the Catholic sacraments, and then sidestepped the entire issue of burial by a full recovery. Mrs. Holzer was then baptized as well. "She wanted to be what he was," explained Elsa. "They understood each other well."

It was professional achievement that mattered to Mr. Holzer, and he meant to steer his children clear of any possible setbacks from minority status. Rudi's father, the respectable businessman, had even been accepted into the order of Freemasons, where Jews were barred. "He wore a long cape and a great big hat—just like the old knights long ago," Mrs. Holzer had bragged to Elsa. "There had been a consensus that Mr. Holzer had to be taken in," Elsa explained, "because he wrote and printed everything there in that region."

Rudi faced high hopes. He was expected to be the family scholar, inherit the family business, and carry on the family name. At age five he was sent to an internationally known Catholic boarding school, exclusively for boys. The only women he saw were those employed to do what the men wouldn't stoop to: cleaning, laundry, cooking. The monks, his parents hoped, could give their son the Catholic education that they themselves could not give, easing his way later among his professional peers. His education was also about anti-Semitism and about how impossible—if imperative—assimilation could be. "Jew-boy, Jew-boy," his classmates called after him. Rumors got around that the skinny little Holzer kid was Jewish.

But Rudi soon went on to responsible positions in the Catholic school. He became an acolyte and a choirboy. By age twelve he knew what he wanted to become: a pedagogical monk, just like his guardians. "If I were the priest, I'd have more power in my region than a king," Rudi explained to his uncle. "The priest rules over everyone, rich and poor alike."

"In his school they kissed even the robes of the priest, and that must have really impressed him," Elsa said. "So he wanted to become a priest. But later he lost interest. He had an eye for the girls and decided he would rather marry after all."

In its eleventh year the Catholic education Rudi loved and once meant to perpetuate fell casualty to world war. A frail seventeen-year-old, he volunteered for the Austrian Army. Rudi's father and each of his uncles had also volunteered for the army—not that they believed in the German and Austrian cause but because they saw little alternative. How else were they to be accepted and prove their patriotic worth?

"Rudi was not at all loyal to the kaiser," Elsa said. "But the preacher, the doctor, and everyone in his village down there, in that little nest, said that well, a young man has to serve his fatherland! So he volunteered! After the war he joined the Communist party because he didn't want another war. He was a Bolshevist. He had got to know war first hand and had decided that communism was the only party that consistently opposed war. It is too."

After the war Rudi returned to Sankt Johann and readied himself to take over his father's business. Mr. Holzer, an ambitious but careful man, had carved out the beginnings for a respectable family press. It did not yet have the reputation of Mosse and Ullstein, the famous Jewish family presses in Berlin. But Erich Holzer's company was already publishing the weekly newspaper for the Pongau region of Austria and a monthly magazine for the fashion-conscious city of Salzburg. Rudi enrolled in printing and typesetting at the academy in nearby Bad Gastein, where he was graduated in three instead of the normal

Rudi Holzer *(third from right)*, **a volunteer at age seventeen for the Austrian Army in World War I, with his sisters and parents.**

four years. "He could read three or four lines at once," Elsa said proudly. Full of self-confidence and new notions, Rudi returned to his father after graduating and proposed major innovations for Holzer Publishing. But father and son no longer saw eye to eye, as Mr. Holzer insisted on "using the same machinery we have." So Rudi left home and country for Berlin.

His uncle Oskar was there, and Rudi determined to start over on his own. Marxist politics notwithstanding, his main goals were not to make revolution but to find a job and get married. For a skilled printer and typesetter, work was easy to find in Berlin when Rudi arrived. By 1926 there were signs that the German economy was recovering. Politically too the world seemed stable. Economic and social disruptions caused by the war had been overcome. The German and other currencies had stabilized, industrial production surpassed that of 1913, and the threats of revolutionaries had been contained and were dying down. Some of the German rancor over the Versailles Treaty, which had ended the war, had faded, in part because of changes in the method and extent of reparation payments required by the treaty. At Locarno Germany accepted key provisions of the treaty, and the next year it was admitted to the League of Nations and installed again in a place of normal economic and political relations in Europe.

Berlin now vied with Paris and Vienna for the cultural, social, and political leadership of Europe, and it was the secular, modern Berlin that interested Rudi. He did not participate in the life of the Jewish Community or in any other way intend to reveal he had been Jewish. Even before the Third Reich, both Elsa and Rudi preferred avoiding religious and political activities. In Berlin, the huge metropolis far removed from home, Rudi was free to create a new identity for himself and settle down. But as Elsa remembered, she was at first only a reluctant partner. It took months before Rudi and Elsa even addressed each other with *Du*, the personal rather than formal German word for "you." Elsa was suspicious. When one night Rudi tried to kiss her on Berlin's Unter den Linden, she refused, saying it was too dark for her to see what was happening! It wasn't Jewishness as much as marriage that Elsa was avoiding. She had a job and felt self-sufficient. She had seen her mother's marriage and knew that wasn't for her.

Rudi, however, felt alone. In his adoptive city the beer drinker was an institution, and he might have joined the boozy Berlin night crowds. Every night on every street corner there was at least one bar filled until early morning with congenial Berliners. But in Berlin the Austrian was still not a Berliner. His coworkers hounded him as "fat-headed" when he went home after work instead of drinking, but Elsa stood up for him. "That's the story of Berlin," she said. "If anyone does something different from the rest, they all laugh."

Ironically, it was what she took to be his "Jewishness" that made her think marriage with Rudi might be for her. It was his even temper that first led her to suppose he was Jewish. "You can rub Rudi the wrong way," she confided to her mother, "and he won't even slap back." This made her think Rudi was well beyond the ordinary. "At our house we were a bit eager to attack each other," she explained. "Rudi was always polite, always smiling. Once I grew loud and angry with him. My father would have slapped me, but Rudi responded calmly. 'We can talk about things. We don't need to shout,' he said. And that's why I asked him, 'Are you Jewish?' "

It was perhaps from her mother that she had learned to see Jews as especially well mannered. Elsa doesn't remember ever having discussed Jews or Judaism with her mother, but now it came up as she explained why she liked Rudi so much. Mrs. Klose agreed that Jews were nice and polite. "When I was young, I had a boss—a Jew," said her mother. "And he was also charming and not at all pushy." If there was a current of German opinion that saw Jews as nicely civilized, there was, in addition to outright hatred of Jews, a more common German sensibility that Jews had their own peculiar appearance. Elsa still shared the common German notion that Jews are swarthy and big-nosed, a picture that made it easier for the Nazis to cast them as a single "race." "Rudi," Elsa said, "didn't look Jewish at all."

When Elsa asked Rudi whether he was Jewish, the question hit him like a bullet. No one in Berlin had asked him that, and from then on he was sure he wanted to marry her. In Berlin Rudi wanted to avoid being identified as a Jew and was afraid Elsa wouldn't want anything to do with a Jew. "I didn't have anything against Jews," she said, "and in 1929 I didn't perceive it as a danger that Rudi was Jewish."

Before the Third Reich neither of Elsa's parents had anything against her marriage. Elsa's father in fact never took Rudi to be Jewish at all, and Elsa confided only in her mother. She sensed that her father was anti-Semitic. And by her own admission, she avoided confrontation if possible. Both Rudi's family and Elsa's church, however, were against the marriage. Elsa's supervisor—never dreaming Rudi might be Jewish—considered Rudi unacceptable both as an Austrian and as a Catholic. "That won't work," she warned, "because God can't bless that."

In Sankt Johann Rudi's father also opposed the marriage. Elsa was neither rich nor statuesque. "Why hang a Berlin clothes rack around your head?" Mr. Holzer wrote to his son. "Come down here. You can have the wealthy Miller daughter. She's also pretty."

Rudi, an amateur photographer, tried to make the bantam Elsa look more appealing for his parents with trick photography. Standing her on a tree stump, he snapped the picture at an angle exaggerating her height, as she looked down her nose. When Rudi wrote that he was ready to marry and settle in the German capital, his father offered him his life's work in exchange for returning. The entire family enterprise would become his, the father pleaded, and he could do with it what he wanted. Rudi was tempted. He could be his own boss and perhaps make lots of money. Wasn't this, after all, what he had wanted in the first place—before Elsa? Could he go with her?

When Rudi proposed to Elsa, he also used economic arguments and elegant images. They would have their own house in Austria and everything to go with it. Elsa would have nothing of it. "No, I'm not going along down there," she replied. Those words are out of character with the devotion she expressed for Rudi in 1989. But they expressed the same strong will with which years later she thwarted the Gestapo.

Günter Grodka, seated at right, with other members of the Socialist party's Reichsbanner, in 1932. The Reichsbanner was the uniformed, unarmed formation of the Socialists that marched at party rallies.

WORKING-CLASS UNION OF JEW AND PROTESTANT

Günter and Wally Grodka were also important witnesses of intermarried life in Nazi Germany. In the mid-1980s they were one of just several living couples who had experienced the Rosenstrasse Protest together—one as inmate, the other as protester. Although they had never had much money, the Grodkas had always had a taste for good neighborhoods and lived in a small house in a thickly settled part of Lichterfelde, a southern section of Berlin adjoining Zehlendorf, where Charlotte now lived. Günter was a plumber, short and stocky, and she was an aspiring writer from a working-class family who shortly after the war published a two-column article in a neighborhood Berlin newspaper about her experiences as an intermarried German. She also made occasional entries in a diary, a slight but rare resource that together with interviews documented the unbelievable disregard and abuse suffered by an intermarried couple at the hands of neighbors and strangers tempted to hostility by their outcast condition.

For Günter and Wally the problem of fitting in was economic as well as racial. When Hitler came to power, Wally had just moved in with Günter and his mother on Waitzstrasse in Charlottenburg, a few minutes by foot from Charlotte. Neither Günter nor Wally was employed, and their only income was the welfare check of Günter's mother. Their friendship was just a few weeks old, and despite the rising clamor of the Nazis, Wally, a Protestant from the working-class Moabit section of Berlin who painstakingly wrote poetry, saw in Günter "a ray of sunshine, a shimmer of hope." If even once it crossed her mind that her new life would bring serious political trouble, she didn't allow it to interfere. Günter, however, a Jewish member of the Socialist Reichsbanner and active in local Social Democratic politics, knew the basic Nazi ideals and might have realized that a non-Jewish partner could be advantageous.

Günter Grodka hated the Germans for Hitler, but he was not especially fond of the Jews. He derided the Germans for supporting Hitler, adding that "this or that Jew also voted for the NSDAP because they hadn't even perceived the Nazis as an enemy."[10] It is the professional (conservative) Jews that Günter as a working-class Jew faulted most for not seeing Hitler as he was. Jews most concerned with building their careers and economic security, he claimed, were the most likely to lack political interests. They felt like good Germans, and they didn't worry about Hitler's seizure of power. Like other Germans, they hoped the Nazis would revive the economy, and they were "unable to imagine what was to follow."

It was not fellow Jews but fellow Social Democrats who most hurt Günter, an active Social Democrat. Up and down the streets, in windows where he had seen Communist or Socialist flags, Nazi flags suddenly went up. Those who had once cried, "*Rotfront*," in salute to the red flag now smartly saluted the swastika (and after the war got angry at him and accused him of harassment when he reminded them of this). Within weeks his former Socialist comrades, the ones he used to play cards and drink with, began to avoid him, a Jew. "Don't be angry at me," some said to him. "We'll stay just like always, but we can't say hello to each other anymore on the streets!"

Suddenly the party's anti-Semitic campaign was an official government effort. On March 13 Joseph Goebbels established the new Ministry for Propaganda and Public Enlightenment and began filling the press and public places with anti-Semitic propaganda. Wally, a rebel by nature, was personally introduced to the new official hatred of Jews and those who stood up for them during the "Boycott Day" of April 1, 1933. Goebbels and the notoriously anti-Semitic Nazi party district leader in Nuremberg, Julius Streicher, organized this boycott of Jewish businesses, announcing on March 31, in the *Völkische Beobachter*, the Nazi party newspaper, that "world Jewry" had poisoned popular opinion and slandered the German people. President Paul von Hindenburg initially opposed the boycott, but Hitler convinced him that the people really wanted it. Goebbels, on the other hand, wanted to use the boycott to convince the civil service that the boycott sprang from a popular outcry and that the people would welcome new anti-Semitic laws.[11]

The boycott was thus supposed to appear to be a popular action. At ten on April 1 brown-shirted young SA men took up posts outside Jewish businesses throughout the Reich. The Propaganda Ministry also planned to catch and prevent boycott violators, relying on social shame and denunciations. Goebbels intended to use the press to scandalize Germans who flouted the boycott. Photographers were on hand to record this, and Goebbels also expected help in enforcing the boycott from clerks, who were expected to name customers in Jewish businesses.[12]

There were lots of Jewish businesses in Charlottenburg, a neighborhood favored by Berlin Jews, and Wally remembered that the street was brown with detachments of SA men when she left her apartment that morning.[13] The SA, with red swastika armbands, stood guard by Jewish businesses with placards that declared DON'T BUY FROM JEWS!

Some of them had cameras and took pictures of customers bold enough to walk past them into Jewish stores. The store where Wally normally shopped was not owned by a Jew, but that day she walked into one marked Jewish by the SA men standing guard at the door. "Don't you know you were with a Jew?" an angry SA man asked her when she came out. As Wally ignored his admonitions, he grew angrier, said she was a sorry excuse for a German woman, and finally threatened to take her to the local party headquarters, to have her arrested. "You'll soon find out where that will lead!" he threatened.

This official boycott of Jewish businesses was not popular among Germans generally, but the centralization of Nazi authority reached through voluntary cooperation is illustrated in this regard by the business sector. Following the April 1 boycott, private trade associations, firms, and individuals made inquiries to the German Trade Association about whether and how they should boycott Jewish merchants. By May, just weeks into the Third Reich, the mounting number of inquiries caused the trade association to refer the question of Jewish boycotts to the Propaganda Ministry. Goebbels responded that Jewish merchants should not be boycotted further because it would be too detrimental to the Nazi effort to rebuild the German economy. Not content with this restriction, the trade association wrote to the Reich Economic Ministry, which thanked the association for its "accommodating" inquiry and seconded Goebbels's opinion.[14] Hitler and the party held that Jewish influence in politics and culture was more damaging than it was in commerce,[15] and for the new regime, crushing Jewish influence in politics and public opinion was a primary concern, while confiscating Jewish property could wait. Interior Minister Wilhelm Frick, one of the small band of Nazi "old fighters," finally responded to the voluntary boycotts with an order of restraint in January 1934.[16] Frick applauded the medical and legal professional associations for their immediate efforts to eject Jews, but he wrote that the unlimited application of the Aryan Clause to business, especially in the textile industry, where Jews dominated, was counterproductive to the national economy.[17]

Unlike Charlotte and Julius Israel, Wally and Günter Grodka did not have a business or even jobs to lose, and because of their lower economic status, they were less affected by the early economic forms of Nazi discrimination against Jews. Wally's father, after four years of fighting during World War I for the German fatherland, had been killed in 1918, and her mother survived on a small widow's pension. Both Wally and Günter had quit school at age fourteen. Günter had had only occasional jobs as a laborer but in 1933 was looking for work

again. Wally had taken an internship as a salesclerk but was also without
a job. The debts piled up. Mrs. Grodka's welfare check was seven marks
and forty-five pfennig per week, hardly enough for even one person.
A meal of chicken kebab cost one mark, but even that was too much
for all but the most festive occasions; the usual meal for Günter and
Wally consisted of two thin frankfurters for twenty pfennig apiece. In
the evenings, sitting at home and dreaming of what they would do if
they had money, they would discuss current movies. Should they
sacrifice the necessary twenty-five pfennig each for a movie at the
Minerva Kino? On their budget it was an act of reckless abandon.
"Reason usually prevailed," Wally said. But when they did splurge on
a movie, they paid by skipping lunch the next day. They saved money
by walking rather than taking the bus, and it was their hunger, Wally
remembered, that made them hate the Nazis. Gazing through the
restaurant windows on the Kurfürstendamm at well-rounded, self-
satisfied Nazis in uniform, who lingered over steaming dishes, "a
terrible hatred came over us, and the wish to eat ourselves full on
something fine," Wally recalled.

The months of unpaid rent accumulated, and when they were
evicted, Günter and Wally dropped their search for work to look for
an apartment, trudging the streets day after day, from Grünewald to
Wittenbergplatz, in search of a landlord who would give an apartment
to an unemployed couple recently evicted for not paying the rent. Wally
schemed that they might interest a landlord if they claimed to have
subleasees, and when they finally found a vacancy on a good street in
the respectable Charlottenburg section of Berlin, Wally tried her ruse.
The landlord demanded to meet Wally's subleasees, so she advertised
and found four: a young man, two sisters, and an old woman. They
all moved into Niebuhrstrasse 67, carrying their furniture piece by
piece the five blocks to their new home. The next month Mrs. Grodka
died. Added to the grief over her death was the loss of her small weekly
check. But Günter had met a man at the local library who arranged
occasional work for him at a paint and lacquer business. It paid just
four marks and forty-five pfennig per week, and Wally too at last took
a job, working part-time in various odd tasks at the Hertie department
store in Wilmersdorf.

III

THE POLITICS OF RACE, SEX, AND MARRIAGE

> What use is reason in such a world?
>
> —The Wife in BERTOLT BRECHT,
> *The Jewish Wife*

A REGIME IN SEARCH OF A RACIAL PEOPLE

In September 1935, after almost two years of frequent government discussions, the Nazi dictatorship finally issued the Nuremberg Laws. Although these laws became a cornerstone of Nazi efforts to "purify the race," they represented a compromise with Nazi ideology, a compromise forced on the dictatorship by general social traditions and Jewish assimilation through intermarriage.

At first the regime had held more ambitious goals for maintaining the purity of the German people. At the outset of the Third Reich German lawmakers considered banning all marriages between Germans and several "other races," including Jews. The justice minister in Thuringia proposed a law that would prohibit marriages between "persons of too great a racial difference."[1] Officials even discussed the problem of tourism and sexual intercourse and considered prohibiting tourists as a necessary measure to protect Germans from sexual liaisons with non-Germans.

German bureaucrats from the Justice, Foreign, and Interior ministries carried on these prurient considerations for several months, before being cut short within a few short weeks by international indignation and boycotts. The conflict erupted in September 1933. The Reuters news service published a story that the Prussian justice minister, Hans Kerrl, was considering a law that would forbid marriages between Germans and "members of foreign races." Reuters had seen a copy of a memorandum from Kerrl that also revealed plans to punish Germans for relations with "niggers" and other "coloreds." Even dancing between these groups would become a punishable offense, as a "violation of racial honor." Kerrl's newly proposed law in fact elevated sexual intercourse between Germans and others members of "foreign races" to the crime of "racial treason," punishable by loss of German citizenship.[2]

Germany's plans on the "racial question" damaged German relations with Ceylon (now Sri Lanka) "more than any other incident of the postwar era," according to the German consulate in Colombo. A number of Sinhalese, including ministers, broke off "useful relationships" with the consulate. Brazil and Japan also made diplomatic protests. The Japanese launched their own "sharp protest" against being counted as "colored," while in Ceylon the parliament was considering a measure to boycott German goods, since the people already were boycotting German goods and even German persons and their parties.[3] The German Heller Company complained to the German Foreign Ministry that all its careful work to build up business relations in Ceylon and South India was being "devastated" by reports of impending German racial codes. Ironically, the proposed measures awakened a racial hatred against the Germans.[4]

Fearing that international public opinion would turn against Germany, the Foreign Ministry fired a telegram to all foreign consulates claiming the Kerrl memorandum did not mean to disparage "other races" and declaring that the German Justice Ministry was *not* preparing a law to prohibit racial intermarriages. The Indian newspaper *Commercial Gazette*, however, claimed in response that "racial arrogance in Germany" was already so high that denials of German racial laws were not to be believed. India had nothing to do with domestic German politics, the *Gazette* claimed, but any such law applied to Asian countries would be "disastrous" for Germany.[5]

"RACIAL TREASON" AND REGIME COMPROMISE

By November 1933 the German ministries were busy with damage control in the offended countries and were limiting their zealous proposals to regulate sexual relations to the most odious offenders at home: Jews married to other Germans. Here too, however, international and domestic opinion and practices constrained the regime. The foundation the regime wanted to build on was widespread social acceptance of Nazi values, and here, partly because of the efforts of the Propaganda Ministry, a cornerstone was already in place. The regime proceeded carefully, pushing its anti-Jewish practices to the limits of social acceptance and compliance. Just months into the Third Reich German officials reported that the overwhelming majority of Germans had already, "thank God, perceived the terrible danger that lay in a further mixing of German blood with Jewish elements." In the dour tones of dutiful ministers, these officials added, however, that some German girls were "allowing themselves to go out with Jews," and some of these couples had even been seen dancing! The Gestapo took some of these couples into *Schutzhaft* (protective custody).[6]

Where National Socialist ideology failed, the Nazis hoped that economic misery and social embarrassment would make divorce seem eminently reasonable. Prior to the Nuremberg Laws, the April 1933 Law for the Restoration of the Civil Service was the regime's most effective wedge for forcing a separation between Jews and other Germans. Observing the widespread effect of the law's Aryan Clause, which banned Jews from the civil service, Prussian Justice Minister Kerrl noted that it had practically the same effect as a direct ban on intermarriage. A man considering marrying a Jew would have to think twice, Kerrl said, considering the limited professional possibilities this would entail for him, to say nothing of what might happen to his sons.[7] Kerrl and other officials initially thought the regime could spare itself a systematic legal approach to these cases of intermarriage, given the Civil Service Restoration Law, and because nongovernment agencies and organizations voluntarily adapted the law's Aryan Clause, which drove Jews out of the civil service to their groups, levying the onerous social and economic pressures on Jews, including those in intermarriages, throughout society. Kerrl was right to anticipate that the Aryan Clause would wreak havoc for many Jews. Others, however, were not affected. Günter Grodka, for example, an economic outsider, had never anticipated having a profession. Although the Nazis pursued intermarried couples from all classes with equal determination, those with a solid stake in society—the middle classes and professionals—were the most affected by the Aryan Clause.

Beginning in early 1933, numerous laws as well as numerous regulations from private organizations discriminated against persons in intermarriages. The first, published on June 30, 1933, required candidates for the civil service to prove that their spouses' ancestors had been "Aryans." Civil servants who married Jews were to be dismissed.[8] In a separate exertion of financial and peer pressure on Germans married to Jews, the Reich finance minister ruled in July that the popular Nazi loans for married couples could not be extended to intermarriages.[9] The Marriage Loan Program of June 1933 awarded loans to women who left the workplace to get married and then reduced the amount of the loan principal by one-fourth for every child the woman bore. The German birthrate began rising, but only racial Germans, not *Mischlinge*, were welcome. Adoptions too, the Interior Ministry announced in December 1933, would not be recognized if the adoptive parents were intermarried.[10]

In August 1933, the Reich labor leader, Robert Ley, demanded that married administrators in the German Labor Front, the monolithic Nazi organization of workers, have German spouses.[11] This regulation, however, exempted public servants already married to Jews, and again it appeared as if the Law for the Restoration of the Civil Service might be sufficient. Interior Minister Frick pointed out to other Nazi authorities that under this law Germans married to Jews could be fired or forced into retirement, on a case-by-case basis.[12] It was left to the Reichsbahn (German railroad) authorities to take the lead in demanding that German workers married to Jews either get divorced or get out. In November 1933 the railroad administrators ruled not only that intermarried Germans were banned from employment but that any German married to a Jew already working for the Reichsbahn would also be fired.[13] A later amendment required all German public servants who entered marriage to prove the "Aryan" ancestry of their fiancées.[14] In October 1933 a federal law required editors, other than those of Jewish publications, to be of "Aryan descent." Editors were also required to have "Aryan" spouses.[15] Within weeks the law had to be amended to clarify that editors married to non-Jews could stay on the job if they had already had their jobs as of the day the "editor law" went into effect. On February 28, 1934, the army introduced its own Law for the Restoration of the Civil Service. Previously, in July 1933, it had decreed that soldiers could not marry Jews.

Especially ruinous for Germany's Jews was the medical and legal professions' readiness to adopt the Nazi racial bias as their own. Both professions consisted of Jews to a far greater extent than the population in general. Although German Jews constituted less than 1 percent of the national population, Jews made up 10 percent of the doctors and 20 percent of the lawyers. In November 1933 doctors, dentists, and dental assistants with non-German spouses were banned from receiving payment by state health insurance, a key to earning a living in these professions. In the future those who married non-Germans would have their memberships canceled.[16] Reich "Regulations for Doctors" were changed so that anyone married to a Jew, as well as Jews themselves, would not receive certification in their professions. As of July 1935, candidates for positions as judges and public attorneys also had to prove that their spouses were "Aryan."[17] Holocaust historian Raul Hilberg writes that "from the first days of the Nazi regime, members of the medical and legal professions were preoccupied with the ouster of their Jewish colleagues."[18]

As the influence of the Aryan Clause spread, high-level bureaucrats continued to spade the ground for the upcoming Nuremberg Laws. In the late summer of 1933 "important German leaders" in Nuremberg publicly heralded the imminent arrival of a law against marriage between Germans and Jews. In October 1933 Minister Kerrl's recommendation of a law forbidding racial intermarriages was being rumored.[19] More and more rumors began to circulate that within Germany intermarriages would be forcibly dissolved.[20] To the chagrin of the state, some couples reacted to the news of an impending law to prohibit intermarriages by rushing to the altar.

Side by side with the ministries, many members of the legal profession—judges, lawyers, legal scholars—also took up the weighty issue of intermarriage and divorce. Although the regime did not change German marriage laws until July 1938, lawyers and courts began to interpret the language of the existing laws in new ways, to complement the regime. Some judges made the radical claim that intermarriages could be prevented on the ground that the maintenance of the purity of German blood was a "binding legal principle."[21] One hotly contested issue was whether the law allowed a couple to divorce merely because one partner was Jewish and the other "Aryan." Some judges made unprecedented rulings that intermarried couples could be divorced merely on grounds that they represented two drastically different races. Influential legal scholars or officials weighed in with articles and arguments published in prestigious legal journals. By September 1933 one common opinion was that intermarried "Aryans" could sue for divorce on grounds that only National Socialism had schooled them in the dangers of marrying Jews and that with this new enlightenment, they needed divorce. In September 1933 Court Assessor Böhrmann, writing an article for the *Deutsche juritische Zeitung* (German legal newspaper) titled "Can Marriages between Aryans and Jews Be Dissolved?," concluded that by April 15, 1933, at the latest, everyone in Germany knew of the "race problem" and "everyone who entered intermarriage knew the consequences, both for himself and for his children."[22] Böhrmann, echoing the opinion of Reich Justice Commissioner Dr. Hans Frank,[23] thought that the rise of Nazism had alerted Germans to the dangers of intermarriage and that "Aryans" who had married Jews after April 15, 1933, should have known they were entering intermarriage but that they were entitled to divorce if they had been deceived or mistaken about the "racial" identities of their partners at the time of marriage.

In the courts the party could count on the support of a number of important sympathizers. Judges, however, were a disparate lot. Some continued to probe the judicial bases for dissolving and preventing intermarriages, while others went on to make independent judgments or ruled only partially in favor of party ideology. In March 1934, without basis in law, the state supreme court granted a divorce in an intermarriage on the ground that the Jewish "character, personality, and perspective on life" were so foreign that intermarriages were "destructive, unnatural, and repugnant."[24] But in July 1934 it refused to annul a marriage of a non-Jew who had married a Jew in 1930. The petitioner wanted a divorce on the ground that only now, thanks to the enlightenment of Nazi ideology, had he become aware of the importance of racial differences.[25] The court held that divorce could be granted only if at the time of marriage the bride or groom did not know the "racial" identity of the marriage partner.

Even after it had grasped control of the levers of state power, the Nazi party was still struggling to impose its will in the crucial areas of racial and eugenics politics. Ministries lent key support in implementing as well as in legitimating Nazi ideology. In addition to the Prussian and German justice ministers, Dr. Wilhelm Frick, a longtime Nazi who in a key position as interior minister had established an office for "racial matters" in his ministry, helped spearhead the party's efforts to implement new racial policies. When a court in Altona found that by existing law intermarriages could not be dissolved merely on the ground of racial differences,[26] Justice Minister Franz Gürtner asked the Foreign Ministry to invite him to a high-level conference on the issue of marriages between "members of different races."[27] Writing in early November 1933, Gürtner said that the issue of intermarriage required a "political decision" since the legal system alone had proved "insufficient." A law forbidding further intermarriages, he suggested, was "legally possible."[28]

Ministries and laws were not the first choice of the party that tried to shape the public perception of norms. To spread the Nazi conscience, the party also tried to display racism as if it had already become the reigning popular opinion. To prevent further intermarriages, the party orchestrated crowds to heckle and interfere at the wedding ceremonies of mixed couples. This task of controlling information and public opinion fell to the first new ministry in the state, the one for propaganda. Propaganda Minister Goebbels organized anti-Jewish crowds to shape the opinion of lawmakers and the general public. The boycott of Jewish businesses on April 1, 1933, for example, had been an effort to convince state ministries that the German people themselves were hostile to Jews and thus that the laws must also be so.[29] In October 1935 a sympathetic court ruled that public pillory of "Jewish friends" was justified because it is "the duty of every German citizen, to do everywhere what he can to push back Jewish influence in public life."[30] The regime was eager to portray racism as the natural, God-given order that laws must mirror.

In some cases the bureaucratic and judiciary defiance of laws and precedents was due to direct party influence on individual bureaucrats and judges. Local party and police officials threatened judges facing the appeals of mixed couples who had been denied marriage licenses.[31] Perhaps as a means of preparing popular opinion for the Nuremberg Laws, the party in early 1935 began pressuring marriage registrars (the German equivalent of the justice of the peace and responsible for civil marriages) to deny requests by mixed couples. The Gestapo also intervened, requesting the registrars to inform them of proposed intermarriages, so that they might "enlighten" the Germans involved.[32] A marriage registrar in Nuremberg named Häberlein denied the application of a German wishing to marry a Jew, claiming the rumored impending law to prohibit intermarriage as grounds. Häberlein's German victim appealed the decision to the German district court, and Häberlein defended himself as "acting according to state intentions."[33] In the city of Mainz the mayor had instructed the marriage registrar to tell him of any applications from mixed couples ("person of German origin" and "racial Jew"). The mayor's office would then inform the regional office of the party, which would "suggest" to the German partners that intermarriage was not in their interest. The mayor also instructed the marriage registry itself to warn these Germans that intermarriage would lead to employment hardships and difficulties for their children.[34] Especially during the summer of 1935, without lawful

authority, registrars denied wedding permits to mixed couples, sometimes citing their "National Socialist consciences" rather than the law.[35]
Even though mixed marriages had been legal for decades, individual
registrars around Germany now refused to marry mixed couples, in
the face of Gestapo pressures, rowdy street demonstrations against
intermarriages, arbitrary arrests of mixed couples, and rumors of a law
that would prohibit this. With the ruling party's position contradicting
the legal one, these bureaucrats were perhaps confused about what
orders they had to follow. Yet it is clearly futile to expect any type of
resistance at all from persons who, even given a legal basis for doing
so, were still unwilling to resist the Nazi will.

Hitler did not think new laws were sufficient to change old customs,
but he dreamed of establishing a mass movement, gathered around
Nazi values. The courts and the ministries symbolized decent, well-
established sources of authority, and getting them to act on behalf of
the new ideology was a step toward redefining Nazi norms as general
German norms. Thus bureaucrats and judges led and helped constitute
the building of a Nazi mass movement. Employees of the state, if less
reliable than those of the party, were also vested, along with the army,
with the responsibility and privilege of forging Nazi principles into
general social practices. When in general usage the word "intermarriage" continued to refer to interreligious marriages, rather than the
interracial ones that concerned the regime, the Interior Ministry in
April 1935 issued regulations: Among officials, "intermarriage" (Mischehe) was now restricted to reference to "racial" intermarriage.[36]

Like the Nazi party, state ministries and the courts encountered
social and cultural limits on their institutional powers, and the shrewder
ones proposed social and economic measures that would push intermarried Germans into "voluntarily" seeking divorce. This, however,
indicates that they were good strategists, not that they were concerned
with curtailing fascism or making it less oppressive. They recognized
that institutional mandates could not reverse norms overnight and
suggested more savvy measures that appeared milder than brutal law
and police force. An article in the Deutsche juritische Zeitung stated
that a legal prohibition of intermarriages was necessary but cautioned
against this because of social customs. Unhappily for the regime, the
author notes, compelling the divorce of intermarriages would pit the
Nazis against "religious and decent order." Legal justification could be
found for allowing Aryans to divorce Jews on racial grounds alone, the
author continues, but a preferable course would be to allow the social
"stuff of conflict," arising from the spreading racism in Germany, to
eat away at these marriages until in time divorce under existing laws

would follow. The next year, in 1934, Interior Ministry bureaucrats manufactured the kind of "stuff of conflict" especially potent for breaking up intermarriages. By issuing a decree prohibiting employees married to Jews from promotions, the ministry forced workingmen to choose between their wives and their careers.[37]

IV

COURAGE
AND INTERMARRIAGE

> What do they want actually? What do I do to them?
> I've never meddled in politics. Was I for Thälmann?
> No, I'm thoroughly bourgeois, a housewife with
> servants and so forth, and now suddenly only
> blondes can do this sort of thing. . . . What's wrong
> with the shape of my nose and the color of my hair?
>
> —The Wife in BERTOLT BRECHT,
> *The Jewish Wife*

NAZIS IN THE FAMILY

From 1933 to 1935, as new pressures on intermarried couples caused some to divorce,[1] rumors that intermarriage would soon be banned hastened some mixed couples into getting married at once. Consider Charlotte and Julius Israel, for example. After Hitler took power, as Charlotte hesitated to discuss wedding plans with her mother, Julius worried that she would abandon him. Then he began hearing rumors that it would soon become difficult or impossible for Jews to marry Germans. "What difference does Hitler make to us?" Charlotte replied to his question of whether she still wanted to marry. "We'll leave Germany if we have to. There are other countries. Where you go, I will go."

Home was the first familiar territory Charlotte would have to leave. The night after Julius told her of a possible ban on intermarriage Charlotte forced herself to face her mother. They would have to marry now, she said. Charlotte had not fully anticipated the fear and fury of her mother's response. If the state wanted to ban intermarriage, how could Charlotte dare do it now? "Unheard of!" Her mother trembled. "Incredible! You can't marry a Jew at this point!" Charlotte knew marrying Julius would bring her trouble, but she had hoped at least for the support of her family. Now, when she told her mother to "stop cursing the Jews," Mrs. Press ordered her daughter never to "show your face here again!"

"My mother was so totally spineless," Charlotte recalled bitterly. "She was a coward. She was this way today and that way tomorrow. One moment she was on my Nazi brother-in-law's side, but if she was in another moment with me, then she was again a little bit less uptight. I found it terrifying that she could be that way and didn't trust her. It's horrible if one cannot trust one's own family, if one can't even trust relatives. I was always afraid. Always. Constantly in fear."

It was only through the encouragement of her new Jewish family that Charlotte returned to her own mother. Julius's mother urged her to reconcile herself with her mother before the wedding, and for Charlotte, there was no one more authoritative than Mrs. Israel. When she left home, thinking she would never return, Charlotte knew where to turn. Like other intermarried non-Jews who spurned the status of Master Race, Charlotte found the support of family from her Jewish in-laws and learned about family solidarity there. Julius's sister had already married a non-Jew, and his parents readily accepted his engagement to Charlotte. "With Julius's family I didn't have a hint of a problem because of intermarriage," said Charlotte. "On the contrary, they praised me to the heavens. Sometimes, when I was with Julius he would introduce me proudly to his friends as 'my future wife'! And they would say, 'I've heard so much about you already, it's a pleasure to meet you.' That was because Julius's mother had told them about me.

"I lost all my non-Jewish friends." She continued. "Little by little they all shook loose. Because I had Julius! It hardly mattered. I had my Jewish family now. I got to know Jewish family life. I belonged to it now. How wonderful their togetherness was. It was only with my Jewish family that I learned how a family holds together. I belonged to it now. How different life can be when everyone holds together!

"My mother-in-law was so steadfast. She wanted to have everything just right. She was a wonderful woman. Very pious. She always spoke of God, always said, 'There's only one God, and all of us have him.' I liked her much more than my own mother." Julius himself wasn't pious, Charlotte recalled, although many of his friends were. Religion wasn't an issue for Charlotte and Julius, and they celebrated

Christian as well as Jewish holidays (Julius was especially adept at trimming the Christmas tree). The Holocaust turned Julius bitter toward religious belief. Still, Charlotte remembered Julius as a deeply spiritual person, at home especially among Jews.

Finally Charlotte agreed to talk with her mother again. She had always been close to her brother, Stefan, and asked him to persuade their mother to come to the wedding. Charlotte's sister, on the other hand, had become an enemy. Her Nazi husband even threatened to have Julius arrested on the way to the marriage license bureau. Charlotte remembers retorting that she would burn his house to the ground if Julius were arrested.

She never told Julius about her brother-in-law's threat. She wanted to protect him, she said, and when they walked the kilometer to the marriage license office, she chatted gaily, thinking for sure that Julius would notice how she stole glances over her shoulder. They arrived safely, to a very cool reception by the marriage registrar. Julius's father insisted on having the family celebration a week later. That way troublemakers appearing after the wedding would have no one to bother.

At the wedding celebration, given at the Israels', Charlotte's mother and brother were in attendance. Somehow Charlotte forgave Stefan for joining the Nazi party. He remained loyal to her during the Nazi years. After the war he too married a Jew. But the marriage didn't last, and Charlotte again sided with him and visited him. After 1933, however, she had no contact with her sister and the Nazi brother-in-law. "We suffered terribly under their harassment," she said.

After marrying a Jew, Charlotte, who had never had an interest in party and institutional politics, took one subversive step after another, as the regime confronted her day after day with a choice between divorce and noncompliance. By the time of their marriage the SA had picketed Julius Israel's tailor shop and harassed his customers until it became impossible for him to stay in business. Although it was unusual at the time for German women to run a business, Charlotte did so. She continued working with Julius as before. But she, rather than Julius, presented the public face of the business. While he worked in the back, she greeted the customers and carried on the relationship with the Office of Business Affairs. Registered in her name, their business became officially "Aryan." Their new place was really an apartment, with a room that could serve as a storefront for customers.

Charlotte's marriage was a direct assault on her brother-in-law's ambitions. Attempting to create unity around Nazi norms (rather than existing practices and legal standards), the Nazi leadership encouraged the general populace to look up to party members. Party members were required to be anti-Semitic in ways the general populace was not, and members of the elite party organs, the SS and SA, were held to even higher standards. From their position of privilege, SS men like Charlotte's brother-in-law were expected to represent ideals of racial purity. Even though it was still legal after 1935 to marry a "quarter Jew," a party member applying to do so "already can prove a lack of racial instinct that precludes a continuation in the NSDAP."[2] Even previous marriages to Jews could lead to "Jewish relations" (and sympathy for Jews) and precluded membership.[3]

In matters of conduct and lifestyle, Heinrich Himmler, who in 1929 had left his chicken farm near Munich to become the head of the SS—then merely a three-hundred-man personal bodyguard for Hitler—established a special Racial Office of the SS in December 1931.

Charlotte Israel, newly married, in 1933, in front of her tailor shop in the Charlottenburg section of Berlin.

Each applicant to the SS had to prove pure "Aryan" descent back to the year 1800; SS officers had to show pure descent back to 1750 (seven to nine generations). The Racial Office was responsible for guaranteeing that all SS marriages and later all sexual relations of SS men would not deviate from Nazi racial standards. Himmler himself handled marriage applications, particularly those in which there was some cause for question.[4] SS men wishing to marry dutifully filled out long applications, responding to questions about the racial heritages, the health and hygiene histories, and the characters of their fiancées. "Is she dependable or undependable?" "Fond of children, or not fond of children?" "Companionable or domineering?" "Thrifty or wasteful?" "Home-loving or inconstant, dressy?" "Is her family economically stable or not?" The right answers of course always indicated parsimony, cleanliness, and docility. Good Nazis transposed language for cleanliness, usually associated with hygiene, onto areas as remote as economics.[5]

In time, after the public had become accustomed to stricter standards for Nazi party members—generally those with status and privilege—these standards were applied to the general public.[6] For example, in April 1935 Nazi party members were expressly forbidden to associate with Jews, and in October 1941 this prohibition became law for the general public.

THE RUSH TO BEAT THE NUREMBERG LAWS

Like Charlotte Israel, Wally Grodka was forced to marry earlier than she might have because of rumors that intermarriage would be outlawed. Four decades later it was difficult for Wally to remember what danger she had sensed in committing to a Jew in 1934. But she believed that she had already begun to reckon that her commitment to Günter might cost her everything. "My premonition was that the worst would happen to us," she recalled, "especially following the rumors that intermarriage was about to be prohibited."

Despite the public actions and propaganda against intermarriage, Wally and Günter Grodka got engaged in February 1934, on Günter's twenty-sixth birthday. It was a normal, personal event that the new Reich invested with momentous political meaning. Günter and Wally were careful to tell only friends, but word got out. Three months later Wally Grodka was summoned to the local Nazi party headquarters on Berlin's Roscherstrasse. Her plans for marriage had become known, an officer said in a friendly way, and he felt responsible for enlightening her about the "evil Jews."

"Well, I'm not marrying a Jew, but a person," Wally replied.

"But how do you think that would work?" The officer persisted. "The Aryan partners of such marriages are expected to be dealt with harshly in the future. The racial problem must and will be addressed by all possible means. We will not hesitate to separate you and your husband by force."

Unable to influence Wally, the Gestapo summoned her mother, Mrs. Rossbach, to appear at local party headquarters in Berlin-Moabit. She was the guardian of Wally's small daughter, born out of wedlock. Now the Gestapo warned Mrs. Rossbach that maintaining contact with Wally would be considered "maintaining contact with Jews." In that case, they cautioned, the small child would be taken from her and

Wally Grodka with her daughter in 1934, just before the Gestapo forcibly separated the two because Wally insisted on marrying a Jew. The separation of mother and daughter continued after the fall of the Third Reich, an anguish Wally said was as great as any other caused by Nazism.

The wedding photograph of Wally and Günter Grodka, June 6, 1935. Rumors that Jewish-German intermarriages would soon be banned caused the Grodkas—like other couples—to marry at once, rather than wait longer, as they had planned.

"taken to the place where it can be raised according to the principles of the Führer." Presented with this choice between her daughter and granddaughter, Mrs. Rossbach cut off relations with her daughter and began to keep her grandchild away from Wally as well.

A year passed as Wally and Günter waited to marry until at least one of them had found full-time work. Then, in May 1935, a friend of Günter's, a Nazi party member named Hans Jüttner, warned him of an impending law prohibiting intermarriage. Wally and Günter began their quest for a marriage license immediately.

Like the Israels and the Grodkas, other mixed couples rushed to marry. In most of these cases the man was Jewish and the woman German.[7] Dr. Walter Grave, another example, wrote a letter to Goebbels in October 1933. Grave was wringing his hands because his (adult) daughter had married a Jew "against our will and despite our urgent warnings." News of the impending law to ban intermarriages had hastened this marriage, he said, and he urgently requested Goebbels to dissolve this particular marriage. If annulment was not possible, could Goebbels please see to it that their daughter not be allowed the normal inheritance? the horrified parents-in-law of a Jew pleaded.[8]

Intermarriage was still legal, although it was not easy to find a cooperative marriage registrar. Finally Wally and Günter found one on Rankestrasse, an elegant street near Bahnhof Zoo in the Kurfürstendamm area, and the wedding date was set for June 6. "We spent the day of the wedding in a trancelike state," Wally remembered, "knowing we had accomplished it despite all hindrances." Wally's father and cousin were witnesses at the wedding. No one in the family had any money, so the wedding meal was an extravagant portion of garden peas and fatty bacon, taken while standing up at Quick, an inelegant *Schnellimbiss stube* (snack bar). Afterward they each had a piece of mocha torte with whipped cream, and in the evening they splurged on a honeymoon visit to the movies, at the Ufapalast near Bahnhof Zoo, just blocks away from their apartment. The next month, on July 17, 1935, the Interior Ministry ordered all requests for intermarriage (between "full Jews" and "full Aryans") to be deferred, in anticipation of a general law on the matter.[9]

V

MISCHLINGE: A "PARTICULARLY UNPLEASANT OCCURRENCE"

Ambiguities about the racial status of *Mischlinge* caused an "unbelievable amount of discussion about *Mischlinge* and Jews in mixed marriages."[1] The clear Nazi racial ideology, when viewed alongside real-life Jewish-German families, appeared simple and impossible to apply. Himmler's staff, exasperated by its attempt to fit these persons into its racial schema, characterized *Mischlinge* as a "particularly unpleasant occurrence."[2] Children of intermarriages like Werner Goldberg were caught between Germans and Jews as anomalies not belonging to either group.

At first Werner Goldberg had no fear of Hitler because he had no idea his father was Jewish. Like his brother, Werner had been baptized at birth in the Grünewald Lutheran Church, at the request of their father. Mr. Goldberg had grown up in Königsberg with Jewish parents, as a member of a Jewish community. But his first adult decision had been to have himself baptized in the local Lutheran church.

Baptism did not necessarily mean that Mr. Goldberg wanted to be a Christian. His was a bid for mainstream assimilation. In 1906, at the age of twenty-five, he left Königsberg for Berlin to pursue a profession and the good life. He began as a bank clerk, and by the end of the war in 1918 he had worked his way up to the position of director and accountant in an insurance agency and to residence in the exclusive Grünewald section of Berlin, west of Charlottenburg. Financially secure, he had finally been married—to a Protestant. For his children, Werner and Martin, born in 1919 and 1920, Mr. Goldberg hoped for achievement and respect within German society. The Jewish identity would be shuffled off, the minority status forgotten. In the Germany of Weimar, it was a reasonable hope, as his sons soon began to prove.

When Hitler came to power, Werner's world was an undifferentiated mixture of Jews and Christians, non-Jews and "non-Aryans." At school in his upscale Berlin neighborhood of Schmargendorf, there were other assimilated Jews and so-called half Jews (persons with one Jewish and one German parent) like him—about 50 percent of his grade school class, Werner claimed in retrospect. That figure sounds high, but it represents the equality among the religious groups in his class that Werner experienced. Every week he attended Sunday school.

The holidays they celebrated together were Christian. One of Werner's classmates, Karl Wolf, was Werner's inseparable friend. Karl, known because of his fiery red hair as the fireman, lived in the Goldbergs' building, and as children he and Werner were often guests in each other's homes. They attended the same church and took the same Protestant religious instructions in school. At ten they both joined the Pfadfinderbund, the German Boy Scouts, which became their second family.

After Hitler took power, Mr. Goldberg still delayed telling fourteen-year-old Werner about the new political meaning of his Jewish background. This was not because he had no reason to, for Mr. Goldberg soon lost his job, as an indirect victim of the Law for the Restoration of the Civil Service of April 1933, which expelled Jews from the civil service. Commenting on why his father lost his job, Werner said that "the organizations, chambers, and associations adopted the so-called Aryan Clause, and the norms of the dictatorship were now perpetrated by the private initiative of these organizations."

With its *Gleichschaltung* program of bringing all government and other groups in line under Nazi party control, the dictatorship set out to bring its politics into the everyday lives of every German and to force each institution and social group to adjust to Nazi ideals. Nazis began popping up as the directors of businesses, trade and professional

Werner Goldberg's parents on their wedding day in 1918. Albert Goldberg was baptized as a Protestant at age nineteen, in 1900, and married a Protestant. Werner did not know his father was from a Jewish family until Hitler took power.

Werner Goldberg (left) and his brother, Günther, in 1930. Werner was eleven, and Günther ten.

associations, ministerial bureaucracies, and private clubs, to promote the new Nazi styles and norms. With the arrival of the Nazis in power, there also arrived in Werner and Karl's school a new principal, adamantly loyal to National Socialism. His immediate career ambition was to make his school *Judenfrei* as soon as possible, and he set out to identify publicly and disfavor the Jewish students. When he ordered, "All non-Aryans, stand up!" Werner watched as some of his classmates rose. Werner remained seated. "Goldberg," Werner remembered the principal's asking him, "are you Aryan?" Werner said he didn't know. "Then I'll tell you: You are not Aryan. So get on your feet." At home that evening Mr. Goldberg explained to his son for the first time what he had hoped would not be necessary: He had been raised in a Jewish home.

Werner's response to being pushed out was to continue to push his way in. Just as they had joined the Boy Scouts together, Karl and Werner now, when they turned fourteen, joined the Hitler Youth. At his age, belonging to the Hitler Youth pained Werner less than not belonging at all. In Socialist Weimar Germany, the German Boy Scouts had been an international organization, attending Boy Scout assemblies in Holland and other European countries. The friendships that German boys formed at these so-called jamborees from around Europe, however, made a very poor basis for Nazi racial propaganda. The motto of the nationalistic Hitler Youth was Führer, command—we follow! To describe his ideal followers, the Führer turned to images of metal and animals: The new German youth was to be "without intellectual training . . . swift as the greyhound, tough as leather, and hard as Krupp steel."[3] The membership regulations of this male branch of the Nazi youth movement excluded not only Jews but youths from other nations as well.

Although *Mischlinge* as well as Jews and Germans married to Jews were precluded from the Nazi party, they were initially allowed into such related groups as the Hitler Youth. The unhappy result of this, Himmler later fretted, was that every "half Jew" had tried to join a party-affiliated organization in an attempt to appear politically dependable or to hide the fact of Jewish heritage. In response the party chancellery contacted the leaders of all party-related groups and clubs and requested them to expel the children of intermarried couples, as well as all Germans married to Jews.[4] Werner was told to leave the Hitler Youth and felt as if he had nowhere to turn.

By 1934 the new principal had forced some Jews out of the school. Still, for Werner, there were some teachers whom he deeply respected and who he secretly knew would never be for Hitler. One of these was

Mr. Schenk, the science teacher. Then one day Schenk invited the bicycle enthusiasts of the class to his home. They were to make an excursion with him outside Berlin that weekend, starting at the Schenk residence in Berlin-Steglitz. Werner recalled his dashed expectations that day. "We all stood with our bicycles, ready to roll. And suddenly, a window at the top of the house opened, a flagpole was shoved through the window, and an enormous flag with a swastika unfurled. And I stood there, fully perplexed to find that something like this was possible, from someone I had never suspected of being a Nazi, someone I admired so highly. I began to cry and got on my bike and went home. That was a big disappointment. Now I suspected that inside everyone a Nazi was hiding."

The fourteen-year-old Werner, however, could still find in the Boy Scouts the friendships and social acceptance that the regime was wresting from him. Then without warning the new leader of his Boy Scout group called Werner in. His voice was not harsh, and he laid his arm gently on Werner's shoulder as he dumped the hard truth on the lad. "I know, Werner, that you are very attached to this club and have done a lot for it," he said. "But you have to understand that for us you are a burden. The Nazis don't want to have any *Mischlinge*. So I have to ask you to leave. Do us a favor, and quit."

At a loss Werner decided to talk with his fellow Boy Scouts. "And it was very interesting," he said, "that suddenly I could not find even one person in this entire group who stood up for me and said, 'No, we won't allow you to be pushed out. In that case we'll all leave.' No. I was fully isolated. Alone. I had the feeling that I could not do a thing. I did not of course foresee what would develop from this anti-Semitism. The beginnings of the persecution were minuscule, but this was the beginning." Werner remembered relying on his father's advice as he decided to leave the Boy Scouts. "If anyone doesn't want you, don't force yourself on them," his father said.

But where was he wanted? By introducing the practice of wearing uniforms to class, Werner's new principal had quickly cut off Jews and *Mischlinge* from the others. In Nazi Germany the prevalence of uniforms, like massive street demonstrations, gave the impression that the majority, or at least the leaders, were on the Nazi bandwagon. At Werner's school "Aryan" boys received Hitler Youth uniforms, and "Aryan" girls received uniforms for joining the League of German Girls. Those without uniforms no longer felt accepted. Even his old friend Karl Wolf, who proudly wore his uniform, was avoiding Werner now. Werner and Karl had taken their steps toward adulthood together, but the camaraderie was over.

Werner decided to leave school. "I wanted to study medicine, but that was no longer possible," he recalled. Mr. Goldberg saw what his son was up against and insisted only that he finish the school year. He even went to Werner's teacher to get his consent.

After leaving school in April 1935, Werner apprenticed in one of the many clothing firms on Königstrasse, near Alexanderplatz, directly across from the Red Rathaus, and around the corner from Rosenstrasse. "My firm was called Schneller und Schmeider, a leather clothing manufacturer, coowned by a Jew and a German," Werner said. "Finally, in Nazi Germany, I would get to know Berlin's Jews." Many of Werner's colleagues were Jews or *Mischlinge*. His boss, Mr. Grohm, was a strictly observant Jew who kept kosher and religiously emptied his pockets of money before his regular visits to the synagogue. It was Mr. Grohm's opinion that the Orthodox Polish Jews who had poured into Berlin by the tens of thousands following World War I were the real cause of the harsh Nazi anti-Semitism. "Throw him down the stairs," he said to Werner about an Orthodox Jew from Berlin's Scheunenviertel, who sold cigarettes on the sidewalk beside the Grohm clothing business. "These Jews are the ones who have made anti-Semitism here so bad."

Werner now confronted the Jewish identity his father had allowed him to avoid. Like many other Germans who would have ignored the Jewish identity of their ancestors, Werner was to become inextricably linked with Jewish associations. During the Nazi period, however, the Jewish Community was often closed to either *Mischlinge* or Jews who were not members. After being fired from his insurance company for being Jewish, Mr. Goldberg turned to Heinrich Stahl, the chairman of the Berlin Jewish Community. "Herr Goldberg," Mr. Stahl said, "you don't belong to the Jewish Community, so I can't do anything for you." Mr. Goldberg eventually got work with a Swiss company, but the visit with Stahl "really shocked my father," Werner recalled. "But you have to understand that Heinrich Stahl probably already had more members than he could take care of."

Official prejudice encouraged anti-Semitism among latent bigots, even when this brutally discriminated against family members. In these cases of social discrimination, *Mischlinge* were often treated as badly as Jews themselves. Werner Goldberg's uncle was an opportunist, who joined the Nazi party and now refused to be seen with the Goldberg family, avoiding even his sister, Werner's mother, the "Aryan."

Erika Lewine, a *Mischling* from the working class in Berlin-

Friedrichshain, had known anti-Semitism in Germany even before Hitler. Her mother's parents, the Krügers, had been enraged when in 1922 their daughter married a Jew. Neither they nor their other four daughters attended the wedding. The problem was not social, for like the Lewines, the Krügers were from the working class. Mr. Lewine worked at the local cleaner, and his bride, the former Ms. Krüger, was unemployed and brought an illegitimate daughter, Mathilde, into the Lewine household. Erika's aunts soon made a show of preferring Mathilde, the "Aryan," over the other Lewine children. Erika remembered that at her aunt's house Mathilde was seated at the table and fed pastries, while Erika, because she "came from Jews," was allowed only to look on from a low stool.

Erika's mother, however, drew closer to her husband's family and his religion. She was a baptized and confirmed member of a Protestant church, but now she registered each of her children at birth as members of the Jewish Community. Even her oldest daughter, Mathilde, who had a German father, was named Lewine and enrolled in the Jewish Community. Every week the entire family went to the Reform synagogue on Ryckestrasse. True to form, Mrs. Lewine, a convert, was a more faithful observer of the Jewish tradition than many born into it, including her husband. She was "more pious than all the rest of us put together," her children used to tell her.

Tensions were high before Hitler, but the Nazi leader's assumption of power in 1933 was the wedge that drove Erika's mother and her aunts apart forever. In an act of defiance Mrs. Lewine actually converted to Judaism in early 1933 and remarried her husband, Erika's father, in a Jewish ceremony. Mrs. Lewine's sister Lena, however, declared her intermarried sister dead, without survivors. Two of Lena's daughters were in love with SS men, and the strict rules of marriage for the SS prohibited relations with Jews.

After 1933 only one of Erika's aunts, Greta, still visited the Lewine family. But her husband, Alfred, a former earnest Communist whom Erika described as a "very mean Nazi who slouched around in a uniform," put an end to that. "Alfred would have a fit if he knew I was visiting you," Greta explained to Erika's mother, explaining why she came and went furtively. But Mrs. Lewine would have none of it. "Take your things and go," she told her sister. "We aren't criminals, and anyone who comes to visit us must come openly or not at all."

Like Charlotte Israel, Erika Lewine discovered warmth and solidarity among her Jewish side of the family, in contrast with brutal treatment from the German side. "All the aunts forgot about us," Erika, the Mischling, recalled. "I never saw the relatives on my mother's side again, since Hitler. But with the Jewish family—with those cousins—there we were always together, like one big family. There we held together tight. The Jews were much more capable of accepting others different from them."

During the Weimar years of unemployment and high inflation, the Lewines had had barely enough to eat; that didn't change now. They could not afford to buy a newspaper. They didn't have a car and often couldn't even afford public transportation. Their time was more expendable than money, and when they visited Erika's aunt in the neighboring Berlin district of Moabit, they walked the mile there and back. But they rarely ventured into the wealthy areas of the Charlottenburg district. The distance Erika felt between herself and Berlin's well-to-do Jews was perhaps wider than that she felt between herself and her non-Jewish working-class neighbors. That difference still sounds clearly in her voice, as she emphasizes that she could never have known Hans-Oskar Baron Löwenstein de Witt, a Jew from a wealthy family from Berlin's fancy Kurfürstendamm, who later shared her fate on Rosenstrasse.

Hans-Oskar Löwenstein de Witt, a descendant on his maternal side of the brilliant constitutionalist de Witt brothers who governed the seventeenth-century Dutch oligarchy, was also the descendant of wealthy Jewish entrepreneurs, decorated for their service in war for Germany. After nearly two decades of living in Israel Löwenstein returned to his hometown Berlin, where his illustrious family tree was traced in a chronology of photographs, portraits, and medallions arching across the living room wall. Another room was half filled with the family's silver dinner sets and jewelry, including antique rings engraved with the family seal, an unused collection draped in protective plastic still awaiting an heir from Hans Löwenstein.

During the 1920s Hans Löwenstein's liberal parents had given him both Jewish and Protestant religious instructions, thinking that he would later choose one or the other as his own. As in Werner Goldberg's case, a zealous Nazi school official convinced Hans-Oskar to leave his public school because he was a *Mischling*. Unable to find another public school, his parents turned to the Jewish Community. The community agreed to enroll him in its school—on condition that he enroll as a member there. It was a fateful choice, for at Nuremberg in 1935 the German state decided to define *Mischlinge* who belonged to the Jewish Community as *Geltungsjuden*. This subjected them to treatment as Jews, in contrast with *Mischlinge* baptized as Christians, like Werner, who, like other Germans, were (initially) allowed to keep their citizenship rights.

VI

SOCIETY VERSUS LAW: GERMAN-JEWISH FAMILIES AND SOCIAL RESTRAINTS ON HITLER

POLITICAL RALLIES, POPULAR OPINION, AND LEGAL MEASURES

Although Hitler hated bureaucrats and traditional government bu-reaucracies—the Interior, the Justice, and other ministries—he could not do without them. To promulgate the Nuremberg Laws of 1935, he relied on them to lend him the trappings of legitimacy and respectable government and to moderate party radicals. On matters of race, Hitler was as radical as anyone. But at Nuremberg the dictatorship's concern with maintaining social quiescence enabled the Interior Ministry to moderate the party's position. Hitler's subsequent responses to the intermarried and *Mischlinge* questions shows he was limited not by these or any other laws but only by concern for his popularity.

The Nuremberg Laws and their public dissemination combined the wiles of propaganda with the sober efforts of lawmakers and their respected institutions. Respectability was important to the party in its alliance with the conservative elite. Most Nazis were upstarts (in a country with its nobility still intact), and they also intended to deviate drastically from the norms. At stake was the fate of hundreds of thousands of Jews who had become embedded in German economic and social life. Some of them had dominated German cultural, political, scientific, and economic development. Would Germans permit these Jews to be deprived of citizenship, then plundered and shoved out of Germany? Hitler solicited the help of lawmakers to make this tragedy look respectable, and together with Goebbels, he also attempted to control directly popular opinion about German Jews.

Hitler's theory that power must build on popular support coincided well with his charismatic authority and his conviction that Germany had lost World War I because the German people had undercut the German Army. His establishment of the Propaganda Ministry at the outset of the Third Reich was the institutional embodiment of this theory. Goebbels, who thought Germans in general had an unfortunate tendency toward a bookkeeping style of bureaucracy rather than leadership, led with mass rallies.[1] In the months preceding the Nuremberg Laws, Goebbels orchestrated mass public outbursts against Jews, hoping to gain support for anti-Semitism by making it seem already the norm. He wanted public demonstrations reserved for the Nazi party alone, not just for "enlightening" the public but as a means for strategic displays of social unrest as well. The Nazi party had a pattern of taking power by force after claiming that uncontrolled social unrest warranted its abrogating existing democratic structures.[2] Goebbels, who had an uncanny habit of standing the truth on its head, typically accused Germany's Jews of causing social disturbances.[3] Through his office's rowdy street actions he hoped to convince established ministries that Germans would welcome tough anti-Jewish laws.[4] In the late summer of 1935 Nazi leaders cited these incidents as an indication that laws were needed to separate Jews from other Germans. Hitler believed that the opportune moment for codifying the party's position in law had arrived.[5]

One of Goebbels's means for staging anti-Jewish incidents and instigating rumors was *Mundfunk* (mouth radio), a network of offices and employees organized around the Reich through the Propaganda Ministry's twelve regional offices.[6] In 1935, during the spring and summer months preceding the Nuremberg Laws, small crowds cropped up here and there across the Reich, harassing and scandalizing Jews. The police suspected the Propaganda Ministry of staging public outbursts against Jews, and the fact that these scattered "individual actions" increased dramatically during 1935 suggests a central source. To the passerby, however, they could have appeared to be spontaneous outbursts. Covertly stimulating actions or rumors at the grass-roots level, Goebbels made them appear to be the authentic voice of the people.

In some areas, rowdies prevented Jews from going to theaters and vacation resorts or boycotted Jewish ice-cream shops.[7] In Bavaria during July 1935, "approximately 15 to 20 young bathers had demanded the removal of the Jews from the swimming bath by chanting in the park which adjoins the baths," according to a police report. "A considerable number of other bathers joined in the chanting so that probably the majority of visitors were demanding the removal of Jews." Three weeks later the spa association posted a notice: "Entry forbidden to Jews."[8] Public brouhaha had been sufficient to persuade the spa to take anti-Jewish actions, but the police surmised that the source of the unrest was not the public but Goebbels.[9]

Goebbels also staged rabble-rousing at the weddings of mixed couples, particularly during the months leading up to the Nuremberg Laws. Even the justice minister insinuated that these public outbreaks against intermarriage had actually been planned by the party.[10] In the midst of the uproar police officers appeared and arrested both bride and groom, taking them into "protective custody," ostensibly for their own protection from the mad crowd.[11] Thus in some cases Goebbels used his crowds to invoke the use of police force; the appearance of popular rage served to set in motion the standard processes of law. In addition, local Nazis, claiming to be angry because there was still no law banning Jewish-"Aryan" marriages, began interfering with public announcements of intermarriages and disrupting wedding ceremonies.[12] Lynch mobs pursued Jews suspected of, or known to be, having sexual relations with non-Jews and made "numerous denunciations" of Jewish-German romances every day.[13] German as well as the Jewish partners of romantic mixed couples were paraded through the streets with signs hung about their necks declaring: I ALLOWED MYSELF TO BE SHAMED BY A JEW or I SHAMED A JEWISH GIRL, or, in another instance, I AM THE BIGGEST PIG IN TOWN, AND ONLY GO WITH JEWS AROUND.[14]

In August 1935 the party determined that "legal measures" were needed to maintain public quiescence.[15] Thus the party disassociated itself from the unruly outbursts of public violence and set the stage for new laws. If Hitler's decision to promulgate the laws banning intermarriage and depriving Jews of citizenship at the party rally in September 1935 seemed to be taken suddenly,[16] it coincided with his habit of waiting for his intuition to inform him that it was the opportune moment to take action. "You must understand that I always go as far as I dare and never further," he said. "It is vital to have a sixth sense which tells you broadly what you can and cannot do."[17] The "legal

regulation of the problem" of Jews in Germany was the only way to
head off these "defensive actions of the enraged population," Hitler
said in justification of the Nuremberg Laws.[18] These laws, a watershed
in the evolution of Nazi racial policy, a major step on the way to the
Holocaust, were to deprive Jews of their citizenship and basic rights.
For the announcement of such a radical departure from recent German
legal and social traditions, what occasion could be more accommodating
than the annual party rally held in Nuremberg? By 1935 there was no
better platform for portraying Hitler as the great charismatic leader,
and on this occasion he aligned his popularity with anti-Semitism by
giving the first major public speech on the Jewish Question since becoming reich chancellor.[19]

Hitler arrived in Nuremberg for the 1935 rally with a new racial
law, drafted by the Interior Ministry and titled the Law for the Protection of German Blood and Honor.[20] According to Hitler, Germany
mingled two "races" so diametrically opposed that one would have to
be expelled. Not just individual fates but the country's strength and
honor were at risk. When the stakes were so high, knowing who was
Jewish and who was not was terribly important. Yet until 1935 there
had been no law to define who in Germany was Jewish (the practice
had been to label anyone with just one Jewish grandparent as Jewish).[21]
Hitler intended to change this by using the customary ministry to draft
a law he would personally sign and by giving a speech on September
15 to the Reichstag assembly, the German parliament that in 1933 had
granted him dictatorial powers.

The Führer, however, rejected the Interior Ministry's proposed
law as "too meager" for the grand scale of his purposes. Feeling inadequate to produce anything grander without their file folders, the
Interior big shots called on their ministry's Jewish expert, Bernhard
Lösener. Back in Berlin, where the government quarters in and around
the Wilhelmstrasse had been abandoned for Nuremberg by anyone of
importance, business had ground to a halt. Lösener was partying at
the office when he got a call from his superiors. With a bundle of
ministry documents on the Jewish Question in his bags, he departed
from Tempelhof Airport for Nuremberg. There he set to work at once
with four of his superiors, feverishly formulating drafts of a new law.
Some members of the drafting team were of more assistance to Lösener
than others. One of them, an assistant to Hitler's deputy Rudolf Hess,
spent most of his time playing with a toy tank in the suite of Interior
Minister Frick, where the team was meeting. The interior minister
himself, who was supposed to review the works in progress, occasionally
emerged from his private room, where he was entertaining Frau Hä-

berlein over wine and lebkuchen, to run each successive draft to Hitler. The draft soon returned with an order from the Führer to change this or that. By afternoon there were what Lösener called "a large number of drafts."[22]

At midnight, after fifteen hours of writing the law that prohibited intermarriage and forbade sexual contact between Jews and Germans, Frick returned with Hitler's latest order: Produce a Reich constitutional law![23] It was due the next day. The distinguished civil servants were incredulous. Had Frick knocked the sense out of Hitler? they wondered. How much thorough preparation and careful consideration should it take to prepare a constitutional law for a Thousand-Year Reich? Frick told the exhausted bureaucrats not to worry; the Führer only wished for a few terse words corresponding to the appropriate portions of his book. With the task thus simplified, Lösener and the others spent the next half hour drafting a brief and vague law on the back of a menu. Hitler finally accepted it at 2:30 A.M.

Obviously Hitler could have written the constitutional law himself. But the Führer wanted the Interior Ministry's cooperation and imprimatur. The charismatic leader did not spurn but rather incorporated the lawmakers. He used the procedure typical of Weimar and decent government. By cooperating with the charismatic dictator, the old bureaucracy presented these extreme, radical measures as mere bureaucratic procedure. The work at Nuremberg on the race law was done largely by improvisation, yet the improvisations in the end only added up to Hitler's will, after he had been assured that the bureaucrats would cooperate with him all the way.

The hard question of how to define a Jew was left open at Nuremberg, to be defined by amendments during the following two months. Hitler, Goebbels, and other Nazi leaders who eventually directed the persecution of the Jews would have preferred to subject all half Jews to the same measures the Jews themselves were to experience. Hitler referred to *Mischlinge* as "monstrosities halfway between man and ape" and claimed that the Jewish blood of a "half Jew" would not "Mendel out" over six successive generations of reproduction with pure Germans.[24] Yet the laws he finally approved in 1935 allowed most half Jews to retain the rights of citizens, which Jews lost.

After the war Interior Ministry officials who had helped draft the racial law claimed credit for the compromises in the law's definition of *Mischlinge*.[25] The ministry did disagree with the party over whether "half Jews" should be treated as Jews.[26] Both these offices, however, waited on Hitler for a decision. At two separate conferences (on September 29, 1935, and on November 5, 1935), Hitler was given the forum to make the final decision on the problem of defining who was a Jew, and the officials expected him to do so.[27] But Hitler dithered here, just as he refused to be associated with any other unpopular or even controversial matter, allowing the Interior Ministry to prevail. Although the Nuremberg Laws and their criteria for determining who was a Jew remained in force throughout the Third Reich, neither they nor the bureaucrats made the critical determination about the fate of *Mischlinge*. In some cases the German bureaucracy facilitated Nazi rule by moderating the positions of Hitler, thus making it more acceptable to the Germans.[28] In the case of the Nuremberg Laws the bureaucrats did moderate the party, but the dictatorship's concern about the reaction of the people ensured that not even this moderate position was fulfilled.

On the last day of the 1935 Nuremberg party rally, Hitler presided over the Reichstag ceremony for the promulgation of the Nuremberg Laws. For the overflow crowd outside, Goebbels broadcast it all, including Hitler's speech on the Jews and his announcement, leading up to the reading of the law itself, that a law regulating Jewish citizenship and interaction in Germany was to be declared. Then directly at the climax of the assembly—the point when the law itself was actually read—Goebbels created an image of a Germany hungry for racial laws, by changing the broadcast from the Reichstag and the reading of the laws to music. The response of the crowd was immediate and made a lasting impression on Lösener, the lawmaker. The people, he recalled, began to call out, "What has been decided? What has been decided?"[29]

WHO'S JEWISH IN NAZI GERMANY?

The Nazis claimed to define Jews as a race, not as a religion, but they also looked to the membership rolls of the Jewish Community; anyone with four Jewish grandparents on the rolls was a "full Jew." Anyone with four grandparents not on Jewish Community rolls was considered a German. But what of those with one, two, or three Jewish grandparents? These the Nuremberg Laws put into a third racial category of *Mischlinge*. During the deportations, when more than seventy thousand German *Mischlinge* lives were at stake every time the term *Mischlinge* was defined,[30] the bureaucrats and party officials argued these points.

The Nuremberg Laws defined anyone with two Jewish grandparents as a *Mischling* of the first degree, or a half Jew, while persons with only one Jewish grandparent, or quarter Jews, were *Mischlinge* of the second degree. During the Third Reich *Mischlinge* of the second degree were allowed to keep their German citizenship but were kept out of positions of power. Professions that limited membership to those with "Aryan" blood, for example, could not accept *Mischlinge* of the second degree. The German Labor Front and the military accepted them for work and armed services, but an order from Hitler on April 8, 1940, barred them from receiving promotions.[31] They could also be barred from high schools or universities if their attendance burdened facilities and created disadvantages for Germans. They were allowed to marry Germans, but not half Jews or Jews, indicating that while hobbling their careers, the regime was hoping to assimilate their children.[32] These second-degree *Mischlinge* could be sure they themselves would not be sterilized or murdered as long as the half Jewish *Mischlinge* had not yet been murdered or sterilized.

Half Jews, or *Mischlinge* of the first degree—persons with two Jewish grandparents—the Nuremberg Laws divided into two groups. One category consisted of those who either had been members of a Jewish Community or were married to Jews. In official Nazi communications, they came to be identified as *Geltungsjuden* (those counted as Jews). According to the Nuremberg Laws, any half Jew was a *Mischling* of the first degree. But only the *Geltungsjuden* were treated like full Jews (as if they had four Jewish grandparents). They were allowed to marry only other Jews or *Geltungsjuden*.

The category of *Mischlinge* of the first degree also included half Jews who had (because of their parents' choice) been baptized either Protestant or Catholic. In official Nazi language these half Jews were generally known simply as *Mischlinge*, in contrast with the other half Jewish Mischlinge of the first degree who were called *Geltungsjuden*. Baptized *Mischlinge* outnumbered *Geltungsjuden* by nine to one, since only 11 percent of *Mischlinge* belonged to Jewish communities. Even before Hitler, many intermarried couples had baptized their children in the hope that this would free them from the difficulties of anti-Semitism in Germany and Europe. In some cases fully Jewish couples shared this hope and reared their children as Christians.[33] Under the original Nuremberg Laws, *Mischlinge* were allowed to keep their citizenship status. But under a series of amendments to the Nuremberg Laws and subsequent laws their rights steadily eroded until they, like the *Geltungsjuden*, were without legal rights.

IMPURE BLOOD: "BIOLOGICALLY [AND POLITICALLY] UNPLEASANT OCCURRENCES"

German bureaucrats who worried about precision found the Nuremberg Laws imprecise. Exacting officials pointed out that a person might fall between categories. A person whose father was Jewish but whose mother was a *Mischling* of the second degree, for example, would be five-eighths Jewish. The preponderance of such a person's blood would flow from Jewish ancestors, they reasoned. But according to the Nuremberg categories, only two grandparents were Jewish, allowing these five-eighths Jews into the category of the *Mischlinge* of the first degree. Himmler's office declared that these Jews should never, in any case, be allowed an "equalization" (a dispensation from Hitler granting a *Mischling* exemption from persecution).[34] Another defect of the Nuremberg Laws encompassed *Mischlinge* who lacked even one full Jewish grandparent (but whose grandparents were *Mischlinge*). Such persons were as much as half Jewish. Associations allowing only racial Germans tried to ban these persons, who under the Nuremberg Laws were not identified as carrying Jewish blood at all.

The Nuremberg Laws also seemed to equivocate on intermarriage. On the one hand, they outlawed further German-Jewish intermarriages and annulled all standing engagements between mixed couples. Persons contracting an intermarriage after the Nuremberg Laws would not be legally married and could be prosecuted for *Rassenschande* (racial shame or defilement). On the other hand, the Nuremberg Laws did not mandate the divorce or annulment of existing German-Jewish intermarriages. Thus intermarried Jews had a relatively privileged position as Jews: They too were deprived of citizenship and rights, but they lived together with Germans who continued to hold these. This condition, as the secret police reported, led to complaints that intermarried couples were living in "legalized *Rassenschande*."[35]

For Goebbels, intermarriages were both tough and delicate. Propaganda effective for separating intermarried couples would have to promote not just anti-Semitism but the dissolution of marriages as well. This was a formidable task. Marriage was a deeply rooted norm, and divorce in Germany of the 1930s was still the exception. The Wilhelmine legal code remained the law during the Third Reich and made divorce very unattractive for women, while making "monogamy and lifelong marriage attractive to men."[36] Both the Protestant and Catholic churches also sanctioned marriage: Catholic dogma opposed divorce, while German Protestant churches had only "cautiously considered the dilemmas of birth control, and sometimes even abortion and divorce."[37] In matters of marriage the churches had recently held sway; only since 1875 was civil marriage in Germany mandatory.

The Nuremberg Laws of 1935 banned all further marriages between Jews and Germans, but given the norm of faithfulness to marriage vows, they did not forcibly separate existing Jewish-German married couples, even though sexual relations between them was a crime.[38] The regime was in a bind: Without force divorce was unlikely, but since divorce was not popular, forcing it upon intermarried couples would also not be popular. Keeping Jews separated from Germans led to a ban on Jewish and intermarried households' employing "Aryan" women under the age of forty-five as house servants, a measure aimed at preventing the birth of *Mischlinge*. Many intermarried couples found the requirement that they release their "German-blooded" domestic servants painful, however, if for reasons other than sexual intercourse. Dozens sought exceptions. Among them was the renowned philosopher Karl Jaspers, who was married to a Jew. Jaspers petitioned various offices, including the Interior Ministry, pleading for permission to keep his household servant, Erna Baer. Because of his work, his poor health, and the poor health of his wife, the release of his domestic servant would have "catastrophic results," he wrote. "We are without children, and don't have any other help." Jaspers even hinted that without Baer he might be forced to stop his "scientific work."[39]

For exceptional cases like Karl Jaspers, top party leaders created the category of *Schutzjuden*—Jews protected from Jewish regulations because of their political or scientific usefulness to the state were. The regime needed the respectability of the ministries and courts but not their specialized perspective. Court rulings on *Rassenschande* also resembled the work of bureaucrats, rather than indicated an understanding of the overall political goals of top Nazi leaders. For party leaders, *Rassenschande* laws were not only an important means of preventing the further births of *Mischlinge* but also a mechanism for the social isolation of Jews from Germans, an important goal in advance of the concentration and expulsion of Jews. Judges sometimes lost this overall perspective, concentrating instead on minutiae.

The party perpetrated the idea, the bureaucracy wrote the laws, and the German courts made the interpretation and enforcement of *Rassenschande* laws more comprehensive and more stringent. By 1937 the claim that the Jewish identity of a partner in *Rassenschande* had not been known no longer satisfied the court (it was the responsibility of every Jew to announce this racial identity to any German interested in sexual partnership). Just the attempt by one person to requite sexual urges was enough for punishment under *Rassenschande* laws, even if one partner had merely "tolerated" the sexual act.[40] Even commencing mutual masturbation was *Rassenschande*, regardless of whether orgasm occurred. A man who claimed he had only moved his genitalia back and forth on that of a woman's and then stopped was guilty of *Rassenschande*. Persons who owned apartments in which mixed couples had sexual intercourse could be held liable as accomplices.[41] A Jew looking at a German woman could be charged with *Rassenschande*. The court held guilty a Jewish defendant arguing that he had not known his partner was German on the grounds that a Jew could not trust a woman who merely said she was Jewish but had the responsibility for obtaining satisfactory documentation that she indeed was.[42] In the Third Reich a relatively high number of those prosecuted for *Rassenschande* were convicted because the courts relied on the barest threads of evidence.[43]

The regime and its institutions drove a wedge between Jews and Germans not already united by family. It is not possible to calculate how much anti-Semitism the regime actually engendered, but Nazi racial ideology had little influence on the divorce rate of Germans married to Jews. A new marriage law of 1938 allowed intermarried Germans a divorce if they could convince the court that they never would have married a Jew had they understood the gravity of the Jewish Question. Only a few Germans took advantage of this new provision,[44] a fact the regime accepted as an indication that it could not legislate an end to a family relationship if the marriage partners wanted to stay together. In late 1944 the regime dropped a proposed new law to loosen divorce standards since police reports showed the people in general would oppose it and because "very many German-Jewish mixed marriages have remained since 1933 despite the divorce possibilities."[45]

In his effort to build a Thousand-Year Reich, Hitler wanted to change German traditions to match Nazi values, but he knew he could not change traditions quickly. Nazi propaganda was unable to alter social norms quickly, nor could it contradict daily experience. Every German, Himmler complained, "has his decent Jew."[46] Daily, personal experience could also limit the regime's capacity to wield violence. For as history shows, "it was hard for even the worst fanatic to be utterly ruthless against someone who had grown up on the same block with him."[47]

Nazi efforts to separate "Aryans" and Jews led to a maze of contradictions. The bureaucrats tended to proceed logically, categorizing Germans according to the party's racial ideals. The top leadership's concern with popular accommodation clashed with this, however, and led to inconsistencies between party ideology and party policies. *Mischling* half Jews had the same amount of Jewish blood as *Geltungsjuden*, for example, but were to be treated much differently. The decree of September 1941 forcing Jews to wear the Star of David applied to *Geltungsjuden* but not to *Mischlinge* of the first degree. The star marked an identity bereft of rights and police protection, and it marked the population initially designated for deportation. Despite the laws, *Geltungsjuden* escaped the deportations to death camps and survived the war because they had non-Jewish family members.

VII

SOCIETY AND LAW: GERMAN-JEWISH FAMILIES AND GERMAN COLLABORATION WITH HITLER

Following the Nuremberg Laws and especially in preparation for the 1936 Berlin Olympics, the public face of anti-Semitism was briefly veiled. With the international focus on Germany that the Olympics brought, the German capital, in the description of the *Mischling* Hans-Oskar Löwenstein de Witt, seemed to exhibit a new "tolerance" and blossom into a "paradise."[1] In shopwindows up and down the streets of Germany's cities and towns, the signs forbidding Jews began to vanish. Although the government had not required these announcements that "Jews are unwanted," they had appeared widely in German businesses after 1933. Some shops had gone beyond banning Jews to taking special pride in their "Aryan" identity, displaying especially virulent anti-Semitic articles and cartoons in their windows.[2] The sudden disappearance of the signs prohibiting Jews indicates the regime was working its will not only through laws and regulations but through informal links as well (threats of boycotts and "other consequences," for example, had cowed some businesses into publicly banning Jews).[3]

Even so, the legal persecution and day-to-day harassment of persons and businesses rolled on. Nazi officials like Hans Kerrl who expected self-interest to prevent Germans from marrying Jews perhaps also thought that the status of Jews would sunder the existing intermarriages. The Nuremberg Laws prohibited Jews from flying the German flag, but as of December 1936 this prohibition was extended to any "German-blooded" person married to a Jew. As the German people united more and more under their Führer and his successes of rearmament and expansion, flag waving had become more and more important socially, and the law forbidding intermarried Germans from raising the flag caused at least one of them to commit suicide, according to his daughter.[4]

The dictatorship used shame as well as force to repress dissent. Hitler integrated the Germans, and to offend ideals Hitler stood for could be a social embarrassment, even if not a legal offense. The Gestapo identified nearly half its cases as "Nonconforming Behavior in Everyday Life." In the twelve Nazi years the Düsseldorf Gestapo called 29 percent of its cases either "Nonconforming Verbal Utterances," or "Nonconforming Work or Leisure Activities"; 17 percent of the cases were "Other Forms of Nonconformity," such as "Acquiring or Spreading Forbidden Printed Matter" and "Listening to Foreign Radio" or "Political Passivity." Since there were not enough officers in uniform to observe the daily activities of eighty million Germans, these cases depended heavily on civilian Germans to bring information to the party, police, or Gestapo.[5] Some people saw it as the duty of friendship to tell others how to avoid getting into trouble.[6] The experiences of intermarried Germans shows that the regime could rely on the general public to enforce its social standards. The German population—with Nazi party members and functionaries often in the lead—did for the regime what it alone could do only imperfectly: pressure those intermarriages to break up.

Neighbors and friends of intermarried Germans continued to abandon, harass, and denounce them in step with a bombardment of legal assaults. Music, theater, literature, radio, print media, visual arts, and film—all were subordinated by Goebbels into the Reich Chamber of Culture, and one by one these were closed to Jews and Germans married to Jews.

- By April 1936 the Reich Press Chamber, one of seven bailiwicks of the Reich Culture Chamber, required all its members—anyone practicing journalism—to prove that they and their spouses were descended from an "Aryan" lineage since 1800.[7]

- At about the same time Goebbels's Reich Publishers' Chamber also required book vendors to prove themselves likewise racially pure.[8]

- In October 1936 the civil service tightened the screws with a ruling that public servants (state and federal) married to Jews could now no longer receive job promotions.[9]

- Two and one-half months later the German Civil Service Law of January 26, 1937, required the resignation of any civil servant married to a Jew.[10]

- Other professions imitated the early decision of the prestigious medical and legal professions and adopted the Aryan Clause for themselves. In February 1937 the civil service hiring practices discriminating against the intermarried Germans were adopted for the notary public profession, shutting out Germans married to Jews as well as Jews.[11]

- Soon thereafter the Association of Surveyors also excluded Jews and Germans married to Jews from their profession.[12]

- In the second quarter of 1937 Hitler's office began a campaign to force *Mischlinge* as well as civil servants married to Jews out of their jobs.[13]

This litany of laws rolls down the page as easily as a shopping list, but for many Germans each was a heavy blow. In August 1935 Goebbels ordered that all German Jewish artists could perform only within the so-called Jewish Cultural Association, under the direction of Hans Hinkel, whose title was "Special Assistant to the Reich Minister for Public Enlightenment and Propaganda for the Control of Non-Aryans Occupied with Cultural and Humanistic Activities in the German Reich Territory."[14] After the Civil Service Law of April 1933, performance opportunities for Julius Israel, Charlotte's husband, the pianist, had dwindled to a trickle as businesses began to ban Jewish performers. Now they stopped completely, increasing again Julius's dependency on Charlotte.

When Hitler came to power, Julius worked together with the musician Günther Schwenn. For a program Berlin Alexanderplatz, they received permission from Heinrich Zille to use one of his motifs. "My husband wrote music texts, but he was actually better at composing," said Charlotte. After the war Charlotte was listening to the radio when she chanced on an interview with Schwenn, who was answering questions about how he had made his career. "I played at Küka" (the artists' cafe next to the Roman café), Charlotte heard him say. "I had a piano player too." Charlotte remembered that Schwenn did not name his piano player. "I was so disappointed," she said. "My husband had helped him up the ladder."[15]

Charlotte became the main breadwinner, and just having enough room to exist quietly at home, with space for Julius to play for their circle of musical family and friends, became a dream. After marriage, Julius had moved in with Charlotte on the ground-floor apartment she rented on Leibnizstrasse, next to the tailoring business. This effort to present Charlotte as the owner of their business quickly fell through when the SA discovered that the Press tailor shop on Leibnizstrasse was really an extension of the Israel tailor business. "I had that new shop exactly one-half year," Charlotte said. "It got out somehow that it was 'under Jewish influence,' and we were boycotted day after day. The SS stood in front of our door and sent the people away: 'Hey, don't buy anything from this Jewish sow here.' It was impossible. I also was afraid. We had to give up the store and the adjoining apartment. So we had no more place to work than place to live."

The Nazi party, eager to spread their boycotts beyond picket lines, posted announcements that Germans going in and out of Jewish stores were being photographed, a trap that would "of course embarrassingly surprise" the unsuspecting offender.[16] When it became impossible for them to maintain their business on Leibnizstrasse, Charlotte and Julius were forced to move into a single empty room within a four-room apartment, on the corner of Kaiser-Friedrich Strasse and Bismarckstrasse. The Israels' new home was shared by two other families. Everyone shared the kitchen and the bathroom. That might have been fine, said Charlotte, if only the fellow tenants had not been Nazis. The Propaganda Ministry brought anti-Semitism into homes around the Reich through radio broadcasts. Speeches of leading Nazis beamed into German homes, where families assembled piously around the radio to receive the word of their leader. Charlotte's neighbors invariably turned their radios up so loud that she could not help hearing what she could not bear to listen to. "I didn't want to hear anything of it," she said. "That was hell for me. I couldn't stand it."

The kitchen also provided an opportunity for the other tenants to make the young couple miserable. "It was a collective living arrangement, and theoretically everyone had the same rights and duties," Charlotte said. "But the others ganged up on us, reciting the anti-Jewish Nazi prejudices even though they didn't have to. We had very few rights because we were a Jewish household. We were at the bottom of the pecking order. The others could always have their way. So it was I who always worked in the kitchen, not my husband. I protected him and always left him a little more in the background."

By chance the Israels found another apartment—at Dahlmann-strasse 22, between Sybelstrasse and Mommsenstrasse, where they were briefly happy in their new privacy. Here Charlotte and Julius started up their tailoring business again. Without a ground-floor shop and a sign to announce their business, Charlotte was officially able to register her business and carry on without the SA's boycotts. In time the business flourished. Even the local government bureaucrats dropped by to have their sleeves lengthened or their hems let out. "We cut and sewed very fine clothing," said Charlotte. "Blouses and shirt blouses were very fashionable then. Through word of mouth our work became known. And the work we did, people needed. So our livelihood was assured, for the time being." Julius could not earn his living by performing, and their business could not prosper. But they lived in their own apartment and could still visit concerts, public exhibitions, and movie theaters. They had their Jewish family and circle of friends.

The Israels also had Julius's music. Julius played piano at home virtually every day throughout most of the Nazi years. Charlotte sang along. Sometimes, seated next to him, she turned the pages for him, while sewing with her free hand. The couple's proudest possession was a gorgeous Bechstein piano Julius's parents had given him as a wedding present. It dominated their small living room, and it was the center of the Israels' social life. "My husband composed his own music," Charlotte said with pride. "He wrote chansons; those were his favorites. Once or twice in the week there was a music evening in our apartment. Our friends were all musical. One played flute, the other cello, or violin; there were singers of all ranges—how wonderful! All our friends came. That was all like a family back then. Really beautiful. And then I always sat beside my husband and sewed buttons and so forth; one always has to work, you know. I sat next to him, turning the page, They were wonderful hours, which I will never forget."

But even as the Israels learned to adjust to an ever-tightening corset of legal and economic restrictions, propaganda against Jews and *Rassenschande* worsened. More and more the words "Forbidden for Jews!" were seen in front of public bars, restaurants, parks, and entertainment centers throughout Germany. So-called *Stürmerkasten*—public exhibits of propaganda from the Nazi paper *Der Stürmer*—were scattered throughout German cities, deriding Jews, portraying them as rapists and defilers of the "Aryan Master Race." On the streets Charlotte and Julius were a striking couple—he the short, dark, and crippled Jew, she the statuesque "Aryan." To the public "keeping a watchful

eye out for Jews who go around with blond girls,"[17] they suggested
Rassenschande.

Perhaps acting on a tip from a neighbor or a customer, the Business
Licensing Office informed Charlotte that her business was "under Jewish influence" and closed it. "When I went to the licensing office to
say I wanted to register my business again," Charlotte said, "they
always told me, 'Get a divorce! Then you can register again.' I always
told them, 'You're no doubt also married. I don't know if you would
divorce so easily. In any case I'm not going to divorce.'

"We were all out of work," said Charlotte, "and depressed. But
then I had an idea. One always has to have ideas. I went to the factory
as a seamstress. I thought this would work, but it was horrible for me.
From the huge hall the sound rose from all those machines like the
noise of hell. No single seamstress sewed an entire piece. That was
boring beyond belief. I, who was used to making the finest tailor-made
pieces, now only sewed on buttons. Again and again. You only made
a little sleeve or something. We made standard sizes, and anyone
buying it who was a little smaller or a little bigger was out of luck! I
could have despaired—and it was also poorly paid. The factory atmosphere got on my nerves, and I held out exactly one day. That was
all.

"On the streetcar coming home that evening, I had only one
thought: From what are we going to live? To myself I appeared worthless. I despised myself. It took about a week until I recovered. I lay in
bed as if in a coma. My husband took care of me. I am not demanding.
I can be very modest. But you have to live from something! That was
always the most important thing for me: that we had enough for one
day in advance."

Finally Charlotte turned to making a living illegally, a terrifying
prospect. A law of April 1938 mandated the imprisonment for not less
than one year of a German who knowingly contributed to the false
representation—to either the public or the authorities—of a Jewish
industry or business as a German business. Anyone with knowledge
of an improperly registered Jewish business was required to tell the
authorities or face charges as an accomplice in deception.[18] Charlotte,
not accustomed to breaking the law, nevertheless wanted to live. She
opened her business secretly but told only Jews about it.

"We wrote to our Jewish customers that we were working again,"
Charlotte recalled. "And they all came. We worked only for people
we knew and trusted. We made changes, took in clothing; the people
grew thinner and thinner because times kept getting harder! Everything
had to be made smaller. We also offered training—sewing lessons. My

husband gave lessons in cutting material. That was for Jews who wanted to emigrate. Even lawyers came to learn this from us. All this in our apartment, always in secret. We lived on the first floor, and you could hear it from outside. Above us too, they could hear it, I thought. We were of course afraid, especially when the doorbell rang.

"I had two sewing machines, and we gave instructions from Monday through Thursday, from two to four in the afternoon. Two marks per hour. Sixteen marks per week. We could live on that. We couldn't make any great strides. But we lived on it. Everything was forbidden for us anyway," Charlotte added, laughing. "We had no opportunity to spend money. Friday I didn't want to work because that was the Sabbath and I wanted to be there for our private life. I accepted the Sabbath."

While some people bent under the pressure of persecution, Nazi racism actually strengthened Charlotte's commitment to Julius. Once she took a bike trip with her brother, to the beach at Ückermünde. "It was a wonderful trip," she said, "always through the woods, in beautiful weather. As we reached the beach, my brother said, 'Isn't that wonderful, the sea?' But I didn't see the sea. At first I saw just a huge sign, placed directly over the beach: FORBIDDEN FOR JEWS. In huge letters, about a yard tall, very high, and broad, so that everyone could read it. My gaze was transfixed. I stared at the sign and didn't go farther. My joy was gone. I was terribly unhappy. I had only one thought, just one wish: To my husband! I took it upon myself never again to travel without my husband. And that's the way it would be from then on too."

Stürmerkasten and other public displays of propaganda were supposed to pull all Germans together, casting the Jews as hideous intruders. They were especially common around bus and trolley stops and anywhere else Germans gathered in clusters. Once while Charlotte was strolling Charlottenburg's Kantstrasse with her friend Paula, they came across some Germans jeering at a *Stürmerkasten* portraying a Jew. Paula Schlesinger was a beautiful Jew who maintained her composure despite the Nazis. Paula went where she wanted to go with her usual vitality and composure. "You don't need to laugh! There are also beautiful Jews," Paula told the jeering group, throwing her head back. "Look at me!"

Separating Jews from non-Jews was urgent for Goebbels since in person Jews might disprove his propaganda. Most intermarried Germans would not be influenced by state anti-Semitic propaganda. Family ties caused them to stand in the way of state purposes. Charlotte had begun her adult life by falling in love with Julius, not as a Nazi resister.

The small sacrifices she made for him at first became enormous later, and her capacity to resist social and political pressures grew in step with the mounting pressures. Still, the words Charlotte Israel had to tell her story remained the same: "horrible, terrible, unbelievable." The words one might use to describe getting caught in a summer thunderstorm or losing the set of keys are the only ones available for describing a victim's fate in Nazi Germany. But the sorrow of Charlotte's loss, the loss of friends and loss of trust in her fellow humans, still lived deep in her voice, as she recalled her friend Paula Schlesinger: "Paula and her entire family were gassed."

Wally Rossbach had married Günter Grodka despite the fact that neither of them had a job. Following their wedding, she began to receive a continuous flow of summons to appear at this or that office of the Gestapo. More often and just as treacherously, neighbors and acquaintances hurled insults at her. She remembered especially being called "Jew sow!" and "Jew whore!" Some spit on her or drove her off the sidewalk. Even the Grodkas' dog was insulted as Jewish, and passersby would warn their dogs sharply to "get away from the Jew dog!"

"I learned to be especially wary of onslaughts whenever two Germans were together," Wally said. One person alone "was too cowardly" to act so cruelly. Other survivors recalled that Gestapo officers were also prone to speak more loudly and act more severely when they were in one another's company. One officer who was "very loud and energetic" became "quiet and efficient" as soon as his colleague left the room."[19] To be a good Gestapo man, you had to scream and shout. A German woman remembered that a Gestapo man conducting a house search in an orderly, even polite way began to fill the air with insults, flinging the contents of dresser drawers around the room and hurling shelves of books to the floor, when a colleague entered the room.[20] A common fear in Nazi Germany was that of standing out in the crowd. Germans together could act heartlessly, sometimes merely to avoid being different.[21]

Wally recalled that low-level party functionaries often instigated the harassments against her and Günter. In almost every house there were party members, and it was often they who traced the coming and going of anyone who went in and out of an apartment where Jewish-German families lived, yelling insults and even spitting on them or dumping waste out of apartment windows as they passed below. Especially important to the party's maintenance of control were its so-called *Blockleiter*. Although these officials ranked lowest in the official party hierarchy, they were the eyes and ears of the leadership at the most mundane, everyday level. They were also responsible for conveying party orders to the grass roots. Since the regime wished to control the levers of institutional power and change social behavior— even the behavior of Germans in bed—it needed a systematic surveillance. *Blockleiter* provided this, investing lots of their time without pay to (among other duties) keeping "household card indexes" on each person living within their particular blocks. They reinforced the Nazi norms by noting who subscribed to the Nazi paper, who used the "Heil Hitler" greeting, who voiced dissent or gave quarter to Jews, passing their information on to the Gestapo or their superiors within the party. Party officials often consulted with the relevant *Blockleiter* when determining the "political reliability" of someone applying for any of the many necessities and amenities that the party controlled.[22] One German writing immediately after the collapse of the Reich claimed these "little men" of the party did more than the Gestapo for "the strengthening of the regime."[23]

In the Grodkas' building the party's snoopers were the Bluts, who lived on the first floor. Mr. Blut was the party *blockleiter*, and Mrs. Blut was the building superintendent. Günter remembered Mr. Blut as a *Goldfasan*, a functionary in gaudy uniform who gave orders and strutted like a peacock. The Bluts were never easy to avoid. No matter how stealthily she came or went, Wally often heard Mrs. Blut's voice filling the air around her with taunts of "Dirty old, flea-ridden Jewish sow!" The Bluts lived beside the courtyard and surveyed the comings and goings of the entire house through their window at the courtyard. The Grodkas lived in the *Hinterhöfe*, the section of apartments behind the courtyard built originally for Berlin's working classes, with narrower, less decorous stairways and smaller apartments. Wally grew to dread each moment she entered or left her place. Propped up on thick pillows at her windowsill, Mrs. Blut engaged house residents in gossip and petty politics. She harassed Jews and anyone visiting Jews, encouraging others to badger Jews as well.

For siding with Jews, intermarried Germans were routinely attacked by their neighbors and strangers, sometimes more than the Jews themselves. At work Wally's boss taunted her, and an inner fury rose inside her as she took from him the money she needed to stay alive. Arriving home, Wally was greeted with hate notes on her door: "Sow—filthy whore—swine." The roaches in her neighbors' apartment, she was told, had arrived with the Grodka family. "I couldn't defend myself," Wally said. "Who would have stood up for me—a filthy, dishonorable Jewified sow?"

The official propaganda and regulations were directed toward Günter, not Wally. He was a Jew, a member of a category that had no choice, considered genetically flawed beyond any remedy. For Wally and other Germans married to Jews there was, however, the chance to join in with the Master Race, through divorce. Wally was assaulted with the fury of a spurned lover for rejecting the notion that Germans were superior. For going against the grain, she was accused of "impudence," "cheekiness," and "lack of shame." "My wife was harassed much more than I was," Günter admitted. "They constantly insulted her."

Despite the hell they went through, Wally, Charlotte, and Elsa all said they never regretted having married Jews. There was the very occasional bright spot, neighbors who maintained their usual friendship. Eventually Mrs. Blut prohibited the Germans of the house from so much as speaking with Jews. "I was considered a Jew, and no one was supposed to talk with me either," Wally said. Nevertheless, three women in her house were not so easily cowed and continued to be her friend. "Only Mrs. Nowakowski, Mrs. Löwe, and Mrs. Prabsch didn't allow themselves to be influenced, and this was my greatest joy in all that pain and suffering," Wally remembered. On the other hand, she has scorn for those who didn't stand fast. "From the deepest part of my heart, I abhor those people who abandoned their [Jewish] partners," she said. "Because they once, when it went well for them, valued [their partners]. Then, when they had less comfortable times before them, they abandoned them, sending them to death."

From 1936 through 1939 Werner Goldberg's experience as a *Mischling* contrasted with the national, public face of anti-Jewish persecution. In 1936 and 1937 private organizations, independent of legal requirements, expelled him. Yet at the beginning of 1938 he was suddenly invited back into the national community, first as a member of the Reich Labor Service and then as a private in the German Army. Having been banished from the fast-track organizations of his boyhood friend Karl Wolf, he had the chance to bounce back. Werner's wildly fluctuating experiences reflected the waffling of the party leadership as it attempted to work out the conflicts between its racial ideology and practical policies.

The annual Nazi party rally in 1935 had set Werner and Karl far apart. That rally known for the Nuremberg Laws had also spotlighted Hitler addressing fifty-four thousand members of the Hitler Youth, who marched before their Führer. Karl, soon to be selected for the most exclusive unit of the SS, was very possibly there to hear Hitler's promise that National Socialism would train dull, degenerate youth to become a new disciplined force. Karl had already had a year of the Hitler Youth training that Hitler said would make young men dominating and brutal. Werner, forced to leave school early, was working among the outcast in a Jewish clothing business, and thoughts of the future filled him with uncertainty.

Immediately following the Nuremberg Laws, Werner experienced persecution mainly by private, rather than state, institutions. Even an institution as old, large, and independent as the Lutheran Church confided to Werner that it could not bear his weight. "I was very active in my church here in Grünewald," Werner said. "I was the treasurer, and I was at church three times a week. I was always there Sunday and during prayer meetings on Thursdays, and I also attended the Bible hour. And one fine day a member of the Church Council approached me and laid his hand on my shoulder. I thought he was about to ask me to do this task or that. But then with amazement I heard him ask me to stop my participation. Because it represented a hardship for the church! He told me this tenderly, with his arm around my shoulder: 'Yes, we like you, Werner. But you have to realize that you're a burden for us. Do us a big favor, and step aside.' "

Werner's church was influenced by the German Faith Movement, a Nazi-instigated Protestant group that synthesized Christian teachings with Nazi doctrine by granting National Socialism and the Führer the divine legitimacy Christianity reserved for church and Christ. Protestantism, so deeply rooted the regime could not eliminate it by force, offered instead this ersatz Christianity. Proselytizing was the regime's best option because, as the Gestapo concluded in a report from 1936, "a resolution of the conflict [between Nazism and traditional Protestantism] through force is not possible—that is already evident in developments to date. All measures of force and restrictive regulations have not repressed the confessing church [the traditional branch of Protestantism] and its forward march."[24] The Nazi-inspired Christians' Faith Movement also adopted Nazi racial beliefs, expelling anyone who could not show pure German ancestory back to 1800, a stipulation that led to Werner's ejection.[25]

Unable to believe his pastor had agreed to his expulsion, Werner wrote to him. "I asked whether he saw eye to eye with the request that I leave," Werner said. "But he never wrote back, never got involved in the matter. He was wonderful, but he probably had too much to do. The church, if it is actually fulfilling its function, must take care of the soul, maintaining independence from the guidelines of other social institutions like labor unions, schools, or the volunteer fire company. Everywhere, all around, I was thrown out—always in a very nice manner, as if it were a favor for me to leave. First I had been very warmly received and accepted, and then all of a sudden I was told I was a 'burden'—with great regret. After I was expelled from church, the tennis club was my only association. There I was allowed to stay. The owner of this club arranged for me to be a member of the Reich Sports Club. And then I was accepted. So I was there at the club a lot. Had a lot of friends there. Felt fine again. At the club no one thought to ask whether I was Aryan. So I was only allowed to stay wherever there were people who didn't go along with the Nazis. In this tennis club there was an attorney general, a man who had been transferred from his court to work for the Volksgericht [the People's Court, a dreaded court the regime established to pronounce quick verdicts—one death sentence after the other—against traitors of the Reich]. And within fourteen days he retired. He said that he could not answer for that work. He refused and wasn't punished in any way. He proved his character. It is because of persons like him that I stayed here in Germany after the war to rebuild."

Suddenly, at the beginning of 1938, Werner was invited back into the ranks of the privileged, at the invitation of the regime, and given a uniform with a swastika. Like other male German citizens, Werner served, at age nineteen, a six-month term in the Reich Labor Service and two years of military service afterward. (This was an identity that placed him, a *Mischling*, above even many full-blooded German females.) Werner was back into the standard eleven-year track of national service for males. At age ten, and after a thorough investigation of his record with special attention to his "racial purity," a boy was initiated on Hitler's birthday into the German Young People. At age fourteen came the Hitler Youth, four years later graduation into the Nazi party, and eventually the SA. Werner and other *Mischlinge* had been cut out of the earlier steps of nazification known to his current comrades in the National Labor Service. His Labor Service uniform, Werner recalled, "had a swastika on an armband." Werner wore it even at home, around his father. He had to wear it on weekends as well, he said, because he had so few civilian clothes. In 1938 Mr. Goldberg photographed his wife together with his son in his Nazi uniform, symbol of a racist Germany that Mr. Goldberg had not sought in his assimilation.

Werner joined the army on December 1, 1938, donning another

Nazi uniform. Now he was really "in." But just before that he was struck by a major shock, another blow that made him feel as though his fate could change again, from one day to the next. The Kristallnacht Pogrom of November 1938 was an attack on the Jews, an attack on Werner's loved ones and a reminder that he too had Jewish blood. As a *Mischling* in the military he experienced the pogrom as a new signal of his precarious position, without a clear race and without a clear place.

For Elsa Holzer the decade following her marriage was her best. These were the only years she and Rudi had to live as they wanted, without regard to politics. Prominent on the landscape of her memory are their trips to the mountainous world of Rudi's childhood. She had refused

Werner Goldberg, in a Reich Labor Service uniform with swastika, standing beside his mother, in a photograph taken in 1938 by his Jewish father. As a *Mischling* Werner was serving his compulsory premilitary service term in the Labor Service.

to move to Austria but found it a splendid place to visit. Rudi's Jewish family in fact became a key to her happiness. "In my experience down there in Jewish circles, the Jews have a marvelous family life," Elsa said. "Rudi's parents were simply good people. Unassuming people. The children were too. Father-in-law was a open man. A modern person. And in addition to that, witty. Charming."

Conversely the key to Rudi and Elsa's happiness was the avoidance of everything Jewish in Berlin. Even before the Third Reich Rudi, a baptized Catholic, had told no one of his Jewish past. The documents he needed to get a marriage license identified him and his parents as Catholic, so no one was suspicious, and if he could avoid trouble by avoiding religious institutions, he would. As Nazism spread throughout Germany, the young couple said nothing of Rudi's Jewish past. Like apolitical Germans, they ignored the hail of Nazi regulations crippling the lives of the Jews around them. "No one in Berlin knew Rudi had Jewish parents," Elsa recalled. "How could they know? They would have needed ties to Rudi's hometown to know."

As anti-Jewish measures thickened, the Holzers clung to their secret. And every year they traveled south to Rudi's family. German citizens crossing into Austria had to pay a prohibitive hundred-mark visa fee per person. But Elsa as a woman had been assigned the citizenship of her husband and was Austrian from the moment she married. With Rudi's family she hiked the Kitzbühel Alps and the Tennen Mountains. Eagerly now she remembers their climbs to heights of nine thousand feet. Half-jokingly the Holzers called Elsa the "little flatlander," as she struggled to match their pace.

Twenty miles to the north of the Holzer home, surrounded by three majestic peaks, was Berchtesgaden, a sleepy town of three thousand with little prospect of achieving fame until Hitler selected it as the site of his elaborate estate, the lofty "eagles' nest." At Berghof Hitler relaxed, received his famous guests, or held court with Goebbels, Goering, and Bormann, whose smaller houses stood nearby. Immediately the area became a sort of place of pilgrimage, with a constant stream of "pilgrims" headed for the Berghof, hoping to glimpse the Führer. Pieces of wood were reportedly taken as relics from Hitler's garden fence, and one woman collected sod where the Führer had trod. Overnight Berchtesgaden swelled to twenty-six thousand inhabitants.[26]

The German annexation of Austria in March 1938 signaled the end of Elsa and Rudi's happiness. Like all non-Jewish Austrians, they became German citizens. Unlike most of these new Germans, they did not celebrate. When German troops marched into Austria, adulation of Hitler and the consensus for his leadership reached high tide. In

Austria itself Hitler and his army were hailed from crowded streets like Roman emperors at their ancient triumphs. Field Marshal Wilhelm Keitel, accompanying the Führer as he rode into his hometown of Linz, reported that "the atmosphere of the whole demonstration was electric and excited beyond belief; I had never seen anything like it before and I was deeply impressed."[27] Leopold Gutterer, Goebbels's deputy for propaganda and director of mass rallies, also accompanied Hitler and the military as they rode into Vienna. Despite whatever hand he might have had in orchestrating the Austrian crowds that greeted Hitler, righteous indignation rose in his voice when he recalled that time. Like Germans whose "Aryan" friends left them because they were married to Jews, and then after the war tried to resume their friendly manner as if nothing had happened, Gutterer felt betrayed—betrayed by Germans who once proudly claimed to be Nazis but since the war have denied it. "You should have seen the great hue and cry as Hitler and the army came riding into Vienna," Gutterer said. "Hundreds of thousands of people screamed. Voluntarily. To force that many people to scream like that, you would have needed millions, each with a whip!"

By this point in Hitler's string of successes, Social Democrats were glumly admitting that any future worthwhile opposition was unlikely since "the country is now fully prepared for the fact that the Führer can do everything he wants to." Enthusiasm for the annexation ran strongest in the border areas between the countries, near Berchtesgaden, for example, and Rudi's home in Sankt Johann. People talked of "the German miracle" and their unlimited trust in Hitler.[28] Catholics in southern Germany were especially jubilant about union with the nearby Catholic regions. In Sankt Johann the Austrians welcomed Hitler because they believed all sorts of nonsense, such as that Germans paid no taxes, Elsa remembered. "Even in the highest mountains they screamed 'Heil Hitler.' We were in Austria again in the summer of 1938, at a hotel, eating lunch when it was announced: 'At half past twelve the dear Führer will give a speech!' Soon the speech started, and all around the table hands went up, and the eating stopped."

The annexation of Austria was popular because it occurred without bloodshed. In Germany there was a notion that Hitler was greater than Napoleon because he gained territory for the nation but without war. The Germans, like other Europeans, were decidedly not eager to go to war again. Goebbels pictured the acquisition of Austria as the "Flower War" since the Austrians had met the Germans not with guns but flowers.[29]

Yet Hitler always planned for war, and his confidence about victory hinged on the German people, as the Czech crisis six months later showed. In contrast with the jubilation about the Austrian annexation, the Berlin populace responded indifferently to the Second Motorized Division as it rolled down Wilhelmstrasse in the direction of the Czech frontier, on September 27, 1938. On the previous evening Hitler had delivered a speech at the Berlin Sports Palace demanding that German troops be allowed to occupy and annex the Sudetenland by October 1. Hitler was willing to go to war to get his way, and the movement of troops toward Czechoslovakia on September 27 reminded some people of the first day of war in August 1914. In 1918 cheering throngs on the same street had greeted soldiers with flowers and kisses and expected war to have the same replenishing effects of a thunderstorm after long weeks of hot, sticky weather. Following Hitler's speech intoning war on September 26, 1938, Goebbels leaped to his feet to declare: "The German folk has once again a feeling of national honor and duty. It

Rudi and Elsa Holzer in Rudi's Austrian hometown, in the early 1930s.

will know how to act accordingly. Never again will a November 1918 be repeated"—a reference to the Nazi belief that Germany had lost that war because the people lacked the will to fight. Hitler seconded Goebbels with a "wild, eager 'Ja!'"

On the morning of September 27 Hitler ordered widespread publicity about the movement of the Second Motorized Division that was to take place in the evening, just as hundreds of thousands of workers poured out of their offices at the end of the workday. William Shirer, the journalist, reported from Berlin that as the division passed by that Monday evening of September 27, 1938, workers and others "ducked into the subways, refused to look on, and the handful that did stood at the curb in utter silence unable to find a word of cheer for the flower of their youth going away to the glorious war." Shirer added that this response to mobilized armed forces "has been the most striking demonstration against war I have seen. . . . What I've seen tonight almost rekindles a little faith in the German people." In contrast with the mood in 1914, "the completely apathetic and melancholy behavior of the Berlin populace, which Hitler observed from a window of the Chancellory, made a deep impression on him," Hitler's translator wrote. The Führer, standing on his balcony to review the troops, turned grim, then angry, then disappeared inside. The deputy of the Reich press chief described the slight crowd of two hundred gathered below Hitler's balcony as "silent and grave" and could not help wondering what they were thinking. According to his translator, Hitler's demeanor following this "disillusioning sight of the crowd" changed from a jaunty "War next week!" to a chastened mood in which he wrote a conciliatory letter to British Prime Minister Neville Chamberlain. In his speeches in Berlin on October 5 and November 6, Hitler, still in a bad mood because of the lack of popular show of enthusiasm for war, protested repeatedly that his strength depended on the people. Even if military conquest did not depend on popular will, Hitler continued, throughout his rule, to believe that it did.[30]

By the fall of 1938 and Germany's annexation of the Sudetenland, Rudi and Elsa's fate was doomed. The Anschluss that the vast majority of Germans and Austrians eagerly embraced Elsa Holzer experienced as the onset of tragedy. When Austrians accepted Hitler, they also accepted racist laws. The Nuremberg Laws and the Aryan Clause, which had already been so devastating for Jews and their families in Germany, were introduced into Austrian law on May 24, 1938. This plunged Rudi's family into catastrophe.

In 1925 Rudi's sister Utta had married Siegfried, a local blond and blue-eyed "Aryan." Siegfried was adrift, so Rudi's father had arranged for him a job with the railroad while he took technical courses that would boost him up the career ladder. Then following the Anschluss with Germany and the introduction of the Aryan Clause, public employees were checked for Jewish blood in their family, including through marriage. "You will have to stay with the railroad and divorce your wife or stay with your wife and leave the railroad," Mr. Holzer's son-in-law was told. He chose the job and found another wife. "He loved his job more than his wife," said Elsa, her voice choked with disappointment. Seeking to understand this, she added that "they were possessed, the Austrians. Given over to Germany and the Anschluss."

Another of Rudi's sisters, Anagrette, who had married a poor weaver, also suddenly became "unbearable" to her "Aryan" husband. As a wedding gift Rudi's father had given this new son-in-law three looms, so that he could gain financial independence and self-respect. When Austria unified with Germany, Anagrette had just presented her husband with their third child. Not long after, her husband found a new wife, non-Jewish, and Anagrette was called in for police interrogation.

Rudi and Elsa had begun to discuss emigration. Then in early 1939 a postcard arrived for Rudi from the Gestapo that inquired, in a matter-of-fact way: "Is Anagrette Schwarz, of Sankt Johann, your sister?" The card ordered Rudi to appear at Gestapo headquarters to prove his "Aryan" identity. "Anagrette had apparently told the police that she wanted to go to her brother in Berlin," Elsa explained. "And the police said, 'Aha, you have a brother?' And then they had us nailed."

The Gestapo's discovery of Rudi was what Elsa refers to as the end of their time together. Following this, all their energies were poured into survival. "We were such a short time together. Then came the iron test. Then we had to prove whether we really thought it was worth it or not, our love. Yes. In my opinion, that can only come from the heart, such a decision. One can't calculate whether it's worth it or not. One is ready, or not. One does it or not. You see, we didn't have children. My family also left the picture. And my husband was my one and only. And it was worth it to live together with my husband."

From the moment he was identified as a Jew, Rudi became a criminal under German law, guilty of hiding his Jewish identity. German Jewish men were required to take "Israel" as their middle names as of January 1, 1939; German Jewish women were ordered to take "Sara" as their official middle names. Every time they identified themselves to police or government bureaucrats, Jews had to display special identification cards, marked with their new names and a large *J*. Rudi had heard of Jews arrested and sent to concentration camp during the

Kristallnacht Pogrom months earlier. Weeks later the survivors had been allowed to return—demoralized and broken, some stripped of hair, with a crude Star of David tattooed onto their foreheads.

"I didn't know I was Jewish," Rudi told the police. "All my documents are Catholic." The police scoffed and sent him to the Berlin District Court for sentencing.

Jews in Germany had been introduced to Nazi anti-Semitism over time, measure for measure, regulation by regulation, but Rudi became an object of terrible persecution overnight. Jews could not travel abroad, so there would be no more trips to Austria for Elsa and Rudi. Certainly Rudi would lose his job, she reckoned. By late 1938 some two hundred federal laws restricted Jews and Jewish households.

Elsa accompanied Rudi to his trial. As they neared the court, she saw as if for the first time the signs proclaiming JEWS ARE PROHIBITED. She had passed them many times before, but now they choked her view in all directions. The courthouse, a huge and decorous building constructed in Gothic Revival style in the Moabit section of Berlin, lay just north of the Hansaviertel, a part of Berlin lined with embassies but also a popular residential section among Berlin's Jews. The prison at the Moabit courthouse was a maximum-security prison where political prisoners were interrogated and detained prior to execution.[31] Several blocks to the east was Bahnhof Lehrter, from which some of Berlin's Jews were soon to depart in freight and cattle cars for the ghettos and the death camps.

Inside, guards in uniforms bustled Rudi briskly into the courtroom, leaving Elsa standing alone in the towering hallway. Above the doorway which had just swallowed Rudi hung a sign: CLOSED TO THE PUBLIC. "I paced up and down like a wounded bird," she recalled. "I could only think about what was going to happen now to us. I wasn't allowed into the courtroom. Then I saw a guard who was drunk—like the servant in *Fledermaus*, a sort of frog. But he let no one into that room."

Elsa pulled herself together and approached the drunken guard, addressing him deferentially. He refused to let her in, but a short while later she thought she saw him signaling that he wanted money. She thought it took about five marks and a promise that she'd be totally silent to bribe him. "Then I went in and was totally alone," Elsa recalled. "My husband was in front, in the box. And in front of him, sitting in red and black robes, were five lawyers. As if there had been a great, big crime! Five men, in pompous robes, against my husband because he didn't have the name Israel on his identification card.

"And then a prosecutor stood up and gave my husband a lecture. About eagles. 'It's very unlikely that you didn't know you were Jewish because your mother's name is Adler. And then he said Jews were pigs and began to scream, 'Sow! Jew! Swine! How have you dared to act this way to Germany?' The card in his hand shook, as if he were speaking of an enormous assassination. And then I saw how my husband went white behind the ears. And I thought, My God, I hope nothing happens to him. Under this stress—and we didn't know what he might yet say. When you knew what power they had over you, you trembled. In the end we got off with a five-hundred-mark fine. But that was a lot of money. Before he had earned a normal salary of about three hundred marks per month. But after this trial he lost his job, and as a forced laborer my husband earned only eighty-eight marks per month."

Elsa recalled an odd fact: It was surprisingly difficult to get Rudi's new court-ordered identification with the name Israel. The police refused and sent her to the marriage registrar. The registrar said he was not responsible and suggested the church. The priest Elsa sought out said that a "higher authority" would have to do the job. "A higher authority would be God, but He hasn't granted any identification cards yet," Elsa reflected later. Finally the Holzers turned to Vinzenz, the "Aryan" husband of Rudi's third sister, the mayor of his Austrian village and the magistrate of the surrounding district, who helped Rudi establish his new official identity.[32]

When the state discovered Rudi's past and defined him as a Jew, he lost the German citizenship he had acquired with the Anschluss. Then he lost his job with Schwarzkopf printers. "Sorry, we've got to let you go," his boss told him. "I know you'll come out of this just fine, though."

The Holzers found their new life hard to fathom. Although movies were now forbidden, they made a plan to attend the theater in Halensee, which showed French films. No one could possibly recognize them there, far from their own neighborhood, they thought. The trip from their Neukölln apartment to the theater required them to change subway and bus lines three times. Who would follow them all the way?

"We had good luck. Let's do that more," Elsa said when they returned. But the next morning a policeman stood at their door. He was an ordinary traffic cop, who recognized Elsa by sight. "Ach, you're the one!" he exclaimed when he saw her. "*Man*, don't do anything stupid," he said. "The next time you'll certainly be punished."

Elsa thinks they were denounced. Although the majority of Germans and former Austrians never imagined a Jewish catastrophe like the Final Solution, it was their support for the regime that made that mass murder possible. Only the people could isolate the Jews socially,

a first step necessarily preceding the expulsion and then murder of the
Jews.

Anti-Semitism was not as important for building the Nazi mass movement as was reemployment and the renewed German national stature,
following Hitler's foreign policy successes and the abrogation of the
Versailles Treaty. Yet Hitler identified anti-Semitism as a force useful
for gaining and expanding political power;[33] Jews served "as the master
symbol of the adversity of the German people . . . to unify the different
evils which beset them."[34] Hitler hoped to transcend party politics,
class differences, and even national borders with racism. Identifying
certain minority groups as hostile outsiders could help consolidate the
support of a majority. The notion that one had some neighbors who
were inferior had become part of everyday life during the fifty years
of the German Second Reich, down to 1933.[35]

    While some Germans victimized Jews for reasons of racial idealism,
some were motivated by career incentives. Paper-pushing bureaucrats,
especially, gave preference to their jobs, regardless of the consequences.
Hans Pfundtner, state secretary at the Interior Ministry, kept doing
his job, even though he had a bad conscience about the results of his
work. Bernhard Lösener, the "Jewish expert" at the same ministry,
claimed after the war that Pfundtner "was, on the inside, in opposition
to the entire anti-Jewish agitation . . . but avoided friction so as not
to endanger his position."[36] Pfundtner was unable even to raise his
voice if it challenged authority. In his key position, to "avoid friction"
was to provide the technical support and the authority of legitimate
office to genocide.

    Lösener himself generally maintained that as the Interior Min-
istry's "Jewish expert" he had little power to make a difference. Yet
he also claimed, in self-justification, that had he advocated sharper
measures against the Jews, he could have advanced his career. "If I
had made proposals back then aimed at sharpening the pressures on
the Jews, they would have fallen on most fruitful ground," he writes,
"and I would have rapidly come into favor with the most powerful."[37]
A secretary in Eichmann's office claimed in a postwar trial testimony
that her boss, a deputy to Eichmann, had not been at all especially
anti-Semitic but that he bristled with career ambitions. He impressed
his superiors by assiduously organizing the transportation to death
camps of Jews from all over Europe.

    Party climbers and career makers knew that anti-Semitism cor-
responded with their self-interest since anti-Semitism was clearly "the

core component of ideology to which the Führer was totally committed."[38] One young careerist eager to make his mark was Georg Dengler,
a thirty-nine-year-old Gestapo officer in Darmstadt whose position was
buried far below that of Adolf Eichmann's deputy on the organizational
chart of administration for the Final Solution. Dengler was charged
with separating and deporting intermarried Jews, a job that he vigor-
ously carried out, according to the judge at his postwar trial, as a possible
way of "ensuring the good will and promotion of his superiors."[39]
Given the means of proving one's Nazi stripes through vigorous anti-
Semitism, the *Mischlinge* and intermarried Germans in the fringe
categories were especially likely to become the targets of lower-level
bureaucrats attempting to prove their Nazi worth. Hitler held back
from giving directives on intermarried Jews that matched Nazi ideology. Given the clear Nazi ideology, lower-level officials who did not
understand the leadership's concern with morale were tempted to act
radically against intermarried Jews and *Mischlinge*.

At his trial in Jerusalem, Eichmann said that he had felt supported,
or at least not opposed, by German society. Individual conscience itself,
as his testimony indicated, is determined by social conditioning. Goebbels portrayed the Final Solution as a fulfillment of the desires of the
German people. This was easier for those carrying it out to believe, as
long as the public looked the other way. Eichmann testified that "the
most potent factor in the soothing of his own conscience was the simple
fact that he could see no one, no one at all, who actually was against
the Final Solution." He "had always been over-awed by 'good society.'
. . . His conscience was indeed set at rest when he saw the zeal and
eagerness with which 'good society' everywhere reacted as he did . . .
his conscience spoke with a 'respectable voice,' with the voice of respectable society around him."[40]

VIII

KRISTALLNACHT: INTERMARRIAGES AND THE LESSONS OF POGROM

November 9, 1938, brought the pogrom known as Kristallnacht. In fifteen hours, on the streets of towns and cities across the Reich, the Germans burned 101 synagogues, demolished 76 others, and destroyed 7,500 businesses. The rampage killed ninety-one people and at least twenty thousand Jews, many from Berlin, were arrested and deported to concentration camps in Buchenwald, Dachau, and Sachsenhausen. Again, Joseph Goebbels was the chief instigator of the violence, and again, he gave instructions to make it seem that this pillaging was the work of the people in general, rather than of the party.[1] This was the last action of public SA-style violence against the Jews, and it was followed by a harsher phase of official sanctions against Germany's Jews, just as three years earlier the great increase in the incidences of boycotts and violence against Jews during the spring and summer of 1935 presaged the Nuremberg Laws and a new phase of persecution.

"Aryanizations," the expropriation or buyout (at cut-rate prices) of Jewish businesses, began the day after the physical destruction.[2]

Again (even though they generally did not support the pogrom and its disorderly destruction),[3] the Germans looked on passively, and their silence allowed Goebbels to declare the pogrom a result of the righteous indignation in the collective German soul, and the regime the direct agent of the people.[4] His claim that popular opinion consistently governed public policy was a fantasy, but he chose this lie because it was best suited to the regime's self-image and aspirations.

KRISTALLNACHT IN BERLIN

Other than those from the Germans married to Jews, there were no significant German protests over Kristallnacht. These protests represent a turning point in the regime's awareness of the tension between two of its most basic goals: maintaining the image of Germans united behind Nazism and isolating and persecuting Jews who were married to Germans.

At the time of the pogrom Werner Goldberg had just completed his term at the Reich Labor Service and was working temporarily at his old firm before beginning his term of military service. Unsuspecting, Werner left for work that morning. As his train passed by Fasanenstrasse, Werner saw that the synagogue there lay in smoldering ashes. On Alexanderplatz he saw entire rows of broken shopwindows. On Königstrasse so much broken glass littered the sidewalk that pedestrians were making their way down the middle of the street. Only one store had been spared, the huge Israel department store, a major Berlin business stretching around the corner from Königstrasse onto Spandauerstrasse, with about forty showcase windows. Werner's employer, Schneller and Schmeider, hadn't been touched because it wasn't on the first floor. When his boss explained that the action was against Jews, Werner was surprised to know that there were so many Jewish-owned shops. The Israel store had been spared because it was owned by a foreign Jew, his boss explained.

As Werner and his fellow workers left their building for lunch, the attack on the Israel store began. People began throwing pavement stones through the store windows. Most marauders were dressed in civilian clothes, but some wore the uniforms and boots of the SA and other party functionaries. Werner remembered thinking that the huge number of stones betrayed the fact that someone had been brought them in especially for this destruction.

It was the lack of action from the police, in particular, that brought home to Werner how vulnerable he was. On the Israel store's corner, as the store was being attacked, a policeman stood directing traffic and refused to intervene. Piles of clothing came flying through the broken windows. On the street the clothing was tossed onto a huge, crackling bonfire. "Within a half hour it was destroyed," Werner said. "People stood there and looked at it and did nothing. No one dared do anything. But it was clear that the people were shocked throughout Berlin. They had their fists balled up in their pockets, but they didn't pull them out. People didn't have the courage. And that's when I really felt it wasn't safe any longer."

Wally Grodka recalled a different fear: Her non-Jewish friends refused to take her and Günter in. How much less likely, then, that any ordinary German would protest? The one German who did try to help the Grodkas was a Nazi. In the early-morning hours the night of the pogrom, Günter's friend Hans Jüttner, a Nazi who had contacts within the SA, warned the Grodkas not to stay home. Günter had learned to trust Jüttner, and he reached his father to warn him too. But Mr. Grodka, with his usual confidence, insisted that nothing could happen to him; he had fought four years for "the fatherland" during World War I and received two medals for bravery. "It was impossible to instill a sense of danger in him," Günter said. "That was really bad. There were other Jewish soldiers who—before the Kristallnacht— thought they were safe, even if other German Jews weren't."[5]

Uncertain of what would come next, Günter and Wally decided to seek cover in Berlin's Grünewald Forest. At dawn, exhausted and miserably cold, they walked the six miles back to Alexanderplatz. Jews on the street turned in fright at the sound of each approaching person or car. On Münzstrasse, near Alexanderplatz, the Grodkas were shocked to find the huge two-story jewelry store beside the theater totally destroyed. Nazis in uniform and others in civilian clothing stood around, tearing off plaster from the building and picking up stones to hurl them into the store. A cheer went up from the crowd each time a stone did an especially large amount of damage. Wally agreed to pass by their apartment to see whether it had been attacked. Günter waited at a distance. At the corner milk store Wally overheard her neighbor Ulla Hensel gloating about the goods she had looted. Despondent and still uncertain about whether it was safe at their apartment, the Grodkas sought shelter with their non-Jewish friends. Not one, including Jütt- ner, would take them in. "They felt that they were under observation and that it would be too dangerous," Wally remembered. "That's the way it was already in 1938."

German women married to Jewish men were in an anomalous position: protected citizens of the Reich and threatened members of "Jewish households." Wally Grodka and Charlotte Israel played a more public, reconnoitering role than their Jewish husbands, and during Kristallnacht both of them surveyed the damage and made assessments while their husbands lay low. Charlotte and Julius's apartment was in the Gartenhaus wing, away from the street, and like Werner, they didn't notice the plunder until the next morning. As they sat down to breakfast, Julius's sister Erna rushed in, pouring out the story. As a Jew Erna had come by hoping for refuge with Charlotte and Julius— or, more precisely, hoping for protection from Charlotte, the German. There was word that the attack on Jews had come as revenge for the act of Herschel Grynszpan, a Jew who two days earlier had assassinated Ernst vom Rath, the third secretary of the German Embassy in Paris. Grynszpan was a seventeen-year-old Jew who in 1936 had left his home in Germany to escape persecution. He hoped for a temporary permit to live in France, but the French denied him this in July 1938. Then in October, during the first forced deportation of Jews from Nazi Germany, the regime packed Grynszpan's family and thousands of other Polish Jews living in Germany into sealed boxcars and shipped them across the border into Poland. There they sat in limbo, under appalling conditions, while the Polish government at first refused to admit them, and then, in compromise, finally agreed to accept seven thousand of the fifty thousand Polish Jews living in Germany. The young Grynszpan, indignant that Jews were being rejected in so many places, went to the German Embassy in Paris and shot the first official who gave him an audience.[6] "The Jews back then were horrified at what Grynszpan had done," said Charlotte. "They said, 'That nut, what has he done to us now!'"

Speaking to the foreign press the day after the pogrom, Goebbels implied that the pogrom was in retaliation for the death of Rath and claimed: "The German government is in this matter in absolute and total agreement with the German people. The Jewish Question will be resolved in short order in a way that satisfies this sentiment of the German people. That's the way the German people want it, and we are only executing their will."[7]

"PRIVILEGED INTERMARRIAGE":
THE MISMEASURE OF WOMAN?

Kristallnacht resulted in only one significant protest—by the German partners of victimized Jews, made directly to high officials. According to one historian, the prominent Jews from intermarriages were among Kristallnacht's victims,[8] and Rudolf Schottländer, a respected intermarried professor in Berlin, heard at the time that Germans married to Jewish victims of the pogrom were indignant. These marriage partners went to the top, complaining to Hermann Goering, head of Germany's four-year economic plan, and the Hungarian statesman Nikolaus Horthy.[9] In the weeks following the pogrom Goering suggested dividing intermarriages into two categories, "privileged" and "nonprivileged" (or "simple"). Privileged intermarriages, he proposed, existed when the wife was Jewish or the couple had at least one child they had baptized as a Christian, rather than enrolled in a Jewish Community. Nonprivileged (or simple) intermarriages involved couples whose Mischlinge children were classified as Jews (Geltungsjuden), as well as childless couples with Jewish husbands. Privileged intermarriages outnumbered nonprivileged ones nearly three to one because the overwhelming majority of Mischlinge were baptized as Christians. Hitler accepted Goering's proposal in December 1938, and most intermarried couples became "privileged."[10]

Nonprivileged intermarried Jews were now to be treated like other Jews, while Jews of privileged intermarriages would be exempted from the worst aspects of the persecution. The regime divided intermarriages to prevent further unrest, by pacifying the segment of intermarried Germans it considered most influential. At this time German leaders were making plans for the forced separation of Jews within major German cities. The people, under influences of the regime, had isolated Jews socially. Now German Jews were to be physically separated, concentrated into houses already owned by Jews. Contained in these Jewish houses, Jews would still be scattered throughout the various districts of urban areas, but the number of Jewish addresses would be greatly reduced. Reinhard Heydrich, as head of the Security Police and the SD, rejected a plan for ghettoizing German Jews into single districts since the "watchful eye of the whole population" kept the Jews under control, "forc[ing] the Jew to behave himself."[11]

Heydrich realized that Germans had gone well beyond merely avoiding Jews to actively denouncing and excluding them. But here too (as with efforts to isolate the Jews socially) intermarried couples were an obvious sticking point. The regime had too much fear of popular and church protest to attempt forcibly to break up marriages and separate families. The regime was no match for the force behind social traditions and religious sanctions upholding marriage and family. Could it then send Germans married to Jews into Jewish houses? On the other hand, could it allow Jews married to Germans to continue living in a racially purified Germany?

The regime responded to this dilemma, as it did to that of the *Mischlinge*, by dividing the problem group into two parts. Relying on the categories at Nuremberg, one criterion for dividing intermarriages was the religious affiliation of children: Were they members of the Jewish Community or baptized Christians (and thus perhaps protected by a church)? Goering was also worried about *Mischling* affiliations with another venerable institution, the military. Unlike *Geltungsjuden*, baptized *Mischlinge* were not Jews according to the Nuremberg Laws. They still served in the military, and the regime could not afford to alienate its soldiers.

The second criterion for dividing intermarriages reflected the traditional sexist notions of the party's leadership that women were weak-willed and best at bearing children. If the Jew in an intermarriage was a woman, the marriage was to be privileged, but if the woman in the intermarriage was German, it was nonprivileged. These new categories increased the participation of intermarried German women in their husbands' fates. If in traditional Germany homemaking was the woman's career, then intermarried women now would feel the brunt of the discrimination borne by men under the earlier regulations that had cut off job and career opportunities for intermarried Germans. Goering still hoped to persuade intermarried women to "return" to the German community and productive childbearing.[12]

Goering's hope and Hitler's decree reflected National Socialism's notion that women were incapable of leadership, either at home or in politics. Reflecting his notion that "women [even German women] were very weak individuals, without wills of their own," Hitler had ordered that only men—Jewish or German—should be punished in cases of Jewish-German sexual relations. Women were to be exempted from punishment for *Rassenschande*.[13]

To be sure, women were important in their own way, but men determined the pattern. Women should be homemakers for German men and bearers of the racial people. "If we say the world of the man is the state, the world of the man is his commitment, his struggle on behalf of the community, we could then perhaps say that the world of

the woman is a smaller world," Hitler explained to the National Socialist Women's Organization at the Nuremberg party congress of 1934.
"For her world is her husband, her family, her children and her home.
But where would the big world be if no one wanted to look after the
small world? How could the big world continue to exist, if there was
no one to make the task of caring for the small world the center of
their lives? No, the big world rests upon this small world! The big
world cannot survive if the small world is not secure."[14]

If women lacked a capacity for political leadership, they were also
subordinate to men even at home.[15] In Nazi Germany the husband
was the official head of the household. Consequently the husband's
racial identity determined that of the household itself. Thus since Rudi,
Julius, and Günter were Jewish, Elsa, Charlotte, and Wally belonged
to "Jewish households," directly in the path of many anti-Jewish
measures.

Basing intermarriage policies on gender roles led to indecorous
compromises in the regime's ideology. It shielded some Jews from racial
persecution while it turned some Germans into its victims. German
women married to Jews were sometimes more vulnerable to persecution
than Jewish women married to Germans. When in 1939 Jews were
concentrated into Jewish houses, intermarried German women were
required by law to move with their Jewish husbands. Intermarried
Jewish women, though, were legally exempted. Later intermarried German women had the Star of David posted on their outside doorways.
Gestapo agents might drop in at any moment to conduct a random
house search, turning the house upside down to find some violation of
this or that law. The star publicly proclaimed a Jewish household.
Jewish women married to German men, however, never wore the Star
of David or had it on their doorways.[16] The government distributed
food ration cards to each household through the house superintendent,
but Jews and intermarried couples had their own distribution centers.
To members of Jewish households, wartime rations were reduced. German women married to Jews received no clothing rations or special
rations for Christmas or to support morale after an especially heavy
bombing. "Jewish women who married Aryans were better off than
I," said Charlotte Israel, who observed the differences closely while
sharing an apartment with a "privileged" intermarried couple in 1944.
"Intermarried Jewish women were protected through their husbands.
But through my husband I was made vulnerable."[17]

Ironically it was the regime's policies that forced intermarried
German women to learn new roles as key wage earners, public representatives of the household, and political dissidents. With Kristall-

nacht the Jewish persecution entered a new phase marked by the Aryanization of Jewish businesses. The day after the pogrom Jewish businesses and trades that had not already been "voluntarily" sold to Germans were compelled by decree to do so.[18] Some intermarried Jews transferred property to their partners, but beginning in 1933, the regime had also kept lists of the financial interests of Germans married to Jews. Jews as well as "German-blooded" spouses of Jews were required to register possessions worth five thousand marks or more.[19]

Intermarried Germans took more responsibility for the financial support of their families as Jewish partners were deprived of their livelihoods. Since nearly one-half of Germany's Jews were self-employed (the German figure was 16 percent), this new measure hit Jews hard. Many were in retailing,[20] and in certain sectors of the textile and clothing industries, Jews owned half the enterprises. Werner Goldberg worked in one of 3,750 Berlin clothing shops under Jewish ownership at the time of November pogrom.[21]

As the regime realized its political goals, the private lives of intermarried German women grew politically important. The regime thought their new status would push these women into divorce. Instead these women perforce assumed new, powerful roles within their marriages. Charlotte Israel, Elsa Holzer, Wally Grodka, and other intermarried German women were never politically active, nor did they ever imagine confonting a ruthless dictatorship, until the Nazis presented them with a choice of political opposition or family desertion.

Charlotte had to learn to use her power as a German. Because she looked like an ideal "Aryan" in offices dominated by men, her blond hair and good looks were of priceless value, she said. "Whenever there was anything to do with official business, my husband always said, 'It's better if you go, Charlotte—you with your blond head.' " Charlotte went for both of them to get a business license, to find an apartment, to fetch ration cards, to do the shopping. In the offices of Nazi police and bureaucrats, she learned to defend herself, she said. It was important to look straight in the eyes of policemen and bureaucrats, asking for what she needed as if it were normal, as if she had nothing to hide. Her basic rule was never to show fear. "In the presence of the Nazi officials, one must never cry. When they screamed at me, 'Why don't you get divorced from your guy?' I said back to them, 'Why don't *you* get divorced?' And when they grew threatening, and said, 'You'll hear from us again,' I turned around and said, 'Sure, do what you want, that'll be my pleasure.' But sometimes I too had no idea what I should do or say."

THE GESTAPO SUGGESTS DIVORCE

The dictatorship's decision to grant privileges to some intermarriages compromised its policies on both gender and race. The division of intermarriages was not successful in eliciting many divorces or in intimidating those in noncompliance and protest. The decision to grant privileges to German men in intermarriages deferred to established, institutional influence. Women's power, however, did not depend much on institutions and connections. Two to three decades earlier German women had relied on protest and public actions to gain the vote and oppose the First World War. Now they were refusing to divorce in higher numbers than men. Their actions in fact were of the kind Hitler advocated for undermining unworthy governments.[22]

An early sign that new pressures in 1938 might fail was the response of intermarried Germans to Gestapo "consultations." The National Marriage Law of July 1938 gave intermarried Germans new opportunities for getting divorced, and especially following Kristallnacht, the Gestapo began a campaign to convince Germans married to Jews to do just that. The Gestapo began to summon intermarried Germans into their offices for consultations. First came a friendly suggestion. Divorce was in the German's self-interest, given the regime's view of race. Some Gestapo agents appeared genuinely perplexed. Why would a blond, good-looking German woman marry and remain married to a Jew? If the intermarried German demurred, the demeanor of the consulting Gestapo man might turn mean. Germans who persisted in unions with Jews would have to share the Jewish fate.

In Berlin Germans married to Jews endured numerous consultations about their marriages. Hans-Oskar Löwenstein said his mother was called several dozen times to the Prinz-Albrecht Strasse Gestapo headquarters, where she was bombarded alternately with saccharine promises and implicit threats.[23] To receive a divorce, the Gestapo pointed out, Mrs. Löwenstein need only admit that National Socialism had so enlightened her that she now saw her marriage to a Jew as a mistake. Mrs. Löwenstein was from one of Europe's noble families, and the Gestapo promised her that upon her divorce, her son, Hans, would be accepted into a prestigious German military academy and trained as an officer.

Hannelore Steudel, a Berliner who had inherited a family estate in Potsdam, Berlin's posh suburb, was persuaded to divorce her Jewish husband.[24] Otherwise the state would confiscate her estate, she was told. So she divorced, held on to the villa, and her Jewish husband moved out. Still, they secretly saw each other until January 1944, when he was deported to the Jewish ghetto in Theresienstadt (after the war they remarried, but the villa was gone, lost to the East German state).

To women with children, the Gestapo drove a harder bargain: Abandon your husband to save your children. Continued marriage would render them a Jewish fate. After a divorce, on the other hand, the state would embrace *Mischling* children as German.

The Gestapo told Erika Lewine's mother she could save her entire family if she got divorced. Like many others, Erika's mother had incurred the scorn of her own family by marrying a Jew. Like others, she had been married for quite a long time, and was accustomed to pariah status. Her family was her meaning, her reason for living. Beyond that Nazi racism led her into active protest, with political meaning. In February 1933, directly following the Nazi assumption of government power, she converted to Judaism. "That was a protest," Erika recalled. "When the Gestapo informed my mother that she should get a divorce," Erika said proudly, "she wouldn't budge. 'Why should I divorce?' she asked. 'I've married my husband, and it hasn't even occurred to me to divorce him.'" Often the Gestapo would suggest that after divorce it would be possible to have another, much nicer marriage, to which one intermarried German, married to the Jewish photographer Abraham Pisarek, retorted: "I've married the best man in the world. Why should I divorce?"[25]

It became known that despite Gestapo promises in the consultations, Jews divorced by Germans were doomed. "There were some [in intermarriages] who under pressure got divorced," Elsa, who was married to a Jew, said. "Yes, yes, that was the worst. The Jew whose partner divorced him, was immediately arrested. We knew a cigar man in the Neukölln section of Berlin, a great big cigar businessman, a Jew. But his Frau was 'Aryan,' and she divorced him. And the man disappeared overnight. Overnight. Gone." In Berlin the Gestapo arrested within twenty-four hours Jews whose German spouses died or divorced them. In Prague they were deported within a month.[26]

Elsa Holzer was among the many, many intermarried Germans who were ordered to appear at the Gestapo offices on Prinz-Albrecht for a consultation. Prinz-Albrecht Strasse No. 9, the former Hotel Prinz-Albrecht, was known simply as the SS House or the SS capital, and No. 8, beside it, concentrated more administrative offices of the Nazi police empire than any other single building. It housed the headquarters of the Gestapo, the central offices of Himmler and his personal staff, and the headquarters of the central agency of Himmler's SS police conglomerate the Reich Security Main Office (RSHA).[27] Approaching the palatial entrance of this colossal building, Elsa wondered what the Gestapo wanted. While she was detained here, might they not arrest Rudi? After a long wait, she was led to her interrogator, a well-mannered man, she said, with a pleasant face, like a family doctor.

He began with flattery: "You're a beautiful woman. Why do you stick to your husband?" He was earnest and seemed genuinely perplexed. "I married my husband because he is supposed to be my husband," Elsa replied. "Yes, but don't you know that a good German doesn't get together with a Jew?" he asked. When she persisted, he got up and left. Another officer entered. He began to insult and then threaten her, asking what she liked so much about her husband and suggesting that he himself would be better. Furious, Elsa demanded to speak to his supervisor. He left the room and left her alone. "Then I thought, Who knows what will happen now?" she said. "I was afraid. *Afraid.* I waited half an hour, shaking with fear, sweating. And then I left. And nothing happened. They only wanted to harass people. Those men weren't even old either, but in their best years.

"If it hadn't been for me, they would have taken my husband. I had such fear that they would do this, and I always wanted to be at home, always there where he needed me. I was his guardian angel for a short time. Now he's mine. Many married for money, and as soon as the money disappeared, so did the love. That wasn't the case for us. My husband was so logical that sometimes it hurt. He told the truth. We married, you could say, because we liked each other and understood each other. What we had would never happen again.

"You see, it was a terrible, bad time. I probably couldn't have held out if my husband had been a beast or a drunk. In that case I could imagine divorce. If I hadn't had anything in common with my husband, I wouldn't have stayed together with him. But I can't say that I regretted or didn't regret having married him. I did what was mine to do. When I could protect him, I protected him."

THE JEWISH RENTAL RELATIONS LAW

With laws prohibiting Jews from concerts, theaters, and cinemas, Germans who remained with Jewish spouses had fewer and fewer opportunities for social and cultural life. Foreshadowing the order of 1941 requiring Jews to wear the Star of David, Jews had their passports marked with a large yellow J. When the war started in September 1939, the regime ordered strict new curfew laws for Jews. Then telephone lines were ripped out of Jewish households,[28] and radios were confiscated.

January 1939 brought Wally Grodka the news that Jews would no longer be protected under the German rental protection laws. From the January 11 edition of *Der Gerichtssaal* Wally clipped an article for her diary: "The District Court in Berlin has further decided: If one partner of a couple that has rented [a place] together is Jewish, rental protection is nonexistent. Whoever is married to a Jew will have to share his fate."[29]

The Berlin court's decision was only a prelude to the Law on Rental Relations of April 30, 1939. Under that law Wally, like all Jews in nonprivileged intermarriages, was ordered to move into one of the Jewish houses, buildings owned by Jews and occupied by Jews. Months later in German-occupied Poland Jews were crowded into ghettos, but within Germany itself the regime's sensitivity to popular opinion helped prevent this.[30] The Law on Rental Relations with Jews established that Jews could conclude rental contracts only with other Jews, so that they would be crammed into the Jewish houses.[31] The leaders of the Berlin Jewish Community, upon oral instructions from the Gestapo, were charged with implementing all aspects of this new housing law. At the community a Housing Advisory Office was created under the direction of Dr. Martha Mosse, a Jew who in 1933 had been expelled from her post within the Prussian police service as a police councillor (*Polizeirat*) in the office of the Berlin president of police. "The leadership of the community was ready to lend assistance under the justified assumption that one would be able to soften many hardships," remembered Dr. Mosse about this new realm of authority.[32] The new Housing Office was created within the Jewish Community for maintaining statistics and carrying on the necessary correspondence.[33] All "Jewish" living space was registered, by provision of the law, with the community. Every arrangement for living space, every change of quarters required the permission of the Jewish Community. Jewish owners of houses and apartments were compelled "at the request of Community authorities to take in other Jews as renters or sublets."[34]

In Wally Grodka's building and neighborhood the campaign to throw Jews out arose suddenly. Wally and her husband, Günter, took in his relatives, who began to arrive on their doorstep after being expelled from their own places. In their house a Nazi named Nikolai appeared at the door of a Jewish couple and demanded that they move out. Nikolai wore the golden Nazi party emblem, reserved for the party's first hundred thousand members and other Nazi notables. A man by the name of Hanke came to another Jewish couple in the

Grodkas' building. Hanke introduced himself as a friend of the Nazi "martyr" Horst Wessel, and demanded: "The dirty Jew will vacate the apartment within three days!" The Jewish couple left, but the Hankes, meanwhile, threw open the windows and waited to move in until the "Jewish stink" was gone. Nikolai moved in with four brats, who spent their days in the courtyard outside of the Grodkas' window, hitting and biting each other, while every now and then Nikolai appeared to interrupt them with loud curses.

On the heels of Kristallnacht, the Rental Relations Law was presented as a measure to clear the way for the new Germanica. Ostensibly it signaled another step toward Hitler's new Berlin. Two years before, his fourth anniversary as chancellor, Hitler had unveiled his vision for an architectural transformation of Berlin and Albert Speer's plan to rebuild the center city. In preparation, venerable buildings throughout the heart of Berlin were razed, and Jews removed.[35]

The Law on Rental Relations stripped Jews of more than 30,000 Berlin apartments.[36] A report requested by Albert Speer from early 1939 identified 1,646 Berlin apartments of five rooms or more, and 267 smaller apartments, as targets of evacuation. About 600 large apartments and 40 smaller ones were in Charlottenburg, more than in any other Berlin district.[37] Hans-Oskar Löwenstein, who together with his father and mother lived in a stylish twelve-room place on Berlin's ostentatious Kurfürstendamm, was forced to take in four Jewish families. "Our apartment was a grand apartment, but we were forced to take in subleasees, until there were twelve of us," he remembered. "It was so crowded that we had to take turns using the kitchen and the bathroom. It went something like: The Schönlange family is allowed to use the kitchen between eight and nine; the Mohnhausen family between nine and ten, and so forth. That was a so-called Jewish house."

THE (POLITICAL) PROBLEMS OF POPULATION POLICIES

As the regime was implementing the Jewish Rental Relations Law, it was just launching another of its racial hygiene initiatives, the Euthanasia program. Racial hygiene initiatives were designed to eliminate all "non-Aryans" first of all. Euthanasia eliminated "inferior" Germans in a program that divided German families and led to protests.

Since July 1933 the regime had sterilized Germans with congenital diseases, arousing little opposition save that of the victims and their families. Germans tended to protest (even if they claimed to object on principle) only after the law had victimized them personally. Seeking cooperation, Nazi propaganda made a slogan out of the Nazi principle "Common good before individual good."[38] Nevertheless, as the sterilization law's victims increased, so did the volume of complaints. Many "bitterly condemned" the state for violating personal freedoms.[39] When its drive for a racially pure nation moved from sterilization to murdering Germans with mental and hereditary illnesses (designated as "life unworthy of living"), the regime acted under a veil of secrecy. No law was promulgated. The Euthanasia program claimed its first victim during the winter of 1938–39,[40] just after Kristallnacht and during the radicalization of anti-Semitic measures.

Hitler said in 1935 that Euthanasia should be postponed until wartime, when the expected opposition from churches "would not play so significant a role in the context of war as at other times."[41] Himmler advocated postponing it until propaganda had convinced Germans to support it openly.[42] But with the start of war Hitler pushed ahead with an order to expand the secret Euthanasia program.

Secrecy proved impossible. Euthanasia revealed the difficulty of separating a family in order to victimize just part of it. Carried out on German soil (some thirty different German hospitals participated), the grim truth slipped out. Euthanasia doctors and bureaucrats made mistakes. They sent two urns of ashes to the same family. Or (along with their sincere regrets) claimed the cause of death was appendicitis when the victim had long since had an appendectomy. Staff members from the Euthanasia asylums, tongues loosened at the local beer hall, occasionally spoke of their grim work.[43] As word began to get around, rumors proliferated, threatening the veil of secrecy around Euthanasia. "Psychological problems" arose, threatening not just secrecy but also public morale.

IX

AT WAR AND AT HOME: *MISCHLINGE* IN HITLER'S ARMY

> Just as we turn into animals when we go up to the [front] line, because that is the only thing which brings us through safely, so we turn into wags and loafers when we are resting. . . . We want to live at any price.
>
> —ERICH MARIA REMARQUE

At dawn on September 1, 1939, Werner Goldberg and some 1,500,000 other German soldiers poured across the Polish border, in the opening aggression of World War II. With stunning speed and efficiency, German troops converged on Warsaw from the north, south, and west. Once again, Werner and his boyhood friend Karl Wolf were soldiers in the same cause. As a *Mischling* Werner Goldberg was back on the inside. But his mission brought him into terrible conflict not just with Poles (and the Jews there) but also with intermarried Germans—like Charlotte or Elsa or even his own parents—who realized that Hitler's victory meant their own personal destruction. Werner went home to a father who was the racial enemy of Germany, while Karl's father was a high-ranking SS officer.

In his Wehrmacht uniform Werner sensed new power. Normally a soldier senses danger about war, but Werner remembers the feeling of safety—safety from the threat to Jews he had witnessed in the

Kristallnacht Pogrom and from his nightmare visions of the police who had refused to stop it. He himself was now behind a gun and within the ranks of the dominant army. The question of race seemed behind him, for as he said, "No one asked whether I should serve in the army. It was a simple fact that for the moment I had reached this safe shore, where I could say to myself, 'Nothing can happen to me now.' "

Once on the inside, Werner was popular again. Had anyone inquired about his Jewish ancestry, he could have referred to the newspaper. One Sunday a friend called. Had Werner noticed that day's edition of the newspaper *Berliner Tagesblatt*? There in the Sunday segment was a picture of the young blond Goldberg in his army uniform, with the caption "The Ideal German Soldier." "Each of us soldiers had to be photographed," Werner remembered. "And the photographer here in Schmargendorf sold my photo to the paper. Everyone chuckled."

On the Polish front, in September 1939, Werner moved behind the armored panzer tank divisions, supported by the Luftwaffe, to breach Polish Army lines. "We had to march behind tanks, forty to fifty kilometers per day, in thick forest. It was half dark, so that no one could see a thing, and all we heard was the dense exchange of gunfire. It wasn't like a maneuver anymore! Polish soldiers sat in trees, tied into place. And from below, we couldn't really tell which direction they were shooting from. That was a lousy situation. Someone discovered one of them and emptied his gun into him, but he didn't drop. They were strapped up there, so that they wouldn't drop if shot and reveal the whole nest. Then a tank pointed its gauge into the trees and let fly. And after that all was silent."

When the Wehrmacht crushed Poland in less than four weeks, Germans in general were exuberant. Charlotte recalled that it became more difficult to oppose Hitler in any way. Even the army officer and later resistance leader Claus von Stauffenberg exulted in Germany's spectacular military defeat of Poland.[3] One exuberant general went so far as to claim that only "the incredulous, the weak, and the doubtful people" had not been converted to Hitler at this point.[4]

In August 1939, just six years into his Thousand-Year Reich, Hitler sensed that his charismatic spell had reached a level he could not sustain. Like any magnetic leader, he measured his popularity by his successes. Contemplating the moment to launch war in August 1939, he remarked that "no one will ever again have the confidence of the whole German people as I have," a circumstance he considered "favorable" for going to war, since it would "no longer prevail in two or three years' time."[1] Hitler needed his charisma to rally Germans behind the war, for in contrast with the mood at the outset of World War I, few Germans were eager for war in 1939. Hitler believed military conquest depended on the popular will to fight.[2] Although he knew Germany was not yet optimally prepared economically and militarily, he pushed ahead, pinning his hopes on short, lightning-fast campaigns that not only won territory and resources for Germany but also maintained morale at home by keeping German casualties low, while avoiding a mobilization of the economy for Total War.

Charlotte found that among family members and neighbors, Hitler's victories proved Hitler's virtue. "When I visited my mother, all she could speak about was the glorious victories of the Führer," Charlotte said. "Once she had the radio on, and there was this continuous boasting jubilation about how Germany was beating France, and I said, 'Mutti, turn that thing off or I'll throw it through the window!' She said, 'I'm glad that Germany won,' but I said, 'To hell with Germany, Mother. What will happen to Julius and me if Germany wins?' Had

The young blond Werner Goldberg, pictured on the title page of a Berlin newspaper in 1939, above the caption "The Ideal German Soldier." Private Werner Goldberg was a *Mischling*, however, and only appeared to be the ideal "racial" German the newspaper took him to be.

the Germans won, then everything would have been over for me and my husband. That would have been our end. I grew more and more distant from my mother."

Werner Goldberg had no long-term view about his fate and that of his family should Germany prevail. For now he found refuge and acceptance in the military, that winter of 1940, even as he suspected that his status as a *Mischling* might hold him back. At Christmas that year Werner experienced what he called "his great success experience." It was not a military feat but the reading, before his regiment, of a poem he had written. In December 1939, Werner explained, his officer had asked him to plan and arrange an Advent celebration for the regiment. Werner had been wondering why ten or twelve of his colleagues had already received promotions on December 1, while he had not, and he took this request as an opportunity to inquire. Was it because he was a *Mischling* that he been kept back?

"The officer was mighty irritated," Werner remembered, "and let me have it. 'That kind of injustice doesn't exist!' he told me bluntly. 'A soldier is a soldier! We don't know a difference here between Aryan and non-Aryan. You're a soldier like all the rest, with rights and duties. And of course you'll be promoted at the time we think that's right.' "

Werner set to work planning the celebration. To cap the evening's program, he wrote a poem. As he read it fifty years later, his voice choked with emotion. At Christmas 1939 he had bathed in acceptance as his regiment cheered the power of his poem to explain their own feelings. "It was as if a bomb had struck," he recalled. "The entire officer corps was up and clapping. 'That's it, young man!' they cried. So I was fully integrated and accepted in my regiment."

But Werner's deep fear soon found new grounds. Like many other Jews, Werner's father had lost his job in the anti-Jewish measures following Kristallnacht, and his health had deteriorated. Suddenly he was bedridden with an illness that was diagnosed as prostate cancer. Werner, the soldier in uniform, had already helped find hospital treatment for his father, who as a Jew had been turned away from the famed Berlin Charitee clinic. So in the early spring of 1940 Mr. Goldberg called again on Werner, now stationed with his company in Trier in preparation for the German assault on France. Werner's mother wrote that her husband had recently been subjected to a row of frightening new regulations. His passport had been stamped to make his Jewish identity obvious. He could no longer travel outside his own neighborhood in Berlin without special permission. He could receive only "Jewish food rations." Jews received food ration cards in sheets just like the Germans, but their cards were stamped with the large yellow *J* to indicate that they could not be redeemed. Jews could not receive meat, white bread, eggs, milk, fish. The final straw for Mr. Goldberg were his orders to report to the Reichsbahn for hard labor.

Werner found this all "somehow totally absurd." He, the son of a person persecuted by the Reich, was a soldier on the front in the service of the Reich. And his father, weak and bedridden, had doctor's orders not to work! Fully convinced of the validity of his case, Werner took the matter to his superior, who referred him up the military chain of command. He shuttled from one superior to the next, as each in turn referred him and his "Jewish matter" on to the next superior officer. Finally, through a colleague who was a nephew of their general, Werner made an appointment to see the general of the Potsdam Garrison, Count Erich von Brockdorff-Ahlefeldt. The general received Werner politely, pacing his office floor back and forth behind his desk as Werner sat pouring out his story: "I'm on the front. And my father isn't allowed to travel, doesn't receive full food rations, and is marked as a Jew. And now the Labor Office has ordered him to report for hard labor."

Werner remembered Brockdorff-Ahlefeldt's response. The general shook his head and came to a sudden stop in front of him as he said: "Herewith I'm granting you a promotion. Take the proper uniform, strap on a pistol, and go to Berlin to arrange things as they should be for a German soldier. You have fourteen days. And if that's not enough, send me a telegram, and I'll renew your leave."

With new faith in justice, Werner set out for Berlin. "First I went to the Labor Office," he remembered. "They were initially unconcerned. But soon I succeeded in convincing them that sending my father to work just wouldn't do. I was in uniform! Then I went to the army headquarters to see that my father received food rations, like all the others. Then I had to go to the Food Ration Office. I was at a whole lot of offices and ministries—all in uniform."

Back at army headquarters Werner got the news: Hitler had ordered all *Mischlinge* and intermarried Germans expelled from the German military.[5] On April 8, 1940, on the verge of Germany's western offensive, Hitler's order expelling all persons of Jewish-German families from military service represented a revocation of the status granted them in the Nuremberg Laws. This new fate for *Mischlinge* also ran contrary to the so-called equalization with German-blooded. Equalizations resolved the conflict between Nazi race ideals and spectacular performances by *Mischlinge* by granting *Mischlinge* equal status with Aryans. The party and the ministries wove a net of regulations against

Mischlinge and then established elaborate, time-consuming procedures for the (few) exemptions of equalizations. The Interior Ministry screened petitions and sent meritorious ones on to Hans Lammers, the Reich chancellor. Lammers decided which ones to forward to Hitler, who sat in ultimate judgment over equalization petitions. Successful petitioners received a pedigree identifying them as German-blooded (printed on bright blue paper, however, to indicate the case of equalization rather than real German stock). Usually their children gained German status too, indicating again the political complications of dividing families. If a person was privileged enough to belong to the exclusive German national community, should he not also be allowed to bring those most important to him along? Just prior to ordering all *Mischlinge* expelled from the army, Hitler had granted a number of equalizations, citing the particular courage of their recipients in battle.[6]

Hitler had strategic as well as ideological reasons to expel *Mischlinge* and intermarried Germans from military service. Some Nazis, including Himmler, considered *Mischlinge* especially undependable, both because of their mixed blood and because of the poor way the state had treated them.[7] Yet if all *Mischlinge* had been undependable, equalizations would have never occurred. Equalizations compromised race ideology; keeping *Mischlinge* out of the military would deprive them of the opportunity to prove themselves.

When Werner learned of Hitler's order that would expel him from the protection of the military, he decided to ignore it. He was still lining up appointments and making his case in the halls of power when he heard the news on the radio: The Wehrmacht had invaded Luxembourg, in the first step of an arching drive around the Maginot Line and into northern France. That was on May 10, 1940, and the radio was also bringing news that Winston Churchill had replaced Neville Chamberlain as prime minister in Great Britain. Werner decided to get back to the front and the "secure shore." He called his company commander, who was also in Berlin, and made the case that it did not make sense for him, the young soldier, to quit in so critical a moment for Germany. His commander agreed. "I have no word yet of this so-called Führer order," Werner heard him say. "I give you my orders to return to the front. At once!"

As Werner left Berlin, he was about to find out the limitations of the army's power within the Reich—or at least of the limitations on the willingness of his superiors to resist the Nazi party. It took Werner six weeks to reach his regiment—more than four weeks longer than his company commander. "On the way I was with various different regiments, guarding prisoners of war, and so forth," Werner explained.

Finally he found his commander, lying in a hammock, at postvictory ease. France had signed an armistice. The ease with which Germany had felled its neighbor stunned the world but injected the regime with fresh confidence. Perhaps his commander would have retained Werner longer if the fighting had been protracted and damaging. But Werner's new orders were waiting for him when he arrived: "Return to Potsdam, take off the army uniform, and go home. You've been released."

Werner remembered that his army commander was sorry to have to expel him and organized a good-bye party for him in his army company. "That was very touching," Werner recalled. "We sang; there were speeches; we drank together. It was really great, a beautiful farewell, like one with good friends, who stood up for me. We were in a boat from which no one could step out. And now someone steps out. Into the water. Can he swim or not? That was very problematic."

The water Werner now had to swim was about to become much more dangerous, and he reacted with an attempt to keep his grip on the shore. Back at company headquarters in Berlin Werner resisted returning to the hunted and persecuted margins of society. He tried to maintain his place in the army. "Of course I tried to keep my uniform as long as possible," he said. But it was no use. He was forced to give it up and return to the leather clothing business, where he had worked under Mr. Grohm. Since Aryanization, the firm was the Feodor Schmeider Company, having changed to delete the Jewish name Schneller.

In Berlin, without his uniform, the young man once pictured as the ideal racial German was continually confronted with questions like "Why aren't you at the front?" Like women, children, and old men not fighting, he now followed the war through the news. In the summer of 1940 Berlin still glowed in the glory of the Wehrmacht's most recent victories. In less than ten months after defeating Poland, Germany had subjugated Norway, Denmark, Belgium, Holland, Luxembourg, and France. Only Britain, the island nation, still resisted, an effort the German press portrayed as a postponement of inevitable defeat. The Nazis swaggered with power, and for the moment Werner was once again an outsider, a man of military age justifying his civilian life as "on leave" from the front.

It is possible that Werner might have been allowed to remain with his company had he not drawn so much attention to his case within state agencies, about the unfair treatment of a Jew. For despite Hitler's order and Germany's defeat of France, commanders and generals more con-

cerned with winning wars than with racial purity sometimes kept
Mischlinge in uniform under their command. An army general did not
have to be sympathetic to Jews to be motivated to do this. Self-interest
sufficed. Unusual capacities in a *Mischling,* concern for the morale of
the troops as a whole, loyalty—these and other grounds might have
sufficed. Thus Hitler's decree for the expulsion of *Mischlinge* and intermarried Germans was only partially fulfilled. Some *Mischlinge,* even
as late as mid-1944—when even some Nazis were looking for opportune
connections to Germany's enemies—preferred remaining in the military, recognizing it as a connection to power and prestige that they
might exchange for exemptions from racial laws. The regime knew
that some military officers were ignoring Hitler's decree and issued a
number of reiterations and clarifications of Hitler's original decree
through October 1944.[8]

Equalizations and other special dispensations became irritating to
some party leaders, including Himmler. Numbers of *Mischlinge* applied
for exemptions, as stepping-stones to achieving equalization. One exemption some *Mischlinge* sought was the license to marry a German
or a *Mischling* of the second degree, someone who was not much
disadvantaged or endangered by Nazism. This was almost as good as
equalization or might lead to it. Thousands of *Mischlinge* petitioned
for permission to marry their way out of their precarious lot, but
virtually none was successful.[9] Himmler's office complained that a
Mischling who had received a special dispensation, even such a small
one as the right to attend a university, would upon graduating want a
job reserved for a German. Having reached that goal, the *Mischling*
would then certainly attempt to marry a German and so forth. An
"equalized" *Mischling,* in fact, was "prone to be satisfied only after
he had succeeded in procuring the status of German for every one of
his relatives, followed by their acceptance in the Nazi Party!"[10]

The number of *Mischlinge* who actually received equalization was
minuscule (fewer than a thousand in all), yet the news of such a
deliverance spread like the news of a single reprieve on death row. New
petitions for equalization flooded in, soaking up time among officials
concerned with precedents in decision making. In the Interior Ministry
officials were expanding their powers by issuing decisions on equalization petitioners that Himmler thought fitted for only the party. It
was usually necessary to deny the requests of *Mischlinge* who petitioned for status as "Aryans," but bleeding-heart Interior Ministry
officials had softened the blow to *Mischlinge* denied equalizations with
promises that they at least would not suffer further career setbacks.

Himmler blamed the bureaucracy for the confusion created by this inconsistent treatment of *Mischlinge*. But Hitler himself continued to grant equalizations and exemptions from his order expelling *Mischlinge*. As of September 10, 1942, the Führer had granted equalizations to 339 *Geltungsjuden* and 394 *Mischlinge* of the first degree. Against his own decree, Hitler had also allowed 238 *Mischlinge* of the second degree to advance to senior positions.[11] The leadership stood above the law. Goebbels, Goering, and even Hitler himself exempted Jews from privation and destruction, as long as they served their purposes. These so-called *Schutzjuden* were important Jews whose businesses, skills, or reputations served the Reich in ways that could not really be replaced.[12] Goering and Goebbels granted a number of special permissions to intermarried Germans, *Mischlinge*, Jewish artists, or even Jews married to popular artists. Comedians were allowed to remain because they were good for the public mood, as were figures so popular their sudden disappearance would have caused an uproar and demanded a public explanation. Hitler reportedly offered his own protection to a Jew he wanted to work for Germany (holding out to the physicist Lise Meitner the offer of his protection and a position as professor if she would return to Germany to help Otto Hahn produce a nuclear bomb).[13] In Berlin alone there were some two hundred of these so-called *Schutzjuden*, protected personally by the highest Nazi officials.[14]

Given the confusion of these special cases and the military's occasional exploitation of *Mischlinge*, it is not surprising that military industries accepted Werner Goldberg's services after he had been expelled from the front. Social organizations continued to ostracize him. Even the Paulus Bund, which had gathered together Christian *Mischlinge*, was forcibly disbanded. "For us *Mischlinge* there were no more organizations," Werner said. "Aryans had their own organizations; the Jews had the Jewish Community. *Mischlinge* had none." He recalled with dread the image *Der Stürmer* used to illustrate his status as a *Mischling*: A Jew sat on a yellow chair, a German sat on a green chair, and in between, without a chair at all, squatted the *Mischling*.

   Expelled from serving the army with a weapon, Werner strove successfully to maintain military contacts, working hard to render his ideas and energy in support of Hitler's military. He quickly made himself useful to the Reich through the clothing business he had learned with Schmeider. Werner's fate, he said, was to be one of the few non-Jews in Berlin who knew something about the clothing industry. Virtually every other able-bodied man had been conscripted into the war, and there were no more Jews working at Schmeider. Werner was given more and more responsibility. The German Labor Front, which determined whether a person could be officially employed rather than put into forced labor, generally accepted *Mischlinge* for work, although Hitler's order of April 1940 barred them from receiving promotions.[15]

"I wasn't allowed to be the director," Werner remembered. "But I did become the soul of the business. Whenever there was a question, people were told to go ask Goldberg, on Königstrasse. That's how I came to work closely together with the German officer corps, on Jebenstrasse, near Bahnhof Zoo." So it happened that at his business on Königstrasse he supervised the production of uniforms for the military. "The navy looked for persons to make clothing, and came across me," he said. "Everyone knew I was a *Mischling*, but everyone else had been conscripted. I was invited to Kiel and given a contract to make navy uniforms, an equal number in black and gray. From the wasted leather I proposed to make gloves for the soldiers on the east front."

As the war demanded more resources, Werner expanded his purview to lecturing and writing on improved efficiency in the use of materials. He had attended the Reich Board of Labor Studies School (REFA, or Reichsausschuss für Arbeitsstudie), where he excelled, and was one of just four of eighty students who passed the test for new REFA teachers. In addition to working, Werner was now a Labor Studies Board lecturer on the clothing business. "I had to give lectures to organizations and lots of industry directors," he said. "And as a little fellow I always had big hang-ups doing this until one day someone told me, 'Man, when you get up and lecture, you must always remember that you are God himself and they are the oxen!' "

Werner continuously sought to expand his services to military officers and business leaders. When he published an article in a weekly publication, *Textilwoche*, on the rationalization of production in the clothing industry, he was invited to give a lecture on the subject for the Organization of German Engineers. He was just about to begin when someone took him aside and said, "Goldberg, tell me, are you an Aryan? No? Well, for Christ's sake, you can't hold a lecture here then! Well, the hall is full now. Go ahead!"

Werner is not ashamed of having served in Hitler's army but understands his action as "us-ism," the rule of survival that required taking care of oneself first of all, a need that might also extend to protecting others one needs.[16] He fought under Hitler's command in an attempt to save himself and, by doing that, those closest to him as well. He said that he could "empathize with those [*Mischlinge*] who tried to find refuge with Aryans," hid their real identity through silence, or sought equalizations. "There were mothers who testified that their [*Mischling*] sons were not from a Jewish father," he said. "Each person tried to save himself."

Many *Mischlinge* tried to save themselves and their families by disappearing into the protective folds of Nazism. A handful were able to cling to their places in the German military until the bitter end. Other *Mischlinge* successfully covered their Jewish identities with papers from their German sides, and with this guise some had even served the Nazi party with particular aplomb. Others sought the more limited compromise, and the more limited protection, of membership in organizations under the wing of state or party. Like Werner, some had initially joined semiparty organizations like the Hitler Youth or the League of German Girls, which Himmler saw as an attempt either to "show himself as being particularly reliable or to cover up his real identity."[17] Rudi's *Mischling* nephew Peter, like Werner, also petitioned to remain in the military despite Hitler's expulsion order, and he was successful. Labeled "unworthy of service" and denied both education and work opportunities, Peter had nowhere to go. So his father, the popular non-Jewish magistrate of his district, arranged for his son (who later became a veterinarian in France) to remain in the German Army. "Peter even went to Russia," Elsa said sadly, "and ended up supporting this nasty war. But he did it only to stay alive. What a tragedy that is."

Elsa summed up the tragedy of Werner, Peter, and other *Mischlinge*'s fate: Their ambiguous racial status at some points afforded them the chance to continue living personally while contributing to the power that was intent on killing their family members and that in the long run would have destroyed them as well. As a single person in a huge worldwide struggle, Werner did not see his work for the military as a significant force prolonging the Germany hegemony, during which hundreds of thousands of Jews (including his grandparents) were murdered.

But he was able to help his father survive the war, more than once. In December 1942, during the peak of the murder at Auschwitz, Mr. Goldberg was admitted to the Bavaria Clinic, a non-Jewish hospital. But the Gestapo raided the hospital and sent Goldberg to the Jewish hospital in Iranischestrasse. The Gestapo refused Werner's request to take his father home since he was "a prisoner of the state." While the Jewish hospital still served as a clinic for Jews, it had also been forced into service as a Gestapo prison. Jews were taken from there to fill the deportation trains headed for Auschwitz. On Christmas Eve, suspecting the Gestapo guards at the Jewish hospital would be drunk or elsewhere, Werner drove up to the hospital and strode businesslike through the door and up the stairs to his father's room. "Please help me take my father home," he pleaded to a nurse. Together they carried his father out to the safety of the waiting car. Two months later Mr. Goldberg was back in the Gestapo's clutches at Rosenstrasse, and Werner was there for him then as well. In April 1943 Mr. Goldberg was summoned for deportation, but Werner insisted that he not show up, and he was saved that time too.

Werner in some ways resembled Oskar Schindler, a manufacturer for the Nazi Reich who is rightly celebrated for saving Jews. Schindler was a cunning and dashing entrepreneur who insisted on exercising his leadership skills despite enormous risks.[18] Such boldness and enterprise could succeed if one had a foothold as a German. On a severely reduced scale, this was true for *Mischlinge* as well.

Rudi Holzer's nephew Peter, a *Mischling* in Nazi uniform. With connections, and because it was the safest place for him, he managed to remain in the army despite Hitler's order of April 1940 that expelled *Mischlinge* and intermarried Jews from the military.

X

RACIAL HYGIENE, CATHOLIC PROTEST, AND NONCOMPLIANCE, 1939–41

> I'm packing because otherwise they'll take away your position as chief surgeon at the clinic. And because they already cut you there to your face and because already you can't sleep at night. I don't want you to tell me not to go. I'm going in a hurry because I don't want to have you tell me I *should* go. It's a question of time. Character is a question of time. It lasts for a certain length of time, just like a glove. There are good ones that last a long time.
>
> —The Wife in BERTOLT BRECHT, *The Jewish Wife*

Following Kristallnacht most intermarried Germans continued to resist rather than divorce. Goebbels was behind a number of the new anti-Jewish measures, such as banning Jews from the German air-raid shelters. As more and more resources were absorbed by the war, Jewish rations were cut. By mid-1942 meat, eggs, milk, white flour, and other foodstuffs had been eliminated entirely from Jewish food coupons. Jews did not receive clothing rations and, after war began, could not even buy a pair of socks. Would their German partners hang on? By the time the regime began to deport German Jews in October 1941 the continuing commitment of intermarried Germans to their families convinced the regime that it should "temporarily" defer the deportation of intermarried Jews and their *Mischling* children.

Beginning in March 1939, after Aryanization had robbed Jews of their businesses, Jews were forced into construction and reclamation projects at rates below even those sufficient to support a single person. Other Jews were placed in factories or took positions in the expanding network of Jewish Community organizations.[1] Forced-labor programs gave Jews no choices about where or when they worked or how much they were paid. Günter's father joined the work force of the Berlin Jewish Community, while Günter was put to work at a textile factory in Zehlendorf, washing the fibers with gaseous chemicals in huge vats. Rudi was forced to work for the Reichsbahn. Julius repaired uniforms. Jews in forced labor received around eighty-eight marks per month, a fraction of what even lower-level employees generally earned.

As conditions worsened, Jews married to Germans grew more dependent on their German partners' loyalty. They never felt safe from the Gestapo but hoped their partners would intervene if so. Their German partners, with their Aryan ID cards, handled public matters. Rudi's food rations barely staved off starvation, so they shared Elsa's. She earned 320 marks per month to his 88.

Intermarried Germans had personal reasons for remaining married, but they had many more and stronger reasons of self-interest to choose divorce. Those who did not abandon their spouses to the Gestapo

Julius Israel's official identification papers. As of 1939 Jewish identification papers were marked with a large *J* (left of photograph), and to identify them readily as Jewish, Jewish men were required to take Israel as their middle name (Jewish women took the name Sarah). Thus Julius Israel's papers identify him as Julius Israel Israel.

risked facing the Gestapo and the fate of the Jews themselves. In addition, these liaisons magnified the stresses of day-to-day life in cities that were war zones. Because Jewish food rations were set at near-starvation standards, these couples were always looking for ways to get food, while enduring the feeling of constant hunger. As Allied bombing raids over Berlin intensified, the separate, unsafe shelters for Jews also brought home to them again and again their insecurity as despised outsiders.

When Rudi was put into forced labor, Elsa took a second job. Since losing his job at Schwarzkopf printing, work for Rudi had been hell. He had first been taken to the printing shop of a huge Berlin company that had belonged to Jews. After Kristallnacht the shop had been hastily Aryanized, but no one knew how to run the equipment. Imported from the United States, the machines represented the latest in printing technology. Under threats on his life Rudi was taken to the shop and told that he had three weeks to figure out exactly how the shop and its equipment functioned. During those weeks of feverish labor Elsa hardly saw him. When Elsa tried to relay Rudi's description of his experiences there, it came out like science fiction, the story of a mad basement scientist racing for his life against dark, otherworldly forces. The machine, bigger than an apartment, was the only one of its kind in Germany. To Rudi it was a horrendous mass of cogs, gadgetry, and metal, but he worked incessantly, dropping off briefly into sleep at work on a pallet. But "Jews are intelligent and can figure out things they don't know," Elsa said, reflecting her continuing positive biases about Jews. Rudi succeeded.

But Rudi's long hours of work away from home had just begun. In 1940 he was pressed into forced labor, along with several dozen Jews, for the Reichsbahn. Many of Rudi's coworkers were from Berlin's intelligentsia—composers, pharmacists, academics, writers, pianists, dentists, doctors. None was used to physical labor.

Under open skies, around the year, they swung heavy picks and carried the enormous railroad ties. In the winter they froze. First their hands and toes slowly succumbed; then the rest turned painful and numb. In summer they sweated under the scorching sun until they longed for winter once more. Very often they also handled the baggage coming into Friedrichstrasse, a central stop on one of the main arteries of the German train system, in the heart of Berlin, one station stop from Alexanderplatz. Almost all soldiers and officers returning from the eastern front arrived at Friedrichstrasse as well.

A train of arriving soldiers would turn the platform gray-green with army uniforms stuffed with self-important officers and aspiring soldiers, returned from the world of heroic struggle. Rudi and his colleagues, downcast in their miserable sweat and wretched clothing, would carry their baggage, careful to strike the right balance between abject humility and eagerness to serve. A smart Jew with an instinct for survival knew almost instantly how to manage the mood of each. A Jew might ingratiate himself by addressing an officer according to his rank, and with just one glance at a uniform and military insignia, an observant baggageman might address an officer properly. The Jews were the lowest, the high officers the greatest, in this German world. Freight car after freight car pulled through, loaded with heavy cartons of goods robbed from the Soviet Union—oil and sunflower seeds, cheese and sugars, caviar and vodkas—luxuries and vanities Berlin Jews had long since forced out of their minds.

Hours too were grueling and unpredictable. Often Rudi worked all night. Elsa never knew what to expect and worried constantly. The psychological torture was a millstone. Jewish workers were allowed to pass only along certain paths, so as not to present an eyesore to the traveling public. They had no rights and could be taunted, heckled, and shoved at will. Some of them began to think of themselves as burdens to families. In the worst moments Rudi must have thought of killing himself. Some of his colleagues did choose suicide. "They threw themselves in front of the train," Elsa remembered. Elsa was normally ironic and sometimes even sweet, but anger narrowed her eyes as she continued. "And the Nazis called this a public nuisance. The Jews who couldn't take it anymore were a public nuisance." The Nazis responded by prohibiting Jews from certain sections of the track, Elsa said.

Elsa, seeking income to supplement Rudi's forced labor income, found a job doing housework and errands for a German writer, Dr. Marlou Droop. "I can't imagine that I had any desire to do more work," she said. "I already had so much around my neck, you know—always something new, always something different, to take care of. Siemensstadt, where I worked, was far away. It took me an hour and a half, with several transfers, just to get to work on the bus and train. We got out at five, and I was home at six-thirty. Then I had to cook and clean. But now Rudi had about a fourth or fifth of his income from Schwarzkopf."

With so much pressure to earn for the household, Elsa was forced to lie about her marriage at work, living in daily fear that she would be discovered. At Siemens, where Elsa worked, the general response to Nazi Germany's war was *mitmachen* (go along). There was pressure to use the greeting "Heil Hitler!," rather than "Good morning" or "hello." Whenever possible, she avoided the "Heil Hitler!" greeting. But it wasn't always possible. To her superiors she said "Heil Hitler," but to colleagues she said "Good day." Every week Elsa was given a complimentary copy of the latest *Der Stürmer*, the violently anti-Semitic Nazi newspaper. As she remembered it, Siemens dismissed intermarried Germans. She was careful not to tell anyone that she was married to a Jew, but once she, along with the other employees, was asked to complete a questionnaire, apparently to determine general reliability in the German cause. A number of inquiries were made about each employee's spouse. "Where does your spouse work? For what income?" Elsa left all the questions pertaining to Rudi blank, hoping to hear nothing more of it. But the personnel director called her in. He asked her all the questions again, in person. She insisted that she didn't know where Rudi worked, or how much he made, and that she never talked with him about it. Each earned money and threw it into an old cookie jar on the mantel, drawing on it as needed, she said. When she left the office, she thought, Now something is sure to happen.

Another time, under the pressure of a colleague's inquiry, she said she was against the war. Soon the vice-president of her division called her in. Was she really against the war? She wanted to have children, Elsa hastened to explain when questioned, and the war made that impossible. Elsa was apprehensive, but no reprisals were taken. Once again, however, what freedom Elsa had, had been bought with the sense that she must live duplicitously, even though her every move was being watched. If she slipped again, she might not be so lucky.

For Charlotte and Julius Israel, life was also a struggle against despair and the regime. To supplement their tiny business, Charlotte took a job at the corner milk store and took her salary in food. Mrs. Statler, the store's owner, had posted a Help Wanted sign, but Charlotte hesitated to apply. Statler might be a Nazi. But each day, as she passed the shop on her way home, she thought again about the positive side: milk for Julius. The longer the sign remained up, the more confident she felt: The shopkeeper wouldn't want to endanger a helper so difficult to come by.

As it turned out, Mrs. Statler was more interested in turning a profit than in causing problems for Charlotte. Mrs. Statler was a miserly sort, who shaved butter from the half pounds and skimmed milk from the kilos, storing the bits she pinched here and there under the table. She readily agreed to Charlotte's requirements that in the store Charlotte be called by her maiden name, Press, and that Charlotte could take her wages in milk, which was forbidden to Jews. When the store was damaged slightly in an air raid, Mrs. Statler confided to Charlotte that there was a profit to be made by reporting a larger loss of groceries than the shop had really suffered. "Just don't tell anyone," she said. "I said, 'Fine, I won't tell, but we'll of course divide the profit fifty-fifty.' "

There were always the bombings, to stretch thin whatever nerves survived the hunger. Nevertheless, unlike the Israels, Wally and Günter Grodka decided to have a child. They were used to having very little, and ever since Hitler had granted privileges to intermarried couples with Christian children, they thought of having children, rather than emigrating, as a possible way to escape some of their misery. Günter had now been conscripted into forced labor, which had actually increased his income.

When Wally went into labor that winter on February 5, 1940, she called on a German neighbor, Mrs. Nowakowski, for help. "She and another woman in the house were always good to me, and I can never forget that," said Wally, who gave birth that day to twins. The tiny babies, however were premature, and the central heating system in the Grodkas' apartment was kaput. Wally attempted to keep them the infants by surrounding them with warm bottles. Still, both got colds and refused to eat. Wally despaired. She was afraid the children would be purposely killed if she took them to the hospital. The neighbors knew their young lives hung in the balance, "but because they were only 'Jew children,' they were totally unconcerned about it," said Wally.

After three days the Grodkas tried to take the twins to a hospital, but the hospitals refused. Finally Günter got the Jewish hospital to take them, but only on condition that the Grodkas enroll at the community as Jewish. He had barely arrived home before the news arrived that both babies had died. Wally knew she couldn't expect sympathy from most of her neighbors, but that night was a new horror as the neighbors celebrated their *Schadenfreude* at the death of her babies. "Mrs. Blut started a jubilee because the Jew bums had finally died," she said. The others in the house were supposed to follow her example.

Nevertheless, the Grodkas determined to have another child. With a child baptized as a Christian, they hoped to gain the status of a privileged intermarriage. That would permit Günter to receive regular food rations and exempt him from other onerous regulations for Jews.

The first German Jews were deported during the night of February 11–12, 1940, from Stettin to three ghettos near Lublin, in German-conquered Poland. Soon thereafter Jews were also taken from neighboring Schneidemühl. News of these forced evacuation of some 1,260 Jews caused a stir among Berlin Jews. Stettin was only about 150 kilometers to the northeast of Berlin, and certainly the Grodkas, with Günter's good connections to the Jewish Community, would have heard about this action. The Nazi gauleiter for Stettin, Franz Schwede-Coburg, eager to prove himself as a radical Nazi, had become the first gauleiter to make his region *Judenfrei* and had deported intermarried non-Jewish women who refused to divorce, along with the Jews.[2]

The Gestapo cited lack of living space as the reason for the deportations. The Wehrmacht was said to need more space.[3] The Central Organization of Jews in Germany (Reichsvereinigung der Juden in Deutschland), established by decree on July 4, 1939, absorbed the Jewish Community in Berlin and was in continuous contact with Jews in Germany, whose community names were now Jüdische Kultusvereinigung. All Jews, including *Geltungsjuden* and those in intermarriages, were required to become members of fourteen branch offices with two to six employees each. Rabbi Leo Baeck led the Central Organization.[4] Initially the Central Organization set out to be an advocate for German Jews, and now Dr. Paul Eppstein, the leading member of its directorate, spoke out against the deportations.

Dr. Eppstein met up to several times a week with Obersturmführer Jagusch, a representative of Adolf Eichmann's office at the Reich Security Main Office. Eppstein's minutes of his meetings with Jagusch indicate that in 1939 and 1940 he continued to maintain expectations that Jews would be treated as a group of people with rights. He made requests, dealing with Jagusch as one person to another, and Jagusch gave reasons when he denied Eppstein's requests.

Following the Stettin deportations, Dr. Eppstein requested that the Jews be returned and that their property be restored to them. He asked for a promise from the RSHA that this deportation had been merely the result of a local initiative and would not happen again. He received the assurance. The Central Organization seemed to be in a position of influence. In April—perhaps in return for the commitment —it sought to soothe the disquiet running through Jewish communities all over Germany by issuing a circular calling for calm.[5]

Soon it became clear, however, that measures against Jews would multiply, while the pleas and proffered bargains from the Central Organization would fall on deaf ears. On June 25, 1940, Eppstein was informed of a German plan to settle all European Jews in a "colonial reserve."[6] At this time, however, even as the regime seriously developed plans to send Jews to the island of Madagascar, Goebbels was developing plans for deporting Jews from Berlin to the east. On July 19, 1940, Goebbels reported to Propaganda Ministry section leaders that he had decided to deport "all of the surviving 62,000 Jews in Berlin . . . to Poland." This he said he would do within a span of just eight weeks, as soon as the war ended (Goebbels then expected this to occur by the end of the summer). In the glow of Germany's defeat of France, Goebbels was making plans on July 19, 1940, for the celebratory receptions of the Berlin divisions, returning from the front. He expected a *Volksfest* to blossom around this event, and through radio broadcasts as well as public receptions he hoped "to emphasize the impression that the whole world is listening." As he described this scenario, his acting deputy, Leopold Gutterer, spoke up to warn his boss that the disrespectful "waltzing pack" could be expected to show up again, on Berlin's Kurfürstendamm. "In this context" Goebbels announced his decision to deport all of Berlin's Jews to Poland. The mood in the western part of the city would continue to be influenced, as long as Jews lived in Berlin, Goebbels warned. Hans Hinkel, Goebbels's special assistant for cultural affairs, who had been charged with overseeing the Jewish Cultural Association, then gave a report on a plan to clear Berlin of all Jews that had been worked out with the police. In conclusion, Goebbels charged Gutterer with taking responsibility for this plan as well.[7] Two months later Hinkel reported at another meeting of Goebbels's deputies that there were actually 72,327 Jews in Berlin. Hinkel noted that a plan to concentrate 3,500,000 Jews on the island of Madagascar had been approved, but Goebbels had other plans for Berlin Jews. Goebbels reiterated that 60,000 of Berlin's Jews would be sent to "the east" within four weeks of the end of the war, and the rest would "also disappear."[8]

In the summer of 1940 Goebbels pushed into law anti-Jewish measures that would facilitate the deportations he planned. As Berlin's Nazi party gauleiter and as Reich minister, Goebbels was taking a leading role in separating Jews from Germans. As Reich minister he shaped anti-Jewish measures in the Reich, sometimes after introducing them first in Berlin. Leading with a new policy in his Berlin gau, Goebbels might follow it up with political pressures on the lawmakers to extend the policy's purview throughout the Reich. "Against the resistance of the Interior Ministry," Goebbels reported to his deputies that summer, the Propaganda Ministry had "finally succeeded" in pushing through measures to strip "all living Jews in Berlin" of their telephones.[9]

Gutterer was Goebbels's executive, at least in the early stages of his boss's efforts to concentrate and deport the Jews in Berlin. In the spring of 1940, as he began formulating plans for sending Berlin Jews to the east, Goebbels formally placed Gutterer in the position of acting *Staatssekretär* (state secretary), his temporary deputy still proving himself. By the end of the summer Gutterer had also come to the attention of his SS superiors. On October 31, 1940, he received a flowery letter of recommendation from Heinrich Heydrich, head of the RSHA (including the security police). Heydrich recommended to Himmler that Gutterer be promoted from *SS-Oberführer* to *SS-Brigadierführer*. No one in any ministry had come close to utilizing and exploiting the secret SD situation reports as much as Gutterer, Heydrich wrote. In press, radio, film, and general propaganda, Gutterer had "in every way conceivable" made appropriate administrative responses to the "wishes, impulses, complaints, and irritation" of the people overheard by police agents, Heydrich enthused. Since taking the position as the liaison between the Propaganda Ministry and Heydrich's RSHA, Gutterer had radically changed relations between the two agencies. The Reich security office now worked closer with the Propaganda Ministry than did any other ministry. Heydrich closed with a dubious boast about how smart Gutterer had looked in his SS uniform while attending the most recent Führer rally.

In preparation for expelling Berlin's Jews, Goebbels, with Gutterer as his hard-driving assistant, intensified the public image of Jews as social misfits. Goebbels separated Berlin's Jews from Germans at their work places by creating *Judenkolonnen*—separate task forces consisting of only Jews. This he did so that coming "separation can be carried out as cleanly as possible." Soon Jews throughout the Reich were separated at their workplaces, following Berlin's precedent. With a decree of July 4, 1940, Goebbels limited the time when Jews in Berlin could buy groceries to between 4:00 and 5:00 P.M.[10] Because like many other German women, Wally, Charlotte, and Elsa did the shopping for both themselves and their husbands, they too were restricted to shopping during this hour. Simultaneously, Goebbels ordered that ration cards allotted to Jews be marked with a large *J*. Jews received the same cards as Germans; only each of the cards marked with the *J* was worthless (another psychological harassment). Now anyone in the shops could know that Elsa Holzer, Wally Grodka, and Charlotte Israel were from Jewish households.

Fraudulent use of the food ration card system in wartime Germany was punishable by imprisonment in a concentration camp and sometimes by death. Allied planes dropped fake food ration cards on civilian centers, but those caught using them would be executed. Yet hunger once drove Charlotte to attempt deceiving a grocer with Julius's cards. She took the train to a grocer in Königswusterhausen, a distant part of Berlin scarcely populated with Jews. To hide the *J* invalidating Julius's meat ration cards, Charlotte laid her own ration cards on top of his and requested meat for two Germans. Without shuffling through the ration cards, the grocer began weighing out meat for two. Charlotte breathed deeply. Then a sudden breeze nudged the cards across the counter, revealing a bold *J*. Charlotte was numb with fright. "The *J* stands for *Jugend*—children," Charlotte hastened to explain. The grocer was kind and gave her the meat. "We couldn't have afforded children," Charlotte said. "We were so poor, and I was nothing more than a bundle of nerves." Yet she never tried this trick again. "Imagine that poor man's surprise when he tried to exchange Jewish cards for the meat he had sold!" she said.

Goebbels necessarily relied on the cooperation of grocers and shoppers to enforce the new Jewish shopping hours. Some shopkeepers went further than the law required, hanging store window announcements that Germans related to Jews were also restricted to buying during hours open to Jews.[11] Clearly there could never be enough uniformed police to ensure that Jews shopped only between four and five. Just as the regime relied on individual Germans to strip Jews of their businesses at cut-rate deals, so too there were civilian Germans who voluntarily policed the new regulations for Jews. Secret police reports indicate that "all circles" of the Germans generally supported strictly limited shopping hours for Jews.[12] Some German women denounced Jews who ignored the regulations because they did not want to be anywhere near Jews. Wally experienced this personally. Mrs. Hensel, a fanatical Nazi in the Grodkas' house, stood in front of the neighborhood store, preventing Jews from entering before or after hours and hitting and screaming at Jews who were even just five minutes late in leaving.

When these new regulations appeared in 1940, Dr. Eppstein pushed back against the anti-Jewish regulations, testing his weight as head of the Central Organization. He attempted to have the shopping period for Jews lengthened to three hours, for Jews who worked.[13] Next he tried to get forty to fifty Jews who were in concentration camps as protective custody cases released. In return, Eppstein promised that the Jews would emigrate within one month. To strengthen his case, he completed necessary questionnaires on behalf of these Jews.[14] All was to no avail. The regime made no deals. Nevertheless, Eppstein pressed on. In May the Central Organization completed its survey of German Jews capable of work. Forty thousand were capable, Eppstein reported, adding a request that weak-bodied Jews and women receive "non-physical labor." The RSHA replied with "We'll see," an indirect denial.[15] By mid-1940 it was becoming clear to Eppstein and other Jewish leaders that measures to keep Jews away from Germans would extend beyond relocation. The state wanted Jews out of German living areas and out of German economics.

At work Günter learned that Jews faced increased danger from air raids. Many Berliners had wanted to believe Air Force Chief Hermann Goering's boasts that his name would turn to "Meier" if ever a bomb struck the Reich capital. Throughout the summer of 1940 the Luftwaffe and the RAF waged the Battle of Britain to determine if Germany would dominate the air over the Channel and southeast England as a prerequisite to invasion. The RAF struck back at Berlin. In Günter's factory the Jewish task force stayed on the floor in the machine rooms during bombings, while others took cover in the basement. "That way we would be destroyed the moment the machines were," Günter said.[16]

GERMANS AND THE JEWISH AIR-RAID SHELTERS

During the summer of 1940 Berliners grew accustomed to RAF bombing raids. Then, in September, the first Berliner was killed by a British bomb. A German national agency responded to the British bombings by forcibly evacuating children from the German capital. Defending his authority as the party leader in Berlin, Goebbels complained to Hitler that this outside interference in his region had caused confusion. The Führer duly sided with Goebbels in this dispute, and Goebbels returned to work eager to ventilate this new claim to power. "I will issue a circular to all Reich authorities, to the effect that in the future I shall not stand for any interference in the Berlin Gau," he declared.[17]

The prerogative Goebbels was guarding concerned not only evacuations from Berlin but the public perception of the war itself. Through German radios, the *Volksempfänger*, which received only Goebbels-approved propaganda, Germans were told that Germany was bombing

Britain into a pulp. Any Luftwaffe victory against Britain was announced on air with a blast of fanfares, followed by the playing of the tune "We're Driving against England," a popular march one of Wally's neighbors found irresistible. As he bellowed along with the radio, Wally felt hot anger. In September the Germans finally abandoned the Battle of Britain, and Goebbels changed his propaganda to match. Britain had once been portrayed as a weak enemy, but propaganda now had to prepare Germans for the idea of a longer war and an consequent adjustment to tighter rations.[18]

Under pressure of continuing RAF raids, Goebbels gave an order through the police president of Berlin barring Jews from using the same air-raid shelters as Germans.[19] Two weeks later the German minister for aviation followed Berlin's suit by ordering Jews throughout Germany to stay out of German shelters during air raids.[20] Perhaps Goebbels thought this would surely tear intermarried couples apart. Companionship was as good an antidote to the terror as any for Germans, as they helplessly traced the course of bombs shrieking earthward, nearer and nearer. In their building in the Britz section of Berlin, Rudi was the only Jew, so he and Elsa spent the terrifying hours of the air raids alone in the dingy "Jewish" corner of the basement. "The air you breathe out, we cannot stand to breathe in," a neighbor explained to Elsa, when exiling her and Rudi to their fear alone in the Jewish shelter.[21]

"An air raid was like an earthquake," Elsa remembered. "First there were flares; then the bombing started in earnest. When a bomb hit once across the street from us, it raised so much dust in our own cellar that I couldn't see my hand in front of my face. Just from the blast! In the next street over, exactly where we had dreamed about moving in, a bomb hit the heating system, and everybody close by in the cellar was scalded. They died anyway. I mean to say, that's something else you can't imagine—what we also happened to experience— and that is war in the middle of a city. I say that's something no one could imagine without experiencing it. We sat downstairs, and when we came up, everything had been reduced to rubble and ashes. By the end of the war we were spending more time in the basement than in our apartment. Because of the bombings alone, Rudi and I didn't know, from one day to the next, whether we would ever see each other again."

Hitler's decree expelling intermarried Germans from the military was a clear signal of their new vulnerability, yet Jewish women married to Germans continued, in some cases, to be less noticeable in public as outsiders than were German women married to Jews. Lotte Paepcke, a Jew married to a German, remembered that learning to be an outsider in Nazi Germany was terribly uncomfortable, like being forced to wear a dress that didn't fit.[22] Yet Jews in privileged intermarriages like Lotte Paepcke could accompany their husbands into the German shelters.

At the Grodkas', the new separate shelter regulations for air raids arrived through Mrs. Blut, the house superintendent at Niebuhrstrasse 67. The cellar in the Grodkas' house had been made into a bomb shelter, using extra supports. The *Blockwart* (block warden), Mr. Blut, had suggested that the Jews not be allowed in the basements at all. "The Jews should stand out in the courtyard," he proclaimed. "Then, when the bombs fall, they'll be the first to go." But the Jews were allowed to wait out the bombs in the coal bin, which had not been reinforced and could easily collapse. Inside the coal bin it was easier to hear the bombs whistling downward and the antiaircraft guns shooting, Wally remembered. Even the most courageous grew timid.

It was not the Bluts but Mrs. Brase, a fanatical Nazi and the local leader of the National Socialist Women's Organization who took it upon herself to keep the Jews and Germans strictly separated, amid bombs that might have killed them all. At the end of each air raid she stood in the doorway of the "Aryan" shelter, stretching out both arms to prevent the Jews from leaving the basement until all the Germans had left. "She made sure no Aryan tenant came into contact with us," Wally said.

The Grodkas did have allies among the Germans. Just as some Germans breathed life into national regulations by denouncing Jews who ignored them, so those who felt sympathy for the Jews did small things to help, often in silence and secretly. In addition to Jüttner, the Nazi whose warnings about the Nuremberg Laws and Kristallnacht had been timely, there were three women in the Grodkas' building who were kind to Wally. Otherwise, an old colleague of Günter's from the Socialist party dared to suffer the consequences of loyalty. A former city councillor invited the Grodkas to his place to listen to illegal British radio broadcasts. At the outset of the war the state had confiscated radios from Jews, but news from London, lending a new perspective on the war, was vital for survival, Günter said.

Goebbels's grasp on public communication so increased that he could seal off the German populace from almost all outside information. Contradictory information or interpretations might discredit his own ministry, instigate dissent, and throw his strategies into question (this was especially true if he could not be sure just what other information his audience had). The need to deceive effectively might compel him to tell the truth so as to maintain credibility. Personally experienced hardships could not be denied, so Goebbels attempted to report air-raid casualties accurately on the local level, while keeping those not personally affected in the dark. Public protests and rumors might also upset Goebbels's depictions, but as long as there were no other sources of information, he could choose to scorn "objective truth" and clarified even sore German military defeats as part of an overall German strategy of conquest. "We listened only to BBC," Elsa Holzer remembered, "because according to our reports on the so-called folk radio, the German Army did nothing but win! They lied. And if the army was pushed back, then they said, 'That's part of conquering! We're loosening them up!' " Günter Grodka remembers hoping "this wouldn't grow into the promised Thousand-Year Reich but would last even less than twelve years. Still, those twelve years seemed to last forever."

Like Elsa and Wally, Charlotte never considered leaving her husband alone in danger. In 1940 a dozen Jewish families were still in their apartment building, so Charlotte joined them. "I of course remained with my husband," said Charlotte. "In the Jewish basement it was sometimes pretty funny. We told Jewish jokes! Why not? We also had humor then. The basement was hidden a little, and I sometimes said, 'Man, if anything happens to us here, no one will dig us out.' They wouldn't have done that, either. A neighbor once asked me, 'When are you finally going to get rid of your guy? Then you can come in here with us.' So I felt better down in the corner with my Jews. There no one glared at us so much!

"It wasn't so simple, though, to get into the basement quickly with my husband. When the air sirens blew, everyone ran, just flew. And he walked normally. His crippled leg was in a splint, from top to bottom. In addition, we had to take valuables along. I sewed backpacks, one for him to carry and one for me. In addition, I carried a suitcase in my left hand. With my right arm I steadied my husband. In his right hand my husband held his cane.

"I always hoped that my husband would be protected through me. Nevertheless, I sewed our names on our backpacks and put necessities in them. We would grab them and flee if we had to. I was ready at every instant to go where he had to go.

"Once I observed that two of our wounded soldiers on the street had special French cane supporters. That way they could move faster. I asked them, 'Where did you get those?' I went to the store to buy some but was told they were only for 'Aryans.' So I looked around to buy them on the black market. I got them too, and then my husband could walk faster and better, and I had one hand free.

"I was always worrying out loud about what to do with Julius if we had to leave our home and flee. How could we move quickly enough?

Finally Julius was tired of listening to me and built a small wagon—quite small, with wheels and all, and a tongue. He sat on it, and I pulled it. There was room enough for a suitcase too, in case we had to escape. Finally I was quieted. That wagon was such a reassurance, and we used it too. I always hoped that my husband would be protected through me."

Sometimes Charlotte and Julius weren't at home when the air-raid sirens announced another bombing. Once the sirens sounded while they were on the train two stops from home. They got off at Berlin's massive train station Bahnhof Zoo and headed for the huge shelter below the station. A police officer came by, checking identification: "IDs!" The only one they could show was marked with a J. That might result in Julius's arrest and deportation, for being present in an "Aryan" air-raid shelter.

"Julius said, 'My wife has the ID,' " Charlotte remembered. " 'No, I don't have it! You must.' I played as if I were angry at him. 'No, you must have it,' said Julius, raising his voice. Then I said, 'I laid it on the table.' And after a few more exchanges I said, 'Come on, I guess we'll just have to leave in that case.' But at this point the policeman, looking at Julius on crutches, said, 'Oh, no, no. Stay here, comrade.' 'Comrade!' he called Julius. He had mistaken Julius for a crippled soldier!"

The longer the war wore on, the less food there was. Starvation loomed, Charlotte thought. On one occasion she managed to barter Julius's wedding suit for an entire ham. There was a waiter who needed a formal suit, but when he arrived at the Israels' with the ham, he refused to come inside the apartment of a Jewish household. Charlotte, on the other hand, refused to part with the suit until she had the ham. After some negotiations they both went into the hallway, where the waiter tried on the suit. The ham, rare delicacy that it was, went with them, along with other valuables, into the air-raid shelter during each bombing. After each raid they nibbled some of the ham, and when only the bone remained, Charlotte made a soup. "Mmm—that tasted just great," she recalled, smacking her lips emphatically.

The one comfort for Charlotte was the company in their despised Jewish cellar. But when the Gestapo began to arrest and deport Jews, the Jewish community in the house grew smaller and smaller. By 1943 Julius was the only Jew left. Charlotte worried that no one would know about them if their cellar collapsed, and she schemed to get into the "Aryan" cellar. She asked the house superintendent, who, as she said, "was no big Nazi." Still, he could agree to let the Israels in the "Aryan" cellar only if everyone else in the house was in favor. Perhaps he feared denunciation, but this gave Charlotte an idea. Charlotte remembered thinking that "all of them are a bit cowardly, and afraid to stand alone. They don't trust themselves." So she started out to get everyone's permission, one by one, by stating, "Everyone else has agreed to allow us into the 'Aryan' cellar. Would that be all right with you too?" Each one agreed in turn, thinking that all the others had already agreed. "I knew exactly how fearful they all were of one another," Charlotte said. "Some of them looked at us a little crossly. But we were now, in any case, in the cellar with the others! We were now in!"

In October 1940 Berlin Jewish leaders and those in touch with the Jewish Community like the Grodkas were faced with cataclysmic news. It came from regions—Baden, Pfalz, and Saarland— where all the Jews—some seventy-five hundred—were deported without warning one night to a camp in Gurs, in unoccupied France. Hitler himself had ordered the deportation.[23] The Gestapo's promise not to deport more Jews had been broken, Jagusch's trust proved unworthy. Two gauleiters had persuaded the Gestapo to join their effort to push Jews from their territory. Among those taken were Eppstein's mother- and sister-in-law, who were from that region of Germany. Eichmann himself accompanied the deportation train, to convince the French border guard that it was a military transport. This was a sort of trial deportation to determine "whether Jews could be made to walk to their doom on their own feet . . . what the reaction of their neighbors would be . . . how a foreign government would react."[24] If it was in these ways a test of reactions, it was also a test of the will of Eppstein and the Central Organization. How would Jewish leaders respond, and must they be taught never to protest or make demands as they had following deportations from Stettin? Although the Jews were not killed in Gurs, Jewish leaders could not be sure because they were denied information. At least as of December 1940 Eppstein's wife had not heard from her mother and sister.

Once again Eppstein moved to protest immediately following the deportations. The Baden deportations caused what was the peak of resistance by the Jewish authorities in Germany. Dr. Otto Hirsch, a director of the Central Organization, complained bitterly to the RSHA and announced that "as a sign of mourning," not as a "protest against the government," the Central Organization had called on all its employees around Germany to fast for one day and to cancel all cultural activities for that day. The RSHA immediately forbade the Central Organization's plans to make an announcement about the fast on the following Sabbath. Dr. Julius Seligsohn was accused of initiating the Central Organization's outcry and was imprisoned. The Central Organization asked to have at least some of the deportees returned and sought to send them care packages. But not even communication was allowed. Eppstein himself was arrested, but he was released by early January 1941.

By January the RSHA representative in charge of receiving the Central Organization's representative in nearly daily meetings was changed from Jagusch to the callous Fritz Wöhrn. Wöhrn announced that any Central Organization member who did not obey would be treated like Seligsohn. Despite pleas for Seligsohn's release, he was held captive (and never heard from again). There would be no more discussions, or talk of reasons, with Eppstein. Long-standing requests would now be denied: Members of the Central Organization would not receive the identification cards they wanted; Eppstein was told that he and other Central Organization leaders would no longer be allowed to emigrate because they were facing a lot of work. "Don't worry, you'll get to leave in good time," Wöhrn said cynically. "Do your work first." Dr. Seligsohn's application for permission to emigrate was denied "in the interest of his still unfulfilled duties."[25]

Eppstein was a broken man. The organization's minutes of early 1941 show him to have changed. He worked. Secretaries in Eichmann's office recalled seeing him, decades later, when testifying in the trial against the former chief of the Berlin Gestapo, Otto Bovensiepen. One remembered calling him "Mr." Eppstein and having been immediately instructed to call him only *Jude* Eppstein. He became the conversation partner of Eichmann and his deputies, the tireless bureaucrat whom the secretaries seemed to like. Hirsch and Eppstein were named assistants to the Central Organization chairman, Leo Baeck (a rabbi who had stayed on despite opportunities to emigrate because he wanted to be with his people, where he could help them), as daily executives.[26] But almost immediately Hirsch was arrested and taken in protective custody to a camp.

Just before his arrest Hirsch had become especially forthcoming. Perhaps he had been warned to shape up.[27] Eppstein remained after Hirsch was taken, and Eichmann, an "obsessed bureaucrat," required Eppstein to produce a written version of the minutes of their meetings within an hour of their dissolution.[28] Eppstein's minutes became carefully typed, reasonably delineated and columned examples of neatness and order, as he too on occasion pointed out possible technical flaws in the Gestapo's orders for deportations. According to a rumor, a direct telephone line connected Eppstein's and Eichmann's offices. Yet Eppstein was most likely "a man who in normal times would have been an efficient administrator, not a saint, not a great leader, but certainly not a villain. A man who had wanted to serve the community, not to harm it."[29]

It was early 1941. The German Jewish deportations were still just a plan, and the spirit of the Central Organization had already been ruthlessly, tragically broken. Thereafter the Jewish leaders were to make few requests for leniency, and perhaps to preempt reprisals, they sometimes instructed the RSHA on how it could act more effectively. Bare-throated appeasement appeared to be their most viable form of hope or power.

ATTEMPTS TO FLEE, ATTEMPTS TO CONVERT

Nazi tyranny forced its opponents to make painful compromises in the interest of surviving and helping others. The most painful compromises were the ones that actually lent assistance to the regime, like those of the *Mischlinge* in the army. The kind of lying Rudi did to the Gestapo was necessarily commonplace. Jewish leaders, motivated to help Jews through a process they considered inevitable, began to take orders from the Gestapo. To both Elsa and Charlotte, the churches seemed utterly out of touch, able to care only about institutional practices rather than the agonizing plights of real people.

Out of fear, and with Julius's as well as her own interest in mind, Charlotte had voted for Hitler. Until the war elections were held in Germany, and all citizens received a ballot in the mail. On the ballot was the question "Do you vote for the Führer?" Beside "Yes" was a big circle, while "No" was next to a very small circle. "I said to my husband, 'Nonsense, why should I vote?' " Charlotte remembered of the first time she received a ballot. "The polls were only open until six, and at five forty-five, our doorbell rang. It was two SS men. I almost fell over unconscious to see such people standing there. We weren't used to that yet. Then one said to me, 'You haven't yet exercised your duty to vote!'

"Ach, you mean it's not too late?" Charlotte replied, playing dumb.

"Oh, yes, there's still time," they assured her.

Charlotte agreed to go, hoping they would be satisfied and leave. But they insisted in going with her to the voting booth. "As I entered the school on Sybelstrasse, no one was there," Charlotte said. "Only the ballot urns and the men sitting there. It was possible to go behind the curtain to vote, but as I turned to do so, they said, 'No, no, you can stay right here! You don't need to go back there.' Then I thought, I've got to make the X now—for Hitler! I am still ashamed of that to this day. My husband was at home sweating and worrying. As soon as I came in, he asked, 'Where did you put the X?' 'Unfortunately in the big circle,' I said. 'Nothing else was possible.' 'I hoped you would' is all he said."

Charlotte and Julius decided to leave Germany, but their efforts were thwarted because they were a mixed couple. At first the regime had encouraged Jews to emigrate from Germany, and this was still possible until the fall of 1941. Adolf Eichmann became proficient at the mass mobilization of Jews as the head of an office in Vienna established to dispossess Jews and expedite their emigration. The Central Organization of German Jews had been charged with a central task of facilitating emigration.

Some German Jews emigrated to Shanghai, a venture Julius and Charlotte considered but rejected because Julius had asthma. Then they chose the United States. "I didn't want to stay here," Charlotte said in Berlin more than forty years later. "But we didn't have the money to emigrate." Julius went to a Jewish organization, the JDC (Joint Distribution Committee), which helped Jews without money to emigrate. But the JDC could not pay for Charlotte's emigration because she wasn't Jewish. "Joint would have sent my husband over, but I would have had to stay here," Charlotte said. "Then he would send for me from America. But we didn't do that because I couldn't imagine life without my husband.

"I spent sleepless nights. And suddenly I again had an idea. 'I'll convert to Judaism,' I told Julius. 'Then they'll have to help me too.' " Julius was surprised, but joyous. "He didn't think I would do that," Charlotte said. "We hadn't talked about religion at all, and he thought I was a real Catholic. Now he was inspired by my idea. We were very happy. I went straight to the synagogue and said I'd like to convert. No problem. The rabbi and I discussed everything—how, where, and when. Twice a week I had to go to him for instructions. It was supposed to take three months."

Before joining the Jewish religion, Charlotte had to leave the church. A woman Charlotte described as a nun looked down her nose at her and asked, "Are you giving up your faith that easily?" Charlotte said she would be gladly keep her religion—if the church would only pay her way to America. She grew indignant when recalling the answer: "The church doesn't have funds for that." Charlotte retorted that the church should "hurry up and do something about that!," adding that "the nun wanted to save souls, but I wanted to save Julius."

By the time the rabbi told Charlotte she could become a member of the Jewish Community, Julius objected. Charlotte was perplexed. "Well, I've thought about it," Julius said. "Look, if the beloved Nazis find out about this—and they always find out about everything—then we both will be lost." He feared that the "beloved Nazis," as he always called them, would judge Charlotte as a Jew after she converted. "And I thought," said Charlotte (in retrospect knowing Julius was wrong), "that if Julius says it, it must be right. For me, he was my gospel. I would have gone to Shanghai, but he couldn't. What he said I accepted as gospel. I simply forgot about converting. And then I said, 'Well, then I've merely learned that for nothing.' and Julius said, 'No, you never learn something for nothing.' "

While Charlotte sought help by converting to Judaism, Elsa sought refuge by converting to Catholicism. She was not religious. But her friend Dr. Marlou Droop convinced her to convert to Catholicism and remarry Rudi in a Catholic ceremony.

"I had worked for Marlou since 1939," Elsa said, fondness coming into her voice. "She wrote books and film scripts. I worked in her house as her secretary. She was a monarchist from a very wealthy family. She joined the Nazi party early and had a very small party number. But she was no Nazi. She could never have even dreamed of destroying the Jews. She joined the party because she thought the Nazis would bring the emperor back.

"We had a long friendship, but of course I called her Dr. Droop and she called me Mrs. Holzer. She was so learned. God, was she learned. In France she had learned French. In England she had learned English. She wrote poems and wouldn't have even had to work. But she made a living by writing. And when she talked, you were fascinated."

Dr. Marlou Droop converted to Catholicism and convinced Elsa to do the same. The church might help rescue Rudi, she said. Elsa was skeptical of religion. "I believe that a person is wondrous," Elsa said, "and I'm amazed each summer that the trees grow full with leaves again. That thrills me half to death. But that there should be a beloved God, who directs everything . . . what God? I don't have anything against belief in God. Indeed, everyone I respect is pious! My Marlou too. But I can't believe. Back then I thought, however, that the Catholic Church might help somehow."

Elsa does not remember her experience fondly. A church official

Elsa remembers as Mrs. Dr. Sommer told her she was living in a "wild marriage," then inquired what religious training they would give their children. "Children were the last thought on my mind," Elsa said. "We wanted children. Rudi liked children a lot. But not then. There wasn't enough even for us."

Nevertheless, the church allowed Elsa to persevere. She went every Sunday to the priest's house to learn the catechism. A twelve-year-old boy and his Jewish father were also studying to convert. "The secretary told me that the priest loved nature and birds," Elsa said. "And I thought, 'Yes, indeed he does. Every Sunday he smells like roast chicken!' And if not to me, then to that little twelve-year-old he could have given some of that chicken.' "

Elsa was a terrible student and even told the priest, "Don't require me to learn anything! You can tell me everything, but don't ask me anything. I haven't remembered it." Still, she converted and received a certificate of baptism. "Only for that stamp did I listen to what the church had to say," Elsa said. "I thought maybe the church can help in this terrible time. I didn't have so much hope. But I thought *maybe* that would help. *Maybe*."

After conversion Rudi and Elsa had a Catholic wedding. This, Elsa said, caused another ruckus. The priest told Rudi he would have to appear at the altar without wearing the Star of David. Elsa nearly went wild and accused him of wanting to kill her husband. "Without the star, as you know, he'll be arrested, and then it's over," she said. So they agreed to get married in their own apartment.

"Well, the church people had been educated as Catholics," Elsa said, changing her tone to a gentler one after a moment's reflection, tempering her anger. "We had the wedding, but that didn't help." She went on. "I told Rudi, 'Rudi, we don't need any religion. We'll believe in ourselves, and neither will hurt the other. Try it,' and we apparently succeeded in doing this."

CATHOLICS (PARTIALLY) AGAINST THE REGIME

On the eve of the Holocaust, public protest curtailed an important forerunner of that genocide. By late 1940 rumors that the regime was killing Germans coursed through Germany. The Nazi racial hygiene program did away with the congenitally insane and sick, even though they were Germans. Innumerable reports and requests for exemptions from this euthanasia revealed that a wide circle of the population in all parts of the Reich were highly disquieted.[30] The Justice Ministry refused to prosecute rumormongers, choosing not to add to the publicity by acknowledging the secret program. Six years earlier Hitler had worried that the church would oppose Euthanasia, and some church leaders had written protest letters.[31] Then in July and August 1941 Clemens von Galen, the Catholic bishop of Münster, in northwestern Germany, made the protest unignorable by publicly denouncing Euthanasia. Following Galen's third blistering sermon, Hitler ordered a stop to Euthanasia in late August.

Galen was the catalyst forcing Hitler to resolve the tension between an important program and the regime's desire for popular support.[32] Hitler's order, although it did not completely stop Euthanasia, did stop public protests. Despite his great power as the feared dictator, eliciting conscious consent to his rule from all the German people remained his basic goal. Regardless of whether the Wehrmacht was triumphing or retreating, this was crucial. Even in August 1941, when there was still no sign of German military defeat on any horizon, Hitler truncated a fundamental part of the dictatorship's drive for racial hygiene, to maintain popularity. J. P. Stern, the British scholar who personally witnessed Hitler and the spread of Nazism, concludes that "it seems beyond any doubt that if the churches had opposed the killing of the persecution of the Jews as they opposed the killing of the congenitally insane and sick, there would have been no Final Solution."[33]

Bishop von Galen, schooled in the power of Catholic opinion by uprisings in 1936 and 1941, could have calculated the risk of publicly opposing the regime in his position. In 1936 the bishop had been among those who successfully opposed a local decree removing crucifixes (and pictures of Luther) from schools in Oldenburg, in mostly Protestant northern Germany. When the Nazi regional leader from Oldenburg issued a decree on November 4, 1936, ordering the removal of crucifixes from public schools, his action resulted in what SD police reports called a "storm of indignation" in the town of Cloppenburg, a Catholic enclave. Prelates of the area supported the protests "with all means," and the "grave unrest" spread even into party circles.[34] A special nine-day church service was held, and church bells were rung in protest every evening. Families began holding their own devotional ceremonies at home. Children went to school with crucifixes around their necks, and protest commissions sprang up to demand the end of the decree. To the consternation of officials in Berlin, the "grave unrest" caused by the crucifix decree spread even into party circles: Nazi administrators put office resources at the disposal of protest groups; the National Socialist Women's Organization refused to carry out certain orders, and even members of the Hitler Youth failed to cooperate. In response to these widespread public outcries, the Oldenburg party leader called a meeting at a large auditorium in Cloppenburg on November 25 to announce that the the decree would be rescinded.[35] The church saw these events as "generally the first victory of the Catholic church over the state."[36] Church activists concluded that the Catholic people would be able to defeat any anti-Catholic state actions as long as they posed a united front.[37]

In April 1941, just months before Germany invaded the Soviet Union and began the mass slaughter of Jews, the success of what had become known as the Spirit of Cloppenburg became an important precedent for another Catholic struggle. This one, in southern Germany, was also against a crucifix decree and also relied on noncompliance and protest. On April 23 the Bavarian minister of education, Adolf Wagner, ordered that crucifixes be removed from schools in his district, that the usual school prayer be dropped in favor of Nazi slogans or songs, and that by the end of the summer holidays Christian pictures be replaced by "pictures suited to the present time." When the local population, along with many local functionaries, protested, Wagner stepped up his timetable. This caused more protests, and within two weeks Wagner was forced to rescind the decree. But in hope of saving face, he did so secretly.

The result was explosive mass disobedience by devout villagers that lasted into the summer and was "greater than at any previous time during the Third Reich in Bavaria," according to Ian Kershaw. Mothers of schoolchildren launched a "mothers' revolt," sending delegations to head teachers or local leaders threatening to remove their children from school if the crucifixes were not replaced. "In many instances," Kershaw writes, school strikes persuaded local authorities that they would have to bow to the pressure, especially since "any form of unwillingness to concede [by them] led to demonstrations by angry groups or crowds of people, prominent among them the women of the village."[38]

Petitions, criticisms, and threats of resignations from the party and the party women's organizations piled up. While Germany fought "godless Bolshevism" on the new eastern front, godlessness was rearing its head at home. Exploiting their intimate link with the the war front, women encouraged one another to write to their husbands about their struggle. The replies—recording their husbands' dismay—were then used as ammunition in the fight for crucifixes. One wife received a letter from her husband saying the news had made him decide to stop concealing how horrible conditions at the front really were.

The Nazi party district leader of Augsburg-Land accused the

church of going on the offensive against the crucifix decree by using Nazi methods, comparing the mobilization of opinion and public assemblies that the Catholic Church used to defeat the party's crucifix decree with the methods once employed by the party to extend its support. Bavarian Governor (Staathalter) Franz Epp complained bitterly about Adolf Wagner's crucifix decree in his region, in 1941. Epp wrote to Reich Chancellor Lammers in late December 1941, reporting that Wagner "has provoked demonstrations, school strikes, and unrest in the entire province. . . . Much worse, the inner devastation of the people and with it the erection of a front of psychological resistance [*einer geistigen Widerstandsfront*] has remained." According to Epp, Wagner's real role as a responsible domestic leader during wartime was to preserve morale on the home front "during the hardships of war and [to avoid] unnecessary strains on that morale since, as every participant in the First World War was aware, morale at home could lift or depress morale at the Front."[39] Once again the authorities relented. Wagner ordered a "stop decree" on the removal of the crucifixes.

The struggle against Euthanasia was coming to a head at the same time. Fought primarily by religious leaders, especially Bishop von Galen, it was influential because it represented widespread fears. In February 1941 an entire village population turned out in a show of sympathy for Euthanasia victims. As mentally deficient patients were rounded up and taken off in buses, "the entire population of Asberg, strongly Catholic, had gathered and watched the scene in tears. . . . Among the weeping spectators were even some party members, and comments were made amid the general uproar which must be classed as irresponsible."[40] Everyone realized the patients were being taken to their deaths. The leadership responded to rumors with orders that the SD make specific, separate reports on "rumors and political jokes," ahead of normal reporting deadlines. The SD was charged to identify the location of these negative rumors and jokes. Were they circulated within an entire region or just among a certain group? Exactly when and where did a rumor first surface, and how far had it spread? SD spies were instructed to follow rumors to their sources. Anyone voicing a rumor was to be interrogated about its origins. If possible, the specific instigator of a joke or rumor should be named.[41]

Within weeks the SD reported that "numerous political jokes and rumors of a character particularly detrimental and hateful to the state, for example, vindictive jokes about the Führer, leading personalities, the party, the army, and so forth, were being spread."[42] In a letter to Reich Chancellor Lammers (who had received many of the written complaints about Euthanasia) of March 4, 1941, Acting Minister of

Justice Franz Schlegelberger said it would not be wise to prosecute people who spread reports about the program because such a process would only spread further reports.[43] Gestapo head Heinrich Müller responded differently (if no more effectively), on March 13, 1941. He promised "to take severest measures against those who spread such detrimental and vindictive jokes and rumors, introducing all necessary countermeasures."[44]

In the late summer Galen preached three sermons, warning against the lawless power of the Gestapo from his pulpit. The bishop reasoned that no one was safe from arbitrary police treatment; according to the logic of a program that sacrificed those who were of no obvious productive use to the state, the state could soon be administering Euthanasia to wounded soldiers as well as cripples, the old, or the weak. Thousands of copies of the bishop's third sermon were printed and circulated.[45] Thousands of believers gathered in silence at Münster Cathedral to demonstrate their support for Galen.[46]

Galen gave voice to the many whispered fears about Euthanasia. As soon as he spoke out against Euthanasia in public, he had public awareness on his side. If he were arrested, the public would know immediately both about his arrest and about the reason for it.

The bishop helped form the opinion that protected him. Martin Bormann, Hitler's personal secretary, and other high officials called for Galen to be hanged. Goebbels, responding to the party chancellery, said that only Hitler could condemn the bishop to die. In wartime hanging Galen would be unusually difficult, even almost impossible, Goebbels added. "If something against the bishop was done, one could forget about receiving support of the people of Münster for the rest of the war," he said, adding that maybe the entire region of Westphalia would no longer support the war.[47]

The purpose of Hitler's order was to stop public protests. Indeed, the gassing did stop, but it was replaced by a decentralized effort, more difficult to blame on the regime. In nineteen months, from January 1940 to August 1941, Euthanasia had claimed some seventy thousand victims, but in the final forty-four months of the greatly reduced Euthanasia program thirty thousand more died. Under a new so-called wild Euthanasia trustworthy doctors were told that it was not undesirable to kill certain handicapped or deformed persons through overdoses of medicine or starvation diets. Cooperating doctors continued to do away with "useless mouths," reporting them as deaths from natural causes.[48] Many of the victims of the new cautionary "wild Euthanasia" had no German families. They were orphans or forced laborers from the East.[49] Racial hygiene, the cornerstone of Nazi politics, stirred up fears when Germans themselves felt threatened. But these victims had no voice among the people.

Galen, on the other hand, survived. He was too widely respected to be eliminated without causing the unrest the regime sought to quell. He made public what the regime tried to hide. The machinery for gassing was now transferred to a much more massive operation, the genocide of Jews.[50]

XI

THE STAR OF DAVID DECREE: THE OFFICIAL STORY AND THE INTERMARRIED EXPERIENCE

> The human facts of life and death and history are so dismaying that only some reflexive numbness or self-mesmerism keeps even the most favored of us from going screaming mad. A good morning's work, a fine afternoon's sailing, half an hour of love, a good dinner and a balmy evening's anchorage divert us, and we may be grateful for such diversion, inasmuch as the python [death] does not go away. It is the sea we sail upon, the warp and woof of ongoing history, the very ground beneath our feet. The wonder then is not that courage, magnanimity, altruism, mercy, and the rest are rare; it is that here in the reptile house they occur at all.
>
> —JOHN BARTH

In November 1939 the German civil administration in occupied Poland required Jews to wear the Star of David, either as an armband or (in Wartheland) as a four-inch yellow patch sewed to the front and back of their clothes.[1] In September 1941 a decree required all Jews in Germany over age six to wear bright yellow Stars of David on their outer clothing, over their left breast.

All persons designated by the Nuremberg Laws as Jews were subject to the new rule except for the few Jews in privileged intermarriages and *Mischlinge* like Werner Goldberg, who were Christian. Jews who had fought for Germany, even officers who had received medals for bravery from Hitler himself, were to be marked. The hospitalized were not exempt.[2] The star was to be sewn on tightly, so that it could not be easily removed and replaced. If a Gestapo officer could wiggle a pencil between star and clothing, it was too loosely attached. Within two weeks a Berlin flag factory manufactured blanket-size patchworks of the gold stars, and the Jewish Community organized their sale at twenty pfennig per star.[3]

Spearheading the effort to initiate the Star of David law was Goebbels, the minister charged with preventing unrest. The star, a Propaganda Ministry press conference announced, would drive the wedge between Jews and Germans deeper. The new regulation marked Jews as dangerous criminals. All Jews, including national war heroes, must now appear to be responsible for the current war. Without protection under law, they would be abandoned like prey on public streets.[4] The Star of David marked the population slated for the death camps.

The decision to require just a portion of the intermarried Jews and *Mischlinge* to wear the star reflected a hope that the regime might gradually deport these persons, beginning with those the star criminalized. Goebbels considered the deportation of these persons a delicate matter. He planned to move slowly and partially—thus avoiding unrest—toward his additional goal of the total elimination of intermarried Jews and *Mischlinge*. Intermarried Jews were a more urgent problem for the regime to solve because they were "full" rather than just part Jews like the *Mischlinge*.

The desire to preserve public morale led Hitler, in early 1941, to refute the efforts of high Nazi party and security police officials to draw *Mischlinge* and intermarried Jews into the impending Final Solution. Despite the Nuremberg Laws (which separated some *Mischlinge* from "full Jews"—those with three or four Jewish grandparents), high Nazi officials agreed in January 1941 to treat *Mischlinge* as Jews. In accord with the Nuremberg Laws, these officials—from the party chancellery, the SD in the Reichsicherheitshauptamt (RSHA), and the Office of Racial Politics—intended to deport the full Jews from intermarriages, including those in privileged intermarriages. On August 13, 1941, in a final meeting before the beginning of the genocide of German Jews, the same Nazi leaders agreed to expand the definition of Jews in occupied territories to include *Mischlinge*. But immediately thereafter, at the time he was meeting with Goebbels, Hitler rejected the party chancellery's plan to count *Mischlinge* as Jews.[5] The Gestapo then received instructions to "defer temporarily" all German *Mischlinge* and all intermarried Jews from the Final Solution deportations, which began in mid-October 1941.[6]

Goebbels, who enjoyed Hitler's confidence as much as anyone, was visiting the Führer in his East Prussian headquarters, where he had persuaded Hitler to issue the Star of David decree. The joint decision to require just a minority of *Mischlinge* and intermarried Jews to wear the Star of David, and to exempt all of them from the Final Solution "temporarily," indicates that Goebbels preferred to subject persons from Jewish-German families to the harshest anti-Jewish measures, testing public reaction along the way.[7]

The dispute about which Nazi principle should prevail—maintaining social peace or purifying the race—was a struggle over power as well as principle. Goebbels had risen swiftly in party politics through power struggles, occasionally forcing Hitler to his side by threatening to resign should he not get his way. In 1933 the intellectual outsider had fought for money and purview for his new ministry within the thicket of long-established ministries and government budgets. Many rumpled old bureaucrats must have felt more irritated than threatened by such a toothless ministry. But Hitler well understood the centrality of propaganda in his search for popular consensus. Goebbels cunningly contented himself with the explanation that his ministry had the final say in all matters relating to the public mood.

High representatives of the party and the SS had not included Goebbels in their Final Solution deliberations in 1941 (when they had tried to project their consensus on intermarried Jews and *Mischlinge* into any future decisions with a determination that all future questions on the Jewish Question would be resolved by the same circle).[8] At first, rather than infiltrate their circle, Goebbels relied on his direct connections to Hitler,[9] staging his own conference. On August 15, 1941, Goebbels's deputy at the Propaganda Ministry Leopold Gutterer hosted forty bureaucrats on the urgent need to mark German Jews publicly.

Gutterer had been in charge of developing Propaganda Ministry schemes to mark the Jews of Berlin publicly since at least April 1941. Gutterer himself perhaps pushed Goebbels to press for the public marking of German Jews.[10] When he chaired the conference on the Star of David, Gutterer had just received a prize for his loyalty and extremely hard work. Hitler had called him at home on his birthday, Gutterer remembered, to tell him he had been named Goebbels's unrivaled deputy at the Propaganda Ministry.

Bernhard Lösener, the Interior Ministry's Jewish expert, had expected a small, quiet conference of experts. Instead he encountered a series of speeches followed by "applause, not like in a conference—but as if it were an election campaign." Lösener, author of the Nuremberg Laws, had drafted this decree as well.

Gutterer opened the conference with several charges against German Jews, all of which the Propaganda Ministry saw as affecting the public mood and thus as matters squarely within its jurisdiction. He concluded that "the fundamental basis for an effective fulfillment of all measures would be the [public] identification of the Jews." The Jews were causing outrage because of their impudent manner, and this was causing anger among soldiers at the front. In Berlin the Jews constituted a rabble-rousing headquarters. Furthermore, they took up important living space and were hogging precious food supplies. Jews, Gutterer charged, were responsible for the shortage of strawberries in Berlin! Their food rations should be reduced, he said, adding that "best of all would be to beat them to death."[11]

The conferees readily agreed on the issue of marking the Jews. Goering, however, through a representative, demanded that all measures regarding the Jewish Question be presented first to him, for his review, and stated that the Interior Ministry was the leading authority on such matters. Gutterer agreed, adding, however, that the Propaganda Ministry had to step in whenever public opinion became "aroused." This claim of aroused public opinion, or the claimed threat of it—which from Goebbels was guaranteed to receive Hitler's attention—became Goebbels's most important basis for asserting his authority over the most important matters of the Jewish Question.

Forty years after the war Leopold Gutterer casually described his role as chair of the meeting as if he had been walking down the hall and, without explanation or responsibility, had been drawn in to sit for a moment at the head of a table that was all set in any case to brand all Jews publicly for the coming death camp deportations.[12]

The first day Jews came out wearing the Star of David, many people were in for a surprise. Jews and Germans alike discovered that neighbors and acquaintances they had known for years and never thought of as Jewish now wore the star. There were still 150,000 Jews in Germany, more than 70,000 of them in Berlin. Charlotte Israel sewed the stars on her husband's coats. "From that moment on he refused to go out on the street. 'I'll wait until all this is over,' he said. 'It can't last that much longer.' All of us said that. Many believed it.

"So I was the only one who went out. I went shopping, and otherwise I stayed there for my husband. After two months of this I finally talked him into taking a walk. It was such a beautiful sunny day. He didn't need to be ashamed; others should do that, I said. So we took a walk. People who saw us looked away. Only one man called out, after he was already past us, 'German woman, shame on you for that Jew.' I didn't react. At other times, if people glared at me, I glared back, until they looked down."

At church services Jews wearing the star caused an awkward stir. In Breslau the church considered holding special services for publicly marked Jews, and in Berlin a priest agreed to marry a couple only if the Jewish bridegroom did not wear the star during the service.[13] Even Jews in privileged intermarriages felt themselves "above" Jews who wore the star and avoided appearing with them in public.[14] Hans-Oskar Löwenstein, the fifteen-year-old *Mischling*, put on the Star of David along with his father. "Of course we were terribly afraid," Hans remembered of his first day wearing the star. "Many persons I knew from the street but never thought of as Jewish now appeared wearing the star! In the first three or four days people looked at us as if we were from another planet. After that it changed. As long as we lived with the Jewish star in Berlin, the Germans looked through us like glass. I knew that if anyone wanted to strike me down, no one would interfere. But only twice did someone spit or yell after me. On the other hand, only twice did I receive kindness from strangers because of the star. Once an old women in the subway stuck an apple in my bag, and once a man, with a strong Berlin accent said: 'Don't worry, things will get better someday.' "[15]

Six months later, in March 1942, all Jewish households were required to post the Star of David beside their outer doors. After that only one German outside the family crossed the Israels' doorstep. He owned a laundry several blocks away on Mommsenstrasse and was Julius's chess partner of several years. Julius loved to play chess, and chess partners of his caliber weren't that easy to find. "When he left, this man always left something behind—sweets or something, on my sewing machine. And after he had gone, I found it there. That was truly touching," said Charlotte, still moved. Such seemingly simple acts meant a lot to Charlotte and Julius, but they were rare for her. Other Jews reported that Germans did show them small favors, slipping food and cigarettes to those wearing the star.[16]

The Star of David and Jewish social isolation were especially hard to explain to children. One of Charlotte's neighbors, a Russian Jew, had a beautiful six-year-old daughter named Nora. Told that she would have to wear a star because she was Jewish, Nora said, "What? I thought we were Russians!" One day in a garden restaurant she suddenly got up to ask a little girl at the next table whether she too was Jewish. Then she continued around the tables, asking other children, "Are you Jewish?" Some of the children didn't know. It was terribly embarrassing for the adults. Respectable society knew its place, positioned conveniently within the folds of etiquette. The regime could avoid discussions on the terrible fate of Jews if the public also preferred silence. "Everyone glared at us as if we were criminals," said Charlotte. "It was terribly hard to explain to a child that she shouldn't do such things." Jewish identity and the fate of Jews were a difficult subject for dinner society.

For Wally and Günter Grodka, their child Ranier was born in time. On May 22, 1941, at a mere four pounds, his birth eventually exempted his father from wearing the Star of David and bestowed on the Grodkas the status of a privileged intermarriage. Although the Nuremberg Laws prevented a *Mischling* of the Jewish Community from converting to Christianity in order to escape the *Geltungsjude* status, the Grodkas found an "anti-fascist" Protestant minister to baptize their new son. Then at the Central Organization of German Jews they managed to procure the status of a privileged intermarriage because of their Christian son.[17] As a Jew in privileged intermarriage, in contrast with his former position as a Jew, Günter now received the same food rations as Germans, along with clothing and cigarette rations. He was permitted unlimited use of public transportation, could leave his neighborhood and the city without special permission, and enjoyed other rights that sharply distinguished his life from that of Jews wearing the star.[18]

Ironically, the new decree could actually improve the lot of Jews in privileged intermarriages. The public was now prone to think that anyone not marked with the Star of David was not Jewish and thus that Günter, for example, was also not Jewish. This inconsistency exemplifies the complications Jewish-German families imposed on Nazi racial politics. In 1941 and 1942 ministry bureaucrats were still spending an enormous amount of time trying to deal with these.

For Günter's neighbors, however, the case remained simple: He was a Jew, Wally was married to a Jew, and their child was a mongrel. The government might recognize the Grodkas as a privileged intermarriage, but this did not change the neighbors' views. The regime had tactical reasons for creating privileged intermarriages, but its coveted goal was a society that, having adopted Nazi values, drove out the Jews and anyone married to them. In their house the Grodkas' neighbors were warned. Mrs. Blut spoke with each tenant, Wally remembered, and warned them that she would denounce anyone who so much as spoke with the Grodkas. "I was forced to realize that this woman would probably think up something, to get me in trouble," she added.

Ranier too was assaulted. Mrs. Blut also instructed everyone in the house to avoid the baby boy. The neighbors' children were taught that he was a "Jew idiot." They spit on him and jeered him, sitting in his stroller, too young to walk. When they pressed against the fence of the Grodkas' garden to get a look at the monster, their father tore them away with "Get away from that Jewish brood!"

Was it possible for Germans to resist Nazism? Much of the Grodkas' experience hardly raises this question, indicating that Germans took to Nazi racial ideals, if need be. Jewish social isolation, a prerequisite of mass murder, was encouraged by the regime, yet only the Germans could accomplish it. Could the regime have pushed anti-Jewish measures to the point of publicly plundering and deporting Jews if the entire German population had even been merely guarded in helping Jews rather than open to isolating them?

Because of their small child, Wally and Günter experienced kindness. Günter remembered that it was women, especially, who, while his wife was shopping, secretly slipped groceries or ration cards into Wally's bag. "We had people who were secretly still on our side and who took a little care of us," Wally said. The grocer Salzmann, for example, slipped little things in the bag for Ranier. He had two children of his own and was sympathetic. There was a bakery too that gave Mrs. Grodka goods. This happened, though, only at certain times, when hardly anyone was in the store—just before the store closed, for example. "Some of these people [who helped us] were members of the Nazi party, but they were not really Nazis," Wally said. "They were

The infant Ranier Grodka, held by his father, sporting a Charlie Chaplin/Adolf Hitler–style mustache. As a baptized Christian Ranier changed the official classification of his parents from a "nonprivileged" to "privileged" intermarriage. The difference was momentous. Because of his son, his Jewish father was exempted from most measures of persecution, including the most severe ones: He did not have to wear the Star of David, and he received normal food and clothing rations rather than the starkly reduced rations for Jews.

party members because they were businessmen or for some other reason, but on the question of the Jews, Nazism went against the grain for some. Of course they didn't fight publicly for Jews because they themselves had families."

The Holzers were not a privileged intermarriage, and the Star of David decree forced Rudi to take on a religious identity he didn't want. It required him to suffer continuous public scorn for a cause he hadn't chosen. When the decree was published, Rudi, like Julius, refused to leave the house. But Elsa persuaded him. "Rudi, we're extraordinary people, we don't belong to these masses," she told him.

"Well, *you* don't belong to them," he replied.

"What do you mean, I don't?" she said. " '*We* don't.' And then he took his briefcase, held it over the star, and we went out," Elsa said. "This star was a bright, glowing yellow. And on a dark coat it would have been horrible. I rubbed it with ashes to make it black, and then you couldn't see it so easily."

When Rudi began to wear the star, Elsa became acquainted with her neighbors in a new way. Perhaps they hated her for being different or reminding them that it was possible to resist Nazi terror. "For us wives of Jews back then it was not at all easy," Elsa said. "People made villains of us." Elsa recalled Mr. Rexi, a giant of a man known throughout Berlin for his flourishing stockyards in the wealthy Halensee part of the city, who was also their neighbor. His legs were so huge he lumbered like an elephant, and Elsa and Rudi called him Liverwurst Legs. Rexi lived on the third floor and always looked out from the window, glaring at them. One day as they left their house, there was a huge crash just behind them. "We jumped for fright," Elsa remembered. "We turned around and saw that it was a great big flower pot. If you had caught that on your head, you would have noticed it. Liverwurst Legs wanted to scare us. Once when we walked by, someone threw a pot of urine out on us. It was really bad, though, when someone put feces all over our doorstep. I hurried out in the morning to catch the train and stepped all over it. And the next day the house superintendent—thank God he liked my husband and wasn't against us—told us that other tenants were saying that the Holzers were tracking shit around the house. Then they came to us and said, 'How is it that you track shit all through our house?'

"Once I was returning home down the stairs at the Neukölln train station, and three old ladies approached me. They were neighbors, and

I looked and greeted them: 'Good day.' And suddenly they spit on me. All three. From top to bottom. Uhhh. *Old ladies.* They didn't say a thing. Only spit. Because I was married to a Jew.

"And the husband of one of those women was also a printer, like Rudi, and got along well with him—before. Before, we all got together on their balcony, in the evenings, spent nice hours there. She had even praised my husband—because he was an engaging soul and had a way with words. And this woman told me once, 'To live with Rudi must be just great!' Then, when it came out that Rudi was a Jew, she was actually furious. So this woman was once quite nice—but false.

**Ranier Grodka
with his mother on
Berlin's Kurfürstendamm.**

"And this same woman changed again later! After the war she was walking with her mother along the street, and as we got closer, she called out, 'Ach, Elsa, how nice!' And I made a face, so that she looked away and walked off out of the picture. Yes, yes, that's humanity. Ha-ha. No, no, no. The other tenants in our building refused to let us in their air-raid shelter, refused to breathe the air we exhaled. But at the end of the war, with the Russians at the edge of Berlin, they approached us nicely and said, 'Here, come in with us.' They wanted to claim that they had protected Rudi, the Jew. But they only wanted to protect themselves. 'No, we're not coming in,' I told them.

"In my family too everyone suddenly knew Rudi was Jewish." Elsa continued. "It went around as fast as if it had been published on the kiosks. And after that we didn't get together with my sisters at all. Do you think they'd want to go around with us, with him wearing a Jewish star? My cousin Jutta also liked getting together with us. But not after this. No more. Once we were taking a walk in Wilmersdorf and almost ran into each other. All of a sudden I saw her. In three more steps I would have said, 'Ach, Jutta, sweetie, how are you doing?' And before, Jutta would have said, 'Man, the Holzers. Man, how are you?'

"No more. As soon as she saw us, Jutta crossed to the other side. Like a rabbit. Gone. From one day to the next she was gone for us. I don't mean that she was against us. But she didn't want to be together with us anymore. That's the way people are. I still find it that way today. One day they love you, and all of a sudden they step on you. Seventy-five percent of the people are that way. My parents too.

"Yes, even my parents," Elsa confided softly, ashamed. "My parents were the worst. That was the worst. Before Hitler, my parents didn't have anything at all against our marriage. But not later. Then I became 'the endangerment of the family.' Because of Rudi. I was the one, however, who was in danger! I never knew whether I'd see my husband again the next day. I might have disappeared too. And I was supposed to be the 'endangerment' of the family.' My parents never wrote or visited us during the war. Not at Christmas, not on birthdays. Never. The entire time I didn't hear a thing from them. And they didn't live two hundred miles away, only twenty minutes by car."

"If only you would divorce, Elsa, everything would be fine again. Then you'd have enough to heat your house," her father told her the last time she saw him during the war. She was there to visit partly on the pretense of getting firewood. Elsa tells the story now with averted eyes. To her it was so shameful she never did bring herself to tell Rudi—not even long after the war. It was just before Christmas in

1941, and even in this early stage of the war, coal rations were shrinking. Two Germans could still live in relative comfort, but ration cards for Jews were virtually useless. Still, Elsa and Rudi would have had enough to live had her family and their friends stood by them. They could have had sufficient rations to eat and to heat their home had German loved ones and acquaintances shared with them. But they were abandoned to fend for themselves.

"Why should I divorce?" Elsa remembered responding to her father. "I've married the man who's supposed to be my husband."

"Rudi is a criminal," he said. "It's in the newspapers now, can't you read?"

"Oh, God, you know Rudi," Elsa said. "We've already been married twelve years, and you know the way he is."

Elsa turned to her mother. She could talk with her mother, who would certainly support her now, Elsa thought. "Mama, you say," asked Elsa. "You know your husband well, and you know his family. and then someone comes along and tells you he is a criminal, you've got to divorce. What would you think?"

"Elsa, I'd take my children and leave him," said her mother.

With nowhere to turn, Elsa remembers that she began to laugh hysterically, so hard she couldn't stop. Her father called her crazy, and she told him that "I have a different relationship to my husband. You perhaps would divorce your wife. Not me!"

Then he screamed at her to get out and never show her face there again. "I've only waited for that," Elsa replied. "I'll never step through this door again. Don't worry." Her mother called after her to take the wood, but Elsa was gone.

In 1941 the regime issued a law providing for imprisonment of Germans who "show a friendly relationship to Jews."[19] Elsa's parents might have feared this law. Yet Elsa's story shows that by remaining loyal to her marriage, she was able to rescue Rudi.

Elsa's strongest memory of that night she left her parents' home was of darkness. Because of British air raids, the government prohibited lights in public spaces and private homes. The train and the train stations were utterly black. Their apartment was dark as a basement. Elsa expected Rudi any minute. How much she needed him now. But that night he didn't come as expected. "Rudi didn't have just eight hours of work but sometimes twelve," she explained. "And sometimes even more than that. Sometimes he didn't come home at all, and I waited the whole time not knowing what had happened to him. So I lived constantly under wrenching pressure. Constantly."

When Rudi arrived, hours later, she told him she looked so terrible because she was getting a cold. Months later he suggested that they should perhaps visit her parents again. "No," said Elsa. "Let's just spend the precious time we have together alone."

"I only wanted to protect him," Elsa explained. "And also I was ashamed of my parents. Ashamed that people—and then *even my parents*—could do such a thing! And the funny thing is that still today no one in our family knows my story. My sisters still live and don't know I was kicked out of our home. I never told the story. After the war, when I began to speak about it, my oldest sister immediately broke in: 'Don't go into that old story. You're trying to make Father look bad. Leave it now, little one.' "

How can we understand a person who defied the Gestapo (knowing this could cost her life), who also could not confront her sisters with their own story? Elsa calmed herself by trying to see it from their side. "They did it out of fear," she reflected. "Out of fear my parents harassed me. They simply wanted me to divorce! Because they were afraid. But out of fear, can you send someone to death? Is that possible?" she added, bending toward me intensely. Alone in her East German apartment she had lived with the memories of Nazi Germany for decades. She wanted to know whether it is a "chapter for itself" or whether she must believe that it teaches lessons about human behavior. "If fear is something everyone experiences, how can killing be its antidote?" She continued. "If I have fear, should I say, 'We have to kill that one, and when he's gone, we'll have no more fear?' " Then, as if feeling herself backed into a suffocating corner, she suddenly concluded: "Let's not talk about this again. Let's make this the last time we talk about this."

When the pain of memories became too great, Elsa asked that I discontinue my interviews. The gulf between us also seemed too great to bridge. I had not been there, and for her the war had brought realities that could never be imagined, could never be understood if not experienced. Most people will act brutally under extreme pressure, she now believed. "Before the war I was certainly a different person," she said sadly, unable to return. "Before the war I would have received everybody with open arms. Hugged them all. I felt warm toward everyone. But now I say, 'You never know what a person will do under pressure. You know a person only in the situation of distress. Then they will step on you! With both hands, they will grab you and strangle you.' "

XII

THE PRICE OF COMPLIANCE AND THE DESTRUCTION OF JEWS

DEPORTATIONS TO THE EAST

About two months after Gutterer's conference, the Final Solution of German Jews began. The first deportation of Berlin's remaining seventy-three thousand Jews left on October 18, 1941.[1] One thousand Jews were crammed onto freight trains headed for "work camps in the East."[2] Within several weeks twenty thousand Jews from old Germany (pre-1938 borders), including several thousand more Berlin Jews, were deported to the Polish ghetto of Lodz.[3]

It is not that Jewish leaders did not try to protest. They had protested in 1940, but their efforts had been met with the most heartless reprisals. Rarely has compliance been so ruthlessly extorted. Jewish leaders were treated only with deception and force.

The Jewish Community was drawn into becoming an arm of the German police in a seemingly innocent way. In relocating and concentrating Berlin Jews in 1939 the Gestapo had first vested authority in the Jewish Community: A Jew renting from a German was required to move when the Jewish Community designated a space for the Jew to move to. But the Jew *had* to move if the Jewish Community ordered the Jew to do so. This was the first step of a long journey. It physically dislocated and concentrated Jews for the first time, but more important, it established materials, administrative officers, procedures, and lists of names and addresses essential to upcoming deportations. Now, two and one half years later, Berlin Jewish leaders were instructed to initiate more "resettlements." This time Jews were going outside Berlin, to the east. The timing of the Gestapo's new orders to Jewish leaders in October 1941 lent a sadistic edge to its characteristic efficiency.

On Yom Kippur 1941 the Gestapo broke news of the deportations to Berlin's Jewish leaders. In the middle of the sermon at the Jewish temple on Joachimstalerstrasse 13, a stone's throw from Bahnhof Zoo in central Berlin, the chairman of the Central Organization of German Jews, Rabbi Dr. Leo Baeck, received a call. It was Scharführer Prüfer, acting as director of the Jewish Desk of the Berlin branch of the Gestapo. Prüfer ordered Baeck to appear at his office on Burgstrasse at once. Upon arriving, the rabbi found his deputy, Philipp Kozower, and Dr. Martha Mosse, the director of the community's Housing Advisory Office, along with one or two others. This news would have to be kept top secret, Prüfer began. Because of a housing shortage exacerbated by the British air raids, some Jews were to be "resettled" on the eastern border of Germany, near Lodz. He called the operation an "action to clear living space." Dr. Mosse recalled Prüfer's saying that the Jews "would be allowed to take along twenty-five kilograms of clothing, toiletries and so forth, and they would be allowed to live a normal life there."[4] Jewish leaders were to assist this evacuation effort.

First they were to prepare a list of names. Prüfer gave the Jewish Community three thousand copies of a questionnaire about age, place of work, size of family, whether a medal of honor had been earned in World War I. Dr. Mosse's office would order three thousand members to come to her office to fill out the questionnaires. The completed forms would be returned to the Gestapo, which from them would in turn compose a list of one thousand of those to be "resettled." Before leaving Prüfer's office, members of the Jewish leaders asked the Gestapo man whether they were permitted to repeat his instructions to other members of the Central Organization's Directorate. It was necessary for carrying out the "resettlement" plans. Prüfer agreed. Now the Jewish leadership would be privy to information denied to other Jews.

Shortly after their meeting with Prüfer, the leaders of the Berlin Jewish Community met with leading representatives of the Central Organization of German Jews. Should they carry out Prüfer's demands?

Perhaps they thought that by cooperating, they might prove themselves and gain some autonomy. Or perhaps they considered the significance their authority as Jewish leaders might have on the efficiency with which Jews would be brought together for an evacuation. No doubt they turned over in their minds the grave results of hesitation. The Jewish leader Otto Hirsch had been taken to the Mauthausen camp, where he died. They did take Prüfer at his word; certainly they could not have imagined the terrible fate awaiting those deported to the east. Their work, the leaders now reasoned, would soften the blows of an evacuation bound to happen anyway.[5]

The Jewish Community selected three thousand names from a list developed for the relocation of Jews in 1939. Additional names and addresses had been gathered through the community's role as the vendor of the Stars of David. Data on persons defined as Jews under the Nuremberg Laws but not registered with any Jewish organization were gathered through notices published in the *Jüdische Nachrichtenblatt*, the Central Organization's paper sent to every German Jew. Throughout the deportations the Gestapo relied on the Jewish Community's list for the names and addresses of Jews. It was the most dependable one, Himmler's statistician wrote in 1943, because the community's work was so thorough and so dependable.[6]

The Gestapo ordered Jewish leaders to make the Levetzowstrasse synagogue ready for one thousand persons and to arrange to send appropriate Jewish Community personnel to serve both night and day shifts there. The Gestapo took those arrested directly to the synagogue, a place many Jews associated with the security of caring community and God's protection. At Levetzowstrasse scores of Jews in blue armbands were deployed to register those about to be deported and to keep order. Jews on hand at the synagogue to keep order and provide meals and medical assistance were called orderlies. There was also a questionnaire to be filled out, devised by the Jewish Community, which inquired into past work experience and work capability with a view toward placement in the work camps in the east. With the Gestapo's permission, Jewish Community leaders provided hot meals. They also convinced the Gestapo to provide those designated for the deportations with medical checkups, to determine their fitness for the journey and work, according to Dr. Mosse. Community doctors administered physicals.[7]

At the synagogue, possessions of deported German Jews were confiscated on allegations that Jews were "enemies of the state." In Berlin the Gestapo confiscated the possessions of those they arrested for deportation and then locked and sealed their residences, which became the property of the Reich. The Berlin Gestapo was supposed to turn over every object and German mark it confiscated to the chief president of finances of Berlin/Brandenburg.[8]

When the Gestapo first ordered the Jewish leaders to compile a list, they envisioned that only a few thousand Jews would have to leave. Many people—particularly Jews with non-Jewish friends—believed that their fate would not get worse, said Dr. Mosse. They believed that it would not be allowed to get worse. But the Gestapo was ordered to remove fifty thousand Jews from the Reich territory (including Austria and the protectorate in the former Czechoslovakia) to Minsk and Riga between November 1 and December 4, 1941,[9] and in the six weeks between the first deportation on October 18 and November 27 there were seven deportations of Berlin Jews, averaging about one thousand per deportation.

The employees of the Jewish Community became increasingly caught up in the enormous amount of work created by the deportations. Jewish leaders were in nearly daily contact with the Berlin Gestapo and the RSHA on organizational matters.[10] In addition to those at the Housing Office and the orderlies, typists, nurses from the Jewish hospital, statisticians, and others were forced to apply their trades to the process of deportations. A list of ninety-six Jews who worked for the Gestapo and were deported in the so-called Orderly Transport of 1943–44 itemizes the jobs they performed. Nearly thirty types of work are listed, including medical care, barbers, electricians, plumbers, secretaries, guards over prisoners, detectives (searching for Jews in hiding), cooks, and administrator of the clothes locker.[11] Jews working for the Gestapo were paid by the Central Organization.[12] Seventeen Jews, in addition to construction workers, worked for the RSHA and were paid according to their most recent employment for the Central Organization.[13]

The Housing Office continued to request Jews to fill out questionnaires from which the Gestapo made the deportation selections.[14] Then the Housing Office sent out postcards advising Jews of their impending evacuation, some five to seven days in advance. A seven- to eight-page list of instructions informed them precisely what and what not to bring for their journey and how much their suitcases could weigh.[15] Receipt of such a card became known colloquially as receiving the list or the card.

The 188 deportations of Jews from Berlin can be divided into four phases, reflecting the methods used to make arrests. The original method of advance notification had to be abandoned within months (or perhaps just weeks) because "too many" Jews fled instead of showing up for deportation. The Berlin District Court concluded that "not just a small number" of Jews successfully evaded deportation this way in Berlin, an enormous city with a relatively large number of possibilities for living "underground."[16] The bombings had destroyed or half destroyed thousands of houses. Along the Spree River there were garden huts rarely used in winter. Sections of the city were barely patrolled by the police. Berlin had received the Nazis with relative reluctance, and some persons might hide Jews out of conviction—or for money.

In the second phase of deportations, the Jewish Housing Office continued to send out questionnaires that targeted persons for deportation. But instead of sending notices, the Gestapo went door to door, seizing the Jews from their homes. The Jews were taken to the synagogue and from there in covered trucks to the train station. This phase continued until the arrival in November 1942 of Alois Brunner, who forced Jews to accompany Gestapo agents as they arrested Jews. As the Jewish population dwindled, and it became difficult to deport the last remaining Jews, the Gestapo's reliance on Jews for the deportations became more ruthless. The final phase of the Berlin deportations coincided with the deportation of the last indigenous Jewish authorities, when the Gestapo employed Jews as "catchers"—armed accomplices of the Gestapo ordered to ferret out the last Jews from their hiding places. Deceit and force in the hands of these few desperate catchers were the means of trapping the last Jews. Günther Abrahamsohn, a catcher who carried a pistol to enforce his authority while employed by the Gestapo, interpreted his crime decades later in an interview as the deeds of a twenty-three-year-old, not yet fully morally formed man, who, although ambitious, had no (other) way to make a career and who was, as a waif from the backwaters of provincial Prenzlau, overawed by the Reich capital and an invitation to serve power, on arriving there.[17]

Officially, intermarried Jews and *Mischlinge*—even those who wore the star—were "temporarily deferred" from the deportations.[18] But once the deportations began, they did face deportation for even the slightest infraction. Denunciations against them were now more likely to lead to death. Mrs. Böhm, a "half Jew" the Nazis considered Jewish because of her marriage to a Jew, had moved in with the Grodkas with her husband and newborn son. Both Böhms received the Jewish food ration cards and could shop only between 4:00 and 5:00 P.M. The Böhms, however, needed more food just to keep the baby alive. In an effort to get German portions, Mrs. Böhm went shopping one day

without wearing the Star of David. Mrs. Hensel, the guardian of practices at the local grocer, was watching. She immediately denounced
her, and a short while after, the Gestapo arrested Mrs. Böhm, leaving
behind her husband and small child. "That was heart-rending to see
how she held the child and loved it, before leaving," said Wally.[19]

The number of Jews in the Grodkas' house dropped weekly. Even
Günter's relatives, who had moved there in 1939, were now deported.
"In the middle of our meal, these poor people are picked up," Wally
wrote. "Panic was thick in the air." Attempting to help Jews instructed
to appear at the synagogue for "evacuation," Wally went with them,
pulling their suitcases on a small hand wagon to the synagogue. "On
the way she was often harassed for helping a Jew. My wife did that
because I myself couldn't be seen much in this kind of way," said
Günter.

"The Gestapo threatened to take me too, for helping the Jews,"
Wally recalled. "When the people insulted me, I simply went on without reacting. It would have been senseless to react. You had to realize
that these insults were hurled to make you lose your cool."

An acquaintance of the Grodkas' was the janitor at the Levetzowstrasse synagogue, who told her what happened inside, where Wally
was not allowed to follow. In the main hall of the synagogue Jewish
orderlies assisted the Gestapo with the registration and search of the
Jews. At one big table names were called out one by one. The person
and the person's suitcase were assigned matching numbers. At a second
table personal information was registered. At a third table personal
possessions not packed in suitcases were stripped away; passports, iden-
tifications, medals of honor, jewelry, and any other valuables, including
food, were taken. Suitcases were searched at yet another table and
robbed of valuable or dangerous items. Jews were required then to strip
for a body search. Each Jew was then given a sign with a number, to
be worn around the neck. Finally, suitcases were numbered and returned.

"It happened like it does at the post office," explained Anton
Loderer, a former Gestapo officer who helped search the Jews in the
synagogue. "In the background there were thirty to fifty Jews [order-
lies] waiting. In addition to me, there were about five or six colleagues
who looked through the baggage, which went from hand to hand, passed
along by one colleague to the next." He and the others, Loderer reported, confiscated valuables under SS supervision, including clothing
in good condition. The Jews were separated by sex, then led one by
one into small rooms, where they were stripped naked and searched
by members of their own sex for any valuables and money other than

the train fare. Dr. Kunze, who directed much of the processing and baggage checks in the Levetzowstrasse, even ordered his assistant to reach into the anus of a man to check for any hidden valuables there. Loderer concluded: "As soon as we finished the task assigned us, we went home. The Jews who had been in the room stayed at the collection center."[20] This process at the synagogue lasted on average about two days, after which the Jews were loaded onto the furniture trucks and taken to the train stations, where they were driven onto the trains like cattle.[21]

By December 1941 rumors were filtering back to Berlin that Jews sent to "the east" and never heard from again were being shot into mass open graves. "During the war I once retold a rumor by a friend that in Lithuania there had been some mass shootings," Mosse told the court. "I didn't believe this rumor, because I could not imagine that such things could happen."[22] Other Jews, even after hearing BBC reports that Jews were being murdered, thought this was enemy propaganda, reasoning among themselves that the regime would at least employ Jews as slave labor.[23] On the other hand, Günter Grodka, whose father and cousin worked for the Jewish Community, claimed after the war that he believed these reports. Grodka's cousin, who reported that members of the Jewish Community accompanied the deportation trains to the east as orderlies, told Günter of the shootings in 1941, "how they were taken from the trains, how they were driven forward, how graves were dug, how behind the Jews the SS was already positioned, who then mowed them down."[24]

Certainly the regime did everything possible to maintain secrecy about the mass murders. It did not want to risk alienating Germans generally, and it needed to prevent Jewish protests and mass noncompliance.[25] The official story persisted: Jews were being taken to work camps. Early deportation directives, held strictly secret, even made provisions for the deported Jews to take along their sewing machines. Many took hope from the opportunity to take their sewing machines and complied, Wally remembered.

Nevertheless, Charlotte Israel and her Jewish friends soon came to know that deportation meant separation forever. Still, as their group of Jewish friends dwindled, the Israels continued to have their "music evenings." Sometimes Charlotte also invited her mother, who through Charlotte had become friendly with a few Jews. She was especially fond of Julius's family friend Mrs. Rosenstiel.

One night after one of Charlotte's get-togethers, before walking home, Mrs. Press slipped into Mrs. Rosenstiel's coat by mistake. It was the coat of a Jew, marked by a bright yellow Star of David. "Mrs. Rosenstiel, the last to leave, noticed her coat was missing," Charlotte said. "And I said, 'If this coat is not yours, then my mother has your coat on! I hope she arrived safely there!' 'Well, it's already dark,' said Mrs. Rosenstiel. 'No one will have noticed the star now.' "

In winter, there was an eight o'clock curfew for Jews, but Mrs. Rosenstiel, the one with experience, knew how to use darkness as protection. "But all was soon well again," Charlotte said. "I sent someone to my mother's, and we exchanged the coats. Everything was fine again," Charlotte concluded.

In constant need herself, Charlotte did what she could. Some Germans cited their families as reasons for taking care only of themselves, but Charlotte sat with panicked Jews through the night or sewed packs for them to take on their trip east. When Mrs. Rosenstiel was

Charlotte and Julius Israel's circle, before the deportations. From left to right they are: Julius, standing in the back, wearing a tie; Charlotte; Heinz Streblow; Charlotte's friend Edith Kopf. Seated in front, from left to right: Julius's niece Inge, with the dog; Mrs. Kopf, Edith's mother; Mrs. Israel, Julius's mother; Trude Rosenthal, holding the small child.

slated for deportation, Charlotte and Mrs. Press spent the last night with her as she cried and pleaded for them to help hide her. "Hide me in the attic, in the cellar," she said. "You're a Christian. You can help. Hide me. I promise I will never come out until the war is over!" Mrs. Press was so touched she was about to agree. But Charlotte didn't allow this. "If my mother had hidden Mrs. Rosenstiel, the Gestapo would have found out about it, and everything would have been over," Charlotte said. In any case Julius would not have agreed. He knew Charlotte was his protection, and when she wasn't there, he feared for his safety. The nights Charlotte spent at Mrs. Rosenstiel's, Julius fretted terribly. "He was a bundle of nerves," Charlotte said. "What was he supposed to think had happened to me? he asked. I should also think about him sometimes! But he wasn't the one directly affected at that moment. Mrs. Rosenstiel was the one then.

"The next morning my husband said, 'Don't go over there to Mrs. Rosenstiel again.' " Charlotte continued. "He didn't want me to help so much because he was afraid that the Gestapo would come and take me too." But Charlotte did go and found Mrs. Rosenstiel dead: She had turned on the gas, and gone to sleep.

"I was totally done for," Charlotte concluded. "Kaput! That was horrible for me. I always presented myself as the strong one, but then afterward I always had fits of weeping and breakdowns. Because of these experiences, I still very often get depressions. I try to fight against them, but such a trauma can't be flushed away. I do receive some government compensation today because of my nerves. But my enemies have more than I do."

1942: OFFICIAL RECONSIDERATIONS OF THE INTERMARRIAGE PROBLEM

Final Solution executives were of course angry about Germans who held to Jews, and by 1942 Charlotte, like Wally, sensed that she also was in danger. Amid the agony of Jewish lives ruined, families destroyed, entire communities rooted out, the struggle over when to deport intermarried Jews and *Mischlinge* continued. Himmler's men pushed for drawing them into the Final Solution while Goebbels held back, waiting, like Hitler, for the opportune moment.

On the issue of these Jews and part Jews, Goebbels's mandate to maintain public passivity brought him into conflict with Himmler, who was in charge of death camps and other aspects of Germany's "racial purification." During the war Hitler sided with both Goebbels and Himmler. Just as he continued to contradict himself on the issue of equalizations and dispensations for *Mischlinge*, his signals on inter-married Jews were not definitive. On a case-by-case basis he stopped the efforts of Himmler's men to draw intermarried Jews and *Mischlinge* into the Final Solution, as they now and then renewed their efforts on this problem. Early in the process of deporting German Jews, Hitler perhaps began to think that the resolution of the *Mischlinge* and intermarried Jews problem would have to wait until after the war.[26] He understood the psychological reasons that led Goebbels to release intermarried Jews arrested for deportation in March 1943, yet in June of the same year he agreed with Himmler that the Jewish problem had to be "radically" solved, indicating intermarried Jews must be deported, regardless of the unrest this might cause. True to his self-proclaimed style, Hitler waited for the right moment to take action.[27]

Goebbels agreed with Himmler's men at the RSHA in theory. On different occasions Goebbels recorded in his diary that far from protecting their Jewish spouses, Germans who chose to marry Jews were incapable of understanding the basic tenet of National Socialism and might well have to share the fate of the Jews with whom they chose to associate. "What is to be done with the half-Jews," Goebbels asked in March 1942. "What with those related to Jews? In-laws of Jews? Persons married to Jews?"[28] Goebbels concluded then (as well as a year later in March 1943) that National Socialism and the situation of war allowed for no indulgence in sentimentality. He did not even consider intermarried Jews to be a question; that was clear. He mused only about whether to murder the non-Jewish in-laws, relatives, spouses as well. Yet these Germans married to Jews, as Goebbels knew, had lots of racial German relatives.

Since dividing families was a delicate matter, Goebbels held back. Himmler's men, impatient to complete the Final Solution, had not included Goebbels in their deliberations. In the occupied eastern territories non-Jews who refused to separate from their Jewish spouses had been deported along with the Jews, a pattern Himmler wanted to apply to Germany. In an October 10, 1941, meeting, Himmler's deputy Reinhardt Heydrich, Eichmann, and other Nazi decision makers concerned with the Final Solution had agreed that an intermarried German who refused to divorce would be deported along with the Jewish partner.[29] This decision, however, was taken without Goebbels, who represented Hitler's special concern about avoiding unrest. The discussion of intermarriages came to the fore again during the Wannsee Conference. Heydrich, who wanted to treat *Mischlinge* just like Jews,[30] did not invite the Propaganda Ministry to participate in that key Final Solution meeting held on the banks of a Berlin resort lake on January 20, 1942.

Hitler had temporarily stopped RSHA efforts to include German *Mischlinge* and intermarried Jews in the deportations. At Wannsee, five months later, about half of this ninety-minute meeting was taken up with the special problems relating to *Mischlinge* and intermarried Jews. Heydrich was willing to make compromises now. Intermarried Jews were to be treated like other Jews, except in special cases where, in consideration of a non-Jewish relative, the Jew would go to Theresienstadt: "It will have to be decided from case to case whether the Jewish part [of intermarriages] will be evacuated, or whether because of regard to the effect of such measures on the German relatives of this intermarriage, the Jew will be sent to an old people's ghetto." Theresienstadt, a camp without means of mass killing or ovens for disposing of corpses, was a disguised component of the Final Solution. Even Jews the military requested be shown mercy were secretly sent from this "privileged ghetto" to Auschwitz.[31] In an instructive example of the regime's fear of domestic unrest, however, the small number of intermarried Jews who were sent there (following divorce, in some cases) were not sent on to the ovens and crematoria of Auschwitz.[32]

The Wannsee Conference concluded with an agreement that the Final Solution in the occupied east must be completed as quickly as possible—"during which, however, stirring up unrest among the population must be avoided."[33] The conferees agreed that German *Mischlinge* would be allowed to remain in the Reich—on condition that they "volunteered" to be sterilized, their other option being deportation. Heydrich expected more resistance from the officials to his proposals. At the end of the conference he was very pleased, he told Eichmann, that he got virtually none.[34]

When a copy of the minutes of the meeting reached his desk, Goebbels demanded representation at all such future meetings.[35] On such delicate matters touching on the public mood, he claimed to be the expert. Accordingly, two propaganda specialists were on hand for the follow-up Final Solution conference, held on March 6, in Eichmann's Kurfürstenstrasse office. Hitler's (and Goebbels's) perspective was represented in the conferees' agreement that the presence of *Mischlinge* in the Reich, even if they were sterilized, would prevent the accomplishment of a Final Solution; nevertheless, because of "political reasons," it would be impossible to do more. Officials rejected a proposed law to compel all *Mischlinge* married to non-Jews to divorce because "the forced breakup of the marriage would lead to considerable disquiet among non-German relatives, which in these cases can and must be avoided."[36]

Decisions to compromise ideology in favor of maintaining the social peace by not deporting intermarried Jews were reserved for the highest level. Interior Ministry State Secretary Wilhelm Stuckart, who claimed to be a man of conscience who protected *Mischlinge*, indicated instead that on matters of intermarried Jews he was a narrowly focused bureaucrat. He proposed that the Interior and Justice ministries promulgate a law mandating divorce for all Jewish-German couples, and the officials at the March 6 meeting agreed. The operative German policy was to exempt intermarried Jews from the deportations, but to deport them immediately if their German partners asked for divorces or died.[37] If the problem was that Germans were not divorcing their Jewish spouses, there should be a law to ensure divorce, Stuckart reasoned.[38]

Stuckart's proposal was rejected by Goebbels and the acting minister of justice, Franz Schlegelberger, an unlikely ally. Goebbels opposed it for "political reasons, particularly the expected reaction of the Vatican."[39] Schlegelberger objected on the ground that such a law would not achieve the desired effect of deporting the Jews while avoiding social unrest: "A forced divorce is useless because even if it would break the legal tie, it could certainly not break the inner ties. . . . In any case, only persons married for a long time, who have withstood long years together, are expected to hold fast to their Jewish partners."[40] Schlegelberger's proposed solution for maintaining the peace and purifying the race was to deport both partners to Theresienstadt. Goebbels suspected, however, that this too might cause protests from German relatives of these couples.[41]

No doubt Hitler wanted to solve this problem as soon as possible in the opportune moment.[42] On July 28, 1942, in any case, Himmler asked that the law to force the dissolution of intermarriages, which at that point existed in draft form, be abandoned: "With all these silly commitments we are only binding our own hands!"[43] Himmler preferred to take action with his police force at the opportune moment. So the regime never did pass a law to force the dissolution of intermarriages. The conclusion of those who met to discuss Stuckart's proposal was to grant a divorce to a German married to a Jew upon request, a policy that continued the regime's dependency on the cooperation of intermarried Germans.

The conflict between the regime's ideals of racial purification and social quiescence could have been solved by social cooperation, the willing decision of intermarried Germans to divorce. The importance of the cooperation that intermarried Germans withheld is illustrated by the regime's struggle, in early 1942, to keep public newspapers from reaching Jews. In January the Reich Press Chamber ordered that Jews throughout the Reich no longer receive newspapers other than the *Jüdische Nachrichtenblatt* and instructed post office and newspaper vendors not to deliver papers to Jews.

Because intermarried German bought newspapers for their partners at the stands or put subscriptions in their own names, the law was ineffective. From January until the end of June a number of agencies occupied themselves with this matter of newspapers and Jews, while German partners in both privileged and nonprivileged intermarriages continued to make newspapers available to their spouses. At first the concerned government agencies agreed to relax the law by allowing only those in privileged intermarriages to receive newspapers (allowing Jews in nonprivileged intermarriages would mean "too much of a violation of the rule"). Then it became clear that the regime had no better means of keeping newspapers from reaching Jews in nonprivileged intermarriages than from Jews in privileged intermarriages. The law was finally abandoned entirely because, "a check on whether someone ordering newspapers or magazines is part of a Jewish mixed marriage, and above that whether the person might be a part of a privileged or nonprivileged mixed marriage, is practically impossible to carry out, since a partner of a mixed marriage is not outwardly apparent as such."[44]

Trouble with the enforcement of the regulation led to a conflict between Himmler and Goebbels. Goebbels claimed authority over newspapers, and Himmler over the Final Solution, and the dispute was over who could tell the Central Organization of Jews what to publish in the Jewish newspaper. Goebbels complained that Himmler's RSHA had made direct orders to the Central Organization, which passed all Reich ordinances on to German Jews in the *Jüdische Nachrichtenblatt*. The RSHA reasoned to the Press Chamber that since Goering empowered its director, Heydrich, with the Final Solution, it too would necessarily deal with the Central Organization.

RESISTANCE, REPRISALS, COMPLIANCE

Ironically the fate of pets led finally to the fear that no Jew would be spared. In May 1942 a decree required Jewish households to have their pets killed by the Animal Protection Association (or a private veterinarian). Intermarried couples of Jewish households were not exempt even if the pet was registered as property of the German partner. The reaction was immediate and bitter. "This decree resulted in a never-ending stream of plea attempts for the exemption of animals," wrote Hildegard Henschel, the Jewish Community director's wife. "Particularly the Aryan partners in intermarriages lined up in entire columns at Iranischestrasse 4, at the Jewish hospital, to plead for their four-legged or feathered house comrades." Some sent photographs of themselves with their animals and spent days at various city and state offices in search of an exemption. The Gestapo, however, bent the rules in only several cases.[45] Charlotte remembered how bitterly she took her canary to the veterinarian to be killed. For her it stood for the innocence of the Nazis' victims as it sang its last beautiful song "from a full throat." What the bureaucracy demanded of her was not the bird itself but merely a certificate that it was dead. Thinking back, Charlotte could not help wondering why the veterinarian didn't just give her the certificate and allow her to take her canary back home. That is of course something Charlotte thought of, but did it ever cross the veterinarian's mind?

There soon followed events with more serious implications. In mid-May a group of young Communists blew up one of Goebbels's anti-Soviet exhibitions, the ironically titled "Soviet Paradise" display, in the famed Berlin Lustgarten. A number of persons were injured. Some of the Communists in the Baum Group—named for its leader —were Jewish. All of them were captured, and most were shot or hanged by early 1943. Herbert Baum reportedly committed suicide.[46]

Ten days later Reinhard Heydrich, the Reich protector of Bohemia-Moravia as well as the director of the Reich Security Main Office, was fatally wounded by members of the Czech resistance near Prague. This resistance was more serious, and authorities blamed the Jews. The day after the attack on Heydrich, Jewish leaders in Berlin, together with the heads of the Jewish communities in Vienna and Prague, were summoned to the RSHA. After waiting hours in icy suspense, they were told that 500 Jews in Berlin had been arrested the previous night and that 250 had been executed. Of those executed, 154 were newly arrested, while 96 were taken from Jews already imprisoned in Sachsenhausen.[47]

Behind the terror, again, was Berlin's gauleiter, who ordered reprisals. On May 27, 1942, Goebbels recorded in his diary: "I shall now likewise complete my war against the Berlin Jews. At the moment I am having a list drawn up of the Jewish hostages to be followed by many arrests. I have no desire to put myself into a position to be shot in the belly by a 22-year-old Jew from the East—such types are to be found among the assassins at the Anti-Soviet Exhibition."

A few days later, following the executions, Goebbels wrote that war was more important than evidence in determining his reaction to the resistance: "We still don't know the background of the plot . . . in any case, we are making the Jews pay. I am having my planned arrest of 500 Jews in Berlin carried out, and am informing the leaders of the Jewish community that for every Jewish plot or attempt at revolt 100 or 150 Jews whom we are holding are to be shot. As a consequence of the attempt on Heydrich a whole group of Jews, against whom we have evidence, were shot in Sachsenhausen."[48]

The RSHA now used threats to stem sabotage. Jewish leaders would be held responsible for sabotage, so they must warn German Jews that resistance would lead to heavier reprisals. Eppstein met repeatedly during the next days with representatives from the RSHA, including Eichmann. If and by what means should the Central Organization inform the Jewish population about the Baum Group act of sabotage? Goebbels was sometimes torn between using acts of reprisal as a means of deterrence and suppressing all communication about acts of sabotage and resistance leading to reprisals.[49] In the end, despite the varied proposals by RSHA officials, any public announcement was forbidden, while letters were sent to relatives of the reprisal victims, informing them of their deaths. Deportation and execution were held up as the price of resistance, and Jewish leaders were warned: Any Jew petitioning high offices for special permission to emigrate would be deported immediately, along with his family.[50] Jewish leaders were firmly in the icy grip of an arbitrary Gestapo.

Throughout the summer of 1942 a steady stream of Berlin's Jews departed on deportations to the "east," from which no Jewish traveler returned. One "east transport" followed another, and with each departing train, there were about one thousand fewer Jews in Berlin. On July 11 deportations to Auschwitz began. Then the intermarriage of Erna, Julius Israel's sister, fell victim to National Socialism. One day, without announcing his intentions, Erna's German husband disappeared. His daughter, Inge, never saw him again, although for a while afterward her eyes would comb the streets to match her fading, early memories of him with the faces she saw. Charlotte recalled that her father was blond, and Inge too looked typically "Aryan," a beautiful young woman with bright blond hair.

Although she was a *Mischling* with a German father, Inge was

Jewish according to the Nuremberg Laws because she had been enrolled in the Jewish Community at the time the laws were issued. As of July 1, 1942, all Jewish schools were ordered closed,[51] and Inge and her friend Sonja began taking sewing lessons at the Israels'. They also sang while Julius played, and Charlotte remembered that she taught them their first dance steps. She was a "real sunshine," Charlotte said of Sonja, who began to dream and talk of opening her own tailoring business.

As she talked about her students of half a century earlier and what she had given them, Charlotte's voice grew happy. Her weariness evaporated. Lovingly she remembered the Jews snatched from her for the gas chambers. One by one Charlotte and Julius's group of friends dwindled. Their music evenings and their sewing school shrank. In this hapless world Charlotte and Julius were an island of hope for the Jews who learned the trade of tailoring at the Israels'. For some it was all the work they had and their means of imagining a happier future. "None of our students survived," Charlotte said. "They all wanted to emigrate, but none made it. All were arrested, all were taken to the gas chambers—except one student. He made it to Shanghai and became very wealthy. But first he had studied with me!"

Somehow Julius's parents hadn't yet received "the list," and Charlotte told herself that the Gestapo would overlook them. They both were in their seventh decade and rarely left their apartment. Charlotte remembered how they had reasoned that the Gestapo would no longer bother with sending Mr. Israel to the "work camps." "We thought to ourselves, now of course *such* persons won't be taken," Charlotte said, looking down. "That's what we thought," she added, as if in self-reproach for too much wishful thinking.

Then, without warning, the fateful day arrived. On September 29, during the week Goebbels and Hitler sat down to talk about completing the deportation of Berlin's Jews, the Gestapo appeared without warning to haul away the old couple. Mr. Israel had been sick all summer with stomach cancer and had just returned home from the Jewish hospital on Iranischestrasse.

At the hospital Mr. Israel's condition had steadily worsened, but nevertheless, Charlotte, as a German, was the only family member who could visit him. Jews needed a special permit to travel outside their own sections of the city, and no permits were granted for visiting sick relatives. Mr. Israel was under the care of Dr. Walter Lustig, an intermarried Jew who had been adviser to the Greater Berlin municipal health department before being displaced by the Aryan Clause in 1933.

In September 1942 Dr. Lustig announced to Charlotte that she should take her father-in-law home because finding a cure for him was hopeless.

At the Israels' home in Charlottenburg, Erna, Charlotte, and Mrs. Weizel, a kindly German neighbor of the Israels', had turned the living room sofa into a bed. It would be less lonely for Mr. Israel than the bedroom, they thought. All the chores she could do at his bedside, Mrs. Israel did there: mending clothes and even peeling potatoes.

When the Gestapo came to take the old couple, Mrs. Weizel heard the ruckus and called Erna at her job. Erna was allowed to leave work and went straight to find Charlotte. The Israel apartment that day made an impression fresh in Charlotte's memory. Cabinet doors hung ajar. Drawers from the bedroom dresser were strewn about. Pieces of clothing littered the floor. Mrs. Israel's chair and footstool still stood at the head of her husband's bed, where she had been working. The potatoes she had been peeling had spilled onto the floor and turned a sullen gray. Since then, Charlotte said, she had not been able to eat potato cakes. In the hallway Mrs. Weizel had watched in pathetic horror. The Gestapo had dragged and slid Mr. Israel down the stairs, shoving him onto the bed of a truck waiting outside. At seventy-five and fatally ill with cancer, he could not walk on his own.

On the kitchen table Charlotte and Erna found a note: "We're in Gerlachstrasse. We have nothing." For Jews, "Gerlachstrasse" had come to designate a former Jewish old people's home in central Berlin. The Gestapo had converted it into a holding center for Jews arrested for deportation and used it as a transit camp for Jews bound for Theresienstadt. Charlotte remembered fighting back the bitter tears as she and Erna pulled together some clothing, food, and toiletries and caught the subway to Gerlachstrasse. As a Jew Erna had to stand while using public transportation, and like many other Jews, she preferred to hide her bright yellow Star of David with a briefcase or by pressing against the wall.

The workday was ending. As Charlotte crossed Alexanderplatz, bureaucrats from Wilhelmstrasse's government quarters seated themselves comfortably. Nursed by state propaganda, a sense of normality often still prevailed in Berlin. To Charlotte, clutching the few things she could bring to comfort her parents-in-law, the square seemed to swim with Nazis. On the eve of its first crippling defeat the German Wehrmacht appeared unassailable. By August 1942 German armies controlled an enormous arc eastward. All summer the Wehrmacht's Army Group South had pushed eastward again, encircling Russian forces west of the Don River. It seemed the Soviet Union would break apart or surrender. In September 1941 the U.S. War Department had planned to create an American army of 213 divisions; now the U.S. General Staff estimated that 350 American divisions were needed to win the war.[52] The Germans now seemed poised to grab their prize, the city of Stalingrad on the Volga, capture of which would cut the Red Army's main supply route and open up to the Germans the main Russian oil-producing region.

At Gerlachstrasse Charlotte received permission to visit the elderly Israels for fifteen minutes. Officially it wasn't allowed, but Charlotte somehow managed. "Mrs. Israel was very happy and said she knew we would come," Charlotte said. "Father-in-law was lying in bed and said to me: 'Charlotte, you will get us out of here.' 'Yes, Papa,' I replied.

"That was a warmhearted lie," Charlotte continued. "Was I supposed to say no? I couldn't have done that. 'Yes, I'll get you out of here,' I said. Then he was so happy, like a small child, and took interest in what I had brought along for them."

Mrs. Israel was resigned but composed. Charlotte described her as very courageous. "We will all meet again," she told Charlotte. "When the war is over. I can work! I'll volunteer." She was seventy. "Papa," she told Charlotte, "will soon pass away. We would have had to reckon with that at home too."

Mrs. Israel had bunions and walked crooked. To gain support, she always wore only shoes with laces. Charlotte's mother had given Mrs. Israel a pair of lace-ups, and Mrs. Israel asked Charlotte to bring them. Charlotte said they needed repair, but Mrs. Israel said they would do that in Theresienstadt. "She was so trusting!" said Charlotte admiringly.

After leaving Gerlachstrasse, Charlotte went straight to the police station on Grolmannstrasse, not far from where she lived. She wanted a permit granting Julius the right to use the subway to visit his parents, and she received it although it was against regulations. Julius's sister, Erna, also asked for one but was denied. "Erna probably whined, and the officers didn't want to hear that," said Charlotte. "I requested it very quietly as if it were a very simple thing. Certainly not with tears. I was always filled with fear but never showed it. I learned that I must make my requests, as if they were fully normal, fully within the law, rather than in a subordinate way, as if I expected them to say no."

But when Charlotte returned to Gerlachstrasse the next day, she was refused entrance. The Israels had brought nothing but the clothes on their backs and wanted things for their upcoming trip. Undeterred, Charlotte took up an inconspicuous examination of the guard by the building's main entrance. It was almost noon, and she hoped for an opportunity at least to hand the food and clothes she had brought for her parents-in-law through their ground-floor window. At twelve the guard left. Charlotte waited to see whether he would be replaced. Nothing happened. About twenty minutes later the guard returned and took up his post again. The next day Charlotte was there again, just before noon, with the things the Israels urgently needed. After the guard had gone, and when no replacement was in sight, Charlotte scurried to the window. Mrs. Israel came when she knocked. "That was dangerous, for me and my mother-in-law," said Charlotte. But at least they knew Charlotte cared. She came every day, for the next five days, always careful to leave before the guard returned.

When Charlotte saw her mother-in-law for the last time on October 4, she asked Mrs. Israel whether she had a warm hat. She had only a small one, whereas Charlotte's was larger and warmer. "Spontaneously I took off my hat and gave it to her through the window," Charlotte recalled. " 'Take mine, Mama, I'll sew a new one,' I said. She was touched. She thought I would sew a new one. But unfortunately I couldn't. I didn't have any material. Then I took my scarf and wrapped it warm around her neck. Then we said farewell, with a handshake and tears in our eyes. 'God's blessing on your soul,' she said. She always said such words. Mother-in-law was a pious woman. 'You have blessed hands,' she always told me.

"After that my husband didn't play the piano anymore," Charlotte said, "and I didn't sing." The handful of remaining friends and relatives were also in mourning for Julius's parents. Julius's niece, Inge, Sonja's friend, was a frightened fifteen-year old. She had heard that some *Mischlinge* like her had received equalizations, which qualified them to be "Aryans" and escape the persecution. "I'll Aryanize myself and move out from the Jewish family," she announced to Charlotte. "Inge, you belong to Julius's family just as much as I do," Charlotte said. "And I'm not getting out." Inge, who lives today in Maine, stayed with her family and was the only survivor of what Charlotte called "my big Jewish family."

There must have been very little strength to summon for meeting new tragedies. But on January 7 there was no sign of Sonja, Inge's friend, who had lately been coming every day to Charlotte and Julius to learn sewing, so that she could open her own shop one day. In the mail the next day they found out why. In hastily scrawled words addressed to "Dear Ischen," as Sonja called the Israels, she belied the truth she had sensed behind her brave talk of plans for her own future tailor shop.

> *Good-bye forever,*
> *Today we will be taken,*
> *Remember me kindly.*
> *Stay healthy and strong*
> *I greet you all heartily*
> > *your Sonja.*

"We were overwhelmed by her lines," Charlotte whispered. "We cried, both of us, as if we had lost a daughter. I never saw her again."

Not surprisingly, the new friends of the Israels', in the last years of the war, were the new outcasts in Germany. In mid-1942 Germany had begun to requisition French laborers for work inside Germany, and as the Jewish population fell, the regime dragooned its eastern conquests for forced laborers. Charlotte now found forced laborers from the east to join her and Julius. Charlotte had a German-Russian friend, who introduced her to his girl friend, Inna, a forced laborer from the Ukraine. She was one of the enslaved Russians and Poles who had been brought to the Reich by the millions, branded with a red marker and the word "east" over their left breasts, and crowded without privacy and dignity into barracks.

"Inna was shut up in barracks and appreciated it so much when she could experience a little atmosphere, a little bit of intimacy, and home comfort," Charlotte recalled. "We began to gather on Sundays again to play music, and I always invited her. Inna had a nice voice. She brought a sort of balalaika and accompanied Julius. In matters of music I always had abundance—through my husband!"

By late summer of 1942 the Berlin Gestapo was under pressure. Goebbels, unhappy with the pace of the deportation of Jews from his gau, thought the Berlin Gestapo worked more like nine-to-five bureaucrats than activists with a cause. The deportations in Berlin had not progressed as rapidly as in Vienna, Berlin's traditional rival. Then the second phase of deportations in the capital was virtually ended with a crippling blow to the Gestapo's Judenreferat—the Jewish Desk—of some two dozen men. In September 1942 the wrath of the SS leadership was visited on the Judenreferat. Although forbidden to steal from their victims, Judenreferat men had commonly pilfered from the Jews they arrested. Certain Gestapo men, in particular, had a reputation for searching through the ashes of Jewish fireplaces for untarnished remnants of jewelry or lumps of paper cash. Some secretly returned after hours to an apartment or house they had cleared of Jews to pillage at greater leisure. Men who otherwise would have never saved enough in a lifetime to buy a five-carat diamond might now scoop up a pocketful of such valuables in weeks. As the practice continued, a number brazenly accumulated their loot in heaps in their office desks, and news of this leaked out.

Early on September 2 the ax fell. The SS police arrived at the Jewish Desk before anyone else and searched each desk for evidence of pilfering. Each astonished suspect was arrested as he arrived for another day at the office. Just about the entire office was empty the next day, a secretary reported. Dr. Kunze, who was in a supervisory position at the Jewish Desk, was also arrested and interred in the SS headquarters on Prinz-Albrecht Strasse, on the charge that he had not paid proper attention to preventing the thefts by the Jewish Desk.[53] Gerhard Stubbs, Prüfer's successor as the head of the Judenreferat, heard of the arrests in time to preempt his own with a fatal shot to the head. Police adviser Karl Lassmann, the director of the household and economics section of the police, also shot himself in the head, with different results. Lassmann, who because of "unusual arrogance" was known as "beloved God," lost his eyesight.

Those arrested were imprisoned and arraigned on charges of stealing Reich property at the SS Police Court in Berlin-Grünewald. Dr. Mosse testified against those charged with pilfering, and according to her testimony, SS prosecutor Dr. Berger promised her immunity from the deportations. A Jewish employee accused of stealing was deported.[54] At least one of the accused Gestapo officers was executed. Four were imprisoned in Berlin and died in an Allied air raid in March 1944. Others were interned in the Dachau concentration camp.[55] The one-eyed Lassmann, feared because of his good connections, survived and died in Berlin in March 1956.[56] Otto Bovensiepen, the Gestapo chief in Berlin and a personal friend of Heinrich Himmler's, was removed from his office at this time as well and ordered to abstain from alcohol for two years.[57]

Himmler himself directly or ultimately sat in judgment of this Berlin scandal. In his Posen speech of October 6, 1943, the SS *Reichsführer* warned his audience that every SS man who stole Jewish wealth would be executed—a sentence, he said, that he had just meted out on about a dozen men guilty of this crime. Himmler wanted none of the goods that the Reich meant to steal itself to be stolen out from under it. The proper SS demeanor, he said at Posen, was machinelike discipline without self-interest. (Following Kristallnacht, twenty-six men who were imprisoned for murdering twenty-six Jews were not expelled from the party, and the justice minister was urged to quash proceedings in the criminal court. But four who raped women were expelled from the party and ordered to face criminal proceedings. The difference, according to Raul Hilberg, was that they showed selfish motives.)[58]

As Berlin's Jewish population dwindled, the methods of rounding up the city's Jews became more and more ruthless. Finding enough Jews to fill the trains grew harder. Some of those left behind were more resourceful in evading the "east transports," as rumors spread that deportations ended in death. In addition, the Jews with German family members were "temporarily exempted." Thus the Jews most difficult to deport made up a growing proportion of those remaining.

The young SS man in charge of the Vienna deportations, Hauptsturmführer Alois Brunner, had caught the attention of Nazi leaders with his speed in getting the Jews out. In Vienna, where there had once been about ten thousand more Jews than in Berlin, the deportation process was very nearly completed. With more than forty thousand Jews remaining in Berlin and the Berlin's Jewish Desk incapacitated, Brunner was called to the capital. He arrived on November 11, 1942, amid rumors among Gestapo men that Hitler himself had chosen Brunner.[59] Employees of the Jewish Community remembered Brunner, at thirty-one, as looking "ridiculously young," a man dark and small, with an expressionless face punctuated by beady eyes. His appearance earned him the nickname among his SS cronies of Sweet Jew, after the protagonist of a Goebbels anti-Semitic film, *Jude Süss*. In Berlin Brunner understood his job as showing "those damn Prussian pigs how to handle filthy Jews."[60]

Brunner, who had been Eichmann's personal secretary in 1938–39, had just married his secretary, and he was a young man in a hurry. His arrival in Berlin was to mark the start of a career as a traveling deportation expert, moving from country to country under orders to render entire regions *Judenfrei* (free of Jews). He had advanced steadily in his career by ruthlessness and treated his job as a calling. Once after an air raid a German doctor attending the wounded had pressed a Jewish doctor into service. Brunner was incredulous and instructed the German that a Jewish doctor treating German patients polluted the German blood. "It would be better if the victims died," he explained. "What would happen to the German ideology otherwise?"[61] To prevent escapes of French Jews rounded up for deportation, Brunner recommended that they be tied together with a long rope.[62]

In Berlin Brunner introduced a new, more brutal phase of deportations. He arrived with a train of Viennese Gestapo agents and four

Jewish orderlies, forced to accompany him like slaves, referred to as "men of Israel" or *Jupo* (Jewish police). Forcing Jews into his employ was a special trademark of Brunner's. Any Jew who did not cooperate faced deportation and death along with their families. Within twenty-four hours of arriving Brunner transformed the Jewish home for old people on Grosse Hamburger Strasse into Berlin's main predeportation collecting center. Günther Abrahamsohn, one of the chief Jewish orderlies, who later carried a pistol in the service of the Gestapo as one of the feared "catchers,"[63] was told to prepare a list of deportees in half an hour. In the hurry furniture was thrown from the windows of the old people's home, and the floors were covered with straw, in preparation for the arrival of twelve hundred to fifteen hundred persons. Brunner ordered that all Jews were to stand and to stay at least two steps away when a German entered their room.[64] Then he declared that the last Jews would be leaving in short order. "It was clear," said Max Reschke, the Jewish Community's director of operations at the Grosse Hamburger collection center, "that all the earlier considerations no longer existed. The community now had no more possibilities for influence."[65]

Hauptsturmführer Alois Brunner, a deportation expert who moved from one location to another to deport local Jewish populations. Brunner arrived in Berlin from Vienna in November 1942.

Brunner required Jews to accompany Gestapo men on their rounds to seize Jews. While the Gestapo waited outside in trucks, Jewish orderlies entered Jewish homes to help the arrested Jews pack the few things they were allowed to take with them to the east, then accompanied them to the waiting trucks. These orderlies saw themselves as helpful to the arrested Jews: "I can only attest to how happy the ones were, who I accompanied, under the command of a [Gestapo] officer. They knew how to appreciate the fact that it was we who helped them pack, shared their last meal in their apartment, gave them advice and attempted to comfort them—us and not a pair of SS men."[66]

Brunner introduced two methods. First, after sealing off entire city blocks, he combed sections of the city block by block. Then he came through house by house. Doors were knocked down, apartments wrecked. The wife of a dentist who lived near the Spandauer Brücke was shot when she did not get out of the bath quickly enough to answer Brunner's knock at the door.[67] This method required the assistance of the regular Berlin police. Soon, however, the furious protests of accidentally arrested non-Jewish Germans forced Brunner to stop this method. Even the Berlin police went "on strike." Brunner then turned to the Jewish Community for the list of addresses of Berlin's Jews.[68]

Brunner and his men also began a practice of grabbing Jews from the streets. Accompanied by German shepherd dogs, he and his men prowled through Berlin streets during business hours. Leaping out of their trucks at the sight of anyone who looked Jewish or wore the Star of David, they chased down hapless victims amid bustling pedestrians and traffic. If the victim was Jewish, or identification was not 100 percent clear, the person was crammed into the truck and carted off for further interrogation to Grosse Hamburger Strasse. On Berlin's Champs-Élysées, the Kurfürstendamm, it was said that people reacted to the "Brunner Actions" with "vehement gatherings and very loud protests," according to an eyewitness.[69]

Both of Brunner's methods resulted in the arrests of intermarried Jews and *Mischlinge*. In Vienna Brunner had deported some of the intermarried Jews despite deportation directives prohibiting this.[70] Georg Zivier, a Jewish journalist married to a German, reported just after the war that Brunner had also deported some Jews in intermarriages from the western section of Berlin. Arrests divided families for the first time.[71]

Brunner's methods invaded Goebbels's "delicate" categories. Brunner, however, was unaccustomed to delicacy and the reasons of popular morale that held the regime back. Taking the documents of a

Mischling, he crossed out *Mischling* and wrote in "Jew." "What? Y'er a *Mischling*?" he said. "Y'er a dirty Jew."[72]

Other lower-level officials like Brunner also occasionally deported intermarried Jews. Their actions corresponded with Nazi ideology and made them appear serious. Every once in a while local Gestapo agents rounded up the few intermarried Jews living in their area and deported them along with other local Jews. Gauleiters, the local party chieftains, were charged with making their territories *Judenfrei* (free of Jews) and also took liberties in their regions. The racial and social ambiguities around "racially mixed" families created confusion and opened up possibilities for power plays. On matters of intermarriage, decision making in the Reich was particularly decentralized. The history of Jewish-German families shows a dictator unwilling to take a firm stand publicly rather than a disciplined bureaucracy flawlessly executing orders from a decisive Führer. When local power players deported persons from German-Jewish families without causing unrest, Hitler did not interfere (and perhaps did not know).[73]

Himmler's RSHA, on Goebbels's requests, meddled in the daily management of the Gestapo in Berlin. From his office in Berlin Adolf Eichmann, who directed the deportation of Jews around Europe at the RSHA, sometimes took action directly against Berlin's Jews. Brunner had a direct relationship with Eichmann's office, and together he and Eichmann's deputy, Hauptsturmführer Rolf Günther, targeted staff members of the Jewish Community itself.

Employment at the Jewish Community became known among Jews as the surest way to avoid being deported, and community authorities strove to keep as many Jews as possible on their payroll. Yet following a directive from Eichmann, Jewish Community employees were to be released and deported in proportion to the number of Jews in general who had been deported. This Eichmann directive was sent to the heads of Gestapo branch offices and to the Central Organization of German Jews.[74] The Gestapo's purpose for allowing the structure of the community to exist was to facilitate deportations, and the fewer Jews there were, the less administration this task should require. Intermarried Jews were exempted from "release," but "little-used" war veterans could be "recommended" for release. Since November 1941 employees of the Jewish Community had been released for the deportations, but Jewish authorities hesitated since release from employment meant deportation.[75]

Throughout 1942 state agencies, including the Propaganda Ministry, demanded more reductions of Jewish employees.[76] Unannounced, Brunner and Günther appeared in uniform one day in late November

Hauptsturmführer Rolf Günther. In postwar court testimony a secretary in Günther's office said he had told her that the Germans did not hate the Jews but were persecuting them only out of obligation. Günther, she testified, ordered the execution of the Jewish leader Paul Eppstein in Theresienstadt.

at the Oranienburger Strasse community headquarters, with three or four assistants. For the next deportation he would need five hundred community employees, Günther said. Every division must give up a certain number.[77]

Günther ordered all employees downstairs to the large assembly room. Most employees were on hand that day, following specific instructions from community leaders.[78] The director of each division, Günther announced, would immediately, personally have to select employees for deportation. The director of welfare, the editor Leo Kreindler, was slow in compiling the list. With trembling hands he finally gave Günther the names. "So, and now put your name on the list, and then it will be ready," said Brunner. Kreindler crumpled and died of a heart attack. "Get that Jew out of here," ordered Brunner. "I don't like the way he's lying there."[79] Dr. Mosse too was hesitating until Günther said, "Mosse is thinking this over for a very long time." After Günther made his remark, she remembered that one of Günther's attendants said to her, " 'Hurry, hurry'—which was, however, well intended."[80]

Günther left, and they all returned to their work sites, except for those selected, who were ordered to a particular room. There Brunner kept the five hundred Jews standing at attention for six hours while he sat casually before them with Eichmann and Günther.[81] In the end Mr. Kozower, on orders, stood on a table and informed the five hundred that they were to be deported. For each person who did not show up for the deportation, he told them, a leading official of the Jewish Community would be arrested and shot. Then the five hundred were dismissed. On the day of the deportation twenty were missing. Finally two showed up late. For the eighteen who had fled into hiding, eighteen hostages were selected; eight were shot, and ten deported.[82] It was the second reprisal for resistance, the last one that was necessary in Berlin.

By November 1942 Final Solution authorities thought the end of their job in Germany was at hand. The RSHA ordered the Central Organization to make a statistical report on all localities with fewer than 100 Jews. Six days later the Central Organization delivered a list of 1,411 areas of this description. Listed were 6,275 Jews.[83] On November 27 the Central Organization also published in the *Jüdische Nachrichtenblatt* an order that all Jews (according to the Nuremberg Laws and including *Geltungsjuden*) not already registered with the Central Organization must now do so, no later than December 1, 1942. Two weeks later it repeated this order, giving Jews "one last summons" to register. Intermarried Jews were required to register "whether they live in privileged or nonprivileged intermarriage."[84]

CONSEQUENCES

Well before the deportations had even begun, the Gestapo had co-opted leaders of the Central Organization of German Jews. For many who faced the concentration camps, Levi's principle of "us-ism" gradually took hold: "selfishness extended to the person closest to you."[85] Charlotte Israel, who found herself in constant need, was also in constant demand by Jews facing deportations. Like Jewish authorities, she could only try to soften the blow as they waited for the Gestapo.

When so many abandoned the Jews, the few who would help were inundated with pleas. Charlotte was thrust unwillingly into deciding whether to remain with her husband or attempt to comfort others. "I myself was kaput, my nerves were shot," she recalled. "I had to do everything not just for myself but also for all the surviving Jews I knew. I was totally overburdened, in every way. Back then I had several breakdowns, just from too much nervousness. I was a witness to everything. I saw my parents-in-law taken. All our friends disappeared. Sometimes persons received 'the card,' telling them they would be picked up on such and such a day. Then they said to each other, 'Go to Mrs. Israel, she helps!' They were beside themselves then. They didn't have a clue about what they should do, what to pack. I always acted so courageous, but I too had terrible fear. One couldn't allow oneself to be intimidated! I helped where I could. I sewed backpacks for many persons about to be taken. That was rumored around, and then everybody had to have backpacks. I packed the backpacks for them, the things that they needed.[86]

Elsa Holzer, who also defied the Gestapo to save her husband, was less able to reach out to defy the principle of us-ism. Every day on her way to work Elsa passed close to Bahnhof Lehrter, the freight train station from which thousands of Berlin Jews were deported. The platform was roped off as the trucks drove up to fill the train with one thousand Jews. But Elsa, like all the other Berliners passing by, saw the agony, the heads pushed toward the tiny openings. Most of these trains leaving Berlin were unheated freight cars.[87] Elsa felt the helplessness. "I didn't even visit any Jews back then," she admitted. "They were all so terribly unhappy. And we were ourselves mistreated so horribly that I couldn't have endured more pain."[88]

In small, seemingly harmless ways Jewish leaders, motivated by a desire to do good, began to help the Gestapo. In due course they lent the Gestapo the weight of their authority as well as technical assistance. Raul Hilberg explains the leadership's compliance as part of the pattern of behavior Jews had learned over two thousand years. Jewish leaders "were reliable agents in the eyes of the German perpetrators while still retaining the trust of the Jews."[89] The community offered a reliable source of information about who was Jewish and where the Jews were, but perhaps most important, Jews were ordered by their religious leaders to report for deportations and to cooperate with every Gestapo order. Every postcard the community sent out to the Gestapo victim carried the weight of religious authority and threat of police reprisals against noncompliance. It was a potent combination.

Some historians fault Jewish leaders for underestimating their own influence, a criticism similar to the one Guenter Lewy made of Catholic bishops.[90] "If the Jewish people had really been unorganized and leaderless, there would have been chaos and plenty of misery but the total number of victims would hardly have been between four and a half and six million people," Hannah Arendt wrote.[91] A decade later the historian Isaiah Trunk argued back that Jewish cooperation did not significantly affect the number of Holocaust victims in eastern Europe. In any case, he added, the motives of Jewish authorities had been good, whatever their results, and the prevailing opinion in Jewish ghettos was that resistance would result in the immediate destruction of the entire ghetto.[92]

From the beginning Jewish leaders made it clear that their tactics would remain within the requirements of German law. The basic assumption of Germany's Jewish leaders was that they could not influence the number of persons deported, but did they underestimate their possibilities for defining this situation? Was encouragement of civil disobedience, including hiding, a possibility for them? "Paradoxically, disappearing into the underground meant that one first had to overcome Jewish representational institutions," wrote the historian Konrad Kwiet. "The [Central Organization] sent out the registration forms and was responsible for ensuring that the transportation of deportees took its 'proper course.' This meant, among other things, that the Jewish officials strongly advised against any refusal to comply with deportation orders."[93] In delivering a new census to the Gestapo in September 1942, Berlin Jewish leaders wrote that its count of intermarried Jews was "obviously too low" since the community did not know of the whereabouts of "many cases" of intermarried Jews who had simply refused to register with the Jewish Community.[94] Rudi Holzer, for example, would have never registered and would not have been caught had his sister not fallen into police custody. Despite published orders demanding that every Jew register, along with a warning that noncompliance would be met with severe penalties of the law,[95] some Jews (as the community's report indicated) had decided to disobey the law, and there was little the Gestapo could do.

In Haifa, on Mount Carmel, Edith Wolf, an intelligent, sensitive, and highly articulate woman in her eighties, looked back at the deportations with anguish.[96] Hannah Arendt wasn't able to comprehend the situation, she said, because she experienced it only at her desk. Then she told her story. As a *Mischling* member of the Jewish Community Wolf was supposed to wear the Star of David. However, an aunt who worked at the Jewish Community in the registration office removed her name from the list of *Geltungsjuden,* an act she said effectively removed her from the persecution. Around 1939 or 1940, during the removal of Austrian Jews to Poland, she went to Vienna and learned that some Jews had not reported to the Gestapo as required. "This idea hadn't even occurred to me," she said. "Of course these Jews had to hide themselves afterward." Back in Berlin she suggested noncompliance to Jewish authorities, including those in charge of emigrations to Palestine. "I said, this is the only means we have for saving people. It is better to save people than to carry out the orders of the Gestapo." But the notion of civil disobedience was repugnant to the Jewish authorities, Mrs. Wolf said. "The authorities of the Jewish Community as well as those at the Palestine Office were against this. They chased me away."

The story of German Jewish leaders is one of the most agonizing sagas. They wanted to help, not harm, the community, and in normal times would have. Their choices were stark: martyrdom or complicity. One might ask whether the Jewish leaders both contributed to what they saw as inevitable and made it more comfortable. But this question risks a failure to understand slow developments that compromised good, well-intentioned people, as it risks empathy with persons forced into acting expediently under threat of death.

XIII

PLANS TO CLEAR THE REICH OF JEWS—AND THE OBSTACLES OF WOMEN AND "TOTAL WAR"

> I am always afraid that they will eventually succeed in discovering some secret which will provide a quicker way of making men die, and exterminate whole countries and nations.
>
> —MONTESQUIEU

For Germany, the climax of the war arrived in midwinter of 1942–43. The Battle of Stalingrad, a large industrial center on the west bank of the Volga River 550 miles southeast of Moscow, was one of the greatest military debacles of all time. Germany's defeat denied Hitler the victory critical to German morale, and it spelled an undeniable need to cut back the living standards on the home front. At the same time, plans to complete the Final Solution focused attention especially on intermarried Jews and to a lesser extent on *Mischlinge*. Defeat escalated the conflict between Hitler's two basic goals of racial purification and maintaining the people's full support. Hitler responded with a decree ordering Total War, an effort that based hopes for victory on increased German efforts. As more and more men left home for the war, women increasingly constituted the home front. Thus the Total War decree called on women, as the largest source of untapped labor, to sacrifice more than men, even as they made up an ever-larger proportion of the home front, the element Hitler considered critical in war.[1]

In the autumn of 1942 the tug-of-war between Goebbels and Himmler's men over German-Jewish families continued. Had inter-married Germans cooperated with Nazi aims, there would have been no fear of social unrest related to the intermarriage problem and no conflict among regime power centers. Now intermarried Jews became increasingly visible as the remaining obstacle to a full Final Solution, urgently highlighting the struggle that divided powerful officials on how and when to draw these Jews into the camps. A military victory might have broken the stalemate, uniting the Germans, boosting morale, and thus reducing the risk of unrest the regime associated with plucking intermarried Jews from their families.

In September 1942 German military victory at Stalingrad seemed possible while the machinery of mass murder cut down its victims at unprecedented speed. Hitler and Goebbels displayed their confidence with unprecedented public statements about the Final Solution. On September 23, 1942, Goebbels became the first key member of the Nazi leadership to speak openly about the annihilation of German Jews. In a speech to sixty German newspaper editors in Berlin on September 23, 1942, the propagandist declared: "There are still 48,000 [Jews] in Berlin. They know with deadly certainty that as the war progresses they will be packed off to the east and delivered up to a murderous fate. They already feel the inevitable harshness of physical extermi-nation and therefore they harm the Reich whenever possible while they live." A copy of this speech was leaked to the British Foreign Office, where a number of leaders, including Foreign Secretary Sir Anthony Eden, read it but did not pass it on to the U.S. or Jewish leaders.[2] On September 30 Hitler delivered one of his rare public excoriations of the Jews, claiming prophetic foresight in his earlier claim that war would result in the extermination of the Jews.[3] With the majority of Ger-many's remaining Jews living in Berlin, the Reich capital would be the first focus of the last deportations.[4]

With military success envisioned, plans for deporting intermarried Jews were on the agenda. The deportations, including *Mischlinge*, had, in any case, been only "temporarily deferred." The military industry still employed thousands of Jews, mostly in Berlin, but their fate did not need to be discussed by the group of officials who sat down to resolve the remaining aspects of the Final Solution, on October 27, 1942.[5] Intermarriages and *Mischlinge* were the agenda items. The con-ferees agreed that intermarried full Jews, as well as intermarried half Jews who wore the Star of David, were to be separated from their partners and deported. This included Jews in privileged intermarriages, a deputy of Eichmann reported after the war.[6]

The significant difference between this decision and that of the RSHA-dominated conference of October 1941 was that intermarried Germans were not to be deported should they not divorce. Euthanasia had shown that dividing families and murdering Germans led to troublesome protests. In May 1942 Himmler's Gestapo director, Heinrich Müller, had dismissed the scheme to deport Germans married to Jews. In a telegram to Gestapo branch offices he wrote that all *Mischlinge* who wore the star (*Geltungsjuden*), the intermarried Jews from "simple" (nonprivileged) mixed marriages, and privileged intermarried Jews whose spouses had died or divorced them would be deported. The Final Roundup of Jews in February 1943 roughly followed this Müller memorandum.[7]

As for *Mischlinge* who did not wear the star, the October 1942 conference favored sterilization. Thus a half Jew could provide labor but would not pass on Jewish blood. "New knowledge" would facilitate mass sterilization. *Mischlinge* were "voluntarily" to agree to sterilization in exchange for being "mercifully allowed" to remain in the Reich. Those who hesitated would be told that the other option, being "pushed out" of the Reich, would be the "sharper measure." To prevent "bad psychological effects," the sterilization procedure would be a deception (one proposal was to shoot radiation onto the genitals of a *Mischling* standing in a specific spot, ostensibly to fill out a questionnaire). "New knowledge" on sterilization did not exist, however, and sterilization on a mass scale proved unfeasible during the war.[8]

Directly following the October 27 conference Himmler ordered that all the concentration camps in the Reich were to be made "free of Jews" and that "*Mischlinge* of the first decree should be counted as Jewish prisoners."[9] He had already given the first limited, exploratory orders for deporting German intermarried Jews and *Mischlinge* on September 29. The chief of police began with women, with an order that the women's concentration camp at Ravensbrück be made *Judenfrei*; female Jews would be sent to the east (Auschwitz) "with their entire families"; in "serious cases," even intermarried Jewish women were to be deported too, "although without family members."[10] In anticipation of the thousands of German women who would be left without partners when intermarried Jews were deported, soldiers were prohibited on September 24, 1942, from marrying women who had previously been married to Jews.[11] On November 7 Paul C. Squire, the American consul in Geneva, was told by Carl Burckhardt that in January 1941 Hitler had signed a decree ordering Germany to be "cleared of Jews" by the end of 1942.[12] Intermarried Jews were now in grave danger, as the historian Uwe Adam concluded.[13]

Goebbels apparently decided to deport intermarried Jews without children.[14] It was his move because most of Germany's Jews and intermarried couples lived in his district. Goebbels's plans to clear Berlin of Jews were a cornerstone of the regime's plans to clear Germany of Jews, not just because so many Jews still remained in Berlin but because Goebbels and the capital city aimed to set policy precedents for others to follow. It fitted the Nazi sense of propriety that deportation precedents for territories occupied by Germany should be set in the Reich, and Berlin should lead the way for the Reich.

The deportation of persons from German-Jewish families without children followed from the Nazi logic of race as well as from the logic of preserving social passivity. Intermarried full Jews were a higher priority for deportation by racial calculations than their children (whom the RSHA also wanted to deport). On the other hand, deporting those without children reduced the number of persons who might complain and cause protest to just the remaining German partners. Nevertheless, Goebbels remained apprehensive.

The leadership's decision in late 1942 to deport intermarried Jews is represented in the Final Roundup of Jews, an attempt to intimidate protest with surprise and a show of force. This solution was an attempted domestic equivalent of the blitzkrieg strategy that the Germans executed so successfully at war, where, according to Hitler, strength was in "quickness and . . . brutality."[15] Hitler's bodyguard division of the SS, which had already logged experience on the war front, was to participate in this sudden mass arrest of Berlin Jews.

The regime's method was to look for opportunities to move quickly and then to present the situation as a fait accompli if questions arose. In his exasperated demand of July 1942 for an end to further discussions on legal solutions to the intermarriage problem, Himmler had betrayed a bias for avoiding policy in favor of acting decisively with force at the opportune moment. When Hitler acted on the intermarriage issue by secret decree, instead of through the public bureaucratic process, he reserved for himself and his coterie the chance to change policy quickly. At Nuremberg the public definition of the Jewish population had been an important step in isolating it. Yet the intermarried Germans who refused to divorce Jews were embarrassing to the regime, and the intermarriage problem would have to be kept out of the public eye as much as possible. By avoiding public disclosure and bureaucratic processes, Hitler could improvise on the timing of his solution to the intermarriage problem, moving quickly when the chance allowed.

Plans for completing the Final Solution were laid in late 1942. But so many German trains were tied up transporting soldiers to and from family holiday celebrations that fewer than normal could be spared for deporting Jews.[16] While Nazi leaders waited to implement plans, Stalingrad fell and Total War was declared. In Finland, where under Nazi policies for western occupied territories popular opinion was also taken into account, the arrests of Jews and Communists at the turn of the year led to a "storm of indignation." "As a result of the protests," deportations were discontinued.[17] Nevertheless, in late January 1943 Hitler and Goebbels agreed again that the Jewish Question in the Reich capital had to be solved as quickly as possible. Goebbels feared a coalition of foreign workers and Jews in revolt. Germany did not have internal security as long as there were still Jews in Berlin, he and Hitler agreed.[18]

TOTAL WAR AND GERMAN WOMEN

By February 1943 the Wehrmacht had suffered a defeat that shook the confidence of many Germans to the core. The entire Sixth German Army was annihilated, its soldiers and equipment lost. Thereafter the Wehrmacht fell into a retreat that Germans began to sense would end only in Berlin and surrender. After Stalingrad, up to one-third of German workers began to doubt Germany would prevail, compared with late December, when "hardly any" workers were uncertain of German victory.[19] Thus the Battle of Stalingrad marked a strategic turning point in the war, both at war and at home. Nazi leaders were forced into a bind between their fundamental principles and policies most likely to reverse defeat. Living standards must be lowered, armaments production increased. German women, who bore the brunt of increased bombings and the rising military casualty rate, now also faced cutbacks in goods and services on the home front. Yet in January 1943 the new labor conscriptions of the Total War decree fell disproportionately on women. So the regime, in early 1943, was particularly apprehensive of unrest among women.

All over the country more Germans now personally experienced the mounting sacrifices of war. More and more women appeared in black, mourning fallen sons and husbands. Families had been divided for more than three years at this point, and the tightening grip of food and coal rations grew harder to bear. Lower rations and higher casualties pressed home just as the specter of terrible defeat became increasingly difficult to ignore. Berliners had sacrificed soldiers to the war at an average of 361 per month during the first year of the war, 467 per month during the second, and 661 during the third. Then in the six-month period from October 1942 to April 1943 soldiers from Berlin died at an average of 1,565 a month; 1,713 casualties were registered in March 1943 alone.[20] Goebbels claimed that a rousing speech by the Führer would have as much good effect on the German morale as a rousing Wehrmacht victory, but Hitler was taken "seriously ill" for the first time. He grew reluctant to meet with party leaders and refused to appear publicly for the duration of the war.

Also at the turn of the year, the Allies stepped up the bombing campaign. At their conference in Casablanca on January 21, 1943, the Allies agreed that only the enemy's unconditional surrender would end the war and that the Anglo-American combined bomber offensive would be a key instrument for breaking Germany's back. Because of major technologicial advances, the British capacity to bomb targets increased about twofold within several weeks. On January 27, 1943, American bombers attacked Germany for the first time. In Berlin the British bombed by night, and the Americans by day. In all Germany, Allied bombs killed between four and five hundred thousand civilians.[21]

Not surprisingly, the regime faced the collapse of public morale. German wartime morale reached its nadir in early 1943.[22] Indicating the leadership's belief that women were the key to morale, Goebbels wrote later that women were "largely responsible" for "our [public] sentiments."[23] Women, an American intelligence report concluded, grumbled the most about news from Stalingrad and the chaos and pain of bombings.[24] Now, too, women were asked to fill in at jobs for men on the front. A "large number" of women went to work in the anti-aircraft service, according to one Berlin newspaper.[25] In Berlin newspapers appealed for women to volunteer as truck drivers, promising there would be no long-distance hauls.[26]

Despite the harsh new situation at home, Goebbels used the defeat at Stalingrad to push for hard changes on the home front. Goebbels, who had once announced "a movement for the organization of optimism,"[27] now calculated that "the war could no longer be won simply by engendering confidence."[28] For the first time he ordered the press not to print cartoons belittling the enemy.[29] To impress on Germans the new gravity of war, he ordered a three-day period of mourning and sobriety. The Total War decree would also be a sign to the people that their government was serious, he argued. The credibility of the leadership was at stake, he claimed (and SD secret agents reported that the public was increasingly questioning the regime's credibility).[30]

Reflecting Hitler's notion that popular will was at least as important as armaments in battle, the German dictatorship had opted to maintain popularity by requiring minimal material sacrifice. Having raised expectations with economic growth, the regime was reluctant to tighten the belt once war began. Although Germany eventually claimed over 60 percent of its GNP for military expenditures, food consumption remained high throughout the war, potential workers were not conscripted, and taxes and wages remained constant. Even as sacrifices became inevitable, the dictatorship continued to picture German society as placid, if not really normal. The regime barely drew upon female labor at all before 1943.

The regime had stepped up mobilization efforts after the Wehrmacht faltered in the winter of 1941–42,[31] but now, in January 1943, Goebbels reasoned that more was needed. The German rout of the British at Dunkirk just months after the war had begun had actually been a disguised blessing for the British by forcing them into full mobilization from the beginning. On the other hand, the string of early German conquests had lulled Germany into taking mere "half measures" for mobilizing war resources. Now Stalingrad would have to serve as Britain's Dunkirk, forcing the regime to check civilian consumption, simplify the fat and counterproductive administrative apparatus, restrict cultural activities, and put women to work in the armaments industries.[32]

In early 1943 the dearth of German women working in industry was the most obvious sign that Germany had not mobilized its resources to the extent that its enemies had. As early as the German invasion of the USSR in mid-1941, Goebbels had proposed to force women out of households into the work force. Hitler had refused. By early 1942, when he became armaments minister, Albert Speer was also making the case for conscripting women. In April 1942 the Führer again refused, speaking abstractly of "German womanhood" and the moral injury that factory work might cause it. Work would damage a woman's "psychic and emotional life" and her ability to bear children. It would also be damaging to morale. Labor Minister Fritz Sauckel subsequently issued a proclamation that "in order to provide the German housewife, above all mothers of many children . . . with tangible relief from her burdens, the Führer has commissioned me to bring into the Reich from the eastern territories some four to five hundred thousand select, healthy, and strong girls."[33] To spare the Germans, material goods were robbed from conquered peoples, while the conquered peoples themselves were pressed into serving the German war industry.

Hitler had wished to conduct war without requiring major changes in traditional ways of living—with women at home. Like Hitler, Goebbels believed "a woman's primary, rightful, and appropriate place is in the family, and the most wonderful task that she can perform is to present her country and people with children."[34] Woman was to be eliminated from public life "in order that her honor may be restored to her."[35] Yet Goebbels was willing to bend principles for the cause of winning war. To save the Reich, the minister in charge of public morale pushed for changes that were expected to depress morale.

For Goebbels and his allies, conscripting women for work was now more important than ever. Total War was not well supported by Armed Forces Chief of Staff Wilhelm Keitel, Hitler's personal secretary, Martin Bormann, and Reich Chancellor Lammers, the "Committee of Three" Hitler appointed to implement Total War measures. They proposed enslaving more foreign workers from conquered territories as an alternative to conscripting women. Goebbels's allies were Economics Minister Walther Funk, Chief of the Labor Front Robert Ley, and especially Armaments Minister Albert Speer, who pointed out that foreign forced laborers could not be trusted as specialists in vital industries because of the danger of sabotage.[36] Austerities and hard facts risked popular alienation, but Goebbels, the expert in lies and deceptions, turned to truth in a desperate effort to wring more effort from the Germans.

On January 13, 1943, Goebbels prevailed as Hitler reluctantly issued a decree ordering "the extreme totalization of the war which he, the minister, has been demanding for the past eighteen months."[37] Through the new conscription of women between seventeen and forty-five, the regime expected to glean 3,500,000 or more women into the work force.[38] Only 13 percent of all German women with jobs worked in industry. Up to 5,500,000 female domestic servants and women without young children remained outside the labor force.[39] Armaments Minister Speer calculated that the conscription of 4,900,000 German women into the work force would bring the percentage of women employed outside the home up to 61 percent, the British quota of women employed outside their homes.

Bringing women into the labor force, however, brought the regime directly into contradiction with its ideology and practice. Women stayed at home to provide havens for men and future soldiers for the military. Hitler's metaphor of two worlds, one big world for men and politics and one housebound world for women who supported men, incorporated women in mass movement politics.[40] His big and small worlds (common in industrial societies) constituted a division of labor in a common enterprise. This paradigm of two worlds was never truer than during war, the greatest national enterprise. Men's wars depended on the weaker women's world. The small world was the core at the eye of the history-making man's world, a refuge to which men might momentarily retire from battle for emotional reconstruction, breeding, and renewed strength.[41] The more strenuous men's wars became, the more important was the supportive women's realm. In addition, morale on the war front was supported by admiration from the home front for the war cause and its victories (in turn morale at home was buoyed by Wehrmacht victories). The state might give a medal for courage in battle, but often it was a mother, lover, or wife who could best make a soldier feel like a hero. Soldiers received encouragement from letters, urging them to be brave, telling that all was well and that their loved ones stood behind them or prayed for their victory.[42] In Nazi Germany, under the peculiar social-political relationship of Nazi mass movement politics, traditional women were already doing important work for the war outside factories if they continued to believe in Hitler and the cause of nation.

With the attempt to rely more on women, the possible political impact of women expanded just as their cooperation became more important. The so-called *Stillegung* (business closure) clause of total war measures also required sacrifices—primarily from women. Germans in civilian businesses unrelated to war were now to be employed for war. Most of these were women. Public places of entertainment and pleasure—"luxury" restaurants, cabarets, bars, and gaming halls—also would be closed under Goebbels's plan. This would make more resources and labor available for war, drying up businesses that promoted frivolity, which the minister in charge of the national mood now deemed counterproductive to war making. Goebbels, who had banned dancing as out of step with the necessary sober demeanor, ordered three days of national commemoration for Stalingrad. Across the Reich entertainment halls, crafts shops, "luxury" restaurants, cookie factories, hotels—all were to shut down by March 15, 1943.[43]

The regime's hopes for regaining control of the war relied more on women than men. Thus in early 1943 German women might have constituted a particularly influential group in any collective effort to oppose the Nazi regime not only because they made up an increasingly large part of the home front and possible labor pool but also because the regime's decision to conscript women caused internal conflict. Total War measures contradicted the noncivic role Nazism had assigned women and ran contrary to the traditional female household roles it had asserted for ten years. From 1933 to 1943 Nazi propaganda, supported by social policies and party organizations for women and girls, had reinforced traditional notions that woman's place was in the home, bearing children and maintaining the home. To preserve quiescence, traditions should not be disturbed. The dictatorship wanted to eliminate any assertions by women of an independent public presence. Hitler sensed that bringing women into the labor force would give them new footing that could be used politically. In fact, by the time Goebbels gave his speech whipping up the public mood for Total War on February 18, there were already reports that masses of women were ignoring or sidestepping Hitler's Total War decree.

Precisely in February 1943, when a disastrous end for Germany was becoming palpable, women were turning unruly and unwilling to bear the war hardships—just as they had done toward the end of World War I, that awful specter in the Nazi imagination.[44] Few, if any, women directly refused to comply as a conscious act of civil disobedience,[45] but SD secret police agents reported increasing signs of defeatism and opposition to war among women. Women in Frankfurt am Main were reported as saying that "if all women got together, then this madness would soon be over!"[46] Across the Reich hundreds of thousands of women reported that they were unfortunately ill and unable to go to work. Massive headaches, sinus flare-ups, chronic back problems, hip ailments, colds that would not go away, even broken bones, and all manner of infections were reported. The Gestapo in Karlsruhe reported that "there are not even as many ailments as those registered here in the Labor Office."[47] Many women reported that they would be traveling, without stating their destinations or the dates of their expected returns. Women with husbands or other family members in the state bureaucracy relied on these men to pull strings. Clearly the Gestapo could not pursue these excuses on a case-by-case basis. Because of the massive noncompliance, Speer called the Total War decree's effort to put women to work a "total failure."[48] The women who disobeyed Hitler were not penalized.[49] Because it reflected ideals the regime had encouraged for a decade, the widespread refusal of women to work is not characterized as opposition to Hitler. It does, however, illustrate that even in the last years of war German noncompliance might go unpunished.[50]

The regime was in a weak position to enforce Hitler's work order. It could not afford to alienate women, especially if they insisted on standing by traditional Nazi ideals. Yet it was not only because of their gender that a mass of women might succeed in a limited public protest but because they were civilians who threatened home front morale.

For Goebbels, influencing Hitler to declare Total War was not an ultimate expression of power but a springboard for courting it. As bad

news poured in, Hitler refused to make the public appearance that
Goebbels considered crucial, so the club-footed demagogue stood in for
the Führer on February 18, as he gave his famed "Do you want Total
War?" speech, at Berlin's Sports Palace. It was an orchestration aimed
at reaching total support through the appearance that total support
already existed. Radios around Germany carried the thunder of Goebbels's audience responding with an echoing "Yes!" each time the minister shouted out, "Do you want Total War?" Albert Speer attended
and said that "except for Hitler's most successful public meetings, I
had never seen an audience so effectively roused to fanaticism."[51]

But Goebbels made the speech not just to arouse the mob but, as
Speer wrote, "to place Lammers and all the other dawdlers [lukewarm
supporters of Total War] under the pressure of the mob." Goebbels
wrote that he would use public opinion as his ally against the Committee
of Three.[52] The established officials at prestigious ministries he wanted
to influence looked down on his upstart Propaganda Ministry. Yet
Goebbels mobilized opinion even in the internecine battles he waged
to expand his own power, at the expense of old-style bureaucrats, who
had a more limited understanding of Hitler's attention to crowds. Speer
reported that in early 1942 Goebbels, through his control of public
images, made Speer, the new armaments minister, "one of the best-
known personages in the Reich . . . [and] in its turn was useful to my
associates in their daily bouts with government and party bureaus."
When Total War measures closed Horcher's restaurant in Berlin, a
famous patron, Hermann Goering, resisted, placing a guard outside the
premises to protect it from "the crazy Goebbels regulations." But
Goebbels had declared that he would not "stand for any interference"
in the Berlin gau and was firm.[53] He instigated a "spontaneous" demonstration outside Horcher's, making it look as though the people too
wanted Horcher's closed. Goering agreed that the restaurant would
remain closed to the public.[54]

Goebbels, whom Himmler's deputy Ernst Kaltenbrunner referred
to at Nuremberg as the second most powerful man of the Reich, realized
that an effective decree reflected the tenor of social practices, and his
ability to whip up popular opinion was the primary reason he had such
close access to Hitler. As he gave his Total War speech, Goebbels also
foreshadowed the coming Final Roundup of Jews. The last of his three
themes in the Total War speech was that the Jews were demonic war
makers "who in bolshevism had constructed a terroristic military
power."[55] There too the crowd shouted in orchestrated agreement.

INTERMARRIAGES IN GRAVE DANGER

By the beginning of 1943 Eichmann was threatening to draw all intermarried Jews and *Mishlinge* into the Final Solution. Under at least the general direction, if not the specific directives, of Hitler and Himmler, Eichmann's office was preparing a series of plans and deceptions. Eichmann might well have implemented all his plans in succession— and received acclaim from the leadership for it—if the Final Roundup had proceeded without drawing the mass protest.

The leadership and the RSHA had come together on their goals, but the drastic reversal in Germany's direction at war indicated how much they were at odds over tactics. Despite Germany's plummeting war fortunes, Eichmann doggedly persisted with plans for completing the Final Solution, by planning to deport persons from German-Jewish families.

Like Alois Brunner, who thought he could resolve the problems around deporting *Mischlinge* by merely changing their documentation to indicate they were Jewish, Eichmann and his officials, from Goebbels's perspective, generally understood neither the concern of the leadership for maintaining morale nor the tactical retreats made to save the war. This attention to detail rather than strategy, according to Goebbels, was typical of Germans.[56] Eichmann's schemes against intermarried Jews and *Mischlinge* were developing as Brunner, working from Eichmann's office, deported some of Berlin's intermarried Jews. A report by Dr. Gerhard Lehfeld from Berlin in mid-March 1943 also coincides with other reports that the RSHA was struggling to find ways to do this at the same time. In January 1943 the RSHA ordered the Gestapo in Frankfurt am Main to begin preparations for deporting intermarried Jews in that area, where more intermarried Jews lived than any other city of old Germany (pre-1938 borders) than Berlin. Having already deported the rest of the Jewish population, the RSHA decided to carry out this "last action" against the Jews as part of the "De-Jewing of the Reich Area."[57] Rather than deport intermarried Jews as a group in the manner of previous deportations, however, the Gestapo arrested intermarried Jews individually on criminal charges and then sent them as protective custody prisoners for three-month sentences to corrective labor camps. There they were to die under harsh conditions or be sent on to Auschwitz after their terms expired.[58] Local Gestapo offices had authority to intern persons as protective custody cases for up to three months, but the RSHA had to authorize longer internments. This method of deporting intermarried Jews as protective custody prisoners thus required the Frankfurt Gestapo to work with the RSHA, implicating the RSHA in a systematic attempt to murder intermarried Jews as a "last action" of the effort to clear the Reich of Jews in early 1943.

The goal of these arrests, according to a postwar German court's judgment, was to "clear the area of Jews," an integral part of the Final Solution.[59] According to the Frankfurt court, the RSHA deported intermarried Jews as criminals rather than as a group to "clothe [it] in a form that appeared to be legal." This was necessary because these Jews had relatives and friends among the German people, wrote the court.[60] The deportation of individual intermarried Jews as criminals, however, depended on a German public that actively collaborated since charging these Jews required denunciations. Jews were burdened with hundreds of regulations so petty that life was impossible without breaking some of them, but detecting breaches of petty regulations in the course of everyday life required not just uniformed police but the wider public. Following a request by Hessen (Frankfurt area) Gauleiter Jakob Sprenger, a flood of denunciations poured in from government offices, including party offices, against intermarried Jews. At the time, in a circular to party offices on October 9, 1942, party Chancellor Martin Bormann had made it a duty of every party member to tell their local leaders (Ortsgruppenleiter) about every known "Jewish offense."[61]

Falling back on the protection of legal procedure, the RSHA had evaded the social unrest the leadership feared from deporting intermarried Jews. But drawing intermarried Jews into the Final Solution one by one through protective custody charges was extremely inefficient. The RSHA restructured the Gestapo office in Darmstadt by creating a full-time Gestapo position to arrest and deport intermarried Jews, but in Darmstadt it took two months to deport twelve Jews this way. In Berlin the Gestapo probably could have avoided mass protests with similar methods, as those affected would have remained isolated, alone, and thus still afraid of voicing protest. But this case-by-case arrest and deportation method would have been far too slow against Berlin's five to seven thousand intermarried Jews.[62]

In the Reich capital there were other plans, according to Lehfeld's report based on information from Minister Director Erich Gritzbach, Goering's personal adviser in the Office of the Four-Year Plan. Gritzbach, an enigmatic figure who in 1940–41 passed some highly restricted information to Gero von Gaevernitz,[63] was interested in the attempt to clear Germany of Jews because this forced industry to replace its Jewish workers. Goebbels had agreed to deport intermarried Jews without children, while Jews in privileged intermarriages were not to be taken. However, in January 1943, as the military situation for Germany "sharply worsened, the [RSHA] radicals pushed also for the compulsory separation of privileged intermarriages and the deportation (i.e., murder) of the Jewish partner." At the same time they devised a plan to send even the *Mischlinge* who did not wear the Star of David to work camps in Poland.[64]

Also in January 1943, Lehfeld reported that the RSHA had "simultaneously made a plan . . . to shove the *Mischlinge* . . . into Poland, by way of work details—without doubt also for the purpose of being annihilated." Eichmann had drafted a law corresponding to this plan. It targeted all the *Mischlinge*, whether or not they wore the Star of David.[65] As a basis for deporting intermarried *Mischlinge*, Eichmann proposed a law grounded in the rationale that sexual intercourse had to be prevented between *Mischlinge* and Germans. Even Germans married to *Mischlinge* who did not wear the Star of David were to be separated.[66]

Eichmann conveyed his intentions to a Protestant minister and Catholic bishop who visited him in his office "at the end of 1942." The two prelates asked Eichmann about the accuracy of "rumors" from Bernhard Lösener at the Interior Ministry that intermarried Jews were soon to be deported. Lösener had reported on "widespread" rumors in different social circles that *Mischlinge* of the first degree would soon be ordered to wear the Star of David and would then be deported. Widespread and serious unrest followed the rumors through society like a "wave of tension."[67] A cloud seemed to fall over Eichmann's demeanor when the prelates asked him about *Mischlinge*. Eichmann, who until then had been quiet and nearly friendly, leaped to his feet and "With an agitated, brutal voice he answered . . . 'I will resolve this question radically, like I have resolved the other questions.' "[68]

Many German industrialists were also interested in preserving Jews. Since the beginning of the deportations Jews working in German armaments industries—along with intermarried Jews and *Mischlinge* —had been "deferred" from the deportations. German firms were reluctant to release their productive Jewish workers in exchange for forced laborers from the east since they cost less in wages and benefits and (under threat of deportation) worked harder to achieve the production levels on which profits depended. "The factory operators snatched up any available Jewish workers. Jews were known as dependable and conscientious workers, and employers hired them much more eagerly than foreigners," recalled the former leader of the Berlin Jewish Community.[69]

In Berlin thousands of intermarried Jews and *Mischlinge* also worked in factories. In December 1942, as industrialists were instructed to replace Jewish workers by March 1, Eichmann made a corresponding decision that the *Mischlinge* law was to be deferred for three months. In the fall of 1942 Hitler himself ordered that arguments of industrialists to the contrary, Jewish workers were now to be deported.[70] Goebbels, who had gotten together with Hitler to reach a decision that every Jew would have to leave Berlin, had also long since wanted to clear Berlin of the Jews industrialists claimed were indispensable.[71]

In Berlin in early December 1942 (as Eichmann deferred his plan) the new director of the Berlin Gestapo's Jewish Desk, Criminal Commissioner Walter Stock, announced that he was going to solve the Berlin Jewish question by March 1, 1943. Stock was a brute who, after driving Jews onto Auschwitz-bound trains, once sat at the station drinking a beer, quipping that the Jews would soon be feeling no more pain at all. To the owners and directors of the Berlin Industry and Trade Works he announced that Berlin Jewish workers, including those married to Germans, would be replaced as fast as possible by forced laborers from the east. Factory bosses were to make plans for this transition.[72]

On February 2, 1943, Goebbels arranged to have Hitler's bodyguard division of the SS, the Leibstandarte Hitler, assist in a massive arrest of Berlin Jews on February 27 and 28, in time for the March 1 deadline. They were to assist the efforts of Gestapo's Judenreferat director in Berlin, Walter Stock, who was constructing the technical and administrative apparatus to carry out deportations on this new large scale. On February 15 the Gestapo ordered Jewish Community leaders to select ninety additional Jews who would be working for a coming "action" to arrest Jews, including, this time, intermarried Jews.[73] The community's personnel director, Siegbert Kleemann, took charge of forming these task forces from the community's various administrative offices. Final Roundup arrests and deportations were supposed to continue day after day, until Berlin's Jews were deported, and then the Jewish Community employees who had been forced to assist in the deportations were to be deported at the very end.[74]

Gestapo preparations for the Final Roundup led to rumors that the pending arrest action also included new efforts to make a census of intermarried Jews.[75] In mid-February the Gestapo ordered the churches to corroborate and update its list of intermarried Jews. By January 1943 Jews in intermarriages and their spouses had already been required to register at the Jewish Community.[76] On February 17 the Relief Help Office of the Catholic bishop of Berlin wrote to Catholic parishes throughout Berlin, requiring each parish to identify its intermarried couples, their children, and, in some cases, their places of work. Most parishes replied by February 27, and a few during early March. The resulting lists, which were given either to the Jewish Community or directly to the Gestapo, contain hundreds and hundreds of names and addresses, identified in separate categories of "Privileged Intermarriages" and "Nonprivileged Intermarriages" and "Catholic Non-Aryan" or "Non-Aryan-Catholic Heads of Households."[77] The Gestapo meant to deport at least anyone wearing the Star of David, as the Gestapo code name Final Roundup implies, and it also wanted to make a complete registration of all Jews in privileged intermarriages if deportation at the moment was not yet feasible.

So at the onset of 1943 the RSHA prepared to complete the deportation of German Jews, beginning in Berlin. Eichmann had prepared several plans, for the treatment of several groupings of intermarried Jews and *Mischlinge*. At the same time his office released a copy of the ordinary deportation directives.[78] But Hitler, Himmler, and Goebbels wanted to complete the Final Solution in whatever way possible, and vagueness or confusion about orders could be an ally in the moment of a quick strike. Orders from the highest level in fact were notoriously vague in order to allow the leadership to deny involvement in controversial matters.

Efforts to register, arrest, and deport intermarried Jews might have been the initiatives of the RSHA, but given Goebbels's increased interest in clearing his district of Jews during these months, it is unthinkable that he did not know about them. Goebbels looked forward to ridding Berlin of Jews as one of his "greatest political achievements."[79] His diary shows that he talked with Hitler as well as Sepp Dietrich about using the SS Leibstandarte Hitler to help in the first two days of the Final Roundup and that the SS also arrested intermarried Jews and *Mischlinge*.[80] The fact that Goering's air force barracks and garage were used for this action also implicates levels above the RSHA in this arrest action. Goebbels himself had a plan for deporting intermarried Jews without children. He referred to the Final Roundup as "our plans," and he instructed editors of the Swedish press in Berlin not to publish anything on the coming mass arrest of Jews.[81]

On February 24, 1943, Hitler commemorated the founding of the Nazi party twenty-two years earlier with a speech promising again that the war would lead to the annihilation of Jews, and the speech played widely in the German press under the title "The Destruction of European Jews."[82] The top Jewish leaders Leo Baeck and Paul Eppstein had been deported to Theresienstadt a month earlier.[83] Brunner too was gone, but the Berlin Gestapo had adopted his ruthless methods and plans for a massive final arrest of Berlin's Jews.[84]

**The director of the Berlin Gestapo's Jewish Desk
Criminal Commissioner Walter Stock.**

By late February rumors of a massive arrest of Jews that would include intermarried Jews this time pulsed through the city. Tensions mounted. On February 26 the Berlin Gestapo's Jewish Desk director Walter Stock attended a meeting with the Wehrmacht's Armaments Division to discuss the replacement of Jewish workers with forced laborers from Poland and Russia. At noon the same day Moritz Henschel, the chairman of the Jewish Community, appeared under Gestapo orders at the Gestapo's Jewish Desk on Burgstrasse. The offices were swarming with hundreds of outside police officers in civilian clothing, waiting for further instructions. After waiting anxiously for hours, Henschel was instructed to prepare new task forces and collection centers for arrested Jews. The Gestapo would need five or six first-aid stations, with Jewish nurses, and a number of secretaries, with typewriters. All these instructions led Henschel to the inevitable conclusion: "An evacuation of large proportions" was imminent.[85]

Goebbels voiced misgivings in advance about trying to force the separation of families, as he engaged Hitler's SS division. He hoped the show of "brawny force" by the SS Leibstandarte Hitler during an arrest action carried out in "grand style" would stifle any outcry the deportation of intermarried Jews might cause. But he worried that following the German disaster at Stalingrad, with the regime pushing for new efforts from the home front, the time was not exactly right for resolving this domestic problem with force.[86]

XIV

COURAGEOUS WOMEN OF ROSENSTRASSE

Liberty, when men act in bodies, is power.

—EDMUND BURKE

Anything more than the truth would have seemed too weak.

—ROBERT FROST

THE LION'S DEN

Before dawn on the twenty-seventh the Final Roundup was under way. Gestapo chauffeurs were at their posts that morning by four for a "big alarm Jewish action." Every covered truck in Berlin was requisitioned for the raid.[1] The SS Leibstandarte Hitler appeared without warning at factories to arrest working Jews while the Gestapo and street police seized Jews from their homes and the streets—even some on visits to Berlin.[2] Erika Lewine, a feisty young woman of eighteen from a hardscrabble working-class family, remembered that day. Erika worked for Siemens, the giant telecommunications firm, where her shift began at six. She had barely arrived when she heard the tramp-tramp of boots crossing militarylike on the floor above. "Yes," she heard her supervisor say. "The SS is taking all of you. We can't do anything about it."

At that moment the SS strode in with horsewhips in their hands and begin whipping and shouting, "All Jews out!" The entire Jewish group, without steps or ladders, scrambled to get onto the truck. Together with thousands of others Erika was penned up in the horse stables of Hermann Goering's air force barracks.[3]

"There were two young women from Siemens with us," Erika said. "And when we arrived at the barracks, they began to talk about making an escape. I told them that this would be stupid, but they didn't listen. They were so much in despair they took off running and were both shot. And then we had to watch the shooting after they were both caught. 'Look at this,' a Gestapo man said, 'so you'll know what happens to those who try to flee.'

"Then the Gestapo sorted the men out from the women." Erika continued. "I saw my aunts and my uncles, and all my cousins, my entire family, for the last time. After that I never saw them again. All my relatives from my father's side were gassed—twenty-two relatives, all from Berlin. All of them were taken in this mass action—except one aunt, who had already been taken in 1942."

In another, distant part of the city Dr. Ernst Bukofzer was also surprised that morning by the SS. He was a Jew who had been practicing law when World War I forced him to the front to share the common German cause with another young soldier, Adolf Hitler. Like Hitler, he returned from war decorated with the Iron Cross medal for bravery. After the war Bukofzer married a German with two daughters and again practiced law until under Hitler this was again interrupted.[4]

Bukofzer had just reached work when the whole Jewish crew was ordered out to the courtyard. The men at first thought they were expected to load a truck, he remembered. Instead an SS man, who gestured wildly, ordered Bukofzer and his coworkers to jump onto the waiting truck. They were given no explanation. In the dark one Jew managed to slip away and under the fence. Six SS men were sent after him, but they finally returned, unsuccessful. Then another officer checked the workers' names against a list, confiscating their work permits and any sharp objects. One of them confiscated Bukofzer's flashlight. An SS man gave a warning that guards sitting at the back of the truck would immediately use their weapons if anyone tried to flee. Then they charged off to the Hermann Goering barracks. Along the way they stopped for more Jews, even stopping at factories with only one Jewish employee. Ferdinand Wolff, a Jew married to a German, was picked up from his job at Warnicke & Böhme.

Upon arriving at the Goering barracks, Bukofzer recalled, "we had to get out of the truck—fast. Then we heard one of the drivers ask a nearby guard, 'Are your guns already loaded?' If before we had been uncertain about our fate, we now believed that our last hour had certainly struck. But the day wore on: noon, afternoon, then evening. There was no food or drink. There were no toilets. Truck after truck rolled up, bringing more and more Jewish workers.

"When in the afternoon a number of us men were commanded to dig trenches in front of the camp, we were convinced that we were shoveling our own grave." Bukofzer continued. "Then the female prisoners were led out in a group. They also thought they were to be shot and buried and began to wail and cry out in fear. Then under the inspection of the SS guards and their gloating catcalls they were forced to relieve themselves in the open trenches."

Neither Charlotte nor Julius noticed the SS and their trucks that morning, or any other signs that this Saturday would be different. Julius had to report to the police to renew his pass for taking public transportation to work. Jews had to walk to work except if work was more than six kilometers (four miles) from home. Driver's licenses had been taken from Jews in 1938.[5] "My husband left at seven in the morning, saying he would be back at ten," Charlotte said. "But he didn't come back!"

Arriving at police quarters, Julius was ordered to take a seat beside two women, each wearing the Star of David. Neither knew any more than he did about what to expect. Then a street policeman, service revolver at his side, entered with two more Jews. District by district, all over Berlin, the regular street police had been requisitioned to help the Gestapo and the SS bring Jews into custody. Without explanation two police officers escorted Julius and the others to a nearby streetcar. "Now they're even taking the cripples!" Julius heard someone mumble as he got on. Jews were prohibited from sitting on public transportation, and Julius steadied himself on his crutches as the car lurched from stop to stop. He schemed about getting word to Charlotte and then decided to trust the stranger who had complained under his breath. He wrote a phone number on a matchbox and pressed it into the stranger's hands. "Would you please call my stepmother and say that you saw me here?" he asked. "She is Aryan."

By noon Charlotte had begun to look for Julius. Across from their house was a grocer with a telephone, and she had an agreement with Julius that he would call there if he needed her. "The store owners were very nice," Charlotte recalled. "They were truly anti-Nazis— secretly, of course." But Julius had not called, and each time Charlotte ran over, there was still no message.

"Then at about two-thirty I saw my mother coming," said Charlotte. Someone had called her mother to say that Julius had been taken with five other Jews to Levetzowstrasse. Fearful, Mrs. Press had first denied knowing any Jews when the stranger called. But when he persisted that a Jew on crutches had given him her number, she knew it was Julius. Charlotte went to the police office for a record of Julius's arrest. A friendly officer who recognized her told her to go to Rosenstrasse.

Across the city center Julius's sister, Erna, was also trying to get in touch with Charlotte, the German in her life who represented a possible connection to safety. That morning, as Erna was walking down Kantstrasse to work, she had been warned by a street policeman to go back home. Erna had recognized this officer instantly. He had been saying hello to her each morning on her way to work, and for anyone wearing the Star of David, a greeting from a German could be a surprise.

The Gestapo, seeking the advantages of surprise, sought to conceal its plans. Yet preparations for the arrests required the Gestapo to give indications to employers and churches, as well as Jewish leaders, and word leaked out. Ursula Braun said her "family always got word of Gestapo actions—through, for example, a Gestapo chauffeur, who always spoke with one of our neighbors."[6] Rumors caused one Jew in a privileged intermarriage to flee Berlin with her daughter, to relatives in Braunschweig.[7] Elsa Holzer's Jewish husband, Rudi, was approached by a friend, Abraham Moritz, who had contacts with the Jewish Community and proposed that the two of them go into hiding together to escape the arrests. Rudi refused, saying he had no money and didn't want to be dependent on Moritz for help.[8] Ingeborg Schneider-Lüschow said she received a warning through her former boss, who had "continuous contact" with the Berlin Gestapo. Another deportation action was about to begin immediately, he informed her, and this time it would include intermarried Jews.[9] Goebbels fumed that shortsighted industrialists had managed to warn four thousand Jews. "Our plans were tipped off prematurely, so that a lot of Jews slipped through our hands," he wrote. "But we will catch them yet. I certainly won't rest until the capital of the Reich, at least, has become free of Jews."[10]

The Gestapo used deception to spread an air of normality until Jews were ensnared. Werner Goldberg's father, Dieter Elkuss, and other intermarried Jews had received orders through the mail to appear at the Labor Bureau on the Fontane Promenade in central Berlin that morning of February 27. Hilda Elkuss had married her Jewish husband in December 1933, after they had heard rumors that intermarriages would be banned. "That was courageous," she said, "because in a way we knew what was coming—and it came too."

On this day Dieter and Hilda thought that he would receive a new work assignment. This was welcomed since Dieter, like Rudi, worked extremely long, hard hours for the railroad. Yet Hilda was on guard. She had formed her social circle mostly from among intermarried couples and knew that other intermarried Jews had received similar orders. "We [intermarried Germans] were like-minded," Hilda said, "and got to know each other from the tennis or the bridge club—even before the war." Hilda and her circle of intermarried German wives decided to go together with their husbands as a group that morning. At the bureau, however, they were forced to split into two groups, one of Jewish men, who were loaded onto trucks, the other of the German wives, who were told nothing.

Those summoned to the Labor Bureau that day were either intermarried Jews or *Geltungsjuden Mischlinge* who wore the Star of David. Gad Beck, a twenty-three-year-old half Jew who had grown up with a strong sense of Jewish identity, was among them and was also expecting a new job assignment. He remembered waiting in the back of the Gestapo's truck at the Labor Bureau until they were a company of forty or fifty men. Then they were driven to Rosenstrasse and unloaded directly into a single room. Gad had grown up in Berlin's Scheunenviertel, the Jewish ghetto of poor and Orthodox Jews from the east, and he knew the area around Rosenstrasse like the back of his hand.

The method of summoning Jews to the Labor Bureau made their arrests convenient, and perhaps it also deceived church and Interior Ministry officials, who had raised concerns about *Mischlinge*. Eichmann ordered that arrested intermarried Jews and *Mischlinge* be separated and interned at Rosenstrasse.[11] "These Jews at Rosenstrasse were supposed to be put on a train, and then no one would have heard from them again," said Siegbert Kleemann, the Jewish Community's personnel director, who had organized the Jewish task forces to assist the Gestapo during the Final Roundup.[12] They were separated to make it seem as if they would not have the same fate as other Jews, and maybe they were to be taken initially to labor camps, where they could be retrieved if complaints warranted it, but from which they were never supposed to return. Goebbels expected some kind of opposition to the forcible separation of intermarried couples,[13] and deception might help throw these opponents off-balance, at least until the Jews had been shipped out. When Hilda and her friends asked the police about their husbands, they were told to return the following day. They waited quietly, but on the following day the police still had no information for them.

Gad didn't remember being afraid when he arrived on the Gesta-

po's truck at Rosenstrasse 2–4, surrounded as he was by a familiar
Jewish context. This, the oldest part of the city, dating back to the
thirteenth century, was where Jews had first congregated in Berlin, in
1348. Accused of spreading the Great Plague, the Jews were driven out
of Berlin, not to reappear for four centuries. By the early twentieth
century there were nearly a quarter of a million Berlin Jews, but now,
in 1943, they were soon to be virtually wiped out once more.[14]

The area around Rosenstrasse was a place of community and
safety, according to Gad. "This area was the center for us Scheunenviertel Jews," he said, combining a sense of irretrievable loss with a
romantic prophetic vision. "It was a Jewish section, something that's
hard for a Berliner today to imagine. The Jews lived and had their
shops there, and that whole area lived from these Jews. There were
only small bakeries and textile shops. Nothing grand. There was also
a café there or two that only Jews used. During the week all the kids
went to the Jewish schools on Auguststrasse or Grosse Hamburger
Strasse. I too went to school around the corner from Rosenstrasse, on
Grosse Hamburger Strasse. Every day I took the train to Hakescher
Market, where I got out, and saw Rosenstrasse. Behind it was the
Heidereuter synagogue, which I attended for years and years. Fridays
and Saturdays this area was ruled by the presence of Jews, as they
filled the streets to and from the synagogue."

Gad was curious when he arrived that Sabbath morning at Rosenstrasse. Who was there? Did he know anyone? "I met one man
who perhaps had associations with the Gestapo," he said. "He wasn't
negative because I knew of a relationship he had to a Jewish family in
the underground. He looked at me and saw I looked very sporty. That
morning I had dressed to make an impression, with long black boots
and riding pants. So this man looked at me and said, 'You will be an
orderly! You will look out here, so that everything stays quiet and the
people remain calm, so that everything here can develop smoothly.' "

The Gestapo requisitioned the help of an unprecedented number
of Jewish Community employees for the Final Roundup. Each received
a yellow "protection ID," signed by the chairman of the Jewish Community, with the script: "The person showing this ID is protected from
this action, because he is employed for urgent reasons. In case of doubt,
call the office of Commissioner Walter Stock."[15] Many employees of
the Jewish Community forced into Gestapo service wore red armbands
stamped with a number, to alert the police not to arrest them for the
duration of this operation, even though they also wore the Star of
David.

"I too became an orderly, with an armband," Gad whispered. He was reminiscing now, back in Berlin, where after eighteen years in Israel he had returned to live. He felt more at home in Berlin, he said (but he brought to mind Robert Frost's line "the heart is still willing to seek, but the feet question whither"). "As an orderly," he continued, "I had the armband and could enter the various rooms in the building. And that's the way I met my sister, Miriam, who was arrested from work at Siemens. And then I found my father, who was also there, and he was totally broken."

Werner's father was also imprisoned that day along with Gad Beck and Dieter Elkuss. When Mr. Goldberg hadn't returned by early evening, Werner and his mother began to fear the worst. Werner set out to find him. The Fontane Promenade in front of the Labor Bureau was deserted, but across the street in a park stood a small group. They told Werner that trucks had taken the Jews away that morning, but no one knew where. So Werner started off again, questioning each person he encountered. Someone said the Jews had been taken to Clou, the recently closed entertainment center. At Clou, however, Werner was hurried on by reports that Jews married to Germans were at Rosenstrasse.

At Rosenstrasse Werner found about 150 to 200 people collected, mostly women. "Outside the building the sidewalk was blocked off," he recalled. "Policemen stood across the street from the crowd that had gathered and prevented anyone from getting through. About twenty policemen, positioned about ten meters from each other, formed a chain across the front of the building. And the people in the crowd waited, hindered from any kind of contact with persons inside. We had virtually no notion at all what was happening inside."

"What's going on?" Werner asked a policeman who stood there. "I think my father is in there."

"Write down his name," the policeman replied. He took the name from Werner and gave it to an SS man at the door.

"Shortly thereafter he came out and nodded," explained Werner. "Now I was certain that Father was behind the wall." Werner called his brother and made arrangements to take shifts with him, standing vigil on the street. From then on Werner and his brother took turns watching the door day and night. There was only one door, and if their father left, he would have to leave through it.

On that first evening of the Final Roundup, Elsa was desperate for news about Rudi. When she searched her memory to locate in time that day when she feared she had lost him, she remembered that they had just celebrated her thirty-ninth birthday. Normally Rudi returned by two o'clock on Saturdays, but she expected him to return as much as an hour later this Saturday. He had an insatiable sweet tooth and bought sugar on the black market from a source near Janowitzbrücke. He would go there after work, he said, but be back by two-thirty.

"Well, it turned three o'clock, and then three-thirty," Elsa said. "Already at that point I had terrible fear. I didn't know where my husband was or where to look. I thought perhaps that he got into trouble for buying sugar. Then I reproached myself, thinking, No! We won't eat sugar anymore! Then I thought I should have asked him exactly *where* at Janowitzbrücke he would be, so I could find him. Then I waited a little longer. We had no phone. I thought I might start out. Then I thought, If I go now, maybe he'll come and I'll be gone. I got sick. I had made potato soup that evening, and since then I have never cooked it again. At ten I simply couldn't stay at home any longer. I pulled my courage together and rode down to Bahnhof Friedrichstrasse, where Rudi worked. There at the station a man came out of the glass booth, as he saw me coming, and said, 'Mrs. Holzer, I've waited for you. Here, take your husband's things.' "

Elsa's intensity grew as she began to recall the strength it took to ask, "*Where is my husband?*" She whispered the question fiercely now, the way she had finally taken action. "The Jews were all taken," she heard him say. "The SS rolled in here like fire trucks and bundled them off. I don't know where to. They're gone now. Please take his things home."

Rudi's winter coat, his street shoes, and his briefcase were still there. There had been no time for Rudi to take them. That meant he had only his wind jacket. On the street Rudi often wore the wind jacket over his winter coat, because his winter coat had no Star of David. At work, among his Jewish colleagues, he always wore the wind jacket with the star. Elsa had smeared it with cinders until its bright yellow turned grayish. She half feared to take his clothes as if admitting that was all that remained. Home at midnight she couldn't rest. "In my head was only 'who, what, when, how, where,' " Elsa said. "I thought I would go mad. Where was I supposed to go find my husband?"

At ninety-three Dr. Ernst Bukofzer still remembered well the night he had spent on the cement floors of the Hermann Goering barracks. There were no windows, and when the huge doors stretching the entire length of the barracks were pulled down, it was pitch-black. Hundreds of people spent the winter night on cement there, without blankets.

Many reckoned with the ends of their lives; a number suffered nervous breakdowns. The sorrowful murmuring and wailing continued throughout the night. Many yearned for word from their loved ones. Bukofzer himself had last seen his mother when the Gestapo took her, tossing her "like a chopped log" on the truck. "At least I knew my wife and children were safe," said Bukofzer. "By contrast, this was the worst for my fellow sufferers, who did not live in intermarriages."

In the morning the huge doors at the Goering barracks were suddenly flung open to the bright light, and the place began to swarm with SS men, lesser officers, and their assistants. Hauptscharführer Karl Krell, an unemployed baker who had found work for Berlin Gestapo, was the director of this detention center. He ordered Jews married to Germans to step to one side. A Jew married to a German who had divorced her in 1939 told Krell that she had three children and that the father was no longer there to care for them. "That doesn't matter," Krell retorted. "Your husband could also be put into a concentration camp!" With that he waved her over to the group that would stay behind.[16] But when his back was turned, she slipped into the group of intermarried Jews, along with Ernst Bukofzer. Around midday the

Hauptscharführer Karl Krell, an unemployed baker who found work for the Jewish Desk of the Berlin Gestapo arresting and deporting Berlin Jews.

intermarried Jews were loaded onto a truck and taken to Rosenstrasse.

There a crowd flooded the streets, spilling back to the Spandauer Brücke. Most people did not work on Sunday and were free to come and go as they pleased. In front of the building people surged back and forth. As Bukofzer got out of the truck on Rosenstrasse, he caught sight of his youngest stepdaughter. "Impulsively I waved," he said. "Thereupon a guard gave me a kick in the seat so hard I almost fell over, and I hurried into the house with the others. But I now knew that my relatives were informed about my fate. That gave me a certain calm. Someone was there for me."

Just around the corner and within earshot of the crowd on Rosenstrasse was Burgstrasse and the Jewish Desk of the Berlin Gestapo. A few salvos from a machine gun could have emptied the square. The law forbade all public gatherings, and the Gestapo registered every incident that looked even faintly like a hostile gathering. Now they searched in vain for organizers of the protest.[17]

On the first day of the Final Roundup the Gestapo, the SS, and the street police seized and imprisoned five thousand Jews. On Sunday, all day long for the second day, heavy trucks plied the streets throughout Berlin, their canvas canopies only thinly veiling the outline of tightly packed human cargo. Coworkers and neighbors lowered their gazes, wrote one Jew who went underground when he saw the caravan of trucks on his way to work that day.[18] Charlotte Israel remembered once seeing people rub their hands in pleasure as the Gestapo shoved Jews on their truck. History was being made, and this was a necessary part of it, the regime promised.

For the Weigert family the story of Rosenstrasse became a collective memory, told and retold. In Mrs. Weigert's Berlin apartment more than forty years later, it brought them together again, as Mrs. Weigert and her children, Horst and Helga, relived it. Occasionally their individual memories contradicted one another, but together they wove a narrative, like a tapestry, from the events each in turn experienced.

Helga Weigert was an eight-year-old *Mischling* at home with her German grandmother when the Gestapo arrived on the second day of the Final Roundup. "Dress the child warmly, and give her some milk to take along," the Gestapo said. While the grandmother dressed Helga, Mr. Weigert arrived. He and Helga's brother were also on the Gestapo's list. But without waiting for the brother, the Gestapo drove off with Helga and her father to the Levetzowstrasse synagogue.

"When we arrived, we had to identify ourselves," Helga remembered. "You were categorized and put with your group." Parents were separated from children; spouses were separated from each other. Jews who tried to move out of their group to meet friends or family were beaten by a Gestapo man with a cowhide whip who screamed "dogs!" and "lousy Jew!" at them. A German man who had come to the synagogue to talk to his Jewish wife made it to the balcony where the group of Jews in intermarriage were held. From there he was kicked so hard he tumbled back down the stairs.[19] *Geltungsjuden* who were married to Jews or were members of the Jewish Community were put with the group of Jews married to Germans.

"After a while we were put into a truck and taken to a building that turned out to be Rosenstrasse," Helga said. She was in the same building with her father but separated. "Some of the children separated from their parents weren't even old enough to go to school yet," she remembered. "One was rolled up, about the size of a soccer ball. Many had been plucked from the street as they played or walked to school. Of course the parents weren't told what had happened." Forty-three abandoned children called the Jewish Community in search of their parents.[20] Julius Lewine, an artist who worked as a helper at the Jewish Community and was himself to die in Auschwitz months later, found two deserted infants. Making the rounds of the various huge collecting centers with an infant in each arm, he called out over and over again for the mother. After a half day's search he finally found her, and reunited them for the trip "east."[21]

Mrs. Weigert was at work that day when she got a call from her mother: The Gestapo had been there to take her husband and small daughter. "I ran, ran, ran back home," she remembered, "and from there I ran to Levetzowstrasse synagogue. I rushed up to go in. I wanted to see if my child was there, and my husband. But I wasn't allowed in! SS men stood in front of the door. One said, 'Get back. People are being transported from here.' 'Where will I see my husband again?' I asked. 'Wherever he goes, I will go. So I have to know.'

"And then I just waited there at a little distance to see what was happening and who was being transported, and then I saw Jewish people were shoved into the truck brutally. I was horrified. I had terrible fear. I tried again to enter the synagogue, saying, 'I've got to find my next of kin.' They stopped me again. Then I tried a third time, and one of the SS men took hold of me by the arm and said, 'If you don't disappear, I will throw you out.'

"And then I withdrew and, in terrible fear, began to make a scene there on the street. I was infuriated and cried out again and again: 'Help! Help! Help! What's going on here!' I myself wasn't sure what was happening to the Jews; one didn't believe it. The street was totally empty there where I was, except for the synagogue. And then a woman approached me and said, 'Hey, don't make a scene here, or it will get much worse! If you want to do something, don't do it here alone. Go to Rosenstrasse. At Rosenstrasse you will find a number of people with the same problem you have, who are gathering together there.'

"So I went there and walked around, looking. And there were many people who were experiencing the same thing I was! And then I saw my sister-in-law. My husband's brother had also been arrested that day, so she had also come to Rosenstrasse. Her family and ours lived in the same house, one above the other. Later we went home together. I had a son there, and my mother, who was already over eighty, and if I hadn't gone back, she wouldn't have known what to do. But my sister-in-law and I agreed to get up at the crack of dawn to return."

All day the Jewish intermarriage partners and half Jews kept pouring into Rosenstrasse 2–4. They were mostly male Jews married to German women and a lesser number of *Mischlinge* who wore the Star of David. About one hundred women or girls were there.[22] Inside, it became harder and harder to move around. Forty men were squeezed into a room of twenty square meters, so that they could only sit or stand in turn. When not standing, most crouched or knelt on bare floors; some had a bale of straw or two, others an old mattress. In one small room the younger prisoners stood the entire time, to give the older ones a chance to sit. An older man, distraught and hungry, died of a heart attack.[23]

Erika Lewine was in a room with other women, including an actress about forty years old. Erika recalled fondly that "once in a while she acted out something or played, so we could laugh. I know she wore a ponytail and had black hair—straight as an arrow. I still see her sitting in front of me on the ground. These are pictures which one never loses. Another woman in the room always whistled tunes for us, so that we were a little bit distracted. She could whistle hundreds of tunes—splendid!

"We didn't have a toilet. Only a bucket, in a sort of closet. All the women got their periods because of the excitement. We couldn't wash ourselves; we had nothing there; we were totally covered with dirt. Then I forced myself to carry the bucket out, nose pinched shut, so I could put one foot in front of another.

"And there I saw my father in the hallway. He almost fell over in fright because he thought I was at home. He said, 'I'll give you my bread.' Our only food the entire time was dry bread with marmalade. I said, 'No, Dad, you eat it please.' "

Ernst Bukofzer was crammed into a small room on the third floor that faced the street. "If I stole a glance through the window I could occasionally catch a glimpse of my wife and daughters among those passing back and forth on the street," he said. "Several times I could also determine that crowds were scattered by the police."[24] Gad Beck remembered being in a room with his father where the floor was so thick with people that "we squatted on the ground, because there wasn't enough room to even lie down. Beside me was a very nice young man, Johann Siegel, very well dressed in comparison to the others. I discovered that this family had a villa in Grünewald and that the man was an accomplished biochemist."

As an orderly Gad Beck was allowed outside the building. "On that first evening of the arrest there was a circle of people on the street—maybe about two hundred," he said. "No massive wall. On the second day there were already more standing there. And there I discovered my mother and her four Christian sisters. All of them bourgeois Germans. They stood beside each other, and said: 'We want our husbands back!' That was the heroic act of their life. They didn't have anything more to lose. Their husbands had just been taken."

Gad's mother had brought a small package of food for Gad, his father, and his sister. Gad took them in. Other family members also brought packages for their imprisoned loved ones—food, toiletries, love notes tucked in butter sandwiches—and kept insisting that someone take them in. Some of them wrote names on their packages and then threw them at the door. Gad, who later became involved in efforts to rescue Jews,[25] recalled that at Rosenstrasse, "I was happy. Everyone looked at me and said, 'He's the orderly; he's the one who comes and goes, in and out, and takes care of business.' "

Among the crowd on the street Werner and his brother had continued a twenty-four-hour vigil. Others also remained through the night. Suddenly an open jeeplike vehicle of the SS Leibstandarte Hitler drove up; four members of the Tall Guys Club—the nickname for the Leibstandarte, which required its members to be at least six feet tall —were supposed to disperse the crowd. There in the front seat sat Werner's old classmate and childhood friend Karl Wolf. Werner rushed over and, taking Karl by the arm, said, "Karl, you've been sent to me from heaven."

"Why?" said his old friend, embarrassed by Werner's reappearance.

"My father is imprisoned in there, and I need your help to get him out. Can you help me speak with him?"

"Look, I can't talk to you here," said Karl. "Here's my card. Call me later."

On the evening of the second day of the Final Roundup, Anton von Kryshak, a regular street police officer who had been at his job since before the Third Reich, received orders in the afternoon to guard a Jewish collection center at Rosenstrasse 2–4. "I had to report at about eight in the evening at the Rosenstrasse detention camp, armed only with my service pistol, to relieve five members of the SS, wearing black uniforms," he said. "I was very astonished that I was not given instructions on how I was supposed to replace the SS. I had the impression that the people had longingly awaited my appearance and wanted to leave the detention camp as fast as possible. The next morning, around eight I was replaced by about twenty members of the city police. They were astounded to find that I had spent the entire night alone, without the least incident."[26]

Kryshak received three days of vacation because there had been no escapes. The story his superiors later told him was that each Berlin police district was supposed to have sent a policeman to Rosenstrasse, but only his did. Perhaps those planning the Final Roundup did not have plans for police guards around Rosenstrasse for more than two days and had to improvise quickly.

On Monday, March 1, the Gestapo continued to arrest Jews at their houses and on the street. Children were also taken. On Uhlandstrasse in Wilmersdorf a nine-year-old child attempting to flee was shot and wounded by an SS man.[27] Wally Grodka wrote in her diary: "Close to Bayernplatz . . . in the evening hours the SS tries to pick up two children, whose parents they already hold. One was thrown into the car. The other ran off. He ran a few steps and lay crying. An SS big shot had shot him in the knee, to hinder him from fleeing."[28]

Gerhard Braun, a nineteen-year-old *Geltungsjude*, was home that Monday when the Gestapo came for him. He had recently gotten engaged and had attended school with Stella Kübler, the infamous Gestapo "catcher."[29] After the war he became a professor in Berlin and together with his then fiancée, Ursula, they raised five children. Like Gerhard, Ursula was half Jewish. But she was not a member of the Jewish Community, was not required to wear the Star of David, and in turn had not been arrested. Gerhard had been sick in bed on Saturday and so escaped the SS arrests at work. Now, amid "wails and cries of my mother," he too was taken.

At Rosenstrasse the minutes passed slowly, uneventfully. To

shorten the hours of uncertainty, Gerhard tore part of the cover from the mattress the Jewish Community had placed in the room and marked it with a pencil like a chess board—a chess board he still had in 1985. Using pebbles as chess pieces, he and his fellow sufferers were able momentarily to forget their plight.[30] To eat there was chopped cabbage, and more cabbage. The Jews waited in line for the food for up to three hours in front of clogged toilets that had no doors. "I have never eaten chopped cabbage again," Gerhard remarked. Another Jewish inmate remembered that there was a lot of confusion. One morning at about six, for example, the inmates received potatoes and sauerkraut.[31] There was no information about what was to happen next. Now and then the Gestapo held roll calls. Occasionally Gerhard also heard the protest outside and took hope. "The Jews inside had already seen their partners holding to them through so much hardship that they were hardly astounded at the action outside. These [German] partners had proven they would hold fast this way on an almost a daily basis, if not in such a public and obvious form as this."

In an attempt to keep people away from Rosenstrasse, where they would see an illegal crowd protesting, the city closed the closest elevated train station, Bahnhof Börse.[32] It was of little use. People willing to defy Gestapo orders and death threats would walk the extra mile. Mrs. Weigert was on Rosenstrasse with her sister-in-law. On the street "there were small groups of family members," she recalled. "Then we spread out on the street, in front of the building, and we marched back and forth. There we said, in chorus, 'We want our husbands back! We want our husbands back!' Yes! We simply wanted to get our husbands back. "My sister-in-law and I weren't even sure if our family members were really there. That was only what we had heard from the general public."

Unsure her husband and daughter were really at Rosenstrasse, Mrs. Weigert chose to protest there anyway. There was solidarity and perhaps safety in numbers. Mrs. Weigert had heard of protest as a form of political influence. She recalled knowing something of Mahatma Gandhi's mass mobilizations, and she was indignant. Her family had been violated. Something had to be done. Some of the women protesting on the street would have known about or even personally experienced the frequent Communist and Socialist street protests during the Weimar period, to say nothing of the specifically women's mass uprisings and politically orchestrated street actions against World War I and on behalf of women's suffrage.

Gerhard Braun's mother had called her son's fiancée, Ursula, at work, and Ursula went as quickly as possible to Rosenstrasse. "On the

street there was never any news about what would happen," she remembered. "And so the only thing to do was to join the crowd and
hope. We were forced to go against the law," said Ursula, who never
before or after that has felt so compelled to disobey the state openly.
She described the energy that caused the women to group together and
protest as the "courage of despair," saying that "it was the most urgent
sense of emergency that drove us. We knew what we were facing too.
I had met Gerhard through my sister, who was married to Gerhard's
brother. My sister and Gerhard's brother were taken by the Gestapo
in 1942, along with their two-year-old son, and we never heard from
them again.[33] I never stopped to consider whether going out on the
street would help bring the men back," she said. "But our motivation
for being there was to have them back! I met a woman there who
didn't know me, and we made an appointment to meet there the next
day."

Evenings in wartime Berlin were dark. In compliance with blackout
regulations that made the city a harder target for RAF pilots to find,
not so much as a single light was permitted to shine through an apartment window.

Looking back, Berliners were to remember the evening of
March 1 as "the first big air raid." It foreshadowed the degree of
bombing to come, but March 1, 1943, was still a loudly proclaimed
"Day of the Luftwaffe," a celebration of Goering's air force. The enemy,
the Royal Air Force (RAF), also knew this.

At about eight-thirty on the evening of the Day of the Luftwaffe,
the air-raid sirens began to sound. Nerve-racked Berliners crept into
basement shelters, as dozens of houses exploded and lit up in the flames.
Hundreds of people were burned, suffocated, or buried under ruins.
Cathedrals, monuments of culture, museums with ancient treasures—
what had taken centuries to establish—disintegrated in minutes.

Rosenstrasse lay in the middle of the city, where most of the
RAF's bombs fell. At the first hint of attack the SS, Gestapo, and police
guards fled the building, having nailed the windows shut. The Jews
stayed put, awaiting the mercy of gravity and chance. Bombs peppered
the vicinity; one explosion followed another. Across the Spree, on
Unter den Linden, the opera house was hit. St. Hedwig's Cathedral,
where the Catholic priest and cathedral provost Bernhard Lichtenberg
had prayed for the Jews in open services, took a direct hit and more
or less disappeared. Nearby, the horse stables of the royal palace were
destroyed. Königstrasse collapsed in a stretch of blazing ruins. A wing

of Goering's nearby Luftwaffe headquarters was struck and burned. In the opinion of an American OSS informant, damage in Berlin on March 1 was greater than in all former air raids combined. One thousand people were reported killed outright, while more than three thousand were thought to be severely wounded. Between three thousand and four thousand homes were destroyed. The raid "resulted in a great deal of anxiety on the part of the inhabitants of Berlin, who realize that only a beginning has been made," wrote the OSS.[34]

The building at Rosenstrasse 2–4 shook and wobbled, the walls shuddered, and the rooms, between short pauses, lit up as brightly as at midday. Like other Jews and intermarried Germans, Gerhard Braun remembered conflicting emotions about the plunging bombs that night. He clearly recalled his terror as he was stuck on the third floor at Rosenstrasse, on one side, while on the other side he hoped that the British bombs would overwhelm his mortal enemy, the German state and its supporters. His fiancée, Ursula, also had clashing feelings. "On the one hand were fury and hate against the Nazis, who deserved the attack, and on the other side there was terrible misery all around each of us—the screaming people, the hellish fires."

For Jews, bombings could come as moments of grace, leveling the extreme social hierarchy. Six hundred thousand German civilians died in the raids, and Jews of course also faced this danger. Yet as long as the bombs fell, the Gestapo were in bomb shelters. The persecutors too were afraid and waited out the bombings helplessly. Cocky Gestapo men eyed the sky nervously and dashed to the shelters the moment the air-raid sirens blew. Some Jews even escaped during these moments, and there was rejoicing among Berlin Jews at the news in 1943 that Prüfer had been killed by a bomb. The death that dropped from the sky might strike anyone and seemed more tolerable for threatening everyone, not just Jews. As Lotte Paepcke wrote, burdens borne by everyone in the community are lighter than solitary burdens that "mark and separate."[35] Like the Jews, Charlotte Israel wanted to see the regime smashed. "I always had such fear about the air raids," she said. "But on that night I thought, That serves them right! I was so enraged. I was together with a few others, who got down on their knees and prayed. I could have laughed in scorn! But then I thought of my husband, who was locked up at Rosenstrasse. I knew they would not be able to leave the building."

After a long hour the bombing was over, for that night. Entire blocks lay in ruins, but somehow Rosenstrasse 2–4 remained untouched, a sign that "God was with us after all," said Erika. Werner Goldberg's father was still lying on the bare floor after the bombing when the door opened and someone with a flashlight stepped through. "Goldberg!" a man called. Without knowing who called, Mr. Goldberg got up and stepped over about thirty people to get to the door. The man with the flashlight grabbed him by the arm and led him down the stairs. There an officer pressed into his hand a folded page that he determined to be a release form. Goldberg and other men from privileged intermarriages—those with children who were baptized members of the Christian Church—were released that night.[36]

The Goldberg family lived to the south in Wilmersdorf, a well-to-do section of the city favored by Jews, miles from Rosenstrasse. It took Mr. Goldberg several hours to get there, picking his way through burning streets, collapsing balconies, and shattered glass. A terrible odor of burning and sulfur hung over the city for hours, and people struggled to pull furniture or other belongings from the burning buildings. "At four-thirty the doorbell rang, and there stood my father, covered with dirt and ashes, unshaven, and almost starved," remembered Werner.

On the morning of Tuesday, March 2, German newspapers inveighed shrilly against the British "terror attack" on Berlin. In their reports, following Goebbels's new tactic of confronting the people with the serious situation, the words "sorrow" and "suffering" occur frequently. An editorial by Goebbels exhorts the people to lighten the burdens by sharing them, declaring again that the welfare of the community transcends that of the individual.[37] He promised that Germany would soon deal the enemy a frightful blow and in his diary that day confides: "We are definitively pushing the Jews out of Berlin. They were thrown together in one fell swoop last Sunday and will now be shoved off to the east in short order."[38] Goebbels was away at Obersalzburg, until March 3, and those reporting to him had not yet informed him of the Rosenstrasse Protest. Goebbels's deputy, Leopold Gutterer, said that those in charge had hoped that the courage of the women would fail and that they would grow weary or become intimidated and leave.[39]

Yet neither the police nor failure of courage seemed able to disperse the demanding crowd. Relatives of those imprisoned continued to stream to Rosenstrasse. In the hours after work the crowd grew larger. It swelled and ebbed as people joined and then departed for work or other urgent business. After work hours the crowd peaked. Following the bombing, some of the women climbed onto the ruins of a neighboring bombed-out house, not yet cordoned off, to peer into the upper-story windows. Alfred Schneider, a skinny, boyish barber turned SS man, as a member of the Berlin Gestapo was in charge of overseeing the Jews at Rosenstrasse 2–4 from his office by the entrance on the ground floor.[40] He always wore his SS uniform, slammed doors, shouted orders, and made extra noise with his boots when walking. Now this "pencil, this nobody who wanted to be somebody," as one of the women protesters later described him, tried to order the protesters to go home. Unsuccessful, he retreated to watch the situation from behind the curtains in a café across the street, which was also host to many protesters warming themselves.

On various occasions the guards brandished weapons and ordered the protesters to "clear the streets or we'll shoot." The protesters ran for the shelter of doorways, and some took refuge under the nearby automobile bridge over Spandauerstrasse. But within minutes they began streaming out again and took their places. Again they were scattered when the SS suddenly leveled their guns and shouted, "Get back or we'll shoot!" Again the troops of protesters soon flooded back onto Rosenstrasse. "When they threatened to shoot," Mrs. Weigert remembered, "we ran in separate directions, so that they couldn't get all of us at once or would think that we really went away. But after five or ten minutes we all appeared again, got together, and began calling out, 'We want our husbands!' But only that. We didn't call out anything else." No one knew for sure whether the Gestapo's threat to shoot was directed at them or their imprisoned loved ones, said Weigert. But Gutterer remembered that "the threat was definitely directed against the women."

Since her father's arrest on the first day of the roundup, Ruth Gross, a ten-year-old *Mischling*, had been coming to Rosenstrasse several times each day. Each time she took a small package of bread in case she could somehow get it to her father. "Sometimes an orderly in civilian clothes took a package of bread from us," she recalled. On the street "people came alone and went off alone again in different directions. You went there in the first place just because you had heard the rumor 'They are there!' So you naturally went there and returned there. Did anyone hear anything? Could you meet someone? Can anyone say something or other, were there any reports? Someone called out, and then the others joined into the group, and into the chorus of voices. We thought: We are Aryans, and if we only stand here and we are only women, perhaps they will become fearful. That was not political resistance, but indeed, it was a protest. That was an attempt to achieve something. Because it was always the case that one was never supposed to be very noticeable—always. Conspicuous it certainly was, and had an effect.

"There I discovered my father behind a window. He saw me too and waved with the little note from the little package we had sent him. So he had received it! At the corner was a kiosk, where I always stood, because there I could always watch precisely that window behind which I could occasionally glimpse my father. When we were scattered [by threats that the police would shoot], I could always stay a little longer at that kiosk because the police didn't come from all sides. They didn't want to arouse any extra excitement by driving away the women."[41]

As more learned of it, the protest continued to grow. The Holzers were not part of the "mouth radio" network among Berlin's Jews and intermarried couples, so Elsa turned to Dr. Marlou Droop, the writer she worked for. Droop, the Nazi, was angered about the news of Rudi, her Jewish friend. "As a Nazi party member she felt responsible for all that happened in the state," Elsa said. "And now she couldn't rest. She tried talking to an old family friend, an army officer. 'You can't do anything about that!' he replied. 'Besides, you shouldn't even mention things to do with Jews—or if you do, you can't be caught doing it!' Then Dr. Droop consulted with her Catholic allies since Rudi was a Catholic. When that didn't work, she went to the Gestapo Jewish Desk on Burgstrasse and finally learned that intermarried Jews were interned at Rosenstrasse."

Elsa told her supervisor she would be late for work the next day. Elsa was a dependable employee no one suspected of intermarriage. The supervisor readily agreed. "I thought I would be alone there the first time I went to Rosenstrasse," Elsa recollected. "I wanted to find out what was going on. I didn't necessarily think it would do any good, but I had to go see what was going on. I thought perhaps there would be a house, and maybe he would peer through the window. But as I arrived, I saw a crowd—at six in the morning already! People flowed back and forth. The street was full. This short little street was black with people. They were like a wave, and they moved like a body, a swaying body."

Elsa thought one of the guards would perhaps accept a small package of food for Rudi. Rudi was especially fond of pumpernickel, and she had made a small butter and pumpernickel sandwich. Between the buttered bread she placed a sheet of waxed paper, with her message: "Dear Rudi, all the best. I love you forever, your Elsa." "There was such uncertainty then," Elsa recalled. "I didn't know whether he would be alive tomorrow or not."

After taking stock, Elsa began to look around for a "human face" among the row of police guards who would help her. Some of Berlin's street police had been employed long before the Nazis, at a time when the Berlin police were heavily members of the Social Democratic party. Now a few police guards gave small signs of encouragement to the Jews, and one appeared in the room of Dr. Kurt Radlauer and told the prisoners, "Don't believe that we're in agreement with this."[42] Mrs. Weigert described the guards as "understanding but not sympathetic." As the women continued to define the setting at Rosenstrasse, one Gestapo agent even took a package from Charlotte and agreed to give it to Julius. Charlotte was standing among the crowd when she saw an orderly she recognized, a Mr. Hirschfeld. She ran up to him. Would he take the package to Julius? The man beside Hirschfeld asked her what was in the package. "No knives?" The next day when she approached Hirschfeld again he exclaimed that she must never try such a thing again. "My God, Mrs. Israel," he said, "that was a Gestapo officer accompanying me."

Suddenly Elsa glimpsed their doctor, Dr. Cohn, who lived in their neighborhood, coming through the door. As a medical orderly he could visit the imprisoned Jews and then return home. Elsa ran up to grab his arm. "I nearly fell over when he told me he had seen and talked to Rudi," she said. Elsa was full of questions about how Rudi was doing. She was excited and asked whether he could take something in to Rudi. But Dr. Cohn was afraid and said he was allowed in only as a doctor.

Finally Elsa approached a police guard who had spoken with another woman. "I didn't know whether he would knock me down or lock me up too if I asked a favor," she said. "But I wanted to let my husband know I was there. The policeman made a long face, but he took the sandwich. Then I was dizzy with the thought that Rudi would know I was there," Elsa recollected. "In the midst of all that fear I felt real joy!"

Hilda Elkuss also arrived at Rosenstrasse only several days after her husband, Dieter, had disappeared. She had been in a panic as the Final Roundup had continued ominously throughout Berlin. Dieter's two sisters and two of his aunts had been deported earlier. One had dropped a postcard from a train on the way to Auschwitz, and that had been the last sign of life from her.

Finally, through "mouth radio," Hilda and her friends found out

A love letter Elsa smuggled to her husband, Rudi, in a sandwich, while
he was interned at Rosenstrasse. After the war, Elsa said, Rudi kept the
note in his wallet as a talisman.

that their husbands were at Rosenstrasse. They went there together
after work and saw that "women were promenading." That first day
they had come for information, but the next day she went, Hilda said,
"to accomplish something. We got together in small groups and called
out, 'We'd like to have our husbands back.' We were really quite
courageous. Of course. We belonged to our husbands. It was actually
this feeling that we belonged there and had the right to be there that
motivated us. It wasn't a law, but it was our right." Like other Germans
of her generation, Hilda had grown up with hardly a thought of disobeying the law.

When she was interviewed, she lived in a tidy apartment in Berlin-
Charlottenburg and was still active in an exclusive tennis club. Hilda's
memories of the protest, like her manners, were of actions disciplined
by proper diplomacy. While other German women married to Jews
remembered being screamed at and threatened by Gestapo men urging
them to divorce, Hilda remembered only polite suggestions. The protest
was a cautious effort to influence the Gestapo. "One has to remember
that we too could have been arrested, and it appeared to us to be more
diplomatic to just get together in small groups," she said, "and walk
back and forth, and always we looked up toward the windows and called
out in a chorus. We waved and hoped that they would look out and
see us. That was a real protest, of course. It was a call for help, a

request for consideration. We had to be cautious. We hoped we would achieve something."

Like Hilda, Mrs. Weigert went with her sister-in-law to Rosenstrasse every evening after work. Also like Hilda, she stressed that she was defending her rights, on the street. "We wanted our husbands and had a right to that," she said. "That was out of self-respect, the protest. The Weigert family has always been a decent family, and we've had a certain pride. So of course I had to do something. That I took for granted. Of course they would have been deported if we hadn't asked questions and demonstrated." Then she added, "When a person is in need, a person is also courageous." Elsa too emphasized that "you wouldn't believe what a person in need is capable of."

Each woman wanted her husband back. Several women emphasized that they had been careful only to call out together for their husbands, nothing else. This would have been a key part of any protest strategy for the women, but it is not certain that they instructed one another on this. A couple of eyewitnesses recalled that a single voice called out "We want our husbands," and then on the repeat, the others joined in.[43] "We cried out for our husbands; we had that in common," said Hilda. "We were not in despair yet. That's why we took action." Mrs. Weigert agreed: "We didn't talk a lot at all or make any agreements. We simply all wanted the same thing there, and we felt we had to do something."

Johanna Löwenstein, Hans-Oskar's mother, also remembered the solidarity. "At first it was as if I were paralyzed," she recalled about hearing the news that her husband and son had been interned at Rosenstrasse. "But it was nothing less than a flood of people that poured into the street, and of course I also joined in. It was a feeling of solidarity with one another that drove us on and gave us courage."[44] Standing beside Mrs. Löwenstein among the protesters on Rosenstrasse was her sister, a longtime party member who was the wife of the head mayor of Potsdam and wore the Nazi party golden emblem.[45]

Gad Beck recalled that at Rosenstrasse his mother had "created an entirely new circle of friends that lasted a lifetime. All at once these women could acknowledge their Jewish relatives there—together, openly, on the streets. It was a public confession of family ties—to Jews."[46]

Clou was Berlin's huge, well-loved concert and pleasure hall. Hitler had held his first speech in Berlin there, on May 1, 1927, but most of

the acts were more playful: dancing, concerts, cabaret, burlesque. Just
days before the Final Roundup, Goebbels, as part of the Total War
measure to close unnecessary businesses, had silenced Clou, and now
it became a detention center for Jews captured in the massive Final
Roundup.

On Monday afternoon, March 3, Clou was a theater of brutality.
As the neighborhood looked on, the Gestapo shoved and beat Jews onto
the ubiquitous fleet of trucks. The SS man of the local Berlin Gestapo's
Jewish Desk in charge of this, Sammellager, was eloquently dressed in
a black pinstripe suit, as though attending a cocktail party. Exuding an
air of superior self-regard, he drove the Jews onto trucks with a whip,
crying, "Faster, faster."[47] From there the Jews headed for the freight
station on Quitzowstrasse—and Auschwitz. Under the swing of horsewhips, 1,736 Jews were driven into open cattle cars.[48] Husbands remained separated from wives, mothers from children. Night fell as the
train steamed into the unknown. No one was there to protest for these
Jews, and not one of them could be saved; a consensus of silence
deadened the pangs of conscience.

To help maintain the official secrecy on the true fate of the Jews,
the Gestapo had striven to arrest and deport them in an orderly and
efficient way without attracting public attention. An SS man who witnessed the deportation of Jews from Clou that day objected. He almost
certainly knew about the fate of the Jews and didn't raise his voice
about that. However, he considered the public view of the treatment
of Jews "politically insane." Public brutalities might upset the people
and cause them to question the regime's claim that Jews were being
sent to work camps.

From his editorial office of the SS newspaper, Das Schwarze Korps,
around the corner from Clou on Zimmerstrasse, Hauptsturmführer
Rudolf von der Rissen looked onto the courtyard. "The Jews stormed
as quickly as possible . . . out of Clou and attempted, as fast as possible,
to get on the truck," he reported to Dr. Rudolf Brandt, a high-ranking
member of Himmler's personal staff. "When about half of the Jews
were on (they couldn't have gotten on faster), a civilian, cigarette in
mouth, swinging a huge dog whip, came galloping out of Clou and
beat like a wild man upon the Jews struggling to get on. I must note
that among these Jews were women with small children in their arms.
The view was at once degrading and humiliating.

"[The man] beat especially the women, so much so that a great
howling arose, whereupon the man bellowed up to the surrounding
houses that the windows were to be closed. . . . A man of the Weapon-
SS had apparently taken a thick walking stick from one Jew and also

beat now from his position just as madly upon the Jews, who were already on the truck, although they could go no farther. A police officer with a smaller stick did exactly the same thing.

"Later I received a call from the Stapo [Berlin Gestapo]. . . . There was supposedly someone from that office who had just been there to oversee the matter. In any case he reported that nothing out of order had happened, and he verified that a dog whip lay on the table.

"I might add that during this incident workers and employees stood at all the windows and doors of the tall surrounding buildings, watching. This [is an] impossible and politically nothing other than crazy method of procedure. . . ."[49]

When Dr. Brandt received this telex, he considered it so important he put a copy in his safe. The SS, at a high level, was moved to assess the events in the capital city, home of foreign journalists, embassies, spies—all people who must be shielded from any details of such a treatment of Jews and any signs of dissent among the Germans. Goebbels could no longer be shielded from details.

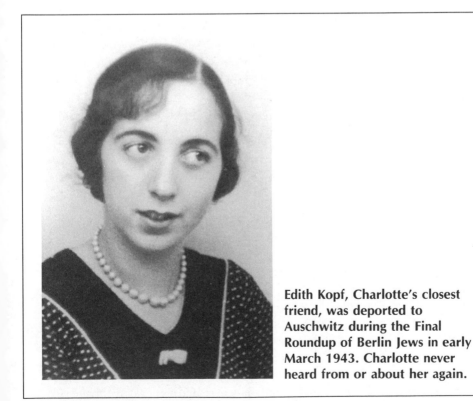

Edith Kopf, Charlotte's closest friend, was deported to Auschwitz during the Final Roundup of Berlin Jews in early March 1943. Charlotte never heard from or about her again.

That day Charlotte Israel went to Clou. She already had her coat on, for as she said, she never removed it, not even at night. She always had to be ready. At home she had received from Edith Kopf, her best friend, a letter that documents the trauma Jews all over Berlin were experiencing, alone.

"Dear Lotte!" Edith began. "Several days ago I tried to call Mother. What's happened to Mama? I am in Clou, Mauerstrasse. Don't have a thing. Send the most necessary—tooth brushes, laundry, etc. My things balcony room. Speak with the nice woman. Bring me please yourself before 7:30, also news of Mother.

"Maybe you can drive by—Aschaffenburgerstrasse 22, Masur, the same for sister-in-law. Come pretty soon, as long as I'm still here. Survived tonight good. Hope you did too. What's Julius doing? (Above all, yarn, needles). Skin cream, mouth water, Band-Aids. All as soon as possible. Much warm thanks, maybe also blankets, pillows, every-thing is there. Eating utensils, plates. Warm kiss. Until we see each other soon, your, Edith."

Charlotte threw together a bundle of what she had and hurried out to Clou, planning to go by Rosenstrasse later. She didn't understand Edith's plea to speak with the "nice woman" but thinks it indicates how Jews hung for hope on Germans who had shown them sympathy. As Charlotte arrived at Clou, she saw huge trucks pulling out, headed for the train station. Perhaps Edith is in there, she thought, on the way to "the east." A guard at the door asked her business and checked his list. "Yes, she has just been taken away," he reported. Then Char-lotte reproached herself for not being there on time. Edith will have thought that I wasn't loyal to her in her last moment, she mourned desperately.

By March 4 the local Berlin Gestapo was acting with force and terror. Criminal Adviser August Schiffer, Walter Stock's superior at the Berlin Gestapo and the third and middle-ranking of three executives in charge of the day-to-day operations of the Final Roundup, reportedly ordered the deportation of some Jews, while brutally torturing one who at-tempted escape. The same day the regime executed the remaining members of the Herbert Baum Group, some of whom were personally acquainted with or related to the families of those protesting at Ro-senstrasse.[50] These resisters, arrested in May 1942 for destroying a Nazi exhibit deriding communism, were executed in Plötzensee, a Ber-lin prison renowned as the site of Nazi torture and death.

The previous day the Gestapo had arrested several intermarried

Jews who were prominent intellectuals. At least one or two of them lived in a privileged intermarriage, which should have protected them during the Final Roundup, but the regime had a particular hatred for anyone who might think independently and shape public opinion. Among the intellectuals taken was Dr. Arenberg, a former employee of the Prussian parliament (Landtagsstenograph), the free-lance writer Wolf, the father of Edith Wolf, and the Jewish poet Arthur Silbergleit. Silbergleit, having heard of the Final Roundup, had just broken his own arm, in hope that this would provide the medical certificate needed to get an exemption from the deportations. The arm was still in a cast.[51] Mr. Wolf, who had lived in the same house with the writer Kurt Tucholsky, had temporarily edited the anti-Zionist newspaper *Toleranz* and had never been able to decide to leave Germany, even under Hitler. Like Silbergleit, Wolf was arrested at home and hauled off to Grosse Hamburger Strasse.

Dr. Arenberg was a courageous man who had helped Jews to safety

Criminal Adviser August Schiffer, Walter Stock's superior at the Berlin Gestapo, who, along with Stock and Rolf Günther, was in charge of the day-to-day operations of the Final Roundup.

August Schiffer and his wife as newlyweds.

by furnishing them with false passports but had stayed on to help others. In the Grosse Hamburger detention center he shared a three-by-four-square-yard space with about thirty-five others. From the first day of the Final Roundup Jews and their pursuers had come and gone continuously. Trucks rolled up, "cries like battle commands" rang out, and hundreds of the Gestapo's victims poured in or were hurried out. Gestapo men strode importantly, dutifully, in and out. Amid the confusion Arenberg decided to attempt escape. Slouching over and scrunching his hat down over his face, he sauntered out the door behind a row of three Gestapo officers, past the entry guards, who checked the identification of all those coming and going, and bolted.

When he got the news, Schiffer was beside himself with rage. He called Felix Lachmuth, the Gestapo's Jewish Desk officer in charge of the Grosse Hamburger center. If Dr. Arenberg was not back in custody by midnight, Lachmuth would be sent to a concentration camp, Schiffer warned. Furthermore, ten randomly chosen Jewish orderlies would be shot in the courtyard of the building. Lachmuth slumped out of his room white as a corpse and related this to the Jewish orderlies in sobs. The Gestapo men and their Jewish orderlies were immediately dispatched in teams of two, and one caught Dr. Arenberg shortly before midnight at a distant Berlin train station, Berlin-Grünau, trying to get out of town.

Arenberg was taken that night to an "interrogation." It was led by Schiffer, who in a Posen prison, in the first year of the war, had killed five priests. First he had shot them in their stomachs with his service pistol so that they screamed horribly, and then, as they writhed in agony and begged him for a "mercy shot," he had shot them all again, one by one, in their buttocks. This he had confessed in a "sobbing voice" while drunk in a bar, claiming "that he nevertheless could never kill children, but indeed, it had to be, because the future avengers had to be wiped out."

A Jewish orderly who saw Dr. Arenberg after Schiffer's interrogation the next morning said that what he saw of the doctor was not capable of being described with human words. Mouth, nose, eyes were no longer to be perceived. Both arms were broken, a leg had been pulled out of its joint, and his whole body wounded from a machine that had whipped him for hours during the night, after the Gestapo had exhausted themselves from the torture and retired to bed. The Gestapo explained that they wanted to make him "understand," Dr. Arenberg told this witness in tortured speech. Dr. Arenberg's tormentors sent him on a stretcher to the gas chambers and ovens of Auschwitz. There are things considerably worse than death. Who, knowing where it would lead, would have the courage to take the course of Dr. Arenberg?

On March 4 the Gestapo deported thirteen Jewish men in inter-marriages from Grosse Hamburger Strasse and five Jewish women from Rosenstrasse to Auschwitz. The intermarried intellectuals too were deported, and like the five women accused of treason, they were never seen in Berlin again.[52] One of the women deported was accused of throwing a treasonous note from her window.[53] Erika Lewine reported that Scharführer Alfred Schneider appeared at the door of their room, assumed a military bearing, and shouted: "I would like to know which one of you threw that treasonous note out the window! If I don't get five volunteers, then I will select them myself." The windows had been nailed shut, so everyone knew this was an outrageous accusation. "But one had to remain absolutely quiet, or you were nailed," said Erika.

By March 4 the Jews who had been taken from Clou the day before had arrived in Auschwitz. On that day in Auschwitz, Obersturmbahn-führer Maurer reminded Auschwitz Commandant Rudolf Höss that these Jews had been employed in the war industry and would be employable at Auschwitz. The arriving Jews were thus brought not to the crematorium but instead to the Auschwitz plant of I. G. Farben, the most powerful business conglomerate of the Third Reich. Farben had permission to fill its labor needs from the arriving Berlin transports, but Obersturmführer Schwarz was not impressed. Only 632 were men, Schwarz complained, and most of the 918 women and children had to be given "special treatment": They were immediately gassed and burned. At Auschwitz the SS main office for economic administration (WVHA) was expecting 15,000 Jews to arrive from Berlin; approximately 8,000 Berlin Jews did arrive, but intermarried Jews and *Mischlinge* were about to be "temporarily deferred" from deportations once again.[54]

The RSHA apparently experienced the protest as a challenge to its power, but Goebbels could see that the women were attempting to keep their families together rather than calling for the collapse of the regime. He was keenly attuned to the politics of women, as well as to that of crowds (some men were among the protesters, but the drive to protest clearly came from the intermarried women, who made up the vast majority there). Even though Goebbels had argued that women should work, he had just rejected proposals to increase cigarette rations for men on the front by reducing cigarettes apportioned to women. "Women's political hatred," Hitler said later in 1944, "is extremely dangerous."[55]

By the time of the protest, reports were abundant that hundreds of thousands of women were simply disobeying or cleverly evading Hitler's Total War decree that ordered them to register for work. The war in combination with Nazism's peculiar mass movement politics and fear of social unrest added weight to any dissent or protest by women. The regime had expanded the political role of women, with conscriptions that left them dominating the home front more than ever, and it relied on them for work. Ominously, defeatism was setting in among Germans after Stalingrad and so much war. For Goebbels the protest represented additional evidence of dissent, a public display that might be seen as indicating an early failure of Total War. The effort to break up intermarriages affected only tens of thousands of Germans, but it caused a public show of opposition when thousands of other women were disregarding Hitler's Total War decree.

Nevertheless, had there been no protest on Rosenstrasse, the Gestapo would have kept on arresting and deporting Jews until perhaps even Eichmann's most radical plans had been fulfilled. Differences existed between Eichmann's office and the leadership on the importance of maintaining social quiescence, during deportations, but this would not have mattered if protests during the Final Roundup had not arisen. Power plays surrounding decision making on intermarried Jews and *Mischlinge* do not so much explain the survival of these Jews as point to the regime's fear of unrest. There would have been no hesitation and no conflict among officials had intermarried Germans cooperated fully with Nazi racial aims. It was, after all, the aggregate noncompliance of intermarried Germans that had caused the leadership to order the "deferment" of intermarried Jews and *Mischlinge* in 1941 despite the RSHA. It was the recalcitrance of intermarried Germans that had made a real issue out of the different positions of the top leadership and the RSHA on the importance of social quiescence in the first place, and it was their protest in 1943 that soon caused Goebbels to revert to the position of temporarily deferring these problem cases.

On or about March 5 the Gestapo took new measures to end the protest. Officers forcibly removed about ten women protesters, and a vehicle was used to disperse the crowd. One of the women forcibly removed reported: "We were escorted single file by the Gestapo to the Labor Bureau, where we peeled potatoes all day and then were released."[56] But those who saw them leave feared for them. "Where these women were taken we didn't know," said Charlotte. "And after that I hung back a little in the crowd. Otherwise I could have been taken too, and then I wouldn't have been able to help my husband either."

Elsa was there when an open jeeplike vehicle drove up to the edge of the crowd. "Two SS men were sitting in front, and two in back," she said, "in black uniforms and steel helmets. The two in back stood up, and I saw that they had machine guns. 'Clear the streets now or we'll shoot,' they cried. And at that moment the truck started toward us. Not slowly either! At the same time I heard a rattle—tat-tat-tat-tat-tat! We ran like wild. Everyone tried to take shelter inside the courtyards of the nearby houses. But they were all locked. The Gestapo had locked us out. The people at the doorways were nearly smashed flat by those pushing from behind. Who wanted to get shot? First we wanted to free our husbands!"

By their insistence the Germans protesting at Rosenstrasse redefined the image of what was occurring. Elsa sensed that she was part of a force that was gaining confidence. She had originally come there for information, but by now, she said, she hoped to have an effect on the fate of her husband. "We expected that our husbands would return home and that they wouldn't be sent to the camps," she said. She understood her action as an ethical, influential act, one she could not escape. "We acted from the heart, and look what happened," she said. "If you had to calculate whether you would do any good by protesting, you wouldn't have gone. But we acted from the heart. We wanted to show that we weren't willing to let them go. What one is capable of doing when there is danger can never be repeated. I'm not a fighter by nature. Only when I have to be. I did what was given me to do. When my husband needed my protection, I protected him. I went to Rosenstrasse every day before work. And there was always a flood of people there. It wasn't organized or instigated. Everyone was simply there. Exactly like me. That's what is so wonderful about it."

Dr. Droop had been to Gestapo offices for Elsa, but many of the women who protested also went directly to the Gestapo to seek the release of their loved ones. Charlotte went repeatedly to the Judenreferat of the Berlin Gestapo on Burgstrasse, after she had gathered courage from the protest on the street. "I went to every office to get him released," she said. "I said, 'You won't really be able to get much out of him. Earlier he played music, and you won't really need that, I guess.' The Gestapo men always threw me out. Well, what else could I have expected?"

Hilda actually entered the Rosenstrasse building—the "den of lions," as she called it. She wanted to find out if her husband was there, and a guard took her in as he checked his list. Dieter was there, and the guard agreed that Hilda could bring a small package for him the next day. "The guard was cool but not unfriendly," she said. "The next day I waited on the first floor as the guard called my husband downstairs, and I gave him the things. What a terrible moment. I had just enough time to give it to him and say a word or two. But at least I knew he was still alive. Whether I would see him again, no one knew. It was dangerous to go into that den of lions."

Mrs. Weigert too went after her husband, into the heart of the Nazi terror system. "At Burgstrasse I spoke with a Führer—in uniform. I was pretty much together, quite calm, not at all rebellious. I spoke to him, he answered, and if he had a question for me, I answered him. And then I also went to Kurfürstenstrasse 116 [Eichmann's office]. All of them told me, 'Developments will be unfolding', or 'We don't know.' So I had to go again. What could I do there?"

Hannah Herzberg was married to Erich, a shoemaker who was one of the intermarried Jews deported to Auschwitz on March 4. The Gestapo of course did not tell her this. When she began inquiring, some officials rebuked her, saying, "Get divorced, and then you'll be rid of the whole can of worms. You'll find another man." Several days after she had last seen Erich, she received a postcard from him. He was on his way to Auschwitz when he managed to toss a postcard out the window in Silesia. "He wrote 'I'm on the way to the east. Chin up.' And then there was another note: 'Request finder to please send this card!'"

With the card Hannah went to the Gestapo offices on Burgstrasse. "I was led to an elderly man on the top floor and told him my story," Hannah said. "'That's not possible!' he replied. 'If your husband lives in an intermarriage, he hasn't been deported.'" The Gestapo also told other women who said that their husbands had been deported from Rosenstrasse that this was not possible. Hannah, however, had the postcard from her husband as evidence. "I laid the card in front of him on the table and said, 'Take a look at this, please,'" she said. "He read the card and in a very official tone said, 'I'd like to know who forwarded this mail!' I said to him, 'People!' He screamed at me, 'Do you mean to say that we too are not people?'"

By midweek Elsa had been late so many consecutive days that her supervisor turned angry and threatening. Elsa had been a model employee for Siemens, "and when someone else was missing, I was always there to help. But after I was late three or four days, my supervisor was mad. But the fact is I only wanted to be there where my husband was." Like Werner and others, Elsa had had to make herself useful to the regime, in order to help her family survive it, but now she was putting her job in jeopardy. To explain why she had been late so often, she finally broke down and told her boss, "I'm looking for my husband, and as a Jew he was arrested."

"He just about fell over when he heard that," Elsa remembered.

"No one knew. At Siemens all intermarried Germans had been expelled. 'Mrs. Holzer,' he said to me, looking pale, 'you haven't told me anything, please. You haven't told me anything. Otherwise I am obligated to inform the director's office. Go as often as you like, but you have to say that you didn't tell me about it.' "

On March 6, in fulfillment of Eichmann's plans, the Berlin Gestapo continued to arrest intermarried Jews, and falling back on Goebbels's plan from late 1942, they also deported twenty-five intermarried Jews without children from Rosenstrasse.[57] One of the men, Kurt Blaustein, recalled noticing or discussing at the time the fact that none of them had children.[58] Another Jew taken that day was Ferdinand Wolff, a Jewish musician. He had been forced out of his profession in 1935, when Goebbels threw all Jews out of the Reich Music Chamber, and since 1941 he had been doing forced heavy labor in construction.[59] On Wolff's seventh day in Rosenstrasse, the Gestapo made a roll call. He and twenty-four others had been singled out for a work detail, Jewish Desk director Walter Stock explained. All twenty-five were taken in the back of a canvas-covered truck to the Putlitzstrasse freight train station, which was cordoned off by officers in uniform.

"We knew by the way we were handled that little or no care was or would be taken for us and that nothing good was planned for us," Blaustein, one of those deported on March 6, remembered.[60] Asked where they were being taken and whether they could tell their wives, Stock told them, "You are going where you will never see your wives again!" By this time many of the relatives of these surviving intermarried Jews had been deported, never to be heard from again. In 1938 Wolff's brother had been arrested during Kristallnacht and taken to the camp at Sachsenhausen, where he died. Another of these twenty-five men, a former businessman, had lost his parents and his sister and nephew in a deportation to Riga in January 1942. "Don't expect to see them anymore," he had been told by a former customer, a soldier who was on vacation after serving in Riga.[61]

At the station, three SS men directed the 25 onto the train, which was already full, and then stepped in as the traveling command unit. They were headed to Auschwitz, along with 665 other Jews. Some managed to throw scribbled notes addressed to their wives out of the train, hoping some kindly person would put them in the mail. Ferdinand Wolff's wife, prevailing against Criminal Commissioner Walter Stock to find out what had happened to her husband, was shown documents that indicated her husband had been taken into protective custody.[62]

Since the beginning of the Final Roundup 7,031 Jews had been deported to Auschwitz.

Günter Grodka was at home that day when the Gestapo arrested him and trucked him off to Grosse Hamburger Strasse. With the Rosenstrasse collection center overflowing, and the one in Grosse Hamburger mostly emptied following deportations there, newly arrested Jews in intermarriages and the *Geltungsjuden* were interned at Grosse Hamburger. The Gestapo was apparently planning a new wave of arrests: They required Günter Grodka to give the names and addresss of five other intermarried Jews living in Berlin. To the Gestapo's frustration, however, German relatives of the Jews at Grosse Hamburger Strasse began streaming into that street there, demanding the release of their loved ones. Wider arrests caused wider protests.[63]

New food ration cards were issued that day, and the Gestapo even arrested all Jews who appeared to renew their ration cards. Rita Kuhn was a witness. Her mother usually picked up the family's ration cards at the ration center in the local schoolhouse. On this day Mrs. Kuhn was told that her husband and *Mischling* daughter would have to pick up their own cards. When they all returned together, the Gestapo unceremoniously locked Rita and Mr. Kuhn in one of the schoolrooms. Throughout the day the Gestapo kept pushing more and more Jews into the room with them. "You can't have my husband and little girl!" Rita heard her mother screaming outside. Mrs. Kuhn was still there in the evening, when the Jews were led out to the Gestapo truck, en route to Rosenstrasse.[64]

At another ration card distribution center on Knesebeckstrasse Wally Grodka noticed that two Gestapo officers posted themselves by each exit. "Anyone with an identity card marked with a *J* receives no food ration cards and is taken into custody by the officers at the door," she wrote in her diary. "It is horrible to have to see all of this without being able to help in the least, to hear the despairing sobbing and screaming of mothers whose children wait at home. There is no turning back—no one is allowed out. The food ration cards are, so to speak, a license to freedom. Apprehension was in the air. The clerks avert their gaze."[65]

At home further trauma awaited Wally. "Two officers are there to pick up my husband. I make an effort to be chipper. I send a spoon, blanket, and something to eat along." Within hours she discovered that her husband was being held at Grosse Hamburger and went straight there. "There are already many, many there—hundreds, men and women," she wrote. "They wait on the street in front of the entrance. I join in with the many other women passing to and fro; we are scattered: the guard approaches us and says, 'Go away or we will shoot'; then we ran, pushed ourselves into the entrances of the various houses there along the street. And yes, indeed, within a few minutes we gather ourselves together again in front of the entryway. Carefully my searching gaze travels along the row of windows, and all at once I see him behind the bars—because he is a Jew. Our glance meets only for a second because they will shoot if someone appears at the window."

It had been six days since Charlotte had seen her husband and taken off her coat. On this day, Charlotte remembered, it was so cold that the tears froze on her face. Once again she stood with her fifteen-year-old brother, Günther, in front of the house where her husband was imprisoned.

On this day, she said, the street was "dark with a sea of heads, a thousand people. I went there every day, and each day there were more and more."[66] The protest had grown to include people who did not have imprisoned relatives, and as Charlotte remembered it, it also took on a more clearly political and anti-Nazi tone that day, as protesters screamed out, "You murderers," and not just, "Give us our husbands." "The situation in front of the collecting center came to a head. Without warning the guards began setting up machine guns. Then they directed them at the crowd and shouted: 'If you don't go now, we'll shoot.' Automatically the movement surged backward in that instant. But then for the first time we really hollered. Now we couldn't care less. We bellowed, 'You murderers,' and everything else that one can holler. Now they're going to shoot in any case, so now we'll yell too, we thought. We yelled 'Murderer, murderer, murderer, murderer.' We didn't scream just once but again and again, until we lost our breath. Then I saw a man in the foreground open his mouth wide—as if to give a command. It was drowned out. I couldn't hear it. But then they cleared everything away. There was silence. Only an occasional swallow could be heard."

RETURN

On March 6 Goebbels gave orders for the release of intermarried Jews and *Mischlinge*. "I will commission the security police not to continue the Jewish evacuations in a systematic manner during such a critical time," he wrote (referring primarily to the defeat at Stalingrad). "We want to rather spare that for ourselves until after a few weeks; then we can carry it out that much more thoroughly." Goebbels complained that the RSHA was a loyal bureaucracy, good at following orders but incapable of adapting to changing circumstances with quick tactical maneuvers. "One has to intervene all over the place, to ward off damages," he wrote about the RSHA's notions of deporting the Jews despite the protest. "The efforts of certain offices are so lacking in political savvy that one cannot let them operate on their own for ten minutes."[67] On April 1, 1943, the American Legation in Bern sent this dispatch to Washington: "Action against Jewish wives and husbands on the part of the Gestapo . . . had to be discontinued some time ago because of the protest which such action aroused."[68]

Goebbels justified releasing the Jews with an excuse about timing. But he released the Jews married to non-Jews because it was the best way to dissolve the protest, said Leopold Gutterer, who in 1943 as Goebbels's chief deputy and representative at the Propaganda Ministry virtually lived at the ministry. "Goebbels released the Jews in order to eliminate the protest from the world," Gutterer said. "That was the simplest solution: to eradicate completely the reason for the protest. Then it wouldn't make sense to protest anymore. So that others didn't take a lesson from [the protest], so that others didn't begin to do the same, the reason [for protest] had to be eliminated. There was unrest, and it could have spread from neighborhood to neighborhood. . . . Why should Goebbels have had them [the protesters] all arrested?" Then he would have only had even more unrest, from the relatives of these newly arrested persons."[69] Nevertheless, according to Gutterer, "every" option of police state force had been a possibility. "They had to reckon at least with being arrested. It would have been no problem to find out who was there; the police could have gone through and demanded identification. They could have been sent to jail, at least, or to a concentration camp. All means could have been used against them."

Gutterer, who claimed National Socialism had wanted to do good until the war drove Hitler mad, recalled that "these women were as persons there. Anyone could recognize who they were. They demonstrated openly and risked their existence [Dasein]. They were very courageous, yes? No doubt about that. . . . But if one or the other [of the protesters] had had a pistol along, then the police would have had to shoot. Of course there was an investigation to find out whether someone was instigating this. But nothing was found. If so, one could have hindered it. [The protest] wasn't organized but spread by word of mouth. It was a spontaneous reaction. A protest against the system never existed. These women didn't want a revolution. They simply couldn't understand. What's going on? What's this supposed to mean? Why? For what reason?"[70]

For Elsa, the quality of the protest arose from the fact that each person acted from the heart rather than on calculations or outside instructions. Gutterer also described the open, public quality of the protest, in contrast with a conspiratorial action, as part of its strength. But the real strength of the protest was that many persons were so deeply motivated to protest that they risked their lives even though there was no central organization or creed. Elsa Holzer said that putting her life at stake was possible only because the protest came from her heart, yet it was the crowd that held her there and kept her coming back. Mass protest erupted, without organization, because the regime attacked an important tradition. Germans could sympathize with persons trying to preserve their families. Spouses were expected to look out for each other, and women traditionally had special jurisdiction in this area. Goebbels realized he could not murder all the people he wanted to murder—the Jewish relatives, spouses, sympathizers. At some point the Germans would have begun to identify with one another rather than with a government that kept demanding ever more human victims.

Goebbels feared that Germans, angered by forced deportations of their partners and children, would begin to question and complain. Unrest about the fate of the Jews could severely hinder the domestic social unity necessary for fighting the war. A parallel development was the increasing need for secrecy around the Final Solution, the revelation of which would have damaged the public morale that the regime strove to nurture, especially during war. A public discussion about the fate of the deported Jews threatened to disclose the Final Solution and thus endanger that entire effort.[71] Goebbels could control the press, but public protests openly communicated that the seamless popular unity he claimed existed only in propaganda. The protesters were communicating dissent about the core of Nazi ideology and might soon be raising questions about the fate of the Jews, a taboo subject.

After the protest the foreign press carried reports that German morale was low and that Germans were deserting the Nazi party. There were related reports and rumors about Germans protesting. Following his pattern of turning the truth inside out for propaganda purposes, Goebbels instructed his deputies to respond to these reports and rumors with the assertion that the "ten thousands" on the street at the time of the protest had been bombed out by the British Air Force! He claimed the people had turned out by the thousands to contribute to a Nazi party street collection on March 3, a collection that had registered a 70 percent increase over the previous year's collection despite the homeless state of the thousands milling about on the street.[72]

The crowd of women who cried out in a chorus for their husbands could not be readily identified as enemies of the state, and to Hitler they were a spectacle summoning up his fear of the protesting domestic crowds whom he accused of having stabbed Germany in the back during World War I. Especially when the German mood was so volatile, the National Socialist theory that popular support was the primary basis of political power established limits on the use of force against a crowd of unarmed Germans. When Goebbels visited the Führer in his *Wolfschanze* (wolf's lair) on March 9, the Führer agreed that Goebbels had responded correctly to the "psychological" pressures of the protest.[73] He told Goebbels he had done the right thing, but that he would still have to make sure the Jews of Berlin "disappeared," Gutterer explained. By March 9 the overwhelming majority of Berlin's remaining Jewish population lived in intermarriage. What Hitler said remained important. He also generally trusted the party gauleiters to govern in their regions, especially Goebbels. "I have never regretted giving him the powers he asked for," he wrote of Goebbels. "In the literal sense of the word, he conquered Berlin."[74] Goebbels rationalized in his diary that he would carry out the deportations within several weeks more thoroughly.

In Berlin, however, where half the intermarried Jews lived, it was not easy to solve the intermarriage problem. Relative to other parts of Germany, support for Nazism in Berlin was not deep, and the party leadership felt somewhat insecure there. In Munich, for example, support for Nazism ran deeper and stronger, and the party leader for Munich, Paul Giesler, would not have worried about tactfulness and popular opinion the way Goebbels did. Gutterer emphasized that the Rosenstrasse Protest could have happened only in Berlin. "That [protest] was only possible in a large city, where many people lived together, whether Jewish or not," Gutterer said. "In Berlin were also representatives of the international press, who immediately grabbed hold of something like this, to loudly proclaim it. Thus news of the protest would travel from one person to the next."

Although there are reports that individuals contacted Goering (or his wife and personal adviser Erich Gritzbach), the release of intermarried Jews cannot be ascribed to this personal, special influence. Goering, Goebbels, and Hitler each personally protected Jews from deportations. In Berlin alone there were one to two hundred of these so-called *Schutzjuden* (protected Jews). The complaints of the few soldiers or influential people affected by the Final Roundup could have been quietly assuaged by the quick addition of their few relatives to this *Schutzjuden* list. There were scattered complaints by church officials, as well as by entrepreneurs, who tried to save Jews for work. Yet these complaints were greatly encouraged, if not completely generated, by the courageous example of open protest on the street. Unlike church officials and entrepreneurs, the intermarried Germans had already had a long record showing they would do everything to protect their family members, including standing in the way with their lives. A letter from a church official here or there or a request from an entrepreneur had virtually no force at all compared with a unified and, above all, public action by Germans who had already shown how much they cared, and thus how much unrest they might cause, should their relatives be deported. Hitler and Goebbels feared protests from the church and Germans related to Jews, but at Rosenstrasse it was not church but popular protests that stayed deportations.

In fact during the Final Roundup factory owners and the military also protested the precipitous disappearance of their Jewish employees, who, working for their lives, had often had excellent records of production. According to the Jewish orderly Max Reschke, charged with overseeing the Jewish staff of workers at Grosse Hamburger Strasse, entrepreneurs and factory foremen appeared at the collection center to show that they had the authorization to employ individual Jews. The Gestapo received "work letters showing military authorizations. . . . From military industrial factories, private firms, and also from the military itself came protests, all with the aim of getting their Jewish workers released again," Reschke reported. "Dobberke [the Gestapo man in charge of the main predeportation detention center in Berlin] took all the work books and the protests into account. They didn't do a bit of good."[75] Like industry, the German military had also made a vain effort to save some of its Jews. In early 1942 the military had prevailed upon the RSHA to deport Jews who had been decorated for their service in World War I to the ghetto at Theresienstadt instead of to one of the death camps. The regime, however, deported these Jews with a military service record from Theresienstadt to Auschwitz.[76] The objections neither of the military nor of the industrialists rescued Jews. But a public protest did rescue them.

Goering's opinion on Rosenstrasse, given his low estimation in Hitler's eyes at the time, would not have mattered so much, but Himmler could have understood. Although he urgently wanted to complete the Final Solution, Himmler, the onetime Nazi party propagandist, would bend ideals for position, and he was somewhat sympathetic to

Hitler's careful attention to social unrest (although he intensely disliked Goebbels).[77] Himmler "felt the pulse of the German people," and to prevent unrest against the Euthanasia murders, he had proposed they be postponed until the public had been educated to accept them.[78] On December 18, 1943, he was to order the deportation of a group of intermarried Jews whose German partners had died or divorced, with the notable exception of formerly intermarried Jews with a child or children who might stir up unrest as a result.[79]

Rosenstrasse was not the first time Himmler and Hitler were willing to compromise principles to maintain power. In late 1942 Himmler had proposed releasing some ten thousand Jews with relatives in the United States in exchange for ransom payments, and Hitler had approved, on condition that it brought in large amounts of foreign exchange. Himmler and Hitler's willingness to exchange Jews for payment indicates that they would compromise the genocide and their ideology, at least if this seemed to help in a critical wartime situation and if the numbers of Jews to be exempted were relatively small.[80] On the other hand, it is conceivable that Hitler might have agreed to exchange twenty thousand Jews for two times as much if it were to ensure military victory or that under pressure the regime might have made concessions larger than the seventeen hundred persons released following the Rosenstrasse Protest in early 1943.

After he ordered the Jews released, Goebbels had to decide what lies to tell in order to hide the fact that a protest had happened and to put him and the leadership in the best light. At the Interior Ministry, where there had been some opposition to the deportation of Mischlinge, officials claimed credit for saving Jews,[81] and even lowly Karl Krell, the unemployed baker turned Gestapo agent for Berlin's Jewish Desk, claimed at his denazification trial after the war that he had ordered the release of two thousand intermarried Jews.[82]

But following the release, the official explanation was that the Berlin Gestapo had abused its power by arresting and deporting persons from German-Jewish families.[83] The leadership and even the RSHA denied responsibility. Given that there was an abuse, there had to be an offender, and the blame was shifted all the way down to Berlin Gestapo Director Schiffer, who oversaw the Jewish Desk. Schiffer was transferred as a reprisal for abusing his power.[84] But if there had been no protest, Schiffer or his superiors would have been roundly rewarded for clearing Berlin of Jews who had caused the leadership so much trouble. Individual Germans inquiring about their deported family members probably still would have been told that the deportation was the work of this or that unruly underling but that (unfortunately) it was now a fact that couldn't be changed. This was the excuse the RSHA had given Jewish authorities when they protested the deportations from Stettin in February 1940.[85]

After all, Goebbels (who had written that Germans married to Jews should also be deported)[86] did not complain about the deportations but only about their timing, rationalizing that he would do a more thorough job of cleaning up in a few weeks.[87] On the same day Goebbels excoriated the SD (the term to designate those in the Reich Security Main Office who made decisions about the deportations) for inflexibly proceeding to follow their orders for deporting Jews despite the protest. "The fundamental malady of our leadership and above all of our administration consists in operating according to Schema F [bureaucratically]," he wrote. "One has the impression that these people, who carry out this or that measure, don't reflect a wit, but rather hang to the written word, whose main value to them is that they thus have their actions covered by orders from above." Confirming Goebbels's hint that the RSHA had received orders from above, Gutterer remembered that "the SD did indeed have an order from Himmler and wanted to carry it out. . . . Goebbels wasn't against it, but he thought that doing it at the moment was foolish."[88] In his postwar trial the director of the Berlin Jewish Desk, Walter Stock, testified that he had deported intermarried Jews on orders of the RSHA.[89] Everyone was shifting the blame around, but Stock's testimony (in self-justification) corresponds with evidence.

At Rosenstrasse the Gestapo immediately began to release Jews, threatening that they would be back very soon. Still, some of the Jews believed they had a new lease on life. Gerhard Braun remembered that one day the Gestapo commanded them to go to the courtyard for a roll call. Uniformed Gestapo men began to torment them with threats. Then they told the Jews to get their things, and the Jews were officially released. "I had to pick up my papers at my old place of work," said Gerhard, "because I was given new work orders for another job. On the way there an old, old woman recognized me as a Jew. There on the open street this woman hugged me, saying something like 'How nice it is that you're here again, young man.' There were such signs of sympathy in Berlin."

Like Gerhard, none of the Jews released returned to their former jobs. "When I left that house, equipped with my official release note and instructions to appear again at the work office for a new job, my wife and both daughters were there, expecting me." Ernst Bukofzer smiled. "They had already been there for hours, patiently sticking it out, and led me home, glowing with happiness. I was exhausted, as if a heavy burden had fallen from my shoulders. There had indeed been hours when I had not expected to return once again to the circle of family.

"Having reached home at last, I had above all the need for a warm bath because I looked like a pig—as one says in good German. It was, however, not so simple to get a good bath because warm water, because of the dearth of coal, was turned off. Every bit of water had to be heated on the stove. But indeed, the friends in our apartment house had already got news of my return and had carried affectionately and

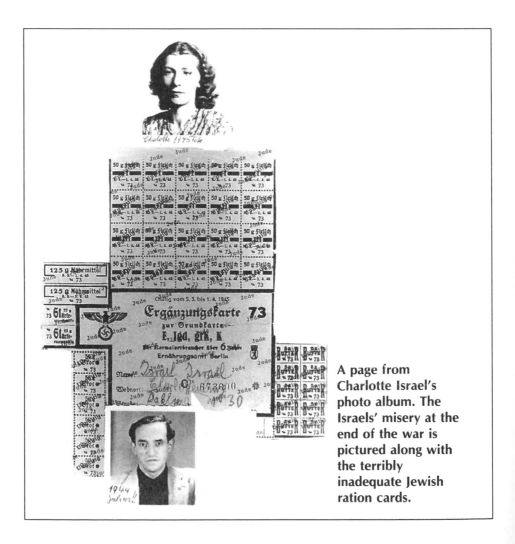

A page from Charlotte Israel's photo album. The Israels' misery at the end of the war is pictured along with the terribly inadequate Jewish ration cards.

cleverly in advance huge vessels of boiling water to us, so that we succeeded in filling the bathtub. Of course I was extremely moved by this show of concern from my Aryan fellow citizens. This bath filled me with a particular sense of comforting feelings."

"Jewish pig, we'll have you in here again soon," one Gestapo man told Charlotte's husband, Julius, as he was released. At home Charlotte had received a note the day before from a Jewish orderly that said her husband would be released the following day. "My brother, Günther, lived in the neighboring street with my mother and came over with a cake," said Charlotte. "And then he wanted to stay there too until my husband came. Well, I didn't want that. I said, 'Go home, Günther.'

" 'No,' he said. 'I was always there in Rosenstrasse, and I want to greet him too.' Then he waited, and my husband didn't come, he didn't come, he didn't come, and then my little brother asked: 'Can I play music?' And I said, 'What will he think if we're playing music here?' 'Okay,' he said, 'then I will play something sad.' And then he put on a record, that I will never forget, from Zarah Leander: 'I know that one day a miracle will happen, and then a thousand fairy tales will come true.' And that was for me a miracle that he returned.

"He was totally sick. He was sick to his soul and smelled horrible. He cried constantly. Cried constantly. 'In that camp one is less than a louse,' he said. 'They take away every ounce of strength.' At the Charlottenburg train station he tarried long enough to shave. He hadn't shaved at Rosenstrasse. Now he was spattered with shaving cream. He absolutely wanted to shave because he was so dark-haired. And hairy. Whenever he wasn't shaved, he said something like 'I absolutely have to get to the barber. I look just like a Jew!'

"Oh, I was so happy that he was there, because for me it was like a present. And I asked him, 'What would you like first?' He said, 'First a bath.' Then I said, 'What would you like to eat? I have everything good here—cake, coffee, meat.' Then he said, 'I want to get a bath, then go directly into bed, and from there I'll have coffee and cake!' When the men came out of Rosenstrasse, I told my husband, 'Now we'll celebrate! We'll make special request concerts and invite friends.' My husband was always agreeable on such matters! And then we thought, Why only one time? One can always celebrate. We were young. And we got together with others Julius had gotten to know in Rosenstrasse.

"At these festive afternoons, there were usually about four pairs. That always happened over malt coffee and oat flake cookies. Without sugar and fat. It was all wonderful because everyone was hungry. Also a nice pudding, so the bread would have some taste. These 'request concerts' were nice; they are for many certainly still a memory. But from this moment on I was on guard. I never again left my husband alone—never. And it wasn't even yet over, the Nazi period. It went on and on, and we still had to survive."

Rudi returned home on March 8. "He looked like a robber, filthy and with a beard so dark it was blue," Elsa recalled. "Of course he told me about finding the note in his sandwich. He did receive that sandwich," she says happily, almost triumphantly. "He always kept that note in his wallet. This little note, the one all fat with cheese and butter, became his talisman."

Upon arriving in Auschwitz, the twenty-five Jews from Rosenstrasse had been immediately sorted out from the others. They were not subjected to the "selection" process determining which Jews were

---

Rudi Holzer's release certificate from Rosenstrasse, signed March 8, 1943. Each of the released Jews received a similar certificate. Considering the severe bombing in Berlin at the time, these certificates testify to German orderliness (note that "the Jewess" has been crossed out in order to identify Rudi as "a Jew" and that his profession is listed below a line noting that he was not given food rations at the time of his release).

Der Jude   H o l z e r , Rudolf Israel
XXXXXXXXX

geboren am 14.10.98 St. Johann   wohnhaft Berlin – Britz,
                                              Bürgerstrasse 28.

wurde am 8.3.43   aus dem Sammellager Rosenstraße 2-4
                              Anruf: 41 67 11

entlassen.

        Es wurden ihm/ihr keine Lebensmittelkarten ausgefolgt
        ----

Buchdrucker/Schweizerdegen.

put to work and which to death. The telex report of March 8 from the concentration camp commanders of Auschwitz to the Central Office for Economic Administration referred to these twenty-five as protective custody cases.[90] Apparently they were slated for "destruction through work." They were sent to I. G. Farben's Buna rubber plant at the adjoining work camp, Monowitz. There they were divided among different barracks, were tattooed on their left forearms, and no longer used their names, only their numbers.

"In Buna we worked twelve hours a day," one intermarried Jew remembered. The guards often shot at inmates, he said, because they were rewarded for stopping escapees with three days of vacation, five marks, and a pack of cigarettes. "Guards loved to grab a prisoner's hat, throw it, and when he had to go bring it back, he was 'shot trying to escape.' "[91] Kapos regularly mistreated inmates, and numerous prisoners committed suicide by electrocuting themselves on the wires surrounding the camp.[92]

On the morning of their twelfth day, just as they were about to leave for work, an SS Führer ordered them to shower and then to report to "medical supervision." There they learned that they were to be sent back to Berlin, on order of "high authorities."[93] They returned on a normal passenger express train. "They couldn't get rid of us fast enough," remembered one. "Someone in Berlin must have hit 'em upside the head."[94] Nevertheless, before leaving, they were commanded under threat of being returned never to mention what they had seen in Auschwitz.

One of the twenty-five from Rosenstrasse had to remain behind because he was too sick to make the trip.[95] The others were joined by eleven Jewish men in intermarriages who survived the deportation from Grosse Hamburger Strasse on March 4. The release of the prisoners was so unexpected by Auschwitz authorities that the prisoners received clothes that were not their own.[96] Rumors of a release spread like wildfire among the Auschwitz prisoners. Johnny Hüttner, a Communist Jew who had been in various concentration camps since 1936, recalled that "we turned it over in our minds whether it was a true 'release.' It could have been a special 'Human Experiment,' we thought."[97]

Hannah Herzberg remembered the day her husband, Erich, returned from Auschwitz. "They gave him clothing from other inmates," she said. "The men arrived half dressed. Horrifying. My husband later told me that the officers in Auschwitz had been in a big hurry, all of a sudden, to get rid of them. They were thrown together, taken to the station, and sent to Berlin on a two-person compartment train. With only one guard! Each of them thought that they were now to be released. 'Don't do anything stupid, you're on your way home!' the guard said. My husband also recounted how each of them was very worried because none of them had any money to catch the bus home from the train station. But in Berlin they were greeted by the SS."

The thirty-five intermarried men released from Auschwitz arrived back in Berlin at the Friedrichstrasse station, accompanied by the guard. The train stopped so "that we stepped directly into a cordon of SS and Gestapo people," remembered one.[98] The Gestapo took them to Gestapo offices on Burgstrasse and locked them into the basement prison cell-blocks, where they spent the night. Stock, Schneider, Krell, and two secretaries, present to take the minutes, interrogated five to eight of them about their experiences in Auschwitz. A "very high-ranking army official" was also on hand to "hear how decent it was in Auschwitz." Stock, who claimed in his defense in a postwar trial that he had done this only out of curiosity about Auschwitz, directed the interrogation. The interrogations lasted about fifteen minutes and, most important for Stock and his henchmen, extracted signed confessions to crimes, including spying, treason, and spreading bad reports. "The Gestapo man started to question me," Erich Herzberg remembered, "and I said, 'I signed a statement declaring I would be completely silent about everything I experienced.' 'Well,' he said, 'then I'll ask you, How was the food?' 'Good,' I replied. "Were you beaten'? 'No, sir!' 'Did you see anyone else being beaten'? 'No, sir.' Na, well, I'm not stupid," he explained. "I was in their power, right? I didn't have anything to say that was against what they wanted to hear."[99] The Berlin Gestapo, however, did not dare to allow those who had seen Auschwitz to mingle with the public again. Arbitrarily charged with crimes punishable by death, they were sent as prisoners in protective custody to the nearby labor camp in Grossbeeren.

"The Gestapo officially informed us that our husbands were back," Erich's wife, Hannah, said. She remembered well the Gestapo's instructions to her and the other wives not to arrive at the Gestapo offices in a large group, reminiscent of protest. "We were ordered to Burgstrasse [Gestapo offices]," she said, in small groups. "According to the Gestapo, our husbands were guilty of espionage and were sent to the camp at Grossbeeren, three hours from Berlin."

In Grossbeeren the Auschwitz survivors were greeted with angry cries from Commissioner Schulz, who shouted, "Now, boys, have you too been allowed to see the sun shine again!" But from this point on their wives could visit them—if they could manage to survive and their wives did not divorce.

For the intermarried Jews released from Rosenstrasse, there was continuing uncertainty. Yet the repercussions of the diminutive Rosenstrasse Protest reached beyond March 1943 and beyond Berlin. Despite Goebbels's promise on March 6 to deport intermarried Jews a couple of weeks later, a decision not to deport them had been reached by March 18. On that day Himmler recorded in his telephone diary the business of a conversation with Gestapo chief Heinrich Müller: "No deportation of privileged Jews."[100] It was about the same day that the Jews from intermarriages who had been deported to Auschwitz work camps during the Berlin Final Roundup were released.[101] On March 20 Goebbels reported to Hitler that "Jews have for the most part been evacuated from Berlin."[102] Many of the Jews, some on advice of their employers in Berlin, began to remove the Star of David from their clothing.[103] "I don't want to see Jews with the Star of David running about in the capital," Goebbels wrote on April 18, 1943. "Either the Star must be taken from them and they be classed as privileged, or they must be evacuated altogether from the capital of the Reich."[104]

On May 19, 1943, Goebbels had declared Berlin *Judenfrei*, and if Berlin was "free of Jews" there should also be no signs of them.[105] There had been no more deportations of Jews in intermarriages or their *Mischlinge* children since the Rosenstrasse Protest. But he was under pressure to have this part of his job as gauleiter for Greater Berlin completed and apparently considered prevarication preferable to the risk of another protest.

On May 21 Adolf Eichmann's deputy Rolf Günther answered a question from the German police in Paris, who had been waiting to hear from headquarters about what to do with French Jews in intermarriages. The treatment of intermarriages and *Mischlinge* cannot be resolved for foreign areas, he wrote, before it is "clarified" in the Reich. The resolution for the Reich had to be made in Berlin, because about half the intermarried Jews lived in Berlin and because it was true to the Nazi sense of propriety that precedents for the Reich be set in the Reich capital.[106] Goebbels thus exercised sway over the fate of all German intermarried Jews not only as propaganda minister but also as party gauleiter of Greater Berlin.

Also on May 21, Himmler's deputy in charge of the Reich Security Main Office, Ernst Kaltenbrunner, issued a memorandum ordering the immediate release from concentration camps of all Jews from intermarriages except for those interned on criminal charges. Then he turned to Himmler's order that every Jew be removed from the Reich by June 30 and listed four categories of Jews who had often been spared up until this point, including those considered "irreplaceable" by weapons industries. The first three categories were now to be deported. But the fourth—Jews in intermarriages—was not: "I order expressly that Jewish intermarriage partners are in no case to be sent. There may also be protective custody arrests and deportations only when they have committed real offenses. Insofar as Jewish intermarriage partners have been deported on general grounds [that is, strictly because of their Jewish identity], they are to be successively released."[107]

In October 1943, following endless ministerial discussions, the bureaucrats submitted the question of intermarried Jews to Hitler for his decision. But the Führer refused to reconsider his position of 1941 that had resulted in the "temporary" exemption of intermarried Jews from deportations.[108] Despite this decision, the RSHA and Organization Todt mounted a few more life-threatening attempts on intermarried Jews. Just as Hitler had refused to determine the definitions for the Nuremberg Laws in September and November 1935, so he refused to take a public stand on intermarried Jews or to arbitrate the dispute between rival power centers. Meanwhile, gauleiters who drew intermarried Jews into the Final Solution (Schwede-Coburg and Sprenger) were to flourish, while the Führer insisted on the completion of the Final Solution and agreed in June 1943 that this would have to done regardless of its political impact.[109]

At Rosenstrasse, police force was not sufficient for separating and deporting intermarried Jews in the face of protest because the regime still hoped to rally the people and save the Reich. In late 1944, when none of the Nazi leaders could have hoped for victory any longer, a plan to use armed force against intermarried Jews failed again. In September 1944 Gustav Nosske, the brazen deputy of Otto Ohlendorf's Einsatzgruppe D who had killed thousands of Jews in cold blood, received orders to round up all the intermarried Jews in the Düsseldorf area and shoot them.[110] Nosske refused. He protested the order, and it was revoked or at least not enforced. Nosske himself was not executed and not even demoted. The noncompliance and protest of intermarried Germans had stayed the death of their Jewish partners until the regime's decision to defer "temporarily" intermarried Jews from the Holocaust had been rendered permanent.

So the Jews released from Rosenstrasse survived the war. For Ruth Gross, the ten-year-old *Mischling* who hung out on Rosenstrasse to catch an occasional glimpse of her father as he was imprisoned on the other side of the line between those allowed to live and those destined for death, her father's release in early March 1943 was a symbol of life transcending death. For her, like all those the Gestapo had tried to separate, it was a matter of utmost importance to get word to her imprisoned loved one facing death that she knew and cared. In that moment those inside and those outside were together, despite the Gestapo. Ruth Gross had sent her father a note of affection concealed in a small package of food, and it was the moment that he waved her note that symbolized for her their togetherness.

"This thing with Rosenstrasse, that was always a bond between us, my father and me," she concluded. "This scene, as he stood right there, and waved at me through the window, that I have always had in my consciousness. It came up again too, as he lay in the hospital during his last two years. I of course visited him every day there, and his room was at the end of a sort of hallway. And each time as I went away, he could still stand up, and he waved at me! Then I thought about that window from before, in Rosenstrasse, where he had always waved just like that. Then, in the hallway, as I was leaving him, I also turned around a few times and also waved at him. We never talked about it. But I have always been convinced, that he too was always thinking about this scene there on Rosenstrasse. About how he stood there and waved."[111]

XV

PROTEST, RESCUE, AND RESISTANCE

INTERMARRIED GERMANS AS RESCUERS

Given the Nazi dictatorship's maximal exploitation of force for political power and its fundamental commitment to the destruction of Jews, why did a street protest of unarmed Germans persuade it to release some seventeen hundred Jews arrested for deportation? This book has sought to find marking points that divided civilian actions that forced the dictatorship to compromise and the regime's capacity to do its will regardless of popular opposition. To what extent did the dictatorship perceive its power to be founded on uncoerced popular accommodation (ranging from enthusiastic support to passive acceptance)? In turn, to what extent could withdrawal of accommodation cause the regime to compromise its ideology and rescind its initiatives? The largest obstacle for this study is the dearth of popular opposition. Scholars have often attributed this acquiescence to Nazi terror, but more recent studies of self-policing and uncoerced conformity question this. One possible means for exploring the regime's degree of control is to look at a sector of Germans who openly refused to obey the regime throughout its twelve years and who actively protested.

Germans collectively were a powerful force, working mostly in favor of Nazism. The regime's anxiety about disturbing its social accommodation caused conflict between its race ideology and its persecution policies regarding intermarried Jews and, to a lesser extent, regarding the *Mischlinge*, those only partly Jewish. The survival of "full Jews" in intermarriage indicates that the sufficient condition for exemption from deportation was German relatives (especially considering that the Interior Ministry in 1942 actually proposed a law for the compulsory divorce of intermarried couples in order to facilitate the deportation of intermarried Jews).[1] It was the people Hitler was concerned with, not the bureaucrats, who, like the military, were, in any case, also compelled to support Hitler in large part because of his enormous widespread acclaim among Germans. Hitler, as recorded in his speeches and by close associates, was deeply affected by the indifferent reception the public gave the Second Motorized Division as it left Berlin for the Czech border in September 1938, and he considered his extraordinary popularity an important basis of German strength at war.[2] After the war members of the Interior Ministry claimed credit for protecting *Mischlinge*,[3] yet the *Mischlinge* also survived because they had German family members. The party wanted to do away with *Mischlinge*,[4] and in the eastern occupied territories intermarried Jews (along with intermarried Germans) were seized and killed, indicating that the exemption of intermarried Jews in Germany from the Final Solution was due to regard for popular opinion at home.[5] In Finland protests in December 1942 against the arrests of Communists and Jews caused the Germans to discontinue deportations. And even in the eastern territories among the population the regime wanted to disregard as *Untermenschen*, it was forced for tactical reasons to take popular morale into account.[6]

Mass public protest was the most powerful form of civilian opposition. Racial hygiene programs raised protests when they divided families and murdered victims. As protests became unignorable, the regime was forced to resolve the tension between racial hygiene and social quiescence. In the case of Euthanasia as well as in that of intermarriage, the regime resolved this problem in favor of popular morale. Although the potential number of Germans victimized by Euthanasia was much greater than those potentially victimized as relatives of intermarried couples, the opposition of intermarried Germans was also successful because it also represented the crucial, unavoidable junction between Nazism's intended victims and members of the "Aryan Master

Race." Families stood up for their victimized members, even though the war, as regime leaders calculated, facilitated genocide and despite the fact that many Germans were radicalized along with the regime during the course of the war.[7]

Comparative cases of church and family protest indicate that civilian (non-Jewish) Germans did circumscribe the regime's power. Civilians did oppose the regime in defense of traditions and family—in spite of Nazi terror. Civilian opposition in certain forms was strong enough to prevent the government from ruling in totality even late in the war. Catholic resistance peaked in 1941, but the opposition of Germans married to Jews indicates that the war increased the dictatorship's dependency on the people and that it remained responsive to public protest at least through early 1943. At Rosenstrasse the fundamental Nazi principle of racial purification clashed with its fundamental need to avoid social unrest and protect secrecy. For even though the regime could not prevent knowledge of the genocide from reaching some Germans, it never stopped striving to keep it secret.

The regime relented to just one protest against deportation of Jews, but there was only one. Would additional protests have slowed or stopped the deportation of German Jews?

The context of any protest would have been critical to its outcome (the venue of Berlin was particularly conducive for the success of even a limited protest, for example).[8] More generally, the opposition that was successful was limited, aimed only at specific initiatives. Certain policies motivated many individuals to object simultaneously. This minimized the need for protest organization and makes it difficult to generalize that opposition organized in the form of protest could have succeeded just as easily. It is possible to see the release of Jews at Rosenstrasse as a small, isolatable exception the regime made in order to move forward with its larger purposes. In this view the Rosenstrasse protesters made an isolated, limited demand the regime could agree to, a calculable cost it could pay. The regime could count the protesters and count their demands: about seventeen hundred Jews. It could be certain that the Rosenstrasse Protest would end with the release of these Jews and that the regime could then proceed with the enormous program of genocide elsewhere, where there were no protests. A more general protest against the Final Solution itself that frustrated all of the regime's will to genocide would have pushed it into responding with brutal force, one might argue. Gutterer implied that the result of the Rosenstrasse Protest did not necessarily indicate that larger protests would have led to further liberations of Jews.

This assessment, however, rested squarely on the fact that no

Germans other than those married to Jews were motivated to protest. The protest and the regime's reaction were "episodic," Gutterer said, because the protest was motivated solely by "personal reasons." Thus Goebbels knew that the "negative effect" the protest was having "on the general populace" would be eliminated by a single release of Jews.[9] We might ask whether German protests could have stopped the death camp deportations of German Jews because these deportations rested on the social isolation of Jews, a process for which German civilians bear primary responsibility. Identification and concentration of Jews, the necessary preliminaries to deportation, depended on civilian cooperation that encouraged the regime to carry its ideology through to genocide, a conclusion the regime's ideology does not explain or guarantee. The year for Germans to protest Nazi Jewish policies successfully was 1933, not 1943. The case of intermarriage indicates that the social isolation of Jews was the critical foundation of genocide. A thesis of this book is that a most decisive context of the Rosenstrasse Protest for determining its outcome was the history of dissent by the intermarried Germans themselves.

Gutterer was emphatic in characterizing Goebbels's decision to release the Jews as the only expected one. With this much unrest concerning an issue that the regime needed to keep secret, that threatened to go from "neighborhood to neighborhood" and "serve as an example," of course Goebbels would look for the quickest way to dispel the protest and then figure out a more favorable way to achieve his goals. The tension the regime had wrestled with when it temporarily exempted intermarried Jews from the deportations remained in Gutterer's mind: The genocide of Jews was a Nazi imperative, but unrest that challenged wartime morale and secrecy must be avoided. Rosenstrasse indicates that a relatively small number of public protesters could exercise disproportionate influence because of their "negative effect on the general populace." The regime could have avoided protest by deporting intermarried Jews one by one, but it could not afford to allocate the resources for doing so. The protest was effective, one could say, because it made the Jews more costly to obtain. A larger-scale protest, then, might have made a larger number of Jews too costly to obtain.

Yet is it not expecting the heroic to require a person to risk life for another (especially an unrelated person)? Intermarried Germans, who protested only for their own family members, were compelled to protest. Each took action for personal reasons but, fortunately for the cause, became part of an aggregate action that appeared organized or at least unified. What event could have amassed other Germans spontaneously, simultaneously? Many Germans, including some married to Jews, refused to believe the incredible reports that Jews were being murdered. This might have compelled some Germans to passivity, but intermarried Germans did not need the motivation of knowledge of genocide to protest. In addition, the general public, the element that most concerned the regime in its release of Jews, might have been more sympathetic toward Germans merely struggling to maintain their families than toward protesting Germans who were unrelated to Jews. Spouses traditionally had responsibility for safeguarding each other, and women, especially, had jurisdiction over home and family, a tradition the Nazis encouraged.[10]

This book has explained the results at Rosenstrasse in its immediate historical context. The dictatorship considered war a conducive context for carrying out Euthanasia and genocide.[11] Yet the ambitions of war required more support from the people than ever before, and this in turn required the government to conduct genocide in secret. Government secrecy is government admission that popular opinion matters. The need for secrecy on any program empowered public dissent against it (although any individual living in Nazi Germany might not have perceived it this way). In early 1943 the aggregate influence of women's dissent potentially increased, since the Total War policy demanded new public roles for women.

Nevertheless, they did not succeed only because they were women. The regime feared public unrest (especially during war), not just women's unrest. Noncompliance and protest among groups of enlisted men also would have been problematic (and the military expelled intermarried Germans and *Mischlinge* to help prevent this).[12] On the other hand, had the women been Jewish, their protest would have been brutally stifled, just like any armed protest or any individual protest, male or female. Nazi leaders did tend to see women's actions as apolitical, and thus women might more easily escape suspicion as political opponents. To punish women for political actions would be to acknowledge a political role for women that National Socialism denied.[13] Yet the regime might have responded ruthlessly to a women's protest against National Socialism itself. German women did use noncompliance and protest more than men in Nazi Germany (and more research should be done on why this was the case).[14]

In giving in to women's demands, the regime was not attempting to stanch a mighty opposition so much as it was trying to maintain the support of a group that Hitler saw as "among his most enthusiastic admirers."[15] If National Socialism's theory of mass movement politics did perhaps force the regime to make unnecessary concessions for the sake of public morale, there can be no doubt that this Nazi theory, in the new mass age, was more important for establishing and maintaining Nazi power than it was in limiting the regime. With this approach, the regime elicited far more support than unrest.

One key to the success of the women at Rosenstrasse was their record of opposition. Their decade of dissent had exacerbated a division among important Nazis on the issue of unrest. For the leaders who feared social unrest, intermarried Germans, by 1943, had a currency that just about all other Germans lacked. They had shown that they would consistently resist the regime on its most important goal when this threatened to destroy their family life. The fear of home front unrest learned from World War I came to life before the dictatorship as intermarried Germans who had refused to divorce protested on the street during war. Under Nazism's repellent race logic, intermarried Jews would have been the first Jews to be deported. Intermarried Jews whose German partners divorced them were deported with dispatch. If all intermarried Germans had divorced or otherwise registered no capacity for noncompliance with the regime's efforts to destroy their families, intermarried Jews and *Mischlinge* would have been sent to the death camps in 1941.

By the time the Gestapo designated intermarried Jews and *Mischlinge* "temporarily deferred" from the deportations in 1941, the intermarried Germans were already well on their way to rescuing them from certain death. Goebbels also wanted to deport even the intermarried Germans along with their Jewish family members, but he feared this would compromise his performance as minister of propaganda. A program that divided families and included Germans among the victims must be kept secret, but this was hardly possible, as Euthanasia indicated.

Goebbels's general claim to authority on Jewish matters was his prerogative on matters of public mood, but this hold on power with regard to the Jewish Question was undermined by a population that ordinarily made few or no signs of protest about the isolation, depredation, and expulsion of Jews. Secret agents carefully monitored popular responses to the disappearance of the Jews, but in general they reported that deportations were proceeding without friction. Only the Germans from Jewish-German families registered the kind of public noncompliance and then protest that pushed the problem of Jewish-German families squarely onto Goebbels's jurisdictional turf. The intermarriage problem had created a power struggle within the elite, but only because intermarried Germans had shown how resistant they were to any measures dividing their families.

Goebbels's mission of maintaining home front support reflected early party theory, elaborated by Hitler, that popular support is the primary pillar of power. For Hitler and Goebbels, force could only stabilize the consensus, the accommodation of the broad masses. Leaders at the RSHA and Martin Bormann were relatively indifferent to the social impact of policies. Himmler was concerned to a lesser extent than Goebbels, but his directives on intermarried Jews and *Mischlinge* did reflect the theory that social unrest was to be avoided.

In Berlin, where power was most closely watched, power was also most closely limited by the public mood. This was the home of foreign observers as well as the bulk of intermarried couples, and the general tension between the regime's basic goal of deporting the Jews and the basic goal of maintaining social accommodation (including the lie about the fate of the Jews) clashed more directly here than anywhere else in the Reich. Goebbels's drive to eliminate all Jews from Berlin coincided with the more general drive in late 1942 to clear all of the Reich of Jews and with the climax of the war. Goebbels could intervene so decisively at Rosenstrasse because he was the party's leader for Berlin (the home of half of Germany's mixed Jewish-German families).

Up until Rosenstrasse the tension between a radical execution of the party's racial purification ideology and the regime's need for social quiescence had been resolved by its "temporarily" deferring the deportation of intermarried Jews and their *Mischling* children. Party ideology demanded the demise of all Jews and *Mischlinge*; the Nuremberg Laws modified this by selecting only some *Mischlinge* for treatment as Jews, while assuming intermarried Jews would be treated like all other Jews. The temporary arrangement to defer all intermarried Jews and *Mischlinge*, regardless of Nuremberg Laws and ideology, remained unproblematic as long as the machinery of destruction was filled to capacity with Jews who were not related to Germans. By late 1942 intermarried Jews became increasingly visible as the remaining obstacle to completion of the Final Solution in Germany.

Still, there was no resolution of the tension that had caused the regime to defer intermarried Jews. Voluntary cooperation of intermarried Germans was not forthcoming, presenting the regime with a choice between not deporting their Jewish partners and using force to do so. The Final Roundup that unleashed the Rosenstrasse Protest indicated that the regime's decision to defer intermarried Jews temporarily was well founded if public unrest was to be avoided.

Intermarried Germans rescued their Jewish and half Jewish family members before and during the Final Roundup, but Goebbels did not want anyone (foreign or domestic) to know this, reiterating that most

Germans were behind regime Jewish policies and that the protesters were civilians without homes following the massive British air raid on March 1. Nazi officials explained the release of Jews from Rosenstrasse as the corrective to unauthorized initiatives of local Gestapo leaders, who in arresting intermarried Germans had "overreached" their authority. But the regime is not entitled to this deception. The Final Roundup was a typical exercise of power by the Nazi elite, an opportunistic ambush, facilitated with deceptions, taken at the right moment, and presented as a fait accompli. Lower-level Gestapo hacks did know that anti-Semitism was the core Nazi ideology, and the lack of overt directives from Hitler on intermarried Jews and *Mischlinge* created a vacuum that tempted them to step in and prove their Nazi worth with radical measures against Jews. Especially the gray, in between category of *Mischling* and intermarried Jews seemed to offer them a chance to prove their mettle, since in this case some party members seemed to hang back in trepidation and uncertainty. The highest Nazi authorities were well known for using oral orders instead of written ones if this helped them reach their goals, and Hitler was well known for requiring deniability—the possibility of denying association with anything controversial—in order to preserve his Führer image, which was so important for the integration of an entire society's energies within the service of Nazi goals.

ROSENSTRASSE AS RESISTANCE?

The history of intermarriage is substantial additional evidence that the Nazi dictatorship backed down when it encountered overt mass protest. It indicates that the regime relented to protest even as late as March 1943 and that it relented, in small numbers, even on the issue constituting the core of its ideology. Regardless of whether the success of intermarried German opposition is dated to the Rosenstrasse Protest or before, it is the noncompliance of intermarried Germans that caused the conflict between Nazi ideology and perceived policy options, influencing Hitler to hesitate and decide temporarily against Nazi ideology on the matter.[16]

The Rosenstrasse Protest occurred near the end of the war. Historians (who have not cited the case of intermarriage) refer to this period, running from 1941–42 to the end of the war, as one "characterized by an acceleration of violence and terror," implying that the increased terror repressed further partial resistance.[17] Survivors have considered intermarried Germans heroes, figures deserving the highest honor because of the Jewish lives they saved and the torments they endured to save them.[18] They are rescuers. But how do they fit within or adjust our picture of resistance, and the potential for German resistance, in Nazi Germany?

Early postwar definitions classified resistance as centrally organized, ideologically motivated efforts to overthrow the regime in its entirety.[19] These were also clandestine and generally armed efforts. By defining resistance as an attempt to overthrow the state, this so-called *Widerstand* definition tended to shift attention away from civilian actions like mass protest and mass disobedience as constituting resistance and also defined power as the purview of prominent institutions—political parties, the churches, armies. Revisionism has led, on the one hand, to scholarship on individuals as resisters[20] and, on the other, to the more prevalent studies of "partial" or "single-interest" opposition, actions of noncompliance and dissidence the late historian Martin Broszat identified within a category of dissidence and noncompliance called *Resistenz*.[21]

Although the consequences of their actions went beyond the protection of their own self-interest, the motivation of intermarried Germans for opposition could be characterized as the reflex of self-defense, their opposition limited to repulsing the regime only when it encroached on their own customs and only to the extent that it encroached. Judged according to the standard definition of resistance, intermarried Germans failed the test. They did not oppose the regime itself or even the regime's Jewish policies as a whole.

The motives of the hundreds of intermarried protesters are not on record, but it is possible to give examples of the motivations that caused Germans to remain in intermarriages. We know that very few, if any, of these intermarried protesters engaged in other actions of resistance, on behalf of other causes. They remained married, at great risk to themselves, for a variety of reasons: love, honor, tradition, habit, social and economic status, family egoism. The sake of struggle, the sake of a life—these too might also have kept them together. Some divorced almost immediately following the fall of the Nazis and the return of their freedom.[22]

Most of those I have talked with described their decision to protest as an involuntary reaction.[23] They had to do something for their loved ones but also to maintain their own integrity. For some it was an issue of basic rights and of living life the way it had been learned (this might be described as a concern for human freedom in general). Although personally motivated, one protester had a sense of social injustice and the political power of protest, and in postwar Germany she fought for a democratic society and against anti-Semitism. Some of the women at Rosenstrasse were from the upper middle class, and one of them implied that she resented the brutish Nazi parvenu out of class hostility.

One eyewitness made an anonymous phone call in response to my request for information. His father had been taken during the mass arrest action that had led to the protest at Rosenstrasse. As an eighteen-year-old he watched his father being prodded onto the Gestapo's truck, and leaping onto the truck beside his father, he joined the other Jewish victims. Despite Gestapo orders, he refused to leave, and the Gestapo drove off with a threat that he would share the fate of the Jews. Without the protest of his mother and the others, it would have been the beginning of a journey to Auschwitz or some other camp. Yet the way this man told his story was no less striking than the story itself. During the entire conversation he referred to Jews simply as "J," explaining, "I am sitting here in my office, and I use 'J' instead of 'Jew' because you never know who might overhear, and whether he might be sympathetic with the Nazis, and what they did to the Jews."

A man who had loyally decided he would not leave his father regardless of where this led was afraid to say the word "Jew" in his office for fear of being overheard. Was this a man of courage? Was this a man who had fought for some sense of truth or ideal? Other intermarried Germans tended to identify Nazism with anyone who was anti-Jewish and declare anyone who was not anti-Jewish to be a non-Nazi even if that person was a Nazi party member. Their opposition to Nazism was as deep as anti-Semitism was fundamental to Nazism, yet it was also no deeper than whether a person had shown anti-Semitism in their presence.

Nevertheless, although the motivation was not generally on behalf of humanitarian politics, some of these women, like Charlotte Israel, came to the aid of victims of the regime who were not family members. The stories of intermarried Germans, like those of other rescuers, indicate that they began by risking little and grew into their roles of greater help and greater risk as pressure from the regime increased. The Third Reich transformed some intermarried Germans who had only wanted a private life into partial political opposition. The protest on Rosenstrasse was itself also transformative. Desperation, an emotion unlikely to produce sustained, effective resistance, did motivate some persons to join the protest.[24] As they returned again and again, and as the Gestapo appeared unable to disperse them, some protesters who initially came to get information began to take hope that the protest could have an impact. And although they came as individuals or in pairs, they became part of a group and acted on behalf of one another in solidarity. Is this resistance?

Although the opposition of intermarried Germans was motivated by a single cause, they cannot be denied the status of resisters for the same reason as other single-issue oppenents. Among the assessments of single-interest dissenters is that they basically made peace with Nazism. Mere partial single-issue opposition, in this view, enabled the regime to rule more effectively, by allowing people to let off steam that otherwise might have built up to a level capable of a more general challenge to the dictatorship. Single-interest dissent has also been associated with mere nonconformism, rather than active struggle,[25] and judged as not having hindered the overall effectiveness of the Nazis to govern.[26] Analysis of single-issue resistance has relied primarily on religious-based dissent in Nazi Germany and fits that history better than it does that of intermarried Germans.[27]

The difference between the opposition of intermarried Germans and that of other single-issue dissenters can be measured by the duration of their opposition, by the significance of the consequences of their opposition, and by their general disposition toward the regime. Intermarried Germans who did divorce showed raw self-concern. On the other hand, given the official and social hatred that intermarried Germans had to endure, the humiliating sense of injustice, and the grueling uncertainty about their fate, did those who remained with Jewish family members act out of self-interest? Their self-defense was the defense of Jews—a noble selfishness.

Intermarried Germans did not support Nazism fundamentally. They could not embrace both Nazism and their families.[28] They knew that only an Allied military victory stood between them and their demise. Intermarried Germans who remained married have more in common with the very small part of the German population that could not identify with any aspect of Nazism at all[29] than they do with other single-issue resisters who supported Nazism generally. Furthermore, the opposition of intermarried Germans was persistent over the course of twelve years. This indicated integrity and willingness to carry on the battle indefinitely. This lack of support for the regime generally did not result because intermarried Germans had greater ideological commitments than other single-interest dissenters but because it was less possible for intermarried Germans to be deluded about the fate of their families and of themselves under the Nazi regime. Not all single-interest opponents generally supported Nazism, in part because not all single issues were of equal concern to the regime. In addition, intermarried Germans were not passive nonconformers. Because they opposed the regime on such a significant issue, they were forced to become active opponents. Remaining married was a continuous, public act of dissent.

It might be sufficient to identify intermarried Germans as rescuers and protesters rather than resisters, as long as they are also not identified with the dissenters historians have typically identified as partial or single-issue opponents. Their example in refusing to divorce was a primary factor in convincing the regime not to promulgate a law aimed at pressuring barren couples to divorce.[30] Thus, although they did not refuse to divorce to save marriages other than their own, intermarried Germans by refusing to divorce did extend their impact beyond their own cause. Thousands of intermarried Germans came to stand for the norm of German behavior, and the regime thus came to expect that the norms on marriage would hold despite whatever laws they made.

Given the diversity of actions that might be considered opposition, historians speak of forms of resistance or varieties of resistance.[31] One definition cannot do justice to the complexity of history. Rosenstrasse, although more important than other single-issue resistance, does help define the crucial characteristics of successful limited opposition. These protesters were protected somewhat by their insistence on caring for family rather than on the demise of the regime. Nevertheless, even their limited opposition, as well as that of the Catholics, was successful only because it took certain forms.

The characteristics of protests essential to their success, like the characteristics that made programs vulnerable to protest, derived from the regime's perceived need to maintain popular accommodation. Successful protests against programs as important to the Nazis as Euthanasia and especially the Final Solution had to be public and sufficiently large enough to convince the regime that it threatened public morale. These protests were also unarmed and collective. In addition, it helped the cause of the protests against Euthanasia and the deportation of intermarried Jews that Catholics and intermarried Germans already had a record as protesters.[32] War and secrecy made the regime more vulnerable to public displays of unrest. Maintaining unity was especially important during war; controversial programs had to be conducted secretly. Protests against secret programs not only displayed dissent but also threatened to unveil what the regime needed to hide. Public protests, especially, threatened secrecy.

For a variety of reasons, public opposition was the most potent form of German opposition. The public display of many people in disagreement with the leadership could open up or exacerbate differences among the leadership. The regime perpetrated an image of the German people as uniformly supportive of Nazism, and many Germans felt helpless alone in their dissent, fearful of standing out in a crowd. The psychological isolation of each individual dissenter was a goal of the regime, and (as Goebbels feared) an action like the Rosenstrasse Protest that showed dissent publicly could spread quickly. The Rosenstrasse protesters represented personal interests, yet the public nature of their opposition wrecked the regime's daily portrayal of reality, while the terror apparatus remained on the sidelines.

In the Third Reich the power of protest to influence the regime stood in relationship to the degree of risk taken by the protesters. In a state that inhibited assembly, controlled information and communication, and portrayed dissidence as a fringe element in an otherwise unified populace, mass public protest was a political force. Public defiance demands public reassurance that the state maintains control. Open protest, including gathering petitions, collective street actions, and other actions intended to force the regime to retreat, poses an even more overt challenge to authority than does noncompliance. It brings the conflict into public view, so that retreat is a public display of impotence.[33]

The degree of force exerted by protest correlated with the degree to which it was public. The protesters used the strongest method available, and their impact verified the degree of the risk they had taken. The late historian Detlev Peukert, positing that the influence of protest depended on the degree to which it was public, devised a scale for measuring resistance. The Peukert scale assesses an act of opposition on a continuum ranging from "nonconformist behavior" through organized, armed attempts to overthrow the regime (*Widerstand*), and from private to more public acts of dissent. The two categories for Peukert between "nonconformism" and *Widerstand* are "refusal" and "protest."[34] The arrangement of Peukert's scale suggests that *Widerstand* is the strongest form of opposition and that protest, refusal, and nonconformism are successively weaker forms. Yet the effectiveness of any one of these forms of actions is dependent on specific historical circumstances; protest at Rosenstrasse, for example, was more effective than armed resistance.

While attempts to overthrow the regime were characteristically conspiracies, single-issue opposition like the Rosenstrasse Protest were done openly. Goebbels's deputy Leopold Gutterer attributed the impact of the Rosenstrasse Protest to its openness and contrasted it with conspiratorial resistance, which the regime could more easily portray as an act against the people and state. Yet no matter how public the challenge, successful German protests were also unarmed. They challenged the regime without giving it an excuse to use force. Unarmed actions avoided the appearance of treason and did not legitimate and unleash the crushing violence of the Nazi regime. Police violence against protesters, rumormongers, or Bishop von Galen only would have exacerbated the panic about Euthanasia, working against the Nazi goal of soothing the public back into submissive support.[35] If the protesters had come to Rosenstrasse armed, the police would have *had* to shoot them, said Gutterer. The structures and aims of family and church opposition caused protest without arms, just as it caused protest only against the particular policies that undercut personal and traditional interests.

At least two of the criteria of successful protest—that it be sufficiently large and public—discriminate against rural regions and smaller urban areas and shift a greater possibility toward Berlin, a huge metropolitan area with the sharp eyes and ears of the foreign press and embassies. A large city not only afforded social possibilities for survival but also produced the conditions for a large yet unorganized protest. The regime could be almost certain that other intermarried protests like that on Rosenstrasse would not arise outside Berlin and, if they did, that they could be more easily managed.

Yet the size and public quality of a protest cannot be measured solely by the number of actual protesters but must take into account persons whom the public protesters represented. At their strongest, protesters appeared to represent not just themselves but an integral part of society. The protesters on Rosenstrasse represented intermarried Germans who were not on the street but who had already defied the laws and braved the fear of ostracism, poverty, and the possibility of sharing the Jewish fate to remain married. Actions against those protesting the crucifix decrees would have alienated many more Catholics than those who personally protested. Bishop von Galen represented tens of thousands.

Protests successful against Nazi programs as important as Euthanasia and Jewish deportations were made by those with earlier records of successful opposition against lesser state initiatives. Divisions within the regime on how to respond to protests were important to the success of opposition. But it is necessary to credit the church, by the time of its Euthanasia protest, and the Jewish-German families, by the time of their Rosenstrasse Protest, with having opened up policy controversies among leaders, by their earlier acts of opposition.

Regardless of when they occurred and whether they opposed fundamentally important or lesser programs, effective acts of opposition were also collective, or at least aggregate.[36] Catholics protesting the crucifix decree of 1936 had learned this, asserting "that every anti-Catholic action of the state must remain unsuccessful if the Catholic people stand united together."[37] People were executed for as little as telling a political joke, for criticizing National Socialism, or for publicly doubting Germany's victory at war—when they acted individually.[38] But when state policies interfered with the traditions of church or family, popular opposition accrued.

In Nazi Germany, Nazi infringements on entire traditions occasionally motivated disparate persons to resist while minimizing the need for resistance organization. The Nazis could hardly isolate and punish as "enemies of the state" either the church as a whole or the tens of thousands in Jewish-German families. Intermarried couples constituted a large and different sector of German society. Faith and family traditions had a social basis in practice broader than that of political parties (which the regime crushed) and were, also unlike political parties, widely respected as practices derived from an even higher authority than that of the state. The tradition and practice of marriage and family rested in religious and social customs that demanded allegiances deeper than those of National Socialism, and the history of intermarriage portrays additional examples of opposition that forced the regime to modify or rescind particular initiatives.[39]

The regime anticipated that the forcible divorce of intermarriages would cause strong protest and unrest among intermarried Germans, but it also had reason to believe that the population would disapprove of such a divorce law. In mid-1938 Germany issued a law that, although not forcing any divorces, made divorce in certain cases considerably easier to obtain. For an intermarried German, it provided for divorce merely on the basis of a claim that the damage to the "Aryan" race from intermarriage had been revealed only by the advent of National Socialism. On the basis of its survey of reactions to this law, the SD warned that it was on the "outer boundaries" of what the public would tolerate. Several years later the regime deliberated a proposed law to compel the divorce of only Jewish-German couples but decided against it, finally, because legal measures would not change the basic social fact that many intermarried Germans would do all they could to protect their families and because the "Vatican" would oppose it.[40] The German episcopacy's postwar claim that it had prevented the compulsory divorce of intermarried couples thus has some credibility.[41] Nevertheless, the church and its traditions alone—without the protest of intermarried

Germans—would have been insufficient to save intermarried Jews, and there is ample evidence that churches also cooperated in critical ways with the regime, even on anti-Jewish measures. The Catholic and Protestant churches were crucial in many ways in identifying Jews while subverting their own ideologies by allowing baptized Jews to be persecuted as "racially" Jewish.[42] "The Church fought for its confessional schools, press and organizations and monasteries and clashed with the government on Euthanasia, successful protests that only highlight its failure to protest the Holocaust. Reports of regional administrators and the Gestapo along with Hitler's dinner conversations and other records amply indicate the church's popularity and the political pitfalls the leadership perceived in proceeding against the Catholic Church. Protest from both churches would have had an impact, but the German nationalism and anti-Semitism of key church leaders actually encouraged Hitler rather than inhibiting him. Church leaders condemned resistance to the state, exhorting obedience and warning against seditious activity, which discouraged '*any* spirit of opposition.' "[43]

However, the Germans as a whole, not just church leaders, *are* implicated in Nazi atrocities. Behind successful opposition by leaders were the people (the July conspiracy against Hitler did not seek or enjoy widespread popular support). In the few, very important instances in which church leaders did take a defiant stand, they did so certain that they had the strength of popular feeling behind them. And in each case the regime backed down. It is true that by the time of war only the top leaders of the churches and the military seemed to command enough weapons or popular allegiance to challenge the regime as a whole effectively. Yet church leaders confronted the regime only after segments of the public were already disaffected. The room for opposition, these leaders, military and church alike, perceived, was limited by Hitler's popular consensus.

Had Germans married to Jews cooperated with the regime, and had they not aggressively protested the imminent deportation of their Jewish partners, these intermarried Jews would have been among the murdered. Intermarried Germans who had not divorced by 1943 had repeatedly demonstrated a capacity to oppose the regime to save their families. They had a track record that had put the regime on guard from early on and lent their street protest influence when it happened. By 1943, however, it was too late for other Germans to convince the regime that a significant sector of the overall population strongly opposed the deportation of Jews. The claim that Germans couldn't have succeeded if they had protested cannot exonerate Germans who did not protest because they had already proved that they were behind the regime, and this in turn buoyed the regime's confidence for continuing harsher policy expressions of its racist ideology.

The significance of partial opposition, relative to actions defined as resistance, which failed entirely, is that it partially limited the regime's policy options. Yet Ian Kershaw argues that these successes hardly mattered since they did not hinder the overall effectiveness of the regime to govern. Hitler's popularity was so great that it neutralized dissent until late in the war, when Hitler began to look like a loser. The escalation of terror in 1944–45 was in large part a reaction to the crumbling popular consensus for the regime, and resistance was limited to the very few willing to put their lives on the line. "If the meaning of 'resistance' is not to be wholly diluted," Kershaw argues, "it seems sensible to restrict it to active participation in organized attempts to work against the regime with the conscious aim of undermining it or planning for the moment of its demise."[44] Hans Mommsen suggests that a resister not only took a great risk but incurred "risk of failure and death in order to restore a humanitarian politics that transcended individual interests."[45] The number of Germans who should be called resisters is certainly very limited, and historians justly fear that broader definitions include "almost any gesture of nonenthusiasm."[46]

Perhaps no Germans hindered the regime's capacity to rule. Yet no Germans curtailed the regime more, or more significantly, than intermarried Germans. Because of their civil disobedience and the threat to public morale that forcing them to cooperate might have developed, intermarried Germans blocked the regime from achieving its most basic goals, offset its drive for "racial purity," and saved thousands. The opposition of intermarried Germans is so significant because it placed a (minuscule) limitation on the aspect most notorious about the regime, genocide. This was a tremendous, crowning achievement.

The opposition of intermarried Germans should be measured against those actions already characterized as resistance rather than against abstract definitions. The Germans who initially enjoyed a status as the personification of the high ideals of resistance are also tainted. Concerning the "fundamental" resistance attributed to Communists during the early years of the regime, Broszat writes that "personal connections and shared hardships often turned out to be more important than ideological conviction or party loyalty" in motivating their resistance.[47] How different were the protesting wives in motivation from the true heroes of July 20? The personal fate of the elites has traditionally been concern with political power; the personal fate of ordinary wives is with home and husband. And Broszat makes the point that the plot and actions of the July 20 conspirators was unrealistic, foundering on "illusory beliefs," false expectations, and a "certain lackadaisical aristocratic style."[48] Did any act of single-issue opposition result in a clearer (temporary) assertion of power by the regime or a reaction more destructive of the resistance than did the thwarted assassination?

Peter Hoffmann, an eminent historian of resistance, disagrees with assessments that the elites began their opposition only after experiencing loss of influence and after coming into possession of privileged information on the dismal prospect of war for Germany.[49] In any case, the open record of limited intermarried opposition caused the regime to delay the deportation of intermarried Jews and opened up the possibility of using a protest rather than arms to show they would continue to risk their lives for family. Although they did not make the ultimate sacrifice, they did put their lives on the line, and they certainly would have been martyred had they used arms rather than protest to force their demands.

Definitions put forward to limit the number of persons characterized as resisters critically rely on the criterion of motivation (political idealism), regardless of how realistic plans and actions to carry out the intention of undermining the regime actually were. Carol Gilligan's work on the moral development of women suggests a parallel assessment of the definitions that restrict resistance to opposition for political ideals. Like intermarried women who protested, Gilligan's morally developed people take life-threatening risks for those they know and care about, rather than political ideals.[50] The Rosenstrasse Protest was especially risky not only because it publicly expressed commitment to a population the regime had portrayed as subhuman but because it came in 1943, during the most treacherous moment for opposition. Risk to life, a characteristic of resistance in standard definitions, is a mark of the Rosenstrasse Protest, just as some other of its characteristics would include it within more recent definitions of resistance as well.[51]

Successful opposition, also when spearheaded by leaders, had significant popular support. No single group of Germans was entirely responsible for the rise of Nazism, suggesting that it is unrealistic to a expect a single faction of Germans acting clandestinely (like the failed military resistance) to overthrow such a popularly based power. Any one group that attempted to topple the entire regime either was martyred or simply went unregistered (lacking impact). Regardless of whether they are called resisters, intermarried Germans who both publicly dissented with the regime's basic ideology over its entire twelve years and risked their lives at the hands of its terror apparatus should be placed in any category of the regime's most important opponents.

For the politics of Jewish-German intermarriages tested the limits of Nazi power, whether through the use of propaganda for changing norms or through the use of force for intimidating dissent.

Perhaps the best term for interpreting the opposition of inter-married Germans comes not from Nazi historiography but from a leading dissident under communism, President Václev Havel of the Czech Republic. "If the main pillar of the system is living a lie," Havel wrote while under Communist police surveillance, "then it is not sur-prising that the fundamental threat to it is living in truth." Com-munism did not perpetrate genocide and world war, but it did, like Nazism, attempt to control entire populations under a single ideology that purportedly spoke for every person. Within these systems most individuals conformed. This allowed the game to go on whether or not these conformers believed in the ideology. This conformity, however, comes at the expense of individual conscience and reason. "Living in truth" is living out one's individual conscience. Nazism and commu-nism attempted to kill both truth and individuality. Within such sys-tems, says Havel, "living in truth" is the primary breeding ground for . . . opposition."[52] On Rosenstrasse the protesters expressed the cul-minating act of years of living according to their own conscience and reason, in defiance of the regime's race ideology. They attempted to live in truth.

The dictator feared social unrest more than he experienced it. According to the intermarried Jewish journalist Georg Zivier, the eyewitness to whom we owe the survival of the story, the Rosenstrasse Protest was a small torch that might have become a general uprising if the public had taken note.[53] The development of the Nazi dictatorship reveals an antithetical relationship between fundamental Nazi ideological tenets and society's most deeply rooted traditions, a widening gap that strained the credibility of state propaganda as well as the state's capacity to mobilize and use armed force. The injurious nature of certain Nazi "population policies" on the German people was destructive of its basis of power. The successes of mass public protest—slight as they were and dependent though they were on Allied military forces—suggest that the German society eventually might have extracted concessions of greater scope.

Yet widespread popular support for Hitler took the wind from the sails of any fledgling resistance, military or otherwise. Even Hitler's power over the army, which he feared especially in 1934 and up until 1938 and then again by 1944, rested on his popular support.[54] On the other hand, civil disobedience did cripple an attempt to draw inter-married Jews into the genocide in September 1944, when Nosske re-fused orders to shoot intermarried Jews.[55] In detention centers within Germany, hardened Gestapo agents refused final orders to kill remain-ing Jewish inmates, who were often *Geltungsjuden,* "catchers," or intermarried Jews.[56] These desperate Gestapo men bargained with the inmates to spare their lives in exchange for testimony from the inmates that might save their lives. The regime could no longer mobilize Noske and these others, who had willingly served when Germany appeared indomitable. Personal motivations that drove some bureaucrats and Gestapo agents now also drove them to abandon ship.[57] Thus the re-gime's apparatus of accelerated terror and violence during its final years was also dependent on cooperation. As the foundation of political power, terror was no match for popular support because the terror apparatus itself was also composed of individuals who lost faith in National Socialism and its Führer as the Wehrmacht lost ground.

Yet history shows that only personal loyalties caused opposition in the form of civil disobedience that saved lives. Protests in Nazi Germany also bring home to us the iron limits of Primo Levi's tragically narrow "us-ism."[58] The history of intermarriage in Nazi Germany points to deep social limitations on the Führer. Regardless of whether Hitler and other Nazi leaders overestimated the force of social unrest, an increased focus on the civilian role in Nazi power and crimes will begin to bring under scrutiny the millions of bystanders who by doing nothing defined that as the acceptable social norm. The history of intermarried Germans who protested is about Germans who challenged that norm, women who risked their lives and whose lives in turn are of great consequence.

EPILOGUE

Following is a brief account of the book's characters, after the Rosenstrasse Protest and the war.

GÜNTHER ABRAHAMSOHN

On March 9, following the Final Roundup, the Berlin Gestapo made a massive arrest of Jewish Community employees at their homes. More arrests followed the next day, this time of workers at the Jewish hospital. The Jewish Community of Berlin was decimated, and on March 12 the employees were deported to Theresienstadt.[1] After the Final Roundup the Jewish Community was required to update its list of Jews. Some Jews had fled, and new names had been turned up. On June 10 the last Jews who had been in offices of authority were deported from Berlin. The second phase of the deportations had ended; virtually the only Jews in Berlin known to the Gestapo were working for the Jewish Community, lived in intermarriages, or were in hiding. The Gestapo now promised some Jewish orderlies a life in Berlin in exchange for their help in catching Jews living illegally underground.

Dr. Walter Lustig remained in Berlin as the Gestapo-chosen head of the Reichsvereinigung (Central Organization of German Jews). His subordinates at the Central Organization were almost exclusively Jewish orderlies who answered also to the Gestapo. Beginning in June 1943, Günther Abrahamsohn carried a pistol to enforce his authority while employed by the Gestapo, working full-time to ferret out the hiding places of Jews and bring them for deportation to the Gestapo, according to his statement to a postwar court.[2] Abrahamsohn's first job was limited to finding the former Reichstag Communist party (KPD) representative Iwan Katz.[3] Abrahamsohn and his partner caught Katz,

Günther Abrahamsohn, holding his Jewish identification papers, more than forty years after the collapse of Nazism. Abrahamsohn was one of the chief Jewish orderlies during the Final Roundup who months later began carrying a pistol in the service of the Gestapo as one of the feared Jewish catchers.

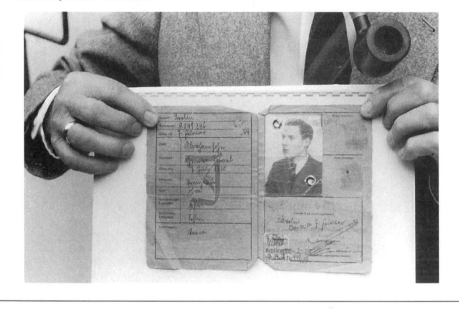

who was sent to Auschwitz but survived to testify against Abrahamsohn. The Jewish "catchers" like Abrahamsohn were very successful, he said. During just the short time he was in the Schulstrasse prison, he said, the *Greifer* (catchers) hauled in about 250 Jews from their hiding places in the underground, 99 percent of whom were sent to Auschwitz. Katz scornfully dismissed Abrahamsohn's claim that he had to work for Dobberke to save his life. Very few of those delivered to the Gestapo agreed to save themselves from liquidation by tracking down others of the persecuted, he said. Out of 8,000, only about 60 did this; the vast majority preferred to allow themselves to sent to Auschwitz. Furthermore, Katz said, Abrahamsohn was a catcher because he got a kick out of it and felt great doing it. One look at Abrahamson, said Katz, made this abundantly clear: There he was—on the other side of the barbed-wire fence from starving Auschwitz-bound prisoners—well fed, neatly clothed, chauffeured in cars around Berlin.[4]

In April 1945, according to Abrahamsohn, he was told by the chief guard of the police (Boch) that the director of the Berlin Gestapo had ordered Abrahamsohn to be shot. Dobberke was to see to it that Abrahamsohn was dead, but Abrahamsohn promised Dobberke that left alive, he would save Dobberke's life when in a few days the Red Army arrived. Abrahamsohn was freed from the Gestapo's Schulstrasse prison along with thirteen others on April 22, 1945.[5] The Russians shot and killed Dr. Lustig when they found his name on a list of persons who received salaries from the Gestapo.

THE HERZBERGS

Many of the coworkers Ferdinand Wolff and his comrades left behind at the Buna rubber plant were worked to death.[6] Following their release from Auschwitz, they went to the labor camp at Grossbeeren, which consisted of about twelve hundred persons, mostly foreigners, many of whom were serving sentences for being "work-shy." Only about thirty Jews, isolated in their own barrack, were there when Wolff arrived. Only fifteen of those thirty-five who came from Auschwitz survived, and they lived for two years in constant awareness that they might die at any moment—and possibly in an extremely painful way. In Auschwitz only three of them had gotten sick, but in Grossbeeren fifteen of them died within two to four weeks. They were the victims of undernourishment, lack of medical care, and inhuman treatment. One died after a "treatment" with a cold jet stream of water. During roll calls they had to stand for hours in temperatures of minus twenty degrees. For no reason at all, the guards might push an inmate into a pit of water. The pit was deep, but not all the inmates could swim. If an inmate made it to the edge to try to save himself, the Gestapo would beat his hands as they grasped at the side, so that he fell back in.[7]

In 1943 the British air raids on Berlin grew so severe that records from the RSHA were moved out of harm's way to an old castle in Wartenberg, Czechoslovakia. Fifteen of the Jews released from Auschwitz to Grossbeeren were now taken along with the documents to Wartenberg. There they finally ripped off the Stars of David they had worn for two years. The new job of the task force was to care for the files that documented the activities of the most murderous Nazi bureaucracy. "Documents, documents, documents," said Erich Herzberg. "We carried them here and there, up and down, and devil knows where else." In 1945, as the Red Army moved close, the Jews were required to burn the Nazi records in huge blazing heaps. "One morning we woke up and there were no more SS there," Erich said of his liberation.

He caught a ride to Berlin on the top of a coal train and arrived home to Hannah on June 4. Erich and Hannah lived then in what was to become East Berlin. But they had no Communist allegiances and were drawn to the zone of the Allies in the West. On the kiosks and elsewhere people posted notices that they wanted to change apartments, trading an apartment in the Soviet Zone for one in the American Zone, or vice versa. The Herzbergs went west.

Then they went even farther west, to the New World, and Nebraska, where Erich got a job in a shoe factory in Omaha. For years afterward on the Great Plains, which seemed so primordial to her and untouched by politics, Hannah tried to assimilate all that had happened to her during those twelve years when she had had no time to reflect. Erich insisted that he alone should be the breadwinner, so she became the traditional housewife who cooked and cleaned. It was already too late for her to have children; the Nazis had won that little conquest even if Erich had been returned from the jaws of death. In the mornings after she took Erich to work, she would drive out onto the open Nebraska plains and ride for maybe a hundred miles, unhindered, and stopping only where she wanted, to look at nature and try to understand what had happened and how they were safe now. She found a special spot there, all alone, surrounded by only water and flocks of birds. After a couple of decades they went back to Berlin to retire. The social welfare was better for them in their old age, they thought (although in Germany they missed the simplicity and directness of the American health care system). The women of this history almost inevitably outlived the men, and after Erich died in the late 1980s, Hannah discovered that he had burned all of his documents that had been saved from the Nazi period, preferring to leave without a trace.

Like Erich Herzberg, Ferdinand Wolff returned home from Auschwitz at the end of the war. He found his wife with a child he knew could not be his. Mrs. Wolff had given sexual favors to the prison guards in order to get care packages to her husband, and, she hoped, to assure that he would be treated better and survive. But Mr. Wolff was impossible to comfort. It was impossible, he said, that she should have let herself have an intimate relationship with Nazi swine. In fury he left her, and they were divorced by 1946, after sixteen years of marriage.

THE ISRAELS

In the early 1950s Charlotte and Julius also divorced, again over a love affair and jealousy. The power balance between them must have become terribly skewed throughout the years when Charlotte was the blond Aryan, he the stooped and despised Jew. But although they got divorced, they really separated. When he died not long thereafter, he died in her arms, and she buried him in Berlin's Jewish cemetery on Heerstrasse. Charlotte was an agnostic, and by the end of the war Julius had also surrendered his religious beliefs. The Heerstrasse cemetery was too far for her to drive to, Charlotte said, but she had Julius buried there because she thought that only a Jewish cemetery was right for him.

Charlotte lived to pass on her father's injunction not to "speak ill of any nation, religion, or any sort of social group; every race has good and bad people." She spoke deliberately, as if surreptitiously, when she said, "That lesson from Father is especially important for our time,

Charlotte Israel (age seventy-nine) in 1989, with her then husband, Mr. Freudenthal, who is holding a blanket-size piece of cloth covered with the Star of David, produced by a Berlin flag manufacturer.

now that we have so many foreigners in Germany." She stole a furtive glance and added, rebelliously, "What Father told me I also spread to others! When someone makes an evil remark about 'foreigners,' I give them a piece of my mind." Living those words in Nazi Germany could have cost Charlotte her life, and seventy years after she first heard them, they sounded to her like a principle that might draw terrible political and social opposition and require enormous sacrifice.

It was the summer of 1990, and Charlotte no doubt had more reasons than many West Berliners to complain about the East Germans and other Eastern Europeans who had flooded into her city since the Wall fell. They jammed traffic to a standstill, forcing a hundred daily adjustments by comfortable West Berliners. Outside her house she was confined to a wheelchair, and the crush of people unaccustomed to Western ways vastly complicated her getting around. On her weekly shopping trips the lines at Aldi supermarket were three or four times as long, and every East Berlin customer had to be personally introduced to the market system of comparison shopping. Charlotte, who had remarried and was now Charlotte Freudenthal, felt impatience and distrust too. But she had also been the victim of extreme political, institutionalized inequality.

Many Nazis also survived their regime. Alois Brunner lived until 1992. He is said to have escaped through Italy to Syria, where he lived in Damascus. He received a couple of letter bombs. Because of them, he lost some fingers and eyesight in one eye. But he had the constant protection of bodyguards from the Syrian government and carried poison at all times, preferring the idea of suicide to sudden kidnapping and prosecution.

The allies executed Alfred Schneider in Italy in 1946 for his part in the mass shootings of Allied soldiers. As result of his "indispensable" work as director of the Berlin Gestapo's Jewish Desk, Walter Stock was never sent to the front. He lived a long life in the West German industrial belt around Essen and, according to German police, recently died. In postwar trials he was sentenced to more than four years in prison but served less than a year. Karl Krell actually took credit for the release of twenty-five hundred half Jews and Jews from intermarriages from Rosenstrasse in his postwar trial, apparently without being contradicted.

LEOPOLD GUTTERER

Leopold Gutterer also lived as of the early 1990s, surviving even his son, who died in 1990 and had remained completely loyal to his father, settling in the same West German city. Obviously I had to be careful about taking what Gutterer, the master of deception, told me. But there were points at which his self-interest did not contradict the record of events. After the war he worked anonymously for two years for a Bavarian farmer, before he was discovered and arrested. He was then sentenced as an "activist," the second of four categories of offenders under American denazification codes, to two years of labor and lifelong suspension of his pension. Since the war Gutterer had never returned to Berlin.

ERIKA LEWINE

Erika Lewine was still a fighter. She recalled her story over cups of dark coffee, from behind a billowing, never extinguished cloud of cigarette smoke, in the small kitchen of her North Berlin apartment. She was still on intimate terms with her inauspicious Berlin origins. But she had tried to keep a finger on the pulse of anti-Semitism and had followed the course of her children's education, watching carefully for anti-Semitism and the treatment of recent German history in the classroom.

THE GRODKAS

The Grodkas lived in Berlin until they died, within a year of each other, in the late 1980s. Wally, a Berliner, was so moved by the construction of the Berlin Wall in August 1961 that she wrote a long poem in praise of the city and in lament of its division. She died within months of the collapse of the Wall. Ranier lived on in Berlin with his wife.

ELSA HOLZER

Elsa Holzer was Berlin. When Elsa said "we," she usually meant "we Berliners." I first met her in early 1985, when the East German government was at a zenith of its self-confidence and international recognition. I met her again, after first monetary and then political unification. The state had fallen around her again and again. She had outlived the kaiser and the Great War, the November revolution and the crises of the German Weimar Republic, the Thousand-Year Reich and the Second World War, the postwar reconstruction and socialism-on-the-way-to-communism under the Socialist Unity party. In a way, in fact, Elsa Holzer, as part of the massive Berlin street protest that dealt the Nazi dictatorship a defeat, even put her imprint on the city's political history.

After the war Rudi and Elsa lived in Britz, in what became the American zone of Berlin. But Rudi was a Communist, certain that communism was the political party that consistently opposed war. They went to the zone of their liberators, the Soviet zone, which became East Berlin, and requested housing there because of their Communist commitments. Party officials told them to "stay where you are and fight for the Revolution," but they moved nevertheless.

Elsa was the only eyewitness from East Germany who responded to my requests on West Berlin radio for eyewitness accounts of the women's street protest in Nazi Berlin. Americans in East Germany were rare creatures, and during our acquaintance she came to refer to me as "my American." For hours at a time we forgot the postwar settlement and the thin Iron Curtain separating our homes in Berlin. Occasionally, however, Elsa made a jarring reference to Nazi Germany with names from postwar East Germany. Describing Gestapo house searches, she said, "House searches were like they are here with the Stasi. If you somehow get a bad reputation, they're immediately there to make a search. Don't you have that where you live?" Her question was sincere. The pervasive police presence during National Socialism together with that in East German socialism had combined to make rights of privacy incredible. There was of course no equivalent in East Germany to the SS and no concentration camps, but for Elsa a continuity of police institutions existed between Nazi and postwar socialist Germany. On another occasion she stated that the guards policing the street as she and others protested the arrest of their Jewish family members were *die SS und VoPo*. The *VoPo*, or *Volkspolizei*, were street police in East Germany, whom Elsa had confused with the *Schupo*, the street police in Nazi Germany. She never transposed Nazi and East German institutions of unequal rank but occasionally used the name of the East German authority roughly equivalent in role to that she meant to designate in Nazi Germany.

WERNER GOLDBERG

Werner Goldberg stayed in Berlin because of the Germans who had the courage not to support Nazi policies, he told me. His father was the only one of his Jewish family to survive the war. "We had a lot of relatives," he said. "Not one survived." Both Werner and his brother have been involved in Berlin politics. As a journalist after the war, Goldberg was a section head of Berlin's SFB radio station and the editor of *Die Mahnung*, the paper of the BVN—League of Victims under the Nazi Regime. He was a member of the Senate of (West) Berlin from 1958 until 1979. This gracious man still lived in the house he grew up in, sixty years ago.

NOTES ON SOURCES
AND DISCOVERY _____

When I arrived in Berlin to write the story of the Rosenstrasse Protest in 1985, no one else was working on the project, and there were merely a couple of dozen written sources, mostly in German, that mentioned the event at all. The longest was a newspaper article; most treated the story in a paragraph or less, as if it were a fluke and had nothing to say about the nature of Nazi power in general. Nazi documentation of the Rosenstrasse Protest, other than that of Goebbels's diary, had apparently not survived the war, and much of the explanation for the Nazi response to the Rosenstrasse Protest had to be drawn from the nature and structure of the National Socialist concept and practice of political power. I was told by a professor at the Free University as well as at the West Berlin Jewish Community that the last survivors of the incident had "just died." But in response to radio interviews and newspaper notices, dozens of eyewitnesses began to call me. Two employees of the West Berlin Jewish Community had shared the experience of the Rosenstrasse Protest without knowing it. Occasionally Germans called to assure me that all eyewitnesses were certainly dead by now.

Although there was not a single scholarly article on the protest, I learned that to claim the protest was successful was to challenge prevailing interpretations. Resistance to interpreting the protest as a force that influenced the regime and saved Jews from death continues. As a means of influence, the protest carries a very mixed message: On the one hand, some Germans did protest the Holocaust, but on the other, if it was possible to do so, why didn't more do this? The German Resistance Memorial Museum of Berlin has scores of pamphlets on topics ranging from grocers who secretly gave Jews more than was officially allowed to the assassination attempt on Hitler, but nothing on Rosenstrasse.

In addition to interviews, many of my sources were from the trial of Otto Bovensiepen, at the Berlin District Court, a fortresslike and decorous building on Turmstrasse, where access was very unusual. Here were the stories, in the form of eyewitness reports, supporting documents, and Gestapo memos of the former chief of the Berlin Gestapo, who together with his henchmen had stood trial in 1969 for the deportation and murder of some thirty-thousand Berlin Jews.

The Bovensiepen Trial was a fractional part of a many-faceted trial directed against the Reich Security Main Office (RSHA), which included various police forces, the Gestapo, the secret police, the SS, and its intelligence branch, the SD. The trial was discontinued, still incomplete, in the early 1970s. But the first step—the collection of evidence—had filled two rooms. The court had embarked on its enormous enterprise with great thoroughness by collecting documents from twenty-five archives and personal collections around the world. Courts had confiscated wartime documents from the privacy of homes. On hand were scores of supporting documents, such as maps, telephone directories, and the complete records of other postwar trials of former Nazis from around Germany. In addition, thousands of pages of transcribed statements from hundreds of witnesses swelled the records. There was testimony from Gestapo men and their secretaries, from Berlin street police and their superiors in the Berlin police hierarchy, from survivors of Auschwitz and other camps and ghettos in the East, and from eyewitnesses. Each document bore one of three colors: Purple folders were those of the victims, green for the accused, orange for other witnesses.

In the court records differences were enormous between testimonies of victims and perpetrators who were hauled in front of the court. The stories from the surviving Jews were always passionate and often full of detail, while the reports of their oppressors were characteristically so lifeless as to suggest that they must have been unconscious in twelve years of Nazi rule. The implication was that the Nazi witnesses had not chosen anything and had taken no initiative during those twelve years (but had somehow managed to make wonderfully big strides in their advancement up the career ladder).

Some of the depositions, culled for the Bovensiepen Trial from earlier postwar trials, were from as early as the late 1940s and early 1950s. Most, however, were from the mid and late 1960s. Early statements made under oath confirmed critical details. Nearly incredible events, like the return of dozens of intermarried Jews from Auschwitz after their deportation to that death camp from Rosenstrasse, were verified in repeated testimonies and integrated into the court's own narrative of events. The multiplicity of sources allowed for the crosschecking of facts, and the court itself had made judgments on issues of cause and effect. The massive collection of documents provided invaluable insight into the operations of the machinelike efficiency of a bureaucracy that was only briefly interrupted by a street protest. Yet the German court, which concluded that the Rosenstrasse Protest caused the Gestapo to release intermarried Jews, had been interested in determining what the men on trial knew about the Final Solution during the Third Reich and whether they had acted "correctly"—without physical abuse—in the process of deportation (a counterproductive inquiry since the assembly line–like efficiency with which the deportation process worked to maximize the number of Jews killed frowned on public abuse of Jews).

Being in Berlin among the victims and perpetrators had brought me much closer to the story. Interviews with eyewitnesses could be another bridge across the decades. Oral history, even when limited by the nature of memory and self-interest of interviewees, had the considerable advantage of allowing the source to respond directly to the historian's most pressing questions.

In interviews I also called for reports from bystanders, but no one in this category replied. So I went to the street of the protest, Rosenstrasse, and began knocking on doors to make inquiries there. This was when it was still East Berlin, but I don't think the new national identity was what caused silence when I asked whether anyone had seen or heard about the protest back in 1943. People seemed bemused or amazed. There were the bombings back then, and people on the street all the time. Rather than bring me closer to the event, my experience in seeking bystanders on the street of the protest made me feel more distant.

Mr. Koblin, the court's archivist, also talked to me about my topic.

He said there had already been too much attention to the Nazi period, and there was no sense in dragging the dirty German history out of the bag (*"Schmutz aus der Tute holen"*). Then one day Koblin came into my room and told me a story. "A Jewish family lived above us on the Wilmersdorferstrasse," he said. "They were called Goldschmidt. One day the SS came by with guns and drove the family out. My mother peeped out the door because there was so much noise. My sister cried because she was scared. We never saw that family again, although we lived there until 1945."

A number of interviewees resisted calling back the bad memories. Very old people could no longer endure it—or no longer wanted to try. People I had talked with in 1985, who had since turned ninety yet were not senile, no longer wanted to talk in 1989. They needed, ultimately, their "rest." Those who talked often did so out of a sense that the story must be passed along. Eventually I became so familiar with some of the Gestapo and Jewish personalities that dominated the life of Berlin's Jews in 1942–43 that I could talk freely with interviewees about a network of names and places that many others had long since forgotten or hoped to forget. As someone willing to listen while they revisited the Nazi past, I was an oddity. In some cases the distance I brought as an American helped initially to open the door, bringing me closer. Often I remained for hours, and in some cases I found no excuse for leaving an interview until that day's last subway train was about to depart.

Once I attempted to get together the remaining eyewitnesses of those intermarried Jews who had been deported to Auschwitz and two weeks later released, while the Rosenstrasse Protest continued. There were two men and three wives who had experienced this. "When are we going to talk about something important?" one asked, tired of my relentless pursuit of the story. A collective interview was impossible. Like many eyewitnesses, each one contradicted what he or she personally had not experienced. Each person in turn had to be given the chance to delve back into the past, alone, during an interview.

Having begun with such eagerness to tell the history of the Rosenstrasse Protest, I always approached in awe the people who could tell me about it. I expected somehow to find them and their place marked and honored among the neighborhood; perhaps there would be a plaque, or perhaps the neighbors would speak respectfully when I asked which apartment was the one. Usually I found interviewees in the most humble circumstances, surrounded by neighbors who did not know their stories.

Where were the former Nazis who knew the story? At least a

dozen secretaries who had worked in Eichmann's office lived in West Berlin. Still living was the secretary who had been present at the notorious Wannsee Conference, but attempts to talk with these secretaries was almost always unfruitful. They had had "other things" in their heads back then.

In the industrial belt around Essen lived at least several very high-ranking members of Eichmann's office. Otto Hünsche, who had become a deputy to Eichmann by 1943, gave me a telephone interview and then invited me to meet him at his home. I arrived with great expectations in his sleepy village late one Saturday morning, when all the townsfolk, it seemed, were involved in the shopping that is the Saturday-morning tradition throughout Germany. But Hünsche would be unable to give an interview after all, he said later, referring to his bad health. Not far away lived a member of the Berlin Gestapo's Judenreferat, Willi Rothe, who after the war became the police chief in his small village. Rothe was actually forthcoming on the telephone, and I was about to make an appointment when his wife broke in. Taking up the phone, she swore at me in no uncertain terms that her husband was old, that the story was ridiculous, that I was *unverschämt*.

Another Nazi, who had been a chauffeur for Eichmann's office, invited me to his home. When I arrived at his place at the edge of the Black Forest, there was a birthday party for him in progress. Family —children and grandchildren—had gathered to honor him in rich measure, and the local newspaper had joined in by printing its congratulations to a man who had become a local social stalwart. All efforts were made to make me feel at home and part of the festivities. At nightfall he drove me the hundred kilometers to my next destination —Calw, hometown of Hermann Hesse, at the eastern edge of the Black Forest. At the wheel, where he had spent so much time in life, he spoke with resentment of what might have happened had Hitler strategically withdrawn the Sixth Army at Stalingrad.

Because of his close association with Goebbels as well as his leading role in work with Heydrich and the SD on domestic espionage reports, Gutterer was potentially one of the best Nazi sources, living or dead, on the Rosenstrasse Protest. I met Gutterer, along with his wife (they were married before 1933) a number of times, over a period of four years, in the Gutterers' West German apartment. The Gutterers of course were good hosts, amid every sign that they enjoyed a rather normal life: caring children, friendly neighbors, entertainment. In her mid-eighties Mrs. Gutterer made an impression of a well-preserved and protective hausfrau, who enthused about Goebbels and the way he used the German language.

Gutterer's mind and memory were still sharp. On the table was a copy of a carefully underscored *Frankfurter Allgemeine Zeitung*, the conservative daily he praised effusively for its correct usage of the German language. Gutterer was matter-of-fact about our interviews, meeting me in his apron with bread dough up to his elbows, inviting me to beer or tea and in turn to a meal. I was, he told me, the first person he had talked to about his activities after 1933.

Gutterer's imagination was still so vivid his hands flew to illustrate the pictures passing through his mind. During our conversations he laughed, cried, and mimicked a Jewish comedian whom Goebbels had protected because of his popularity and positive effect on public morale. He repeatedly grew so loud that his wife finally shut the living room window, lest the neighbors overhear. Gutterer then excused himself by saying he could not help becoming overwhelmed when talking of his and the Nazi movement's dizzying climb to positions of prominence in modern world history. "Children," he cried, giddy from memory, "I can't help it if I get so excited."

Although he loved to recall very interesting tales about his power back then—particularly of his private or semiprivate meetings with Hitler—Gutterer became increasingly concerned with shaping his own profile. He still came across as a National Socialist, however. Gutterer described power in dramatic, definitive terms characteristic of an authoritarian. He praised Israel for making the deserts bloom and, like Holocaust deniers, said that Germany could not have killed six million Jews because there were so many remaining. The overall conception he painted of his own role was of a very important man who as a modern political organizer got involved with a noble cause, whose leaders went increasingly mad during the war. "Believe me, Mr. Stoltzfus," he said, reflecting on the divided Germany and communism, "after those results, I am no longer a believer in Hitler!"

Gutterer's interpretation of the evils of National Socialism is that Goebbels, like Hitler, became inflexibly attached to extreme notions in the course of the war. National Socialism was originally good and wanted to do good for the people, he contended. In the fall of 1944 Gutterer was pushed out of the Propaganda Ministry and into the army as a tank commander in Belgium. The only reason the German army lost at the Bulge and the surrounding region, he claimed, was that it ran out of gasoline.

Gutterer was a vain man whose self-image remained tied to memories of power. Clearly I would, as the Germans say, have to "enjoy carefully" my interviews with him. Yet where his self-justifications did cross paths with credible testimony, he was an invaluable source of information on the Rosenstrasse Protest and its context, the relationship between the population and the Nazi leadership.

In 1947 Gutterer, who had been in hiding on a Bavarian farm, was captured and tried under the American denazification processes. Because records were not available—especially the minutes of Goebbels's meetings with his deputies at the Propaganda Ministry, which arrived at the Potsdam, East German, archives from the Soviet Union in the mid-1950s—Gutterer was merely sentenced as an "offender," the second of five categories of offenders under denazification codes (category one was "major offender). He was sentenced to two years of labor and lifelong suspension of his pension.

In postwar West Germany, research on wartime Germany pointed across the Wall to the other Germany. Among the court documents in West Berlin was a letter, written in October 1948, from the part of the city that had become part of East Germany. A couple of sentences in the letter, written by the "Magistrat von Gross-Berlin [City Council of Greater Berlin, for the Main Office for the Victims of Fascism]" filled me with excitement and sent me on a mission to find documents in East Germany that was to last for years: "We are by chance in possession of memos, which extend from 14 November 1942 until the end of January 1943, of Hauptsturmführer Brunner, who was in charge of deportations during this time period up until March/April of 1943. Because of Brunner's appearance the deportations grew much worse and culminated in the Big-Action of 27 February 1943." Brunner was the deportation expert who, having deported Vienna's Jews with record speed and brutality, was rewarded in November 1942 by an order to move to the Reich capital and do the same there. If his files existed, they would undoubtedly be the single most valuable archival source on the Rosenstrasse Protest since other Nazi documents had been destroyed.

I had initially written to the state archives administrative offices in East Germany in March 1985. Citing East Germany's own guides, I specified the documents I needed to see at the East German National Archives in Potsdam. In July 1985, following my second letter to the archive administration, I received my first answer: "Despite vigorous research no sources in archives under our jurisdiction concerning your research subject could be discovered. Thus we unfortunately cannot confer the desired usage permission." Through an acquaintance, an important person high up at the Academy of Sciences, a German immigrant to the United States who had left the United States during the McCarthy era, I persevered and soon received a second letter from the same person at the National Archive Administration inviting me to a preliminary discussion. During this visit I was invited to begin re-searching. The archivist who had informed me the archives had nothing of interest to me did not seem the least bit embarrassed to extend the invitation; saving face was not important in a state with as equally meager respect for the individual as for truth.

In search of documents, I returned to live for seven months in East Germany on a grant from the International Research and Ex-changes Board (IREX). In a state that ruled by monopolizing initiative, it was especially important to have a Western sense of enterprise in getting access. I never did see the Brunner memos. The archivists suggested that someone had apparently destroyed the documents since 1948. But by the momentous year of 1989 I was promised access to the documents of the Central Organization of German Jews. This offer was repeated again on October 25, 1989, when on the invitation of the Humboldt University I gave a lecture about a street protest in a cen-tralized and closed German governmental system, just around the cor-ner from Humboldt, on Rosenstrasse (no one questioned whether the story of protest in 1943 was in any way parallel to those of the con-temporary upheaval). Two weeks later the Berlin Wall burst open, and the people I had been petitioning for access to documents lost their power to control access. In June 1990 I finally saw in Potsdam the last of the documents I had requested in 1985, but they bore no revelations.

In both Germanys I was very often asked why I had chosen to research such a depressing history. I would answer that from the se-curity of an armchair it offers a chance to consider the most fundamental dilemmas of human existence: about torture and conscience, collusion and compromise, altruism and selfishness. Or that in light of the mon-strous evils Nazi Germany presented, I had learned how minimal were my own difficulties. The story also held hope.

When I began interviewing Germans who had protested on Ro-senstrasse, I approached them as sources of information. I was con-cerned with getting facts, and focused on the event of the Rosenstrasse Protest. But I received more than I knew how to ask for. These survivors had adventures to tell, memories that did not necessarily address my questionnaire. Yet it seemed that to discard all information from in-terviews that did not make a direct argument for the effect of the protest was to confuse wheat for chaff. The story consisted not only of facts my interviewees relayed; the facts themselves had been determined by the interviewees, and the story was also about their personalities, their loyalties, their characters. Personal stories gave me a sense of depth and detail, without necessarily proving any theories. No two people told the same story the same way, and I was never sure the details of any particular biography were representative. But no generalization or theory could ever negate the significance of any personal experience. Instead of dismissing the stories not directly related to the Rosenstrasse Protest I decided my task was to embody them in a larger, unifying structure that would not diminish the emotional intensity of each story. The stories were so moving I was convinced that my task was to stay out of the way (once I had access to them), to let the events reveal themselves.

ENDNOTES _____

ABBREVIATIONS

AA	Auswärtiges Amt (Foreign Office)
BA	Bundesarchiv (National Archives)
BA Potsdam	Bundesarchiv Abteilung Potsdam (National Archives at Potsdam)
BDC	Berlin Document Center
BVB	Berliner Verkehrs-Betrieb (Berlin Public Transportation Authority)
CDJC	Centre Documentation Juive Contemporaine (Center of Contemporary Jewish Documentation)
DAF	Deutsche Arbeitsfront (German Labor Front)
Gestapo	Geheime Staatspolizei
IfZ	Institut für Zeitgeschichte (Institute of Contemporary History)
KB	Kammergericht Berlin (Berlin Supreme Court)
LB	Landgericht Berlin (Berlin District Court)
NA	National Archives
ND	Nuremberg Trial Document
NS	National Sozialismus (National Socialism)
NSDAP	Nationsozialistische Deutsche Arbeiter-Partei (National Socialist party)
LBI	Leo Baeck Institute
OSS	Office of Strategic Serivess

Pr. GSta.   Preussische Geheime Staatsarchiv (Prussian Secret State Archives)
ProMi   Propaganda Ministerium (Propaganda Ministry)
RAF   Royal Air Force
RGBl   *Reichsgesetzblatt* (Reich law gazette)
RJM   Reichsjustizministerium (Justice Ministry)
RMdI   Reichsministerium des Innern (Interior Ministry)
RSHA   Reichsicherheitshauptamt (Reich Security Main Office)
SA   Sturmabteilung (Storm Troopers)
SD   Sicherheitsdienst (Security Service)
SS   Schutzstaffel
VGH   Volksgerichthof (People's Court)
ZSA   Zentrales Staatsarchiv Potsdam (Potsdam Central State Archives)
ZSdL   Zentrale Stelle der Landesjustizverwaltungen (Central Office of the State
             Administration of Justice)

INTRODUCTION

1. Statement of Else Hannach (who escaped Germany in July 1944), July 26 and 31, 1944, Bovensiepen Trial, Supporting Document 30 (Dr. Wolfgang Scheffler Collection).
2. On their field gray army uniforms they wore a small band with the script "Leibstandarte SS Adolf Hitler." Two were officers. They were wearing war medals. Statement of Karl Hefter, October 28, 1955, in the trial of Josef ("Sepp") Dietrich, I P Js 3767.65, Staatsanwaltschaft Berlin.
3. Walter Stock, the former head of the Judenreferat of the Berlin Gestapo, referred exclusively to the mass arrest action (which later became popularly known as the *Fabrikaktion*) as *Judenschlussaktion*, or derivatives of this, including *Abschluss der Juden Aktion* and *Schlussaktion gegen die Juden.* LB, Strafsache gegen Walter Stock (PkLs 3/52), Interrogation of Walter Stock, August 13, 1951.
4. Statement of Dr. Martha Mosse, July 24, 1958, Bovensiepen Trial.
5. Warned that running meant getting shot, the Jews were crammed face forward into the backs of the persons in front of them. Statement of Else Hannach, July 26 and 31, 1944, Bovensiepen Trial, Supporting Document 30.
6. "Die Lage der 'Mischlinge' in Deutschland, Mitte März 1943," a four-page unpublished report from Berlin in mid-March 1943 by Dr. Gerhard Lehfeld, from the archives of Robert A. Graham, SJ, La Civiltà Cattolica, Rome, Italy. Dr. Lehfeld's source was Erich Gritzbach, Hermann Goering's personal adviser at the Office of the Four-Year Plan.
7. Indictment, trial of Otto Bovensiepen, 135, lists these, substituting the old people's home on Gerlachstrasse for the one on Grosse Hamburger Strasse. Rosenstrasse 2–4 housed "*die Schulverwaltung, das Wohlfahrts- und Jugendamt, das Jugendpflegede-zernat, ein Büro fur Winterhilfe, ein Büro für Berufsumschichtung,*" according to a Berlin telephone book from 1942. The indictment gives a summary of the Final Roundup and Rosenstrasse Protest, based on court testimony from victims as well as the Gestapo, LBI, Anklageschrift [indictment] in der Strafsache gegen Otto Bovensiepen et al. (1969), Microfilm Reel 239, 207–217.
8. "Das Ende einer Gemeinde," an anonymous report from a former nurse at the Berlin Jewish hospital, reported from Lausanne at the end of 1943, in Gerhard Schoenberner, ed., *Wir haben es gesehen* (Im Bertelsmann Lesering: n.d.), 313–317.
9. Forty-three abandoned children called the Jewish Community in search of their parents, according to a statement of Dr. Martha Mosse, July 23 and 24, 1958, Bovensiepen Trial.
10. Hysterical men and women, clamoring to reach a child or spouse in another corner of the building, pressed forward out of their designated category, only to fall back under the whips and curses of SS men, who cried out, "You damned Jews are supposed to stay in your group." Statement of Dr. Kurt Radlauer, November 10, 1966, Bovensiepen

Trial, which reported that upon arriving at the synagogue, he was immediately received by two Jewish orderlies and a Gestapo man standing behind them. The twenty-five Jews from his truck were divided at once into groups. Radlauer went with intermarried Jews one flight of stairs up to the gallery, overlooking the huge first floor of the old synagogue.

11. Hildegard Henschel, "Aus der Arbeit der jüdischen Gemeinde Berlin, 16. Oktober 1941–1943." Leo Baeck Institute, New York, Max Kreuzberger Research Papers, AR 7183/box 13, folder A, 9.

12. Lehfeld, "Die Lage der 'Mischlinge.' " Lehfeld reported that Eichmann planned to use nine thousand people from intermarried couples to "build a wall" on the front, language that mirrors the language used later to describe the activity of *Mischlinge* and intermarried Jews forced into hard labor under the auspices of Organization Todt. Holocaust expert Raul Hilberg writes that hundreds of intermarried French Jews were sent to hard labor and that in 1945 "heavy work schedules were also in store" for intermarried Jews from Vienna and Frankfurt. Raul Hilberg, *Perpetrators, Victims, Bystanders: The Jewish Catastrophe, 1933–1945* (New York: 1992), 132.

13. Interview with Vera Breitwieser, March 26, 1985, Berlin. Only privileged intermarried couples were allowed to have telephones, however, so this chain was probably of little use to most of the concerned families.

14. Jewish women married to German men were considered "Aryan" households and were designated by Hitler in 1938 as privileged intermarriages. Jews in privileged intermarriages did not wear the Star of David, and very few were arrested during the Final Roundup. Jewish men married to Germans, on the other hand, were called Jewish households. These men from nonprivileged intermarriages wore the Star of David and were arrested.

15. Interview with Charlotte Israel Freudenthal, February 1985, and statement of Charlotte Freudenthal in Bezirksverordnetenversammlung von Charlottenburg, *Schon damals fingen viele an zu schweigen* (Berlin: 1986), 197.

16. On a map from 1648 Rosenstrasse is one of about two dozen streets pictured. In 1583 it was called Hurengasse (Prostitute Alley). *"Es klang ironisch und sollte erzierisch wirken."* Heinz Knobloch, *Meine liebste Mathilde: Das unauffällige Leben des Mathilde Jacob* (Berlin: 1986), 273.

17. With the permission of the Gestapo, the Jewish men arrested during the Kristallnacht were received at Bahnhof Friedrichstrasse by the Jewish Welfare Committee (Jüdische Hilfskommittee) and brought to Rosenstrasse to be clothed and given medical care. In Sachsenhausen the surviving Jews had witnessed deaths by freezing and heart attacks. Statement of Norbert Wollheim, July 6, 1966, Bovensiepen Trial. The deportation to Buchenwald was the "first large-scale action against the alleged anti-social elements among the Jews . . . persons who had been previously punished for a single, small misdemeanor." A "large number" left the camp; others languished for years and died there. Ernst Bukofzer, *Laws for Jews and Persecution of Jews under the Nazis* (Berlin, 1946), 6, 7.

18. Moritz Henschel, "Die letzten Jahre der jüdischen Gemeinde Berlin" (a lecture given September 13, 1946), Yad Vashem, Jerusalem, 01/51.

19. Statement of Charlotte Rosenthal from February 21, 1955, LBI, Wiener Library microfilms (AR 7187/Reel 600). This microfilm contains eyewitness statements and a list of women participants in the protest. I have interviewed twenty-one participants of the Rosenstrasse Protest, eight who were released from the collecting center because of the protest (including two sent first to Auschwitz and then released about two weeks later), Goebbels's chief deputy at the Propaganda Ministry, a former assistant to Adolf Eichmann, and two members of the Berlin Gestapo.

20. Interview with Giesela Weigert, June 21, 1985.

21. Interviews with Charlotte Israel Freudenthal, February 10 and 25, 1985.

22. Annie Radlauer interviews, March 12, 1985; May 29, 1985.

23. Georg Zivier, "Aufstand der Frauen," *Sie* (December 1945).
24. In the East German Communist party newspaper Inge Unikower wrote that "foreign news sources reported at the time of 400 to 600 . . . including London Radio." Although she titled the article "Silent Protest," Unikower reported that protesters called out, "Give us our husbands back. We want to have our husbands again." Inge Unikower, "Stummer Protest," *Neues Deutschland*, no. 46 (November 14, 1964), 2. Ruth Andreas Friedrich, whose diary was for years the most accessible reference to the protest, writes that there had been six thousand protesters, a possible sum total of persons who participated. Ruth Andreas Friedrich, *Schauplatz Berlin: Ein Tagebuch aufgezeichnet 1983– 1945* (Reinbeck bei Hamburg: 1964), March 1943. Considering that some two thousand Jews were imprisoned at Rosenstrasse and that the vast majority of those who protested were their family members, this would indicate that each person imprisoned had been represented on the street by three family members sometime during the course of the protest. One interned Jew reported that seven of his family members participated in the protest (interview with Gad Beck, January 28, 1985), but it was more common for a prisoner to be represented by just one or two protesters.
25. Zivier, "Aufstand der Frauen."
26. Interview with Rita Kuhn, April 26, 1989, Berkeley, California.
27. Statement of Sartorius, December 13, 1965, Bovensiepen Trial.
28. Interview with Leopold Gutterer, August 19, 1986. Gutterer, who made a career out of deceiving people, can hardly be taken at face value, yet parts of his testimony are reliable because his self-justifications at points coincided with the truth. According to the historian Peter Hoffmann, Gutterer was a relative of Maurice Bavaud, the Swiss student who tried to kill Hitler in 1938. See Peter Hoffmann, "Maurice Bavaud's Attempt to Assassinate Hitler in 1938," in *Police Forces in History*, ed. G. L. Mosse (London: 1975), 173ff.
29. Lehfeld, "Lage der 'Mischlinge,' " 4. I found no references to this arrest and protest in the Swedish press.
30. Ibid., 2, 3.
31. Hitler and the NSDAP hardly grasped power by votes alone. Jürgen Kocha and Hans-Ulrich Wehler, among others, have contended that still-powerful preindustrial forces in Weimar politics made possible the *Machtergreifung* (seizure of power). Hitler rose because of these "feudal remnants"—and the crisis of the Great Depression. Jürgen Kocha, "Ursachen des Nationalsozialismus," *Aus Politik und Zeitgeschichte* (June 21, 1980), 9–13; Hans-Ulrich Wehler, *The German Empire, 1871–1918*, trans. Kim Traynor (Leamington Spa, England: 1985); A. J. P. Taylor, *The Course of German History: A Survey of the Development of German History since 1815* (London: 1945). Another school of thought has argued that economics alone—the crises inherent in capitalism —destroyed the Weimar Republic. See especially David Abraham, *The Collapse of the Weimar Republic: Political Economy and Crisis* (Princeton: 1981). Karl Dietrich Bracher and Otto Kirchheimer emphasize errors in the Weimar constitution itself that were likely to produce a collapse into dictatorship. Karl Dietrich Bracher, *The German Di-lemma: The Relationship of State and Democracy*, trans. Richard Barry (New York: 1975), and Otto Kirchheimer, "Weimar and What Then?", in *Politics, Law and Social Change: Selected Essays of Otto Kirchheimer*, ed. Frederic Burn and Kurt Shell (New York and London: 1969), 33–74.
32. Goebbels's six children, who called Hitler Uncle, were special favorites in the Führer's private circles. See Joseph Goebbels, *The Goebbels Diaries: 1939–1941*, ed. Fred Taylor (New York: 1984), including photographs, 174ff.
33. Some historians have emphasized the role of storm trooper violence and intimidation in the Nazi seizure and consolidation of power, while Richard Bessel has argued that the role of this SA violence against the German left in 1933 was not so much to bring the Nazis to power as it was to demonstrate that "no real battle still needed to be fought." Richard Bessel, "Political Violence and the Nazi Seizure of Power," in *Life*

in the Third Reich, ed. Richard Bessel (New York: 1987), 6. See also Richard Bessel, *Political Violence and the Rise of Nazism: The Storm Troopers in Eastern Germany 1925–1934* (New Haven: 1984).

34. Karl Dietrich Bracher, *The German Dictatorship: The Origins, Structure, and Consequences of National Socialism*, trans. Jean Steinberg (New York and Washington, D.C.: 1970), 87.

35. Anthony Rhodes, *Propaganda: The Art of Persuasion: World War II* (Secaucus, N.J.: 1987), 16. These demonstrations usually took place at about 8:00 P.M., "when people's resistance was at its lowest ebb, and their minds most open to persuasion," writes Rhodes.

36. Joseph Goebbels, *Final Entries 1945: The Diaries of Joseph Goebbels*, ed. and introduction Hugh Trevor-Roper, trans. R. H. Barry (New York: 1978), xviii. Gutterer's title was *Reichshauptstellenleiter für Grosskundgebungen*.

37. "Verordnung zur Aufrechterhaltung der öffentlichen Ruhe und Sicherheit vom 20. Mai 1933," excerpted in BA Potsdam, 50.01 (ProMi), 63, 2ff.

38. Pr. GSta., Rep. 90 P, 12.

39. Joseph Goebbels, *The Goebbels Diaries, 1942–43*, ed. Louis Lochner (New York: 1948), entry for March 6, 1943, 276.

40. Eleanor Hancock, *The National Socialist Leadership and Total War, 1941–5* (New York: 1991), 48.

41. Officials at the Final Solution conference of March 6, 1942, expressed concern that a compulsory divorce of intermarriages "would lead to considerable disquiet among non-German relatives." Summary of conference, ND NG-2586-H. In 1942 the Interior Ministry when considering policies on *Mischlinge*, continued to express concern about the large number of German relatives each *Mischling* had. Stuckart to Klopfer, et al., March 16, 1942, ND NG-2586-1. And even in 1943 the regime was still tailoring its policies on intermarried Jews to the fact that they had non-Jewish relatives and friends. Hessisches Hauptstaatsarchiv, judgment against Heinrich Baab (51 Ks 1/50).

42. The regime continued an effort to cover up the Final Solution, maintaining the secrecy of euphemisms, restricted correspondence on the matter, and prohibitions against speaking of it, etc. It is arguable that by sometime in 1943 segments of the German population knew that "terrible things" were happening to Jews in the east. It is arguable that this knowledge tended to intimidate opposition, rather than stir up dissent. The main point for elucidating the release of Jews at Rosenstrasse, however, is that regardless of what the Germans knew, the regime continued to strive to conduct genocide in secrecy. Awareness that Germany was acting barbarically against Jews might have stiffened the resolve of Germans to win the war, for those who feared that losing would bring revenge for German atrocities. The case of Gustav Nosske and others, discussed below, however, indicates that some Germans were willing to commit atrocities for Germany only as long as Germany was winning the war.

43. Out of 5,837 of these, fewer than half, about 2,500, were sent to the work camps.

44. The Nazis used the term "Aryan" to identify a group of Indo-Germanic people, excluding, most prominently, Jews and Gypsies. For National Socialism, this group represented a race, the Master Race. Aryan is thus a term as offensive as it is irrational, and I have used the word "German" to refer to those Germans whom the Nazis called Aryans. Jews were Germans too, of course, at least until the Nuremberg Laws of 1935 stripped them of citizenship. But given the Nuremberg Laws, the racial-nationalistic meaning Nazism gave to the term "Aryan," and the general usage patterns in histories of Nazi Germany, I have used the term "German" in the place of "Aryan" and contrasted with the term "Jew." Occasionally, however, to emphasize the racial implications of that word, I use the term "Aryan." By 1944 Himmler's office specifically stated a preference for using the term "German-blooded" in place of "Aryan." Report from Himmler's personal staff titled "Behandlung von Mischlingsangelegenheiten" (undated report from mid-1944), BA, NS 19/3335.

45. An inmate at Rosenstrasse estimated that there were 2,000 imprisoned there (Statement of Ferdinand Wolff, May 4, 1951, Trial against Walter Stock, Landgericht Berlin, PkLs 3/52, hereafter cited as Stock Trial) while a police officer who spent one night there estimated only 1,000. Statement of former street policeman Anton von Kryshak, Bovensiepen Trial, 1968. Hauptscharführer Karl Krell, the unemployed baker turned Gestapo agent for Berlin's Jewish Desk, claimed at his denazification trial after the war that he had ordered the release of 2,000 intermarried Jews. Statement of Karl Krell, 4 SpLs 16/47 Bielefeld, BA, Koblenz. There is in any case a difference between the number of intermarried Jews and *Mischlinge* released as the result of the protest and those released from Rosenstrasse, given that some *Mischlinge* and intermarried Jews arrested in the Berlin Final Roundup were released from other collection centers during or following the protest. Thus some *Mischlinge* were released from the Clou collection center, and an intermarried Jew, Walter Baron, was released from a collection center at Auguststrasse 17, a Jewish school. Interview with Baron's daughter, Mrs. Bieversdorf, May 24, 1985, who still has her father's certificate of release, dated March 13, 1943, and signed by Walter Dobberke. The number of intermarried Jews arrested would not exceed the number of officially registered Berlin Jews in nonprivileged intermarriages, but it would also likely be very close to this amount. On September 1, 1942, in preparation for plans to clear the Reich of Jews, the Berlin Jewish Community made a "final report" to the Gestapo on the number of Jews still in Berlin. "Final report" of the Berlin Jewish Community's Registration Office (Kataster Verwaltung), BA Potsdam, R 8150, September 1, 1942. The community's Office of Registration reported to the Gestapo on September 1 that there were 1,436 Jews in nonprivileged intermarriages (those who wore the Star of David). These Jews in the community's "final report" were arrested, either at work or at home, during the Final Roundup. In its report to the Gestapo community authorities admit that the number of intermarried Jews in their lists is "apparently too low, because in many cases" intermarried Jews remained "unknown" and unregistered. Subsequently Jewish authorities under orders from the Gestapo printed in the Jewish newspaper *Jüdische Nachrichtenblatt* demands that all still-unregistered Jews in intermarriage must now register. These announcements apparently were of little use, however, since at the end of the war there were still 1,451 Jews in nonprivileged intermarriages—the same group, by and large, that was imprisoned and released at Rosenstrasse.

    In addition to the 1,400-plus intermarried Berlin Jews who wore the star, a small number of Berlin Jews from privileged intermarriages wore the star. The community's "final report" of September 1, 1942, identifies 24 Jews from privileged intermarriages as wearing the Star of David, and in fact there were a number of Jews in privileged intermarriages who were arrested and then released from Rosenstrasse before the others, on the night of March 1–2, 1943.

    In addition to intermarried Jews, some children of intermarried couples—*Mischlinge*—were arrested in the Final Roundup. These were *Mischlinge* who wore the star, those enrolled in a Jewish community or those married to Jews. This was the minority of the *Mischlinge*, since nationally only 11 percent of German *Mischlinge* were enrolled in Jewish communities. According to estimates from eyewitnesses, there were some 200 or more *Mischlinge* imprisoned at Rosenstrasse. On the basis of these figures, and considering that some persons arrested were released not from Rosenstrasse but from other collection centers, it is safe to estimate that about 1,700 *Mischlinge* and intermarried Jews were released because of the street protest.

46. Statistics of the Central Organization of Jews in Germany (Reichsvereinigung der Juden in Deutschland) show that as of September 1944 there were 13,217 officially registered Jews in Germany. All but 230 lived in intermarriage. BA Potsdam, R 8150, 32. (The archives of the Central Organization of Jews has been made public and reorganized at BA Potsdam since the author read them in the private O. D. Kulka collection.) There

were also Jews in intermarriage who had never been detected and officially registered as Jews, and other Jews survived in hiding.

47. Ralf Georg Reuth, ed., *Joseph Goebbels, Tagebücher*, vol. 4, *1940–1942* (Munich and Zurich: 1942), entry for March 7, 1942, 1763.

48. Statement of Helmut Brinitzer, August 18, 1970, Bovensiepen Trial.

49. Marion A. Kaplan, *The Making of the Jewish Middle Class: Women, Family, and Identity in Imperial Germany* (New York and Oxford: 1991), 81.

50. Bruno Blau, "Mischehe im Nazireich," *Judaica* (April 1948), 46. See also Monika Richarz, ed. *Jüdisches Leben in Deutschland: Selbszeugnisse zur Sozialgeschichte, 1918–1945* (Stuttgart/New York: 1982), 466.

51. Ursula Büttner, *Die Not der Juden teilen: Christich-jüdische Familien im Dritten Reich* (Hamburg: 1988), 14, citing Herbert Strauss, "Jewish Emigration from Germany: Nazi Policies and Jewish Responses," *Leo Baeck Institute Year Book*, vol. 25 (1980), 317.

52. Kaplan, *Making of the Jewish Middle Class*, 81, and 258 n. 117. See also Der Preussische Minister des Innern an den Reichsjustizminister, October 28, 1933, BA Potsdam, 30.01 (RJM), BA Potsdam, 30.01 (RJM), 1389/1 ("Mischblütige Ehen"), 30. The minister noted that intermarriages in 1933 were observed "particularly in Frankfurt/Main and Wiesbaden."

53. Regierungspräsident in Wiesbaden to the Prussian Interior Minister, October 28, 1933, BA Potsdam, 30.01 (RJM), 1389/1, 30.

54. Claudia Koonz, *Mothers in the Fatherland: Women, the Family and Nazi Politics* (New York: 1987), 192.

55. Bukofzer, *Laws for Jews*, 16.

56. Raul Hilberg, *The Destruction of the European Jews* (New York/London: 1985), 169.

57. Report by SS statistician Richard Korherr, April 19, 1943, ND NO-5193.

58. BA Potsdam, R 8150, 32.

59. See Blau, "Mischehe im Nazireich," 52. According to an official Reich census of December 1942, there were 16,760 intermarriages in old Germany (report by Reich Inspector for Statistics Richard Korherr, April 19, 1943, ND NO-5193.) The discrepancy between the figures taken in 1939 and those recorded at the end of the war does not mean that 5,000 Jews in intermarriages were killed in the Final Solution. Jews could still emigrate from Germany until 1941; others died after being sent to hard labor camps on criminal charges; still others died in Allied bombing raids or from ostensibly natural causes or committed suicide.

60. This figure on German Jews who survived does not include the 1,499 *Geltungsjuden*, whom the Nazis counted as Jews in Germany as of the autumn of 1944, nor does it count the 1,200 to 1,400 Jews who survived Hitler as *U-boots*, hidden in the underground. On underground Jews in Berlin see Carolin Hilker-Siebenhaar, *Wegweiser durch das jüdische Berlin: Geschichte und Gegenwart* (Berlin: 1987), 361–369.

61. See the discussion among top ministries from February 16, 1943, into early 1945, about changing divorce laws to increase births. BA Potsdam, 30.01 (Justice Ministry), 10118.

62. Bernhard Lösener, "Als Rassereferent im Reichsministerium des Innern," *Vierteljahreshefte für Zeitgeschichte*, vol. 9 (September 1961), 278.

63. Jeremy Noakes has argued that the Nazi policy toward the *Mischlinge* was "formed by the contradictory pressures and changing priorities" of conflicts between ideology and politics. Jeremy Noakes, "Wohin gehören die 'Judenmischlinge'? Die Entstehung der ersten Durchführungsverordnungen zu den Nürnberger Gesetzen," in *Das Unrechtsregime: Internationale Forschung über den Nationalsozialismus*, ed. Ursula Büttner (Hamburg: 1986), vol. 2, 69, 70. Policies toward intermarried Jews represented an even greater conflict between Nazi ideology and policy, since these were not "half" but "full" Jews.

64. Many of the laws were concerned with blocking careers of Germans married to Jews. See Büttner, "Introduction," *Die Not der Juden teilen*.

65. Dirk Blasius has speculated that this is the case. Dirk Blasius, *Ehescheidung in Deutsch-land, 1794–1945* (Göttingen: 1987), 192.
66. Ursula Büttner estimates on the basis of statistics from Hamburg and Baden-Württem-berg that 93 percent of intermarried Germans remained married. Büttner, *Not der Juden teilen*, 57. Some intermarried Germans did divorce, sometimes by common consent, if the Jewish partners felt they were too much of a burden—see, for example, Irene Runge, *Onkel Max ist jüdisch: Neun Gespräche mit Deutschen die Juden halfen* (Berlin: 1991), 102—even though in some cases the partners secretly remained together as couples and later remarried. Interview with Charlotte Steudel, August 8, 1985, Berlin.
67. Lösener, "Als Rassereferent," 268." See also Büttner, *Not der Juden teilen*, 12, for further evidence that the party leaders wished to eliminate *Mischlinge*. On the regime's *Mischlinge* policies in general, see Jeremy Noakes, "Nazi Policy towards German-Jewish Mischlinge," *Yearbook Leo Baeck Institute*, vol. 34 (1989), 291–354; John A. S. Gren-ville, "Die 'Endlösung' und die 'Judenmischlinge' im Dritten Reich," *Das Unrechtsre-gime*, loc. cit., 91–121; Uwe Dietrich Adam, *Judenpolitik im Dritten Reich* (Düsseldorf: 1972); Uwe Adam, "An Overall Plan for Anti-Jewish Legislation in the Third Reich?", *Yad Vashem Studies*, vol. 11 (1976); and "Nazi Actions Concerning the Jews between the Beginning of World War II and the German Attack on the USSR," in *Unanswered Questions: Nazi Germany and the Genocide of the Jews*, ed. Francois Furet (New York: 1988).
68. Reuth, *Joseph Goebbels, Tagebücher*, entry for March 7, 1942. Far from protecting their Jewish spouses, Goebbels wrote, intermarried Germans were incapable of under-standing the basic tenet of National Socialism and should share the fate of those with whom they chose to associate.
69. Goebbels ordered his ministers to address problems with solutions that were within the realm of what pleased the popular sentiment (BA Potsdam 50.01, 1d, August 13, 1940) and warned them against being "psychologically unrefined," which he defined as that which would "never find any understanding" among the people. BA Potsdam 50.01, 1h (undated). The attempt to orchestrate the public mood with the way he thought would lead to the most productive German effort in wartime led Goebbels into detailed directives about what composers should be played on which radio programs and even into previewing the recipes read on the *Women's Program* (BA Potsdam 50.01 1d, 15 July 1940). Psychological problems would arise when overly celebratory music was played or when recipes for which ingredients were not available during wartime were recommended. Goebbels also dealt with "psychological questions," such as how often to play the national anthem for maximum effect, taking into account such intricate considerations as not overplaying it for fear that it would become commonplace and thus ineffective (playing it too often depleted its value for "emphasis," and it should rather be saved for punctuating the highest victories). BA Potsdam, ProMi, 1g, April 11, 1941.
70. Report by Himmler, 1944, Berlin Document Center, File 0.240 11.

I: HITLER'S THEORY OF POWER

1. "There has been a tendency to suppose that the 'police state' relied on an extraordinarily large police force, which in turn could count on the collaboration of an army of paid agents and spies." Robert Gellately, *The Gestapo and German Society: Enforcing Racial Policy, 1933–1945* (Oxford: 1990), 5.
2. Ian Kershaw, *The "Hitler Myth": Image and Reality in the Third Reich* (Oxford/New York: 1987), 52, 53.
3. Marlis Steinert, *Hitler's War and the Germans: Public Mood and Attitude during the Second World War*, ed. and trans. T. E. J. de Witt (Athens, Ohio: 1977), 1. On the social bases of political power, also see Barrington Moore, *Injustice: The Social Bases*

of *Obedience and Revolt* (White Plains, N.Y.: 1978). The sociologist Georg Simmel, a German, expounded on this point and concluded that "even the most miserable slave . . . in some fashion at least, can still in this sense react to his master." Kurt H. Wolff, ed. and trans., *The Sociology of Georg Simmel* (Glencoe, Ill.: Free Press, 1950), 250, quoted in Gene Sharp, *The Politics of Nonviolence*, vol. 1, *Power and Struggle* (Boston: 1973), 17. Sharp, in his influential work, lucidly describes the theory that governments rely on the support of those they pretend to govern. Although the Nazi regime was concerned about popular mood and opinion, this does not indicate that each person acting alone could have made a difference or even that most people at the time perceived the regime as very concerned about avoiding unrest.

4. Adolf Hitler, *Mein Kampf*, ed. John Chamberlain and Sidney B. Fay (New York: 1939), 764, 765. This concept of power was an elaboration of an opinion characteristic of the Nazi party. Hitler writes that "as early as 1919 we [the party] realized that the new movement has to carry out, first, as its highest aim, the nationalization of the masses." *Mein Kampf*, 465.
5. Like a stillborn child, this attempt "will certainly not be able to live," Hitler concludes. Ibid., 872–873.
6. Ibid., 464.
7. Ibid., 465.
8. Goebbels urged restraint from illegal, violent activity because it would be fruitless and implied that the natural affinity between the racial people and their true representative, the Nazi party, pointed to the electoral path in any case. Hitler agreed, stating, "In these days, only one desire dominates the longing of the enemies of Germany: would that it could work out, so that the National Socialists get agitated, and in turn their masses loose their nerves and break the laws. The Emergency Decree must be obeyed by all party comrades and party officials, SA and SS members in the most precise and thorough way." Hitler supported the emergency decrees not only because he wanted to appear acceptable to decent society and steer clear of damaging violations of law but also because he considered SA violence counterproductive. SD police reports confirmed that SA violence alienated support for Hitler. Lagebericht (Nuremberg), October 21, 1932, BA Potsdam, 15.01 (RMdI) 26093, 335. One impression of SA rabble-rousing was that the Nazis had turned to violence because they had gathered all the votes they could collect by other means. Henry Ashby Turner, Jr., in rejecting claims that big business was primarily responsible for the rise of Nazism, has made the case that it was grass-roots volunteers who buoyed the successful Nazi campaigns. Fanatic devotion to the party, Turner contends, compensated for funds the party lacked. SA violence hurt the public image of the party, but orderly demonstrations were also welcomed for financial reasons. Henry Ashby Turner, Jr., *German Big Business and the Rise of Hitler* (Oxford and New York: 1985), 115–119.
9. "What you are, you are through me, but what I am, I am through you." Adolf Hitler, *Die Kunst im Dritten Reich*, vol. 2, no. 6 (June 1939), 163. See also Hitler's speeches from October 5 and November 6, 1938, in Max Domarus, ed., *Hitler: Reden und Proklamationen, 1932–1945* (Munich: 1991), 923–938. See Norman H. Baynes, ed., *The Speeches of Adolf Hitler, April 1922–August 1939* (New York: 1969), vol. 1, 616–636, on Hitler's continuing expectations for the role of the Nazi movement in undergirding his power.
10. Kershaw, "Hitler Myth."
11. Fighting other ministries for funding, Goebbels addressed a meeting of radio officials on March 25, 1933, and, comparing his task at propaganda with that of the Armaments Ministry, said that "the mobilization of the mind is as necessary as, perhaps even more necessary than, the material mobilization of the nation." Quoted in Jeremy Noakes and G. Pridham, eds., *Nazism, 1919 to 1945: A History in Documents and Eyewitness Accounts* (New York: 1983), 383. Not arms "but the forces of the will" are decisive, Hitler wrote. "The best weapon is dead, worthless material as long as the spirit is

lacking which is ready, willing, and determined to use it," he added. "Therefore, the question of regaining Germany's power is not, perhaps, How can we manufacture arms? but, How can we produce that spirit which enables a people to bear arms? Once this spirit dominates a people, the will finds a thousand ways, each of which ends with arms!" Hitler, *Mein Kampf*, 460. Hitler of course did not deny the significance of arms but rather proclaimed that "an ardent national will for self-preservation" was the primary attribute that would both produce armaments and lead to their use in acts of "heroic death-defying courage."

12. Rosenberg, who had first ruled against this, argued by mid-1943 that German soldiers should be allowed to intermarry with Estonians. "I am of the opinion," he wrote in May 1943, "that under the current circumstances, due to general political reasons, [German-foreigner] marriages should not as a rule raise doubts." In the absence of a decision from Hitler, the burden of proof was now on those who wanted to forbid such marriages. Rosenberg (Leibbrandt) to Reichskommissar Riga, May 31, 1943, BA Potsdam, 11.01 (Ostgebiet) 49, p. 182. As in the controversial decisions concerning German-Jewish intermarriages, Hitler stayed on the fence, for Rosenberg's rules apparently stuck, despite the anger they caused among SS and party officials. Goebbels wrote as early as mid-1942 that treatment in the eastern territories must change. "The inhabitants of the Ukraine were more than inclined at the beginning to regard the Führer as the savior of Europe and to welcome the German Wehrmacht most cordially," he says. "This attitude has changed completely in the course of months. We have hit the Russians, and especially the Ukrainians, too hard on the head with our manner of dealing with them. A clout on the head is not always a convincing argument." Goebbels, *Goebbels Diaries, 1942–43*, ed. Lochner, entry for April 25, 1942, 185. Goebbels adds that "if they are treated right something can be done with them [the Ukrainians]." There was no disagreement about goals, only about tactics, among the Nazi leadership. Reich Commissioner Heinrich Lohse was pressed to teach Goering a lesson from his own experience, at a meeting of Nazi notables in August 1942. Lohse was on the defensive about not having produced as many goods from his territory as he had initially expected. "I have no police and no other means of controlling the territory at all," Lohse told Goering. "When I want to use force or compulsion, the people laugh about it, for I have no means of getting through." Goering retorted, "But you are getting [police] battalions!" Lohse reminded Goering that there weren't enough police to compel each unwilling person in his territory: "Those few battalions in an area as big as Germany!" Goering then asked, "If you get police forces, do you believe you can get more out of [the region]?" Lohse responded by sharpening his point: "On the contrary. I believe, we will get still less if we use force." At an earlier meeting of his staff, Lohse had pointed out that the use of force was not only ineffective but also unsophisticated: "So long as a people is peaceful, one should treat it decently. To make political mistakes and to hit people over the head—anyone can do that." Quoted in translation in Alexander Dallin, *German Rule in Russia, 1941–1945* (New York: 1957), 187, 188.

13. ND PS-739, cited ibid., 498.

14. Gellately, *Gestapo and German Society*, 7.

15. Detlev Peukert, *Die KPD im Widerstand: Verfolgung und Untergrundarbeit an Rhein und Ruhr 1933 bis 1945* (Wuppertal: 1980), 123, quoted in Gellately, *Gestapo and German Society*, 64.

16. William Sheridan Allen, *The Nazi Seizure of Power: The Experience of a Single German Town, 1925–1945* (New York and London: 1965, rev. 1984), 189. According to Allen, Nazi terror worked for the party before 1933 because even though the party was a major cause of the street fighting and chaos characteristic of the late Weimar Republic, the people saw Hitler as a strong figure who could impose order. By the time Hitler became chancellor, the public was "inured" to violence and stood still as various Nazi party organs used violence to consolidate Hitler's power.

17. Ibid.

18. Gellately concludes that denunciations from the public were in "many cases . . . well in advance of what the regime actually expected." Gellately, *Gestapo and German Society*, 140.

19. By the summer of 1935 these Nazi party–instigated disturbances grew so large that observers described them as demonstrations. IML, Lagebericht (Allgemeine Übersicht über die Ereignisse im Monat Juli 1935), St3/673.

20. Minutes of the meeting of officials following the Kristallnacht Pogrom, Nuremberg Trail Documents, PS-1816, quoted in Hilberg, *Destruction of the European Jews* 168.

21. Hannah Arendt described the deportation of seventy-five hundred Jews from Baden, Saerland, and Pfalz to the camp in Gurs, France, as a sort of trial deportation to determine, among other things, "what the reaction of their neighbors would be." Hannah Arendt, *Eichmann in Jerusalem* (New York: 1963), 156. In late 1941, when the systematic deportations of Jews from all over Germany began, Heydrich's secret police continued to keep their ears to the ground. The secret police reported that the initial deportation of four hundred Jews from the area of Minden in December 1941 was "welcomed by a large majority of the population." Although the Gestapo carried it out in secret, the fact that the Jews were "sent away" was soon a topic of discussion in all parts of the population, the report continued. The advantage of this was the opportunity it gave the secret police to report on, rather than merely speculate about, public opinion on the overnight disappearance of Jewish neighbors and coworkers. Some expressed themselves to the effect that the Führer was surely to be thanked for "freeing us from the pest of Jewish blood." A worker said that deportations of Jews should have been done fifty years before, an act that would have saved the Germans from two world wars! The only thing that "astonished" the townspeople was the Gestapo's bad taste in using the well-furnished public city buses to transport the Jews to the train station! The report continues that the only dissenting voices, as the SD had "come to expect," came from religious circles: "One went so far in spreading wild rumors as to say that all the Jews were being pushed into Russia . . . where the workers were put into factories and the old and sick were shot." SD Main Branch Office (Hauptaussenstelle) Bielefeld to RSHA, III B I (Central SD Office in Berlin), December 16, 1941, Heydrich to the Foreign Office, October 1940.

22. BA Potsdam, 50.01 (ProMi) 1d, entry from September 30, 1940. Because secret police reports from September 1940 showed that publicizing cases of recrimination and threats of recrimination had found "no uniform reception among the populace," Goebbels suspended them until he could consult with Hitler. In this case Goebbels was concerned not with whether a mere majority of the populace was sympathetic to his propaganda, but with the much higher standard of whether the public uniformly approved of it (this was early in the war, however, when it was still widely popular).

23. Quoted in Noakes and Pridham, *Nazism*, 381.

24. Hitler, *Mein Kampf*, 467, 468, 485, 486. The flaw of democracy was the weakness of pluralism. As a characteristic of an uncomplicated focus, intolerance was good. "The future of [the Nazi] movement is conditioned by the fanaticism, even more the intolerance, with which its adherents present it as the only right one," Hitler writes. Complexities were the "germs of an inner weakening."

25. Noakes and Pridham, *Nazism*, 379, 409. Goebbels eventually abandoned the project of producing a National Socialist art, resigned instead to a pragmatic production of "innocuous and undemanding" entertainment rather than political indoctrination.

26. The business closure program of the Total War, measures beginning January 1943, showed the regime was far from achieving its ideal of individuals sacrificing for the community. The public in general welcomed business closures as a program that would help Germany win the war. But as soon as people personally were required to close shop or report for work, they grew restless, jealous, and suspicious. Everyone seemed reluctant to make a greater sacrifice than his or her neighbor and ready to believe the neighbor was doing less. Local leaders agreed that as a national measure *Stillegung* was

good but were reluctant to close shops in their area. Their own shops, they claimed, were necessary to supply the people properly. Heinz Boberach, ed., *Meldungen aus dem Reich, 1938–1945: Die geheimen Lageberichte des Sicherheitsdienstes der SS* (Neuwied: 1984), vol. XII, entry for February 18, 1943, 4828, 4829; and entry for March 11, 1943, 4939.

27. Allen, *Nazi Seizure of Power*, 301.
28. Kershaw, *"Hitler Myth"* indicates that the Germans accepted Hitler as their great leader without necessarily internalizing the Nazi ideology.
29. Goebbels, *Berliner Börsener*, April 26, 1940. Goebbels published this statement in response to criticism from a Swiss newspaper in April 1940. For Goebbels it was the press that would "bind the people and hold them in the right attitude."
30. "In an hour when a national body is visibly collapsing and to all appearances is abandoned to the most serious oppression—thanks to the activity of a few scoundrels—obedience and fulfillment of duty towards these people mean . . . pure lunacy, whereas by refusal of obedience and of 'fulfillment of duty' it would be made possible to save a people from its doom." Hitler, *Mein Kampf*, 780, 781. The Nazis threw their support behind the German noncooperation with the French occupation of the Ruhr in 1923, and given the French failure, their popular emphasis in theater and elsewhere on Albert Schlageter, a victim of the French occupation, was not just the glorification of a martyr but a celebration of actual power. See for example, BDC, file of Leopold Gutterer. Gutterer listed his activities on behalf of the "passive resistance" as part of his Nazi credentials. For more on Schlageter, see Jay W. Baird, *To Die for Germany: Heroes in the Nazi Pantheon* (Bloomington, Ind.: 1990), 13ff.
31. Hitler, *Mein Kampf*, 465.
32. Hitler did not blame the working masses for their crippling lack of support so much as he faulted Marxism's heresies. Marxism taught internationalism and class unity when it should have taught classless national unity. The Nazi ideology of national unity and national defense could have forced victory to Germany's side, Hitler brooded. "If, as regards matters of consideration of matters of self-defense, they [German trade unions] had acknowledged their German nationality just as fanatically [as the fanaticism with which they declared the international workers' interests] and with the same ruthlessness . . . then the war would not have been lost." Hitler, *Mein Kampf*, 466.
33. Mason has contended that Hitler was not always a strong dictator and that a key determinant of the dictator's thought and actions was the lesson he took from the revolution of 1918 about the dangers of working-class unrest. Timothy Mason, "Intention and Explanation: A Current Controversy about the Interpretation of National Socialism," in *The "Führer State": Myth and Reality: Studies on the Structure and Politics of the Third Reich*, ed. Gerhard Hirschfeld and Lothar Kettenacker (Stuttgart: 1981), 35. For an analysis of Hitler's fearful interpretation of 1918, see Timothy Mason, "The Legacy of 1918 for National Socialism," in *German Democracy and the Triumph of Hitler*, ed. Anthony Nicholls and Erich Matthias (London: 1971), 215ff, and also *Sozialpolitik im Dritten Reich* (Opladen: 1978), 15ff. Walter Langer's wartime diplomatic report portrayed Hitler and the National Socialists as overwhelmingly concerned both with winning the confidence of a wide cross section of the people and with identifying with the aspects of the everyday life ordinary people experienced. Every effort was made to present Hitler as "extremely human, with a deep feeling for the problems of ordinary people." Walter Langer, *The Mind of Adolf Hitler* (New York: 1973), 74, 58.
34. "In the long run, government systems are not held together by the pressure of force, but rather by the belief in the quality and the truthfulness with which they represent and promote the interests of a people." Hitler, *Mein Kampf*, 388.
35. R. A. C. Parker, *Struggle for Survival: The History of the Second World War* (Oxford and New York: 1990), 108.
36. Goebbels said that "in 1914 we had been mobilized in material terms as no other nation

had—what we lacked was the mobilization of the mind within the country." Quoted in Noakes and Pridham, *Nazism*, 383.

37. Records of Goebbels's daily meetings with his deputies, where he met to form strategies for controlling the press and public opinion. BA Potsdam, 50.01 (Pro Mi), passim.

38. Henry Picker, *Hitler's Tischgespräche im Führerhauptquartier* (Stuttgart: 1963 and 1976), entry for May 21, 1942, 325.

39. Steinert, *Hitler's War and the Germans*, 342.

40. Blau, "Mischehe im Nazi Reich," 47, 48.

41. Wolfgang Benz, *Die Juden in Deutschland, 1933–1945: Leben unter nationalsozialistischer Herrschaft* (Munich: 1989), 751.

42. Siegbert Kleemann, former personnel director for the Berlin Jewish Community, states in a report titled "Jüdische Organizationen in Berlin 1939–1945," of June 2, 1957, that in Berlin German women married to Jews were forced into this *Mischehe Aktion* labor before men. Bovensiepen Trial, Supporting Document 30 (Dr. Wolfgang Scheffler Collection).

43. Interview with Günter Grodka, August 25, 1985.

44. Bukofzer, *Laws for Jews*, 8.

45. Lotte Paepcke, *Ich wurde vergessen: Bericht einer Judin die das dritte Reich überlebte* (Freiburg im Breisgau: 1979), 24.

46. Allen, *Nazi Seizure of Power*, 16. Allen reported that Northeim had one club per every sixty residents, in light of the proverb "Two Germans, a discussion; three Germans, a club."

47. In 1938, for example, a newspaper in Danzig gave laudatory coverage to a congregation of Mennonites that collectively had done the ancestory research entitling each member to the Aryan ID. *Danziger Vorposten*, No. 134, June 11, 1938, in BA Potsdam, 62 DAF 3, 17372, 113.

48. Benz, *Die Juden in Deutschland*, 739–741. On April 22, 1933, both the Teachers' Association and the German Association of Pharmacists adopted the Aryan Clause, and three days later so did the German Sports and Gymnastics Union. Other important associations like those of the medical and legal professions, as well as major employers like the Reichsbahn, soon complied.

49. Kurt Pätzold, *Verfolgung, Vertreibung, Vernichtung: Dokumente des faschistischen Antisemitismus 1933 bis 1942* (Leipzig: 1983), 72.

50. Fritz Stern has pointed out that a range of motivations, not just opportunism, was behind the German social support for Nazism. Fritz Stern, *Dreams and Delusions: The Drama of German History* (New York: 1987), 147ff.

51. In Germany the primitive sociopsychic mechanism of playing favorites against an outsider had conditioned people to accept the idea that some of their neighbors were second-class citizens, according to the eminent historian Hans-Ulrich Wehler. Bismarck's use of the "enemy of the state" category helped prepare the Germans psychologically for the physical destruction of the Jews: "Once Bismarck had established the technique of 'negative integration' in party politics, his successors continued to make use of the strategy." Wehler, *German Empire*, 91, 93. Two generations before Hitler became Führer, Bismarck had attempted to strengthen his own domestic support as chancellor in the Second Reich by a vicious, mendacious campaign against Germany's small, newly formed Social Democratic party. By inflaming the differences between those allegedly loyal to the Reich and those who opposed it, Bismarck managed to maintain a majority while his base of support kept shifting in time to the changing coalitions thrust together to sustain him.

52. Noakes and Pridham, *Nazism*, 547.

53. Pätzold, *Verfolgung, Vertreibung, Vernichtung*, 57, 58, 72. This official boycott day was not popular among Germans in general.

54. Gellately, *Gestapo and German Society*, 158.

55. Hessisches Hauptstaatsarchiv, Wiesbaden, judgment against Georg Albert Dengler (2a

Ks 1/49), 26. The judgment in a separate trial was that "in view of what we know today and the current sources of information, there is no doubt that these actions of early 1943 [against the Jews in intermarriages], though disguised as cases of criminal activity, were aimed against the remaining Jews in Germany." Only one of the twelve intermarried Jews taken into protective custody survived. Of the nineteen intermarried Jews from Offenbach arrested and sent to the labor camps, only four survived the war. Hessisches Hauptstaatsarchiv, sentence of Joseph Hedderich and Johann Schmitz, 2, 29.

56. Hessisches Hauptstaatsarchiv, judgment against Heinrich Baab (51 Ks 1/50).

57. Peter Hayes, "Profits and Persecution: Corporate Involvement in the Holocaust," James S. Pacy and Alan P. Wertheimer in *Perspectives on the Holocaust*, (Boulder, Colo.: 1995), 54. According to Hayes, many such denunciations from 1933 to 1935 are to be found in Brandenburgisches Landeshauptarchiv, Potsdam, Pr.Br.Rep. 60: Staatskommissar/Staatspräsident Berlin, Akten 505–09.

58. Büttner, *Not der Juden teilen*, 20. In a seventy-page introduction to a book about the writer Robert Brendel, Büttner has written on the Nazi persecution of intermarried couples. With his characteristic lucidity Raul Hilberg has also written a chapter on the special anxieties and vulnerabilities of intermarried couples, taking into account official policies toward them. Hilberg, *Perpetrators, Victims, Bystanders*. This book, *Resistance of the Heart*, is concerned primarily with the political impact of intermarriages and less so with questions about family bonds, assimilation, class, and religious identities and gender relations, which others have addressed. See Marion Kaplan, ed., *The Marriage Bargain: Women and Dowries in European History* (New York: 1985) and Monika Richarz, ed., *Burger auf Widerruf: Lebenszeugnisse deutscher Juden, 1780–1945* (Munich: 1989).

59. Lothar Gall et al., *Die Deutsche Bank, 1870–1995* (Munich: 1995), ch. 1. Not only Germans are inculpated. The writer Dr. Claude Levy estimated that about one-half of those in Vichy France who denounced their Jewish fellow citizens to the Germans did so for career reasons. They were doctors or other professionals, he said, who did not like the professional competition of their neighbor Jews. Documentary film *The Sorrow and the Pity*, Part II.

60. Büttner, *Not der Juden teilen*, 31.

61. Koonz, *Mothers in the Fatherland*, 240.

62. Ursula Büttner makes an estimation of the number of divorces throughout Germany based on statistics from Hamburg and Württemberg-Baden. Büttner, *Not der Juden teilen*, 57.

63. The merits for and the problems of using the term "popular opinion" in the context of the Third Reich, and the sources for judging it, were presented in 1970 (trans. 1977) by Marlis Steinert, *Hitler's War and the Germans*, 2–18. See also Ian Kershaw, *Popular Opinion and Political Dissent in the Third Reich: Bavaria 1933–1945* (Oxford and New York: 1983), 4, 5.

64. Hans Bernd Gisevius, *Bis zum bitteren Ende*, vol. 1, *Vom Reichstagbrand zur Fritsch-Krise* (Zurich: 1946), 143. "*mit rauhem Nachdruck, aber irgendwie doch freiwillig und spontan*" (with raw pressure, but somehow indeed voluntary and spontaneous).

65. Ibid., 140, 147. "*Gewiss, es wird viel erobert, aber mehr noch wird preisgegeben.*" (Certainly there was much conquest, but even more was simply surrendered.)

66. Ibid., 141. "*Erst dieser plötzliche, dunkle Drang, der die siegreiche Bewegung binnen Tagen und Wochen unübersehbar anschwellen lässt, is es, der den enuen Gewalthabern frische Impulse verleiht, ihre Kruafte verstärkt und ihnen jenen letzten verwegenen Wagemut einflösst, kurzentschlossen aufs Ganze zu gehen.*" (Primarily it was this sudden dark pressure, which within days and weeks undergirded the victorious movement in an incalculable wave, that gave those in power the impulse to strengthen their power and inspired them to dare quickly to ask for everything.)

67. Allen, *Nazi Seizure of Power*, 300. This refusal does represent a compromise since the Nazi leadership did eventually abolish all church schools in Northeim.

68. Ibid., 290.
69. Hitler, *Mein Kampf*, 465.
70. Albert Speer, *Inside the Third Reich*, trans. Richard and Clara Winston (New York: 1971; 1st ed., 1970), 287. To maintain support and avoid social unrest, the Nazi dictatorship made numerous concessions. Ian Kershaw, *The Nazi Dictatorship: Problems and Perspectives of Interpretation* (London: 1985, rev. 1993), 76, 77. See also Ian Kershaw, "Social Unrest and the Response of the Nazi Regime, 1934–1936," in *Germans against Nazism: Nonconformity, Opposition and Resistance in the Third Reich*, ed. Francis R. Nicosia and Lawrence D. Stokes (New York and Oxford: 1990), where Kershaw discusses at length the implications of the "Provisions Crisis" and the priority Hitler gave food provisions over armaments in 1935–36.
71. Pr. GSta., Rep. 90 P, 16.
72. Steinert attributes lack of protests to "blind trust in Hitler, lack of imagination, indifference and ignorance of the most elementary rules of politics [including ignorance of the potential of popular protest]." Steinert, *Hitler's War and the Germans*, 342.
73. Guenter Lewy, *The Catholic Church and Nazi Germany* (New York and Toronto: 1964); John S. Conway, *The Nazi Persecution of the Churches* (New York: 1968); Kershaw, *Popular Opinion and Political Dissent.*
74. Timothy Mason, *Arbeiterklasse und Volksgemeinschaft: Dokumente und Materialen zur deutschen Arbeiterpolitik* (Opladen: 1975).
75. Martin Broszat, "A Social and Historical Typology of the German Opposition to Hitler," in *Contending with Hitler: Varieties of German Resistance in the Third Reich*, ed. David Clay Large (Cambridge, England: 1992), 26. Broszat classifies the German resistance in three stages to support a claim that "acts and attitudes of opposition . . . were often dependent upon the rule played by the Nazi authorities at a particular time" and that "significant and fundamental resistance arose only in the initial and final phases of Nazi rule." The regime's response to the euthanasia protests supports Broszat's conclusion that the regime while popular and winning could be generous, but the Rosenstrasse Protest does not.
76. Hans Mommsen, *From Weimar to Auschwitz: Essays in German History*, trans. Philip O'Connor (Princeton: 1991), 158.
77. The Nazi party district leader of Augsburg-Land suggested that the politics of mass support was distinctive of the Nazi movement when he accused the Catholic Church of going on the offensive against the Nazi removal of crucifixes from schools in Bavaria in 1941 by mobilizing popular opinion and expressing it in demonstrations. He compared the mobilization of opinion and public assemblies that the church used to defeat the Nazi German state's crucifix decree with the methods employed by the Nazi party to extend its support. Kershaw, *Popular Opinion and Political Dissent*, 354.
78. Hitler, *Mein Kampf*, 787.
79. Franz Neumann, *Behemoth: The Structure and Practice of National Socialism* (New York: 1963), 98.
80. Ian Kershaw, " 'Widerstand ohne Volk': Dissens und Widerstand im Dritten Reich," in *Der Widerstand gegen den Nationalsozialismus*, ed. Jügen Schmädeke und Peter Steinbach (Munich: 1985), 779–798. Kershaw prefers the word "dissent" to describe the spectrum of popular pressures on the regime.
81. See, for example, Claudia Koonz, "Choice and Courage," in *Contending with Hitler*, loc. cit., 50.
82. On August 13, 1941, in a final meeting before the beginning of the genocide of German Jews, officials—from the party chancellery, the SD in the Reichsicherheitshauptamt (RSHA), and the Office of Racial Politics—agreed to expand the definition of Jews in occupied territories to include *Mischlinge*. Lösener, "Als Rassereferent," 297. See also Peter Longerich, *Hitlers Stellvertreter: Führung der Partei und Kontrolle des Staatsapparates durch den Stab Hess und die Partei-Kanzlei Bormann* (Munich: 1992), 220, 221. But immediately thereafter, at the time he was meeting with Goebbels, Hitler

rejected the party chancellery's plan to count *Mischlinge* as Jews. Lösener heard of Hitler's decision on August 16. Lösener, "Als Rassereferent," 304. The Gestapo then received instructions to "temporarily defer" all German *Mischlinge* and all intermarried Jews from the Final Solution deportations, which began in mid-October 1941.

83. Some historians have suggested that Hitler had decided by 1942 to defer the deportation of intermarried Jews until after the war. They base this on a file of fragments from the Justice Ministry known as the Schlegelberger Minute (which is discussed further below). In part this minute states that "Reich Minister Lammers reported that the Führer had repeatedly told him he "wished to have the solution of the Jewish question deferred until after the war." Thus the contention that Hitler had at this point already decided to defer deporting intermarried Jews until after the war rests on interpreting the phrase "Jewish question" in this case to mean only "intermarried-Jewish question." BA, "Behandlung der Juden," R 22/52. If the Schlegelberger Minute does refer only to intermarried Jews, it indicates how painstaking research on the matter is, given the subtle use of language. The term "Jews" here is interpreted to mean only the "intermarried Jews," and elsewhere in Nazi documents intermarried Jews are classified under the category of *Mischlinge*, or, alternately, all intermarried Jews are referred to as "privileged," when formally only some of them had this designation.

84. Regarding intermarried Jews, Hitler was following his habit of waiting for his intuition to inform him of the opportune moment for taking action. "You must understand that I always go as far as I dare and never further," he said. "It is vital to have a sixth sense which tells you broadly what you can and cannot do." Noakes and Pridham, *Nazism*, 550.

85. Goebbels, *Goebbels Diaries*, ed. Lochner, entry for March 9, 1943, 288ff., and interview with Gutterer, August 17, 1986; December 10, 1989.

86. NA, T-175/R 94/2615097. In Himmler's words, Hitler said that "the evacuation of Jews was to be radically carried out in the next three to four months, despite the still developing unrest." This is a small part of a larger memorandum, much of which concerns the east. Hitler's statement, however, should be interpreted as a general policy for Europe.

II: STORIES OF JEWISH-GERMAN COURTSHIP

1. Samuel P. Oliner and Pearl M. Oliner, *The Altruistic Personality: Rescuers of Jews in Nazi Europe* (New York: 1988). Interview with Helena Jakobs (commemorated on Israel's Walk of the Righteous), May 29, 1985, Berlin.

2. On the *Lebensborn* program see Koonz, *Mothers in the Fatherland*, 398–400.

3. Gerhard Paul, *Aufstand der Bilder: Die NS-Propaganda vor 1933* (Bonn: 1990), 42. Paul concludes that during its so-called *Kampfzeit* Nazism was more a propaganda than an ideological movement, Hitler being convinced that visual images were far more powerful for the masses than the written word.

4. Joseph Goebbels, *Vom Kaiserhof zur Reichskanzlei: Eine historische Darstellung in Tagebuchblättern* (Munich: 1934), entry for January 30, 1933. See also the report of the French ambassador in Berlin. Within twenty-four hours of Hitler's appointment as chancellor the party in Breslau celebrated with a huge demonstration of about fifty thousand people; "the center of Breslau, the largest city in eastern Germany, became a sea of swastika flags and marching columns of brown-shirted storm troopers." Richard Bessel, "Political Violence and the Nazi Seizure of Power," in *Life in the Third Reich*, loc. cit., 3.

5. Gisevius, *Bis zum bitteren Ende*, 140, 141, 143, 146.

6. Kershaw, "*Hitler Myth*," 52.

7. Richard Breitman, *The Architect of Genocide: Himmler and the Final Solution* (New York: 1991), 232.

8. Cited in Lucy Dawidowicz, *The War against the Jews, 1933–1945* (New York: 1986), 10, 65.
9. See Bundesamt für Statistik, *Die Ergebnisse der Österreichen Völkszählung vom 22. März 1934* (Vienna: Verlag der Österreichischen Staatsdrückerei, 1935).
10. The Organization of National German Jews, a small group of just several thousand German Jews, did in fact support Hitler early in the Third Reich despite the fact that it "means hardship for us." A statement of the group from 1934 said that "we have always held the well-being of the German people and the fatherland, to which we feel inextricably linked, above our own well-being. Thus we greeted the results of January, 1933 even though it has brought hardships for us personally." See Benz, *Juden in Deutschland*, 22.
11. Hilberg, *Destruction of the European Jews*, 98.
12. Nora Levin, *The Destruction of European Jewry, 1933–1945* (New York: 1973), 43.
13. With 27,013 Jews in 1935, Charlottenburg had a larger Jewish population than any other section of Berlin. Wilmersdorf, with 26,607, was a close second. Berlin, *Grüner Post*, April 14, 1935.
14. Pätzold, *Verfolgung, Vertreibung, Vernichtung*, 57, 58.
15. Hayes, "Profits and Persecution," 57, citing chapter 11 of *Mein Kampf*, the NSDAP's twenty-five points, and principal internal party documents on the Jewish Question prepared through April 1933.
16. Pätzold, *Verfolgung, Vertreibung, Vernichtung*, 72.
17. For a lengthier discussion of the tug-of-war between the regime and the private sector over whether Jews should be boycotted, see ibid., 67–69, 101–103.

III: THE POLITICS OF RACE, SEX, AND MARRIAGE

1. Chief Government Counselor Schraut to Reich Justice Minister, August 8, 1933, BA Potsdam, 30.01 (RJM), 1389/1, 9.
2. German Consulate in Colombo to Foreign Ministry, October 11, 1933, BA Potsdam, 30.01, Nr.1389/1, 67; "Forderung eines Verbots der Rassenmischung," *Frankfurter Zeitung*, October 10, 1933, BA Potsdam, 30.01, 1389/1, 78. Particularly serious offenders would be those who had procured sex or contracted marriage by withholding information or deceiving their partners about their "foreign race" identity.
3. Ibid., 67, 73. Indignant Sinhalese women wondered whether the Prussian minister's proposals indicated that they would no longer be invited to the nice German parties at the consulate (this was at least the report of the concerned German men). A Siemens official sulked that women of color had boycotted the officers' ball and that various private parties had to be given up altogether after the natives had boycotted them in a huff! Siemens-Schuckertwerke Aktiengesellschaft to the Foreign Ministry, October 19, 1933," BA Potsdam, 30.01, 1389/1.
4. Firma Accumulatorenfabrik Aktiengesellschaft to the Foreign Ministry, October 28, 1933, BA Potsdam, 30.01, 1389/1, 35, 37, 38; German Consulate in Colombo to Foreign Ministry, loc. cit., 67, 71.
5. Foreign Ministry to Reich Justice Minister," Berlin, October 21, 1933, BA Potsdam, 30.01, 1389/1, 18; and "telegram of the Foreign Ministry of October 31, 1933 to all Foreign Consulates," 23, 24. Foreign Ministry to Justice Minister, Interior Minister, Economic Minister, Propaganda Minister, and Prussian Justice Minister, November 16, 1933, BA Potsdam, 30.01, 1389/1, 81, 82.
6. Schutzhaft für Verkehr mit Juden, September 29, 1933, BA Potsdam, 30.01, 1389/1, 56.
7. Ibid., 8.
8. RGBl, I, 433. See Bruno Blau, *Das Ausnahmerecht für die Juden in den europäischen Länder, 1933–1945* (New York: 1952), 22. The second amendment to the Law for the

Restoration of the Civil Service of September 28, 1933, indicated that this restriction on persons married to Jews also applied to workers and clerical workers (*Arbeiter und Angestellte*). RGBI, I, 678, cited in Blau, *Ausnahmerecht*, 24.

9. Reichsanzeiger No. 199, cited ibid., 22.

10. Reichsminister des Innern, Ministerialblatt, 1473, December 18, 1933. The regime presented childbearing as a duty and claimed that more and more Germans were joining into the newborn *Gebürtenfreudigkeit* (joy of birthing), as Hitler called the response to their "struggle against slumping birthrates." Picker, *Hitler's Tischgespräche*, 99, 100, entry for January 28, 1942. The German national birthrate had been falling since 1890, a decline "the Nazis attributed . . . to the poisonous atmosphere of the liberal era." Leila Rupp, *Mobilizing Women for War: German and American Propaganda, 1939–1945* (Princeton: 1978), 33–34.

11. Benz, *Juden in Deutschland*, 740.

12. Reich Interior Minister Frick to Reichsbehörden, Reichsstatthalter, Reichsregierungen, January 17, 1936, BA Potsdam, 23.01 (RdDR), 1201a (889), 223, 224.

13. Benz, *Juden in Deutschland*, 740.

14. RGBI, I, 575, of August 8, 1933.

15. RGBI, I, 713, as amended December 19, 1933 (RGBI, I, 1085), cited in Blau, *Ausnahmerecht*, 24.

16. This applied in cities of more than one hundred thousand inhabitants. RGBI, I, 983, November 20, 1933, as amended May 17, 1934 (RGBI, I, 399) and February 13, 1935 (RGBI, I, 192), cited ibid., 24.

17. RGBI, I, 812, July 26, 1935, cited ibid., 28.

18. Hilberg, *Perpetrators, Victims, Bystanders*, 66. Hilberg wrote a chapter on physicians and lawyers (65 ff).

19. Forderung eines Verbots der Rassenmischung, "Abendblatt . . . der Frankfurter Zeitung," October 10, 1933, BA Potsdam, 30.01 (RJM), 1389/1, 78.

20. Director of the District Court to the Dresden Ministry of Justice, November 26, 1933, BA Potsdam, 30.01, 1389/1, 34.

21. Noakes and Pridham, *Nazism*, 533.

22. Excerpted in BA Potsdam, 30.01 (RJM), 1408, 137.

23. Böhrmann's article was a summarization of an article by Dr. Frank printed in *Deutsches Recht*. See the discussion of these two articles in *B.Z. am Mittag*, November 4, 1933, in BA Potsdam, 30.01, 1389/1, Mischblütige Ehen, 21.

24. Pätzold, *Verfolgung, Vertreibung, Vernichtung*, 76. See also Klaus Moritz and Ernst Noam, *NS-Verbrechen vor Gericht, 1945–1955* (Wiesbaden: 1978), 57, for the case of the court's granting divorce to the intermarried couple. The revision of the marriage laws in July 1938 made divorce for intermarriages easier. Büttner, *Not der Juden teilen* 31.

25. Noakes and Pridham, *Nazism*, 533.

26. *Deutsche Justiz-Zeitung* from November 1933, BA Potsdam, 30.01 (RJM), 1389/1, 79, 80.

27. Reich Justice Minister to Foreign Ministry, November 11, 1933, BA Potsdam, 30.01 (RJM), 1389/1, 64.

28. *Deutsche Justiz-Zeitung* from November 1933, loc. cit.

29. Hilberg, *Destruction of the European Jews*, 98.

30. "*Aufgabe eines jeden deutschen Volksgenossen, überall das Seine zu tun, um den jüdischen Einfluss im öffentlichen Leben zurückzudrängen.*" (The duty of every German citizen to do what he can everywhere, to push Jewish influence from public life). Büttner, *Not der Juden teilen*, 20, 21.

31. Lösener, "Als Rassereferent," 278.

32. Noakes and Pridham, *Nazism*, 533.

33. Marriage Registrar Häberlein to the Government of Upper Franconia and Central Franconia, Nuremberg, August 9, 1933, BA Potsdam, 30.01, 1389/1, 15–16; and Transcript,

Government of Upper and Central Franconia, August 22, 1933, BA Potsdam 30.01, 1389/1, 17.

34. Kommission zur Erforschung der Geschichte der Frankfurter Juden, *Dokumente zur Geschichte der Frankfurter Juden 1933–1945* (Frankfurt am Main: 1963), 216, 217.
35. Pätzold, *Verfolgung, Vertreibung, Vernichtung*, 97.
36. Reichsminister des Innerns, Ministerblatt, April 26, 1935, 652.
37. Pätzold, *Verfolgung, Vertreibung, Vernichtung*, 83. Germans married to Jews in positions to influence popular opinion, like those who worked for radio, were forced out almost immediately. See the account of one intermarried radio journalist forced out of work by June 1933 in Noakes and Pridham, *Nazism*. Not only Jews but *Mischlinge* were to "disappear" from radio.

IV: COURAGE AND INTERMARRIAGE

1. Blasius makes this speculation in *Ehescheidung in Deutschland*, 192.
2. BA, NS 19/3335, 34. According to Himmler, maintaining a tough line was necessary for the party and its organizations because a soft party position on race matters would result immediately in even weaker positions by the "politically less composed" offices of the state and the army. BA, NS 19/3335, 24. Party members could be held responsible for intermarriages that they could prevent. Thus any party members whose children married anyone of Jewish blood indicated that they had failed to educate their children correctly, casting doubt on their own political reliability. BA, NS 19/3335, 41.
3. BA, NS/3335, 15.
4. Breitman, *Architect of Genocide*, 34.
5. In making his case for marriage, Hauptsturmführer Alois Brunner characterized his fiancé as "extremely domestic" and her family as having a "clean and orderly situation of stable income." BDC, file of Alois Brunner.
6. SS marriage standards became a model for broader civilian racial legislation, and during the 1930s the Racial Office became involved in certifying civilian marriages. Robert Proctor, *Racial Hygiene: Medicine under the Nazis* (Cambridge, Mass.: 1988), 137–139.
7. Government president in Wiesbaden to the Prussian interior minister, October 28, 1933, BA Potsdam, 30.01 (RJM), 1389/1, 30.
8. Dr. Walter Grave to Propaganda Minister Joseph Goebbels, October 5, 1933, BA Potsdam, 30.01 (RJM), 1389/1, 22.
9. Noakes and Pridham, *Nazism*, 217, 218.

V: *MISCHLINGE*

1. Hilberg, *Destruction of the European Jews*, 1014.
2. BA, NS 19/3335, 4.
3. Louis Snyder, *Encyclopedia of the Third Reich* (New York: 1976), entry for "Hitler Jugend."
4. BA, NS 19/3335, 16.

VI: SOCIETY VERSUS LAW

1. "We Germans just do not know the art of running a large people or a large country from a few key positions," Goebbels complained. "We are much too thorough and are always in danger of administering instead of leading." Goebbels, *Goebbels Diaries*, ed. Lochner, entry for December 16, 1942, 246.

2. This was the pattern of the Nazi takeover of governments in individual German states in 1933 and of the Anschluss annexation of Austria in 1938. Typically the Nazi party initiated, or used the press to exaggerate, the ruckus it claimed as the cause for forcibly removing governments from territories it wanted to control.

3. Goebbels and Hitler agreed on this matter. In a speech on September 15, 1935, Hitler claimed the provocative behavior of German Jews had stirred up widespread complaints and demands for action. Kershaw, *"Hitler Myth,"* 236. "The Germans," Hitler told Goebbels at the end of May 1942, "take part in subversive movements only when Jews have tricked them into it." Quoted in Ernest K. Bramsted, *Goebbels and National Socialist Propaganda 1925–1945* (East Lansing, Mich.: 1965), 396.

4. See, for example, Goebbels's motives for organizing the one-day boycott of Jewish businesses on April 1, 1933. Hilberg, *Destruction of the European Jews*, 98.

5. Noakes and Pridham, *Nazism*, 533–535. At the end of July Reinhard Heydrich, a close associate of Heinrich Himmler's, announced on behalf of the political police that the public outcry against Jewish-German sex and marriage required that "the prevention of mixed marriages be legally fixed" and "extramarital sexual relations between Aryans and Jews should be punished." A rationale that local radicals used for their rowdy attacks on Jews was that there was no law defining and excluding Jews from citizenship.

6. Interview with Leopold Gutterer, August 17, 1986. By floating rumors through the "mouth radio" system, the regime could test popular response to possible initiatives.

7. Pätzold, *Verfolgung, Vertreibung, Vernichtung*, 95ff.

8. Noakes and Pridham, *Nazism*, 531.

9. IML, St3/673, 54–56.

10. BA Potsdam, 30.01 (RJM) Nr. 1389, 176.

11. Noakes and Pridham, *Nazism*, 533.

12. Pätzold, *Verfolgung, Vertreibung, Vernichtung*, 95ff.

13. By the summer of 1935 these Nazi party–instigated disturbances grew so large that observers described them as demonstrations. IML, Lagebericht (Allgemeine Übersicht über die Ereignisse im Monat Juli 1935), St3/673.

14. Helmut Eschwege, ed., *Kennzeichen J: Bilder, Dokumente, Berichte zur Geschichte der Verbrechen des Hitlerfaschismus an den deutschen Juden 1933–1945* (East Berlin: 1981), 44, 70–72. Meanwhile, graffiti denouncing Jews and *Rassenschande* appeared in public, especially on Jewish businesses. The slogans "Get the defilers of race out of all German countries!" and "Jews out—race polluters!" were smeared overnight in August 1935 on a Jewish shop. This was perhaps the work of a party organization, but if so, it was done unofficially to make it appear like a spontaneous private outburst against sexual relations between Jews and Germans.

15. Lösener, "Als Rassereferent," 213.

16. Hitler had probably originally scheduled a foreign policy address for the high-profile moment he used to announce the Nuremberg Laws. Noakes and Pridham, *Nazism*, 535.

17. Ibid., 550.

18. Quoted in Kershaw, *"Hitler Myth,"* 236.

19. Ibid., 235.

20. For the text of the Nuremberg Laws see RGBI I, 1146, or Noakes and Pridham, *Nazism*, 535–537.

21. Hilberg, *Destruction of the European Jews*, 66.

22. Lösener, "Als Rassereferent," 276.

23. "Grundgesetz, ein Reichsbürgergesetz," Lösener, "Als Rassereferent," 275.

24. Dawidowicz, *The War against the Jews*, 65.

25. Deputy of the Interior Ministry Wilhelm Stuckart to Klopfer et al., ND NG-2586-1. Later, when the Interior Ministry (in the person of Stuckart) proposed a law to compel intermarried couples to divorce, the party (Joseph Goebbels) rejected this measure, in consideration of popular traditions. The argument that *Mischlinge* should be saved

because of the one half of their blood that was German was made by Stuckart. Hitler and those closest to him, however, clearly disagreed with this sentiment, and it is unlikely that they would have allowed the opinions of a state secretary and his assistant to influence them on something as important as the Final Solution. Stuckart claimed to be the Interior Ministry's voice of conscience on Jewish matters, but if he had carefully planned and executed a sabotage mission to destroy various copies of the regime's records (addresses, etc.) on Germany's Jews—and from his position he might have received the key collaboration for such a destruction—he would have been more effective in rescuing Jews. In any case, Stuckart proved both lack of concern for Jewish-German families and incapacity in the ways of power, by ineffectively proposing a law for the compulsory divorce of intermarried couples in March 1942.

26. The later exemption from the Final Solution of all *Mischlinge* contradicted the bureaucrats and their categories in the Nuremberg Laws, which marked a portion of the *Mischlinge* for treatment as Jews. *Mischlinge* were racially ambiguous in a way that did enable some officials to make tentative proposals for exempting some of them from the Final Solution. For example, Acting Justice Minister Schlegelberger argued that *Mischlinge* of the second degree should be fully integrated into German society. This meant, in turn, that those of the first degree (the parents of the second-degree *Mischlinge*) must also go unscathed because second-degree *Mischlinge* whose parents had been deported on the ground that they were inferior would surely themselves feel inferior, a condition that would block their full integration into German society. Schlegelberger to Klopfer, Stuckart, Heydrich, Neumann, Luther, Meyer, and Hofmann, April 8, 1942, ND NG-2586-1.

27. Noakes and Pridham, *Nazism*, 538.

28. The eminent historian Hans Mommsen writes that the bureaucracy's capacity in this regard declined with the life of the Reich. Mommsen, *From Weimar to Auschwitz*, 159. Although the Nuremberg Laws identified some half Jews for persecution as "full Jews," and although the Interior Ministry later proposed a compulsory divorce of intermarried Jews in order to draw them into the Final Solution, the bureaucrats ultimately had their (harsher) way with neither the intermarried Jews nor the half Jews.

29. Lösener, "Als Rassereferent," 276.

30. The German census of 1939 counted 72,738 persons with two Jewish grandparents and 42,811 persons with one Jewish grandparent. Census of May 17, 1939, BA, R 18, Nr. 5520.

31. H. G. Adler renders and discusses the text of this decree in *Der Verwaltete Mensch: Studien zur Deportation der Juden aus Deutschland* (Tübingen: 1974), 294–295.

32. BA, NS 19/3335, 4.

33. Blau, "Mischehe im Nazi Reich," 46.

34. NS 19/3335, BA, 4, 5.

35. Boberach, *Meldungen aus dem Reich*, vol. 9, 3245–3248, entry for February 2, 1942, reports that the public complained of "privileged *Rassenschande*" after the regime introduced the category of "privileged intermarriage," while Lotte Paepcke, an intermarried Jew, reports quips against "legalized *Rassenschande*." Paepcke, *Ich wurde vergessen*, 20.

36. Koonz, *Mothers in the Fatherland*, 192.

37. Ibid., 267. In general Protestant and Catholics welcomed German-Jewish intermarriages if the Jewish partner had converted to Christianity.

38. Nuremberg Laws, Reichsgesetzblatt Teil I, 1935, 1146, 1333. A ban on intermarriages was also not out of keeping with German social traditions since Germany was the European colonial power to ban marriage of its citizens with those of a colony.

39. BA Potsdam, R 8150, Minutes of the Central Organization's Directorate, Professor of Philosophy Karl Jaspers, M.D., to the Central Organization of German Jews, Heidelberg, August 31, 1942.

40. *Jahrbuch des Deutschen Rechts* (1937), 757.

41. *Jahrbuch des Deutschen Rechts* (1938), 302, 303.
42. Hilberg, *Perpetrators, Victims, Bystanders*, 72.
43. Hilberg, *Destruction of the European Jews*, 162, 163.
44. Ibid., 169.
45. The discussion among top ministries about changing divorce laws to increase births continued from February 16, 1943, into early 1945. BA Potsdam, 30.01, 10118.
46. Hilberg, *Destruction of the European Jews*, 1027.
47. Allen, *Nazi Seizure of Power*, 299.

VII: SOCIETY AND LAW

1. Interview with Hans-Oskar Löwenstein de Witt, November 8, 1984.
2. Interview with Günter Grodka, August 25, 1985.
3. Especially after 1938 businesses hung signs banning Jews. Bukofzer, *Laws for Jews*, 6. In June 1935 a Socialist party contact man reported from southwest Germany that "The owners of pubs are compelled—with the threat of boycotts and 'other consequences' —to put up notices with the inscription: 'Jews are not welcome here.' The majority of pubs already have these notices." Noakes and Pridham, *Nazism*, 547.
4. Reichsminister des Innern, Ministerial Blatt 1631, December 7, 1936.
5. For statistics on Gestapo cases on "Non-conforming Behavior in Everyday Life" see Gellately, *Gestapo and German Society*, 47. Gellately's material is partially taken from the study by Reinhard Mann, *Protest und Kontrolle*. Mann's study and the quoted figures are only for those of the Gestapo in Düsseldorf.
6. Allen, *Nazi Seizure of Power*, 189.
7. Anordnung des Präsidenten der Reichspressekammer über die Abstammung Mitglieder, April 15, 1936, cited in Blau, *Ausnahmerecht*, 35.
8. Benz, *Juden in Deutschland*, 743.
9. RGBI, I, 893, October 14, 1936, cited in Blau, *Ausnahmerecht*, 35.
10. RGBI, I, 39, January 26, 1937, cited in Benz, *Juden in Deutschland*, 744.
11. RGBI, I, 191, Reichsnotarordnung of February 13, 1937.
12. RGBI, I, 115, Berufsordnung of January 20, 1938.
13. Longerich, *Hitlers Stellvertreter*, 214.
14. Anordnung des Präsidenten der Reichskulturkammer über den Reichsverband der jüdischen Kulturbünde, August 6, 1935, See *Völkische Beobachter*, August 7, 1935, and Blau, *Ausnahmerecht*, 28.
15. Schwenn had apparently found it easier not to mention the problem of working with a Jew in this interview, and Charlotte, who had rescued her husband from the Nazis but never considered calling the radio station to say whom Schwenn had worked with, also felt powerless to set the record straight in Germany after the war.
16. Eschwege, *Kennzeichen J*, 47.
17. IML, Lagebericht (Allgemeine Übersicht über die Ereignisse im Monat Juli 1935), St3/673.
18. Verordnung gegen die Unterstützung der Tarnung jüdischer Gewerbebetriebe (order against the support of the camouflage of Jewish businesses). Reichsgesetzsblatt Teil I, 404, April 22, 1938. There was no general law that required Germans to denounce Jews or anyone else.
19. Statement of Walter Freund, May 22, 1967, Bovensiepen Trial.
20. Interview with Mieke Monjau, December 3, 1984.
21. The German essayist Eike Geisel describes the German problem as "The Banality of the Good People," a banality of people who sought to be good by being obedient to authority. Eike Geisel, *Die Banalität der Guten: Deutsche Seelenwanderungen* (Berlin: 1992).
22. Especially after the start of war, block leaders "intensified their control over every

German man, woman, and child at all levels of everyday existence: in the street, on the apartment stairs, and more and more, in the air-raid shelter." Michael Kater, *The Nazi Party: A Social Profile of Members and Leaders, 1919–1945* (Cambridge, Mass.: 1983), 222.

23. Erich Kordt, *Wahn und Wirklichkeit* (Stuttgart: 1948), 48, quoted in Gellately, *Gestapo and German Society*, 73.

24. Pr. GSta., Rep. 90 P, Band II, 1. The Gestapo attributed the success of the Confessing Church (a Protestant movement opposed to the German Faith Movement) to the fact that it "proceeds clearly without compromise." As of this report (April 1935), the Confessing Church claimed 150,000 members against only 30,000 for the German Faith Movement, which the Nazis attributed to "greater resolution and a clearer position." As an example, the police pointed to political pulpit statements from the Confessing Church. The Nazis at first banned these but because ministers had continued the practice despite the ban, the police were now silently tolerating them.

25. In 1936, the Protestant (Lutheran) Church in Berlin helped the regime identify Jews by completing a card index dating back to 1800 and reaching to 1874, including changes of names. Götz Aly and Karl Heinz Roth, *Die restlose Erfassung* (Berlin: 1984), 70, 71.

26. Kershaw, "Hitler Myth," 60, 61.

27. Wilhelm Keitel, *The Memoirs of Field-Marshal Keitel*, trans. David Irving (Göttingen: 1961), 59.

28. Kershaw, "Hitler Myth," 131, 132.

29. Ibid., 131.

30. Reports on the Berlin response to the Second Division and its impact on Hitler are in William Shirer, *Berlin Diary: The Journal of a Foreign Correspondent* (New York: 1961), 109, 110, and Paul Schmidt, *Hitler's Interpreter* (New York: 1951), 105. For a rendition of Hitler's speech and his response to this incident, see Domarus, 923–938.

31. Johannes Steinhoff, Peter Pechel, and Dennis Showalter, *Voices from the Third Reich: An Oral History* (Washington, D.C.: 1989), 537.

32. After the Anschluss the Nazis displaced Vinzenz with their own district magistrate. An Austrian married to a Jew could not be left in power. But the people loved Vinzenz. He had taken care of their needs, and they had learned to trust him. According to Elsa Holzer, the people made such a disturbance about the Nazi move to oust him that Vinzenz was officially reinstated.

33. *Proceedings of Nuremberg* (*Law Reports of Trials of War Criminals*, 1948), vol. XIX, 437–438. Hitler had surmised that anti-Semitism would be a way of gaining support. Leo Kuper, *Genocide: Its Political Use in the Twentieth Century* (New Haven and London: 1981), 43, 136.

34. Talcott Parsons, *Essays in Sociological Theory: Pure and Applied* (Glencoe, Ill.: 1949), 337.

35. Wehler, *The German Empire*, 94.

36. Lösener, "Als Rassereferent," 266. The example of Einsatzgruppen men who shot Jews face-to-face is in some cases more complicated to explain as opportunism.

37. Lösener concluded that he would have "thrown himself immediately from the saddle" by open opposition or appeals to moral reasoning and determined that he had to limit himself to the argumentation which would have an impact on the decision makers in charge of the Final Solution. Lösener, "Als Rassereferent," 266. Lösener passed off responsibility for the Nazi genocide of Jews to Eichmann's office in the Reich Security Main Office, which he said had "perpetrated the most evil Jewish persecutions." Lösener, "Als Rassereferent," 267.

38. Noakes and Pridham, *Nazism*, 550.

39. Hessisches Hauptstaatsarchiv, Wiesbaden, Judgment against Georg Albert Dengler (2a Ks 1/49), 26. The court also included anti-Semitism as a possible motive for Dengler's

rigorous actions against intermarried Jews. Hessisches Hauptstaatsarchiv, judgment against Georg Albert Dengler, 5.
40. Arendt, *Eichmann in Jerusalem*, 113, 126.

VIII: KRISTALLNACHT

1. Report of Walter Buch to Hermann Göring, February 13, 1939, ND PS-3063.
2. Systematic Aryanization began in late 1938. Raul Hilberg, ed., *Documents of Destruction: Germany and Jewry, 1933–1945* (Chicago: 1971), 25.
3. Ian Kershaw, "The Persecution of the Jews and German Popular Opinion in the Third Reich," in *The Persisting Question: Sociological Perspectives and Social Contexts of Modern Antisemitism*, ed. Helen Fein (Berlin and New York: 1987), 336, 337. Some Germans objected not so much to action against Jews as to the disorderliness of the pogrom. Steinert, *Hitler's War and the Germans*, 37.
4. German press, November 12, 1938.
5. The Reichsbund jüdischer Frontsoldaten was proud of the disproportionately large number of Jews who had died for Germany during World War I. Their national leader, in October 1933, had encouraged them to stay in "our German fatherland" out of a sense of "old soldierly discipline, until the last." Benz, *Juden in Deutschland*, 22.
6. Hilberg, *Destruction of the European Jews*, 394, 395; Dawidowicz, *War against the Jews*, 100, 101.
7. German press, November 12, 1938.
8. Büttner, *Not der Juden teilen*, 40.
9. Interview with Rudolf Schottländer, East Berlin, July 17, 1987. Some Jews were well connected; in the later nineteenth and early twentieth centuries some Jews, especially those from nouveau riche families of banking and other professions, had married families from the German nobility or other high-status Germans.
10. Report of Goering, December 28, 1938, ND PS-69. In April 1943 there were 17,375 nonprivileged Jews and 14,393 Jews in nonprivileged intermarriages in the German Reich. At the end of the war in Berlin there were 3,339 registered Jews in privileged intermarriages and 1,451 registered as living in nonprivileged intermarriages. Richarz, *Jüdisches Leben in Deutschland*, 466.
11. Minutes of the November 12, 1938, Nazi leadership conference following Kristallnacht, ND PS-1816, quoted in Hilberg, *Destruction of the European Jews*, 168.
12. ND PS-69; Hilberg, *Destruction of the European Jews*, 170.
13. Hilberg, *Destruction of the European Jews*, 160. Heydrich gave secret orders to have Jewish women guilty of *Rassenschande* sent to a concentration camp, but German women remained immune from internment for this crime.
14. Adolf Hitler, Speech to the National Socialist Women's Organization, Nuremberg party rally, September 8, 1934, quoted in Timothy Mason, "Women in Germany, 1925–1940: Family, Welfare, and Work," *History Workshop Journal* (January 1976), 74.
15. A theme of German as well as American writers on women's resistance is that the regime did not expect anything politically intelligent from women and tended to interpret their actions as apolitical. See, for example, Vera Laska, ed., *Women in the Resistance and in the Holocaust* (London: 1983), 7. "In Hitler's view of the world, men were powerful and dangerous, women passive," writes Koonz. "In the Third Reich the second sex was beneath suspicion. The regime that defined women as incapable of political participation did not readily perceive them as sufficiently intelligent or independent to commit treason." Koonz, *Mothers in the Fatherland*, 335 (see also 310).
16. Intermarried Jewish women might have worn the star if (in rare cases) their children were enrolled as Jews.
17. Experiences of Jewish women married to German men who did not divorce them also varied somewhat. For one example see the account of Paepcke, *Ich wurde vergessen*.

In general, they were not sent to camps or hard labor; German women married to Jews, however, were forced into collective hard labor in 1944.

18. A definition of "Jewish enterprise," from a decree dated June 14, 1938, which defined the term very broadly, was used for ferreting out the targets of Aryanizations. Hilberg, *Destruction of the European Jews*, 95.
19. Levin, *Destruction of European Jewry*, 43, and Büttner, *Not der Juden teilen*, 37.
20. Hilberg, *Destruction of the European Jews*, 94. Jews had pioneered and owned a large sector of the department store business.
21. Richard Grunberger, *A Social History of the Third Reich* (London: 1971), 174.
22. Hitler, *Mein Kampf*, 780, 781.
23. Interview with Hans-Oskar Löwenstein de Witt, August 20, 1989.
24. Interview with Mrs. Steudel's daughter, Charlotte, May 20, 1985.
25. Interview with Mrs. Gross, April 4, 1986.
26. Ältestenrat der Juden, Prag (Jewish Council of Prague) to Central Office for the Governing of the Jewish Question in Bohemia and Moravia, June 19, 1944, Bovensiepen Trial, Supporting Document 94.
27. Reinhard Rürup, ed., *Typographie des Terrors: Gestapo, SS, und Reichssicherheitshauptamt auf dem "Prinz-Albrecht-Gelände"* (Berlin: 1987), 82, 83.
28. Regime leaders such as Goebbels ruminated about the danger of Jewish sabotage (see his diary entry for March 9, 1943, for example), but in line with the Nazi logic that women's actions were not political actions, Jewish women married to German men in privileged marriages had telephones.
29. According to Wally Grodka's diaries, this appeared in *Der Gerichtssaal*, January 11, 1939.
30. Benz, *Juden in Deutschland*, 632. According to Büttner, *Not der Juden teilen*, 45, this law was implemented only in Berlin.
31. Blau, *Ausnahmerecht*, 64 ff.
32. Statement of Martha Mosse, July 23 and 24, 1958, Bovensiepen Trial.
33. Statement of Martha Mosse, April 9, 1968, Bovensiepen Trial.
34. Ibid.
35. Gerhard Weiss, "Panem et Circenses: Berlin's Anniversaries as Political Happenings," in *Berlin: Culture and Metropolis*, ed. Charles W. Haxthausen and Heidrun Suhr (Minneapolis: 1990), 244.
36. Benz, *Juden in Deutschland*, 631, 32.
37. BA Potsdam, 46.06, Generalbauinspektor für die Reichshauptstadt Berlin, Nr. 157, 17, 18, 19.
38. Taken from the Nazis' twenty-five points, reprinted in Barbara Miller Lane and Leila J. Rupp, eds. and trans., *Nazi Ideology before 1933: A Documentation* (Austin and London: 1978), 41–43.
39. Proctor, *Racial Hygiene*, 107. The sterilization law is published in RGBI I, 529, July 14, 1933. The state promulgated regulations for the filing of complaints about the program (RGBI 33, 529, 25.7.1933), and courts ruling on the law were bound to secrecy. State statistics from May 1935 showed that Germans who complained that a physical examination had not led to sterilization were more successful in reversing court decisions than those who complained that they had been unjustly sterilized. Proctor writes, however, that only a small minority of Germans asked to reverse decisions that deemed sterilization unnecessary.
40. Noakes and Pridham, *Nazism*, 1005, quoting the Nuremberg Trial testimony of Dr. Karl Brandt.
41. Ibid., 1004, citing L. Gruchmann, "Euthanasia und Justiz im Dritten Reich," in *Vierteljahrshefte für Zeitgeschichte* (1972), 228.
42. Gerald Reitlinger, *The Final Solution: The Attempt to Exterminate the Jews of Europe—1939–1945* (New York: 1961), 140.

43. Noakes and Pridham, *Nazism*, 1029. Michael Burleigh, "Euthanasia and the Third Reich," *History Workshop Journal* (February 1990), 12, 13.

IX: AT WAR AND AT HOME

1. Donald Cameron Watt, *How War Came: The Immediate Origins of the Second World War, 1938–1939* (New York: 1989), 35, citing ND 248-PS.
2. See Hitler's response to the indifferent response in Berlin to the Second Motorized Division on September 27, 1938 described above, taken from: Shirer, *Berlin Diary*, 109, 110. Schmidt, *Hitler's Interpreter*, 105. For a rendition of Hitler's speech and his response to this incident, see Domarus, *Hitler*, 923–938. According to Hitler, the will to fight was more decisive than armaments. Hitler, *Mein Kampf*, 460.
3. Interview statement of Charlotte von der Schulenburg, in the documentary film *The Restless Conscience*, by Hava Beller, released 1991.
4. Quoted in International Military Tribunal, *Trial of the Major War Criminals* (Nuremberg: 1947–49), 28: 389.
5. Adler, *Verwaltete Mensch*, 274, 275, gives a history of this order.
6. Lösener, "Als Rassereferent," 310. Hitler also granted equalizations to some *Mischlinge* for outstanding service in the Nazi party, but this could happen, ironically, only in cases where these persons could claim ignorance of their own *Mischling* identity since a prerequisite of party membership was pure Aryan ancestry back to the year 1800.
7. Himmler's position, compatible with Hitler's, is given in Breitman, *Architecht of Genocide*, 232. In an attempt to gain an exemption from Hitler's order, Erich Vogel, a German lawyer married to a Jew, pleaded to the Gestapo that his *Mischling* son loved his country. "That might be, but by now we have treated the *Mischlinge* so poorly that they will certainly be against us," Max Graustück of the Berlin Gestapo replied. Graustück added that the *Mischlinge* were in any case congenitally unreliable, since they possessed the "most dangerous bloodstream." Statement of Erich Vogel, PStg20, Bovensiepen Trial.
8. The party chancellery on October 20, 1942, and again on June 23, 1943, in addition to an instruction of the chief of the armed forces of October 24, 1942, reiterated the order to expel all *Mischlinge* from the army, without exception. In October 1944 the regime acknowledged that there might still be *Mischlinge* in the military with an order barring *Mischlinge* of the first degree and the intermarried Germans (including Germans married to *Mischlinge* of the first degree) from receiving medals honoring distinguished military service. Abschrift of October 21, 1944, from general military notices, Nr. 593 (Auszeichnung von jüdischen Mischlingen I. Grades), BA NS 19/3335.
9. Marriages between *Mischlinge* of the first degree and Jews were allowed. BA, NS 19/3335, 2, 9. But permissions to *Mischlinge* of the first degree to marry anyone other than *Mischlinge* of the first degree or Jews were almost never allowed. Lösener, "Als Rassereferent," 275. During the five months from January 1, 1940, to May 22, 1940, alone, 1,630 *Mischlinge* applied to the Interior Ministry and the Nazi party chancellery for special exemptions to the marriage laws, but only about a dozen petitions were granted. As of March 1942, all such marriage requests were automatically denied for the duration of the war. Lösener, "Als Rassereferent," 283.
10. BA, NS 19/3335, 26, 27.
11. Lösener, "Als Rassereferent," 310. By mid-1944, however, Hitler had grown less generous, turning down a *Mischling*'s request to serve in the military even though he was a "very deserving former party member." Without realizing his characteristics as a *Mischling*, he had served the party particularly well for years, and had even served a term in prison as a Nazi before 1933. BA, NS 19/3335, 34.
12. Before Nazism, cultural attainments in the most varied areas had been a "true domain of Judaism," Himmler said, and one measure of this Jewish infestation of culture was

that, an entire decade after the Nazis took power, a "disproportionately large number of *Mischlinge* and intermarried artists still work in theater and film today." This "Jewish influence" was to be snuffed out as much as possible—a problematic proposition, since a number of these Jews had already received "special permission" to carry on as artists, Himmler noted. BA, NS 19/3335.

13. Gutterer said he arranged a meeting with the Nobel Prize-winning Otto Hahn, Goebbels, and Hitler to discuss the building of the nuclear bomb, and Hitler promised to bring the banished Hahn's Jewish assistant back to Germany under his personal protection and award her the highest honor of the land (*Ritterkreuz*) if she would successfully help Hahn build this bomb. West Germany, interview with Gutterer, August 19, 1986.

14. A report from Himmler's office noted that the party chancellery would have to be contacted before measures were taken against any intermarried artists, because some of them were protected. BA, NS 19/3335, 37. In Berlin new members of the Gestapo's Jewish Desk, which was responsible for deporting Jews, were instructed during their first hours on the job about the matter of *Schutzjuden* and the seriousness of deporting any by mistake.

15. During the war *Mischlinge* and intermarried Germans were also to be kept out of crafts and cultural production. "Moreover they should not be put in positions as supervisors over Germans or foreign workers . . . because, for these positions they in general do not possess the particular political reliability necessary." BA, NS 19/3335, 35, 36.

16. "I chose the third path, that of selfishness extended to the person closest to you, which in distant times a friend of mine appropriately called us-ism." Primo Levi, *The Drowned and the Saved*, trans. Raymond Rosenthal (New York: Vintage Books, 1989), 80. Levi used this term to describe the conditions at Auschwitz, but in the Reich, among those who might at any moment be sent to a camp, it applied more loosely as well.

17. BA, NS 19/3335, 16.

18. Thomas Keneally, *Schindler's List* (New York: Serpentine Publishing Co., 1982).

X: RACIAL HYGIENE, CATHOLIC PROTEST, AND NONCOMPLIANCE, 1939–1941

1. Hilberg, *Destruction of the European Jews*, 145, 45.

2. Else Rosenfeld and Gertrud Luckner, eds., *Lebenszeichen aus Pialski: Briefe Deportierter aus dem Districkt Lublin 1940–1943* (Munich: 1968), 23. The authors report that these non-Jewish wives were given a brief moment to decide whether to divorce and then were deported. There is some controversy about the date of these deportations and the exact number of those deported. Esriel Hildesheimer, *Jüdische Selbstverwaltung unter dem NS-Regime: Der Existenzkampf der Reichsvertretung und Reichsvereinigung der Juden in Deutschland* (Tübingen: 1994), 181. Hildesheimer, 180–184, gives a history of the deportation of Jews from Stettin and Schneidemühl.

3. Vermerk, Deputy of the Foreign Ministry, March 21, 1940, Yad Vashem, Microfilm JM/2248.

4. BA Potsdam, R 8150, Minutes of the Central Organization's Directorate, by Eppstein, February 26, 1941.

5. The circular was sent following a report that the deportation of Jews from Stettin had caused unrest among the Jews, who had begun to move from one area to another. BA Potsdam, R 8150, Minutes of the Central Organization's Directorate, by Eppstein, April 4, 1940.

6. Hildesheimer, *Jüdische Selbstverwaltung*, 186, 187.

7. BA Potsdam, 50.01, Id, July 19, 1940. That sixty thousand Jews lived in Berlin was an underestimation or indicates that ten thousand more Jews were discovered to be living in Berlin by October 1941, including those who moved to Berlin by that time. Goebbels's concern about Jewish influence in Berlin concentrated on the Kurfürstendamm and the

"western" section of Berlin. In late 1942 Brunner arrested intermarried Jews in the western section of Berlin.

8. BA Potsdam, 50.01, Id, September 6 and 17, 1940. Hinkel reported on this date that the "Madagascar project" had been approved, and would concentrate 3,500,000 Jews on that island. Hitler himself had apparently approved the Madagascar plan by July 12, 1940. Director of the Generalgouvernement (German-occupied Poland) Hans Frank disapproved of attempts to send more Jews to his territory and had spoken of deporting "superfluous Poles" farther to the east, "after the victory." Hilberg, *Destruction of the European Jews*, 206–211.
9. BA Potsdam, 50.01, 1d, July 19, 1940.
10. Benz, *Juden in Deutschland*, 748.
11. Büttner, *Not der Juden teilen*, 47.
12. Boberach, *Meldungen aus dem Reich*, vol. IX, 3286, entry for February 9, 1942.
13. Jagusch reported that Jews who worked would get three hours to shop, but this did not happen. BA Potsdam, R 8150, Minutes of the Central Organization's Directorate, by Eppstein, July 25, 1940.
14. Ibid., April 18, 1940.
15. Ibid., May 15, 1941.
16. With his keen Socialist attention to class differences, Günter claimed that money divided Jewish solidarity, pitting Jew against Jew. The work supervisor, Mr. Tusche, loved to play skat and allowed the Jews with money to play instead of work: "Instead of forcing them to work, he allowed them to play because they always allowed him to win. On the other hand, if any one of us didn't suit him or irritated him in the slightest way, that person he kicked in the pants and screamed, 'You dirty sow!' "
17. Goebbels, *Goebbels Diaries*, ed. Taylor, entry for October 4, 1940, 130.
18. Goebbels, *Goebbels Diaries*, ed. Lochner, entry for October 4, 1940, 130.
19. BA Potsdam, 50.01, 1d, September 1940.
20. Benz, *Juden in Deutschland*, 748.
21. Interview with Elsa Holzer, August 16, 1989. For descriptions of air raids over Berlin, see Shirer, *Berlin Diary*, entries for August 21, 1940, onward.
22. Paepcke, *Ich wurde vergessen*, 24.
23. This account of the deportations from Baden, Pfalz, and the Saarland is taken from Hildesheimer, *Jüdische Selbtsverwaltung*, 192–202.
24. Arendt, *Eichmann in Jerusalem*, 156.
25. BA Potsdam, R 8150, Minutes of the Central Organization's Directorate, by Eppstein, April 25, 1940.
26. An Eichmann assistant called Baeck the Jewish Führer in Berlin. Hilberg, *Destruction of the European Jews*, 448.
27. Hirsch had begun acting as a troubleshooter for the RSHA. Perhaps to preempt reprisals (should Wöhrn find out on his own), Hirsch reported in mid-February that Jews were using envelopes designated for non-Jews, which is "of course undesirable." Wöhrn ordered Hirsch to put a stop to this with a general order to each of the Central Organization's fourteen branch offices. Hirsch replied that merely instructing the branch offices would not work, that only a published notice in the organization's paper (*Jüdische Nachrichtenblatt*) would. Wörhn then gave permission to publish a notice, adding that Hirsch must "tell the branch offices too." BA Potsdam R 8150, Minutes of the Central Organization's Directorate, by Hirsch, February 15, 1941.
28. Landgericht Frankfurt am Main, 50 Js 36019/84, gegen Alois Brunner, statement of Norbert Wollheim, April 10, 1986.
29. Walter Laqueur, *The Missing Years* (Boston: 1980), 147, 151.
30. ND PS—681. Secret trials would be just as problematic as public ones, Acting Justice Minister Schlegelberger wrote, because the regime would still have to explain "the particular elements of offense [that] would unfurl the entire problem." A letter from an attorney general in Berlin (Herder) to Schlegelberger on May 19, 1942, shows that

the regime was still preferring secrecy to prosecution more than a year later. The attorney general reported that he had found copies of Bishop von Galen's letters to Reich authorities protesting the Euthanasia action in the desk of a woman accused of treason, but that in agreement with Berlin police headquarters, he was not going to include these in the trial against her. LB, Sondergerichthof Akte, Sondergericht IV, Pk. KLs 2/42.

31. Noakes and Pridham, *Nazism*, 1004. The regime could ignore protest letters from church leaders, but a series of denunciations from the pulpit was problematic.

32. The relationship between Galen's sermons and Hitler's decision is the subject of debate. See Michael Burleigh, *Death and Deliverance: "Euthanasia" in Germany c. 1900–1945* (Cambridge, England: 1995), chapter 5, on German responses to Euthanasia. Burleigh contends that Hitler did not give his order because of local difficulties with a bishop but because the Euthanasia (T-4) team of murderers was needed to implement their techniques in the Aktion Reinhard death camps. But does it follow that this transfer of Euthanasia personnel means that Galen was not the precipitating factor behind Hitler's order? Galen's key influence and the transfer are mutually compatible. Furthermore, it is difficult to contend that the T-4 program stopped because it had already slightly exceed its projected target figure of victims. Many historians (of the functionalist school) agree that the regime improvised, feeling its way toward some policy expressions (not determined in advance) of its ideology. Furthermore, unlimited, extended victimization is a distinguishing mark of the Nazi dictatorship. Galen was right in proclaiming that by its logic, Euthanasia could be extended to an expanding part of the population.

33. J. P. Stern, *Hitler: The Führer and the People* (Berkeley and Los Angeles: 1975), 116. Lewy, *Catholic Church and Nazi Germany*, 266, 267 made a similar conclusion ("Had German public opinion shown a similar response against other crimes of the Nazi regime committed on an even greater scale, such as the extermination of the Jews of Europe, the results might well have been similarly telling"), as have others writing more recently, including Conor Cruise O'Brien, "A Lost Chance to Save the Jews?," *New York Review of Books* (April 27, 1989), 27ff. The history of intermarriage undergirds this hypothesis.

34. Pr. GSta., Repositur 90 P, 14, 15.

35. Jeremy Noakes, "The Oldenburg Crucifix Struggle of November 1936: A Case Study of Opposition in the Third Reich," in *The Shaping of the Nazi State*, ed. Peter Stachura (New York: 1978), 212. Noakes has written the history of the crucifix struggle in Cloppenburg in rich detail, evaluating it as a case study for illuminating the possibilities and limitations of opposition to the regime and beyond that as an illustration of relations between Catholics and the state and the way popular opinion could severely criticize local Nazi leaders and specific day-to-day policies, while lauding Hitler and even the regime in general.

36. Galen sent a pastoral letter to be read in all the churches of his diocese, assuring that word of this struggle would become widely known. "We will avoid all companionship with those who are enemies of the Cross of Christ," the bishop wrote. "We will read no books or papers which disgrace the Cross of Christ and we will not tolerate them in our houses, in shop windows or in show-cases. And if, for the sake of the Cross, it becomes our fate to suffer disgrace or persecution with Christ the crucified, then we do not want to be cowardly or shrink back." The German police interpreted the actions of the church as a direct challenge to state power. Quoted in Lewy, *Catholic Church and Nazi Germany*, 311.

37. Pr. GSta., Rep. 90 P, 16.

38. Kershaw, *Popular Opinion and Political Dissent*, 343. This history of Wagner's crucifix decree is taken from Kershaw, *Popular Opinion and Political Dissent*, 340ff. Crucifix struggles also ensued in the Ermland and Saar Palatinate. David Blackbourn, *Marpingen: Apparitions of the Virgin Mary in Bismarckian Germany* (New York: 1993), chapter 12.

39. Kershaw, *Popular Opinion and Political Dissent*, 353, 354.
40. Ibid., 338, quoting from ND D-906/7–18.
41. RSHA (gez Gengenbach) to directors and leaders of the SD, August 28, 1941. BA, R58/990, 43–46.
42. Müller to directors of the Gestapo and the heads of the SD offices, March 13, 1941, BA, R58/990, 42–43.
43. ND PS—681, quoted in Ernst Klee, ed., *Dokumente zur "Euthanasie"* (Frankfurt: 1985), 213–216.
44. Müller to directors of the Gestapo and the heads of the SD offices, March 13, 1941, BA, R58/990, 42–43.
45. Noakes and Pridham, *Nazism*, p. 1039.
46. Martin Broszat and Elke Fröhlich, *Alltag und Widerstand: Bayern im Nationalsozialismus* (Munich: 1987), p. 62.
47. Heinrich Portmann, ed., *Bischof Graf von Galen spricht!* (Freiburg im Breisgau: 1946), 194–96. Tiessler argued with Goebbels that the regime would only have to publicize and correct the low-down (*hundsgemein*) propagandistic lies of the bishop.
48. Ernst Klee, *"Euthanasia" im NS-Staat: Die Vernichtung lebensunwerten Lebens* (Frankfurt am Main: 1983), 431, 432.
49. Hans-Walter Schmuhl, "Die Selbstverständlichkeit des Tötens: Psychiater im Nationalsozialismus," *Geschichte und Gesellschaft*, vol. 16, No. 4 (1990), No. 4, 412, 413; and Burleigh, "Euthanasia and the Third Reich," 13. Under the modified Euthanasia program, "the goal to strive for is to make indistinguishable, in all but a few exceptions, death by Euthanasia and natural death." Quoted in Hans-Walter Schmuhl, *Rassenhygiene, Nationalsozialismus, Euthanasie: Von der Verhütung zur Vernichtung "lebensunwerten Lebens" 1890–1945* (Göttingen: 1987), 223.
50. On origins of genocide in euthanasia, see Henry Friedlander, *The Origins of Nazi Genocide: From Euthanasia to the Final Solution* (Chapel Hill, N.C.: 1995).

XI: THE STAR OF DAVID DECREE

1. Hilberg, *Destruction of the European Jews*, 216.
2. BA Potsdam, R 8150, Minutes of the Central Organization's Directorate, by Eppstein, September 27, 1941.
3. Ibid., September 17 and 20, 1941, LBI, microfilm 66.
4. Kammergericht Berlin, indictment trial of Friedrich Bosshammer. I Js 1/65, 78, citing an anonymous record from the end of August 1941, summarizing a press conference of the Propaganda Ministry held August 20, 1941.
5. Lösener, "Als Rassereferent," 297, 304. See also Longerich, *Hitlers Stellvertreter*, 220, 221. Heydrich did propose to exclude from the Final Solution (and sterilize) those *Mischlinge* married to Jews who had children, as well as the very few who had received special dispensations from the highest levels. Lösener, "Als Rassereferent," 299.
6. Bovensiepen Trial, Supporting Document 96. The five sets of deportation directives (concerning which categories of Jews should be sent to which camps) issued between October 1941 and February 1943 ordered *Mischlinge* and intermarried Jews to be "temporarily" exempted from the deportations. When Hitler ordered the first wave of fifty thousand Jews to be deported from the Reich in the fall of 1941, intermarried Jews were to be excluded. In their directives on deportation to branch Gestapo offices, RSHA officials explained that these Jews were being "temporarily deferred"—*vorläufig zurückgestellt*—from deportations. Notes from a meeting in Berlin on October 23, 1941, chaired by Adolf Eichmann, ZSdL, Film no. 43. Dr. K. Ventner for the Geheime Staatspolizei, Staatspolizeileitstelle Düsseldorf to branch offices, October 11, 1941, directed that "Jews living in intermarriage . . . are, however, *not* to be evacuated."
7. "Reich Minister Goebbels several days ago raised the question of the marking of the

German Jews to Hitler, and received a decision from him that the Jews in German should be marked." 52AA (Bonn), Inl. 11 g 172. Report from AA, Berlin, August 21, 1941, signed by Under State Secretary Luther.

8. Lösener, "Als Rassereferent," 297.

9. The close confidential relationship between Goebbels and Hitler, thrown briefly on the rocks by Goebbels's near divorce during his affair with a Czech actress, Lida Baarova, rebounded as Hitler accepted Goebbels's claims that his propaganda ploys to demoralize French troops featured prominently in Germany's dazzling blitzkrieg conquest of France in 1940, according to Gutterer. Interview with Gutterer, July 16, 1987.

10. At a meeting with his section chiefs in April, Goebbels said that publicly marking Berlin Jews "had been proposed to him," and he assigned Gutterer the responsibility for carrying out this measure. BA Potsdam, Pro Mi, lg, April 21, 1941.

11. Lösener's account of the August 15 meeting is in "Als Rassereferent," 303–305. The Propaganda Ministry announced this important conference only one day before, a maneuver to present Goebbels's agreements with Hitler as a fait accompli and to steer the conversation by unprepared fellow ministries, preempting any further discussions on the matter.

12. Heinrich Himmler, October 31, 1940, "Betr. Vorschlag, Ministerialdirecktor SS-Oberführer Gutterer im Reichsministerium für Volksaufklärung und propaganda . . . zu befördern." BDC, personal file of Leopold Gutterer.

13. Hilberg, *Destruction of the European Jews*, 179, and interview with Elsa Holzer, December 10, 1989.

14. Richarz, *Jüdisches Leben in Deutschland*, 466.

15. Statement of Hans-Oskar Löwenstein de Witt, *Schon damals fingen viele an zu schweigen*, 184.

16. David Bankier, *The Germans and the Final Solution: Public Opinion under Nazism* (Oxford and New York: 1992), 124, 125, registers German responses to the introduction of the Star of David. District Court Director Ernst Bukofzer and others reported after the war that Berliners had generally responded with a "mixture of sympathy and shame" to the Star of David. In 1946 Dr. Bukofzer, who assisted the prosecution at the Nuremberg Trials, asserted that Germans typically showed Jews small favors, giving them food, cigarettes, etc. *Bukofzer, Laws for Jews*, 13. Nazi secret police agents, however, reported that "overall" the population had responded "favorably" to the requirement that Jews wear the star and wished that it would be more consistently required. Boberach, *Meldungen aus dem Reich*, vol. 9, 3245–3248, entry for February 2, 1942.

17. Minutes of the Central Organization's Directorate, Mannheim, to Paul Eppstein, June 23, 1942, BA Potsdam, R 8150, indicates that as the result of the birth of children, some nonprivileged intermarried couples were being transferred to a status as privileged intermarriages, even as late as 1942.

18. On the rights of Jews in privileged intermarriages, see Richarz, *Jüdisches Leben in Deutschland*, 465.

19. Benz, *Juden in Deutschland*, 750.

XII: THE PRICE OF COMPLIANCE AND THE DESTRUCTION OF JEWS

1. Statement of Martha Mosse, July 11, 1967, Bovensiepen Trial. This number is verified in a Gestapo report in Frankfurt am Main of October 22, 1942, *Dokumente der Frankfurter Juden*, 474–75. Hans Hinkel, BA-Potsdam, Pro Mi, Id, September 17, 1940, reported that there were 72,327 Berlin Jews in September 1940. The Justice Ministry, however, was under the impression that there had been 84,000 Berlin Jews (see ND NG-151. A memorandum to Acting Justice Minister Schlegelberger from a Justice Ministry expert reported that 7,000 Jews had been "shoved out" while 77,000 remained).

2. This was the first of what became 188 deportations of some thirty-five thousand Berlin

Jews to the ghettos and death camps. See Henschel, *"Aus der Arbeit,"* loc. cit., 1.

3. Indictment, 178, Bovensiepen Trial.

4. Statement of Martha Mosse, February 26, 1948, Pr. GSta., Rep. 335, Fall II, Nr. 29, 2597 ff., and statement of Martha Mosse, Military Court Nr. IV, Fall XII, Nuremberg. "We had to summon community members and to advise and support those who came and filled out the questionnaires. The choice of whom to summon would be left to us."

5. "Finally one came to the conclusion, that it would be better to undertake the tasks, because it appeared that in this way still greater hardships would be avoided," remembered Dr. Mosse. Statement of Martha Mosse, July 11, 1967, Bovensiepen Trial. In 1946 the former director of the Berlin Jewish Community spoke to those who would always ask, "How did you [assist the Gestapo], why did you do this?" Community Director Moritz Henschel replied that "the thought that led us was: If we do these things, they will always be carried out in a better, milder way." Without the Jewish Community's presence the deportations would have been "awfully raw." Moritz Henschel, "Die letzten Jahre der Jüdischen Gemeinde Berlin," (a lecture given September 13, 1946), Yad Vashem, 01/51. From his perspective in 1965, Jacob Jacobson, a former employee of the Jewish Community in Berlin, was more critical. "In hindsight, almost more than at the time which I too experienced, the relaxed, stoical quiescence with which the highest administrative body of Jewish autonomy allowed the National Socialist leaders to bring it into the deportation machinery appears to be astonishing." Statement of Jacob Jacobson, December 9, 1965, LBI, Max Kreuzberger Research Papers (AR 7183).

6. Report by Reich statistician Korherr, April 19, 1943, ND NO-5193.

7. Indictment, 182, Bovensiepen Trial, citing the testimony of Dr. Martha Mosse.

8. Indictment, 166, Bovensiepen Trial.

9. Notes from a meeting in Berlin on October 23, 1941, chaired by Adolf Eichmann, dated October 24, ZSdL, Film no. 43. See K. Drobisch, R. Goguel, and W. Müller, *Juden unterm Hakenkreuz: Verfolgung und Ausrotung der deutschen Juden, 1933–1945* (Berlin: 1973), 292.

10. According to Dr. Mosse, she was in "continuous contact with the officers of the Berlin Gestapo entrusted with the deportations. I had frequent conferences concerning matters of housing as well as in efforts to have Jews exempted from the deportations." Statement of Martha Mosse, July 13, 1965, Bovensiepen Trial.

11. "Ordner Transport 1943/44," Bovensiepen Trial, Supporting Document 28b. Only nine of these ninety-six persons deported to Theresienstadt survived.

12. BA Potsdam, R 8150, Minutes of the Central Organization's Directorate, by Kozower, July 21, 1942.

13. BA Potsdam, R 8150, Minutes of the Central Organization's Directorate, by Eppstein, September 17, 1942.

14. After the Gestapo prepared each successive deportation list, the Jewish Community sent each member of the list a card ordering him or her to appear at the Levetzowstrasse synagogue, on a certain day. But after a "few months" the Gestapo called this off, because too many Jews were going underground instead of reporting to the synagogue, reported Mosse, statement of July 23 and 24, 1958, and indictment 183, Bovensiepen Trial.

15. Statement of Willi Königsfeld, September 7, 1965, Bovensiepen Trial.

16. Indictment (citing Martha Mosse), Bovensiepen Trial, 183.

17. Interview with Abrahamsohn, August 16, 1986. Abrahamsohn told his story as a thriving architect and president of the architects' association in an important West German city. Beginning in June 1943, when the only Jews left in Berlin other than those from intermarriages were underground, Abrahamsohn had worked full-time to ferret out the hiding places of Jews and brought them for deportation to the Gestapo. Peter Wyden has written a book on the most notorious "catcher," Stella Kübler. Peter

Wyden, *Stella: One Woman's True Tale of Evil, Betrayal, and Survival in Hitler's Germany* (New York: 1992).

18. With only a few early exceptions, the *Geltungsjuden*—half Jews who were members of the Jewish Community or were married to Jews—were exempted from the evacuations to the east. LBI, letter of Siegbert Kleemann in defense of Martha Mosse, June 12, 1947.

19. Just before her trip to Auschwitz, Mrs. Böhm wrote Wally a letter she kept until her death. "Every person who reads this letter is terribly impressed by what this woman writes," said Wally. "To me, it seems that in Germany we're forgetting too fast what has happened, and anti-Semitism is flaming up again."

20. Statement of Anton Loderer, October 28, 1965, Bovensiepen Trial, and statement of Kurt Grünewald, November 18, 1965, Bovensiepen Trial.

21. Statement of Max Reschke, Supporting Document 30 (Dr. Wolfgang Scheffler Collection), May 4, 1959, Bovensiepen Trial.

22. Statement of Martha Mosse, April 9, 1968, Bovensiepen Trial. Helmut Brinitzer also reported hearing by early 1942 that those deported would not be seen again. Statement of Brinitzer, August 18, 1970, Bovensiepen Trial.

23. Interview with Hans-Oskar Löwenstein de Witt, November 8, 1984. The BBC began reporting on the mass murder of Jews by mid-1942 and on the systematic extermination of the Jews in Poland and Russia by the end of 1942. Walter Laqueur, *The Terrible Secret: Suppression of the Truth about Hitler's "Final Solution"* (New York: 1980, rev. 1982), 73, 222–223.

24. Interview with Günter Grodka, August 25, 1985.

25. To prevent unrest and disobedience among the Jews still to be deported, Jewish Community authorities, especially, were not to be given reason for doubting the official story that Jews were being sent to work camps in the east. In this regard, deportation directives were to be painstakingly followed, Eichmann warned the Gestapo. The Jewish Council from Riga in 1942 made complaints to the Nazi gauleiter that forty to fifty Jews who did not meet the Gestapo's directives for deportations were nevertheless deported. Heydrich was drawn into this discussion. The majority of those whose deportations the council contested had actually been deported according to the Gestapo's directives, Eichmann told the Gestapo. Nevertheless, this kind of complaint by Jewish authorities was under all circumstances to be strenuously avoided, he continued. "Bericht über die am 6.3.1942 im Reichsicherheitshauptamt—Amt IV B 4 stattgefundenen Besprechung." ND, NG-2586-H.

26. In the remnants from the Justice Ministry known as the Schlegelberger Minute Reich Chancellor Hans Lammers reported that the Führer repeatedly told him he "wished to have the Solution of the Jewish Question deferred until after the war." Thus in Lammers's opinion, the "current expressions" on the matter had merely "theoretical value." Lammers cautioned, however, that he would have to take care to prevent "other offices" from making a "fundamental decision" on the matter without his knowledge. BA, "Behandlung der Juden," R 22/52. The historian Eberhard Jaeckel published an article about this minute, "Der Zettle mit dem schlimmen Wort," in *Frankfurter Allgemeine Zeitung*, June 22, 1978, 23, in which he seems to date it April 10, 1942. At the time Schlegelberger was considering a proposed law from the Interior Ministry that would compel the divorce of all intermarried couples. A two-page report from Schlegelberger in the same file on this matter is dated April 5, 1942.

27. Goebbels, *Diaries*, ed. Lochner, entry for March 9, 1943, 288ff. and interview with Gutterer, August 17, 1986, December 10, 1989. In Himmler's words, Hitler said at their meeting on June 19, 1943, that "the evacuation of Jews was to be radically carried out in the next three to four months, despite the still-developing unrest." Himmler's memorandum of his meeting with Hitler, much of which concerns the east, should be interpreted as a general policy for all Europe. The practice of referring to the deportation of intermarried Jews or *Mischlinge* as radical reflects the vocabulary of Eichmann,

who said that he would "radically resolve" the question of German *Mischlinge*. NA, T-175/R 94/2615097. Himmler's calendar (NS 19, 1444) for June 19, 1943, shows that he got a haircut at ten-thirty and met with Hitler at Obersalzburg between three and seven on June 19, 1943.

28. Reuth, *Goebbels, Tagebücher*, entry for March 7, 1942, 1763.
29. Summary of the Final Solution conference of October 10, 1941, Israel Police Document 1193.
30. Heydrich did propose to exclude from the Final Solution (and sterilize) those *Mischlinge* married to Jews who had children, as well as those very few who had received special dispensations from the highest levels. Lösener, "Als Rassereferent," 299.
31. At the Final Solution meeting, held on March 6, 1942, Eichmann said Theresienstadt was established to give soothing false appearances. Summary of Conference, ND NG-2586-H. Theresienstadt, a camp in Czechoslovakia without gas chambers and crematoria, was generally known among the Jews as the preferred "evacuation" destination and was reserved by deportation directives for Jews over sixty-five and a lesser number of "privileged" Jews, such as the leaders of Jewish organizations and Jews from intermarriages whose spouses had died or divorced them. The vast majority of Theresienstadt inmates were sent to Auschwitz. In response to the military's requests that Jews who had fought with high honors in World War I be protected, the RSHA promised to send them to Theresienstadt but secretly deported them from there to Auschwitz.
32. Gestapo Director Heinrich Müller ordered branch Gestapo offices to send four categories of Jews to this "old people's ghetto," two of which were from Jewish-German families: Jews over sixty-five or those in especially ill health over fifty-five; privileged intermarried Jews whose German spouses had died or divorced them; *Geltungsjuden* who were not married to Jews; and Jews decorated with war honors from World War I. Müller to Gestapo offices, May 21, 1942, Internationaler Suchdienst HO 308/103 from Bovensiepen Trial, supporting document 100. Each of these categories, other than those from Jewish-German families, was sent from Theresienstadt on to Auschwitz. Reich officials made the decision to deport Jews honored for their service in World War I and received serious complaints from the military about it. Those in charge of the Final Solution then deported each category of Jews—*except* intermarried Jews—on to Auschwitz and the gas ovens after they had arrived in Theresienstadt. Hilberg, *Destruction of the European Jews*, vol. II, 438, quoting H. G. Adler, *Theresienstadt 1941–1945*, 2d ed. (Tübingen: 1960), 37–60, 725.
33. Summary of the Wannsee Conference, Nuremberg Trial Document NG-2586-E.
34. Testimony of Adolf Eichmann at his trial, Jerusalem, June 23 and 26, 1961, July 24, 1961, quoted in Hilberg, *Documents of Destruction*, 101–105.
35. R. Hilberg, *Destruction of the European Jews*, 421.
36. Summary of the conference of March 6, 1942, ND NG-2586-H. The problem Eichmann faced was drawing a line between cases where unrest was avoidable and where it wasn't, but in addition, given the objectives of both "racial purification" and avoidance of domestic unrest, he was pressed to extract in deportations the greatest amount of Jewish blood in exchange for any given amount of unrest. In deciding not to compel the divorce of intermarried half Jews, Eichmann was establishing minimal standards and drawing an easy line since there were still full Jews married to Germans who refused to divorce.
37. The RSHA directives for the deportation of German Jews to Auschwitz (see, for example, those of June 4, 1942, and February 20, 1943) ordered the deportation of all Jews except for several categories that were to be exempted. These included the privileged mixed-marriage Jews whose spouses had divorced or died; this indicates that the nonprivileged intermarried Jews whose spouses had divorced them or died were being deported. In December 1943 Himmler ordered that as of that point the privileged intermarried Jews whose spouses had divorced them or died could also be deported—with the exception of cases where deporting a Jew would cause too much unrest because of his or her children. Order of Heinrich Himmler to all Gestapo branch offices other than those in

the Protektorat, December 18, 1943, Bovensiepen Trial, Supporting Document 29. The Gestapo in Berlin arrested Jews whose non-Jewish spouses died or divorced them within twenty-four hours, and in Prague they were deported within a month. Ältestenrat der Juden, Prag (Jewish Council of Prague) to Central office for the governing of the Jewish question in Bohemia and Moravia, June 19, 1944, Bovensiepen Trial, Supporting Document 94. See also Langericht Berlin, I P Ks 1/57, Stella Kübler Trial. Kübler was sentenced for working for the Berlin Gestapo and accused by witnesses of arresting Berlin mixed-marriage Jews within twenty-four hours of the death of a non-Jewish spouse. See also the circular letter of the Central Organization of German Jews' confidential spokesman B. O. on matters of "privileged mixed marriage Jews" in the Württemberg and Hohenzollern areas, of July 14, 1942, from Stadtarchiv Ulm, Bestand H, Teil 16.

38. Stuckart had been present at the Wannsee Conference, but he apparently did not understand the anxiety expressed then about German spouses who would be terribly aggrieved by the deportation of their Jewish partners. (Stuckart had apparently not cleared the proposal with the Justice Ministry in advance even though he proposed it as a joint Interior-Justice Ministry project).

39. Compulsory divorce was not a delicate enough instrument for dealing with the wide variations represented in the thousands of German intermarriages, according to the calculations of the Propaganda Ministry. ND NG-2586-H.

40. In such cases, concluded Schlegelberger, the recalcitrant German spouse must accompany the Jewish partner to the ghetto in Theresienstadt. Schlegelberger to Bormann, April 5, 1942, ND 4055-PS.

41. West Germany, interview with Leopold Gutterer, August 17, 1986.

42. See the Schlegelberger Minute, BA, "Behandlung der Juden," R 22/52, which indicates that Hitler had decided to put off solving the "Jewish Question" (not specifically the matter of intermarried Jews) until after the war.

43. Himmler to Berger, July 28, 1942, Bovensiepen Trial, Supporting Document 108, or Bundesarchiv NS 19/1415.

44. Correspondence among the above-named agencies and others between January 13 and June 25, 1942, YIVO Institute for Jewish Research, Nr. G 57.

45. Henschel, "Aus der Arbeit," 5.

46. The story and details of this event is told in Hildesheimer, *Jüdische Selbstverwaltung*, 221–227. For an analysis of the Baum Group and its fate, see Wolfgang Scheffler, "Der Brandanschlag im Berliner Lustgarten im Mai 1942 und seine Folgen," in *Jahrbuch des Landesarchiv Berlin*, ed. Hans Reichhardt (Berlin: 1984), 91–118.

47. BA Potsdam, R 8150, Minutes of the Central Organization's Directorate, by Kozower, May 31, 1942.

48. Bramsted, *Goebbels and National Socialist Propaganda*, 397.

49. Goebbels was constantly involved in the affairs of the Final Solution, and the Central Organization sent three copies of each of its circular letters to the Propaganda Ministry. BA Potsdam, R 8150, Minutes of the Central Organization's Directorate, December 6, 1941.

50. BA Potsdam, R 8150, Minutes of the Central Organization's Directorate, June 25, 1942.

51. Benz, *Juden in Deutschland*, 72.

52. R. Parker, *Struggle for Survival*, 144.

53. Statement of Kurt Grünewald, November 18, 1965, Bovensiepen Trial. In contrast with other areas of the Reich, where the government president provided the authority of confiscation, the Gestapo in Berlin worked both as the evacuation and the confiscation authorities. Anklageschrift, 166, Bovensiepen Trial.

54. When several weeks later Alois Brunner entered Mosse's name on the list of those to be deported, she successfully petitioned Berger to intercede. Dr. Mosse remembered that a Jewish Community employee, Mr. Reichenheim, had also been accused by Jews

of stealing. By a decision of the community leadership, he was released from his job and deported. Statement of Martha Mosse, April 9, 1968, Bovensiepen Trial.

55. Statement of Gerhard Schmidt, August 22, 1966, Bovensiepen Trial.
56. Auszüge aus dem SS und Pol. Gefängnis, Berlin Schöneberg, Grünewaldstrasse 68, Supporting Document 66, Bovensiepen Trial.
57. Pursuant to letters dated March 8–10, 1943, Bovensiepen was removed from Berlin to Kassel. Bovensiepen Trial, Supporting Document 66.
58. Hilberg, *Destruction of the European Jews*, 47 (footnote).
59. Statement of Schnapp, IfZ, Wiener Library Files, WZS.
60. Mary Felstiner, "Alois Brunner, 'Eichmann's Best Tool,' " *Simon Wiesenthal Center Annual*, vol. 3 (1986), 9.
61. Landgericht Frankfurt am Main, 50 Js 36019/84, Trial against Alois Brunner, statement of Norbert Wollheim, April 10, 1986.
62. Hilberg, *Destruction of the European Jews*, 657, citing an order by Knochen and Brunner, April 14, 1944, ND NO-1411.
63. Interview with Abrahamsohn, 16 August 1986.
64. BA Potsdam, R 8150, Minutes of the Central Organization's Directorate, by Kozower, November 14, 1942.
65. Bovensiepen Trial, Beistuck 30, interview statement of Max Reschke, May 11, 1959.
66. Jacob Jacobson, December 9, 1965, LBI, Max Kreuzberg Collection.
67. Statement of Schnapp, IfZ, Weiner Library Files, WZS, 5.
68. Henschel, "Aus der arbeit," 8.
69. One eyewitness spoke of "forceful collections of people and very loud protests." Statement of Harry Schnapp, BA, Bovensiepen Trial, April 27, 1965.
70. Felstiner, "Alois Brunner," 9.
71. Zivier, "Aufstand der Frauen."
72. Statement of Max Reschke (assistant to Dobberke), May 4, 1959, Supporting Document 30 (Dr. Wolfgang Scheffler Collection), Bovensiepen Trial.
73. When Hitler gave no clear public signal, local chieftains felt as if they had to decide or had the opportunity to decide. Before the Nuremberg Laws, writes Lösener, every district and county party leader interpreted the term "Jew" according to his own whim, making even one-eighth Jews their victims. Lösener, "Als Rassereferent," 278. Lösener himself, as the Interior Ministry's adviser for Jewish matters, urged in September 1942 that the fate of *Mischlinge* be left up to Hitler. Affidavit from Lösener, October 17, 1947, ND NG-2982. Later various gauleiters decided on their own to deport Jews from their areas, including those in intermarriages. Longerich, *Hitler's Stellvertreter*, 218. Lesser Gestapo officials in charge of rounding up Jews for deportation also occasionally herded a single intermarried Jew or two onto the trains bound for the camps. Petty Gestapo officers understood little of the Nazi concept of power and "psychological problems." Some advanced by showing "radicalism" on issues of importance to National Socialism, and the deportation of the intermarried Jews suggested to them an obvious way to appear radical on the issue that was the most important litmus test of true National Socialist belief. In February 1940, before deportation directives were issued, the Nazi party gauleiter Franz Schwede-Coburg, perhaps seeking acclaim among his colleagues as a radical Nazi, deported Jews to German-occupied Poland from Stettin and Schneidemühl, including some Jews married to Aryans as well as several non-Jewish wives of Jews. See the story of the deportation of Jews from Stettin and Schneidemühl in Rosenfeld and Luckner, *Lebenszeichen aus Pialski*, 23ff, and in Hildesheimer, *Jüdische Selbsverwaltung*, 180–184. Martin Gilbert, in *Atlas of the Holocaust* (New York: 1993), identifies several German Jews from intermarriages who were deported to death camps, and the histories of individual Jewish communities around Germany contain other examples.
74. Central Organization leaders were informed of this policy by Hauptsturmführer Gutwasser of Eichmann's office. Minutes of the Central Organization Directorate's meeting

on March 21, 1942, by Eppstein, March 23, 1942, LBI, microfilm 66 (original in BA Potsdam R 8150).

75. BA Potsdam, R 8150, Minutes of the Central Organization, by Eppstein, November 7, 1941. In July 1942 Berlin Jewish Community Director Moritz Henschel was also told again that Jews in intermarriages should not be released from community employment. BA Potsdam, R 8150, Minutes of the Central Organization's Directorate, July 2, 1942, by Henschel. Jews released from employment were deported to Theresienstadt.

76. In March 1942 the Propaganda Ministry demanded a further reduction of Berlin's Jewish Community employees—excluding anyone over fifty-five and anyone in an intermarriage. BA Potsdam, R 8150, Minutes of the Central Organization's Directorate, by Eppstein, March 5, 1942. Those released were not to be sent to the Work Office for further work, but a list of them was to be sent to the Berlin Gestapo.

77. "Our administration was of course somewhat bloated, because employment at the Jewish Community could initially protect a person from deportation," said Mosse. The Gestapo repeatedly pressed the leadership of the Jewish Community to release superfluous employees. The leadership responded only hesitatingly to this pressure, "so as to protect our co-workers as much as possible from deportation." Statement of Dr. Martha Mosse, April 9, 1968, Bovensiepen Trial.

78. Felstiner, "Alois Brunner," 9. The day before this so-called Community Action, Dr. Mosse had been instructed by the community directors Moritz Henschel and Philipp Kozower to make sure everyone in her housing section was on the job the following morning. Statement of Dr. Martha Mosse, April 9, 1968, Bovensiepen Trial. There is some disagreement in reports as to the exact date of this "Community Action." See also Henschel, "Aus der Arbeit," 7.

79. Felstiner, "Alois Brunner," 9, and Inge Unikower, *Suche nach dem gelobten Land* (Berlin: 1978), 246.

80. Statement of Dr. Martha Mosse, 9 April 1968, Bovensiepen Trial. In her postwar testimony Mosse tended to protect the former Gestapo officers as men under pressure of orders who had no choice. Her interpretation of Günther's statement as well intentioned probably meant that he was doing her a favor by warning her.

81. Felstiner, "Alois Brunner," 9.

82. Mosse, April 9, 1968, Bovensiepen Trial.

83. The list was categorized according to the local Gestapo branch offices, which would be taking responsibility for their deportations. BA Potsdam, R 8150, Minutes of the Central Organization's Directorate, November 19 and 27, 1942. The November 27 report exceeds one hundred pages.

84. *Jüdische Nachrichtenblatt*, November 27 and December 11, 1942, or "Neue Bestimmung," *Judentum und Recht*, vol. 6, no. 24 (December 15, 1942).

85. Primo Levi, *The Drowned and the Saved* (New York: 1980), 80.

86. Interview with Charlotte Israel Freudenthal, June 22, 1990.

87. Indictment, 149, Bovensiepen Trial.

88. Interview with Elsa Holzer, Berlin, April 7, 1985.

89. Hilberg, *Destruction of the European Jews*, 1038.

90. The historian Guenter Lewy writes that the bishops "underestimated the strength of their position [to influence Nazi policies], especially during the war period," Lewy, *Catholic Church and Nazi Germany*, 313.

91. Arendt, *Eichmann in Jerusalem*, 125.

92. Isaiah Trunk, *Judenrat: The Jewish Councils in Eastern Europe under Nazi Occupation* (New York: 1972), xxxv.

93. Konrad Kwiet, "Resistance and Opposition: The Example of the German Jews," in *Contending with Hitler*, loc. cit., 73.

94. Final Report" of the Berlin Jewish Community's Registration Office (Kataster Verwaltung), BA Potsdam, R 8150, September 1, 1942.

95. See the example in "Neue Bestimmung," loc. cit.

96. Haifa, Israel, interview with Edith Wolf, April 8, 1986. Wolf told her story of the removal of her name from the list at the Jewish Community in her unpublished memoirs, Yad Vashem, 01/247.

XIII: PLANS TO CLEAR THE REICH OF JEWS—AND THE OBSTACLES OF WOMEN AND "TOTAL WAR"

1. Eleanor Hancock has written an excellent treatment of Total War, including the problems of compulsory labor registration for women. Hancock defines Total War as "the complete orientation of society in its political, economic and social life to the pursuit of the war effort." Hancock, *National Socialist Leadership and Total War*, 2.
2. London, London Public Records Office, FO 371/34454. Sol Littman of the Simon Wiesenthal Center recently discovered this speech.
3. "In my Reichstag speech of September 1, 1939, I have spoken of two things: first, that now that the war has been forced upon us, no array of weapons and no passage of time will bring us to defeat, and second, that if Jewry should plot another world war in order to exterminate the Aryan peoples of Europe, it would not be the Aryan peoples which would be exterminated, but Jewry. . . . At one time, the Jews of Germany laughed about my prophecies. I do not know whether they are still laughing or whether they have already lost all desire to laugh. But right now I can only repeat—they will stop laughing everywhere, and I shall be right also in that prophecy." German press, September 30, 1942, quoted by Raul Hilberg, *Destruction of the European Jews*, 407. As Hilberg points out, the Reichstag speech of 1939 that Hitler made reference to was actually given on January 30 rather than on September 1 of that year.
4. More than one-half of those still in the Reich as of January 1, 1943, lived in Berlin. Report by Reich statistician Korherr, April 19, 1943, ND NO-5193.
5. Summary of October 27, 1942, conference proceedings, ND NG-2586-M. Seventeen officials were on hand at the October 27 meeting, liberally representing the RSHA, the party and Reich chancelleries, the general government, and the Office of the Four-Year Plan. In addition, four major Reich ministries were represented, but conspicuous for its absence was the Propaganda Ministry.
6. Otto Hünsche, Eichmann's deputy, who was present at this conference, said in an interview that the intention of the conferees at the time of the conference was to deport Jews married to Germans, including Jews in privileged intermarriages. Interview (telephone) with Otto Hünsche, August 11, 1986.
7. This was the position of the RSHA-dominated conference of October 10, 1941. Himmler's deputy Reinhard Heydrich, Eichmann, and other Nazi decision makers concerned with the Final Solution had agreed that an intermarried German who refused to divorce would be deported along with the Jewish partner. Hilberg, *Destruction of the European Jews*, 402, Israel Police Document 1193; Longerich, *Hitlers Stellvertreter*, 220, 221.
8. Hilberg, *Destruction of the European Jews*, 424–426, citing ND NG-2982 and NG-2586-M.
9. Kammergericht Berlin, trial of Fritz Wöhrn, document vol. 7, 18, and indictment, trial of Fritz Wöhrn, 147.
10. Indictment trial of Fritz Wöhrn, 101, 147.
11. In early March 1943, on the heels of the Final Roundup, party members were prohibited from marrying Germans who had previously been married to Jews. Following the loss of millions of German men in the war, party members, like soldiers, were expected to find better mates than those once married to Jews. BA, NS 19/3335, 32.
12. Paul C. Squire interview with Dr. Carl J. Burkhardt, November 7, 1942, NA RG 84, American Consulate, Geneva, confidential file 1942, 800. Richard Breitman has discussed this document at more length in *Architect of Genocide*, 152, 154. See also Laqueur,

Terrible Secret, 63. Burckhardt had not seen the decree himself but had two very well-informed German sources, officials in the Foreign Ministry and Wehrmacht.

13. In late 1942 the *Mischlinge*, and in particular the Jews in intermarriages, were in very high danger of being deported, as Uwe Adam has concluded. Adam, *Judenpolitik im dritten Reich*, 316, 317, 329.

14. Lehfeld, "Die Lage der 'Mischlinge,' " 1.

15. Hitler said this at the outset of the blitzkrieg in a secret speech of August 22, 1939, to the commanders of the armed services, according to the so-called Lochner version of the speech. Louis Lochner, *What about Germany?* (New York: Dodd, Mead, and Co., 1942), 1–5; printed also in Office of U.S. Chief of Counsel for Prosecution of Axis Criminals, *Nazi Conspiracy and Aggression* (Washington, D.C.: 1946), vol. VII, 752–54, L-003.

16. BA Koblenz, NS/19, 2655, SS Obergruppenführer Krueger to Heinrich Himmler, December 5, 1942.

17. Laqueur, *Terrible Secret*, 37. Unlike in the east, Nazi policies for deportation and attention to popular opinion in western occupied territories were similar to those in Germany itself.

18. BA NL 118/51, Goebbels diary, entry for January 28, 1943.

19. NA, RG 226, 134, February 24, 1943. An OSS report from the same source added the next day that the sinking mood among the workers was nevertheless the highest in Germany: "It is clear that the morale of German upper classes is worse than that of the middle classes, which in turn is worse than that of the lower classes (those working in war industries, including railroads)." NA, RG 226, 134, February 25, 1943.

20. Stadtarchiv (East) Berlin, Rep. 016B, Nr. 2946, 96–172.

21. The British-American agreement called for the "progressive destruction and dislocation of the German military, industrial, and economic system and the undermining of the morale of the German people to a point where their capacity for armed resistance is fatally weakened." Parker, *Struggle for Survival*, 155. On the rapid improvements in Allied bombing and firepower and precision from December 21 to March 5, 1943, see Martin Middlebrook and Chris Everitt, *The Bomber Command War Diaries* (New York: 1985), 334–338. See the study on the impact of the Allied bombing within Germany is by Olaf Groehler: *Bombenkrieg gegen Deutschland* (Berlin: 1990).

22. NA, RG 226, 33008, March 1943.

23. Hitler's left arm and leg began trembling, as they had after his failed putsch. Picker, *Hitler's Tischgespräche*, 174. See also Hancock, *National Socialist Leadership and Total War*, 48. "The low is now behind us," Goebbels wrote in September. "The women are largely responsible for an essential improvement of our sentiments . . . owing chiefly to the fact that the arguments advanced in the Führer's speech of September 1943 appealed particularly to women's feelings." Goebbels, *Goebbels Diaries*, ed. Lochner entry for September 12, 1943, 447.

24. NA, RG 226, 36790. The "unnatural segregation of the sexes caused by total mobilization . . . was causing mass hysterical conditions among women," another OSS report claimed. NA, RG 226, 501, April 29, 1943.

25. Reported from the *Berliner Illustrierte Zeitung*. NA, RG 226, 858.9111/673, March 5, 1943.

26. Reported from the *Berliner Nachtausgabe* and the *Deutsche Allgemeine Zeitung*, NA, 862.9111/1091, March 2, 1943.

27. Gabriele Huster, "Das Bild der Frau in der Malerei des deutschen Fashismus," in *Frauen unterm Hakenkreuz* (Berlin: 1983), 64.

28. Speer, *Inside the Third Reich*, 335.

29. Goebbels, *Final Entries*, Trevor-Roper, ed., introduction, xxiii.

30. Speer, *Inside the Third Reich*, 335.

31. The historian Charles S. Maier concludes that "the number of German women employed may actually have dropped slightly." Maier concludes, however, that the British mo-

bilized for war more capably than did the German dictatorship, that "there is still reason to believe that mobilization of labor and the diversion of productive resources [by Germany] were relatively lackadaisical." Charles S. Maier, *In Search of Stability* (Cambridge, England: 1988), 106–109.

32. Goebbels, *Final Entries*, ed. Trevor-Roper, xxii–xxiii.

33. Speer, *Inside the Third Reich*, 294, 295. One problem with this plan, reported Speer, was that Soviet men requisitioned for labor in Germany preferred "taking to the forests and joining the partisans." The German news bureau requested on September 21, 1939, that news concerning "employing women in the war industry" not be published, "so as not to cause any new unrest in the women's world." Martin Broszat, Elke Fröhlich, and Anton Grossmann, *Bayern in der NS-Zeit*, vol. III, *Herrschaft und Gesellschaft im Konkflikt*, Teil B (Munich: 1981), 575. Goering wrote to Lammers in June 1940 that ordering women into the work force would "carry all too much unrest into the populace." Quoted by Marie-Luise Recker, "Zwischen sozialer Befriedung und materieller Ausbeutung," in *Der zweite Weltkreig*, ed. Wolfgang Michalka (Munich: 1989), 432.

34. Michael Burleigh and Wolfgang Wippermann, *The Racial State: Germany 1933–1945* (Cambridge, England, 1991), 242. In *Nation at War* the Nazi artist Schmitz-Weidenbrück portrays women's faces as serene, in contrast with the awestruck expressions of the farmer and worker. Women should wait quietly, passively accepting the deaths of war. Schmitz-Widenbrück depicts the German mother as holding a letter that she is apparently about to add to the box at her feet (which to German women must have suggested news from the husband or son at war). The young soldier imagines his wife or mother at home, holding his letter and thinking about his performing the heroic acts of war.

35. "Women's proper sphere is the family," Goebbels told a group of women leaders in 1934. "There she is a sovereign queen. If we eliminate women from every realm of public life, we do not do it in order to dishonor her, but in order that her honor may be restored to her." Cited in Rupp, *Mobilizing Women for War*, 16, 17.

36. Speer, *Inside the Third Reich*, 294.

37. Goebbels, *Final Entries*, xxiii. On debates about Goebbels's intentions for Total War, see Hancock, *National Socialist Leadership and Total War*, 69. Although he was the one who sent Hitler a memorandum proposing Total War measures in December 1942, Goebbels was not the only Nazi leader in favor of them. Goering and German Labor Front leader Robert Ley supported conscripting women and closing German cultural societies, for example. The historian Dieter Rebentisch has argued that historians have given Goebbels too much credit for the overall concept of Total War, claiming that Hitler himself, not Goebbels, was the originating force, a difficult argument given that Goebbels had in 1941 unsuccessfully pressed Hitler to conscript women. Hancock, citing Richard Overy as well as Rebentisch, argues that the main dispute between Goebbels and the Committee of Three was mostly over how to implement Total War measures. Goebbels had wanted one person in charge of implementation, rather than a committee. Hancock, *National Socialist Leadership and Total War*, 50–54, 69, 70.

38. Broszat et al., *Bayern in der NS Zeit*, 574. Deputy Secretary Syrup of the Labor Ministry had presented a plan for mobilizing 5,500,000 unemployed women for war production. Speer, *Inside the Third Reich*, 675, footnote 10.

39. Koonz, *Mothers in the Fatherland*, 395, 396.

40. Adolf Hitler, speech to the National Socialist Women's Organization, Nuremberg party rally, September 8, 1934, quoted in Mason, "Women in Germany," 74.

41. See Koonz, *Mothers in the Fatherland*, 399 and passim.

42. One letter from the battlefront to the home front suggests that family members might have portrayed their conditions as more positive than they were in order to keep up a bold facade and create comforting images. Kershaw, *Popular Opinion and Political Dissent*, 350, 351.

43. Goebbels, *Final Entries*, xxiii. In Hanover alone, a city of about five hundred thousand, eighty candy stores were closed. Boberach, *Meldungen aus dem Reich*, vol. XIII, entry for March 11, 1943, 4942.

44. Women, especially the pacifists, wrote Susanna Dammer, "were made responsible for losing the war in the context of the 'stab in the back' legend." Susanna Dammer, "Kinder, Küche, Kriegsarbeit—die Schulung der Frauen durch die NS-Frauenschaft," in *Mutterkreuz und Arbeitsbuch*, 216. Ute Daniel argues that the struggle for survival in Germany after the winter of 1915–16 worked against the state's effort to employ women in the war industry and that economic hardships were at the core of the state's inability to sustain popular support, leading to its collapse in 1918. Women had developed subversive strategies for the survival of their families that "irrevocably destroyed the wartime societal consensus between rulers and ruled," according to Daniel. Working women were the key agents of the state's disintegration. Ute Daniel, *Arbeiterfrauen in der Kriegsgesellschaft: Beruf, Familie und Politik im Ersten Weltkrieg* (Göttingen: 1989), 232.

45. Broszat, et al., *Bayern in der NS-Zeit*, 587.

46. Burleigh and Wippermann, *Racial State*, 264.

47. Boberach, *Meldungen aus dem Reich*, entry for March 11, 1943, 4934.

48. "We must record a total failure to mobilize German women for work in the war effort," Speer's Armaments Department reported by December 1943. Quoted in Mason, "Women in Germany," 21.

49. Here again, although the regime's lack of resolve contributed to the success of women in massively ignoring Hitler's Total War decree, the women who refused to obey Hitler cannot take credit for opening up that lack of resolve and thus are not in the same position as those at Rosenstrasse for being defined as resisters.

50. The women's noncompliance was reinforced by, if not based in, the ideals and encouragement of the first ten years of Nazi rule. It seems to indicate that the majority of women had not yet accepted work as a normative, for as Claudia Koonz writes, women "adapted rather easily to Nazi rule" because they held "a deep belief in women's separate Lebensraum" and were intensely nationalistic. Koonz, *Mothers in the Fatherland*, 310.

51. Speer, *Inside the Third Reich*, 337. To Speer, Goebbels's outburst seemed spontaneous, but after his speech Goebbels calmly analyzed it as a mere technical exercise. As the new Reich minister for defense in early 1942, Speer had difficulty getting the attention and resources he needed for speeding armaments production. When in the summer of 1942 Goebbels at Speer's request turned up the volume of sympathetic newsreel and newspaper coverage on Speer, not only Speer but his associates as well became powerful "overnight." *Inside the Third Reich*, 84. Hitler still limited Goebbels's growing power in 1943, however, deciding in March of that year that Rosenberg's Reich ministry for the occupied eastern territories rather than the Propaganda Ministry would be responsible for propaganda in the east. Hancock, *National Socialist Leadership and Total War*, 49.

52. Goebbels diaries, January 28, 1943, BA NL 118/51.

53. Goebbels, *Goebbels Diaries*, ed. Taylor, entry for October 4, 1940, 130: "I issue a circular to all Reich authorities, to the effect that in the future I shall not stand for any interference in the Berlin Gau."

54. Goebbels, *Final Entries*, xxiv. Horcher's was reopened only as a private club for the Luftwaffe. Speer, *Inside the Third Reich*, 338. Goebbels did apparently have the support of Hitler, who "criticized the continued existence of luxury restaurants such as Horchers." Hancock, *National Socialist Leadership and Total War*, 57.

55. Kaltenbrunner made this assessment as a defendant at the Nuremberg Trials. Office of the U.S. Chief of Counsel for Prosecution of Axis Criminality, *Nazi Conspiracy and Aggression*, Supplement B (Washington, D.C.: 1948), 1297.

56. Goebbels, *Goebbels Diaries*, ed. Lochner, entry for March 6, 1943. On German attention to detail and lack of leadership see entry for December 16, 1942, 276.
57. Hessisches Hauptstaatsarchiv, judgment against Heinrich Baab (51 Ks 1/50).
58. According to the secretary for the director of the Berlin Gestapo's Judenreferat, on Burgstrasse, Jews sent to work camps as protective custody cases survived "as a rule" only three, four, or maybe six months. Statement of Margaret Schindler, Bovensiepen Trial (no date). Sending Jews to the so-called corrective work camps represented in itself a contradiction to Nazi ideology since Jews, irreparably sullied by their blood, were incapable of any change for the better. In general, a Jew in custody was not to be released, and the overwhelming majority of these Jews never returned.
59. Hessisches Hauptstaatsarchiv, Wiesbaden, judgment against Georg Albert Dengler (2a Ks 1/49), 26.
60. Hessisches Hauptstaatsarchiv, judgment against Heinrich Baab (51 Ks 1/50).
61. BA, Anklageschrift, trial against Fritz Wöhrn, 106. Many of the charges on which Jews in intermarriages were arrested were fabricated. One Jew, for example, was charged with association with conspirators against the Nazi state on the basis of a list of names found in his desk, which was actually a list of poor people his family helped every year at Christmas. Hessisches Hauptstaatsarchiv, trial of Joseph Hedderich and Johann Schmitz (4 Ks 2/53), testimony of Luise Wenig, August 11, 1950.
62. Although the close associates of the Jewish Community estimated that there were 7,000 intermarried Jews in Berlin as of 1943–44 (statement of Else Hannach, July and September 1944, Supporting Document 30 [Dr. Wolfgang Scheffler Collection], Bovensiepen Trial), the Jewish Community had registered only 4,723 as of September 1942, noting that this number was "apparently too low, because in many cases" intermarried Jews simply had not registered with the community. "Final report of the Berlin Jewish Community's Registration Office (Kataster Verwaltung), BA Potsdam, R 8150, September 1, 1942.
    The RSHA did set up the Darmstadt Gestapo to wipe out the intermarriages in January but did not activate this new section until March 7, 1943, the day after Goebbels released Jews at Rosenstrasse.
63. On the activities of Gaevernitz, see Walter Laqueur and Richard Breitman, *Breaking the Silence* (New York: 1986), 71–73, 238–239.
64. Lehfeld, "Die Lage der 'Mischlinge,' " 1, 2. Dr. Lehfeld's report that by January 1943 RSHA officials wanted to deport even the Jews in privileged intermarriages coincides with a 1959 memory of Max Reschke, the head Jewish orderly at the Grosse Hamburger Strasse collection center: In early 1943 Jews in privileged intermarriages, as well as their partners, were ordered to register at Grosse Hamburger Strasse as well as at the Jewish administration building on Rosenstrasse. Perhaps this registration was the initiative of those at RSHA who pushed to complete the Final Solution immediately, in preparation for the Final Roundup. The registration of these Jews would not be controversial, as their actual deportation would be, but names and addresses of privileged intermarried Jews were essential if the opportunity for quick action against them should present itself. However, the less radical plan to deport only Jews without children was the one the RSHA followed when under pressure of the street protest, it did deport some thirty-six intermarried Jews to Auschwitz in early March, during the course of the Final Roundup. Interview with Kurt Blaustein, November 4, 1985.
65. This corresponds with Himmler's decree of November 5 to send *Mischlinge* in German concentration camps to either Auschwitz or the labor camp at Lublin. KB, trial of Fritz Wöhrn, Dokument Band 7, 18, or Anklageschrift, trial of Fritz Wöhrn, 147. Sending persons to work camps rather than directly to the gas chambers would have required separating those designated for work camps from the others, and it is possible that intermarried Jews and *Mischlinge* arrested in the Final Roundup were slated for work camps rather than for immediate destruction. (The fate of the thirty-six intermarried Jews without children whom the Gestapo did deport to Auschwitz work camps in early

March indicates the flexibility this left open to the Reich: These Jews were returned to Berlin within two weeks on orders of a "high Reich official.") Statement of Johanna Heym, PSt h 60, XIX, 127 ff., summarized in Anklageschrift, 214, Bovensiepen Trial. Heym was told that the Jews had been deported by "mistake" and that the main executive of the action, Criminal Director August Schiffer, was punished (transferred) for it. Heym's report on Schiffer is confirmed by a statement of Walter Stock, August 13, 1951, Stock Trial.

66. This report of deporting *Mischlinge* on a legal basis corresponds significantly with an interaction between Himmler and Hitler sometime between early December 1942 and late January 1943. Himmler asked Hitler what to do about the "half Jewish race defilers," and Hitler responded: "Sterilization." The search for a legal basis for the deportation of *Mischlinge* mirrors the efforts of Jakob Sprenger to murder intermarried Jews in his district of Hessen after arresting them as criminals and also indicates that the regime was considering taking cover against the possibility of social unrest under the shield of respectable law and legal procedures.

67. Lösener, "Als Rassereferent," 298. In September 1942 new rumors began to circulate in the Interior Ministry that the RSHA was preparing to deport *Mischlinge*. Hilberg, *Destruction of the European Jews*, 423.

68. Statement of Adolf Kurtz, 28 June 1961, Israel Police Document 144. In July, because "the material" to fill the deportations was dwindling, the Berlin Gestapo (Dobberke) had made an inquiry on whether Jews in forced labor as well as those in intermarriages should now also be deported. BA Potsdam, R 8150, Minutes of the Central Organization's Directorate, July 29, 1942.

69. Henschel, "Die letzten Jahre der Jüdischen Gemeinde Berlin."

70. International Military Tribunal, *Trial of the Major War Criminals* (Nuremberg, 1947–1949), 42 vol., testimony of Armaments Minister Albert Speer, vol. XVI, 519.

71. Even before the deportations in Germany began, Goebbels complained about industrialists' claims that certain Jews were indispensable. BA Potsdam, 50.01, Ig, 21 April 1941.

72. Landgericht Berlin, PkLs 3/52, Stock Trial, statement to the court of Alexander Rothholz, May 2, 1951. Rothholz said his boss returned from a meeting to which Stock had summoned all Berlin factory owners and told him Stock had given this speech at the meeting around the middle of December.

73. Minutes of the Central Organization, February 15, 1943. All of Germany was to be cleared of Jews by Hitler's birthday on April 20. See Mira and Gerhard Schoenberner, *Zeugen sagen aus: Berichte und Dokumente über die Judenverfolgung im Dritten Reich* (Berlin: 1988), 296.

74. In fact, the Final Roundup did conclude Berlin's so-called thousander deportations— the deportation of Jews in shipments of one thousand each—and at its conclusion the Gestapo shut down the Berlin Jewish Community, sending its last employees (about one thousand) to Auschwitz and Theresienstadt on March 12, 1943. Henschel, "Aus der Arbeit," 12. The Berlin court called the arrests of the Berlin Jewish community employees "*offenbar den Abschluss der sog. 'Fabrikaktion.'*" Kammergericht Berlin, Vermerk, Bosshammer Trial.

75. "Final report" of the Berlin Jewish Community's Registration Office (Kataster Verwaltung), BA Potsdam, R 8150, September 1, 1942. During the Final Roundup the Gestapo forced arrested intermarried Jews to divulge the names and addresses of five other intermarried Jews they knew of. Interview with Günter Grodka, August 25, 1985.

76. Statement of Max Reschke, Supporting Document 30 (Dr. Wolfgang Scheffler Collection), June 1, 1959.

77. Library, Jewish Community, Berlin (Fasanenstrasse). This is an unmarked folder from the Berlin Jewish Community, titled "Lists due to the Forced Deportations." The lists are carefully marked with checks, slashes, and crosses. The correspondence on hand is between Catholic offices, but the Protestant Church, under official orders, was almost

certainly doing similar work to identify and locate all Berlin Jews who had converted to Protestantism at this time.

78. Seven days before the Final Roundup (carried out in Berlin and elsewhere in Germany, notably Breslau), the RSHA wrote new deportation directives "temporarily" exempting intermarried Jews and *Mischlinge* from the deportations, as had become customary. The deportation directives, written by the civil servants under Eichmann, were "secret" not-for-circulation documents but had been used, at least to some extent, to deceive (directives in 1942, for example, listed in detail what work instruments, including sewing machines, the Gestapo should allow deported Jews to take with them to their new "work camps"). On occasion the RSHA amended its own regulations to fit particular situations, such as on November 8, 1941, when the RSHA sent a telegram to the Gestapo in Nuremberg-Furth supplementing the deportation directives, and on April 17, 1942, when Eichmann sent out a telegram to all Gestapo offices amending the deportation directives. Even lower-ranked officials acted in a way tantamount to amending the directives. In mid-1942 the RSHA, because of pressure from the military, released a new deportation directive ordering that Jews decorated highly for their service in World War I must be deported to Theresienstadt instead of to Auschwitz, but the Düsseldorf Gestapo disregarded this directive on the basis that they received it after they had already made plans for a specific deportation that they did not want to "undo." The branch office at Düsseldorf was excused by the RSHA. The "mistakenly" deported Jews were not retrieved. We cannot be sure that they were released to the Berlin Gestapo in time for their arrests on February 27. In any case, Hitler's SS division, which arrested Jews in the Final Roundup, would hardly have taken instructions from the deportation directives, but these directives could then be used to calm institutions like the Interior Ministry amid the rumors that intermarried Jews and *Mischlinge* were about to be deported. A surprise arrest would have even more of the advantage of ambush if official policy had announced in advance that it was not to happen. The real advantage (which those responsible ultimately fell back on) was that it preserved a way for the leadership to deny that it had ordered these persons deported. At a trial eight years later Berlin Gestapo Chief Walter Stock claimed he had deported intermarried Jews from Rosenstrasse in 1943 on orders of the RSHA, which in turn had blamed the Berlin Gestapo and transferred its director, August Schiffer, as punishment. Stock Trial, PkLs 3/52, statement of Stock, August 13, 1951.

79. Goebbels, *Goebbels Diaries*, ed. Lochner, entry for March 9, 1943, 278ff.

80. Goebbels, diary entry for February 2, 1943, BA NL118/95, and Goebbels, *Goebbels Diaries*, ed. Lochner, entry for March 9, 1943, 288.

81. Lehfeld, "Die Lage der 'Mischlinge,' 4. On March 2, 1943, Goebbels wrote: "Our plans were tipped off prematurely, so that a lot of Jews slipped through our hands." Goebbels, *Goebbels Diaries*, ed. Lochner, 261. A report that a representative of Himmler attended a meeting the day before the Final Roundup to discuss the replacement of Jewish workers with forced laborers also implies planning at the level of the Reich minister if this representative was from his personal staff rather than the RSHA. Statement to the court of Alexander Rothholz, May 2, 1951, Stock Trial.

82. German press, February 25–26, and statement of Richard Hartmann, June 24, 1968, Bosshammer Trial.

83. Baeck survived Theresienstadt. Eppstein did not. He was executed. Perhaps seeking an indication that he would be treated with consideration, he had asked for and was granted permission to have his piano sent with him from Berlin to the ghetto. According to a secretary working for Eichmann, Eichmann's deputy Rolf Günther ordered Eppstein's execution. Statement of Margarethe Reichert, October 18, 1967, Bovensiepen Trial. Reichert called Günther "raw and without feelings." He explained to her that the Germans did not hate the Jews but were merely doing a job that had to be done.

84. Brunner was forced to leave Berlin on January 28. Brunner, a loner, had trouble getting along in Berlin. Eppstein, who had met with him and Eichmann in Brunner's office,

said that Brunner suffered under an inferiority complex, as an Austrian in Berlin, and overcompensated. As an Austrian he had a *"Schnürschuh Komplex"* and tried with all his might to prove himself with harshness and vigor. Landgericht Frankfurt am Main, 50 Js 36019/84, Alois Brunner Trial, statement of Martin Friedländer, June 3, 1986. One of Brunner's assistants testified in 1956 that "Brunner und [his assistant] Gerbing disappeared one day, returned fighting with Berlin people [Gestapo], and we got orders to get ready for a return trip to Vienna." Statement of Brunner assistant Gerö, November 7, 1968, Bovensiepen Trial.

85. Henschel, "Aus der Arbeit," 9.
86. Goebbels, diary entry for February 2, 1943, BA NL 118/95.

XIV: COURAGEOUS WOMEN OF ROSENSTRASSE

1. In the very early hours Erwin Sartorius, a member of the team of drivers, was awakened by the police station and ordered to report immediately to the garage on Magazinestrasse. Statement of Sartorius, December 13, 1965, Bovensiepen Trial. U.S. intelligence services reported that a "responsible" source said "all closed lorries in Berlin were requisitioned" for a deportation action that was to make Berlin free of Jews by mid-March. NA, RG 226, March 13, 1943.
2. Lehfeld, "Die Lage der 'Mischlinge,' " 4.
3. Interview with Erika Lewine, March 19, 1985. At job sites throughout the Reich Jews had been isolated together in Jewish crews, an arrangement simplifying the SS roundup.
4. Interviews with Dr. Ernst Bukofzer, May 29 and June 24, 1985, Berlin, along with one of his stepdaughters, who now lives near Tampa, Florida, and owns a tropical fish farm. In the 1980s Bukofzer lived in Berlin-Zehlendorf a half mile from Charlotte, and although their fates crossed and were determined at Rosenstrasse 2–4, they never met. At ninety-five he was the oldest witness I interviewed.
5. Driver's licenses had been taken from Jews on November 11, 1938. Benz, *Juden in Deutschland*, 747.
6. Interview with Ursula Braun, June 6, 1989.
7. Interview with Vera Breitwieser, February 6, 1985.
8. Interview with Elsa Holzer, December 10, 1989.
9. Ingeborg Schneider to author, April 14, 1985. Schneider wrote that her boss offered, in case of need, to hide her and her endangered relatives in a basement of his office.
10. Goebbels, *Goebbels Diaries*, ed. Lochner, entries for March 2 and 11, 1943, 261, 294.
11. Lehfeld, "Die Lage der 'Mischlinge,' " 2.
12. High-level Jewish officials like Mr. Kleemann were well situated to know Gestapo plans because of the Gestapo's reliance on the Jewish Community for all kinds of technical assistance during deportation actions. Kleemann was an intermarried Jew who had worked for the Jewish Community since 1933 and had been present during the predeportation processes in the Levetzowstrasse synagogue, as well as at the train stations when Jews were deported. Interview with Kleeman, April 26, 1985.
13. *"Man hat wohl vermutet, dass Proteste gegen . . . die Trennung der Ehen laut werden würden,"* Lehfeld, "Die Lage der 'Mischlinge.' "
14. Laqueur, *Missing Years*, 125, 126.
15. Statement of Alexander Rotholz, October 29, 1965, Bovensiepen Trial. Rotholz was arrested twice during the Final Roundup but released because of this paper. See also statement of Rotholz, May 2, 1951, Stock Trial.
16. Statement of Stella Borchers, July 14, 1966, Bovensiepen Trial.
17. Goebbels's state secretary, Leopold Gutterer, said that the Gestapo did search for leaders of the protest. Interviews with Gutterer, August 17 and 19, 1986.
18. Zivier, "Aufstand der Frauen."

19. When the Jewish Community was finally able to deliver a kettle of cabbage soup to the synagogue, the Gestapo man, whose hat slumped under a sweat-soaked brim, whipped whoever came to it, so that despite their gnawing hunger, the Jews stayed back. Then he bellowed: "Everyone to the kettle for food!" When most stayed away, he and two others beat them for disobeying. Statement of Dr. Kurt Radlauer, November 10, 1966, Bovensiepen Trial.

20. Dr. Martha Mosse, July 24, 1958, Bovensiepen Trial.

21. Interview with Mieke Monjau, December 3, 1984 (telephone).

22. Interview with Erika Lewine, March 19, 1985.

23. Interview with Ursula Braun, November 1, 1989.

24. Helga Weigert was eight and does not remember seeing anyone on the street but vaguely recalls that there was talk going around about "some people outside fighting or calling for freedom." Interview with Helga Weigert, June 21, 1985.

25. Gad Beck, *Und Gad ging zu David: Die Erinergungen des Gad Beck, 1923–1945* (Berlin: 1995).

26. Statement of former street policeman Anton von Kryshak, Bovensiepen Trial, 1968.

27. Statement of Karl Hefter, October 28, 1955, in the trial of Josef ("Sepp") Dietrich, I P Js 3767.65 St.A. Berlin.

28. Unpublished diary of Wally Grodka, and interview with Grodka and her husband, Günter, August 25, 1985.

29. Peter Wyden has written a book on Stella Kübler. Peter Wyden, *Stella* (New York: 1992).

30. Interview with Professor Gerhard Braun, May 23, 1985.

31. Interview with Kurt Blaustein, August 3, 1985.

32. Telephone interview with Jerry Monasch, September 29, 1985, Berlin to Lubbock, Texas.

33. Although their siblings were also each half Jewish, they had been deported as Jews. Because Gerhard's brother had been raised as a Jew he was classified as a *Geltungsjude*. Thus Ursula's sister, according to Nazi regulations, had become a Jew when she married him.

34. Woods to Harrison, 22 March 1943, NA, RG 84, Zurich Confidential File, Box 5.

35. Paepcke, *Ich wurde vergessen*, 23.

36. Statement of Kurt Blaustein, November 4, 1965, Bovensiepen Trial, and interview with Werner Goldberg, December 6, 1985. See also the story and release certificate of Siegfried Wexberg in Heinrich Fink, ed., *Stärker aus die Angst* (Berlin: 1968).

37. Laqueur, *Missing Years*, 122.

38. Goebbels, *Goebbels Diaries*, ed. Lochner, entry for March 2, 1943.

39. Interviews with Gutterer, August 17 and 19, 1989.

40. Statement of Wolff, November 15, 1968, Bovensiepen Trial.

41. Hazel Rosenstrauch, ed., *Aus Nachbarn wurden Juden: Ausgrenzung und Selbstbehauptung, 1933–1942* (Berlin: 1988), 130, and interviews with Ruth Gross and her mother, April 1986, Berlin.

42. Statement of Dr. Kurt Radlauer, November 10, 1966, Bovensiepen Trial. Dr. Radlauer was a baptized Jew born in Posen in 1884, who worked from 1919 to 1932 as an adviser (*Oberregierungsrat*) in the Foreign Office, until the Nazis forced him to retire. He was arrested during the Kristallnacht Pogrom and imprisoned at Sachsenhausen from November 10 to December 16, 1938. Afterward, as a forced laborer, he worked with Dr. Kaufman in a group making false passports and ration cards for Jews. He met Annie Radlauer, his wife, in 1913, and died at age ninety-seven.

43. Interview with Ursula Braun, June 6, 1985.

44. Leon Brandt, *Menschen ohne Schatten: Juden zwischen Untergang und Untergrund, 1938 bis 1945* (Berlin: 1984), 126.

45. Interview with Hans-Oskar Löwenstein de Witt, November 8, 1984.

46. Interview with Gad Beck, January 28, 1985.

47. Interview with Günther Ruschin, March 10, 1985.

48. Indictment, Bovensiepen Trial, 9, 208. Among the 1,736 were 160 Jews from Norway, whose transportation had been carefully arranged with the Kriegsmarine and the Reichsbahn. Israel Police Document 1621 and 1622.

49. BA, NS 19/3492.

50. Leo Baeck Institute, New York: Wiener Library microfilms (AR 7187/Reel 600).

51. Statement of Gertrude Trede, May 5, 1951, Stock Trial.

52. Ibid. Trede said that someone recognized her husband, the well-known Mr. Silbergleit, on March 4 at Güterbahnhof Quitzowstrasse, about to be deported.

53. Interview with Heinz Klum, November 22, 1985, Berlin. Klum's mother was deported from Rosenstrasse and never returned.

54. "If the transports from Berlin continue to have so many women and children as well as old Jews," Schwarz wrote in a stern tone on March 5, "there would be no guarantee of increased production." Auschwitz Calendar, March 4, 1943. See also Hilberg's account in *Destruction of the European Jews*, 918. After this message about 80 percent of the men from the successive arrivals of Jews from the Final Roundup action were sent to work in Auschwitz.

55. Quoted by Koonz, *Mothers in the Fatherland*, 335.

56. Interview with Hildegaard Kremczuk, one of those arrested and made to peel potatoes, July 14, 1990.

57. Lehfeld, "Die Lage der 'Mischlinge,' " 1.

58. Statement of Blaustein, November 4, 1965, Bovensiepen Trial.

59. Statement of Ferdinand Wolff, November 14, 1968, Bovensiepen Trial.

60. Statement of Blaustein, November 4, 1985, Bovensiepen Trial.

61. Statement of Brinitzer, August 18, 1970, Bovensiepen Trial.

62. Interview with Kurt Blaustein, November 4, 1985, and statement of Wolff, November 14, 1968, Bovensiepen Trial; statement of Alexander Rotholz, May 2, 1951, Stock Trial.

63. Interview with Günther Stegner, May 1, 1985, East Berlin, who was there to search for his arrested father.

64. Interview with Rita Kuhn, April 26, 1989. See also Kuhn's story in Alison Owings, *Frauen: German Women Recall the Third Reich* (New Brunswick, N.J.: 1993).

65. Interview with Wally Grodka, January 22, 1986, Berlin.

66. Gisela Weigert too said that there could have been a thousand there on the street. Interview with Weigert, June 21, 1985.

67. BA, NL 118/96, diaries of Joseph Goebbels, entry for March 6, 1943. Goebbels, on March 15, 1943, at a press conference in Paris, responded to a question with a qualification that might have been an attempt to explain the Rosenstrasse Protest to anyone who might have heard of it. In response to a French reporter (who addressed Goebbels as well known for being one of the main proponents of the Jewish Question), Goebbels said: "The vast majority of the German people wants a solution to the Jewish Question of total proportions. You can't allow yourselves to be confused due to the opinion of a few doctors or lawyers on the Kurfürstendamm; they are not the German people. The German people thinks differently, the broad masses of our people have another conviction in these things." German press, March 16, 1943.

68. NA, RG 226, April 1, 1943.

69. Interviews with Leopold Gutterer, August 17 and 19, 1986.

70. Interview with Gutterer, July 16, 1987.

71. Raul Hilberg concludes: "The Jews in mixed marriage were finally made exempt because in the last analysis, it was felt that their deportation might jeopardize the whole destruction process. It simply did not pay to sacrifice the secrecy of the whole operation for the sake of deporting 28,000 Jews, some of whom were so old that they would probably die naturally before the operation was over." Hilberg, *Destruction of the*

European Jews, 430. Ursula Büttner writes that the Nazis exempted Jews in intermarriages from the deportations because this would cause social unrest. Büttner, *Not der Juden teilen,* 14.

72. BA Potsdam, 50.01, 1g2, from March 24, 1943, 12.
73. Hitler agreed with Goebbels's "proceedings on the Jewish Question." Goebbels, *Goebbels Diaries,* ed. Lochner, entry for March 9, 1943, 278ff. Hitler had nevertheless again commissioned Goebbels with clearing Berlin of Jews, and Goebbels wrote on March 9: "When Berlin is free of Jews, I shall have completed one of my greatest political achievements."
74. Goebbels, *Final Entries,* xix. Goering's influence on Hitler was at a nadir after his promises to save Stalingrad for Germany with his air force proved to be a dream. Goering was withdrawn and depressed. Hitler talked of dismissing him on March 9, 1943, and fumed that his portly deputy was no more interested in air warfare against Britain than in an excellent lunch or dinner. See Goebbels's report on Hitler's opinion of Goering, Goebbels, *Goebbels Diaries,* ed. Lochner, entry for March 9, 1943, 279.
75. Statement of Max Reschke (assistant to Dobberke), Supporting Document 30 (Dr. Wolfgang Scheffler Collection), May 4, 1959, Bovensiepen Trial. Else Hannach, interviewed a little more than a year after the Final Roundup (in July 1944 by Dr. Meisel and in September 1944 by Dr. Ball), confirmed Reschke's memory. "The heavy industry moved heaven and earth in order to retrieve those [employees] taken from the factories. But it was no use," she said. Supporting Document 30, Bovensiepen Trial.
76. Jews with German family members constituted the only category of Jews who, if deported to Theresienstadt, were not taken from there to Auschwitz.
77. Breitman, *Architect of Genocide,* 54.
78. Reitlinger, *Final Solution,* 140.
79. "Bovensiepen Trial, Supporting Document 29, order of Heinrich Himmler (by Müller) to inspectors of the security police and the SD, and all Gestapo branch offices other than those in the Protectorate, December 18, 1943.
80. Breitman, *Architect of Genocide,* 241.
81. Lehfeld, "Die Lage der 'Mischlinge,' " 4.
82. BA, Statement of Karl Krell, 4 SpLs 16/47 Bielefeld, Koblenz.
83. Statement of Johanna Heym, summarized in Anklageschrift, 214, Bovensiepen Trial. Lehfeld, "Die Lage der 'Mischlinge,' " corroborates this.
84. Anklageschrift, 214, Bovensiepen Trial.
85. BA Potsdam, R 8150, minutes of the Central Organization's Directorate, by Eppstein, April 4, 1940; Hildesheimer, *Jüdische Selbstverwaltung unter dem NS-Regime,* 180ff.
86. Reuth, *Joseph Goebbels, Tagebücher,* entry for March 7, 1942, 1763.
87. Goebbels, *Goebbels Diaries,* ed. Lochner, entry for March 6, 1943, 276.
88. Interview with Gutterer, December 10, 1989.
89. Statement of Stock, August 13, 1951, Stock Trial, PkLs 3/52. Dr. Lehfeld also reported in March 1943 that the RSHA had ordered the Berlin Gestapo to deport the intermarried Jews and *Mischlinge.*
90. The telex is reprinted under the title "Menschenfracht für Buna" in *Die Jüdische Allgemeine,* No. IX/49, March 11, 1955, 3.
91. Yad Vashem, 01/258, statement of Ksinski, deported from Breslau to Auschwitz on about March 7, 1943. Ksinski reported that the deportation of Jews and Gypsies from Breslau on February 27, 1943, was ordered by Goebbels.
92. Statement of Ferdinand Wolff, November 14, 1968, Bovensiepen Trial.
93. Ibid.
94. Interview with Erich Herzberg, August 22, 1985, Berlin.
95. Statement of Ferdinand Wolff, November 14, 1968, Bovensiepen Trial.
96. Interviews with two of these twenty-five men, Kurt Blaustein and Erich Herzberg, together with their wives, August 3, 1985, Berlin.
97. Interview with Johnny Hüttner, December 27, 1985, East Berlin.

98. Statement of Ferdinand Wolff, November 14, 1968, Bovensiepen Trial.
99. Interview with Erich Herzberg, August 22, 1985, Berlin.
100. BA, NS 19/1440, Telefongespräche des Reichsführer-SS am 18. März 1943.
101. Interviews with two of these men, Kurt Blaustein and Erich Herzberg, together with their wives, August 3, 1985. The story of these men deported from Rosenstrasse to Auschwitz, and their return, is also summarized from testimonies in the indictment, Bovensiepen Trial.
102. This report greeted the Führer on his first day of a three-month stay at his "eagle's nest," prescribed by his doctor. Picker, *Hitler's Tischgespräche*, 174.
103. Interview with Gad Beck, January 28, 1985. Charlotte Israel also reported that she "Aryanized" her husband by removing the star from his clothing. This removal of the star was perhaps reluctantly accepted by Goebbels, who after declaring Berlin *Judenfrei* wanted no signs of Jews to contradict that proclamation.
104. Goebbels, *Goebbels Diaries*, ed. Lochner, entry for April 18, 1943, 335.
105. At the end of May 1943 the whole of Greater Germany was officially *Judenfrei*. Reitlinger, *Final Solution*, 173, 180.
106. Paris, CDJC, xxv, 101, Rolf Günther to the SD in France, May 21, 1943. In July Sturmbannführer Günther quashed another attempt to set precedents on intermarried Jews outside the Reich itself, this time from the occupied Netherlands. The security police in the Netherlands had proposed to deport all childless intermarried Dutch Jews, while the Reich commissioner for the Netherlands, Arthur Seyss-Inquart, had a plan to exempt from anti-Jewish measures any intermarried Jews who could prove they were sterile. Sterile intermarried Jews were even to be allowed to remove the Star of David from their clothing. But Günther saw these plans for Dutch Jews as a problem of bureaucratic subordinates getting out of line. Until the RSHA had worked out the compulsory divorce and deportation of German intermarried Jews, Günther explained, intermarried Jews in the Netherlands were in no case to be deported. In such matters the Reich had to be exemplary (*vorbildlich*). Hilberg, *Destruction of the European Jews*, 589, 590.
107. Bovensiepen Trial, Supporting Document 29 or Internationale Suchtdienst (Arolson, Germany), HO 308/242, Ernst Kaltenbrunner order, May 21, 1943.
108. Summary of conversation between Lammers and Bormann, October 6, 1943, ND NO-1068. See also Hilberg, *Destruction of the European Jews*, 430.
109. Memorandum by Himmler of his meeting with Hitler on June 6, 1943, NA, T-175/R 94/2615097.
110. Trial against the Major War Criminals, Case 9 (*U.S. v. Ohlendorf*), in *Trials of War Criminals before the Nuremberg Military Tribunals* (Washington: 1949–1954), vol. 558–59.
111. Interview with Ruth Gross, April 4, 1986.

XV: PROTEST, RESCUE, AND RESISTANCE

1. Summary of March 6, 1942, conference, ND NG-2586-H.
2. Reports on public view of the Second Division, which William Shirer called "a striking demonstration against war," and its impact on Hitler are in Shirer, *Berlin Diary*, 109, 110, entry for September 27, 1938, and Schmidt, *Hitler's Interpreter*, 105. Hitler's notion that the confidence the Germans had in him was a favorable condition for war is cited in Watt, *How War Came*, 35, ND 248-PS. See also Hitler's *Mein Kampf*, 460.
3. Deputy of the Interior Ministry Wilhelm Stuckart to Klopfer et al., ND NG-2586-1.
4. See Büttner, *Not der Juden teilen*, 12, for evidence of Nazi intentions to treat *Mischlinge* like full Jews, as well as Lösener, "Als Rassereferent," 268. Nazi racial purification required that anyone with any Jewish blood could not be part of Germany.
5. U.S. Holocaust Memorial Museum Archives, Washington, D.C. Orders of the *Reichs-*

kommissar for the Eastern Occupied Territories concerning the "treatment of Jewish Mischehe," Riga, October 7, 1941.

6. By mid-1943 Rosenberg turned to methods of Goebbels for ruling German-occupied Poland. After the pattern of the SD within the Reich, Rosenberg ordered his Reich commissioners to report to him twice a month on the mood and activities in his territory. BA Potsdam, 11.01 49, 36. Estonians could have made strong allies against Bolshevism if only they had been shown a clear goal for taking up the fight, Rosenberg lamented. To strengthen its belief in Germany, Estonia should receive autonomy, he argued. Furthermore, to avoid the appearance both domestically and abroad that Germany was granting autonomy only because it was faring so poorly in the war, this autonomy had to be granted at once. BA Potsdam 11.01 49, 14.

7. On this radicalization, see the study of Omar Bartov, *Hitler's Army: Soldiers, Nazis, and War in the Third Reich* (Oxford and New York: 1991).

8. Yet the Rosenstrasse Protest has not been the subject of scholarly analysis and has appeared in historical writing like a fluke. Perhaps it is for this reason that Lewy devotes only a paragraph in his book to this unique protest, and like other distinguished scholars and writers, he did not study it in comparison with Catholic resistance to strengthen suggestions and claims about the force of popular opinion in relation to the genocide of German Jews. Konrad Kwiet mentions the Rosenstrasse Protest in his work on Jewish resistance, but not in comparison with Catholic resistance: "The successful outcome of this protest suggests that similar actions—if repeated across the country on a broad scale—might well have altered National Socialist policies toward Jews." Kwiet, "Resistance and Opposition," 67.

9. Interview with Leopold Gutterer, August 19, 1986.

10. Nevertheless, one could argue on a theoretical plane that the regime relented to the protest out of tactical rather than humane considerations and that the influence the Rosenstrasse protesters had on the general public morale derived from their status as Germans, not necessarily from their identity as intermarried Germans. Himmler decided in December 1943 to deport only those divorced, formerly intermarried Jews whose children would not make dissent noticeable and discussion of the Final Solution more probable—a decision indicating that the agitation of at least the *Mischlinge* children, as well as the troublesome objections of Germans married to Jews, could save Jews from deportation.

11. Reuth, *Joseph Goebbels, Tagebücher,* entry for March 7, 1942; 1763; Noakes and Pridham, *Nazism,* 1004.

12. Führer order of April 8, 1940, Adler, *Der Verwaltete Mensch,* 274, 275.

13. "Had the police rounded up masses of women, eventually people would have realized that women suffered at the hands of the Nazis," Koonz writes in explanation of why women protesting as a group were not arrested. "This would have undercut the official image of the Gestapo as 'clean' and 'noble' by unmasking male brutality toward the 'weaker sex.' In addition, arrests of women would have demonstrated that women could act independently outside 'feminine' roles." Koonz, *Mothers in the Fatherland,* 334. Under the *Nacht und Nebel* orders, women, unlike men, were not executed except for acts of murder and terrorism. H. W. Koch, *In the Name of the Volk: Political Justice in Hitler's Germany* (New York: 1989), 14.

14. Men had also been conscripted in new ways by the Total War decree, but only women, in great numbers, were resourceful in excusing themselves from Hitler's order, and it was women who constituted the core and drive of the Rosenstrasse Protest.

15. Joachim Fest, *The Face of the Third Reich: Portraits of the Nazi Leadership,* trans. Michael Bullock (New York: 1970), 389. Hitler said that in speeches he had systematically adapted himself to the taste of women and tried to counter bad morale with arguments addressed primarily to the "female mind."

16. If we accept the problematic claim that Hitler had made a decision by 1942 to defer deportation of intermarried Jews until after the war, it would follow that the release

of Jews from the Rosenstrasse following the protest in early 1943 was taken on the basis of his decision, rather than because of the protest. Thus the protest itself could no longer be considered resistance. Even if this claim were valid, it would only indicate that intermarried Germans had already successfully opposed the regime by the date of this decision, that Germans related to Jews had already rescued their Jewish family members from certain death as of the date Hitler made the decision.

17. Broszat, "A Social and Historical Typology," 26. Broszat classifies the German resistance in three stages to support a claim that "acts and attitudes of opposition . . . were often dependent upon the rule played by the Nazi authorities at a particular time" and that "significant and fundamental resistance arose only in the initial and final phases of Nazi rule." The regime's response to the Euthanasia protests supports Broszat's conclusion, but the Rosenstrasse Protest, coming in early 1943 against even the fundamental premise of Nazism, does not.

18. See for example Blau, "Mischehe im Nazireich."

19. See Peter Hoffmann, *Widerstand gegen Hitler und das Attentat vom 20. Juli 1944*, 2d ed. (Munich and Zürich: 1984). In his preface, Hoffmann states that the definition of resistance as an attempt to overthrow the state is made for the purpose of his study, but he does not say that resistance can be described only by these criteria. In Chapter 2, Professor Hoffmann represents, as far as possible, all other forms of resistance, organized and unorganized.

20. The historian Klemens von Klemperer characterizes resistance in Nazi Germany as a matter of individuals, not groups, and as an extraordinary leap for these persons into an existential situation. Resistance could be politically calculated only up to a certain point and, given the totality of state control, was often just a gesture. Klemperer, " 'What Is the Law That Lies behind These Words?' Antigone's Question and the German Resistance against Hitler," *Journal of Modern History*, vol. 64 (December 1992), S106, 107. For a more complete version of Klemperer's perspective, see his book *German Resistance against Hitler: The Search for Allies Abroad, 1938–1945* (New York: 1992).

21. Michael Geyer has identified and analyzed these two trends of revisionism in "Resistance as Ongoing Project: Visions of Order, Obligations to Strangers, Struggles for Civil Society," *Journal of Modern History*, vol. 64 (December 1992), S222. On the development of *Resistenz* scholarship, see Kershaw, " 'Widerstand ohne Volk,' " 794, and "Hitler Myth," 80.

22. This sample of motivations was not selected scientifically but rather consists of those who agreed to talk with me. "There existed no such thing as a 'happy' Jewish-German intermarriage during the Nazi terror," said a man whose father, a Jew, and mother, a German, had held together in an icy truce. Another "half Jewish" son of an intermarriage added that "there were no heroes [among the street protesters], just dirt in underwear. People were driven in despair to defend what they saw as essential to themselves, and their acts only now appear to be acts of great courage."

23. Seeking eyewitnesses of the protest, I had radio interviews in Berlin and wrote notices for newspapers in Germany, Jerusalem, and the United States. I interviewed all the dozens of persons who responded. Thus this is not a scientifically selected sample of protesters.

24. The brother of one protester, a committed Social Democrat, came to participate in the demonstration as an opportunity to express pent-up rage at the regime as a whole. But his action, even though politically motivated, was not as risky or persistent as that of the core of protesters who had created the opportunity for him to protest.

25. Klemperer, " 'What Is the Law That Lies behind These Words?,' " S107, 108.

26. Kershaw, "Widerstand ohne Volk," 779–798.

27. Despite its clashes with the regime over specific policies that violated church traditions, the church never abandoned its line of cooperation with the regime. Like Hitler, some Catholics shared the Nazi leaders' theory that a stab in the back had brought Germany

to its knees in World War I (see, for example, Lewy, *The Catholic Church and Nazi Germany* 319, 279), and like the regime's leadership, they could have been expected to try to avoid public uproar and protest, especially as it became clear that Germany was losing the war. Bishop von Galen was steadfastly opposed to any attempts to cause a German defeat. Even in his speeches denouncing euthanasia he said that "our soldiers will fight and die for Germany" and that he was in no way calling for revolt: "We Christians . . . will continue to do our duty in obedience to God out of love for our German people and fatherland." Sermon of July 20, 1941, in Portmann, *Bischof Graf von Galen*, 57.

28. To be opposed to Nazism is not enough to identify someone as a resister, but inter-married Germans who protested also opposed Nazism in general. Germans who were persecuted as spouses of Jews still identify hatred of Jews as the quintessential characteristic of a Nazi. They still refer to some nonparty members as Nazis, while insisting that some of those who wore the party insignia were not Nazi at all, if, for example, they had slipped extra groceries into Jewish hands. East Berlin interview with Elsa Holzer (married to a Jew), July 16, 1987, and Berlin, Erika Lewine (*Geltungsjude*, half Jew), March 19, 1985.

29. Kershaw, " 'Widerstand ohne Volk,' " 794, and "*Hitler Myth*," 80.

30. Throughout 1943 and into late 1944 high-ranking ministers (from Interior, Justice, Propaganda, RSHA) convened to discuss a proposed law that promised to increase the German population by loosening divorce laws so that barren couples could form more fertile unions. This plan, however, was scrapped for two reasons: SD secret police reports showed that popular opinion would strongly oppose looser divorce standards, and the noncooperation precedent of the Jewish-German intermarriages showed that such laws helped very little anyway. BA Potsdam, 30.01, 10118.

31. See Peter Hoffmann, *Widerstand, Staatsstreich, Attentat: Der Kampf der Opposition gegen Hitler*, 4th ed. (Munich: 1985), Chapter 2. The first edition of this book was translated into English by R. H. Barry as *The History of the German Resistance, 1933–1945* (Cambridge, Mass.: 1977), (chapter 2 is titled "Forms of Resistance"). See also Large, *Contending with Hitler*, 2.

32. This not only opened up divisions within the leadership but also convinced it that these groups were deeply motivated to protest and would continue to cause trouble, even at great risk to themselves.

33. Germans who hid Jews sometimes saved them, but they did not resist openly and so had no chance of forcing the regime to modify a policy, as did the Rosenstrasse protesters.

34. Detlev Peukert, *Volksgenossen und Gemeinschaftsfremde: Anpassung, Ausmerze und Aufbegehren unter dem Nationalsozialismus* (Cologne: 1982), 97.

35. The spirit of the Führer, represented by his picture, which was used to replace crucifixes in schools, was the Nazis' chosen weapon for quelling dissent in Oldenburg.

36. Aggregate protest that appeared collective (like Rosenstrasse) would be more likely in large urban areas. The simultaneous arrest and concentration of intermarried Jews provided a fortuitous collecting point for intermarried Germans, a point that had never been experienced by other Germans and that allowed each individually motivated intermarried German to become part of an aggregate and thus influential action.

37. This was the conclusion of Catholics following their victory at Cloppenburg, according to police reports. Pr. GSta., Rep. 90 P, 16.

38. Koch, *In the Name of the Volk*, 5, 6. Listening to foreign radio programs or reading foreign newspapers as well as telling jokes against Hitler could draw the death penalty (for which there were five thousand death sentences between 1941 and 1945, mostly imposed under Roland Freisler at the People's Court, through 1944).

39. Although intermarried couples constituted a tiny minority while church members represented vast segments of the population, the regime's decision in each case was to postpone its persecution in both cases for the duration of the war.

40. ND NG-2586-H and ND 4055-PS.
41. Lewy, *The Catholic Church and Nazi Germany* 289. It is unlikely that the Catholic Church alone, without the much more vibrant protest and unrest of intermarried Aryans to be affected by compulsory divorce, could have prevented the compulsory divorce law. One German episcopate, Archbishop Bertram, did specifically request the German Justice and Interior ministries to withdraw proposals for compulsory divorce of inter-marriages, but he did so well after Himmler and Goebbels had already decided, in early to mid-1942, that there should be no such law (Goebbels argued that it would cause unrest, and Himmler said it would only bind the regime's hands and limit its options).
42. The success of any thorough state program to determine who was Jewish and who "Aryan" depended on church cooperation, for example, since the churches possessed the only records of births and marriages in Germany before 1874. The churches made their records available, implying that their members should complete the forms the regime requested Germans to prove their "Aryan" heritage.
43. Lewy, *The Catholic Church and Nazi Germany*, 309, 313, 314. The historian Guenter Lewy wrote this assessment in 1964, but by now the Vatican is slowly coming to admit its complicity in Nazi genocide. "From the time Hitler came to power all the German bishops began declaring their appreciation of the important natural values of race and racial purity," Lewy has documented. Hitler, aware of the church's long anti-Jewish record, merely intended to do more effectively what the church had long since attempted, he told Bishop Berning and Monsignor Steinmann on April 26, 1933. There was no public voice of dissent from within Germany and the episcopacy against the Nuremberg Laws and their infringement on the spiritual jurisdiction of the church in the matter of marriage. Some prelates welcomed the laws and implied that from the church's point of view, there could be no objection to legal discrimination against Jews. Ibid., 274–275, 281–282.
44. Kershaw, " 'Widerstand ohne Volk,' " 779–798. Kershaw asks whether any of the limits that any of these *Resistenz* actions set on the Nazi system seriously encumbered the capacity of the regime to rule. He looks at different areas and concludes that there was no effective resistance in this sense. Even the church did not achieve this. The church in 1934, 1936–37, and 1941 had temporarily and partially disturbing effects on the regime. But he says in conclusion that this hardly weakened the capacity of the system of leadership to function.
45. Mommsen, "The Political Legacy of the German Resistance: A Historiographical Cri-tique," in *Contending with Hitler*, loc. cit. 162. Political motivations that transcend individual interests are also problematic, however, such as cases of Germans who refused to help anyone who did not belong to their political party.
46. Charles S. Maier, "The German Resistance in Comparative Perspective," in *Contending with Hitler*, loc. cit. 143. Maier has used the term "selective disapproval" to characterize the "mixture of acceptance and rejection" under *Resistenz*. Charles S. Maier, *The Unmasterable Past: History, Holocaust, and German National Identity* (Cambridge, Mass., and London: 1988), 93. For more on this perspective, see also Klaus Tenfelde, "Workers' Opposition in Nazi Germany: Recent West German Research," in *The Rise of the Nazi Regime*, ed. Charles S. Maier, Stanley Hoffmann, and Andrew Gould (Boulder, Colo.: 1985), 107–114.
47. Broszat, "A Social and Historical Typology," 28.
48. Ibid., 31.
49. Claus von Stauffenberg, *Widerstand*'s central figure, was jubilant about the prowess of the Wehrmacht in the sweeping German decimation of Poland, the opening aggression of World War II. Interview statement of Charlotte von der Schulenburg, in the doc-umentary film *The Restless Conscience*, by Hava Beller, released 1991. Peter Hoffmann points out that this enthusiasm for military success, however, does not indicate Stauf-fenberg was enthusiastic about National Socialism. Hoffmann characterizes Stauffen-berg's resistance as early, especially considering his age and lowly rank. Hoffmann also

writes that Stauffenberg's condemnation of Hitler and call for his assassination were based exclusively on Stauffenberg's knowledge of the murders of Jews and others at a time when he still approved of Hitler's military leadership. Peter Hoffmann, *Claus Schenk Graf von Stauffenberg und seine Brüder* (Stuttgart: 1992), 177–181, 177–181, 249–251. (A version of this book is scheduled for release by Cambridge University Press in 1995.) In his *German Resistance to Hitler* (Cambridge, Mass.: 1988), Hoffmann identifies the murder of the Jews as the deciding motive for Stauffenberg, Tresckow, and others for joining in active conspiracy against the regime.

50. Gilligan contrasts women's moral development with Lawrence Kolberg's stages of moral development, abstracted from an all-male study. Kolberg's moral development requires allegiance to abstract ideals rather than to specific persons (the moral person values life and in a life-threatening situation would not attempt to save even an intimate partner before a stranger). Gilligan writes that women tend to take risks for those they know and care about (like the German women married to Jews), contending that this also represented moral development. Carol Gilligan, *In a Different Voice: Psychological Theory and Women's Development* (Cambridge, Mass.: 1982).

51. There is an important distinction to be made between opposition motivated by conscience and that motivated by circumstances. Yet it is difficult to separate these categories completely. For the historian Klemens von Klemperer, resistance in Nazi Germany was a matter of individual action because it resulted from character, not group identity, and because resistance at home was often seen as treason. Moreover, the Gestapo severely limited the communication and other resources necessary for the organization of resistance. A resister, Klemperer writes, is a "solitary witness . . . the individual acting in solitude and following the commands of his or her own conscience," an extraordinary leap for such a person into an existential situation. Resistance could be politically calculated only up to a certain point and, given the totality of state control, was often just a gesture. The emphasis here is on personal integrity, so that questions of organization as well as questions of consequence are of lesser importance. Defense of family by intermarried persons would not be resistance by this definition, unless it was simultaneously the defense of fundamental principles, the response to a moral imperative. Klemperer, " 'What Is the Law That Lies behind These Words?,' " S106–108.

52. Václev Havel, "The Power of the Powerless," in *The Power of the Powerless*, ed. Václev Havel et al (Armonk, N.Y.: 1985), pp. 40, 41.

53. Zivier, "Aufstand der Frauen."

54. General Beck's decision not to resist in 1938 resulted, however, from foreign cooperation with Hitler at Munich.

55. Trial against the Major War Criminals, Case 9 (*U.S.* v. *Ohlendorf*), *Trials of War Criminals before the Nuremberg Military Tribunals*, vol. 558–59.

56. Trial of Günther Abrahamsohn, statement of Günther Abrahamsohn, January 11, 1947; LB, trial against Abrahamsohn (1 PkLs 7/52). (Since the trial Abrahamsohn has changed his name to Abrahamson.) Noske's noncompliance indicated that allegiance to the racial ideology was second to his own survival and dependent on the survival of the state.

57. Even Heinrich Himmler, the dreaded chief of police, tried to escape his fate at the end of the war by dressing in civilian clothes and using the identification of a victim of National Socialism, Heinrich Hitzinger. Breitman, *Architect of Genocide*, 8.

58. Levi, *The Drowned and the Saved*, 80.

EPILOGUE

1. H. Henschel, "Aus der Arbeit," 12. The Berlin court called the arrests of the Jewish Berlin Community employees "the end" of the Final Roundup. Kammergericht Berlin, Vermerk, Bosshammer Trial.

2. "The new Gestapo director of the Jewish collection center, Dobberke, ordered the Jewish

director of the collection center [Max] Reschke to select two persons for the special task of getting information on the unclear addresses," Abrahamsohn testified. "I immediately accepted, sensing first of all an opportunity to evade the hell of the camp machinery, and secondly, I instinctively grasped that here was a chance, in contrast to the general paralysis of the spectator, to do something positive against the Gestapo. Every day there were about 15 addresses to investigate, and a short report to write about them. . . . It was suggested neither from the side of the Gestapo nor from the Jewish side that these notations would be exploited for purposes of uncovering Jews in the underground." Statement of Abrahamsohn, January 11, 1947, Abrahamsohn Trial.

3. Abrahamsohn said there was no place for him to turn, and no chance to say no to Dobberke. "For me, at twenty-two years old, the question was 'what was I to do?' " he said. The challenge, which took all his intelligence and nerve, he said, was to win the trust—or rather allay the mistrust—of Dobberke. He was able to bribe Dobberke with gopher work and alcohol. Also in his favor, Abrahamsohn said, was the fact that he had known Dobberke since the first deportation. Dobberke trusted him so much, he remembered, perhaps partly because he was from the same rural region as Dobberke and "could easily put myself into Dobberke's peasant psyche." Dobberke Abrahamsohn, January 11, 1947, Abrahamsohn Trial.

4. Statement of Iwan Katz, December 26, 1947, LB, trial of Abrahamsohn.

5. After the war Abrahamsohn began studies as an architect. His trial, on grounds of crimes against humanity, dragged out from 1947 until 1952. His sentence was five months in prison and court costs.

6. At least twenty-five thousand of the thirty-five thousand inmates who passed through Buna died. Hilberg, *Destruction of the European Jews*, 930, 931.

7. Statement of Helmut Brinitzer, August 8, 1970, Bovensiepen Trial. After the war Brinitzer lived for fifteen years in New York City, before returning to Hamburg.

BIBLIOGRAPHY

ARCHIVES CONSULTED

Berlin. Berlin Document Center.
Berlin. Charlottenburger Heimatsmuseum.
Berlin. Geheimes Staatsarchiv Preussischer Kulturbesitz.
Berlin. Landesarchiv.
Berlin (former GDR). Stadtarchiv.
Berlin (former GDR). Archives des ZK des SED, Institut für Marxismus/Leninismus.
Cambridge, Massachusetts. Houghton Library, Harvard University. Oral History Collection of German immigrants, with an introduction and guide, Harry Liebersohn and Dorothee Schneider. Reports of Robert Breusch, Paul Diel, and Eva Wysbar.
Jerusalem, Israel Hebrew University. Personal collection of Professor O. D. Kulka.
Jerusalem, Israel. Yad Vashem.
Koblenz, Germany. Bundesarchiv.
London. Wiener Library.
Ludwigsburg, Germany. Zentrale Stelle der Landesjustizverwaltungen.
Munich. Institut für Zeitgeschichte.
Munich. Staatsarchiv.
New York. Leo Baeck Institute.
New York. YIVO Institute for Jewish Research.
Palo Alto. Stanford University, Hoover Institution on War, Revolution, and Peace.

Paris. Centre de Documentation Juive Contemporaine.
Potsdam, Germany. Bundesarchiv Abteilungen Potsdam.
Rome. La Civiltà Cattolica. Private archives of Robert A. Graham, SJ.
Vienna. Resistance Documentation Archives.
Washington, D.C. US. Holocaust Memorial Museum Archives.
Washington, D.C. National Archives

COURT TRIALS CITED

Berlin. Landgericht (District Court) Berlin. Otto Bovensiepen et al. I Js 9/65.
Berlin. Landgericht. Berlin. Günther Abrahamsohn. 1 PkLs 7/52.
Berlin. Landgericht Berlin. Josef ("Sepp") Dietrich. I P Js 3767.65.
Berlin. Landgericht. Berlin. Stella Kübler. I PKs I/57.
Berlin. Landgericht Berlin. Walter Stock. PkLs 3/52.
Berlin. Landgericht Berlin. Walter Stock. 4 Sp Ls 832/47.
Berlin. Landgericht Berlin. Special Court Document, Special Court IV Pk. KLs 2/42.
Berlin. Kammergericht (Supreme Court) Berlin. Friedrich Bosshammer. I Js 1/65 (RSHA).
Berlin. Kammergericht Berlin. Fritz Wöhrn. I Js I/65 (RSHA).
Koblenz. National Archives. Karl Krell, 4 SpLs 16/47.
Frankfurt. Landgericht Frankfurt am Main. Alois Brunner. 50 Js 36019/84.
Nuremberg. Nuremberg Trial Documents.
Wiesbaden. Hessisches Hauptstaatsarchiv (Hessen Main State Archive). Josef Hedderich. 4 Ks 2/53.
Wiesbaden. Hessisches Hauptstaatsarchiv. Georg Albert Dengler. 2a Ks 1/49.
Wiesbaden. Hessisches Hauptstaatsarchiv. Heinrich Baab. 51 Ks 1/50.
Wiesbaden. Hessisches Hauptstaatsarchiv. Joseph Hedderich and Johann Schmitz. 4 Ks 2/53.

INTERVIEWS
(Interviews were conducted on tape and in Berlin, unless otherwise noted)

German women who protested for their Jewish spouses

Braun, Ursula. June 6, 1985; August 28, 1989; October 30, 1989; November 1, 1989 (television).
Elkuss, Hilde. May 21, 1985; July 31, 1989; August 8, 1989.
Israel (Freudenthal), Charlotte. February 10, 1985; February 12, 1985; February 25, 1985; August 11, 1985; August 22, 1989; August 25, 1989; December 7, 1989; June 22, 1990; July 2, 1990; August 5, 1991.
Grodka, Wally (interviewed with her husband, Günter). August 25, 1985.
Gross, F. (interviewed with her daughter, Ruth). April 4, 1986.
Hain, Erna. March 21, 1985.
Heyn, Charlotte. April 30, 1988.
Holzer, Elsa. April 7, 1985; July 16, 1987; August 16, 1989; August 17, 1989; December 10, 1989; July 20, 1990; July 21, 1991; August 4, 1991.
Radlauer, Annie. March 12, 1985; May 29, 1985.
Weigert, Giesela (together with her son and daughter). June 21, 1985.

Mischlinge who protested for Jewish family members

Goldberg, Werner. February 6, 1985; February 8, 1985; December 6, 1985; November 3, 1989; December 11, 1989 (television).
Gross, Ruth. April 4, 1886.
Kremczuk, Hildegaard. July 4, 1990 (telephone).
Larsen, Daisy (interviewed with her stepfather, Dr. Ernst Bukofzer). June 20, 1985; June 24, 1985.
Loeben, Inge. August 23, 1989; December 11, 1989; June 20, 1990.
Mannheim, Rita. July 23, 1987 (telephone).
Michaelis, Herbert. March 20, 1985.
Reknagel, Ruth. December 10, 1989.
Rosen. Jenny. July 25, 1989.
Steudel, Charlotte. August 8, 1985.

Protesters without relatives incarcerated at Rosenstrasse

Matzanke, Paul (*Mischling*). March 21, 1985.
Schwersensky, Frieda (had a Jewish husband in hiding). November 15, 1989.

Jews and *Mischlinge* incarcerated at Rosenstrasse

Beck, Gad. December 13, 1984; January 28, 1985; August 23, 1989.
Beck, Margaret. April 1, 1986 (Tel Aviv).
Braun, Gerhard. June 6, 1985; August 28, 1989; October 30, 1989; November 1, 1989 (television).
Bukofzer, Ernst. May 29, 1985.
Kuhn, Rita. April 26, 1989 (Berkeley, California).
Lewine, Erika. March 19, 1985; July 28, 1989; August 14, 1989; December 9, 1989 (television).
Löwenstein de Witt, Hans-Oskar. November 8, 1984; August 20, 1989.
Weigert, Helga. June 21, 1985.

Jews deported to Auschwitz during the Berlin Final Roundup and returned after about twelve days

Blaustein, Kurt. August 12, 1985.
Blaustein, Kurt (with his wife, Mary); Erich Herzberg (with his wife), and Mrs. Brinitzer (wife of a deceased Jew who had been deported from Rosenstrasse to Auschwitz and returned): August 3, 1985.
Herzberg, Erich (with his wife, Hannah). August 22, 1985; August 25, 1989. Mrs. Herzberg alone, (television), November 1989.

Related interviews

Abrahamsohn, Günther (*Mischling* "catcher" for the Gestapo). August 16, 1986; December 13, 1989 (telephone); July 16, 1992 (telephone).
Anders, Günther. March 23, 1986.
Bieversdorf, F. (father incarcerated at Rosenstrasse). May 24, 1985.
Breitwieser, Vera (*Mischling* who fled Berlin with her mother to avoid the Final Roundup). February 3, 1985; February 6, 1985.
Heinemann, Peter. December 4, 1988.
Heym, Johanna (former secretary for the Berlin Gestapo Judenreferat). August 23, 1985.

Hüttner, Johnny (Communist Jew incarcerated in various Nazi concentration camps from 1936 until 1945). February 19, 1986.
Jacobs, Helena (commemorated on the Walk of the Righteous). May 29, 1985.
Jakob, Rolf (nephew of Mathilda Jakob). March 19, 1985.
Kaiser, Helga (father incarcerated at Rosenstrasse). March 15, 1985; August 10, 1989.
Kleemann, Siegbert (former personnel director of the Berlin Jewish Community). April 26, 1985.
Klum, Heinz (mother incarcerated at Rosenstrasse). December 4, 1988.
Monasch, Jerry (father incarcerated at Rosenstrasse). September 29, 1985 (telephone); January 17, 1986 (telephone).
Monjau, Mieke. December 3, 1984 (telephone).
Radziewsky, Hans (Auschwitz survivor). February 12, 1985.
Rushin, Günther (deported to Auschwitz during the Final Roundup). March 10, 1985; October 17, 1989.
Schottländer, Rudolf. July 17, 1987.
Stegner, Günther (father incarcerated during the Final Roundup at Grosse Hamburger Strasse). May 1, 1985.
Tallert, Harry (*Mischling*). July 1, 1990 (Bad Honnef).
Weigert, Horst (father incarcerated at Rosenstrasse). December 2, 1989.
Wiesenthal, Simon. March 22, 1986.
Wolf, Edith (*Mischling*): April 8, 1986 (Haifa).

Interviews with former Nazi officials

Gutterer, Leopold. August 17, 1986; August 19, 1986; July 11, 1987; December 5, 1989; June 30, 1990 (West Germany).
Hünsche, Otto. August 11, 1986 (telephone).
Lachmuth, Felix. August 9, 1986 (telephone).
Rothe, Willi. August 12, 1986 (telephone).
Ventner, Kurt. July 7, 1985 (correspondence).

UNPUBLISHED WORKS CITED

Grodka, Wally. Diaries.
Lehfeld, Gerhard. "Die Lage der 'Mischlinge' in Deutschland, Mitte März 1943."

PUBLISHED WORKS CITED

Adam, Uwe. *Judenpolitik im Dritten Reich*. Düsseldorf: 1972.
Adler, H. G. *Der Verwaltete Mensch: Studien zur Deportation der Juden aus Deutschland*. Tübingen: 1974.
———. *Theresienstadt 1941–1945*, 2d ed. Tübingen: 1960.
Allen, William Sheridan. *The Nazi Seizure of Power: The Experience of a Single German Town, 1922–1945*. New York: 1965, revised, 1984.
Aly, Götz, and Karl Heinz Roth. *Die restlose Erfassung*. Berlin: 1984.
Arendt, Hannah. *Eichmann in Jerusalem*. New York: 1963.
Baird, Jay W. *To Die for Germany: Heroes in the Nazi Pantheon*. Bloomington, Ind.: 1990.
Bajohr, Stefan. *Die Hälfte der Fabrik: Geschichte der Frauenarbeit in Deutschland, 1914–1945*. Marburg: 1979.
Bankier, David. *The Germans and the Final Solution: Public Opinion under Nazism*. Oxford/Cambridge, Mass.: 1992.

Bartov, Omar. *Hitler's Army: Soldiers, Nazis, and War in the Third Reich.* Oxford and New York: 1991.
Baynes, Norman H., ed. *The Speeches of Adolf Hitler, April 1922–August 1939*, vol. 1, pt. 2. New York: 1969.
Beck, Gad. *Und Gad ging zu David: Die Erinergungen des Gad Beck, 1923–1945.* Berlin: 1995.
Benz, Wolfgang. *Die Juden in Deutschland, 1933–1945: Leben unter nationalsozialistischer Herrschaft.* Munich: 1989.
Bessel, Richard, ed. *Life in the Third Reich.* Oxford/New York: 1987.
———. *Political Violence and the Rise of Nazism: The Storm Troopers in Eastern Germany 1925–1934.* New Haven: 1984.
Bezirksverordnetenversammlung von Charlottenburg. *Schon damals fingen viele an zu schweigen.* Berlin: 1986.
Blackbourn, David. *Marpingen: Apparitions of the Virgin Mary in Bismarckian Germany.* New York: 1993.
Blasius, Dirk. *Ehescheidung in Deutschland, 1794–1945.* Göttingen: 1987.
Blau, Bruno. *Das Ausnahmerecht für die Juden in den europäischen Länder, 1933–1945.* New York: 1952.
———. "Mischehe im Nazireich." *Judaica* (April 1948).
Boberach, Heinz, ed. *Meldungen aus dem Reich: Aus den geheimen Lageberichten des Sicherheitsdienstes der SS 1939–1944.* Neuwied: 1965.
———. *Meldungen aus dem Reich, 1938–1945: Die Geheimen Lageberichte des Sicherheitsdienstes der SS.* Herssching: 1984. 17 vols.
Bracher, Karl Dietrich. *The German Dictatorship: The Origins, Structure, and Consequences of National Socialism*, trans. Jean Steinberg. New York/Washington, D.C.: 1970.
———. *The German Dilemma: The Relationship of State and Democracy*, trans. Richard Barry. New York: 1975.
Bramsted, Ernest K. *Goebbels and National Socialist Propaganda, 1925–1945.* East Lansing, Mich.: 1965.
Brandt, Leon. *Menschen ohne Schatten: Juden zwischen Untergang und Untergrund, 1938 bis 1945.* Berlin: 1984.
Breitman, Richard. *German Socialism and Weimar Democracy.* Chapel Hill, N.C.: 1981.
———. *The Architect of Genocide: Himmler and the Final Solution.* New York: 1991.
Bridenthal, Renate, Atina Grossmann, and Marion Kaplan. *When Biology Became Destiny: Women in Weimar and Nazi Germany.* New York: 1984.
Broszat, Martin, and Elke Fröhlich. *Alltag und Widerstand: Bayern im Nationalsozialismus.* Munich: 1987.
———, ———, and Anton Grossmann. *Bayern in der NS-Zeit*, vol. III, *Herrschaft und Gesellschaft im Konkflikt*, Teil B. Munich: 1981.
Bukofzer, Ernst. *Laws for Jews and Persecution of Jews under the Nazis.* Berlin: 1946.
Burleigh, Michael. *Death and Deliverance: "Euthanasia" in Germany c. 1900–1945.* Cambridge, England: 1995.
———. "Euthanasia and the Third Reich." *History Workshop Journal* (February 1990).
———, and Wolfgang Wippermann. *The Racial State: Germany 1933–1945.* Cambridge, England: 1991.
Büttner, Ursula, ed. *Das Unrechtsregime: Internationale Forschung über den Nationalsozialismus.* Hamburg: 1986. 2 vols.
———. *Die Not der Juden teilen: Christlich-jüdische Familien im Dritten Reich.* Hamburg: 1988.
Childers, Thomas. *The Nazi Voter: The Social Foundations of Fascism in Germany, 1919–1933.* Chapel Hill, N.C.: 1983.
Conway, John S. *The Nazi Persecution of the Churches.* New York: 1968.
Craig, Gordon A. *Germany 1866–1945.* Oxford/New York: 1978.
Dallin, Alexander. *German Rule in Russia, 1941–1945.* New York: 1957.

Daniel, Ute. *Arbeiterfrauen in der Kriegsgesellschaft: Beruf, Familie und Politik im Ersten Weltkrieg.* Göttingen: 1989.

Dawidowicz, Lucy. *The War against the Jews, 1933–1945.* New York: 1975, 1986.

De Grazia, Victoria. *How Facism Ruled Women: Italy, 1922–1945.* Los Angeles/Berkeley: 1992.

Domarus, Max, ed. *Hitler: Reden und Proklamationen, 1932–1945.* Munich: 1991.

Drobisch, K., R. Goguel, and W. Müller. *Juden unterm Hakenkreuz: Verfolgung und Ausrotung der deutschen Juden, 1933–1945.* Berlin: 1973.

Eschwege, Helmut, ed. *Kennzeichen J: Bilder, Dokumente, Berichte zur Geschichte der Verbrechen des Hitlerfaschismus an den deutschen Juden 1933–1945.* East Berlin: 1981.

Fein, Helen, ed. *The Persisting Question: Sociological Perspectives and Social Contexts of Modern Antisemitism.* Berlin and New York: 1987.

Friedlander, Henry. *The Origins of Nazi Genocide: From Euthanasia to the Final Solution.* Chapel Hill, N.C.: 1995.

Friedrich, Ruth Andreas. *Schauplatz Berlin: Ein Tagebuch aufgezeichnet 1938–1945.* Reinbeck bei Hamburg: 1964.

Gall, Lothar, et al. *Die Deutsche Bank, 1870–1995.* Munich: 1995.

Geisel, Eike. *Die Banalität der Guten: Deutsche Seelenwanderungen.* Berlin: 1992.

Gellately, Robert. *The Gestapo and German Society: Enforcing Racial Policy, 1933–1945.* Oxford: 1990.

Gilbert, Martin. *Atlas of the Holocaust.* New York: 1982.

Gilligan, Carol. *In a Different Voice: Psychological Theory and Women's Development.* Cambridge, Mass.: 1982.

Gisevius, Hans Bernd. *Bis zum bitteren Ende,* vol. 1, *Vom Reichstagbrand zur Fritsch-Krise.* Zurich: 1946.

Goebbels, Joseph. *Vom Kaiserhof zur Reichskanzlei: Eine historische Darstellung in Tagebuchblattern.* Munich: 1934.

———. *The Goebbels Diaries, 1939–1941,* ed. and trans. Fred Taylor. New York: 1984.

———. *The Goebbels Diaries, 1942–43,* ed. and trans. Louis P. Lochner. New York: 1948.

———. *Final Entries 1945: The Diaries of Joseph Goebbels,* ed. and introduction trans. Hugh Trevor-Roper, R. H. Barry. New York: 1978.

———*Joseph Goebbels, Tagebücher,* vol. 4, *1940–1942,* ed. Ralf Georg Reuth. Munich and Zurich: 1992.

Grunberger, Richard. *A Social History of the Third Reich.* London: 1971.

Hancock, Eleanor. *The National Socialist Leadership and Total War, 1941–5.* New York: 1991.

Václev Havel et al., eds. *The Power of the Powerless.* Armonk, N.Y.: 1985.

Haxthausen, Charles W., and Heidrun Suhr, eds. *Berlin: Culture and Metropolis.* Minneapolis: 1990.

Hayes, Peter. "Profits and Persecution: Corporate Involvement in the Holocaust." In *Perspectives on the Holocaust,* ed. James S. Pacy and Alan P. Wertheimer. Boulder, Colo.: 1995.

Hilberg, Raul. *The Destruction of the European Jews.* New York/London: 1985. 3 vols.

———. *Perpetrators, Victims, Bystanders: The Jewish Catastrophe, 1933–1945.* New York: 1992.

———, ed. *Documents of Destruction: Germany and Jewry, 1933–1945.* Chicago: 1971.

Hildesheimer, Ezriel. *Jüdische Selbstverwaltung unter dem NS-Regime: Der Existenzkampf der Reichsvertretung und Reichsvereinigung der Juden in Deutschland.* Tübingen: 1994.

Hilke-Siebenhaar, Carolin, *Wegweiser durch das jüdische Berlin: Geschichte und Gegenwart.* Berlin: 1987.

Hinz, Berthold, *Art in the Third Reich,* trans. Robert and Rita Kimber. New York: 1979.

Hirschfeld, Gerhard, and Lothar Kettenacker, eds. *The "Führer State": Myth and Reality: Studies on the Structure and Politics of the Third Reich.* Stuttgart: 1981.

Hitler, Adolf. *Mein Kampf,* trans. and ed. John Chamberlain and Sidney B. Fay. New York: 1939.

Hoffmann, Peter. *Claus Schenk Graf von Stauffenberg und seine Brüder.* Stuttgart: 1992.

———. *Widerstand gegen Hitler und das Attentat vom 20. Jul. 1944,* 2d. ed. Munich and Zurich: 1984. First edition translated into English by R. H. Barry as *The History of the German Resistance, 1933–1945.* Cambridge, Mass.: 1977.

———. *German Resistance to Hitler.* Cambridge, Mass.: 1988.

Huster, Gabriele. "Das Bild der Frau in der Malerei des deutschen Faschismus." In *Frauen unterm Hakenkreuz.* Berlin: 1983.

Jaspers, Karl. *Die Schuldfrage: Ein Beitrag zur deutschen Frage.* Zurich: 1946.

Jochheim, Gernot. *Protest in der Rosenstrasse.* Stuttgart: 1990.

Kaplan, Marion, ed. *The Marriage Bargain: Women and Dowries in European History.* New York: 1985.

Kater, Michael. *The Nazi Party: A Social Profile of Members and Leaders, 1919–1945.* Cambridge, Mass.: 1983.

Keitel, Wilhelm. *The Memoirs of Field-Marshal Keitel,* trans. David Irving. Göttingen: 1961.

Keneally, Thomas. *Schindler's List.* New York: 1982.

Kershaw, Ian. *Popular Opinion and Political Dissent in the Third Reich: Bavaria 1933–1945.* Oxford and New York: 1983.

———. *The "Hitler Myth": Image and Reality in the Third Reich.* Oxford/New York: 1987.

———. *The Nazi Dictatorship: Problems and Perspectives of Interpretation.* London: 1985, revised 1993.

———. " 'Widerstand ohne Volk': Dissens und Widerstand im Dritten Reich." In *Der Widerstand gegen den Nationalsozialismus,* ed Jürgen Schmädeke and Peter Steinbach. Munich: 1985.

———. "Social Unrest and the Response of the Nazi Regime, 1934–1936." In *Germans against Nazism: Nonconformity, Opposition and Resistance in the Third Reich,* ed. Francis R. Nicosia and Lawrence D. Stokes. New York/Oxford: 1990.

Kirchheimer, Otto. "Weimar and What Then?" In *Politics, Law and Social Change: Selected Essays of Otto Kirchheimer,* ed. Frederic Burn and Kurt Shell. New York/London: 1969.

Klee, Ernst, ed. *Dokumente zur "Euthanasie."* Frankfurt: 1985.

———. *"Euthanasia" im NS-Staat: Die Vernichtung lebensunwerten Lebens.* Frankfurt am Main: 1983.

Klemperer, Klemens von. "What Is the Law That Lies Behind These Words?" *Journal of Modern History,* vol. 64 (December 1992).

———. *German Resistance against Hitler: The Search for Allies Abroad, 1938–1945.* New York: 1992.

Knobloch, Heinz. *Meine liebste Mathilde: Das unauffällige Leben des Mathilde Jacob.* Berlin: 1986.

Koch, H. W. *In the Name of the Volk: Political Justice in Hitler's Germany.* New York: 1989.

Kocha, Jürgen. "Ursachen des Nationalsozialismus." *Aus Politik und Zeitgeschichte* (June 21, 1980).

Kommission zur Erforschung der Geschichte der Frankfurter Juden. *Dokumente zur Geschichte der Frankfurter Juden 1933–1945.* Frankfurt am Main: 1963.

Koonz, Claudia. *Mothers in the Fatherland: Women, the Family and Nazi Politics.* New York: 1987.

Kuper, Leo. *Genocide: Its Political Use in the Twentieth Century.* New Haven/London: 1981.

Kwiet, Konrad, and Helmut Eschwege. *Selbstbehauptung und Widerstand: Deutsche Juden im Kampf um Existenz und Menschenwürde.* Hamburg: 1984.
Lane, Barbara Miller, and Leila J. Rupp, eds. and trans. *Nazi Ideology before 1933: A Documentation.* Austin and London: 1978.
Langer, Walter. *The Mind of Adolf Hitler.* New York: 1973.
Laqueur, Walter. *The Missing Years.* Boston: 1980.
————. *The Terrible Secret: Suppression of the Truth about Hitler's "Final Solution."* New York: 1980, revised 1982.
————, and Richard Breitman. *Breaking the Silence.* New York: 1986.
Large, David Clay, ed. *Contending with Hitler: Varieties of German Resistance in the Third Reich.* Cambridge, England: 1992.
Laska, Vera, ed. *Women in the Resistance and in the Holocaust.* London: 1983.
Levi, Primo. *The Drowned and the Saved.* New York: 1989.
Levin, Nora. *The Destruction of European Jewry, 1933–1945.* New York: 1973.
Lewy, Guenter. *The Catholic Church and Nazi Germany.* New York and Toronto: 1964.
Longerich, Peter. *Hitlers Stellvertreter: Führung der Partei und Kontrolle des Staatsapparates durch den Stab Hess und die Partei-Kanzlei Bormann.* Munich: 1992.
Lösener, Bernhard. "Als Rassereferent im Reichministerium des Innern." *Vierteljahreshefte für Zeitgeschichte.* vol. 9 (September 1961).
Ludwig-Uhland Institut für empirische Kulturwissenschaft der Universität Tübingen. *Als die Deutschen demonstrieren lernten: Das Kulturmuster "Friedliche Strassendemonstration" im preussischen Wahlrechtskampf 1908–1910.* Tübingen: 1986.
Maier, Charles S. *The Unmasterable Past: History, Holocaust, and German National Identity.* Cambridge, England: 1988.
————, Stanley Hoffmann, and Andrew Gould, eds. *The Rise of the Nazi Regime.* New York: 1986.
Mason, Timothy. *Arbeiterklasse und Volksgemeinschaft: Dokumente und Materialien zur deutschen Arbeiterpolitik, 1936–1939.* Opladen: 1975.
————. *Sozialpolitik im dritten Reich.* Opladen: 1978.
————. "Intention and Explanation: A Current Controversy about the Interpretation of National Socialism." In *The "Führer State": Myth and Reality: Studies on the Structure and Politics of the Third Reich,* ed. Gerhard Hirschfeld and Lothar Kettenacker. Stuttgart: 1981.
————. "Women in Germany, 1925–1940: Family, Welfare and Work." *History Workshop Journal* (January 1976).
————. "Zur Lage der Frauen in Deutschland, 1930–1940: Wohlfahrt, Arbeit und Familie." *Gesellschaft: Beiträge zur Marxistischen Theorie* (June 1976).
Middlebrook Martin, and Chris Everitt. *The Bomber Command War Diaries* New York: Penguin, 1990.
Mommsen, Hans. *Beamtentum im Dritten Reich.* Stuttgart: 1966.
————. *From Weimar to Auschwitz: Essays in German History,* trans. Philip O'Connor. Princeton: 1991.
Moore, Barrington. *Injustice: The Social Bases of Obedience and Revolt.* White Plains, N.Y.: 1978.
Moritz, Klaus, and Ernst Noam. *NS-Verbrechen vor Gericht, 1945–1955.* Wiesbaden: 1978.
Mosse, George, ed. *Police Forces in History.* London: 1975.
Neumann, Franz. *Behemoth: The Structure and Practice of National Socialism.* New York: 1963.
Nicholls, Anthony, and Erich Matthias, eds. *German Democracy and the Triumph of Hitler.* London: 1971.
Nicosia, Francis R., and Lawrence D. Stokes, eds. *Germans against Nazism: Nonconformity, Opposition and Resistance in the Third Reich.* New York/Oxford: 1990.
Noakes, Jeremy. "Wohin gehören die 'Judenmischlinge'? Die Entstehung der ersten Durchführungsverordnungen zu den Nürnberger Gesetzen." In *Das Unrechtsregime: In-*

ternationale Forschung über den Nationalsozialismus, ed. Ursula Büttner. Hamburg: 1986. vol. 2.

———. "The Oldenburg Crucifix Struggle of November 1936: A Case Study of Opposition in the Third Reich." In *The Shaping of the Nazi State,* ed. Peter Stachura. New York: 1978.

———, and G. Pridham, eds. *Nazism, 1919–1945: A History in Documents and Eyewitness Accounts.* New York: 1983.

O'Brien, Conor Cruise. "A Lost Chance to Save the Jews?" *New York Review of Books* (April 27, 1989).

Office of United States Chief of Counsel for Prosecution of Axis Criminality. *Nazi Conspiracy and Aggression,* supplement B. Washington, D.C.: 1948.

Oliner, Samuel P., and Pearl M. Oliner. *The Altruistic Personality: Rescuers of Jews in Nazi Europe.* New York: 1988.

Owings, Alison. *Frauen: German Women Recall the Third Reich.* New Brunswick, N.J.: 1993.

Pacy, James S., and Alan P. Wertheimer, eds., *Perspectives on the Holocaust.* Boulder, Colo.: 1995.

Paepcke, Lotte. *Ich wurde vergessen: Bericht einer die das dritte Reich überlebte* (Freiburg im Breisgau: 1979).

Parker, R. A. C. *Struggle for Survival: The History of the Second World War.* Oxford and New York: 1990.

Parsons, Talcott. *Essays in Sociological Theory: Pure and Applied.* Glencoe, Ill.. 1949.

Pätzold, Kurt. *Verfolgung, Vertreibung, Vernichtung: Dokumente des faschistischen Antisemitismus 1933 bis 1942.* Leipzig: 1983.

Paul, Gerhard. *Aufstand der Bilder: Die NS-Propaganda vor 1933.* Bonn: 1990.

Peukert, Detlev. *Volksgenossen und Gemeinschaftsfremde: Anpassung, Ausmerze und Aufbegehren unter dem Nationalsozialismus.* Cologne: 1982.

Picker, Henry. *Hitler's Tischgespräche im Führerhauptquartier.* Stuttgart: 1963 and 1976.

Portmann, Heinrich, ed. *Bischof Graf von Galen spricht!* Freiburg im Breisgau: 1946.

Proctor, Robert. *Racial Hygiene: Medicine under the Nazis.* Cambridge, Mass.: 1988.

Reitlinger, Gerald. *The Final Solution: The Attempt to Exterminate the Jews of Europe 1939–1945.* New York: 1961.

Rhodes, Anthony. *Propaganda: The Art of Persuasion: World War II.* Secaucus, N.J.: 1987.

Richarz, Monika, ed. *Jüdisches Leben in Deutschland: Selbszeugnisse zur Soizialgeschichte 1918–1945.* Stuttgart and New York: 1982.

———. *Burger auf Widerruf: Lebenszeugnisse deutscher Juden, 1780–1945.* Munich: 1989.

Rosenstrauch, Hazel, ed. *Aus Nachbarn wurden Juden: Ausgrenzung und Selbstbehauptung, 1933–1942* Berlin: 1988.

Runge, Irene. *Onkel Max ist jüdisch: Neun Gespräche mit Deutschen die Juden halfen.* Berlin: 1991.

Rupp, Leila. *Mobilizing Women for War: German and American Propaganda, 1939–1945.* Princeton: 1978.

Rürup, Reinhard, ed. *Typographie des Terrors: Gestapo, SS, und Reichssicherheitshauptamt auf dem "Prinz-Albrecht-Gelände."* Berlin: 1987.

Scheffler, Wolfgang. "Der Brandanschlag im Berliner Lustgarten im Mai 1942 und seine Folgen." In *Jahrbuch des Landesarchiv Berlin,* ed. Hans Reichhardt. Berlin: 1984.

Schmädeke, Jürgen, und Peter Steinbach, eds. *Der Widerstand gegen den Nationalsozialismus.* Munich: 1985.

Schmidt, Paul. *Hitler's Interpreter.* New York: 1951.

Schmuhl, Hans-Walter. *Rassenhygiene, Nationalsozialismus, Euthanasie: Von der Verhütung zur Vernichtung "lebensunwerten Lebens" 1890–1945.* Göttingen: 1987.

Schoenberner, Mira and Gerhard. *Zeugen sagen aus: Berichte und Dokumente über die Judenverfolgung im Dritten Reich.* Berlin: 1988.

Sharp, Gene. *The Politics of Nonviolence.* Boston: 1973. 3 vols.

Shirer, William. *Berlin Diary: The Journal of a Foreign Correspondent.* New York: 1961.

Speer, Albert. *Inside the Third Reich,* trans. Richard and Clara Winston. New York: 1970.

Stachura, Peter, ed. *The Shaping of the Nazi State.* New York: 1978.

Stephenson, Jill. *Women in German Society 1930–1940.* London: 1975.

Steinert, Marlis. *Hitler's War and the Germans: Public Mood and Attitude during the Second World War,* ed. and trans. T. E. J. de Witt. Athens, Ohio: 1977.

Steinhoff, Johannes, Peter Pechel, and Dennis Showalter, *Voices from the Third Reich: An Oral History.* Washington, D.C.: 1989.

Stern, Fritz. *Dreams and Delusions: The Drama of German History.* New York: 1987.

Stern, J. P. *Hitler: The Führer and the People.* Berkeley/Los Angeles: 1975.

Strauss, Herbert. "Jewish Emigration from Germany: Nazi Policies and Jewish Responses." *Leo Baeck Institute Year Book,* vol. 25 (1980).

Taylor, A. J. P. *The Course of German History: A Survey of the Development of German History since 1815.* London: 1945.

Trunk, Isaiah. *Judenrat: The Jewish Councils in Eastern Europe under Nazi Occupation.* New York: 1972.

Turner, Henry Ashby, Jr. *German Big Business and the Rise of Hitler.* Oxford/New York: 1985.

Unikower, Inge. "Stummer Protest." *Neues Deutschland* (November 14, 1964).

———. *Suche nach dem gelobten Land.* Berlin: 1978.

Watt, Donald, C. *How War Came: The Immediate Origins of the Second World War, 1938–1939.* New York: 1989.

Wehler, Hans-Ulrich. *The German Empire, 1871–1918,* trans. Kim Traynor. Leamington Spa, England: 1985.

Wyden, Peter. *Stella: One Woman's True Tale of Evil, Betrayal, and Survival in Hitler's Germany.* New York: 1992.

Zivier, Georg. "Aufstand der Frauen." *Sie* (December 1945).

INDEX

Abrahamsohn, Günther, 166, 184, 279–81, 330n, 353n
accommodation to Nazi norms, 44–49, 58–60, 65–75, 76–77, 277
  self-interest and opportunism in, 10–12, 96–97
  and success of Nazi regime, 4, 7, 13, 75, 258, 259, 261, 269
  see also collaboration; denunciations
"action to clear living space," deportations of Jews as, 163–91
Adam, Uwe, 194
air-raid shelters:
  German, 124, 138–39
  Jewish, 126, 134–39
Allen, William Sheridan, 13–14, 308n

Allies, bombardment of Germany by, 134–39, 197, 224–26, 281, 337n
American Legation, 244
Angriff, Der, xxii
Animal Protection Association, 174
Anschluss (annexation of Austria), 89–90
anti-Jewish measures, see specific measures
anti-Semitism:
  baptism of Jews and, 71
  career incentives for, 96–97
  in Charlotte Israel's family, 18, 21, 22, 26, 51, 52–53
  as core of Nazi ideology, 13, 96–97, 264

anti-Semitism (*continued*)
early exposure of Rudi Holzer to, 32
in Erika Lewine's family, 62–63
Hitler encouraged by church leaders
on, 273
Hitler's political use of, 96–97
Nazi party members held to "higher
standard" of, 53–54
in Northeim, 13–14
in propaganda, xxii, xxiii, 38, 65–70,
80–81
of Sankt Johann villagers, 30
of shopkeepers, 76–77
in *Stürmerkasten* portrayal of Jews,
80
in Werner Goldberg's family, 62
see also Final Solution; Holocaust;
Jewish Question
Arenberg, Dr., torture and death of,
235–37
Arendt, Hannah, 189, 190, 309*n*
armaments industry, German:
Jews in, 205–6, 256
protests against Jews in, 247, 346*n*
women conscripted into, 196,
197–201
Army, German (Wehrmacht), 178–79
in Battle of Stalingrad, 192, 196
Berliner casualties in, 196–97
deportation of Jewish war heroes protested by, 247, 332*n*
expulsion of *Mischlinge* from, 118–19
Mischlinge in, 87–88, 112–13
Army, Soviet, 281
Army, U.S., 179
bombardment of Berlin by, 197
Aryan Clause of the Law for the Restoration of the Civil Service, 39
adopted by Austria, 92–93
adopted voluntarily by business and
trade organizations, 10, 39, 43–45,
78, 311*n*
as direct ban on intermarriage, 43
intermarried Germans and, xxvii, 44,
45
middle-class intermarried Jews affected by, xxvii, 10, 43–45
"Aryan households," 9, 104, 301*n*
"Aryan" Identification Cards, 10

Aryanization of Jewish businesses, 12,
118, 124
in aftermath of Kristallnacht program,
99, 104–5
"Aryans," "Aryan" descent, 303*n*
equalizations between *Mischlinge* and,
116–17, 119–20, 180
as grounds for divorcing Jews, 45–46
and membership in SS, 26
production of, through SS *Lebensborn*
program, 19
Asberg, 147
Auschwitz, 11, 122, 172, 176, 194, 219,
229, 237, 280
intermarried Jews without children
sent to, 240, 241–42
Jewish war heroes from Theresienstadt sent to, 247
Jews from Clou sent to, 232, 237,
241–42
protective-custody prisoners sent to,
11, 203–4
Rosenstrasse Protest in release of intermarried Jews from, 252–54, 291
Rosenstrasse returnees sent to Grossbeeren from, 254, 281
work detail at, 253, 340*n*–41*n*
Austria:
German annexation (Anschluss) of,
89–90
Germany's racial laws adopted by,
92–93
Jews of, 30–32, 92–93, 165

Baeck, Leo, 130, 140, 163, 207, 342*n*
Baden, Pfalz, and Saarland deportations,
139, 140
Bahnhof Börse, 223
Bahnhof Lehrter, 94, 189
Barnes, Julian, 17
Barth, John, 150
Battle of Britain, 134, 135
Battle of Stalingrad, 192, 196, 198,
200
Beck, Gad, 213–15, 221, 231
Berchtesgaden, 89
Berlin:
Allied bombardments of, 134–39,
197, 224–26, 281, 337*n*

Charlottenburg district of, 37, 38, 64
East, 282, 284, 286, 291
foreign press in, xxii, 245, 264, 271
German Army casualties from, 196–97
Goebbels's mandate of *Judenfrei* and, 131, 195–96, 206–8, 212, 226, 255, 264, 347n
indifference to Sudetenland annexation in, 90–92
Kristallnacht pogrom in, 99–101
majority of Germany's intermarried couples in, 264
Olympics in, 76–77
as Reich policy precedent-setter, 131, 195, 255
Rosenstrasse in, xvii–xviii
Rosenstrasse Protest and, 246, 264, 271
Scheunenviertel section of, xvii, 21, 213, 214
Weimar, 19, 21
West, 282, 284, 285, 286, 295
Berliner Tagesblatt, 113
Berlin Industry and Trade Works, 206
Berlin Jewish Community, xix, xvii–xviii, xix, 62, 63
deportation of employees of, 186–87, 279, 341n
destruction of, 279
in Final Roundup of Jews, 206, 208
Gestapo deportations dependent on lists of, 163–64
Housing Advisory Office of, 109, 163, 165
leadership of, 139–41, 162–66, 176, 188–91, 207, 208
Lewine family membership in, 63
punished for acts of noncompliance, 176, 187
see also Central Organization of Jews in Germany
Berlin Jews:
deportations of, 162–91, 231–37, 329n–30n
Final Roundup of, xv–xxv, 195, 202–57, 265, 300n
first expulsion of, 214
phases in deportations of, 165–66

population of, 153
Berlin Sports Palace, 91, 202
Berlin Wall, 285, 296
Bismarck, Otto von, 311n
Blaustein, Kurt, 241
blockleaders (blockleiter), 83, 84, 136, 320n–21n
Böhm, Mrs., 166–67
Bormann, Martin, 148, 199, 204, 264
Bovensiepen, Otto, 140, 182, 290–91
boycotts of German businesses:
international, to protest handling of "racial question" abroad, 42
threatened to intimidate owners, 76–77
boycotts of Jewish businesses, 38–39
cooperation of German businessmen in, 11, 39
Julius Israel's shop targeted in, 52, 79
as represented by Hitler as "popular" action, 38
used by Goebbels to influence German bureaucrats, 38
Brandt, Rudolf, 232, 233
Braun, Gerhard, released from Rosenstrasse, 2–4, 249
Braun, Gerhard and Ursula, 222–24
Braun, Ursula, 212
in Rosenstrasse Protest, 223–24
Brazil, 42
Brecht, Bertholt, 41, 50, 124
British Broadcasting Company (BBC), 137, 168, 331n
British Foreign Office, 193
Brockdorff-Ahlefeldt, Erich von, 116
Broszat, Martin, 266, 274–75, 313n, 349n
Brunner, Alois, 166, 284, 342n–43n
in charge of Berlin deportations, 183–87, 295
Jewish community employees arrested by, 186–87
methods used by, to arrest Jews, 185
Mischlinge and intermarried Jews arrested by, 185–86
Vienna deportations headed by, 183
Buchenwald, xviii, 98
Bukofzer, Ernst, xxvii, 210–11, 217–18, 221

Bukofzer, Ernst (*continued*)
  in release from Rosenstrasse, 2–4,
    249–50
Buna rubber plant:
  deportees from Rosenstrasse sent to,
    253, 340n–41n
  survival rate of workers at, 353n
Burckhardt, Carl, 194
bureaucrats, collaboration of, 48, 65–75,
  96, 319n
Burke, Edmund, 209
businesses, German:
  Aryan Clause of the Law for the Res-
    toration of the Civil Service
    adopted voluntarily by, 10, 39, 43–
    45, 78, 311n
  boycotts of, *see* boycotts of German
    businesses
  closure (*Stillegung*) measure of Total
    War and, 200, 232, 309n–10n
businesses, Jewish:
  Aryanization of, 12, 99, 104–5, 118,
    124
  boycotts of, *see* boycotts of Jewish
    businesses
  collaborations by, 39, 43–45,
    76–78
  Holzer family publishing business,
    33–34
  Israel clothing business, 20, 21, 81–82
Business Licensing office, 81

"catchers" (Greifer), Jews employed as,
  166, 184, 277, 279, 280
Catholic Church, 14, 260, 269
  on crucifix decrees, 145–47, 272,
    313n, 327n
  on Euthanasia program, 144–45, 147–
    49, 259–60, 272
  identification of intermarried Jews by,
    206
  single-issue opposition of, 144–49,
    327n
Central Organization of Jews in Ger-
    many, 130–34, 141, 155, 163, 296
  civil disobedience discouraged by,
    189–91
  dealings with RSHA by, 130, 133–34,
    139–41, 165, 174, 176, 186, 187

  facilitation of Jewish emigration by,
    142
  Gestapo cooptation of leadership of,
    130, 162–68, 188–91, 279, 326n,
    330n
  ineffectual protests against deporta-
    tions by, 139–40, 162
  see also Berlin Jewish Community
Ceylon, German relations with, 42
Chamberlain, Neville, 92, 117
children, Star of David worn by, 154–
  55
churches:
  collaboration with regime by, 10, 272,
    321n, 349n–50n, 351n
  compulsory divorce opposed by, 272
  Mischlinge as concern of, 205, 213
Churchill, Winston, 117
civil disobedience:
  advocated in *Mein Kampf*, 8, 310n
  discouraged by Jewish organizations,
    189–91
  German, at end of war, 277
  in opposition to crucifix decrees, 145–
    47, 272, 327n
  see also dissent; mass rallies, Nazi;
    noncompliance; protests; protests,
    mass
Cloppenburg, 145–46
Clou, xvi, 231–34
  brutality toward Jewish detainees at,
    232–33
  deportations of Jews to Auschwitz
    from, 232
collaborations, collaborators:
  bureaucratic, 48, 65–75, 96, 319n
  by churches, 10, 273, 321n, 349n–
    50n, 351n
  conformity (fear of nonconformity),
    6, 10, 138–39
  in deportations of Jews from Frank-
    furt am Main, 203–4
  forms and levels of collaboration, 6,
    10–14, 38–39
  in gradual compromise with regime,
    17–18
  by medical and legal associations, 44,
    45
  motivations for, 5–16, 76–77, 96–97

regime's need for, 11
by trade associations and businesses, 39, 43–45, 76–78
voluntary, 6, 11–13, 77, 133, 261
see also accommodation to Nazi norms; denunciations
collection centers for Final Roundup of Jews, xvi–xvii, 208, 215, 218, 219
Grosse Hamburger Strasse, xvi, 184, 236, 237, 242
Levetzowstrasse synagogue, xvi, 164–65, 167–68, 218, 219
Commercial Gazette, 42
"Committee of Three," 199, 202
Communist party, Communists, 24, 276
demonstrations against Nazi party by, 25–26
in Finland, 196
Herbert Baum Group of, 175
1918 revolution and, 8, 9, 29, 92
Rudi Holzer's membership in, 33
concentration camps, 7, 134, 188, 194
intermarried Jews in protective custody sent to, 11–12
release of intermarried Jews from, 252–54
see also individual camps
confessing church, 86, 321*n*
conversions:
to Catholicism, 30–32, 143–44
to Judaism, 63, 107, 142–43
courts:
compliance of, in murder of intermarried Jews, 11–12
divorce of intermarried couples as interpreted by, 45–46, 48–49
prosecution of Jews in, 93–95
Rassenschande as interpreted by, 73–74
crucifix decrees, 145–47, 272, 327*n*
curfew laws, for Jews, 108, 169
Czechoslovakia:
assassination of Heydrich in, 175
German annexation of Sudetenland in, 90–92
RSHA records moved to, 281
Czech Republic, 276

Dachau, 98
Dammer, Susanna, 339*n*
Daniel, Ute, 339*n*
Darmstadt, deportation of intermarried Jews from, 204
Day of the Luftwaffe, 224
Decentralization of Power in Third Reich and the intermarriage problem, 16, 186
"De-Jewing" of Reich, *see Judenfrei*
demonstrations:
against crucifix decree, 145–47
Goebbels's belief in, for gathering power, xxi, 8–9, 14–15
Goebbels uses to promote the appearance of anti-Semitism, 47
Nazi ban on, xxiii–xxiv
orchestration of, 66–67
Rosenstrasse Protest, xx–xxii, xxiv–xxv
see also civil disobedience; dissent; mass rallies, Nazi; noncompliance; protests; protests, mass
Dengler, Georg, 97
denunciations:
business expropriations through, 12
for career reasons, 12, 312*n*
enforcement of racial policies through, 4, 6, 11–13, 102, 204
for infractions of Nazi laws, 133, 166–67, 204
intermarried Jews as targets of, 11–12, 167, 204
as a reflection of the regime's popularity, 12
by voluntary collaborators, 6, 11, 13, 77, 133
deportations:
of Berlin's Jews, 162–91, 231–37, 329*n*–30*n*
of Berlin's Jews, phases in, 165–66
Brunner as Berlin's head of, 183–87
Brunner's methods in rounding up Jews for, 185
directives used to deceive Jews and others about, 168, 331*n*
of intermarried Germans, 130, 194, 259, 334*n*

deportations (*continued*)
  of intermarried Jews, xvii, xxi–xxii,
    xxvi, 16, 97, 107, 124, 151, 168,
    170–71, 173, 185–86, 193, 194–95,
    205–8, 237, 241–42, 244, 255, 334n
  of Jews from outside Berlin, 130–33,
    139, 203, 249, 256
  of *Mischlinge*, 170–72, 194, 203, 205,
    340n–41n
  of *Mischlinge*, temporary deferment
    from, 15, 16, 151–52, 193, 205,
    237, 238, 259, 263, 264, 313n–14n,
    319n
  RSHA and, *see* Reich Security Main
    Office
  trial, 6–7, 139–41, 309n
  "us-ism" of, 121–23
  wearing of Star of David as prelude
    to, 75, 151, 153, 193
  of widowed or divorced intermarried
    Jews, xxvi, 173, 248, 263, 332n–
    33n, 348n
  see also Final Solution; Holocaust
detention center, Clou used as, xvi,
    231–34
  see also collection centers for Final
    Roundup of Jews
Deutsche Bank A.G., 12
Deutsche juritische Zeitung, 46, 48
de Witt, Hans-Oskar Löwenstein, 64, 76
Dietrich, Sepp, 207
dissent:
  anti-Kristallnacht, in Northeim,
    13–14
  of Catholic Church, 14, 49, 144, 206–
    7, 260, 269, 272, 327n
  Final Solution secrecy due to, xxiv,
    168, 232–33, 238, 245, 254, 260,
    261, 262, 303n, 331n, 345n
  history of, among intermarried Ger-
    man women, xxvi, 261, 263, 268,
    269, 271, 273, 275
  shame used in repression of, 77
  single-interest, 266, 268–69
  unified, 272
divorces:
  compulsory, churches opposed to, 272
  intermarriage as grounds for, 45–46,
    48, 74, 272

of intermarried couples, xxvi, xxvii,
    xxviii, xxix, 9, 12, 43, 74, 107, 173,
    259, 263, 272
  intermarried Germans and, 9, 106–8,
    125–26, 173–74, 195, 268
Dobberke, Walter, 247, 280–81, 352n–
    53n
Droop, Marlou, 127, 143, 228
Dunkirk, Battle of, 198
Düsseldorf, 256

eastern occupied territories, 5, 17
  forced laborers from, 181, 198, 199,
    205, 206, 208
  intermarried couples murdered in, 259
East German National Archives, 295
"east transports," 162–63, 176, 183,
    234
economic sanctions
  against intermarried Germans, 43, 44,
    77, 78
  against Nazi Germany, 42
Eden, Anthony, 193
"editor law," 44
Eichmann, Adolf:
  in Final Roundup of Jews, 203–7,
    342n
  Jewish community employees de-
    ported by, 186–87, 341n
  Jewish emigration expedited by, 142
  Mischlinge deported by, xxvii, 205,
    206, 207, 213
  plans of, to deport intermarried Jews,
    xvii, xxii, 97, 203, 241–42
  trial deportation of Jews carried out
    by, 139
Einsatzgruppe D, 256
Elkuss, Hilda, in Rosenstrasse Protest,
    229–31
Elkuss, Hilda and Dieter, 212–13,
    239–40
Emergency Decree, 307n
emigration, Jewish:
  to Shanghai, 142, 143, 177
  to U.S., 142
Epp, Franz, 147
Eppstein, Paul, 139–41, 176, 188,
    207
  execution of, 342n

negotiations on behalf of Jewish
    Community by, 130, 133–34
equalizations (*Mischlinge* with
    "Aryans"), 116–17, 119–20, 171,
    180, 324*n*
Essen (Germany), 284, 293
Euthanasia program, 15, 110–11
    Catholic Church opposed to, 144–45,
        147–49, 272
    family protests against, 259–60
    as precursor of Final Solution,
        149
    secrecy of, 111, 144, 148
    "wild," 148, 328*n*
exemptions, 119–20
eyewitnesses, author's interviews of,
    291–97

Factory Action, *see* Final Roundup of
    the Jews
Final Roundup of the Jews, xv–xxv, 202,
    206–57, 265, 300*n*
    Berlin Jewish Community employees
        used in, 214–15
    Berlin police help in, 211
    Braun arrested in, 222–23
    brutality of, 231–37
    Bukofzer arrested in, 210–11
    children arrested in, 218–19, 222
    Clou used as detention center in,
        231–34
    collection centers for, xvi–xvii, 164–
        65, 167–68, 184, 208, 215, 218,
        219, 236, 237, 242
    and deportation to Auschwitz, 232,
        237, 241–42
    Eichmann in, 203–7, 342*n*
    Goebbels in, 207–8
    Goldberg's father arrested in, 215
    Hermann Goering barracks as collec-
        tion center in, xvi, 207, 210,
        216–17
    intermarried Jews in, xv–xxv, 195,
        206–57
    Julius Israel arrested in, 211–12
    Mischlinge arrested in, xvii–xx, 203,
        210, 213, 220, 304*n*
    number of people arrested in, xxiv,
        218, 242

protests by factory owners and mili-
    tary against, 247
Rosenhstrasse 2–4 as collection center
    in, xvi, xviii, xix, 213–15, 218,
    219–29
separation of families in, 210, 213
separation of Jews and intermarried
    Jews in, 217–18
shooting of escapees in, 210
suicides in, xvi–xvii
updating church lists as prelude to,
    206–7
warning of, leaked to Jews, 212
Final Solution, xxiv, 6, 162–91, 195,
    203, 207, 290–91, 329*n*–30*n*
    inclusion of intermarried Germans in,
        171–72, 259
    inclusion of *Mischlinge* in, 151, 170–
        72
    intermarried Jews "temporarily ex-
        empted" from, xxi–xxii, 15, 16,
        170, 193, 205, 237, 238, 259, 263,
        264, 313*n*, 328*n*
    lack of German protest, 145
    Mischlinge temporarily exempted
        from, 15, 16, 193, 205, 237, 238,
        259, 263, 264, 313*n*–14*n*, 319*n*
    RSHA role in, xx–xxii, 130–33, 139–
        41, 151, 165, 186
    rumors of, 168
    secrecy of, to preserve public morale,
        232–33, 245, 254, 260, 261, 262
    secrecy of, to prevent Jewish noncom-
        pliance, 168, 331*n*
    secrecy of, to prevent noncompliance
        of relatives of Jews, xxiv, 16, 193,
        238, 259, 263, 264, 303*n*, 345*n*
    tactical differences between regime
        and RSHA in, xxii, 85–86, 203–5,
        207, 243–44
    see also Final Roundup of Jews;
        Holocaust; Jewish Question
Finland, 196, 259
"Forbidden for Jews!," 80, 82, 94
forced laborers:
    from conquered territories, 181, 198,
        199, 205, 206, 208
    Jewish, 125–27, 129
Four-Year Plan office, 204

Frank, Hans, 46
Frankfurt am Main, 203–4
Freemasons, 32
Free University (Berlin), 289
Frick, Wilhelm, 39, 44, 68–69
Friedrich I, King of Prussia, 29
Frost, Robert, 209, 215
Funk, Walther, 199

Gaevernitz, Gero von, 204
Galen, Clemens von, 145–49, 349n–50n
  as opponent of euthanasia, 145, 148,
    271, 327n
gauleiter(s), 130, 139, 186, 204, 246
  for Berlin, Goebbels as, xxii, xxiii,
    131, 175, 195, 246, 255, 264
Gellately, Robert, 4
Geltungsjuden, see Mischlinge
genocide, *see* Final Solution; Holocaust
Gerichtssaal, Der, 109
German Army, *see* Army, German
German Boy Scouts (Pfadfinderbund),
  58–60, 61
German Faith Movement, 10, 86
German Labor Front, 44, 71, 121
German Resistance Memorial Museum,
  290
German Trade Association, 39
Germany:
  Allied bombing of, 134–39, 197,
    224–26, 281, 337n
  annexation of Austria by, 89–90
  armaments industry of, 196, 197–201,
    205–6, 247, 256, 346n
  businesses in, *see* businesses, Ger-
    man; businesses, Jewish
  East, 282, 284, 285–86, 291,
    295–96
  international protest over handling of
    "racial question" in, 42
  Jewish population in, 153
  1918 revolution in, 8, 29, 92
  Weimar, 19, 21, 23–24, 64
  West, 282, 284, 285, 287, 295
Gestapo:
  advancement in, through show of
    "radicalism," 96–97, 186, 334n
  arrest of Berlin Jewish community
    employees by, 279

arrest of Holzer by, 93–94
Berlin, Jewish Desk (*Judenreferat*) of,
  181–83, 206, 208, 239, 249, 293,
  300n
collaborators with, 6, 11–13, 77, 133,
  261
cooptation of Jewish leadership by,
  130, 162–68, 188–91, 279, 326n,
  330n
deportation of intermarried Jews in
  Frankfurt am Main by, 203–4
deportation of widowed or divorced
  intermarried Jews by, xxvi, 107,
  173, 248, 263, 332n–33n, 348n
in Final Roundup, xv–xxii, 206–57,
  265
In Final Roundup, official blame for,
  248–49, 265
intermarried couples pressured to divorce by, 9, 47, 48, 106–8
intermarried Jewish intellectuals arrested by, 234–37
interrogation of Rosenstrasse returnees by, 254
Jewish hospital in Iranischerstrasse
  used as prison by, 122–23
measures taken by, to end Rosenstrasse Protest, 238–39, 243
nonconforming behavior prosecuted
  by, 77
pilfering by, 181–83
release of intermarried Jews by, 243–
  46
Stock as head of Jewish Desk of, 206,
  208, 249, 300n
threat to separate Wally Grodka from
  daughter by, 55–56
Giesler, Paul, 246
Gilligan, Carol, 275, 352n
Gisevius, Hans Bernd, 25
Gleichshaltung, 25, 58
Goebbels, Joseph, xx, xxii–xxv
  on annihilation of Jews, 193
  aroused public unrest seen as threat
    by, 7–9, 153
  boycotts of Jewish businesses pro-
    moted by, 38–39
  call for Total War by, xxiv, 197,
    201–2

claims popular opinion as basis of
Nazi persecution of Jews, 98, 99
conscription of women seen as vital to
war effort by, 199–201
decision to deport Berlin's Jews by,
131–33
deportation of intermarried Germans
sought by, 263, 306n
deportation of intermarried Jews by,
195, 204–5, 243–44, 255
in disagreement with Himmler over
timing of deportations, 170–72,
193, 195, 244, 249
in favor of better treatment of eastern
territories, 5, 308n
in Final Roundup of Jews, 207
as gauleiter of Greater Berlin, xxii,
xxiii, 131, 175, 195, 246, 255,
264
Hitler's relationship with, 152, 171,
246
as instigator of Kristallnacht pogrom,
98–99, 101
intermarried Jews and *Mischlinge* released from Rosenstrasse 2–4 by,
243–45, 261
Jewish air-raid shelter order of, 135
Judenfrei Berlin mandated by, 131,
195–96, 206–7, 212, 226, 255, 264,
346n
as a leading progenitor of anti-Jewish
measures and Final Solution, 124,
130–31, 132, 133, 151, 152
mass rallies seen as vehicles to control
behavior by, xxiii–xxiv, 14–15
Nazi party role of, xxii–xxiv
orchestration by, of public outbursts
against Jews, 66–67
propaganda to shape public opinion
used by, xxii–xxiii, 65–70, 152,
306n
Reich Chamber of Culture headed by,
77–78
reprisals for assassination of Heydrich
ordered by, 175–76
Rosenstrasse Protest as viewed by,
xxvi, xxv, 237, 246, 264–65
Star of David decree initiated by,
151–53

strikes feared by, 8
Total War speech as power play of,
202, 338n
unrest seen in division of intermarried families by, xxii, xxv, xxix,
72–73, 171, 185
Wannsee conference and, 171–72
war news controlled by, 134–35, 197,
200, 226
Goering, Hermann, 134, 153, 202, 207,
224, 225, 246, 247, 308n
intermarriage categories of, 102–3
Goldberg, Werner, 57–62, 85–88, 287
anti-Jewish restrictions on father of,
58, 62, 115–16
army service of, 87–88, 112–13, 115–
18
assimilated upbringing of, 58–60
Boy Scout membership of, 58–60, 61
expelled from Lutheran Church, 86
father's life saved by, 122–23
internment at Rosenstrasse 2–4 of father of, 215, 221
as member of Hitler Youth, 60–62
post-army work of, 120–21
Reich Labor Service duty of, 87
Goldschmidt family, 292
Gritzbach, Erich, 204, 246
Grodka, Günter, 125
arrest of, in Final Roundup, 242–43
social isolation of, 38
view of conservative Jews by,
37–38
Grodka, Ranier, 155–57, 158,
285
Grodka, Wally and Günter, 37–40, 83–
85, 109–10, 129–30, 285
apartment-hunting strategy of, 40
German friends of, 129, 136
Kristallnacht experience of,
100–101
marriage of, 54–56
neighbors of, 10, 77, 83–85, 129
working-class status of, 37, 39–40
Grodka, Wally Rossbach:
"Boycott Day" memories of, 38–39
daughter separated from, 55–56
threatened by Gestapo, 167
Gross, Ruth, 227–28, 256–57

Grossbeeren labor camp:
  Auschwitz returnees imprisoned at,
    255, 281
  inhumane treatment of prisoners at,
    281
Grosse Hamburger Strasse, 253
  Collection Center at, 184, 236, 237,
    242, 247
  protests at, 242–43
Grynszpan, Herschel, 101
Günther, Rolf, 186–87, 255, 342*n*
  execution of Eppstein ordered by, 188,
    342*n*
Gurs, 139, 309*n*
Gutterer, Leopold, xx, xxi, 90, 226, 285,
    293–95, 302*n*
  as assistant to Goebbels, 131, 152
  as liaison between Propaganda Minis-
    try and RSHA, 132
  mass rallies organized by, 24–25
  on Rosenstrasse Protest, 244–45,
    260–61, 270–71
  Star of David conference chaired by,
    152–53

Hahn, Otto, 120
Hancock, Eleanor, 336*n*, 338*n*
Havel, Vàclav, 276
"Heil Hitler" greeting, 84, 128
Henschel, Hildegard, 175
Henschel, Moritz, 208, 330*n*
Herbert Baum Group, 175, 234
Hermann Goering barracks, xvi, 207,
    210, 216–17
Herzberg, Erich:
  interrogation of, 254
  in release from Auschwitz, 253–54,
    281–82
Herzberg, Hannah and Erich, 240, 282
Hess, Rudolf, 68
Heydrich, Reinhard, xxi, 102–3, 132
  fatal attack on, 175
  Mischlinge policy of, 171–72, 332*n*
  reactions to trial deportation moni-
    tored by, 6–7, 309*n*
Hilberg, Raul, 45, 183, 189, 301*n*, 312*n*,
    326*n*, 336*n*, 345*n*, 347*n*
Himmler, Heinrich, xxix, 16, 26
  Berlin Jewish Desk Scandal and, 182

  as critical of equalizations granted to
    Mischlinge, 119–20
  deportations of divorced and widowed
    intermarried Jews ordered by, 248,
    332*n*–33*n*, 348*n*
  in disagreement with Goebbels over
    deportations, 170–72, 193, 195,
    244–45, 249
  Judenfrei order of, 255–56
  Mischlinge seen as undependable by,
    117, 324*n*
  postponement of Euthanasia program
    proposed by, 111, 248
  Racial Office of SS established by,
    53–54
  ransom of Jews for foreign currency
    proposed by, 248
Hindenburg, Paul von, 25, 26, 38
Hinkel, Hans, 78, 131
Hirsch, Otto, 164, 326*n*
  as director of Central Organization of
    Jews, 139–40
Hitler, Adolf:
  annihilation of Jews by end of war
    predicted by, 193, 207, 336*n*
  anti-Semitism of key church leaders
    as encouraging to, 273
  attempted assassination of, 273, 274–
    75
  as attuned to popular opinion, 16, 65–
    66, 151, 153, 171, 259, 307*n*
  Berchtesgaden estate of, 89
  characterization of *Mischlinge* by, 69
  charismatic authority of, 66, 68
  church opposition feared by, 111
  civil disobedience as political force ad-
    vocated by, 8, 310*n*
  "Committee of Three" appointed by,
    199, 202, 338*n*
  completion of Final Solution urged
    by, 16, 172, 256
  cooptation of bureaucracies by, 68–70
  equalization petitions granted by, 117,
    120, 171, 334*n*
  Euthanasia stop order given by, 145,
    327*n*
  expulsion of *Mischlinge* and inter-
    married Germans from Army by,
    116–17

Goebbels's relationship with, 152,
171, 246, 329n, 339n
indecisive *Mischlinge* and intermarriage orders given by, 16, 69–70,
171, 256
indifferent public response to Sudetenland annexation by, 90–92, 259
intuition of, 67
Jewish Question and, 16, 68, 196,
331n
Judenfrei decree of, 194
limits of force and terror recognized
by, 5–6, 307n, 308n
political use of anti-Semitism by, 96–
97
popularity of, 16, 113–15, 274
popular opinion used by, 38
popular support as seen by, 4, 14–15,
66
power of will as seen by, 8, 307n
power theory of, 3–9, 246, 264, 307n
temporary deferment of *Mischlinge*
by, 16, 151–52, 172, 256, 313n–14n
women's role as viewed by, 103–4,
198–99, 262–63
workers' unrest feared by, 8, 246,
310n
see also National Socialism; Nazi
party; Nazi regime
Hitler Youth, 60–62, 145
Hoffmann, Peter, 275, 302n, 349n,
351n–52n
Holocaust:
deniers of, 294
failure of churches to join protest of,
145, 273, 348n
Nuremberg Laws as precursor to, 68
popular support of regime resulting
in, 95–96
social isolation of Jews as prerequisite
for, 3, 5–7, 9–16, 77, 95–96, 102,
154, 156, 261, 273, 277
see also Final Roundup of Jews; Final
Solution; Jewish Question
Holzer, Elsa and Rudi, 27–36, 88–96,
157–61, 285–86
courtship of, 34–36
family opposition to marriage of, 35–
36

first meeting of, 29–30
neighbors' harassment of, 157–59
relegated to Jewish air-raid shelter,
135
Holzer, Elsa Klose, 189, 219
Catholic conversion of, 143–44
as family breadwinner, 127–28
father's relationship with, 28
Jews as viewed by, 35, 126
nationalistic upbringing of, 28–29
as pressured by Gestapo to divorce,
107–8
in Rosenstrasse Protest, 228–29, 240–
41
as shunned by family, 159–61
Holzer, Rudi:
army career of *Mischling* nephew of,
122
army enlistment of, 32–33
arrested for hiding Jewish identity,
93–95
arrested in Final Roundup, 215–16
Catholic education of, 32
Communist party membership of, 33,
286
conversion to Catholicism of family
of, 30–32
early exposure to anti-Semitism of,
32
emigration to Berlin by, 34
family publishing business of, 33–34
father of, 30–32
forced labor of, 125, 126–27
racial laws' effect on family of, 92–93
relationship with in-laws of, 89
release from Rosenstrasse of, 2–4,
252
Star of David worn by, 157–61,
216
warned of impending Roundup, 212
Horcher's restaurant, 202
Horthy, Nikolaus, 102
Höss, Rudolf, 237
Housing Advisory Office (Berlin Jewish
Community), 109
in Jewish deportations, 163, 165–66
Humboldt University, 296
Hünsche, Otto, 293
Hüttner, Johnny, 253

identification cards, Jewish, 93, 138
I. G. Farben, 237, 253
Interior Ministry:
  equalization petitions screened by,
    117, 119
  Nuremberg Laws drafted by, 68–70
  proposal of compulsory divorce law
    by, 259
  Star of David Decree drafted by,
    152–53
intermarriage, 305n
  Aryan Clause as in direct ban on,
    43
  effect of Nuremberg Laws on, xxvi,
    xxvii, 72–75, 264
  as form of open dissent, xxvii–xxviii
  as gauge of limits of regime's power,
    276
  impending Nuremberg Laws as goad
    to, 45, 50–52, 54, 56, 212
  Jewish assimilation and, xxvi
  Nazi race creed vs., xxv–xxix, 41–49
  nonprivileged, 102–3, 156, 301n,
    304n, 322n
  privileged, 102–3, 106, 151, 155, 156,
    193, 194, 225–26, 301n, 304n,
    322n, 340n
  propaganda against, xxiii
  "racial," as grounds for divorce, 45–
    46, 48, 74, 272
  regime's criteria for categories of, 103
  rejection of notion of "Master Race"
    through, 85
intermarried couples:
  ban on employment of young "Ar-
    yan" women by, 73
  bans on, in legal profession, 44–45
  baptism of children of, 71
  Berlin as home to majority of, 264
  cultural avenues closed to, 77–78
  denunciations of, 6
  divorces of, *see* divorces
  German friends of, 85, 129, 136, 250–
    51
  in Gestapo's protective custody, 43
  identified in church lists, 206–7
  intermarried friends of, 213
  laws against, 77–78
  marriage permits denied to, 47–48

murder of, in Eastern occupied territories, 259
public shaming of, 67
neighbors of, 9–10, 77, 79–80, 155,
  157–59
Nuremberg Laws on status of, 72–75
profile of, xxv–xxvii
regime fearful of unrest in division
  of, xxii, xxv, xxix, 72–73, 151,
  171–72, 185, 194, 247, 261–62, 263
Rental Relations Law and, 108–10
resilient marriages of, xxv–xxvi
social isolation of, 9–10, 157–61
staged public outbursts at weddings
  of, 67
see also intermarried Germans; intermarried Jews
intermarried Germans:
  anti-Semitic propaganda and, 82
  anti-Semitism in families of, 18, 21,
    22, 26, 51, 52–53, 62–63
  Aryan Clause and, 44, 45
  bans on, in medical profession, 44–45
  birth families of, xxv–xxvi, 10, 18, 23,
    26
  as breadwinners, 104–5
  definition of "Nazi" by, 267
  deportations of, 130, 194, 259, 334n
  divorces of, 125–26, 173–74, 195,
    268
  in Final Solution, 171–72, 259
  handling of couple's public matters
    by, 125
  history of opposition by, xxvi, 261,
    263, 268, 269, 271, 273, 275
  job discrimination and, xxvii, 12
  Kristallnacht protested by, 102
  laws against, xxv–xxix
  limitation to genocide placed on re-
    gime by, 274
  March 1, 1943 bombing of Berlin and,
    225
  motivations of, for protest, 266–67
  and Nazi pressure to divorce, 9, 74,
    81, 85, 106–8, 263
  Nazism as fundamental challenge to
    families of, 268–69, 350n
  neighbors' harassment of, 10, 77, 79–
    80, 83–85, 129

newspaper delivery ban overcome by, 174
profile of, xxv–xxvii
as regime's most important opponents, 275
Reichsbahn ban on, 44
remaining married as an act of dissent for, 269
as rescuers, 258–77
Rosenstrasse Protest's effects on, 267–68
single-interest dissenters vs., 268–69
see also intermarriage; intermarried couples; intermarried German women; intermarried Jews
intermarried German women:
in "Jewish households," xxvii, 9, 101, 104, 126, 132–33, 156, 301n
loyalty of, xxvii, 82–83, 125, 223
persecution and realization of new roles for, 104–5
pressure on, to divorce, 106–8
in Rosenstrasse Protest, xx–xxv, 215–57, 239–41
widowed or divorced soldiers prohibited from marriage to, 194, 336n
intermarried Jews, xv–xxix, 277
assimilation of, xxvi, 58
deportations of, xvii, xxi–xxii, xxvi, 16, 97, 107, 124, 151, 168, 170–71, 173, 185–86, 193, 194–95, 203–4, 205–8, 237, 241–42, 244, 255, 334n
in Düsseldorf, 256
Dutch, 347n
emigration of, xxvi, 142
female, xxvi, xxviii, 9, 10, 104, 107, 135, 301n
in Final Roundup, xv–xxv, 195, 206–57
French, 255, 301n
Hitler's indecisive orders about *Mischlinge* and, 16, 69–70, 171–256
as last obstacle to completion of Final Solution, 264
laws against, xxvii, xxviii, 65–75, 43–45, 76–97

as members of "Aryan households," 9, 104, 301n
official Nazi explanation for release of, 248
in protective custody, 253, 311n–12n, 340n
regime's fear of unrest due to treatment of, 172, 173, 193, 204
registration of, with Central Organization, 187, 340n
release of, as result of Rosenstrasse Protest, 243–57, 291
Rosenstrasse Protest by spouses of, xv–xxv, 215–57
Rosenstrasse 2–4 as collection center for *Mischlinge* children of, xviii–xix
survival rate of, xxv, xxvii, 256
as targets of denunciations, 11–12, 204
"temporary deferment" in deportation of, xxi–xxii, 15, 16, 170, 193, 205, 237, 238, 259, 263, 264, 313n, 328n
warned of impending roundup, 212, 342n
see also intermarriage; intermarried couples; intermarried Germans
International Research and Exchanges Board (IREX), 296
Israel, Charlotte and Julius, xvii, 18–27, 78–82, 154, 283–84
anti-Semitic housemates of, 79–80
courtship of, 21–27
deportation of Jewish friends of, 168–70, 177, 234
and deportation of Sonja, 177, 180–81
emigration plans of, 141, 142
first meeting of, 20
and impending ban on intermarriage, 50–52
in Jewish air-raid shelters, 137–39
religious beliefs of, 51–52
Israel, Charlotte Press, 239
anti-Semitism in family of, 52–53
"Aryan" appearance of, 19
conversion plans of, 142–43
deportees offered help by, 188–89, 267

Israel, Charlotte Press (continued)
  as employee of Julius Israel, 21
  father's relationship with, 19–20
  German victory feared by, 114–15
  illegal reopening of business of, 81–
    82
  Jewish in-laws' relationships with, 51
  loyalty of, despite persecution, 82–83
  as main breadwinner, 79, 128–29
  on March 1, 1943 bombing of Berlin,
    225
  mother's relationship with, 22–23, 26,
    50–51
  prejudice absent in, 21
  ration card deception of, 133
  registration of shop in name of, 79,
    80
  in Rosenstrasse Protest, 243
  vote for Hitler by, 141–42
Israel, Julius, 125
  arrest of, 211–12
  childhood of, 20
  clothing business of, 20, 21
  deportation of parents of, 177–80
  musical talent of, 20–21, 78–79, 80
  niece of, 176–77, 180
  patriotism of family of, 26
  in release from Rosenstrasse 2–4, 251
  Star of David worn by, 153
Israel department store, Kristallnacht
  destruction of, 99–100

Jagusch, 130, 140
Japan, 42
Jewish Community, Nazi definition of
  "Jew" as enrolled member of, 70,
    71
  see also Berlin Jewish Community
Jewish Desk, see Judenreferat of
  Gestapo
Jewish Cultural Association, 78, 131
Jewish-German couples, see intermar-
  ried couples
"Jewish households," xxvii, 9, 101,
    301n
  wartime rations of, 104, 115–16, 124,
    126, 132–33, 155, 156, 242
Jewish property, confiscation of, 164–
    65, 167–68

see also Aryanization
Jewish Question, 16, 68, 101, 153, 196,
    331n, 345n
Jewish Relief Committee, xviii, 301n
Jews:
  air-raid shelters for, 126, 134–39
  assimilated, xxvi, 58
  Austrian, 92–96
  ban on newspaper deliveries to, 173–
    74
  baptism of, 71
  baptized, identified by churches for
    persecution, 273
  Berlin, see Berlin Jewish Community;
    Berlin Jews
  boycotts of businesses owned by, 11,
    38–39
  as "catchers," 166, 184, 277, 280
  as concentrated in Jewish houses, 102,
    104, 109–10
  confiscation of property of, 164–65,
    167–68
  conservative, early support of Na-
    tional Socialism by, 37–38, 315n
  coopted as orderlies, 164, 167–68,
    184, 185, 214–15
  cultural avenues closed to, 77–78
  curfew laws for, 108, 169
  denunciations of, 4, 6, 11–13, 77, 102,
    133, 166–67, 204, 312n
  deportations of, see deportations
  encouraged to emigrate, 142
  Final Roundup of, xv–xxv, 206–57,
    265, 300n
  Final Solution and, see Final Solution
  in Finland, 196
  in forced labor programs, 125–27, 129
  in German armaments industry, 205–
    6, 247, 256, 346n
  German social unrest attributed to,
    66, 318n
  German vs. Polish, 62
  "half," 71
  Himmler's ransom proposal for,
    248
  identification cards of, 93, 138
  illusions of safety held by, 100
  intermarried, see intermarried Jews
  killing of pets of, 174–75

Kristallnacht pogrom against, xviii, 88–101, 104–5, 301n
lack of German response to, 263
leadership of, coopted by Gestapo, 130, 162–68, 188–91, 279, 326n, 330n
Madagascar as, 131
March 1, 1943 bombing of Berlin and, 225
middle class, affected by Aryan Clause, xxvii, 10, 43–45
murders in, 168
Nazi definition of, 68, 69, 70–71
Nazi propaganda against, xxii, xxiii, 38, 65–70, 80–81
Nuremberg Laws' effect on, 65–75, 77
orchestration by Goebbels of mass public outbursts against, 66–67, 70
orthodox, 62
in performing arts, 78
popular compliance in measures against, 3, 10, 43–45, 76–97, 133
"protected" (*Schutzjuden*), 73, 120, 247, 325n
"quarter," 70–71
regime's definition of, 69–71
reports by BBC about murders of, 168, 331n
and reprisals for Heydrich assassination, 175
Rosenstrasse Protest as open resistance to persecution of, xix–xx, xxiv–xxv, 270–71
in Scheunenviertel Section of Berlin, xvii, 21, 213, 214
secular, 30–31
social isolation of, 3, 5–7, 9–16, 73–74, 77, 80–81, 95, 102, 154, 156, 261, 273, 277
Star of David decree directed at, 75, 150–61
trial deportation of, 6–7, 139–41, 309n
working-class, 37–40, 63–64
job discrimination, intermarried men and, xxvii, 12
Joint Distribution Committee (JDC), 142
Judenfrei, 60, 183

as decree of Hitler, 194
gauleiter role in, 130, 186, 204
as goal for Berlin, 131, 195–96, 206–7, 212, 226, 255, 264, 347n
Judenkolonnen, 132
Judenreferat (Jewish Desk) of Gestapo, 206, 208, 239, 249, 293, 300n
scandal at Gestapo's, 181–83
Jude Süss, 183
Jüdische Nachrichtenblatt, 164, 174, 187
Jupo (Jewish police), 184–85

Kaltenbrunner, Ernst, 56–57, 202
Katz, Iwan, 279–80
Keitel, Wilhelm, 90, 199
Kerrl, Hans, 42, 43, 45
Kershaw, Ian, 15–16, 146, 274, 351n
Kleemann, Siegbert, 206, 213, 343n
Klemperer, Klemens von, 349n, 352n
Koblin, Mr. (court archivist), 291–92
Kolberg, Lawrence, 352n
Koonz, Claudia, 339n, 348n
Kopf, Edith, 233, 234
Kozower, Philipp, 163, 187
Kreindler, Leo, 187
Krell, Karl, 217, 248, 254, 284, 304n
Kristallnacht Pogrom, xviii, 8, 94, 98–101, 301n
Aryanization of Jewish businesses after, 99, 104–5
in Berlin, 99–101
destructive violence of, 98–99
inaction of police in, 100
intermarried Germans in protest against, 102
in Northeim, 13–14
as "will" of German people, 99, 101
Kryshak, Anton von, 222
Kübler, Stella, 222, 332n–33n
Kuhn family, 242
Kwiet, Konrad, 190, 348n

Labor Bureau, 212, 213
labor camps, 253, 255–56, 281, 312n, 340n
protective-custody prisoners sent to, 203–4
Lachmuth, Felix, 236
Lammers, Hans, 117, 147, 199

Lassmann, Karl, 182
League for the Protection of Mother-
   hood, 12
League of German Girls, 61
Lebensborn program, 19
legal profession, bans on intermarriage
   in, 44–45
Lehfeld, Gerhard, 203, 204–5, 340*n*
Leibstandarte Hitler, xv, xxii, 195, 206,
   208, 209, 221
Levetzowstrasse synagogue, 218, 219
   confiscation of property of deported
      Jews at, 164–65, 167–68
Levi, Primo, 188, 277, 325*n*
Lewine, Erika, 62–64, 285
   arrested in Final Roundup, 209–10,
      220, 237
   relationship with Jewish side of fam-
      ily of, 63–64
Lewine, Julius, 220
Lewine, Mrs. (Erika's mother), 63, 107
Lewy, Guenter, 189, 327*n*, 348*n*, 351*n*
Ley, Robert, 44, 199
Lichtenberg, Bernhard, 224
Loderer, Anton, 167–68
Lodz ghetto, 162
Lohse, Heinrich, 308*n*
Lösener, Bernhard, 96, 205, 321*n*
   Nuremberg Laws drafted by, 68–70
   Star of David decree drafted by, 152
Löwenstein, Hans-Oskar, 106, 110, 154
Löwenstein, Johanna, 231
Luftwaffe, 134, 135
Lustig, Walter, 177, 279
lynch mobs, anti-Jewish, 67

Madagascar, plan to expel Jews to, 131,
   326*n*
marriage:
   as deeply-rooted German social norm,
      19, 72–73, 172–73
   of SS officers, Nazi racial standards
      upheld in, 54, 55, 63, 317*n*
Marriage Loan Program, 44
Marxism, 310*n*
mass rallies, Nazi, xxi, xxiii–xxiv, 14–
   15, 24–25, 68–70, 202
Master Race, xiv–xxv, 259–60, 303*n*
   see also Aryans

Mauthausen, 164
medical profession, bans on Jews and intermarried Germans in, 45
Mein Kampf (Hitler):
   on sexual relations with non-
      "Aryans," 26–27
   theory of popular support in, 4–5
Meitner, Lise, 120
Ministry for Propaganda and Enlightenment, *see* Propaganda Ministry
Mischlinge:
   ambiguous racial status of, 57–64, 69,
      122, 319*n*
   anti-Semitism in families of, 62–63
   arrested by Brunner, 185–86
   churches' concern over fate of, 205,
      213
   citizenship status of, 64, 71
   counted as Jews (*Geltungsjuden*), 64,
      71, 75, 155, 190, 194, 213, 220, 277
   definition of, xvii, xxviii, 69–72
   equalizations between "Aryans" and,
      116–17, 119–20, 180
   expelled from army, 116–17
   in Final Roundup of Jews, xvii–xx,
      203, 210, 213, 220, 304*n*
   first-degree, 70, 71
   in German Army, 87–88, 112–23,
      324*n*
   Heydrich's policy on, 171–72, 332*n*
   Himmler on, 117, 119–20, 324*n*
   Hitler's characterization of, as "mon-
      strosities," 69
   Nuremberg Laws on, 69–72, 264
   privileged intermarriage status of,
      102–3, 151, 155, 193
   release of, as result of Rosenstrasse
      Protest, 243–67
   Rosenstrasse Protest by, 227
   second-degree, 70–71
   social isolation of, 61, 120
   Star of David decree and, 150–52,
      154
   sterilization of, 172, 194
   temporary deferment from deporta-
      tion of, 15, 16, 151–52, 193, 205,
      237, 238, 259, 263, 264, 313*n*–14*n*,
      319*n*
   "us-ism" of, 121–23

mixed couples, *see* intermarried couples
Moabit Courthouse, 94
Mommsen, Hans, 274
Monowitz, 253
Montesquieu, Charles-Louis de Secondat, Baron de la Brède et, 192
Moritz, Abraham, 212
Mosse, Martha, 109, 163, 165, 168, 182, 187, 330*n*
Mosse and Ullstein, 33
Müller, Heinrich, 147–48, 255, 332*n*
deportation directive of, 194, 256
"mouth radio" (*Mundfunk*), 66–67, 228, 229

National Archive Administration (E. Germany), 295–96
National Labor Service, 87
National Marriage Law (1938), 106
National Socialism, xxii–xxiii, 171, 294
Jews as seen by, xxvii–xxviii
Jews as supporters of, 37–38
mass rallies used by, xxii, xxiii–xxiv, 14–15, 24–25, 70, 202, 314*n*
popular support as primary basis of political power in, 246
see also Nazi ideology; Nazi party; Nazi regime
National Socialist Women's Organization, 104, 136, 145
Nazi ideology:
anti-Semitism as core of, 13, 96–97, 264
conscription of women in conflict with, 198–201
German Faith Movement and, 86
Mischlinge as threat to, xxviii
Mischlinge policy in conflict with, 74–75, 116–17, 305*n*
racial purification in, 260
Nazi party, 4, 302*n*
anti-Semitism as means of advancement in, 97
Blockleiter as eyes and ears of, 84
boycott of Jewish businesses instigated by, 11, 38–39
claims of social unrest in power grabs of, 8–9, 318*n*
Goebbels's role in, xxii–xxiv

"higher standard" of anti-Semitism expected from members of, 53–54
Kristallnacht pogrom as organized action of, 99–101
position on mixed marriages of, 47–48
SA and, 5, 25, 307*n*
twenty-five points of, 5
Nazi regime:
bureaucratic collaboration with, in promotion of laws, 48, 65–75, 96, 319*n*
characteristics of successful protests against, 260, 269–72
criteria of, for categories of intermarriage, 103
definition of "Jew" by, 69–71
emigration of Jews encouraged by, 142
Euthanasia program of, 15, 110–11, 148–49
Final Solution secrecy maintained by, 232–33, 245, 254, 260, 261, 262
German collaboration as gradual compromise with, 17–18
German social norms vs. norms of, 15, 19, 48, 52–54, 65–68, 72–75, 103, 110–11, 144–49, 259–60, 272, 276
intermarried Germans fundamentally opposed to, 268–69
marriage laws reinterpreted by, 45–46
myth of unified populace fostered by, 270
popular accommodation in success of, 4, 7, 13, 75, 258, 259, 261, 264, 265, 269
protests feared by, 8–9, 13–15, 103, 145–49, 168, 246, 260, 263, 265, 269–70
public morale essential to popularity of, 197–98, 259, 261
racial hygiene programs of, 15, 110–11, 144–45, 147–49, 259
racism portrayed as normal by, 47
respectability sought by, 65–66
on Rosenstrasse Protest, xxiv, xxv, 237, 244, 260–61

Nazi regime (*continued*)
  social unrest feared by, xxi–xxiii,
    xxiv–xxv, 3–9, 262, 313*n*
  unrest among families of intermarried
    couples as concern of, 72–73, xxi–
    xxii, 65, 151, 171–72, 194, 237–38,
    247, 261–62, 263
  unrest among women as troubling to,
    196–201, 238, 339*n*
  use of shame by, 77
  use of terror by, 4, 5–7, 274, 277,
    308*n*
  women's role as viewed by, 103–4,
    197, 199–201, 262–63, 322*n*, 338*n*,
    348*n*
Noakes, Jeremy, 305*n*, 327*n*
noncompliance:
  with crucifix decrees, 145–47, 272,
    327*n*
  discouraged by Jewish organizations,
    189–91
  of intermarried Germans, 173–74,
    258–77, 265
  of women with labor conscriptions,
    201, 237
  see also accommodation; civil disobe-
    dience; denunciations; protests
nonprivileged intermarriages, 102–3,
    156, 301*n*, 304*n*, 322*n*
  deportations of Jews in, 194
Northeim, 13–14
Nosske, Gustav, 256, 277, 303*n*
NSDAP, *see* Nazi party
Nuremberg Laws, xxvi, xxvii, 45, 65–
    75, 256, 303*n*
  adopted by Austria, 92
  on definition of *Mischlinge*, 69–72,
    264
  and denial of marriage permits to
    mixed couples, 47–48
  on employment of young "Aryan"
    women, 73
  Hitler's justification for, 67–68
  imprecise language of, 72
  intermarriage under, 72–75,
    264
  Interior Ministry role in drafting of,
    68–70
  as precursor to Holocaust, 68

  and rise of intermarriages, 45, 50–52,
    54, 56
  Nuremberg rally, 68–70

Ohlendorf, Otto, 256
Olympics (1936), 76–77
orderlies, Jewish, 164, 167–68, 214–15,
    229, 236, 247
  coopted as Jewish police, 184, 185,
    236, 279–80
Orderly Transport of 1943–44, 165
Organization of National German Jews,
    315*n*
Organization Todt, 9, 256, 301*n*

Paepcke, Lotte, 135–36, 225
Paulus Bund, 120
"People's Court," 87
pets, killing of, 174–75
Peukert, Detlev, 271
Pfundtner, Hans, 96
Plötzensee, 234
police:
  in Final Roundup, 211
  inaction of, during Kristallnacht, 100
  regular, Rosenstrasse 2–4 guarded by,
    222, 229
Press, Mrs. (Charlotte Israel's mother),
    169, 170, 211–12
  anti-Semitism of, 18, 21, 22, 51
  Charlotte Israel's relationship with,
    22–23, 26, 50–51
privileged intermarriages, 102–3, 155,
    301*n*, 304*n*, 322*n*
  as compromise with Nazi ideology,
    106
  deportation of Jews in, 151, 193, 194,
    340*n*
  release of Rosenstrasse 2–4 internees
    in, 225–26
  see also nonprivileged intermarriages
propaganda, 7
  anti-Semitic, xxii, xxiii, 38, 65–70,
    80–81
  Goebbels's role in, xxii–xxiii, 65–70,
    134–35, 152, 197, 200, 226, 306*n*
  against intermarriage, xxiii, 47, 72–73
  radio used as tool for, xxiv, 79, 134–
    35, 202

Propaganda Ministry, xxii–xxiv
  and boycotts of Jewish businesses,
    38–39
  as embodiment of Hitler's theory of
    power, 66, 152
  rivalry between other ministries and,
    202, 307n
  staging of anti-Jewish outbursts by,
    66–67
  see also Goebbels, Joseph
"protected" Jews (*Schutzjuden*), 73, 120,
    246–47, 325n
"protection ID," 214
protective custody (*Schutzhaft*), 253,
    256, 311n–12n
  fate of prisoners in, 11, 203–4, 312n,
    340n
  mixed couples taken into, 43
protests, 270, 271
  by army, against deportations of
    Jewish war heroes to Auschwitz,
    247
  against deportations of Jewish work-
    ers, 247
  motivations of intermarried Germans
    for, 266–67
  see also civil disobedience; demon-
    strations; dissent; mass rallies,
    Nazi; noncompliance; Rosenstrasse
    Protest
protests, mass:
  against arrests of Jews and Commu-
    nists in Finland, 196, 259
  against Euthanasia, 145–46, 147–49,
    259–60, 272
  large city as ideal site for, 271, 350n
  Nazi regime fearful of, 4, 8–9, 13–
    15, 66, 147, 168, 244, 245, 246,
    247, 263, 269–70
  successful, characteristics of, 269–72
Prüfer, Scharführer, 163–64,
    225
public morale:
  popularity of Nazi party dependent
    on, 197–98, 259, 261
  public brutality toward Jews as dam-
    aging to, 232–33
  racial hygiene programs resolved in
    favor of, 259–60

  and secrecy about Final Solution,
    232–33, 245, 254, 260, 261, 262
  women as key to, 197–201

racial hygiene programs, *see* Euthanasia
    program
racial identification, collaboration of
    churches in, 10
Racial Office, SS, 53–54
racial policies:
  denunciations used in enforcement of,
    4, 6, 11–13, 102, 204
  equalizations as compromise with,
    117, 119
  and intermarried German women,
    104–5
  international protest of, 42, 315n
  intermarried couples threatened by,
    xxv–xxix, 41–49
  in reflection of rulings in divorce
    cases, 45–46, 48
  see also Aryan Clause of the Law for
    Restoration of the Civil Service;
    Nuremberg Laws
Racial Politics, Office of, 151
racial purification, 260
racial purity, 41–42
racial treason, 41–43
radio, as propaganda tool, xxiv, 79, 134–
    35, 202
Radlauer, Annie, xx
Radlauer, Kurt, 230, 300n–301n,
    344n
rallies, mass, xxi, xxiii–xxiv, 14–15,
    314n
  Gutterer as organizer of, 24–25
  at Nuremberg, 70
  for Total War, 202
  see also demonstrations; protests;
    protests, mass
Rassenschande (Racial Shame) laws,
    xxviii, 6, 80–81
  effect on women of, 103
  as interpreted by courts, 73–74
  social isolation of Jews through, 73–
    74
Rath, Ernst von, 101
rations:
  German, 156, 196

rations (*continued*)
   Jewish, 104, 115–16, 124, 126, 132–
     33, 155, 156, 242
Ravensbrück, 194
Reich Board of Labor Studies School
   (REFA), 121
Reich Chamber of Culture, 77–78
Reich Economic Ministry, 39
Reich Labor Service, 85
Reich Music Chamber, 241
Reich Press Chamber, 174
Reichsbahn:
   Aryan Clause for, 44
   forced labor by Jews for, 126–27
Reichsbanner, 36
Reich Security Main Office (RSHA), xxi
   deportation of Jews by, xxi–xxii, 130–
     33, 139–40, 151, 165, 203–5, 209–
     57
   documents of, moved to Czechoslova-
     kia, 281
   Final Solution and, xxii, 185–86,
     203–5, 207, 243–44
   release of intermarried Jews in con-
     centration camps by, 255–56
   Rosenstrasse Protest and, xx–xxii, 237
   SD of, xxi, 151, 249
   on trial, 290–91
   see also Final Roundup of the Jews;
     Final Solution
Reichstag, burning of, 25
Reichstag Communist party (KPD), 279
Relief Help Office (Catholic Church),
   206
Remarque, Erich Maria, 112
Rental Relations Law, 108–10
Reschke, Max, 184, 247, 340*n*, 352*n*–
   53*n*
resistance, 265–77, 340*n*, 352*n*
   Catholic, 14, 260, 269, 348*n*
   condemned by churches, 273
   definition of, 266, 275
   motivation of intermarried Germans
     and, 266–67
   Peukert scale of, 270
   varieties of, 269
   see also demonstrations; protests;
     protests, mass
Resistenz, 266, 351*n*

Reuters, 42
revisionists, 266
Rosenberg, Alfred, 5, 348*n*
Rosenstrasse, description of, xvii–xviii
Rosenstrasse Protest, xv–xxv, 215–57,
   260–61, 267–68, 270, 275, 290
   as Berlin phenomenon, 246, 264, 271
   as cautious effort to influence Ge-
     stapo, 229–31
   confidence gained by participants in,
     239–41
   disclosures about, at Bovensiepen
     Trial, 291
   Gestapo and, 238–39, 243
   Goebbels's role in, 243–44, 246
   Mischlinge in, 227
   as open resistance to persecution of
     Jews, xix–xx, xxiv–xxv, 270–71
   regime's reaction to, xxiv, xxv, 9, 15,
     245, 246, 261
   relatives of intermarried Jews in, xvii–
     xxii, xxiv–xxv, 214, 219–22, 223,
     226–31, 238–43
   release of intermarried Jews and
     Mischlinge as result of, 243–57,
     291
   RSHA and, xx–xii, 237
   solidarity among protesters in, xx,
     223–24, 231, 239, 244–45, 268
   spontaneity of, 239
   SS guards in, 227, 229
Rosenstrasse 2–4, xviii–xix
   as center of Jewish Community ser-
     vices, xviii
   as collection center, xvii–xx, 213–14,
     215, 219
   number of people imprisoned at, 304*n*
   RAF bombardment and, 225
Rosenstiel, Trude, 168–70
Rothe, Willi, 293
Royal Air Force (RAF), bombardment of
   Berlin by, 134–39, 197, 225,
   281

SA (*Sturmabteilungen*), 5, 25
   in boycotts of Jewish businesses, 38–
     39, 79, 80
   Kristallnacht pogrom carried out by,
     98–101

Sachsenhausen, 98, 175, 176, 241, 301*n*, 344*n*
St. Hedwig's Cathedral, 224
Sankt Johann, village of, 30
Sauckel, Fritz, 198
Scheunenviertel, xvii, 21, 213, 214
Schiffer, August, 234–37, 248, 340*n*–41*n*
Schindler, Oskar, 123
Schlegelberger, Franz, 147, 173, 319*n*
Schneider, Alfred, 237, 254, 284
    as guard at Rosenstrasse 2–4, 227
Schneider-Lüschow, Ingeborg, 212
Schulstrasse prison, 280–81
Schutzjuden, 73, 120, 246–47, 325*n*
Schwarze Korps, Das, 232
Schwede-Coburg, Franz, 103, 256, 334*n*
Schwenn, Günther, 78–79
Second Motorized Division, German Army, 91, 92, 259
Selbstgleichschaltung, 13
Seligsohn, Julius, 139–40
Shirer, William, 92
shopping hours, Jewish, 132–34
Siemens, 127, 209, 210, 215, 240, 315*n*
Silibergleit, Arthur, 235
single-issue opposition, 266
    of Catholic Church, 144–49, 327*n*
    of Hitler's would-be assassins, 274–75
    of intermarried Germans, 268–69
social clubs, exclusion of intermarried couples from, 10
Social Democratic party, 23–24, 37, 38, 90
social norms, German:
    marriage and, 72–73, 103, 245, 262, 269, 272
    values of Nazi regimes vs., 15, 19, 44–49, 52–54, 58–60, 65–75, 76–77, 103, 110–11, 144–49, 259–60, 272, 277
Speer, Albert, 14, 110, 201, 202
    as armaments minister, 198, 199, 339*n*
Spirit of Cloppenburg, 146–47
Sprenger, Jakob, 204, 256, 341*n*
Squire, Paul C., 194
SS (*Schutzstaffel*):
    in Final Roundup, xv, xxii, 195, 206, 207, 209–57
    Nazi racial standards applied to marriages of, 54, 63, 317*n*
    proof of Aryan descent needed for membership in, 26
    prosecution of Gestapo pilferers by, 181–83
    Racial Office of, 53–54
Star of David, xvi, 169
    and Berlin as *Judenfrei*, 255
    decree, 75, 150–61
    on doorposts of Jewish households, 9, 104, 154
    Jews marked for deportation by, 75, 151, 153, 193
    worn by children, 154–55
    worn by men in Jewish households, 301*n*
Stauffenberg, Claus von, 113, 351*n*–52*n*
Stern, J. P., 145, 327*n*
Sternsches Konservatorium, 20
Stettin, 130, 249
Steudel, Hannelore, 106–7
Stillegung (business closures) measure, of Total War, 200, 231–32, 309*n*–10*n*
Streicher, Julius, 38
Stock, Walter, 215, 234, 241, 284
    interrogation of Rosenstrasse 2–4 returnees by, 254
    as head of *Judenreferat* of Berlin Gestapo, 206, 208, 249, 300*n*
strikes, Nazi regime's fear of, 8
Stuckart, Wilhelm, 173, 318*n*–19*n*
Stürmer, Der, 80, 120, 128
Stürmerkasten, anti-Semitic portrayals of Jews in, 80, 82
suicides:
    in Final Roundup of Jews, xvi–xvii
    by forced laborers, 127

terror, Nazi use of, 4, 5–7, 274, 277
Theresienstadt, 107, 172, 188, 207, 247
    deportation of employees of Berlin Jewish Community to, 279, 332*n*
    as "show" camp, 332*n*

Third Reich, 4–5, 291
  see also Hitler, Adolf; National So-
    cialism; Nazi party; Nazi regime
Toleranz, 235
Total War, xxiv, 192, 196–202, 336n
  business closure (Stillegung) measure
    in, 200, 202, 309n–11n
  Goebbels's call for, xxiv, 201–2
  and Hitler's "Committee of Three,"
    199, 338n
  women and, 192, 196–202, 262
trade unions, 8
Trunk, Isaiah, 189–90

"us-ism," 121–23, 188, 277, 325n

Versailles Treaty, 34
Vienna, Austria, 90, 142
  deportations of Jews of, 181, 183
Völkische Beobachter, 38

Wagner, Adolf, 146–47
Wannsee Conference, 171–72, 293
Wehler, Hans-Ulrich, 311n
Wehrmacht, see Army, German
Weigert, Mrs., 219–20, 223, 231, 240
  in Rosenstrasse Protest, 223, 231
Weigert family, 218–20
Weimar Republic:
  Berlin in, 19, 21
  constitution of, 23, 25
West Berlin Jewish Community, 289–
  91
"wild" Euthanasia, 148, 328n
Wöhrn, Fritz, 140, 326n

Wolf, Edith, 190–91
Wolf, Mr. (editor), 235
Wolff, Ferdinand, 210, 242, 281, 282
women:
  in "Aryan households," 9, 104, 301n
  conscription of, into labor force, 196,
    197–201, 338n
  in "Jewish households," 9, 101, 104,
    301n
  as key to public morale, 197, 199–201
  Marriage Loan Program for, 44
  Nazi fear of unrest among, 196–201,
    237–38, 339n
  Nazi view of roles of, 103–4, 199–
    201, 262, 322n, 338n, 348n
  noncompliance with labor conscrip-
    tions by, 201, 238, 339n, 348n
  protest at Rosenstrasse 2–4 by, xvii–
    xxii, xxiv–xxv, 215–57
  on World War II German homefront,
    192, 196–202
work camps, see labor camps
World War I, 4, 8, 66, 147, 246, 263
World War II:
  Battle of Britain in, 134, 135
  Battle of Stalingrad in, 192, 196, 198,
    200
  German-occupied eastern territories
    in, 5, 171
  German women on homefront in,
    192, 196–202
  Hitler's popularity linked to victories
    in, 16, 113–15, 274

Zivier, Georg, 185, 276